THE PAN-AFRICAN
PANTHEON

MANCHESTER
1824

Manchester University Press

THE PAN-AFRICAN PANTHEON

Prophets, Poets, and Philosophers

Edited by Adekeye Adebajo

Manchester University Press

First published in South Africa by Jacana Media in 2020

This edition published in North America (excluding West Indies), United Kingdom, Europe, Asia (excluding India), Australia and New Zealand by Manchester University Press
Altrincham Street, Manchester M1 7JA

www.manchesteruniversitypress.co.uk

British Library Cataloguing-in-Publication Data
A catalogue record for this book is available from the British Library

ISBN   978 1 5261 5681 5   hardback

ISBN   978 1 5261 5682 2   paperback

The publisher has no responsibility for the persistence or accuracy of URLs for any external or third-party internet websites referred to in this book, and does not guarantee that any content on such websites is, or will remain, accurate or appropriate.

Printed in Great Britain
by TJ Books Ltd, Padstow

Contents

Acknowledgements

The ancient Chinese proverb tells us that the journey of a thousand miles begins with the first step away from the ancestral home. To edit a 38-chapter book with 37 prominent African, Afro-Caribbean, and African-American scholars represents a real labour of love. This three-year project was supported by the University of Johannesburg (UJ) in South Africa, and implemented through the Institute for Pan-African Thought and Conversation (IPATC) which I direct. The volume seeks to make a substantive contribution to contemporary global transformation debates in an era of "Rhodes Must Fall" and "Black Lives Matter". It also aims to contribute to transforming fossilised Eurocentric curricula, which have insisted for centuries that "dead white men" continue to occupy the central position in global epistemologies on almost every subject under the sun.

I would like firstly to acknowledge the patience, perseverance, and passion of all the committed scholars of "Global Africa" who contributed to this volume. The many sacrifices they made were clearly not in vain, and this book represents the fruits of their labour. Unfortunately, one of our authors – Nigerian scholar, Abiola Irele – died in Boston in July 2017 before the book was published. His chapter on Senegalese poet-president, Léopold Senghor, in this volume will remain an enduring legacy to his rich scholarship. A deep thinker and fluent writer who was endearingly nicknamed *olohun iyo* (the praise-singer), Irele was undoubtedly the foremost prophet of Négritude to which he devoted his intellectual career for five decades. He shared both Senghor and Martiniquan poet-politician, Aimé Césaire's love of the French language and culture, but was also deeply immersed in his own traditional African cultures. "Prof" fervently believed that Négritude and Pan-Africanism would be the essential foundations for the reconstruction of a new African identity. The ultimate cultural bridge-builder, he consistently interpreted the francophone world of black poetry and prose for an anglophone audience. The Black Orpheus and last prophet of Négritude finally entered After Africa's "Dead Poet's Society" in 2017. This book honours his memory, and that of another much younger author in this book, African-American scholar-theologian, Dr Alease Brown, who sadly joined the ancestors in March 2020.

In true African tradition, it takes a village to pull off such a large collective venture. We would, therefore, like to thank the three external reviewers who took the time to provide substantive and useful comments for revising this volume. I thank Russell Martin for his sharp copy-editing skills, and Christopher Merrett for both his thorough indexing and incisive proof-reading. Jacana Media in South Africa has remained an activist, independent publisher for two decades. I would like to thank its formidable publishing director, Bridget Impey, who consistently came up with creative solutions. Founder, Maggie Davey, was the artistic muse who – along with publicide – ensured that the book cover elegantly reflected the Pan-African red, green, and gold of this griot's tale. Glenda Younge and Aimée Armstrong meticulously ensured that we had a clean text, while Shawn Paikin completed the layout. At Manchester University Press (MUP), we would like to acknowledge the efforts of senior commissioning editor, Jonathan de Peyer, and particularly his successor, Thomas Dark, ably assisted by assistant editor, Lucy Burns, who ensured that this book reaches a wider North American and European audience. Other editions will reach Nigerian and Caribbean readers.

Finally, I would like to thank all of my colleagues at the Institute for Pan-African Thought and Conversation in Johannesburg, who contributed to the success of this project over three long years. They also deserve to share in the credit for the publication of this book. We hope that this volume will be read not just by scholars, but also by members of civil society and the general public across Africa and its Diaspora and beyond. While acknowledging these 36 historical and contemporary figures as members of a "Pan-African Pantheon", these critical essays of prophets, poets, and philosophers are not hagiographic, but often point out areas where these figures may have fallen short. The volume seeks, above all, to rebuild the bridges of Pan-Africanism by encouraging intellectual dialogue and mutual exchange between Africa and her siblings in the Diaspora, from Bamako to Bahia to Birmingham to Bordeaux, and from the Bahamas to Bridgetown to Baltimore. God bless Africa!

ADEKEYE ADEBAJO,
JOHANNESBURG, NOVEMBER 2020

LIST OF CONTRIBUTORS

Adekeye Adebajo is a Professor and the Director of the Institute for Pan-African Thought and Conversation (IPATC) and the Institute of Global African Affairs (IGAA), both at the University of Johannesburg (UJ) in South Africa. He was Executive Director of the Centre for Conflict Resolution (CCR) in Cape Town between 2003 and 2016. He served on United Nations (UN) missions in South Africa, Western Sahara, and Iraq, and was Director of the Africa Programme at the International Peace Institute (IPI) in New York. Professor Adebajo is the author of six books including *Building Peace in West Africa*; *The Curse of Berlin: Africa after the Cold War*; *UN Peacekeeping in Africa*; *Thabo Mbeki: Africa's Philosopher-King*; and *The Eagle and the Springbok*: *Essays on Nigeria and South Africa*. He is co-editor or editor of 10 books on Africa's international relations. Professor Adebajo holds a doctorate from Oxford University in England, and is a columnist for *Business Day* (South Africa), the *Guardian* (Nigeria), and the *Gleaner* (Jamaica).

Jerome Afeikhena is the Special Advisor to the Commissioner for Rural Economy and Agriculture, African Union (AU) Commission in Addis Ababa, Ethiopia. He is also a Visiting Professor of Economics at Igbinedion University in Nigeria. He has held several distinguished positions including Visiting Scholar at the International Monetary Fund (IMF); Visiting Fellow at the World Bank; and Senior Associate member at St Antony's College at Oxford University. He co-edited *African Development in the 21st Century: Adebayo Adedeji's Theories and Contributions*.

Kweku Ampiah is a political economist and an Associate Professor of Japanese Studies at the University of Leeds in England. His research and teaching interests include Japanese foreign policy and Japanese politics. He is the author of *The Political and Moral Imperatives of the Bandung Conference of 1955*, and co-author of *Rethinking Japan: The Politics of Contested Nationalism*. He obtained his doctorate from Oxford University.

Ada Uzoamaka Azodo is a Visiting Assistant Professor of French and Women's Studies, and an Adjunct Professor of Minority Studies at Indiana University Northwest in the US. She is author of *L'Imaginaire dans les romans de Camara Laye*; guest editor of *African Feminisms: Ideology, Gender and Development*, and *OFO: Journal of Transatlantic Studies*. She was co-editor of *Gender and Sexuality in African Literature and Film*, and has published six other volumes in the African World Press "Emerging Perspectives" series. Dr Azodo earned her doctorate from the University of Lagos (UNILAG) in Nigeria.

Hilary Beckles is a Professor and Vice-Chancellor of the University of the West Indies (UWI). He is Vice-President of the International Task Force for the United Nations Educational, Scientific, and Cultural Organisation (UNESCO) Slave Route Project; a Consultant for the UNESCO Cities for Peace Global Programme; an adviser for the UN World Culture Report; and an advisor to the UN Secretary-General on Sustainable Development. Professor Beckles previously acted as Chair of the UWI Press, as well as serving on the Caribbean Community's (CARICOM) Commission on Reparation and Social Justice. He has lectured extensively in Europe, Africa, Asia and the Americas, and published over ten scholarly books.

Ama Biney is an independent scholar with over twenty years of teaching experience in Britain and Ghana. Her publications include *The Political and Social Thought of Kwame Nkrumah*; and *Speaking Truth to Power: Selected Pan-African Postcards of Tajudeen Abdul-Raheem*, as well as several academic articles. She is a former editor-in-chief of the Pan-African weekly electronic newsletter, *Pambazuka News*. Dr Biney holds an undergraduate degree from the University of Birmingham, in England. She obtained her master's and doctorate from the School of Oriental and African Studies (SOAS) at the University of London.

Alease A. Brown was a Post-Doctoral Fellow at the University of the Western Cape's Desmond Tutu Centre for Religion and Social Justice in South Africa. She previously practised as an attorney in New York. Dr Brown published in international journals. Her research interests lay in the intersection of religion and progressive social movements in the South African context, as seen through the lenses of Black and feminist theology. She obtained a doctorate in theology from Stellenbosch University in the Western Cape, South Africa.

Selwyn R. Cudjoe is a Professor of Africana Studies at Wellesley College in Massachusetts, US. He previously taught at Harvard, Cornell, Ohio, and Fordham universities. He is the author of *Caribbean Visionary: A.R.F. Webber and the Making of the Guyanese Nation*; *V.S. Naipaul: A Materialist Reading*; *Beyond Boundaries: The Intellectual Tradition of Trinidad and Tobago*; *Resistance and Caribbean Literature*; and, most recently, *The Slave Master of Trinidad: William Hardin Burnley and the Nineteenth Century Atlantic World*. He also co-edited *C.L.R. James: His Intellectual Legacies*. Professor Cudjoe has written for the *New York Times*, *New Left Review*, and *Harvard Educational Review*. He is a weekly columnist for the *Trinidad Express*.

Lee A. Daniels is a journalist who previously worked for the *Washington Post* and *New York Times*, among other US media organisations. He is a former editor of the National Urban League (NUL) publication, *The State of Black America*, and a former Director of Communications at the National Association for the Advancement of Coloured People's (NAACP) Legal Defence and Educational Fund. Mr Daniels is the author of *Last Chance: The Political Threat to Black America*.

Seamus Duggan is a Senior Analyst at the Johannesburg office of Control Risks in South Africa, where he provides political, operational, and security risk analysis on southern Africa. His research interests lie in how Pan-Africanism has shaped responses to conflict resolution and continental integration, with a particular emphasis on the roles of, and relationship between, South Africa and Nigeria. He holds a doctorate in international relations from Oxford University.

Louisa Uchum Egbunike is an Associate Professor in African Literature at Durham University in England. She earlier lectured in Contemporary African Literature at City University of London and SOAS, where she completed her doctorate. Dr Egbunike has published in a number of academic books and journals including *African Literature Today* and *Matatu*. She was a curator of the art exhibition *Legacies of Biafra*, and co-writer and producer of the documentary film *In the Shadow of Biafra*. Dr Egbunike is one of the founders and conveners of the annual International Igbo Conference.

Janice Golding is a programme specialist on climate and environment at the United Nations Development Programme (UNDP) in Tshwane (Pretoria),

South Africa. She served the State Secretariat for Economic Affairs of the government of Switzerland in South Africa, and previously worked as a South African public servant overseeing capacity-building development projects across southern Africa. Dr Golding edited *Southern African Plant Red Data Lists*, and wrote a chapter on Wangari Maathai for the book *Africa's Peacemakers: Nobel Peace Laureates of African Descent*. She obtained her doctorate from Oxford University.

Colin Grant is a historian and an associate fellow of the Centre for Caribbean Studies at the University of Warwick, in England. He writes for *The Guardian*, *Times Literary Supplement (TLS)* and the *New York Review of Books*. His publications include *Negro with a Hat: The Rise and Fall of Marcus Garvey and His Dream of Mother Africa*; and *Homecoming: Voices of the Windrush Generation*.

Clinton A. Hutton is the Director of the Institute of Technological and Educational Research (ITER) at Mico University College in Kingston, Jamaica. He previously lectured at the University of the West Indies for 25 years. His publications include *The Logic and Historical Significance of the Haitian Revolution and the Cosmological Roots of Haitian Freedom*; and *Colour for Colour, Skin for Skin: Marching with the Ancestral Spirits into War Oh at Morant Bay*. Professor Hutton was the lead editor of and contributor to both *Leonard Percival Howell and the Genesis of Rastafari*, and *Rupert Lewis and the Black Intellectual Tradition*.

Abiola Irele died in July 2017, while an Associate at the Hutchins Centre for African and African American Research at Harvard University in Massachusetts, US. Professor Irele served as the Provost of the College of Humanities at Kwara State University in Nigeria. He taught at the universities of Ibadan, Dar es Salaam, Ghana, Ohio State, Tulane, and Harvard. He was the author or editor of: *Selected Poems of Léopold Sédar Senghor*; the *Cambridge History of African and Caribbean Literature*; *The Négritude Moment*; and *The African Scholar and Other Essays*. He obtained his doctorate from the University of Paris, and was an editor of *Transition* and the *Savannah Review*.

Maureen Isaacson is an independent writer, researcher, and editor. She was the literary editor of the *Sunday Independent* (South Africa), and worked most recently for the Foundation for Human Rights (FHR) in Johannesburg as programme manager for participatory democracy. She is currently based in Stockholm, Sweden. She has published a short story collection, *Holding Back Midnight*, and her short stories have been published in a variety of anthologies and journals. She has researched and edited two books: *The Fifties People of South Africa*, and *The Finest Photographs from the Old Drum*.

Adele L. Jinadu is an Adjunct Professor in the Department of Political Science at the University of Lagos in Nigeria. He has served as President of the African Association of Political Science (AAPS) and as Vice-President of the International Political Science Association (IPSA). His publications include *Fanon: In Search of the African Revolution*; *Structure and Choice in African Politics*; *Social Science and Development in Africa: Ethiopia, Mozambique, Tanzania and Zimbabwe*; *Ethnic Conflict and Federalism in Nigeria*; *Intellectuals, Democracy and Development in Africa*; and *Explaining and Managing Ethnic Conflict in Africa*.

Gilbert M. Khadiagala is the Jan Smuts Professor of International Relations and Director of the African Centre for the Study of the United States (ACSUS) at the University of the Witwatersrand in Johannesburg, South Africa. He has published widely on African politics, foreign policy, security, mediation, conflict resolution, and governance. He is the editor of *War and Peace in Africa's Great Lakes Region*, and author of *Regional Cooperation on Democratization and Conflict Management in Africa*, and *How Can Democratic Peace Work in Southern Africa? Trends and Trajectories after the Decade of Hope*.

W. Andy Knight is Professor of International Relations in the Political Science Department at the University of Alberta in Canada, and a Fellow of the Royal Society of Canada (FRSC). He has written and edited several books on global politics, the United Nations, building sustainable peace, and regional integration movements. His most recent books include *Female Suicide Bombings: A Critical Gendered Approach*, and *Remapping the Americas: Trends in Region-Making*.

Dr Malesela John Lamola is a Senior Research Associate at the Institute of Intelligent Systems (IIS) at the University of Johannesburg, and a Senior Lecturer in Philosophy at the University of Pretoria, both in South Africa. He researches and teaches on African social philosophy and African philosophy of technology. Dr Lamola has published widely in international scholarly journals and anthologies on Marxian postcolonial theory, applications of Sartrean existential anti-colonial philosophy, and the representation of Africans in the technologies of the Fourth Industrial Revolution. He holds an MBA degree from Embry-Riddle Aeronautical University, Florida, in the US, and a doctorate from the University of Edinburgh in Scotland.

Vladimir Lucien is a writer, actor, and critic. His writing has been widely published, including in an anthology of Caribbean poetry and prose entitled *Beyond Sangre Grande*. His debut collection, *Sounding Ground*, won him the OCM Bocas Prize for Caribbean Literature in 2015. He is also the co-editor of the anthology *Sent Lisi: Poems and Art of St. Lucia*. He was the screenwriter of the documentary *The Merikins*, which premiered at the Trinidad and Tobago Film Festival in 2013.

Zine Magubane is a Professor of Sociology at Boston College in Massachusetts in the US. She teaches courses in postcolonial studies, race, ethnicity, and popular culture. She earned her doctorate in sociology from Harvard University in the US. She is the author of *Bringing the Empire Home: Race, Class and Gender in Britain and Colonial South Africa*; and co-editor (with Reitu Mabokela) of *Race, Gender and the Status of Black South African Women in the Academy*; as well as editor of *Postmodernity, Postcoloniality, and African Studies*.

Annita Montoute is a Lecturer in the Institute of International Relations (IIR) at the University of the West Indies in Trinidad and Tobago. She was a Research Fellow at the European Centre for Development Policy Management (ECDPM) in Maastricht, in the Netherlands. She is a co-editor of the volume *The ACP Group and the EU Development Partnership: Beyond the North-South Debate*, and co-author of *Changing Cuba–U.S. Relations: Implications for CARICOM States*. She obtained her doctorate in international relations from the University of the West Indies.

Aldon D. Morris is the Leon Forrest Professor of Sociology and African-American Studies at Northwestern University in Illinois in the US. He is a former Chair of the Department of Sociology, and Director of Asian-American Studies and Interim Dean of the College of Arts and Sciences at Northwestern University. Professor Morris was elected President of the American Sociological Association (ASA) in 2019. He was a consultant for the award-winning film *Eyes on the Prize*, as well as the author of the award-winning book *The Origins of the*

Civil Rights Movement. His book *The Scholar Denied: W.E.B. Du Bois and the Birth of Modern Sociology* has received a dozen awards.

Nomsa Mwamuka is a media and communications specialist, focusing on African art, culture, education, and socio-economic development issues. She has curated, facilitated, and contributed to various events and festivals including the United Nations Development Programme's "Unite to End Violence Against Women" Film Festival; African Synergy artist exchanges; and the Southern African International Film Festival. She is the co-author of *Makeba: The Miriam Makeba Story*; a co-compiler of the anthology *Township Girls: The Cross-Over Generation*; and worked on a multi-media project titled *Acts of Activism: Profiles of African Women Cultural and Political Activists*.

Sabelo J. Ndlovu-Gatsheni is a Professor and the Director of Scholarship in the Department of Leadership and Transformation in the Principal and Vice-Chancellor's Office at the University of South Africa (Unisa). He was founding head of the Archie Mafeje Research Institute for Applied Social Policy (AMRI) at Unisa. He has published over 100 peer-reviewed journal articles and book chapters, as well as eight single-authored and nine edited books. His major publications include *Epistemic Freedom in Africa: Deprovincialization and Decolonization*, and *Decolonization, Development and Knowledge in Africa: Turning Over a New Leaf*.

Bongani Ngqulunga is the Director of the Johannesburg Institute for Advanced Study (JIAS) based at the University of Johannesburg in South Africa. A sociologist and a biographer, he holds a doctorate from Brown University in the US. He is the author of *The Man Who Founded the ANC: A Biography of Pixley ka Isaka Seme*, which won three literary prizes, including the prestigious Alan Paton Award. He previously served in the Office of the Presidency in the South African government.

Sola Olorunyomi is a Lecturer in cultural studies and African/Africa-diaspora literature at the Institute of African Studies (IAS) at the University of Ibadan (UI) in Nigeria. He is the author of *Afrobeat: Fela and the Imagined Continent*, and has published widely on related themes in his research on West Africa, the Caribbean, and Nicaragua. He is editor of *Glendora Review*, an African quarterly journal on arts and culture.

Kwabena Opoku-Agyemang is a Lecturer in the Department of English at the University of Ghana in Legon. He has edited special issues of the journals *Hyperrhiz: New Media Cultures*, and *Journal of Gaming and Virtual Worlds* (*JGVW*). His work has also appeared in *Research in African Literatures*. He obtained his doctorate from West Virginia University in the US.

Sanya Osha is a Research Fellow at the African Studies Centre, Leiden (ASCL), in the Netherlands. His work has appeared in *Transition, Socialism and Democracy, Research in African Literatures, QUEST: An African Journal of Philosophy, Africa Review of Books*, and the *Blackwell Encyclopedia of Twentieth Century Fiction*. He is the author of *Kwasi Wiredu and Beyond: The Text, Writing and Thought in Africa; Ken Saro-Wiwa's Shadow: Politics, Nationalism and the Ogoni Protest Movement; Postethnophilosophy*; and *African Postcolonial Modernity: Informal Subjectivities and the Democratic Consensus*. He is also editor of *The Social Contract in Africa*, and a co-editor of *The Africana World: Fragmentation to Unity and Renaissance*.

N. Barney Pityana is the retired Principal and Vice-Chancellor of the University of South Africa. He is a human rights lawyer and a theologian. He is Secretary-General of the Network of African Academies of Science (NASAC), and Vice-President of the Academy of Science of South Africa (ASSAf). Professor Pityana served as Chair of South Africa's Human Rights Commission (SAHRC), and worked closely with Steve Biko in the Black Consciousness Movement.

Reiland Rabaka is the Chair of the Department of Ethnic Studies at the University of Colorado in the US, and a Research Fellow in the College of Human Sciences at the University of South Africa. He is the author of more than 50 scholarly articles, book chapters and essays, as well as more than 12 books including *Du Bois's Dialectics; Africana Critical Theory; Against Epistemic Apartheid: W.E.B. Du Bois and the Disciplinary Decadence of Sociology; Forms of Fanonism: Frantz Fanon's Critical Theory and the Dialectics of Decolonization; Concepts of Cabralism: Amilcar Cabral and Africana Critical Theory*; and *The Négritude Movement*.

Rhoda Reddock is an Emeritus Professor and academic specialising in gender, social change, and development at the University of the West Indies, and was a former Deputy Principal of the UWI St Augustine Campus in Trinidad and Tobago. She has written over 70 peer-reviewed articles and book chapters, and her eight book publications include *Women, Labour and Politics in Trinidad and Tobago: A History*; *Elma Francois, the NWCSA and the Worker's Struggle for Change in the Caribbean*; *Interrogating Caribbean Masculinities*; and *Sex, Power and Taboo*.

Pearl T. Robinson is an Associate Professor in the Department of Political Science at Tufts University in Massachusetts, US. She is currently a member of the US Council on Foreign Relations, and was previously President of the US African Studies Association, Director of Tufts University's International Relations Programme, and a board member of TransAfrica. She has authored more than 40 articles and book chapters on African and African-American politics. She is co-author of *Stabilizing Nigeria: Sanctions, Incentives, and Support for Civil Society*; and *Transformation and Resiliency in Africa*.

Alison E. Stone Roofe is Undersecretary at the Bilateral, Regional and Hemispheric Affairs Division in the Jamaican Ministry of Foreign Affairs and Foreign Trade in Kingston. She previously served as Jamaica's first resident Ambassador to Brazil and was concurrently the country's non-resident Ambassador to Argentina, Chile, Uruguay and Paraguay. Ambassador Roofe has worked for over 28 years in the Jamaican Foreign Service, primarily in the area of trade diplomacy. She has taught in the Department of Government at the University of the West Indies. She holds an MPhil in international relations from the University of Oxford in England.

Cheikh Thiam is the Dean of Africa South of the Sahara at the School for International Training (SIT) in Vermont in the US. He is a founding member of the Dakar Institute of African Studies (DIAS), in Senegal, and an editor of *African Studies Review*. Dr Thiam has also served as an Associate Professor of African-American Studies, African Studies, and French at the Ohio State University, Columbus, in the US. He is the author of *Return to the Kingdom of Childhood: Re-envisioning the Legacy and Philosophical Relevance of Négritude*.

Ndirangu Wachanga is Professor of Media Studies and Information Science at the University of Wisconsin in the US. He is the authorised documentary biographer of Micere Mugo, Wole Soyinka, Ngũgĩ wa Thiong'o, and Ali Mazrui.

Professor Wachanga was a Visiting Professor at Princeton University in the US, and a Carnegie African Diaspora Programme Fellow and Visiting Professor at the United States International University–Africa, in Nairobi, Kenya. His most recent publications include *Ngũgĩ: Reflections of His Life of Writing*; and *Growing Up in a Shrinking World: How Politics, Culture and the Nuclear Age Defined the Biography of Ali A. Mazrui*.

PART 1

INTRODUCTION: THE ROOTS AND ROUTES OF PAN-AFRICANISM

1
———

Pan-Africanism: From the Twin Plagues of European Locusts to Africa's Triple Quest for Emancipation

Adekeye Adebajo

"The Trans-Atlantic slave trade paved the way for colonialism in
several ways. It integrated the economy of several African peoples
into that of the Americas and Europe, and thus into a capitalist
world economy dominated by western Europe ... The overall result
was underdevelopment ... the legacy of wars ensured that Africans
could not unite to protect their interests in the way that Europeans
were able to coordinate their plans for the partition of Africa at the
Congress of Berlin."[1]

J.F. Ade Ajayi, Nigerian historian

"Seek ye first the political kingdom, and all other things will be added unto
it." The famous biblical injunction of Kwame Nkrumah, founding Ghanaian
president and Pan-African prophet, of the 1950s continues to reverberate across
Africa and its diaspora in the Caribbean and the Americas[2] seven decades after
it was first uttered. Having achieved Nkrumah's political kingdom by 1994 with
the liberation of South Africa, Africa and its diaspora found, however, that all
other things were not added unto it. Africans and their descendants are still on
a painful quest for three magic kingdoms: peace and democratic governance;
socio-economic transformation; and cultural equality. This epic griot's tale of
prophets, kings, divas[3] and marabouts will thus focus on the elusive quest of
Africa and its diaspora to attain these three magic kingdoms over the past five
centuries.

3

Pan-Africanism can be defined as the efforts to promote the political, socio-economic and cultural unity, emancipation and self-reliance of Africa and its diaspora. The ideology argues that Africans on the continent and around the globe share a common history and destiny.[4] Pan-Africanists in the Caribbean and the Americas felt physically dispossessed by slavery, while those on the continent felt economically, socially and mentally dislocated through colonialism. They were therefore seeking to affirm their sense of worth and dignity. Blacks in the diaspora had deeply internalised a racism born of four and a half centuries of European slavery, and suffered from a profound sense of low self-esteem and self-loathing. The concept of Pan-Africanism developed amid the sweltering oppression of slavery in the Caribbean and the Americas, and was transported back to Africa by its students who went to study in the US and Europe.[5]

The subject of Pan-African political thought is one that has historically been under-researched. One of the first contemporary attempts to synthesise these ideas into a single volume was the Malian-Frenchman Guy Martin's *African Political Thought*, which was published in 2012.[6] More recently, Hakim Adi, a British historian of Nigerian origin, published *Pan-Africanism: A History* in 2018.[7] Our own book on *The Pan-African Pantheon* covers 36 Pan-African figures, and is similar to Hakim Adi and Marika Sherwood's *Pan-African History: Political Figures from Africa and the Diaspora since 1787* (2003), which covers 40 Pan-African figures.[8] A key difference, however, is that while Adi and Sherwood's very useful compendium has 3–5-page biographical sketches of each of these figures, our volume has more substantive, 15–20-page essays that go beyond the short biographies of these figures to examine the struggles in which they were involved within a broader historical and contemporary context.

Another contemporary volume is African-American scholar, Reiland Rabaka's edited 36-chapter 2020 *Routledge Handbook on Pan-Africanism*.[9] Though comprehensive in its coverage, this book is organised thematically rather than biographically or regionally. It covers issues as broad-ranging and diverse as black internationalism, black feminism, queer Pan-Africanism, black nationalism, Black Consciousness, Africanisation, Afrocentrism, African social movements, and Pan-African aesthetics. The book therefore does not compete directly with our volume which focuses instead on 36 Pan-African figures, and examines their struggles within the fields in which they wrote or were active.

Our volume does not attempt to develop any theory or philosophy of Pan-Africanism. Instead, we set out the history of Pan-Africanism and the evolution, interaction and intellectual ideas and impact of the 36 Pan-African figures covered in this book. We have thus not imposed any theoretical or philosophical framework on any of the authors. The book provides short, readable, multidisciplinary biographical essays about the intellectual thinking and contributions to Pan-Africanist ideals of unity and liberation of these 36 prophets, poets, and philosophers. Even in the Pan-African context, many of these figures have been forgotten, and are not widely studied. The main thrust of this volume is thus to create a Pan-African canon composed of well-known figures and less well-known ones, including many marginalised female figures. This book consistently stresses the importance of African agency, and views history from a Pan-African perspective. The focus on slavery and colonialism in this Introduction is to provide a necessary historical background for undergraduate and graduate students often lacking in such knowledge, and to underline the fact that Pan-Africanism was a reaction to, and outcome of, both slavery and colonialism. The struggle for reparations addressed near the end of the Introduction flows logically from this history of Pan-African emancipation, and the issue of reparations has become one of the major movements that is redefining a new Pan-Africanism.

This book on the Pan-African pantheon has conceptualised Pan-Africanism broadly, and not narrowly. Seventeen of its subjects were pioneers or proponents of Pan-Africanism and would define themselves as Pan-Africanists. The other 19 figures were shaped by Pan-Africanist ideals, whether they were conscious of them or not. They all broadly believed in the dignity of Africans on the continent and its diaspora. Some may argue that figures such as Jamaican-Briton Stuart Hall and St Lucia's Derek Walcott cannot be regarded as Pan-Africanists, but we consider this a parochial and limited understanding of the term since they were both shaped by the ideas and sensibility of their African heritage, even if these were expressed in diverse ways.[10]

This is particularly true after the concept of Pan-Africanism had ceased largely to be part of a civil society-led movement by the 1960s, and had become part of intergovernmental regionalism in Africa. By incorporating issues of race, gender and hegemony into Cultural Studies, and by criticising race prejudice in the Western media, Stuart Hall championed ideas that were intimately connected to causes and issues championed by Pan-Africanists. Likewise, Derek Walcott, a Nobel Prize-winning playwright and poet, wrote lyrical poetry about his native Caribbean that celebrated the beauty and integrity of his African-derived culture. Many Pan-Africanists have embraced his work, as he has embraced theirs. Walcott, in fact, noted that his book *Omeros* "tries to say the same sort of things that [C.L.R.] James said so often, so steadily, before my own generation of writers".[11] Pan-Africanism is thus not a monolithic but a diverse concept, a broad church of many faiths.

We are not necessarily saying that all of our 36 figures are direct proponents of the ideology of Pan-Africanism. We insist, however, that these figures are Pan-Africanists in the sense that they are intellectually and geographically the major figures from Africa and its diaspora in their respective fields of politics, activism, social science, philosophy, literature and music. For example, while not directly espousing Pan-Africanism, Kenyan Nobel peace laureate Wangari Maathai lived it by waging her environmental struggles not just in Kenya, but across East Africa. Egyptian United Nations (UN) secretary-general Boutros Boutros-Ghali may not widely be considered to have been a Pan-Africanist, but he was fiercely outspoken about protecting the continent's security interests as a prophet of Pax Africana. While Nigerian Nobel literature laureate Wole Soyinka may not explicitly have espoused Pan-Africanism as his guiding philosophy, he wrote and preached against autocracy across Africa, and lived for a while in Ghanaian exile while editing the Pan-African journal *Transition*. The Ghanaian-British philosopher Kwame Anthony Appiah, in fact, criticises early Pan-Africanism as essentialist, and the chapter in this book, in turn, critiques Appiah's own approach to Pan-Africanism. But it is still important that Appiah engaged in Pan-African debates as a Ghanaian-Briton based in the diaspora.

This book is particularly timely in seeking to ensure that Pan-African knowledge production forms part of, and influences, mainstream global thinking. It comes at a time of increasing interest in Pan-African thought and Africa's international relations. The volume also responds to current efforts to decolonise university curricula across the globe and to create civil society movements in support of contemporary Pan-Africanism. Diverse and key figures of Pan-Africanism from Africa, the Caribbean and America are covered in these 38 chapters. While acknowledging the contributions of these figures to Pan-Africanism, these essays are not just celebratory, but also critical in areas where their subjects may have fallen short of their ideals.

There are three unique features about this volume. Firstly, as the 38 essays are written by African, Caribbean and African-American scholars largely based in their regions, the book contributes substantively to efforts to transform curricula in all three regions and across the globe; secondly, the book covers 36 major Pan-African figures in a bid to build a contemporary Pan-African canon; and thirdly, the volume encourages a cross-generational dialogue between scholars, as well as between past figures of Pan-Africanism and more contemporary ones with whom current students would already be familiar.

This Introduction begins by tracing the origins of Pan-Africanism historically to the twin scourges of European slavery and colonialism. We argue that the brutal humiliation of these two epic events conducted over five centuries forced Africans to conceive the concept of Pan-Africanism in the Caribbean and the American diaspora, as well as eventually on the mother continent, as a way of coping with, and challenging, the pervasive racism and repression that these two scourges represented. Africa and its diaspora thus embarked on three quests for self-emancipation in the areas of governance and security, economics, and culture. The results of these three continuing quests have been mixed owing to the terrible legacy of the tragic inheritance of Africa and its descendants. Before concluding and summarising the 37 other chapters in the book, we briefly assess the role of contemporary debates on reparations for slavery and colonialism in contributing to rebuilding Pan-Africanism as a civil society movement.

In using the formulation of a mother continent and its African diaspora in this chapter, I diverge from Barbadian scholar Hilary Beckles's idea of "Global Africa" to describe both Africa and its diaspora in order to move away from a "centre–periphery" discourse (see Beckles in this volume). My usage of Africa as mother country does not connote a hierarchical system that places Africa above its diaspora in the Caribbean and the Americas. It is simply the recognition of a historical fact of the origins of these enslaved descendants of Africa. This depiction is, for me, especially appropriate, given the historical disconnection that occurred between Africa and its diaspora when Pan-Africanism returned home in the 1960s. There is still a wide geographical, political, economic and cultural gulf between the continent and its descendants, which we cannot wish away.

I. The Original Sin: Europe's Enslavement of Africa

The Transatlantic Slave Trade

Slavery was undoubtedly Europe's "original sin" against Africa. European locusts – explorers, slavers, merchants, missionaries, imperialists – arrived in Africa in the fifteenth century, and for the next five centuries ravaged the continent. In the process, they spread destructive plague and pestilence. As with the biblical locusts, the agricultural sector, in which most Africans found sustainance, was destroyed; famines proliferated; and the greatest migration in human history was enforced, with enchained human cargo being transported to the Caribbean and the Americas as chattel in totally degrading circumstances. In comparing European slavery to a plague, this phenomenon can be likened in its destructive socio-economic impact to the "Black Death" (1346–53), which killed over 50 million of Medieval Europe's 80 million people: an astonishing 60 per cent of the population.[12] But there is an important difference: while the Black Death was a natural disaster that lasted eight years, the slave trade was a human act that endured for four and a half centuries.

Colonialism was the continuation of slavery by other means, with enslavement dehumanising Africans globally and providing the racist justifications and economic methods to implement alien rule on the basis that Africans could not yet stand on their own feet in the difficult conditions of Western "civilisation". Four and a half centuries of European enslavement of Africans (1450–1888) to work on plantations in the Caribbean and the Americas thus created one of the world's largest diasporas, and flowed seamlessly into a century of European colonisation of the African continent. Both systems involved profit-driven exploitation – cloaked under the perverse justifications of a *mission civilisatrice* – which blamed their African victims for their own misfortunes, while the whole project was legitimised by Western leaders, capitalists, churches and scientists.

Aside from numerous slave revolts in the Caribbean and the Americas, there were many cases of African resistance to European colonialism. One of the most famous was the seventeenth-century Queen Njinga, who ruled the Ndongo kingdom in contemporary Angola for three decades. She bravely resisted Portuguese colonisers through adroit diplomacy and military prowess, and by forging effective alliances.[13] Pan-Africanist movements emerged by the eighteenth century to provide African resistance to the evils of slavery. It was no coincidence that Pan-Africanism was born in the United States and the Caribbean as a response to European slavery. This struggle was led by the descendants of African slaves in the diaspora fighting for both their freedom and that of Africans on the mother continent. The Haitian Revolution, which created the world's first black republic, was achieved in 1804 as a result of a slave revolt.

Between 1450 and 1888, between 12 and 15 million Africans were transported to the Caribbean and the Americas in the notorious transatlantic slave trade. The slavers involved mostly European states, merchants and plantation owners from Britain, France, Portugal, Spain, the Netherlands, Denmark, and Sweden. By the seventeenth century, slaves were being exported by these European nations to work on sugar plantations in Caribbean islands like Jamaica, Cuba, Haiti, Trinidad and Tobago, Martinique and Barbados, as well as South American countries like Brazil, Mexico, Peru and Colombia.

The US, which had been born out of the European genocide of indigenous populations, was also deeply involved in the trade, having inherited sugar and coffee, tobacco and rice-growing slave plantations with 700,000 enslaved people from former British overlords in 1776. Slavery eventually spread through states such as Virginia, Alabama, Mississippi, Texas, South Carolina and Maryland, where cotton plantations were established by the eighteenth century to feed British textile factories. These became the heart of the American economy, greatly enabling its own industrialisation.

These slaves came mostly from contemporary African countries like Senegal, Gambia, Ghana, Nigeria, Benin, Côte d'Ivoire, Mali, Guinea-Bissau, the Democratic Republic of the Congo (DRC), Cameroon, Gabon, Congo-Brazzaville, Angola, Tanzania, Malawi, Mozambique and Zambia. The captives were mostly kidnapped in wars between African kingdoms and principalities, while some had been convicted of domestic crimes of a sometimes dubious nature. About 80 percent of the slaves were exported to the Americas in the eighteenth and early nineteenth century.[14] An estimated 25–35 per cent of these slaves died en route, while about 30 per cent were thrown overboard to their deaths in the Atlantic.[15]

On their arrival in the New World, the slaves were typically branded with a hot iron, given European names, and – in the US especially – often denied the right to speak their own languages or practise indigenous African religions. They were also significantly prevented from learning to read and write. Within three years, 25 to 33 per cent of the slaves taken to Jamaica had died from the inhumane 16–18-hour work days, and few lived for more than nine years, as they were literally worked to death.[16]

Millions of the most productive African men and women (typically between the ages of 15 and 35) were enslaved in their prime, and an entire continent was depopulated of some of its most productive workforce. Africa's population stagnated between 1650 and 1850, with ecological damage caused in some depopulated areas where the tsetse fly forced populations to migrate. African agriculture suffered greatly, and famines increased in some areas, as slave hunters and warriors were prioritised over farmers and entrepreneurs.[17] Slavery effectively arrested human development, socio-economic development and intra-regional trade across Africa. The inhuman trade provided the capital for Europe's and America's industrial revolutions. The West's industrialisation was thus literally built on the back of African slavery.

The Portuguese were among the earliest slave traders from the fifteenth century. Britain, however, soon became the largest slave-trading nation after establishing colonies in the Caribbean and the Americas by the middle of the seventeenth century, along with France, based largely on exports from slave-holding sugar plantations. As they had done in the US, Europeans annihilated most of the indigenous Amerindian population in the Caribbean by the seventeenth century in another historical act of genocide. Britain's Royal African Company was created in 1672, and given a monopoly of the African trade, transporting, on average, 5000 African slaves a year to Caribbean plantations between 1680 and 1686. This monopoly ended 26 years later under pressure from the "plantocracy" of British merchants and planters in the Caribbean, who both pushed for free trade in slaves. In 1750, the Company of Merchants – slave traders based largely in Bristol, London and Liverpool – took over this sordid commerce, and greatly accelerated it. Between 1680 and 1786, over 2 million African slaves were shipped to British colonies in the Caribbean in vessels with names like *Enterprise*, *Fortune* and *Lottery*.[18]

This slave trade laid the foundations of contemporary British industry and banking, and had widespread support within its society. As Trinidadian scholar-politician Eric Williams noted in his seminal 1944 study of slavery and capitalism, until 1783 "the monarchy, the government, the church, [and] public opinion in general supported the slave trade".[19] Slave traders also included British parliamentarians, the Barclay and Baring banking families, and several prominent Boston families in the US such as the Seavers, the Shirleys, the Eustices, the Lamberts and the Welds. The British further supplied an estimated 500,000 slaves to Spanish and French sugar plantations in the Americas. British colonial rivalry with the French in the eighteenth century revolved largely around African slaves and Caribbean sugar. French slave traders operated out of the ports of Nantes, Bordeaux, La Rochelle and Le Havre.

Aside from the Caribbean, a Gallic slave presence was also established on plantations in Mauritius and the Seychelles. European priests blessed slaves boarding vessels. The British government and British churches went along with the planters' insistence on denying slaves the right to religious worship, while Moravian missionaries in Jamaica themselves held slaves. The church also marched in step with the devil in Spanish colonies, being involved in both slave-holding and sugar-growing. But the system of slavery contained the seeds of its own destruction, as the industrial capitalism of the nineteenth century, which had been financed by the proceeds of slavery in the preceding four centuries, rendered the slave trade obsolete.

Although there was internal slavery in African societies, this phenomenon had never formed the basis of the social system, and there was often social mobility within this structure. These were not "slaves" in the European sense in which human beings totally lost their freedom and became the property of slave masters.[20] Though many African chiefs and merchants from kingdoms such as Oyo, Benin, Dahomey and Asante shamefully took part in providing slaves to European slavers and profited from this trade,[21] they were not its main beneficiaries and were a tiny cog in a much larger European wheel. Most African leaders also eventually opposed the slave trade, and some were killed and their territories destroyed for obstructing the trade.[22] The goods that these African traders obtained in exchange for slaves were also often of inferior quality: old pots and kettles, sub-standard gunpowder, cheap gin, trinkets, cloth, and beads.[23]

This was a grossly unequal exchange, and slavery's main profiteers and the trade's initiators and promoters were based in Europe and America, not in Africa. Chiefs who were unwilling to provide slaves were put under tremendous pressure, and European slavers often used force against uncooperative Africans.[24] The insatiable European demand for slaves, in fact, fuelled conflicts in African societies, as chiefs sought to capture prisoners of war to sell into serfdom. Pressure also led to more widespread kidnapping and wider definitions of crime in African societies in order to be able to provide sufficient slaves to satisfy the gluttony of Western slavers.[25]

African Resistance to Slavery

Despite the horrors of the transatlantic "Middle Passage", there were many acts of African resistance during the four and a half centuries of slavery, representing the first stirrings of Pan-Africanism. Mutinies and slave revolts occurred throughout the age of slavery, while many slaves escaped, particularly from the American South to the North. Slave revolts had started in the Americas by 1522. In the Caribbean, the famous Maroon community (descended largely from Ghanaian slaves) resisted British colonialism right from its start in 1655.

They launched major rebellions from their hilltop dwellings in 1673 and 1685, which involved waging guerrilla warfare to destroy plantations and to free slaves. An estimated 400 slave revolts occurred in Jamaica, Britain's richest Caribbean colony. The Maroon War (1729–39) saw local guerrillas launch hit-and-run strikes against British colonisers and their local militias. London was eventually forced to sue for peace, and agreed a treaty allowing the Maroons to continue ruling themselves in their enclaves – and not shelter escaped slaves – in exchange for a British pledge not to enslave them.[26]

There was another major confrontation in Jamaica in 1760 when over a thousand slaves confronted the British planters for six months, resulting in the killing of about 60 whites and the execution of an estimated 600 slaves. The second Maroon War erupted in 1795 when London sought to renege on the previous accord. The Maroons again killed members of the local British-backed militia, and 556 Maroons were deported to Canada. There were three major slave rebellions in Jamaica, Suriname and St Vincent in the early 1770s; the Bussa rebellion was staged in Barbados in 1816, while other slave rebellions took place in Trinidad and Tobago in 1819, 1825 and 1829, and in Antigua and Jamaica in 1831.

The success of the Haitian Revolution (1791–1804) gave enslaved African populations throughout the Caribbean and the Americas a sense of dignity and self-worth, and struck great fear in white plantation owners throughout the hemisphere. This was the most famous black rebellion, and the only successful one, which created the first black republic in the world and only the second free country in the Americas. At the same time as European revolutionaries were rising up against the absolutist rule of monarchs in countries like France, Haitian revolutionaries were rising up against the arbitrary and brutal reign of terror of French and Spanish slave masters. The revolt was led by such figures as Toussaint L'Ouverture and Jean-Jacques Dessalines. The Trinidadian author C.L.R. James memorialised the revolution in his seminal book, *The Black Jacobins* (1938).[27] Several thousand African Americans migrated to Haiti from Philadelphia and other cities soon after the revolt. On the cultural front, Haitians also used their African roots to develop the religion of Voodoo, which was employed to assist the revolution.

In the US, slave revolts took place throughout the 246-year period of the existence of this institution. A large rebellion occurred in Virginia in 1800. Twenty-two years later, slaves revolted in South Carolina. In 1831 the African-American preacher Nat Turner's slave rebellion in Virginia became the bloodiest black revolt in American history, killing over 60 whites, before being halted and its perpetrators executed. The draconian Fugitive Slave Act of 1850 forced Americans in the slave-free North to hand over any escaped slaves to their Southern masters, thus making free blacks vulnerable to kidnapping and enslavement. The notorious 1857 *Dred Scott* decision saw the US Supreme Court argue that black slaves were not American citizens, and upheld the Fifth Amendment, which stated that the enslaved were the property of their owners. About 500,000 slaves risked their lives to escape from Southern plantations to the North during the American Civil War (1861–65), with an estimated 200,000 joining the Union army. During their own war of independence, blacks suffered about 40,000 fatalities.[28]

African-American abolitionist Harriet Tubman was born into slavery in the American South, but escaped in 1849 by walking a hundred miles from Maryland to Pennsylvania. She then joined the Anti-Slavery Society to become a "conductor" on the Underground Railroad: an intricate network used by escaping slaves. She returned 19 times to free at least 70 slaves. During the American Civil War, Tubman became the first female commander, leading an all-black battalion to free over 700 slaves in South Carolina. The pioneering activist also campaigned for women's rights as part of the suffragette movement.

In the Americas, there was also widespread resistance to slavery. A large slave rebellion took place in Cuba in 1812, while over 200 Muslim slaves in the Brazilian city of Salvador – inspired by the Haitian Revolution – staged the Revolt of the Malê in 1835.

The Cultural Impact of Slaves on Societies in the Americas

Resistance to slavery also took cultural forms. Kenyan scholar Micere Mugo has highlighted the importance of orature – the art of the spoken word – which was used by artists and activists to bring about social change in society. As she noted: "When Africans were taken into slavery in the Americas and the Caribbean islands, they not only utilised orature across the Middle Passage to resist and survive terror, but recreated it, emerging with new oratures that spoke to the realities they were encountering and wrestling with under enslavement. Song, dance, music, stories, myths, legends, proverbs, ritual incantations and oracy were the most commonly used genres ..."[29]

Much of this orature was reflected in the "Negro" spirituals characteristic especially of slaves in the American South and captured so eloquently by

W.E.B. Du Bois in his book *The Souls of Black Folk* (1903).[30] Such songs as "Go Down, Moses", "Deep River" and "Swing Low, Sweet Chariot" evoked slaves seeking succour in Christian tales of deliverance from the bondage of autocratic European pharaohs. These lamentations thus represented a call for a black Moses to lead Africans from the clutches of slavery back to the Promised Land of their ancestral homelands.[31] As African-American intellectual Amiri Baraka noted: "blues could not exist if the African captives had not become American captives."[32] Blues and jazz both emerged directly from slavery, based on the rhythmic West African traditional work songs that the slaves sang on the Southern plantations. The improvisational nature of jazz is also tied to this same slave culture.[33] It is no exaggeration to note that America's popular music, from jazz to Motown to hip-hop and rap, had its roots in this slave tradition. It is also no surprise that some of the saddest people in the world invented the singing of the blues, underlining African-American writer Maya Angelou's insight about "why the caged bird sings".[34]

On the cultural front, slaves in Jamaica sought, to the extent possible under these difficult circumstances, to maintain their African cultures by enacting religious rituals and by reciting folktales. Slaves believed that they would return to the ancestral homeland after death, and their funeral rites involved African drumming, dancing and singing. The practice of African religions was eventually banned in Jamaica. Black Baptist preachers, however, emerged by the eighteenth century, and African religions were then often incorporated into their preaching, while literacy among slaves was increasingly encouraged.

The slave system in countries like Brazil and Cuba was, in some aspects, less repressive than in the US, in the sense that slaves were frequently allowed to remain with their families and ethnic groups, and could buy their freedom more easily. This enabled them to retain more of their African cultures. Portuguese-ruled Brazil imported about 5.1 million slaves, the largest number in the Americas. Cuba imported about 778,000 enslaved people, which was the largest for any Spanish colony. Both countries thus accounted for around 40 per cent of all Africans who were forcibly transported during the transatlantic slave trade.[35] Slavery was only abolished in Cuba and Brazil in 1886 and 1888 respectively, and both countries used slaves to produce sugar and coffee. Most of these slaves came from West and Central Africa, bringing traditional religions that were later fused with Catholicism. In both countries, slaves were baptised, and many joined Catholic lay brotherhoods.[36]

In Brazil, plantations had been established from Rio de Janeiro to Porto Alegre, and enslaved populations produced much of the crafts in the country.[37]

14

African cultures greatly influenced Brazilian religion, the arts, literature, music and social institutions, and in 2020 the over 100 million black and brown Brazilians represented the third-largest black population in the world after Nigeria and Ethiopia. Yoruba cosmology and *orishas* (deities) like Obatala, Sango, Ogun and Yemoja were fused with Catholic saints to form the Afro-Brazilian religion of Candomblé, which is still strongly practised in 1,100 temples across Salvador, the capital of the black-majority Bahia state. The Brazilian music and dance form of Capoeira was also originated by African slaves, who used it as a disguised form of self-defence. In 1832, the Society for the Protection of the Needy was founded by free black Brazilian slaves as a civil society movement, which purchased the freedom of fellow enslaved people. But, despite the prominence of black Brazilian footballers such as Pelé, Garrincha and Ronaldinho, impoverished *favelas* (ghettos) like Rio de Janeiro's "City of God" – immortalised in a 2002 movie – in which a disproportionate number of blacks live, are a constant reminder of the racial inequalities that continue to prevail in this mythical "racial democracy". Affirmative action programmes for blacks in Brazilian universities were only initiated in 2003.[38]

In Cuba, slaves worked plantations, from Havana province to La Isabelica. These African slaves contributed to national religions such as Santeria, Palo-Monte and Voodoo, with African deities – as in Brazil – fused with Catholic saints to produce a Cuban national identity. The Abakuá male secret society (originating from south-west Cameroon and Nigeria's Old Calabar) became one of the country's most important social institutions. Its members were prominent in social events like carnivals, and many of these black Abakuá took part in rebellions and other demonstrations throughout the nineteenth century.[39] Enslaved individuals fought in Cuba's war of independence (1868–78), but were marginalised after the war by a racist Spanish-descended elite. African religious and cultural expressions were banned until the 1920s, when *son* music – a blend of African percussions and vocals, with Spanish strings – became popular again. Afro-Cubans benefited from Fidel Castro's 1959 revolution in terms of free education and health care, but prejudice against blacks still remains rife.[40]

Despite four and a half centuries of European dehumanisation and the enslavement of Africans on their continent and in the Caribbean and the Americas, these African slaves showed incredible resilience just to have survived these horrors. Not only did they survive, however, they also left an indelible mark on the mainstream cultures of countries across the Western hemisphere.

15

II. The Curse of Berlin: European Colonisation of Africa[41]

The link between slavery and colonialism is inextricable. European powers perfected the system of colonial rule in the Caribbean and the Americas during three centuries of slavery, before formally applying it to Africa for a century.

Bismarck's Sorcery and Africa's Century of Pestilence

Africa suffers from a curse invoked in Berlin. The Berlin Conference of 1884–5, which was overseen by German Chancellor Otto von Bismarck, dealt with the issue of free trade in the Congo and the Niger as well as the status of protectorates, effectively setting the rules for the partition of Africa. Berlin represented the compromises of avaricious European imperialists rather than the political and economic interests of Africans. The European curse of artificial nation-states has thus caused untold suffering in post-colonial Africa – and the Caribbean – resulting in unviable, dependent economies, artificially imported political systems, weak and Balkanised states, and insecure borders.

Bismarck was undoubtedly the Grand Wizard of the Berlin Conference. The effect of his colonial policies was that the German sorcerer and his European apprentices employed the Western wizardry of the technology of the Industrial Revolution – scientific and technological advances, mass production of goods, global finance, expansion of railways and roads, the telegraph and the Maxim gun – to set the rules for the "Scramble for Africa". Bismarck used his political magic wand to cast a spell on Africa, having earlier done the same in Europe. The German Chancellor united Germany and Europe, while dividing Africa.[42]

Bismarck's quarrels with London were also a way of Berlin getting closer to Paris. German industrialists advocated a German Reich (empire) in Africa as a means for the country to relocate its surplus population abroad, in an early incarnation of Adolf Hitler's *Lebensraum* (living space) argument for the conquest of Eastern Europe. In the British context, the imperialist businessman-politician Cecil Rhodes also championed the idea of acquiring African colonies to settle surplus British populations and to create new markets for British goods.[43] If German unification had been a question of "blood and iron", the European partition of Africa was one of "blood and treasure".

The Conference of Berlin

The "New Imperialism" that erupted into the "Scramble for Africa" by the 1880s was often described in terms of a game that frequently appeared to be played by petulant and pampered public schoolboys in the English tradition. Bismarck often talked derisively of the *Kolonialtummel* (the colonial whirl), while the French talked of *le grand jeu* (the great game). By the time the gun was fired before the dawn of the "Naughty Nineties", avaricious *fin de siècle* European imperialists were pursuing the "race to Fashoda", "blind man's bluff", the colonial "steeplechase", and the "gambler's kick". They sought their own "place in the sun", an African sun that, it was said, would never set on the British Empire. This imperial drama involved squabbling colonial governments; devious explorers of Africa's four great river systems – the Niger, the Zambezi, the Nile and the Congo – like Heinrich Barth, David Livingstone, Henry Stanley and Pierre Savorgnan de Brazza; vicious capitalist-politicians like Cecil Rhodes and Belgium's King Léopold; and sanctimonious Christian missionaries too numerous to mention. As has often been noted, Africa was conquered by the white man carrying the Bible in one hand and the gun in the other.

Africa was notoriously declared a *res nullius* – a no man's land – by European imperialists. Since the continent was inhabited by "uncivilised savages" who were considered subhuman by many European leaders and scholars, the land could simply be seized and exploited by white colonialists. As German-American political philosopher Hannah Arendt succinctly noted in 1968: "Imperialism would have necessitated the invention of racism as the only possible 'explanation' and excuse for its deeds, even if no race-thinking had ever existed in the civilised world."[44]

British explorer David Livingstone described colonialism in the apparently benign terms of the "three Cs": Commerce, Christianity and Civilisation. The more malign "three Ps" may, in fact, have been more accurate: Profit, Plunder and Prestige. As English poet Hilaire Belloc so memorably put it: "Whatever happens, we have got the Maxim gun, and they have not."[45]

As late as 1880, very few African territories had come under direct European rule (though Portugal had occupied Angola since 1575), and 80 per cent of the continent was still ruled by its own leaders. In 1880, the French colonised Algeria.[46] A year later, Paris declared a "protectorate" over Tunisia, and a year later over Porto-Novo in Dahomey (now Benin).[47] The British occupied

Egypt in 1882. Even before sending out invitations to the Berlin Conference in October 1884, Bismarck himself had extended the *Reichsschutz* (the protection of the Reich) to South West Africa (now Namibia) and acquired that territory along with Cameroon and Togo by August 1884. A day after the end of the Berlin Conference in February 1885, he acquired German East Africa: clear evidence, if any were needed, that the Berlin Conference was indeed about how to ensure an orderly partition of Africa.

That conference began in snow-filled Berlin in November 1884. Fourteen largely Western powers (Germany, France, Britain, Portugal, Belgium, Spain, Italy, Russia, Austria-Hungary, the United States, Denmark, Sweden/Norway, the Netherlands and Turkey) attended the meeting. This conference, at which Africa's fate was effectively sealed, was held at Bismarck's official residence in Wilhelmstrasse. Significantly, no African representatives were present around the horseshoe table, even as delegates discussed the continent's future with a map of Africa in the background of the room.[48]

Echoing Livingstone, Germany's "Iron Chancellor" disingenuously argued that the conference aimed to promote the "civilisation" of the "natives" by opening up Africa's interior to commerce and Christianity. He outlined the three main goals of the meeting: to promote free trade in the Congo, ensure free navigation of the Congo and the Niger, and agree on rules for the future annexation of African territories. One of the most significant outcomes of the Berlin Conference was the German Chancellor's successful support of Belgian King Léopold's annexation of the Congo. This triggered the start of one of the most sordid episodes in European imperialism, with widespread atrocities and forced labour on rubber plantations overseen by Belgian colonial authorities, resulting in an estimated 10 million African deaths.[49] On the final issue of setting rules for the "effective occupation" of African territories, the conferees agreed that this term should apply only to coastal areas and exclude protectorates. The General Act of Berlin was thus sealed in February 1885.

This landmark conference would prove to be a watershed in African history: it had set the rules for trade, navigation and control of Africa to avoid conflicts among European nations. Berlin had fired the starting gun for the imperial partition, and in the next two and a half decades almost the entire landmass of Africa would be parcelled out among European powers. Berlin represented an avaricious banquet at which gluttonous European imperialists feasted on territories that clearly did not belong to them. They sought in the process to cloak the fraudulent scheme under the patronising and paternalistic moral platitudes of a "civilising" mission.

It would be hard to find examples in world history in which a single meeting had such devastating political, socio–economic and cultural consequences for an entire continent. As the *Lagos Observer* noted in February 1885: "The world has perhaps never witnessed until now such highhanded a robbery on so large a scale. Africa is helpless to prevent it … It is on the cards that this 'Christian' business can only end, at no distant date, in the annihilation of the natives."[50] In similar vein, Nigerian nationalist leader Herbert Macaulay noted in 1905: "The dimensions of the 'true interests of the natives at heart' are algebraically equal to the length, breadth and depth of the whiteman's pocket."[51]

III. Long Walk to Freedom: Pan-Africanism Returns Home

It is important to note that it was the cumulative efforts, over nearly two centuries, of Pan-African activists, which began in the diaspora that would eventually liberate Africa and the Caribbean from European enslavement and colonial rule, and lay the foundation for the successful African-American struggle for civil rights. The fact that the Pan-Africanist movement was born in 1900, 15 years after the partition of the continent was sealed and 24 years after black Americans had had their civic rights revoked after the brief period of Reconstruction, was no coincidence.[52]

This section examines the emancipation efforts of Pan-African activists from the eighteenth century, focusing particular attention on Edward Blyden, widely considered to have been the greatest theoretician of Pan-Africanism. We then assess the Pan-African Conference of 1900, and the five Pan-African Congresses between 1919 and 1945, which led to the movement being handed over from Africans in the diaspora to Africans on the continent.

The Emergence of Pan-African Civil Society

Pan-African civil society activism can be traced back to the 1770s, when an African Baptist Church movement became active in the US state of Georgia, in the Caribbean and in Canada, seeking to challenge the pervasive racism towards Africans around the globe. In 1773, Phillis Wheatley, a former slave purchased from West Africa by a Boston family, became the first African-American woman to publish a book of poetry which was widely read, and helped to promote a more positive image of the black world.[53] As she wrote:

> Some view our sable race with scornful eye
> Their colour is a diabolical die'.
> Remember Christians, Negros black as Cain
> May be refin'd, and join th' angelic train.[54]

In the 1780s, Olaudah Equiano and Ottobah Cugoano – former Nigerian and Ghanaian slaves, respectively – established the Sons of Africa organisation in Britain to campaign for the abolition of slavery. They lobbied the British parliament, wrote in newspapers, and worked with like-minded groups. In the American city of Boston, African-American activist Prince Hall established the first African Masonic lodge in North America in 1784 to fight racism in the US, and to build bridges to Africa. By 1787, an African Church movement – eventually involving the African Methodist Episcopal (AME) Church – had emerged out of Richard Allen and Absalom Jones's Free Africa Society in Philadelphia and Baltimore. By 1793, George Liele had established the Ethiopian Baptist Church in Jamaica. All these civil society groups sought actively to challenge racist Western views of Africans, and to portray a positive image of their homeland.[55]

Emigration from the Americas to Africa also increased, with former slave Thomas Peters leading a thousand freed slaves from Canada to the new British colony of Sierra Leone in 1792. An estimated 8000 Afro–Brazilians and Afro–Cubans also made the reverse trip across the Atlantic back to West African cities like Lagos and Porto-Novo. The creation of Fourah Bay College in Freetown by 1867 further attracted university students from across West Africa, helping to forge a sense of Pan-Africanism.[56]

Blyden as Pan-Negro Prophet

One of the most significant figures in Pan-Africanism, who came to symbolise its return to the ancestral continent, was Edward Wilmot Blyden. His Trinidadian-American biographer Hollis Lynch described Blyden as "the greatest Negro champion of his race in the nineteenth century".[57] Originally from St Thomas, which was part of the Caribbean colony of the Danish Virgin Islands (now the US Virgin Islands), Blyden trained as a priest, but was denied entry into American theological schools. He thus emigrated to Liberia where he became a scholar-diplomat and educationist, also living in Sierra Leone. One of the advantages that Blyden had over later Pan-African prophets like W.E.B. Du Bois and Marcus Garvey was that his ideas were based on actual lived experiences on the continent, often leading to more nuanced perspectives. With his priestly background, Blyden promoted Africa's regeneration through often patronising Christian "civilisation".

The scholar-activist has sometimes been referred to as the "father of Pan-Africanism" and is widely considered to have been the single most important conceptualiser of the ideology. His two most important ideas were of a triple African heritage of Christianity, Islam and indigenous cultures;[58] and of a unique "African Personality". Blyden was also a forerunner of regional integration in West Africa, calling for its territories to form a federation, though under British and American tutelage. He championed the concept of "Ethiopianism", which envisioned an African regeneration based on biblical Scriptures. As Blyden noted, "Africa may yet prove to be the spiritual conservatory of the world."[59] Ethiopianism urged African Americans in the diaspora to return to Africa to help develop the continent. This idea was also linked to Abyssinia's historic role as an independent African kingdom which would later defeat an Italian army at the Battle of Adowa in 1896.

Blyden was further credited with developing the concept of the "African Personality", which he saw as "the sum of values of African civilisation, the body of qualities which make up the distinctiveness of the people of Africa".[60] Through this concept, African cultures would take their equal place among global cultures, African people would make a unique contribution to the world, and Africans would rediscover their own soul by returning to their indigenous values. As Blyden somewhat patronisingly put it: "if we are to make an independent nation – a strong nation – we must listen to the songs of our unsophisticated brethren as they sing of their history, as they tell of their traditions, of the wonderful and mysterious events of their tribal or national life, of their achievement of what we call their superstitions".[61] These ideas of "African Personality" were credited by later prophets of Négritude like Senegal's Léopold Senghor as having provided the intellectual foundations for their ideology in the 1930s.

Blyden also strongly believed in the European *mission civilisatrice*, talking – in the context of African-American-led Liberia incorporating Asante and Dahomey – of bringing "those barbarous tribes under civilized and enlightened influences".[62] He further bizarrely saw the early years of slavery as positive in "civilising" Africans, and condoned the atrocities of King Léopold in the

Congo, insisting that the Belgian king was a philanthropist. Blyden encouraged the partition of Africa by European powers, and collaborated with these powers.[63] Despite these flaws, he made a tremendous intellectual contribution to the development of Pan-Africanism, and had a great influence on African nationalists such as J.E. Casely Hayford, John Mensah Sarbah, Samuel Ajayi Crowther, Mojola Agbebi and Nnamdi Azikiwe.

The Pan-African Conference, 1900

Fifteen years after the Berlin Conference of 1884–5, the Pan-African movement was born when Trinidadian lawyer-prophet Henry Sylvester Williams – who is credited with having coined the terms "Pan-African" and "Pan-Africanism"[64] – became the moving force behind the first Pan-African Conference in Westminster Town Hall in London in July 1900. Williams had founded the African Association in London in September 1897 to lobby the British parliament and public opinion to oppose the violence of European colonial rule in Africa, the lynching of black men in America and the economic exploitation of the Caribbean.[65] He was assisted by an African-American bishop of the AME Zion Church, Alexander Walters. By this time, African-American and Caribbean churches were also inspiring Africa's Ethiopian Church movement to set up their own independent churches on the continent.

The 1900 London Conference was the occasion where African-American scholar-activist W.E.B. Du Bois uttered the remarkably prescient prophecy: "The problem of the twentieth century is the problem of the colour line."[66] The attendees of the conference from the US, the Caribbean, and Africa addressed a message to Queen Victoria at the end of their deliberations, complaining about the ill treatment of blacks in South Africa and Rhodesia. They also farsightedly called for reparations to Africa and Africans for slavery and colonialism, self-government, and recognition of the rights of women. Two African-American female activists – Catherine Impey and Jane Cobden Unwin – spoke at the conference.

The Five Pan-African Congresses, 1919–1945

Between 1919 and 1945, five Pan-African Congresses took place in various European capitals and New York, with W.E.B. Du Bois as the moving spirit.[67] The powerful Western media mostly heaped derision and ridicule on these efforts.[68] The First Pan-African Congress was held in Paris in February 1919, simultaneously with the Versailles Peace Conference after the First World War. Du Bois was a dominant figure in Paris, along with the Senegalese-born French parliamentarian Blaise Diagne, and the 57 delegates also comprised black American soldiers and black African public office-holders in the French government. The Congress called for the abolition of slave labour and the passing of laws to protect Africans and their land, and demanded that Africans have the right to education and to take part in their own government.[69]

Even as the supposedly liberal, but deeply prejudiced, American president Woodrow Wilson,[70] meeting with European statesmen in Versailles to redraw the map of Europe after the First World War, passionately championed the right to self-determination of subjugated Central European minorities, Pan-Africanists meeting nearby sought to remind him of his denial of the most basic rights to his own African-American subjects, whom he steadfastly refused to acknowledge as full citizens.

The Paris Pan-African Congress of 1919 occurred at a time when Jamaica's Marcus Garvey – "the Black Moses" and one of Pan-Africanism's most charismatic, colourful, and controversial figures – was mobilising huge crowds of black Americans in New York's Harlem and across the country with his "Back to Africa" movement and his evocative slogan of "Africa for the Africans." Garvey, through his Universal Negro Improvement Association and African Communities League (UNIA-ACL), proclaimed himself to be the "Provisional President of a Racial Empire in Africa". He met with the Ku Klux Klan, and was jailed after money from his Black Star shipping line was misappropriated. He died in London in June 1940 and, being blocked by European colonial powers, ironically never visited the Africa to which he had enthusiastically urged his followers to emigrate.[71] In a remarkable act of national restitution, Jamaica transported Garvey's remains back from London to Kingston in November 1964, and gave him a befitting state funeral.[72] He is now regarded as a national hero and has a huge following among Jamaica's Rastafarian movement. Garvey also inspired Kwame Nkrumah to use the colours of his Black Star shipping line to design Ghana's post-independence flag and to name its soccer team.

The Second Pan-African Congress took place simultaneously in London and Brussels in August–September 1921, with the main demand made on behalf of the "Negro race" by "their thinking intelligentsia" being "local self-government for backward groups". This language again underlined the patronising mindset of the movement's middle-class diaspora leaders. Du Bois himself was not free of some of these prejudices, often describing Africans as "backward peoples" in need of a *mission civilisatrice*.[73] Demands in London and Brussels also included establishing indigenous political institutions and democracy. The Third Pan-African Congress took place simultaneously in London and Lisbon in November 1923. The meetings mainly called for Africans to "have a voice" in running their own affairs. The Fourth Pan-African Congress was held in New York in August 1927. It was at this meeting that the towering intellectual prophet of Pan-Africanism, Trinidad's George Padmore, lambasted white communists for trying to discredit black Pan-African organisations that they could not control.[74]

By the time of the Fifth Pan-African Congress in Manchester in October 1945, the movement had shifted its centre of gravity from the diaspora to Africa. The conference was now dominated by future African "kings" like Ghana's Kwame Nkrumah, Kenya's Jomo Kenyatta, and Malawi's Hastings Banda. Other Africans in Manchester included Joe Appiah (Ghana); Obafemi Awolowo, Jaja Wachuku, H.O. Davies and S.L. Akintola (Nigeria); Wallace Johnson (Sierra Leone); Peter Abrahams and Mark Hlubi (South Africa). George Padmore was the major organiser of the congress with Kwame Nkrumah, while his fellow Trinidadian, C.L.R. James, and Jamaica's Amy Ashwood Garvey also participated. Among the 200 delegates were representatives of African trade unions, farmers, cooperative societies and students.[75]

Africans were now speaking directly for themselves in a Western idiom of self-determination, and their demands were unequivocal: immediate self-government and independence for African states, and the waging of armed struggles to liberate colonial territories, if necessary. A policy of non-alignment with East and West was declared, as well as a call for the liberation of both Africa and Asia from the European colonial yoke.[76] At Manchester, the 77-year-old Du Bois symbolically passed the torch of Pan-Africanism to a 35-year-old Nkrumah. Both Du Bois and George Padmore subsequently worked as advisers to Nkrumah's government in independent Ghana after 1957, living out their last days in the country where both now lie buried.

The major European imperial powers – Britain and France – were exhausted and vastly weakened by the Second World War (1939-1945), and two new superpowers – the US and the Soviet Union – emerged, employing anti-colonial rhetoric to find converts to their competing ideologies. India's independence in 1947 set off an inevitable chain reaction for the liberation of Asia and Africa. The historic struggles in the 1950s of Mau Mau rebels in Kenya and Algerian freedom fighters against brutal British and French imperialists, were significant events that signalled the impending demise of colonialism in Africa.

Three Competing Visions of Pan-Africanism: Nkrumah, Nyerere and Senghor

Pan-Africanism moved from Manchester back to Africa, and became mostly an ideology of governments and no longer one of civil society. A historic battle was waged for its soul between a "radical" Casablanca minority bloc led by Kwame Nkrumah (and also including Guinea, Mali, Egypt, Algeria and Morocco), and the majority of more conservative African states, grouped in the Brazzaville and Monrovia blocs, whose leaders favoured a more gradualist approach to continental unity. Nkrumah called for a "United States of Africa" by Africans for Africans, in which countries would pool their sovereignty in the areas of economics, security and foreign policy as a way of achieving industrialisation. The Ghanaian leader envisaged a continental authority to oversee integrated planning and transport systems, and advocated the building of a vast road and railway network, a great increase in air links, and a massive upgrading of continental ports. Nkrumah regarded the association agreement between francophone African countries and the French-led European Common Market as "collective colonialism" designed to make Africa a permanent supplier of primary products for European markets. He called instead for the establishment of an African Common Market with a common currency and a common policy for intra-African and extra-continental trade.[77]

An alternative vision to Nkrumah's was provided by Tanzania's socialist leader, Julius "Mwalimu" (Teacher) Nyerere. He offered the most cogent intellectual opposition to Nkrumah in calling for a more gradualist approach to regional integration involving the use of sub-regional bodies such as East Africa's British-inherited federal institutions as building blocks, before federating with a larger continental group. As Nyerere noted: "African unity is at present merely an emotion born of a history of colonialism and oppression. It has to be strengthened and expressed in economic and political forms before it can really have a positive effect on the future."[78] Though, like Nkrumah, Nyerere also advocated a federal "United States of Africa" as a final goal, he kept stressing – unlike the impatient Nkrumah – the need to convince newly sovereign countries, through patient persuasion, to take the necessary steps for integration willingly, and argued that they be allowed to travel at their own pace, and be given the space for local self-expression. Nyerere thus urged an approach of what in more contemporary terms would be called "variable geometry" in which different forms of integration occurred in different sub-regions. He focused on a federation of Tanzania, Kenya and Uganda as a first step towards attaining a United States of Africa.[79]

A third vision of Pan-African cooperation was provided by francophone leaders like the Senegalese poet-president Léopold Senghor. He advocated cooperation on economic, financial, cultural, technical and scientific issues, while pursuing minimalist political cooperation in which African states harmonised their foreign policies. Insisting that Africa must not be placed out of a global historical context, Senghor argued that "Colonialism has had its dark moments and its moments of light. If it destroyed some of the values of our civilization, Europe sometimes brought its substitutes, almost always fertile ones: *complementary* ones."[80] Unlike Nkrumah, Senghor was prepared to see positive aspects in colonialism and to attempt a synthesis between Africa and Europe. For the Ghanaian leader, however, colonialism was the very antithesis of everything that African liberation stood for.

Senghor suggested that Europe might have destroyed African values, but for him it also brought technical skills to Africa. Where Nkrumah urged Africa to harness its own resources for development, Senghor promoted a pragmatic use of European – in this case, French – financial resources and scientific knowledge to promote socio-economic development. He insisted on seeing the former European colonial rulers as "our friends", and proudly touted the fact that Senegalese students, soldiers, civil servants, agriculturists, engineers, doctors and veterinary surgeons were sent to France for training. Such views often left many francophone leaders – seemingly championing a subservient system of *Françafrique* – vulnerable to charges of neo-colonialism. Most of these countries supported French policies in multilateral forums, even on issues involving the liberation of Algeria. In an unsubtle dig at Nkrumah, Senghor urged the need to avoid demagoguery and threats of violence.[81]

Nkrumah's vision of a "Union Government of African States" would have involved a common currency and monetary zone, an African military command, and a common foreign policy. In May 1963, 32 African states met in the ancient Ethiopian empire's capital of Addis Ababa to sign the Organisation of African Unity (OAU) Charter, which clearly reflected the triumph of Nyerere's gradualist, evolutionary path over the speedy, revolutionary course that had been proposed by Nkrumah. The document rendered the OAU's executive and administrative branches ineffective by according them only limited powers.[82] As these states struggled to transform themselves into viable nations, the link between Pan-Africanism and civil society was broken, and the Caribbean and

American diasporas were effectively abandoned as an ally of solidarity and development. Resolutions of the OAU Assembly were not legally binding, and the body lacked implementation mechanisms. Diallo Telli, the genial Guinean technocrat and prophet and first substantive OAU secretary-general between 1964 and 1972, noted that Pan-Africanism had been born into an atmosphere of "complete alienation, physical exploitation and spiritual torment".[83] Telli would himself be starved to death in monarchical Guinean leader Sékou Touré's prison in March 1977.

But despite its shortcomings, the OAU deserves some credit for its firm and consistent commitment to decolonisation and the anti-apartheid struggles in southern Africa, to which the African diaspora in the US, the Caribbean and Europe contributed massively. The continental body doggedly and uncompromisingly pursued African liberation struggles, furnishing military and diplomatic support to the continent's liberation movements.

IV. Africans, African Americans, and the Avuncular Sam[84]

Before assessing the quest of Africa and its diaspora for emancipatory governance and security, economic transformation, and cultural equality, we next turn our attention to the crucial historical and contemporary role of African Americans in influencing American policy towards their ancestral homeland. In 2019 black Americans made up about 13 per cent of the US population, constituting 42 million out of 328.2 million people.

The Flawed "Founding Fathers"

America's deeply flawed slave-owning "Founding Fathers" George Washington and Thomas Jefferson pushed forcefully for the repatriation of black Americans to the Caribbean and Africa, and never regarded them as full citizens to be integrated into US society.[85] Repatriation movements sprang up in the early nineteenth century urging skilled blacks to return to Africa to develop the continent, and escape the suffocating racism of the US. Inspired by the 1804 Haitian Revolution, self-made black Boston-based businessman Paul Cuffe – working with Daniel Coker, Lott Cary and John Russwurm – funded the repatriation of 38 black Americans to Sierra Leone in 1815. But this was not – as with Marcus Garvey – an appeal for mass emigration but for elite emigration to provide an "enlightened" leadership class for African nations.

The American Colonization Society (ACS) – financed largely by slave-holders who feared the impact of freed slaves on their black workers – had transported the first black American settlers of largely freed slaves from the antebellum American South, to Liberia between 1822 and 1847, when the independent republic was declared. An Americo-Liberian oligarchy, constituting only 5 per cent of the population, established an oppressive autocracy that repressed the indigenous Liberian population. A bloody *coup d'état* in 1980 by low-ranking soldiers, led by Master-Sergeant Samuel Doe, would eventually topple this ruling clique.

Abraham Lincoln and other American politicians who supported the ACS had naively hoped that this might resolve their own country's racial problems. Lincoln – often portrayed in hagiographic accounts by American scholars as the "Great Emancipator" of slaves – had asked the US Congress for funds to repatriate Africans to Central America. As he told a black delegation to the White House in August 1862: "Your race suffers greatly, many of them, by living among us, while ours suffer from your presence. In word we suffer on each side. If this is admitted, it affords a reason why we should be separated."[86]

Emerging Black Civil Society

Black civil society movements in America developed throughout the nineteenth century to champion the Pan-African cause: the African Methodist Episcopal Church, the Free Africa Society and the Africa Society. The AME Church had created a branch in Pretoria, South Africa, in 1896, while the African-American National Baptist Church provided scholarships to students from southern Africa to study at black colleges in the US. These civil society efforts to tackle racism in South Africa would be mirrored by the prominent African-American role in the anti-apartheid struggle seven decades later.

Martin Robinson Delany led the Emigrationist movement in the nineteenth century, travelling to West Africa in 1859 with Robert Campbell, and advocating the "regeneration of Africa" through its children in the diaspora. As Delany put it: "Africa for the African race and black men to rule them."[87] Delany also had the vision of a railroad being built from East to West Africa. Even before Cecil Rhodes's idea of a railway line from the Cape to Cairo, more genuine Pan-Africanists had visions of uniting the continent through peaceful means, rather than through imperial wars of conquest. Alexander Crummell, a Christian evangelist, who founded the American Negro Academy in 1897, compared African slavery to the Babylonian bondage of the Jews, though he also talked of Africa and Africans being covered in "gross darkness".[88] Bishop Henry McNeal Turner of the AME Church also pushed forcefully for African-American emigration to the motherland, on the grounds that "Africa is shrouded in heathen darkness".[89] These advocates for Africa sometimes adopted a patronising Western "civilising mission" towards Africa, demonstrating the totalising hegemony of Western culture.

The post-American Civil War Reconstruction era (1865-1877) saw much progress for the four million African Americans in the form of holding political office, as blacks were rewarded especially for the brave role that their military regiments had played in reuniting the country. Socio-economic progress stalled, however, with President Andrew Jackson reneging on the government's promise of "40 acres and a mule", leading to the reversal of voting rights in much of the South, and widespread penury and a return to virtual slave labour for many blacks.[90] An estimated 4,000 black Americans were lynched in the South between 1877 and 1950.[91]

From Chicago to the Congressional Black Caucus

The Chicago Congress on Africa was held in the "Windy City" in 1893, and attended by such leading black figures as Frederick Douglass, Alexander Crummell and Henry McNeal Turner. Their approach was very much about promoting Western "civilisation" and commerce in Africa. Two years later, a similar Congress was held in Atlanta, at which Liberian female activist Etna Holderness delivered a speech. This second meeting occurred just five years before the Pan-African Conference in London in 1900 and, in a sense, contributed to the six Pan-African meetings of the twentieth century. After the birth of the Pan-African movement in 1900, African-American civil society groups criticised the barbaric brutalities of King Léopold's rule in the Congo; opposed Italian Fascist dictator Benito Mussolini's occupation of Ethiopia between 1936 and 1941; and, from 1948, vociferously condemned the inhumane treatment of blacks in apartheid South Africa.[92]

By the 1950s, African-American scholar-activist, actor and singer Paul Robeson and writer James Baldwin both played a strident role in condemning racism in America and pushing for the civil rights of black Americans. Both intellectual activists lived for long periods in European exile. Robeson paid the price for his outspoken activism when his own government prevented him from travelling abroad for eight years.[93] The Black Power movement, which emerged in the 1960s, was led by personalities like Trinidadian-born Stokely Carmichael, with adherents glorifying black cultural pride and adopting a more militant stance to black liberation than the mainstream civil rights movement.[94] The historic battle between the gradualism of the intellectual Du Bois and the radicalism of the activist Marcus Garvey in the 1920s was replicated in the 1960s by the divergent approaches to civil rights adopted by Martin Luther King Jr (integrationist) and the early Malcolm X (separatist). That historical divide continued with charismatic and popular black leaders such as the fiery Louis Farrakhan – brought up in Boston by a mother, Sarah Manning, from St Kitts and Nevis – whose Nation of Islam preached a gospel of self-sufficiency and self-pride. It is doubtful, as African-American scholar Henry Louis Gates Jr noted, that any other black leader could have mobilised the mass support that Farrakhan achieved during his "Million Man March" in Washington DC in October 1995.[95]

The Congressional Black Caucus (CBC) and TransAfrica had their greatest success in influencing US policy towards Africa when sanctions were imposed on South Africa's apartheid regime in 1986 after two-thirds of the US Congress had overridden a reactionary Ronald Reagan presidential veto. This followed years of daily protests in front of the South African embassy in Washington DC, led by TransAfrica, and involving African-American legislators like Ronald Dellums, Charles Rangel and Julian Dixon. African-American leaders like Randall Robinson, Walter Fauntroy, Mary Frances Berry and Eleanor Holmes Norton also founded the Free South Africa Movement to lead the drive for imposing sanctions on South Africa. Significantly, influential white legislators like Edward Kennedy, Nancy Kassebaum and Stephen Solarz were in the forefront of the legislative struggle for sanctions. The African-American Reverend Leon Sullivan's famous "principles" also imposed a code of conduct on American companies operating in South Africa, forcing many of them to divest, and dealing a serious blow to the South African economy.[96]

In Search of a Post-Apartheid Role

In contrast to its success with South Africa in the 1980s, the African–American lobby was spectacularly ineffectual in efforts to impose sanctions on Nigeria's military regime in the 1990s. During the brutal regime of General Sani Abacha (1993–8), several members of the Congressional Black Caucus campaigned to impose oil sanctions on Nigeria. In 1997, Congressman Donald Payne introduced the "Nigeria Democracy Act" calling for a freezing of American investments in Nigeria and the imposition of an oil embargo on the military junta. But some members of the CBC opposed the measures. Congressman William Jefferson, for example, described the Democracy Act as "unimaginative" and "wrong-headed". Both Senator Carol Moseley Braun and Louis Farrakhan also visited Abacha in Nigeria, demonstrating the ignorance and insensitivity of some members of the African-American leadership in embracing African autocrats who brutalised their own people.

One of the strangest silences from the African-American policy community was the failure to put pressure on the cynical Bill Clinton administration to support the 2500-strong UN mission – which Clinton forced to be withdrawn – during the 1994 Rwandan genocide in which about 800,000 people perished. There is still a lack of a powerful, cohesive domestic constituency on Africa in the US which could wield the influence of the Jewish-American or Cuban-American lobbies. US policy towards Africa is, furthermore, not yet based on consistent Congressional support, and instead seeks ad hoc coalitions in support of specific policies. It is thus important that African-American lobbyists work closer with the plethora of Washington-based non-governmental organisations (NGOs) in fields as diverse as human rights, famine, AIDS and the environment to influence Uncle Sam's policies towards Africa. The tens of thousands of highly educated Africans in the American diaspora must also be involved in building a new constituency for Africa in the US, based on the successes of past mobilisations.

Barack Obama: A Wasted Opportunity?

Despite the historic presidency of Kenyan-Kansan Barack Obama (2009–16), there was eventually a disappointing realisation across Africa and its diaspora that the first African-American president in the White House continued in the malign tradition of his 43 predecessors. On his visit to South Africa, Senegal and Tanzania in June–July 2013 (having briefly visited Egypt and Ghana in July 2009), the unrealistic expectations that the first black president would radically transform US policy towards Africa and the Caribbean did not even come close to being fulfilled. In Africa, Obama deployed drones in Somalia and Libya, and surveillance drones were also used in Mali. In the Caribbean, the US president visited Trinidad and Tobago in April 2009; he went to Jamaica in April 2015, taking in a visit to the Bob Marley museum; and he made a historic trip to Cuba (the first in nine decades by a US president) in March 2016, sealing a remarkable rapprochement between Washington and its former communist enemy. The Obama administration further provided important support on HIV/AIDS to Africa and the Caribbean.

In Africa, Obama, however, reinforced rather than challenged the idea of France and Britain being left to oversee continuing European neo-colonial "spheres of influence", and serious questions were raised about his commitment to democratic governance in countries like Egypt, Uganda, Chad and Rwanda, as well as the continued militarisation of Africa policy through the American obsession with its never-ending "War on Terror".[97] Despite initial euphoric talk about a post-racial America, Obama not only failed to remake US policy towards Africa and the Caribbean (with the notable exception of Cuba), but he also failed fundamentally to transform race relations in his own country. This was clear from the continuing brutality of white police killing unarmed black men such as Trayvon Martin, Michael Brown and Eric Garner, spawning advocacy groups like "Black Lives Matter".

V. Pax Africana: The Quest for the Governance and Security Kingdom

This next section will assess Africa's governance and security challenges, as well as the state of democratic governance in the Caribbean. It is argued that these challenges in both regions prevented a more effective Pan-Africanism emerging between Africa and its diaspora.

Africa's Governance and Security Challenges

From the late nineteenth century, European imperialists employed policies of "divide and rule" to sow the seeds for many of Africa's post-independence challenges by hastily transplanting institutions from the West without first adapting them to fit African conditions. The British preservation of the Emirates of Northern Nigeria, the Kabakaship of Buganda, and the Sultanate of Zanzibar – which all resembled English monarchical institutions – would later lead to

32

instability in post-independence Nigeria, Uganda and Tanzania.[98] As South Sudanese scholar Francis Deng perceptively noted: "If an African nation's constitution and its attendant governing framework are to embody the *soul* of that nation ... they must reflect the essential cultural values and norms of all of the nation's people and build on *their* worldview."[99]

There was no serious long-term preparation of Africans for self-government,[100] and much of the constitutional engineering and leadership training on the continent occurred in the decade after the end of the Second World War. European colonial powers also tended to favour certain African groups and regions, thus creating political and socio-economic disparities in development, as well as marginalising groups and areas in countries like Nigeria, Sudan, Côte d'Ivoire, Senegal, the DRC, Rwanda and Burundi, which later erupted into post-independence conflicts.

In Africa's quest for the security and governance kingdom, the threat of foreign intervention in the heart of Africa was tragically symbolised by the martyrdom of prophetic Congolese leader Patrice Lumumba in January 1961, with Belgium and the US implicated in, and benefiting from, his assassination. This led to a recognition of the need for what Kenyan scholar Ali Mazrui described as a Pax Africana: a peace created, cultivated and consolidated by Africans themselves.[101] The OAU's aspirations for Pax Africana were, however, destroyed by the "proxy wars" waged by the US and the Soviet Union in Africa, and the pyromaniac military interventions – over 50 – of France in its former colonies.

At the time of the creation of the OAU in 1963, Nkrumah was in a minority of one in calling for the establishment of an African High Command. The OAU's leaders, however, rejected his idea and sought instead to freeze the map of Africa that had been crafted by Europe's colonial powers. Several post-independence African leaders subsequently failed to protect their own populations, committing gross human rights abuses, such as massacres in Rwanda, Burundi and Uganda, that resulted in hundreds of thousands of deaths. Military "marabouts" – the "Men on Horseback"[102] – rode onto Africa's national stage 72 times between 1960 and 1990, urging citizens to "stay by their radios" following *coups d'état* that distorted politics. But despite the illusion of military "magic", the soldiers were no more successful than civilian autocrats in achieving the socio–economic transformation of their countries.

The legacy of European-led slavery and partition weighed heavily on Africa. In retrospect, Africa's post-independence "monarchs" also did not do enough to reverse the blighted legacy of colonialism and to develop indigenous systems for managing diversity effectively. Crafting federations and conceding autonomy to "minority" groups were rejected by most nation-builders, who argued instead that one-party states were the only means to avoid destabilising wars and to preserve the unity they needed. Only in Sierra Leone did a ruling party lose power in Africa between 1960 and 1990, and just seven leaders voluntarily stepped down from power. Ethno-regional differences were thus exacerbated by nepotism and favouritism in appointments to military, political and bureaucratic positions.

One of the early prophetic champions of African democracy was the only black Nobel Prize winner in economics, St Lucia's Fabian intellectual, William Arthur Lewis. He served as the economic adviser to Ghana's Kwame Nkrumah, who was ironically one of the early pioneers of one-party rule on the continent. Already in the 1960s, Lewis called for multiparty democracy in Africa's diverse states involving proportional representation, coalition government and federalist devolution. [103] But, only in the post-Cold War era, did prominent African statesmen and scholars start to advocate a dilution of absolute sovereignty. Tanzania's Salim Ahmed Salim was the OAU secretary-general from 1989 to 2001. As the Cold War was coming to an end, he warned African leaders of the need to observe human rights, and to stop regarding the notion of state sovereignty as absolute. Salim further advocated the use of African culture and social relations in managing conflicts on the continent: a call echoed by the first two post-Cold War African UN secretaries-general, Egypt's Boutros Boutros-Ghali and Ghana's Kofi Annan.[104]

There has been some progress in Africa's post-Cold War security and governance architectures. Unlike the OAU Charter, the African Union's Constitutive Act of 2000 allows for interference in the internal affairs of its member states in cases of unconstitutional changes of governments, egregious human rights abuses, and conflicts that threaten regional stability. The organisation has also identified the African diaspora as a sixth sub-region in its structures. This idea has, however, been devoid of substance, and the solidarity forged in the crucible of the anti-apartheid struggle through the efforts of the Cuban military, as well as the Congressional Black Caucus, TransAfrica and other civic groups has all but dissipated, and is in serious need of rebuilding by genuine and concrete civil society initiatives between Africa and its diaspora.

There are some grounds for optimism in Africa's quest for the democratic kingdom: regular elections now take place across the continent; the technology-wielding youths of the "Afro-Arab Spring" famously toppled mummified pharaohs in Tunisia, Egypt and Libya in 2011, with the harmattan winds blowing south to help a popular uprising oust the 27-year-old autocracy of former military marabout Blaise Compaoré of Burkina Faso three years later; and *alternance* of political parties has occurred in countries like Ghana, Senegal, Zambia, Malawi and Nigeria. Though democratic governance has generally improved, polls are still sometimes unfree and unfair, and military brass hats and securocrats continue to wield influence in Egypt, Algeria, Madagascar, Ethiopia and Lesotho. Elections themselves have also sometimes become a way of waging war by other means, with ethnicity, history, race, or religion mobilised to devastating effect, resulting in violent polls in Nigeria, Kenya, Zimbabwe and the DRC.

Libya, under its mercurial leader Muammar Qaddafi, launched the vision of a "United States of Africa" in 1999 that would be loosely modelled on the European Union (EU). Qaddafi came closest to Nkrumah's Pan-African vision, calling for an appointed president and ministers, as well as a central bank. Like Nkrumah's vision four decades earlier, Qaddafi's ideas were, however, overwhelmingly rejected as quixotic by other African leaders. Nevertheless, the Libyan strongman did more than any other head of state to transform the OAU into the AU, hosting several meetings between 1999 and 2001. In 2011, Qaddafi became a casualty of the North Atlantic Treaty Organisation's (NATO) "regime change" intervention in Libya, and he was murdered like a sacrificial ram in his home town of Sirte.

The 15-member AU Peace and Security Council (PSC) has been active, while the 40-member African Peer Review Mechanism (APRM) is a potentially useful governance monitoring mechanism, though it lacks teeth and is grossly underfunded. The New Partnership for Africa's Development (NEPAD) also clearly lacks the resources and capacity to develop the continent. The Pan-African Parliament (PAP) remains a "talking shop", while the Economic, Social and Cultural Council (ECOSOCC) has failed to provide genuine civil society participation in the AU's institutions. African "kings" can still routinely ignore the unenforceable judgments of the African Court on Human and Peoples' Rights (AfCHPR).

Democratic Governance in the Caribbean

Moving from Africa to the Caribbean, as a result of five centuries of slavery and colonialism, both Africa and the Caribbean emerged crippled and deformed from the European yoke that had ruthlessly exploited their economic resources, failed to build human capacity and sufficient infrastructure, and scarred their post-independence governance. Leaders in both regions amassed illicit wealth (though kleptocracy was much worse in Africa) and used public agencies and corporations to reward loyalists. Political parties were also often mobilised as vehicles to fulfil the ambitions of powerful leaders.

Post-independence rulers in Africa and the Caribbean often dismantled internal federations that could have helped to enhance the viability of their states. Local leaders broke up several inherited joint regional services like airlines. European colonial linguistic differences still continue to frustrate attempts at regionalism. Post-independence leaders in both regions have also spectacularly failed to create effective regional integration schemes that could have reduced trade from former colonial masters and increased trade among themselves. After two decades of economic growth in the 1960s and 1970s, in which advances were made in education and health, both regions experienced severe economic crises by the 1980s. In both cases, the Cold War had a negative impact: US interventions in the Congo, Somalia, Ethiopia, Angola, Mozambique and South Africa were mirrored by pernicious interventions in Cuba, Guyana, the Dominican Republic and Grenada. Russia also supported local proxies in both regions.

Powerful leaders in the Caribbean towered over the political landscape. Jamaica's political scene was dominated for decades by Michael Manley and Edward Seaga, while Trinidad and Tobago's Eric Williams spent 19 years in power. Post-independence politics in the region have, however, differed from Africa in one critical respect: most Caribbean countries were able to maintain a multiparty system of government, and few descended into Africa's post-independence one-party states or military dictatorships. Every former British colony in the Caribbean has had a change of government as a result of elections. Barbados, Antigua and Barbuda, and the Bahamas, particularly, maintained stable economies and improved living standards.[105] Politics, though, tended, as in much of Africa, to be dominated by personal rule, and despite regularly held and generally free and fair elections, the lack of proper checks and balances meant that powerful, charismatic leaders could still dominate institutions such as the judiciary, the legislature, the media, and the civil service.[106]

Some powerful leaders in the Caribbean were democratically elected, but then abused their office to act as unaccountable "kings". Haiti's François "Papa Doc" Duvalier ruled as president-for-life between 1957 and 1971, unleashing his fearsome Tontons Macoutes ("Bogeymen") on the populace, before his son, Jean-Claude "Baby Doc", continued to rule with an iron fist until forced to flee into French exile, in a US transport plane, in 1986. As in Africa with Zaire's Mobutu Sese Seko, Somalia's Siad Barre, and Liberia's Samuel Doe, another Western-backed Cold War dictator had outlived his strategic usefulness as a bulwark against communism.[107] Autocratic rule was also evident in Cuba (Fidel Castro) and the Dominican Republic (Juan Bosch and Joaquin Balaguer), and all three Caribbean states experienced the authoritarian rule of *caudillos* in the Latin American tradition.

VI. The Wretched of the Earth: The Quest for the Socio-Economic Kingdom

How Europe Underdeveloped Africa

In assessing the second quest of Africa and its diaspora for the socio-economic kingdom whose absence prevented an effective post-independence Pan-Africanism, it is important to link our discussion to the deleterious impact of slavery in the Caribbean and the Americas examined earlier. The search for new markets amidst a global Great Depression in the early 1880s was a widespread concern that spurred on imperialism.[108] In Africa, modern scientific techniques were introduced into colonial territories that led to the production of minerals and cash crops including cocoa, coffee, palm oil, rubber, cotton, phosphates, diamonds, gold and tobacco. African economies were thus structured – as the economies in the Caribbean and the Americas had been for two centuries – to produce crops to meet European consumer needs. This both increased the dependence of African economies on metropolitan economies and, in many cases, negatively impacted on the ability of African populations to produce their own food. Africans imbibed Western consumption patterns without acquiring Western production methods.

The fact that self-rule and university education were mostly introduced to African territories after the Second World War was a clear sign of the lack of priority given to such critical sectors. Most independent African countries therefore had very few trained personnel to run the administrative systems inherited from colonial rule. The creation of small, unviable states and the

37

existence of 16 landlocked territories due to the arbitrary European partition, further contributed to the difficulties of socio-economic development after independence. Imperialism also negatively affected intra-African trade, greatly disrupting traditional patterns of commerce.

The fall of the Berlin Wall in 1989 marked the end of the division of Germany and of Europe. But events in Berlin would once again have an enormous impact on Africa, as the curse of Africa's ancestors represented by the division of Germany and of Europe was finally lifted. The earlier Bismarckian curse of Berlin, however, remained to haunt Africa's future. Conflicts and disputes, some resulting from the colonial legacy of Berlin, continued between countries such as Ethiopia and Eritrea, Somalia and Ethiopia, Libya and Chad, and Nigeria and Cameroon. Other conflicts had more immediate internal roots. Whereas Africa had once feared intervention during the Cold War, marginalisation had now become a greater concern in the post-apartheid era. Attention, aid and investment shifted to the emerging democracies of Eastern Europe, and resources were later diverted from managing African conflicts to reconstruction efforts in Afghanistan and Iraq by 2003. Africans had failed to overcome the colonial legacy of Berlin, as economic and political systems were still tied to those bequeathed by imperial statesmen in Berlin. In six decades of independence, African leaders had also failed to create effective regional integration schemes to overcome the limitations of the boundaries inherited from the era of the Berlin Conference.

Though the percentage of Africans living in absolute poverty fell from 58 to 41 per cent between 2000 and 2016, and primary school enrolment had increased from 60 to 80 per cent, most of the poorest economic performers in the UN's human development index remained African countries. Caribbean countries were also stuck at the bottom of these league tables. The flattering Western narrative of "Rising Africa" had thus been dramatically halted by the collapse of the commodity boom, which resulted in a 16 per cent fall in sub-Saharan Africa's terms of trade by 2016.[109] By 2020, about a third of Africa's countries were heavily indebted.

In his famous treatise *How Europe Underdeveloped Africa* (1972), the prophetic Guyanese scholar-activist Walter Rodney (who taught in Julius Nyerere's Tanzania), traced the roots of African underdevelopment to the 1884–5 Conference of Berlin. He lamented the consumerist rather than productive nature of African economies and the general lack of savings across the continent. Rodney bemoaned Africa's declining terms of trade, unequal exchange, and exploitation by both European colonial powers and the US, which had integrated African economies into their capitalist economies on vastly unequal terms in a system built during the slave trade. Rodney thus called for African self-reliance and self-sustainability.[110]

Adebayo Adedeji, the Nigerian scholar-prophet who headed the UN Economic Commission for Africa (ECA) between 1975 and 1991, was Africa's most renowned visionary of economic integration. He oversaw the creation of regional integration schemes in West, eastern, central and southern Africa: the Economic Community of West African States (ECOWAS); the Common Market for Eastern and Southern Africa (COMESA); and the Economic Community of Central African States (ECCAS). Adedeji also pushed the OAU to organise an economic summit in 1980 at which he championed – like Walter Rodney – the collective self-reliance and self-sustainability principles of the 1980 Lagos Plan of Action (LPA), which he had crafted with his team. He further led the production of an alternative plan to the World Bank and the International Monetary Fund's (IMF) Structural Adjustment Programmes (SAPs) in 1989. The Bretton Woods institutions conducted cuts in education, health and employment across the continent in an utterly unaccountable manner that often undermined democratic governance and fuelled social unrest.

Adedeji's plans were enthusiastically adopted by African leaders, but were then left to gather dust. Intra-African trade accounted for only about 17 per cent in 2019, and regional integration has generally been an abysmal failure across the continent. However, ECOWAS did make impressive progress on the free movement of persons, while the revived East African Community (EAC) increased trade significantly among its members. In creating the African Union in 2002, African governments, however, failed to recognise that economic development could not simply be legislated into existence. The key document of the tenure of the South African diva and former chair of the AU Commission, Nkosazana Dlamini-Zuma (2012–16), was *Agenda 2063*, a 50-year vision for Africa produced in 2013 that, more than any other initiative, symbolised the alchemy at the heart of the AU Commission. This vision represented a modern-day African effort to replicate the failed alchemic efforts of medieval Europeans to turn lead into gold. It was a triumph of hope over experience. It is almost as if – as in the days of the OAU – by African leaders making a "solemn" declaration on its 50th anniversary and adopting *Agenda 2063*, a religious sanctity could be achieved to ensure its implementation. The vision's more euphoric aspirations included eradicating poverty in two decades; creating a continental free-trade area by 2017 (which was declared in 2019, despite having failed to build on the continent's sub-regional economic pillars); doubling intra-African trade by 2022; "Silencing the Guns" by 2020; and eliminating all forms of oppression, impunity, corruption and youth unemployment by 2050. Many of these ideas appeared to be quixotic, and did not take structural obstacles and the root causes of these challenges into proper account. This was a magical, mystical world of diplomatic marabouts, fetishes and incantations.

The Disintegration of the West Indies Federation

As in Africa, regional integration has proved difficult to achieve in the Caribbean owing to the insularity within its small, mono-crop (mostly bauxite, sugar and agriculture) and tourism-dependent islands that have consistently asserted their own identities over regional ones. The sole exceptions are the West Indian cricket team and the University of the West Indies. Colonial identities have been strongly defended in a context of cultural imperialism that provoked Jamaican historian Franklin W. Knight to complain of the anglophone middle-class West Indian having been converted, through colonial education, into a "coloured English gentleman".[111]

Half of the population in the anglophone Caribbean in the 1950s consisted of Jamaicans, but the country spectacularly failed to provide leadership for regional integration efforts. Its role in the break-up of the West Indies Federation between 1958 and 1962 was a tragic one. Jamaican premier Norman Manley famously chose to "stay home" because of an unnamed anti-federation "conspiracy" rather than lead efforts to preserve the region's British-inherited federalist institutions. He called a referendum in 1961, which effectively doomed the federation. Both of the country's major parties argued that a common West Indian external tariff would destroy Jamaica's industrialisation programme. Interest groups like the Jamaican Chamber of Commerce and the Jamaica Manufacturers' Association also lobbied hard against any customs union. Kingston's decision to establish an oil refinery was further detrimental to any regional development plans, given Trinidad and Tobago's growing oil industry.[112]

Furthermore, regional politicians in the Caribbean argued about the location of the capital of the still-born federation. The deeply entrenched protectionist economic interests of Jamaica, Barbados, and Trinidad and Tobago also played a major role in stalling the federal project in the West Indies. There was thus a drive to have as weak a federal government and federal civil service as possible, so as not to constrain the power of individual states to raise taxes, regulate trade unions and enact their own laws. St Lucia had argued for strong central control of expenditures for the East Caribbean federation in 1965, but met with strong resistance from Barbados. The free movement of labour essential to the success of any customs union was met with hostility by wealthier countries like Trinidad and Tobago. The disintegration of the West Indian federation in 1962 in fact mirrored the disintegration of the East African Community in 1977, in which the more industrialised Kenya was felt by Tanzania and Uganda to have benefited disproportionately from the inherited British institutions. Such economic and later ideological differences led to a cessation of meetings and the eventual demise of the East African common market in 1977, without even being given a decent burial.[113]

The Continuing Travails of Regional Integration in the Caribbean

The Caribbean's micro-states, with a total population of about 20 million, will inevitably have to cooperate to be able to attain the economies of scale needed to achieve industrialisation. Within three years of the disintegration of the British-inherited West Indies Federation, the Caribbean Free Trade Association (CARIFTA) was established in 1965, though it enjoyed only limited success. The 15-member Caribbean Community and Common Market (CARICOM) was therefore born in 1973. It consists today of Antigua and Barbuda, the Bahamas, Barbados, Belize, Dominica, Grenada, Guyana, Haiti, Jamaica, Montserrat, St Kitts and Nevis, St Lucia, St Vincent and the Grenadines, Suriname, and Trinidad and Tobago. The 1973 global "oil shock" combined with continuing economic disparities between CARICOM members, ideological divergences and competing external alliances to make a difficult birth an even more painful infancy.[114] Owing to the tortuous experiences of the 1960s, "federalism" had become a dirty word in the West Indies.

CARICOM has not achieved much integration in the last five decades. Efforts to create a Single Market and Economy (CSME) began in 1993, and a Single Market was euphorically declared in 2006, but its directives have not been fully implemented by national governments in key areas such as the free movement of people and completing the single economy. The Assembly of Caribbean Community Parliamentarians became moribund because of a lack of funding and interest, and the CARICOM Charter of Civil Society was effectively rendered a dead letter as a result of similar challenges. CARICOM leaders did not meet at all between 1976 and 1982, though a revival of engagement occurred in the 1990s with the collapse of socialist experiments in Jamaica, Guyana and Grenada. By 2001, biannual meetings had resumed, but progress still lagged in the coordination of fiscal, monetary and macroeconomic policies.

More positively, the CARICOM Regional Negotiating Machinery (CRNM) – now the Office of Trade Negotiations (OTN) – has functioned fairly well, while CARICOM played an active role in mediating political crises in Guyana, St Vincent and the Grenadines, and Haiti.[115] In the 2001–7 period, CARICOM's intra-community trade was 14.5 per cent, having increased from 8.3 per cent in the earlier 1973–9 period, but 88 per cent of this trade came from Trinidad and Tobago, and was linked to its energy sector.[116]

More recently, CARICOM has continued to suffer from external shocks such as the "Great Recession" of 2008–9, which led to the demise of some of the region's prominent institutions such as Trinidad and Tobago's Colonial Life Insurance Company Limited (CLICO) and its parent company CL Financial. Haiti's disastrous earthquake in 2010 also killed about 230,000 citizens, and destroyed much of its economy. By this time, unemployment exceeded 10 per cent across the Caribbean. In 2012, the CARICOM Secretariat reported that compliance by its member states in implementing its programmes was only 64 per cent, with only 3 per cent compliance in the vital services sector, which accounted for 70 per cent of the Gross Domestic Product (GDP) of 10 of the 14 CARICOM members at the time.

By 2013, over 80 per cent of CARICOM's market was still largely externally oriented towards North America and Europe, with energy-rich Trinidad and Tobago accounting for 70 per cent of regional and international exports. Jamaica's imports of 34 per cent of CARICOM goods and $957 million trade deficit with the region were a further source of tension. In recognition of the need for closer collaboration in key sectors, the Caribbean Regional Public Health Agency (CARPHA) and the Caribbean Disaster and Emergency Management Agency (CDEMA) were established, while the Caribbean Court of Justice (CCJ) has been increasingly used by Barbados, Belize, and Guyana.[117]

By 2015, CARICOM states had identified four key priorities: building social, economic, environmental and technological resilience; strengthening community governance and foreign policy coordination; enhancing the organisation's identity and spirit; and promoting research and innovation. CARICOM continued, however, to struggle with limited technical and financial capacity to engage in complex external negotiations.[118]

Caribbean states also started, from the 1990s, looking to their own hemisphere to engage with larger blocs, with some members joining the Union of South American States while others joined the Venezuela-led Bolivarian Alliance for the Peoples of our America. Engagement further increased with Cuba, as well as Latin American states like Colombia, Mexico and Costa Rica. The Community of Latin American and Caribbean States (CELAC) emerged in 2010 involving all 33 countries in both regions, but the amorphous body has struggled to define its mandate and to craft concrete projects.[119] As St Kitts and Nevis scholar Jessica Byron put it: "CARICOM has shown inadequate flexibility, speed or capacity in responding to either global or hemispheric developments."[120]

The Caribbean Forum (CARIFORUM) is widely believed by critics to have agreed a new partnership accord with the EU, which they perceive to be detrimental to the region. Such critics argue that the Caribbean could face renewed and unequal competition from Europe stemming from coordinating and harmonising regimes in investment, sanitary and phyto-sanitary measures, intellectual property, and government procurement in which CARICOM has not yet even established many of its own region-wide policies.[121] African and Caribbean states thus need, in future negotiations with groups like the EU, to rediscover the Pan-African "spirit of Lomé" of 1975. The incredible cooperation and solidarity demonstrated during this era led to the creation of the African, Caribbean and Pacific Group (ACP), renamed the Organisation of African, Caribbean and Pacific States (OACPS), now 79 strong, in December 2019. At a policy seminar in Barbados in March 2019, former Guyanese foreign minister and prophet of Caribbean regional integration, Shridath Ramphal, undertook a nostalgic journey down memory lane in describing his instrumental role in the 1975 Lomé Convention, which guided trade between 46 ACP states and the nine-member European Economic Community (EEC). Lomé provided duty-free access to the European market for most ACP agricultural products and minerals, as well as preferential access for sugar, rum and beef.

Ramphal noted how Caribbean states had first built regional consensus before joining with African and Pacific negotiators. A Caribbean delegation visited key African countries and regional organisations – ECOWAS and the EAC – between 1972 and 1974, to forge a common negotiating position. The significant lesson for Ramphal was the unified bargaining approach of the ACP. Shortly after Lomé, the Guyanese foreign minister hosted the creation of the ACP Group through the 1975 Georgetown Agreement. Ramphal noted during his 2019 Barbados keynote address that the Lomé trade negotiations had been characterised by creativity and solidarity, and praised the intellectual leadership and sacrifices that were demonstrated by the global South, which he saw as sorely lacking in contemporary interactions between the ACP and the EU.[122]

As the Cold War ended by 1990, globalisation accelerated and other parts of the world in Europe and the Americas formed large trade blocs. This, in turn, forced Africa and the Caribbean to revive their charters and institutions. In the end, though, as Nigerian scholar-administrator Adebayo Adedeji perceptively noted in 2004, it will be politics, and not economics, that will determine the success of regional integration efforts.[123] This is as true in Africa as it is in the Caribbean.

VII. Black Orpheus: The Quest for the Cultural Kingdom

The third and final magic kingdom on which Africa and its diaspora have been forced to embark in the last six decades by the legacy of slavery and colonialism has been that of cultural equality. Early movements of black cultural influence, of course, started with the art of Africa itself, which involved Benin bronzes, wood carvings, face masks, terracotta sculptures and the ruins of ancient Egypt and the Great Zimbabwe. Some of this art was looted by European imperialists and carted off to museums in London, Paris, Lisbon, Brussels, and Berlin. Other cultural movements in the diaspora involved Cuba's *negrismo* from 1921; Haiti's Indigenist Revolt movement from 1927, which was a direct forerunner of Négritude poetry in the 1930s; and America's Black Power movement of the 1960s.

Initially, the demands of early Pan-Africanists were limited to education for Africans, economic development and racial equality. Eventually, however, Pan-Africanism came to emphasise not only the worth of African cultures, but also called for African unity so that these cultures might flourish unhampered by the denigrating influences of Western hegemony.[124] Pan-Africanism, therefore, represented the reaction by the black African diaspora to the indignities that blacks had suffered from Euro-Americans. Some sought refuge in an idealised African past, free of slavery, colonialism and racism. In the francophone world, writers like Martinique's Aimé Césaire and Senegal's Léopold Senghor developed the idea of Négritude, which glorified black culture, looking back nostalgically at a rich African past, and affirming the worth and dignity of black people across the globe.[125] As Aimé Césaire mused:

> My Négritude is no tower and no cathedral
> It delves into the deeper red flesh of the soil. [126]

Nigeria's Wole Soyinka famously ridiculed what he considered the romanticism of this apolitical, moderate approach to Pan-Africanism in wryly noting that "The tiger does not profess its tigritude, it pounces."[127]

Africa and its diaspora have made great strides over the past six decades in efforts to achieve recognition of their cultural equality. The Harlem Renaissance of the 1920s was an era of incredible artistic creativity that produced great African-American prophetic poets like Langston Hughes, who visited Africa. He expressed well the essence of Pan-Africanism:

> We are related – you and I.
> You from the West Indies,
> I from Kentucky,
> We are related – you and I.
> You are from Africa,
> I from these States.
> We are brothers – you and I.[128]

Tanzania's philosopher-king, Julius Nyerere, famously translated Shakespeare's *Julius Caesar* into Swahili in 1963 to demonstrate that an African language could carry a classic Western tragedy. The post-independence era also produced six Nobel literature laureates: Nigeria's Wole Soyinka, Egypt's Naguib Mahfouz, and South Africa's Nadine Gordimer and J.M. Coetzee, and, in the diaspora, St Lucia's Derek Walcott and America's Toni Morrison. Nigeria's Ben Okri and Nigerian-Briton Bernadine Evaristo won the Booker prize. A younger generation of African writers led by Zimbabwe's NoViolet Bulawayo and Nigeria's Chimamanda Ngozi Adichie are making literary waves, as are diaspora citizens such as Zadie Smith and Aminatta Forna. Classics such as C.L.R. James's *The Black Jacobins*, Ralph Ellison's *Invisible Man*, Bessie Head's *A Question of Power*, Mariama Bâ's *So Long a Letter* and Tayeb Salih's *Season of Migration to the North* should surely be part of the Pan-African canon, taught at schools and universities across Africa and its diasporas in the Caribbean and the Americas.

In the realm of music, Africa and its diaspora need to find ways of reviving the remarkable solidarity of the 1950s Highlife era of Ghana's E.T. Mensah and Nigeria's Victor Olaiya; the Congolese musicians of the *belle époque* of the 1950s and 1960s, led by Joseph "Le Grand Kalle" Kabasele and his African Jazz collaborators; the radical reggae rhythms of Jamaica's Bob Marley, as well as the rebellious Afro-jazz percussions of Nigeria's Fela Anikulapo-Kuti, who finally achieved global immortality through the 2008 Broadway musical *Fela!*, which was directed by African–American Bill T. Jones. The pursuit for the recognition of cultural equality has also been evident in the anti-apartheid melody of South Africa's Miriam Makeba; the fiery calypso rhythms of the Jamaican–Martinican American Harry Bellafonte; the powerful renditions of Egyptian diva Umm Kulthum; the soul of Motown and the sultry jazz of Duke Ellington, Louis "Satchmo" Armstrong, Dizzy Gillespie, Charlie "Bird" Parker, Ray Charles and Miles Davis. South Africa's Lira and Nigeria's Asa could represent the voice of a new generation. More recently, Angolan immigrants have globalised the dance-music fusion of *kizomba* with its potential of gaining the popularity of tango and salsa.[129]

In the world of cinema, Denzel Washington brought the life and times of martyred South African hero Steve Biko to a global audience in the 1987 *Cry Freedom* and, in the process, contributed to the anti-apartheid struggle. Haitian-American director Raoul Peck produced tragic tales about Patrice Lumumba (the 2000 film *Lumumba*) and on the Rwandan genocide (the 2005 film *Sometimes in April*). The South African 2005 film *Tsotsi* (with the Kwaito beats of Zola) won the best foreign film Oscar, using township *patois*. African–American Forest Whitaker gave a spectacular, nuanced Oscar-winning portrayal of Uganda's Idi Amin (*The Last King of Scotland* in 2006). Oscar-nominated Beninois actor Djimon Hounsou won widespread acclaim for his role in the 1997 slave epic *Amistad*. More recently, Nigerian-Briton Chiwetel Ejiofor and Oscar-winning Kenyan Lupita Nyong'o teamed up with Grenadian-Trinidadian British director Steve McQueen to produce the Oscar-winning best film of 2013, *12 Years a Slave*. Nigerian-Britons David Oyelowo and Carmen Ejogo played the roles of Martin Luther King Jr and Coretta Scott King respectively in the 2014 film *Selma*. Six years later, Nigerian-Briton Cynthia Erivo was nominated for an Oscar for her portrayal of the nineteenth-century abolitionist Harriet Tubman (in the 2019 film *Harriet*). The 2018 Afro-futuristic blockbuster, *Black Panther*, thoughtfully examined the tensions between Africa and its diaspora in the mythical, technologically advanced African kingdom of Wakanda. If more diaspora directors could make films about Africa for a global audience with genuine human characters, this would do more to change negative global media stereotypes about the continent than any other action.

The phenomenon of Nigeria's prolific film industry – Nollywood – has attracted the most recent positive international attention to Africa's most populous country. In 2019, Nollywood was the second-largest film producer in the world behind India's Bollywood, and ahead of America's Hollywood. This industry already employed an estimated one million people by 2006, making it the second-largest employer in Nigeria.[130] Nollywood films are widely available from Kinshasa to Kingston to Kansas, and have inspired film production in Kenya, Uganda, Tanzania and South Africa. The movies have influenced the dress of Kenyan politicians, Congolese tailors, pastors and architecture, and the accents of South African students.

Unlike the French-funded annual film festival in Ouagadougou, FESPACO (Festival Panafricain du Cinéma et de la Télévision de Ouagadougou), which is based on a spirit of French benevolent neo-colonialism, Nollywood has been more self-funded, more commercial, and more unabashedly authentic. As Matthias Krings and Onookome Okome noted: "Nollywood … has become the most visible form of cultural machine on the African continent … Nigerian video films travel the length and breadth of the continent connecting Africa, particularly Nigeria, to its diverse and far-flung Diasporas elsewhere."[131]

Nollywood's cultural reach has expanded as far as Barbados, an island of 250,000 largely Africa-descended inhabitants. By 2006, with the launch of *Blood Sisters*, Nollywood movies were ubiquitous on the island, selling hundreds of DVDs a week. The University of the West Indies hosted African and Caribbean film festivals from 2002, and featured famous Nollywood director Tunde Kelani in 2004. The Barbadian and Guyanese audiences in Barbados have involved both middle-class and working-class citizens. The movies were seen by many as authentic in presenting genuine African lifestyles with which many of the island's Hollywood-obsessed movie-goers had not previously been familiar. Barbadians and Guyanese migrants have also been impressed to see Africans in starring roles in movies for the first time. Many can relate to the African lifestyles in the films, and admire the luxurious homes, and some have even started wearing dresses sewn in the style of Nollywood actresses. Many also identify with the Pentecostal religion – similar to the charismatic churches across the Caribbean – often on display in Nollywood movies. Caribbean beliefs in Obeah (similar to Voodoo) also found resonance in the supernatural spirit world frequently depicted in Nollywood. Many Barbadian and Guyanese women further identify with the assertive feminism on display in Nollywood movies, and are attracted by the fact that several of the glamorous actresses have figures of ample proportion contrary to Western ideals of beauty.[132]

Nollywood may be leading the way to the first authentic African cinema with wide appeal across Africa and its diaspora. It has unquestionably become one of the few true cultural representations of "Global Africa".

VIII. Three Prophets of Reparations

In concluding Africa's three quests for emancipation, we next address the related issue of reparations for slavery and colonialism by examining three prophets of reparations in the US, the Caribbean and Africa.

As the 400th anniversary of American slavery was commemorated in 2019, the thorny issue of reparations for descendants of this exploitative system of unpaid labour has once more come to the fore. Similar campaigns also exist in Africa and the Caribbean. Rather perversely, it was slave-owners – and not the slaves themselves or their descendants – who were compensated by the American and British governments for the loss of their "property". The British government, for example, paid the contemporary equivalent of £200 billion to slave-owners after the abolition of slavery in the nineteenth century.[133] Democrats in the US House of Representatives and Senate have now belatedly embraced the cause of reparations, and some institutions like Brown, Harvard and Yale universities that benefited from the slave trade have started to acknowledge their role in this sordid commerce, and begun putting programmes of restitution in place.

The most articulate African-American crusader of reparations has been the activist Randall Robinson. He has consistently argued for reparations in order to close the 246-year gap between white and black Americans created by plantation slavery. As Robinson correctly noted: "the black holocaust is far and away the most heinous human rights crime visited upon any group of people in the world over the last five hundred years".[134] He urged America's largely white ruling class to redress these historical wrongs, if the country is to have a future as a united people.[135] Robinson further noted that Germany paid Jews reparations for the devastating but much shorter Holocaust (1933–45) – estimated at $60 billion – while Japanese Americans interned in concentration camps by President Franklin Roosevelt during the Second World War (1939–45) were also compensated with a $1.2 million payment. He further observed that indigenous populations received land and money for the Australian government's genocidal campaign against them, as did members of the Canadian Inuit group ($700 million) (see Knight in this volume on the estimates).[136]

To understand the structural impact of slavery to which Robinson is alluding, one should note that during the "Great Plague" of the 2020 Corona virus, American citizens of African descent were disproportionately included among its fatalities, accounting for 30 per cent of deaths though constituting only 13 per cent of the US population. In Louisiana, 70 per cent of people who died, by April 2020, were black Americans, though they made up just a third of the state's population. Though African Americans constituted only 15 per cent of Illinois's population, they accounted for 43 per cent of deaths from the Corona virus in April 2020. Black Americans, with 14 per cent of Michigan's population, made up 40 per cent of deaths.[137] Even American public health experts conceded that this "aristocracy of death" could be attributed directly to historical structural inequalities: the fact that blacks generally have lower-paying menial jobs – in hospitals, nursing homes, hotels, restaurants, and animal slaughter plants, and on buses and subway trains – that often put them on the front lines of the spread of this deadly virus. African Americans also often live in poorer, densely populated urban neighbourhoods in which it is much harder to practise "social distancing". They are, furthermore, less likely to have health insurance and access to good medical facilities. Their diet is often poor, making them more susceptible to diabetes and other chronic illnesses such as hypertension, heart disease, obesity, asthma and lung disease that render them more vulnerable to fighting the Corona virus. The past – it seems – is not yet past.

In the Caribbean context, Barbadian historian Hilary Beckles similarly noted that "slavery and genocide in the Caribbean are lived experiences despite over a century of emancipation. Everywhere their legacies shape the lives of the majority and harm their capacity for advancement."[138] Modern ailments common among Caribbean citizens like diabetes and hypertension can be traced directly to the bad diet and sugary drinks inherited from the era of European slavery and colonialism. Beckles thus called for an apology and the need for Britain to take responsibility for its crimes against humanity committed in the Caribbean. Reparations should, he argued, be paid by the British state, its banks, merchant houses, insurances companies and the Church of England, which all benefited directly from slavery.

The West Indies had, after all, as Beckles noted, been the "hub of the British Empire" where most of its wealth had been generated, particularly after losing the US as a colony in 1776. A 2004 estimate of the cost of the slave trade to the

Caribbean arrived at a figure of £7.5 trillion. Beckles therefore urged Britain and other European states involved in the slave trade – Spain, Portugal, the Netherlands, France, Denmark, and Sweden – to pay reparations to Caribbean nations in order to repair this damage.[139] He also chaired the CARICOM Reparations Commission, established in 2013, to pursue reparations from European nations for the transatlantic slave trade, and national committees on reparations have been established in CARICOM states to achieve this goal.

In August 2019, Glasgow University in Scotland agreed to raise £20 million to establish a joint Centre for Development Research at the University of the West Indies to start to atone for having benefitted from the wealth of Scottish slave traders in the Caribbean. Oxford University's All Souls College in England also announced an annual scholarship for Caribbean students, and provided a £100,000 grant to Codrington College in Barbados, for having received funding from an eighteenth-century slave trader in the Caribbean, Christopher Codrington, after whom the main college library was named.[140]

In the African context, the late Nigerian historian Ade Ajayi was a member of the OAU Eminent Persons Group on Reparations in 1992–3, which – through the 1993 Abuja Declaration – demanded that the West recognise its moral debt to Africa and its diaspora for slavery and colonialism, and pay these populations full monetary compensation. Ajayi was among the most eloquent continental advocates of reparations until his death in August 2014. As he noted in 1993: "The Crusade for Reparation is … to seek to understand the African condition in depth, to educate the African and the non-African about it, to seek an acknowledgment of wrongs which have impaired the political and socio-economic fabric of Africa and, through restitution or reparation, to attempt to give Africa and Africans a fresh start."[141]

Ajayi noted that discussions about the contributions of the slave trade to the West's industrialisation have been neglected, and also criticised the ambiguous or indifferent attitude of African scholars to this issue. He argued that a major motive of European colonial rule was to keep African labour in a cheap state akin to slavery, using methods perfected during two centuries of Caribbean colonialism. He further noted that about one million Africans had died defending their European colonial masters during two World Wars between 1914 and 1945. Ajayi thus called for four key measures to achieve reparations: domestic education and mobilisation in African societies; documentation and research on the costs of slavery and colonialism; making a cogent case for reparations; and agreeing on the strategy, manner and mode of reparations, having placed the issue on the agenda of the United Nations.[142]

We have now come full circle, having started the Introduction from the "original sin" of slavery and its devastating impact on black populations in Africa, the Caribbean, and the Americas; focused on European colonialism in Africa and the Caribbean; and ended by engaging in debates about potential ways to repair the five centuries of pernicious damage wrought by European slavery and colonialism.

IX. Chapter Summaries

Having provided a background to the quest of Africa and its diaspora for security and governance, economic transformation, and cultural equality in order to vanquish the twin demons of slavery and colonialism, we need briefly to investigate some of the key interactions, ideas and activism that linked together the 36 Pan-African figures in this book who waged many of these battles.

Edward Blyden greatly influenced Marcus Garvey, Kwame Nkrumah and George Padmore. His triple formulation in the 1887 classic *Christianity, Islam and the Negro Race*,[143] was adopted by Kenyan academic Ali Mazrui for his 1986 nine-part documentary *The Africans: A Triple Heritage*, one of the most educational works ever produced on Africa.[144] The inspirational idea of an "African Renaissance" or the "Regeneration of Africa" from the late nineteenth and early twentieth centuries had also been formulated by such figures as Blyden, before Pixley Seme, Kwame Nkrumah, Nnamdi Azikiwe, Cheikh Anta Diop and Thabo Mbeki adopted it. We have further noted the great impact that Blyden had on Léopold Senghor and the Négritude movement, just as Marcus Garvey had a tremendous influence on Nkrumah and Bob Marley.

The role of female activists has often been overlooked in the Pan-African pantheon. Amy Ashwood Garvey was, for example, instrumental in the activities of the UNIA, driving fundraising and creating a Ladies Division, as well as working with her then husband, Marcus Garvey, as chief assistant in the New York branch, editing *Negro World*, and serving as secretary of the Black Star shipping line. This book focuses on such female activists as Amy Ashwood Garvey, South Africa's Miriam Makeba and Ruth First, Kenya's Wangari Maathai and Micere Mugo, Senegal's Mariama Bâ, America's Maya Angelou and Nigeria's Buchi Emecheta in waging feminist and liberation struggles.

Jamaican prophet Dudley Thompson was a Pan-African lawyer and close associate of Kwame Nkrumah, Julius Nyerere, George Padmore, and C.L.R. James. He put together the legal team that defended Kenya's Jomo Kenyatta from charges of being an instigator of the Mau Mau rebellion against British colonial rule in 1952, and was a founder member of the Tanganyika African National Union (TANU). Thompson was later, along with Ali Mazrui, one of the members of the OAU Eminent Persons Group, leading the movement for reparations for the effects of slavery to citizens of Africa and its diaspora.

In seeking to rebuild bridges between Africa and its diaspora, authors such as the African-American diva Maya Angelou, an activist, writer, poet, singer and actress, who identified deeply with Africa, are important. One of the most fascinating of her autobiographies described her three-year sojourn in Ghana between 1962 and 1965, entitled *All God's Children Need Travelling Shoes*. The book captured a memorable visit to Accra by Malcolm X, who did much to try to mobilise African leadership in support of the struggle for civil rights in apartheid America.[145]

Jamaican-British sociologist and cultural theorist Stuart Hall, who was one of the pioneers of the Birmingham School of Cultural Studies, inspired activists like African-American diva Angela Davis. Hall incorporated issues of race, gender and hegemony into cultural studies, while his theory of encoding and decoding urged readers not to be passive receivers of texts, particularly race prejudice in the Western media. Similarly, Trinidad's C.L.R. James was a pioneering voice in post-colonial studies, working closely with George Padmore, Kwame Nkrumah and Jomo Kenyatta in exile in London.

Africa and its diaspora also produced noteworthy philosophers. Martinique's Frantz Fanon was a political theorist of democracy and a political sociologist of development, as well as a Marxist advocating revolutionary change in Africa, based on his direct experiences in the Algerian war of liberation from France (1954–62) and, later, as a roving ambassador across Africa for the Algerian regime. His critique of the first generation of post-independence African leaders was unflinchingly devastating. Bissau-Guinean revolutionary Amílcar Cabral was greatly influenced by Fanon in formulating critical theories of revolutionary decolonisation and revolutionary re-Africanisation, insisting on a "return to the African source" to draw on indigenous cultural resources. Fanon also greatly influenced Steve Biko's philosophy of Black Consciousness.

After my Introduction to *The Pan-African Pantheon*, Hilary Beckles – one of the Caribbean's most renowned historians – concludes the first section by arguing that African delegates at the UN World Conference on Racism in 2001 in Durban betrayed the African and Caribbean cause for reparations for slavery and colonialism, and consequently calls for a reorientation of the relationship between Africa and its diaspora. The second section assesses the contributions of six Pan-African pioneers. Kenyan scholar Gilbert Khadiagala analyses the contributions of scholar-diplomat Edward Blyden, to the Pan-Africanist movement. Leading African-American sociologist Aldon Morris, who wrote the seminal contemporary biography of W.E.B. Du Bois, examines the towering African-American intellectual's contributions to the movement, especially between 1919 and 1945. Jamaican-British thinker Colin Grant, who wrote the seminal contemporary biography on Marcus Garvey, traces his subject's struggles in leading a "Back to Africa" movement.

South African analyst Seamus Duggan then examines the career and contributions of Trinidadian intellectual George Padmore to the Pan-African movement, as well as Padmore's activism within the Communist International. Trinidadian feminist Rhoda Reddock examines the contributions of Amy Ashwood Garvey to the UNIA, her feminist activism, and her travels in Africa and the Caribbean. South African intellectual Bongani Ngqulunga, who wrote an award-winning biography of his subject, then assesses the life and times of Pixley Seme, the ANC's president-general between 1930 and 1936.

The third section analyses four politicians of Pan-Africanism. Ghanaian scholar Ama Biney assesses the Pan-Africanism of Ghana's Kwame Nkrumah within the context of the controversial 1966 article by Kenyan scholar Ali Mazrui, who argued that Nkrumah will be remembered more as a great Pan-African than a great Ghanaian. Nigerian scholar Adekeye Adebajo, who has published a biography of his subject, examines the Pan-Africanism of former South African president Thabo Mbeki, comparing him with Kwame Nkrumah, before examining his efforts at building AU institutions and engaging the African diaspora in the Caribbean and the Americas. Barbadian-Canadian scholar Andy Knight then examines the Pan-African career of Jamaica's Dudley Thompson, while Adekeye Adebajo analyses the peacemaking of the first African and first Arab UN secretary-general, Egypt's Boutros Boutros-Ghali.

The fourth section assesses the contributions of six Pan-African activists. African-American former *New York Times* journalist Lee Daniels examines the civil rights struggles of Malcolm X and his efforts to promote Pan-African unity through travels to Africa with his Organisation of Afro-American Unity (OAAU). African-American scholar Alease Brown next analyses the activism of Maya

Angelou, while St Lucian academic Annita Montoute assesses the contributions of Guyanese scholar-activist Walter Rodney, who consistently argued for a Pan-Africanism of people rather than of governments. South African journalist Maureen Isaacson then examines the Pan-African scholarship and activism of South Africa's Ruth First, through her intellectual work on Namibia and analyses of military *coups d'état* in Egypt, Libya, Nigeria and Ghana, as well as her activism in Mozambique. South African policy intellectual Janice Golding assesses the environmental and human rights activism of Kenyan Nobel peace laureate Wangari Maathai, focusing particularly on her Green Belt Movement. African-American academic Pearl Robinson concludes the section by analysing the activism of African-American civil rights lawyer Randall Robinson on US policy towards Africa and the Caribbean.

A fifth section examines the Pan-African contributions of five social scientists. Trinidadian scholar Selwyn Cudjoe assesses the activist career of C.L.R. James in order to "reclaim" him for the Caribbean, while Jamaican scholar-diplomat Alison Stone Roofe assesses the activist scholarship of the Nobel laureate in economics Arthur Lewis. Zimbabwean scholar Sabelo Ndlovu-Gatsheni analyses the Pan-African ideas of Kenyan political scientist Ali Mazrui, while South African sociologist Zine Magubane assesses the work of Jamaican-British cultural theorist Stuart Hall. Nigerian economist Afeikhena Jerome concludes this section by analysing the Pan-African career of Nigerian scholar-technocrat Adebayo Adedeji.

In the sixth section, the contributions of six Pan-African philosophers are examined. Nigerian academic Adele Jinadu analyses the philosophy of Martinique's Frantz Fanon; African-American scholar Reiland Rabaka assesses the philosophical thoughts of Bissau-Guinean revolutionary Amílcar Cabral; South African scholar-activist Barney Pityana examines Steve Biko's philosophy of Black Consciousness; South African academic John Lamola focuses on the Pan-Africanist philosophy of Beninois scholar-politician Paulin Hountondji and his critique of ethnophilosophy; Senegal's Cheikh Thiam and Ghana's Kwabena Opoku-Agyemang jointly examine the philosophy of Congolese intellectual V.Y. Mudimbe; while Ghanaian scholar Kweku Ampiah interrogates the critique of Pan-Africanism by Ghanaian-British philosopher Kwame Anthony Appiah.

The seventh section contains six essays on Pan-African literary figures. The late Nigerian academic Abiola Irele assesses the work of Senegal's Léopold Senghor and his development of the idea of Négritude. Nigerian scholar Sanya Osha examines the work and activism of Nigerian Nobel literature laureate

Wole Soyinka, whom Osha views as an innovator and bard of the Yoruba deity of creativity, Ogun. St Lucian intellectual Vladimir Lucien assesses the career of Nobel literature-winning playwright and poet Derek Walcott, including an analysis of Walcott's discomfort with the proponents of Black Power in the 1960s and 1970s. Nigerian academic Louisa Egbunike examines the work of pioneering Nigerian writer Buchi Emecheta on women's liberation and related themes concerning the Caribbean diaspora in London. Another Nigerian author, Ada Uzoamaka Azodo, assesses the work of another pioneering feminist, Senegal's Mariama Bâ, through her two major novels, which call for the development of a liberated, egalitarian and progressive African society that is free of patriarchy. Kenyan academic Ndirangu Wachanga then examines the work and activism of Kenyan writer Micere Mugo to conclude this section.

The eighth and final section of the book contains essays on three Pan-African musical activists. South African-Zimbabwean analyst Nomsa Mwamuka assesses the Pan-Africanist activism of South African singer Miriam Makeba, who used her music and speeches to campaign against apartheid at the UN and other international forums. Jamaican academic Clinton Hutton investigates how Bob Marley used reggae as a weapon for preaching a liberation gospel that advocated the decolonisation of southern Africa and the unity of Africa and its diaspora. Finally, Nigerian academic Sola Olorunyomi examines the Pan-African and civil rights struggles of the radical anti-establishment Nigerian musical activist, Fela Anikulapo-Kuti.

Concluding Reflections

In concluding this introductory voyage that has stretched from Addis Ababa to Abuja through Atlanta and Antigua, it is important to note that the Pan-African solidarity forged in the crucible of five centuries of slavery, colonialism, and the decolonisation and anti-apartheid struggles, has dissipated. Pan-Africanism is thus in urgent need of revival. The ideology will need to build a new civil society-led movement with bridges to Africa and the diaspora that goes beyond the sterile Pan-Africanism of governments, to re-embrace a Pan-Africanism of peoples. This book seeks to contribute to catalysing these efforts.

In order to achieve a new Pan-Africanism, it is also vital that some flesh be added to the skeletal bones of the diaspora as the sixth AU sub-region, so that new bridges can be built between Africa, the Caribbean and the Americas. Entrepreneurial members of the African-American diaspora have invested heavily in countries like South Africa and Liberia, and Africans in the diaspora now contribute more money annually in remittances to their ancestral homes than do foreign donors. The millions of highly educated Africans in the diaspora can further be mobilised to build a viable constituency for Africa.

When in 1989 civil rights stalwart Jesse Jackson urged his black compatriots to embrace the term "African Americans" – as Irish Americans, Italian Americans and Polish Americans had earlier done – this suggestion triggered a firestorm of criticisms in some quarters. Though many politically conscious African Americans like tennis player Arthur Ashe welcomed the identification, Oscar-winning actress Whoopi Goldberg exclaimed: "Don't call me an African American ... It diminishes everything I've accomplished and everything every other black person has accomplished on American soil ... no, I am not an African American. I'm not from Africa. I'm from New York."[146] In similar vein, fellow Oscar winner Morgan Freeman – whose genealogical roots have been traced to Niger, and who played African hero Nelson Mandela in the 2009 movie *Invictus* – refused to use the term, noting, "I'm not African. I'm American."[147] These angry, ahistorical responses reflect the refusal of many black Americans to embrace an African identity which, for them, is often still associated with shameful stereotypical images of their ancestral continent of war, starvation, disease and drought, which is the staple diet of the mainstream American media and Hollywood.

The African-born population in the US astonishingly doubled every decade between 1970 and 2020 to reach 2.4 million by 2019. Most have come from Nigeria, Ethiopia and Ghana.[148] Nigerians are now a model minority population in the US in terms of being among the most educationally qualified groups. This development has sadly led to divisions between African immigrants in the US and African-American descendants of slavery. In 2004, prominent black scholars Henry Louis Gates Jr and Lani Guinier questioned the phenomenon of more confident black Africans and West Indians from middle-class backgrounds benefiting more from "affirmative action" programmes in US universities than slave-descended Americans.[149] The same fierce debates erupted between the same group of students at Cornell University in New York, and descended into ugly acrimony. Urgent dialogue is therefore needed if such discourses are not to drive a permanent wedge between two groups that have historically pursued the same struggles of emancipation, and still share many of the same interests and goals.

Over 155 years after American slavery should have ended with the conclusion of the country's civil war in 1865, there is still a stubborn persistence of racism in the US, and the country seems unable to rid itself of the ghosts of slavery.[150] Until her death in August 2019, African-American Nobel laureate Toni Morrison continued to bemoan "the layers of scar tissue that the black-body has grown in order to obscure, if not annihilate, the slavebody underneath".[151]

In the Caribbean, identification with Africa has grown tremendously as a result of Nollywood movies and from its populations seeing cultures and people with whom they can identify. But the level of social interaction and trade between both regions is abysmally low, despite periodic high-level intergovernmental summits. The geographical pull of the US, where many Caribbean students study and desire to study, and the overwhelming American cultural pull, still remain strong influences throughout the Caribbean.

It is now time to bring this griot's tale to an end. So, who uttered the paradoxically immortal words: "Death is an exercise in Pan-Africanism"? These were the words of Abiranja, one of Ali Mazrui's characters in the author's haunting novel *The Trial of Christopher Okigbo* (1971). The book "tries" Nigeria's greatest poet for putting ethnicity before nation, and for betraying his art by swapping the pen for the pistol. Mazrui's novel was set in a "Hereafter" called "AfterAfrica" that formed the background of the traumatic, bloody disunity of the Nigerian civil war of 1967–70, which threatened the disintegration of Africa's Gulliver.[152] Algerian freedom fighter and founding president Ahmed Ben Bella – who was instrumental in creating and funding the OAU's Liberation Committee at its inaugural summit in 1963 – had similarly implored his fellow leaders in Addis Ababa: "So let us agree to die a little or even completely so that the peoples still under colonial domination may be free and African unity may not be a vain word."[153] Having united to attain Kwame Nkrumah's political kingdom, Africa and its neglected diaspora must now collaborate to reach Walter Rodney's socio-economic kingdom and Maya Angelou's cultural kingdom, by building a new people-driven Pan-Africanism, from Benin to Bahia through Baltimore and Bridgetown.

THE GREAT DURBAN BETRAYAL: GLOBAL AFRICA, REPARATIONS, AND THE END OF PAN-AFRICANISM

Hilary Beckles

FOR OVER THREE HUNDRED YEARS, the global political and philosophical thinking of African liberation has revolved around the organising concept of Pan-Africanism. The enchainment and chattel enslavement of Africans by Europeans in particular, on the continent and in its many diasporas, engendered pedagogies of on-site resistance and cosmologies of return. Over time, displaced Africans, at home and abroad, formulated fictions and fellowships of bonding and belonging, and developed cultural practices seeking reattachment and solidarity with strong ontological underpinnings of identity. This was inevitably a two-way process in which "continent" and "castaway" communities spoke a complex language of mutual recognition of historical pain and future gain. "Pan-Africa" was invented, and battles – both bloody and bookish – were waged in its name. As the formative period of enslavement morphed into the general expanse of colonialism, these intellectual energies and physical encounters took different forms and shapes, but intentions revolved around a common set of core visions.

The Pioneers of Pan-Africanism

Long before the first Pan-African Conference was convened in London in 1900 – organised by a prominent citizen of Trinidad and Tobago, Henry Sylvester-Williams – and five subsequent congresses were held in Paris, London, Brussels,

Lisbon, New York and Manchester in the first half of the twentieth century – the global struggle for black freedom from slavery and colonialism had espoused concepts of African social solidarity and cultural identification. This movement had deep historical and political pedigree. Africans resisted their entrapment. The "Middle Passage" heralded a culture of maritime rebellion and maroonage. The colonial plantations became sites of endemic revolutionary warfare. Every generation of enslaved Africans in the Americas rose up in mass rebellion. In this way, Africans gave to the "New World" its first foundation in the politics of fighting for freedom and political equality.[1]

The diasporic anti-slavery wars between the sixteenth and nineteenth centuries were also designed and described within African redemption discourses that served to hold the "Motherland" aloft against the denigration of European colonisation and chattel brutalisation. "All Haitians are black," President Jean-Jacques Dessalines wrote into the 1805 national independence constitution. All black people, the constitution further provided, were free; and all black people who arrived in Haiti as maroons and runaways would not only be free, but legally empowered with automatic citizenship. This constitutional posture served to enshrine a Pan-African vision into the realpolitik of Caribbean nationhood, and established Haiti – the American hemisphere's first free republic – as the ancestral site, not only of popular democracy, but of institutionalised Pan-Africanism.[2]

Before the seismic Haitian enterprise, there had been many embryonic efforts. When, for example, the Asantes defeated their Dutch enslavers in battle in Berbice (part of contemporary Guyana) in the grand rebellion of 1763, their political leader, Kofi, was enstooled in a state of chair as the Asantehene of the first Afro-Caribbean kingdom. The Ghanaian-descended Asantes and other Africans within the kingdom boasted about their military skills and celebrated their African cultural roots and identity. The ruling Asante also moved to have African cultural institutions deeply embedded within the governance model of the kingdom.[3]

King Kofi's leadership vision was shaped by his Asante ethnicity, but the presence of other African groups – and Creoles – in his kingdom gave impetus to an inevitable black empowerment of all Africans. In championing the freedom from enslavement for all Africans, Kofi's Pan-African credentials should be recognised as a precursor to the eruption of Haiti's General Toussaint L'Ouverture and President Jean-Jacques Dessalines half a century later.

At the core of incipient Pan-Africanism was the Caribbean diaspora, home to an emerging global capitalism that had cornered the market in Europe's criminal transatlantic trade in African bodies.[4] The vast majority of the estimated 15 million Africans who survived the *maafa* – the Holocaust of the Middle Passage – had been extracted from West and Central Africa. The sons and daughters of "Guinea" – as Europeans then referred to African communities – collectively built the cultural matrix now referred to as the "Black Atlantic".[5] This relatively new world hosted old African identities that were rooted in a traditional vision of community, civil relations of justice, and the moral authority of Africa's ancestors. The Middle Passage for survivors was therefore more than a bloodthirsty ocean: it was also a bridge over which travelled some of Africa's best and brightest youths who brought with them their communities' finest thoughts.

Pan-Africanism, then – despite the long-established practice of African enslavement beyond the Sahara into the Mediterranean and the Middle East and across the Indian Ocean into Asia – emerged as a Black Atlantic political paradigm built around the ideal of freedom for all Africans, as well as the decolonisation of the African continent. That the trade in black bodies was also a movement of African epistemologies served to secure the intellectual and political consciousness necessary for the monumental, multi-continental Pan-African movement. Thus was reconstituted in the wider Atlantic the African aversion to bondage and the idealisation of the Motherland as the site of salvation. This gave the Pan-African ethos an unrelenting energy for liberation.

Pan-Africanism, then, as a political construct, took shape and gathered unto itself dispersed diasporas that were hell-bent on forging paradigms of persistent revolution in opposition to European colonialism. The very ideas of black collectivism, of African global identification, and the cultural idealisation of Africa were, in themselves, sufficient to frame Pan-Africanism as a struggle for freedom. Political activation of the belief that Africa must be free of colonial rule and all forms of European military domination and be restored to its prior historic trajectory was a commitment to disrupting the imperial world. The global dispersal of enslaved Africans by Europeans and Arabs provided the fuel that fanned the flames of Pan-Africanism. The fire was not confined physically to plantation diasporas, but blazed a vision of black liberty beyond the sites of enslavement.

Diasporas as sites of Pan-Africanism demanded definitions of all Africans as dichotomised persons existing in a "home and exile" paradigm. Politics and anthropology provided the main tools for explanatory frameworks that produced militant Pan-African camaraderie for everyday life. The diaspora cultivated the "Creole" as the ethnically disconnected but spiritually stimulated and recentred African. Separated by oceans of oppression and deemed "detribalised", diasporas fought back with identity cutlasses that gave birth to cultural "retention" studies. Pan-Africanism required that Creoles be classified in categories that measured degrees of retention of African culture. It also stereotyped diasporas as "dreamscapes". But Creoles rejected notions of distance and dissipation. Instead, they set aside notions of dilution, and declared themselves inauthentic.

However, the double description of the diaspora as "detribalised" and "Africanless" drove some early Pan-Africanists such as African-American sociologist W.E.B. Du Bois (see Morris in this volume) to descend deeper in the disrespected dimensions of the dichotomy. Forced to come to terms with their own "Creolisation", "detribalisation", "inter-tribalisation" and "trans-Africanisation", diaspora Pan-Africans asserted the notion of their "double identity". The concept of Creole Pan-Africanism also served to resist the claim of enslavers that their African "chattels" in the colonies were lesser peoples without language and culture. These Pan-Africans clung to performance culture and took to woods, mountains and caves to save remnants and elements of Africanness that could not be stored in their souls. At every turn, these founders of Pan-Africanism prayed and fought for the restoration of their respected Motherland.

The "mother–child" paradigm underpinned Pan-Africanism at its outset and required little clarification, since the break in cultural lineage and legacy was clear for all to see. The "mother" had been raped and plundered, and her children manacled and murdered. The pain was stored in the cargo holds, and tears filled the Atlantic before they flowed into its rivers, lakes and lagoons. The "hot springs" of the soul bubbled until, at the beginning of the twentieth century, Pan-African congresses erupted as a show of confidence and commitment, and a declaration of unity for the onward march to freedom.

The diaspora's refusal to accept its Creolity as "cultural inferiority", lesser than and therefore reduced, enabled early Pan-Africanists to keep faith with the child-like idealisation of the "Mother". Even in the face of the Mother's occasional ontological scorn, the child looked beyond itself and identified its political maturity within the mantra of her maternity. As Pan-Africanism took shape, Creole siblings promoted their own rivalry, and language quickly came into being which also reflected the divisive thinking of the enslaver. The Creole, said the enslaver, was "detribalised". "We agree," retorted the Creole voice, "but look out for my sword at your throat." In this way, the black skin was stretched to the limit to give life to the Pan-African vision of political unity.

The magnitude of the solidarity project suppressed the separatists. The praxis of Pan-Africanism demanded discipline and, to some degree, denials of fractures and the fomenting of inner differences. Powerful minds tapped into the spirit wells of the many, and called forth a politics that took centre stage in the early twentieth century as a prominent revolutionary force. Marcus Garvey's emergence from plantation Jamaica – as Igbo (the major ethnic group in eastern Nigeria) a place as can be imagined – was fuelled by feelings of unity that had not been buried under the burden of bondage. "A new tribe," he said, "had come into being." Speaking the languages of the enslaver, this new "tribe" had but one overriding mission: to tear off the chains of the "homeland" and restore its injured ancestral matrimony.

The Struggle for African Liberation

Pan-Africanists called for an international war – by all means necessary, to paraphrase Malcolm X (see Daniels in this volume) – in order to redeem the dream of an Africa free from the white man's plunder and disrespect. All struggles, in all communities where Africans existed, were considered tributaries flowing into the mighty river that had but one direction and one destiny. There was no time or place for distractions and details that complicated the plot. All Africans – "Creole and crystallised" – were called upon to focus on the main agenda: a free and independent Africa. There was a call for talk of ethnic identities in the colonies to be condemned, and for the drivel in Africa about "detribalised diasporas" to be consigned to the dustbin of history. The goals of the early Pan-Africanists were focused, determined and diametrically opposed to obvious ethnic divisions.

W.E.B. Du Bois and Marcus Garvey had their political differences, but their ideological offspring refused to become deeply involved in the issue. As Pan-Africanists, Trinidadians C.L.R. James and George Padmore and Martinique's Frantz Fanon (see Cudjoe, Duggan and Jinadu in this volume) connected to Guinea-Bissau's Amílcar Cabral, Ghana's Kwame Nkrumah (see Rabaka and Biney in this volume), South Africa's Nelson Mandela and Congo's Patrice Lumumba to frame the fight as a cerebral missile with a clearly defined target. There was no time for the tensions beneath the surface and the differences still being promoted on diaspora plantations and in the villages of the homeland. Feelings of distance, and of disconnection and loss, had to be set aside – even if temporarily – until the war had been won.

For these reasons, Pan-Africanism could not have been, and was not intended to be, a "popular grassroots movement" or an ideology rooted in the common reality of everyday life. It was not framed as a philosophy for social living, but as a call to arms. Its purpose was intended to be primarily political rather than socio-cultural, and its life expectancy was always going to be defined in the pragmatism of the struggle that had called it into being. This conceptual legitimacy of Pan-Africanism meant that its leaders would be tied to its deliverables: these were not peace-time community leaders, but temporal mobilisers for a mission of liberation.

This understanding of their identity produced in Pan-Africanists, by necessity, a level of political passion forged deep in the arms of violent struggle amid the pressing presence of death and destruction. These Pan-African pioneers worked in a space fraught with treachery and euphoria. They were prepared to die for the project, for Africa, for black people. They were messianic men and women, such as Edward Blyden, Amy Ashwood Garvey and George Padmore (see Khadiagala, Reddock and Duggan in this volume), who were singular in purpose and idealistic in attitudes.

On the ground in the diaspora, and in Africa, such men and women were not recognised as heroes of theoretical causes. They were unrealistic, possessed of impractical minds, driven to madness by a mission too remote to be reasonable. To die for a distant place, and for a race that knew death as its popular culture, was in itself an expression of personality disorder. Rushing off to defend Abyssinia (Ethiopia) from Mussolini's terror in the 1930s, for example, and returning to the Caribbean as Rastafarians in the image of Rastafari – Ethiopia's King Haile Selassie (see Hutton in this volume) – was ample proof and compelling evidence, many said, of this loss of mind.[6]

But for over three hundred years, the diaspora went to its death in defence of Africa. Martinican intellectual Frantz Fanon's fate in Algeria as strategist of a savage peasant war waged against the fanatical French[7] served as a symbol of the state of mind that spawned Marcus Garvey. The war for Ghana's freedom also honed the minds of two fellow Caribbean Pan-Africanists – C.L.R. James and George Padmore – both invited back to the ancestral "home" by Nkrumah to help him rebuild the colonial Gold Coast after liberating the country from British colonialism. Both symbolised the power of Pan-African intellectualism, and both lie buried in the deep soil of Ghana today.

Finally, the decision by Cuba's Fidel Castro to send Caribbean women and men to fight to their death in southern Africa – Angola, Mozambique and Namibia – in the 1980s in order to drive the racist apartheid apparition out of

"Azania"[8] confirmed the Caribbean as a diasporic place not to be trifled with within the Pan-African liberation project. Caribbean citizens went to war for a century in support of Africa, the homeland. They joined with their brothers and sisters on all sides of the Mississippi, and those in the anterior of the Amazon, to tear down, burn down and bomb out the albinocratic structures that had long held their "Mother" captive.

The Great Betrayal: The 2001 World Conference against Racism

Then came "Durban", and the betrayal of the diaspora, in the building it had helped to construct – a free South Africa – by those leaders who had benefited the most from the great sacrifices of those who came before them. It was in August–September 2001, at the United Nations World Conference against Racism, Racial Discrimination, Xenophobia and Related Intolerance, that "old Pan-Africanism" was finally laid to rest, without being given a decent burial. A global audience was gathered to examine the legacies of chattel slavery, native genocide and colonialism that remained in place, still defining the post-liberation era of African history. Hosted by South Africa's president Thabo Mkebi (see Adebajo in this volume) – the heir who had inherited the Pan-African mantle of the saintly Nelson Mandela – the diaspora arrived in Durban with its agenda to discuss reparatory justice for the historical crimes committed against humanity during five centuries of slavery and colonialism.

It was a grand reciprocal moment when the diaspora expected –and had good cause to celebrate – the epic Pan-African continuation of black solidarity. We expected the liberated "Mother" to stand cheek to chest with its Creole children in embracing the case for collective justice in order to soothe the sorrows of slavery. It was, however, not to be. Up to the designing of the Durban gathering, the expression of Pan-African solidarity was vocal and sometimes vociferous. Reparations would, however, turn out to be the key that slammed African doors in the face of the diaspora.

The "West" – the United States, Canada and Western Europe – stood in solidarity with each other. Africa broke with its own diaspora, joined with the former enslavers and colonisers, sending shivers down the spines of Pan-African soldiers and scholars. Thus was shattered the Pan-African solidarity that had so painstakingly been constructed over half a millennium. One by one, African leaders told the West that it had nothing to fear from the diaspora, now cast in the diplomatic dungeon as disruptors of the Durban peace. Nigeria – which had lost about five million souls to the sugar plantations of the West Indies – joined with the West against the West Indies. Ghana – which was first gutted by the British slave trading companies owned by the royals of Westminster in the late seventeenth century[9] – joined with the descendants of these former monarchs against Barbados, the first Ghanaian diaspora. Senegal – where it had all begun on the island of Gorée, the place that had sent first shipments from Gambia to the galleys of the slave ships – was aggressive in its betrayal of its enslaved ancestors. Its president, Abdoulaye Wade, dismissed claims for reparations as "childish".

South African host Thabo Mbeki presided over the Durban debacle that sent the diaspora home bewildered in its isolated reality. The Caribbean feared that it could no longer count on Africa to reciprocate within Pan-African solidarity. Reparations were officially expunged from the agenda, and placed in non-binding brackets in the conference documents so that Western governments could walk away from their unspeakable historical crimes. In post-apartheid South Africa, then, West African states and West Indian nations parted ways. The Durban conference, as a result of this unbridgeable rift, agreed to a resolution to be adopted by the UN, that the enchainment and enslavement of Africans in the diaspora *should* have been a crime. The treachery of the word "should" stood as clear testimony of the betrayal that had driven a sharp wedge through the heart of Pan-Africanism.

For participants at this inter-governmental forum – including this author – the Pan-African ideal had died a painful death in Durban at the hands of African leaders who were clearly not representing the popular views of their own civil societies and 800 million-strong populations. From Senegal to South Africa and from Banjul to Bamako, civil society groups stood in solidarity with the diaspora. They too had been betrayed by their political leaders. They too had had the scales removed from their eyes, as their rulers' compromises on the most violent crimes committed against humanity stood in stark contrast to how the West had dealt with the Nazi Holocaust, which had killed an estimated six million Jews between 1933 and 1945.

The diasporic dream of Pan-Africanism thus descended into a nightmare that became the "Durban delusion". This paved the way for the official approach to post-apartheid amnesia. The description of the diaspora as "naive" in its expectations of support for the cause of reparatory justice only added insult to injury. "Sold from Africa" had been the old diaspora song; "Sold out in Africa" now became the new jingle. Jazz gave way to the blues, and the lady was no longer singing.

Pan-Africanism was resoundingly rejected in Durban in 2001 in the language of African political leaders who saw their future responsibility for Africa as having little or no relevance to the diaspora. For sure, the latter had hoped that the reparatory justice movement would create for Pan-Africanism a new frame of reference, adjusted and more relevant to the liberation agenda of the twenty-first century. It was expected to rekindle the same passion and purpose that had characterised its twentieth-century antecedent. This was, however, clearly not the thinking of African leaders. They proposed to the world body a different vision and language. Rolled out instead was the concept of the "African Renaissance", a nebulous alternative to global "reparatory justice" that sought to delegitimise the diaspora by winning Western support, aid and investments (see also Adebajo on Mbeki in this volume).[10]

Mbeki's African Renaissance was effectively a general reformulation of the World Bank's development strategy for Africa in which the continent's dependence on foreign direct investment and financial assistance, largely from the West, was considered the only option available. Steeped in Western dependency, the African Renaissance lacked any moral or intellectual integrity or authority, and used a weak rationale for rejecting the diaspora's vision for the deepening of Pan-Africanism and the continuation of African liberation.[11]

After Durban: The Birth of "Global Africa"

What has unfolded in the two decades since Durban speaks to the weakening of solidarity within Pan-Africanism. The state of Africa's political leadership no longer inspires the diaspora, and there is a growing belief that what the Caribbean sees as African liberation is not what Pan-Africanism itself had imagined. The diasporic betrayal at Durban is now read, in hindsight, as a necessary step to unhinge the leadership of Africa's growing dependency – as well as its neo-colonial politics and policies – from the vision of Pan-Africanism. Furthermore, Durban is seen across the diaspora as the first salvo to free African governments from any moral obligation to diaspora nations by foreclosing any request for reciprocity.

The evidence of this rupture and the rescinding of historical obligations is found in the data that show, for example, Angola's extraordinary high levels of direct foreign investments from Portugal, the coloniser that bled its people dry,[12] while Luanda has attracted no investments of any significance from Cuba, which had paid the greatest human price in blood for its liberation. Likewise, South Africa, despite its post-Mandela euphoria, has not promoted much development in "New World" diasporas that had campaigned vigorously for its liberation over decades of bloody sacrifice. The tepid designation of the diaspora as Africa's sixth region by the African Union (AU) in the aftermath of Durban,[13] and the effective marginalisation of "global Pan-Africanism" within the AU, reveal how "shadow politics" have replaced the real life centrality of "Global Africa".

In the absence of a legitimate Pan-Africanism to guide its ideological emergence, Africa and its 55 nation-states of one billion people have drifted into neo-colonial idealisms that invite the cultural and political recolonisation of the continent. Many minor reversals have had a snowball effect, each with its own weakening impact upon the consolidation of liberation movements. Africa's rising middle classes find reasons to crave and celebrate "Europeanness" in their midst. The collapse of continent–diaspora solidarity at Durban signalled, in many respects, the beginning of the end of twentieth-century versions of Pan-Africanism. It also brought to a close the traditional ideological hierarchy that had structured the vexing "pure and Creole" and "core and castaway" paradigms.

Furthermore, Durban discredited the legitimacy of the call in Pan-African discourses for diasporas to accept their subordinate status and play a supportive role in the service of the Motherland. Instead, what reached full maturity was the notion that "continent and castaways" were now on an equal footing, both home to nation-states that were equal in the new Pan-African community.

Concluding Reflections: Towards a New Pan-Africanism?

The rupture of expectations in Durban in 2001 was initially received as a major setback in Pan-Africanist circles. In a short time, however, the event was understood as the forceful coming of age of the diaspora, a growing up, so to speak. Jamaica, for example, was no longer a distant diaspora of Nigeria, but a nation-state equal in status within the evolved Pan-African political cosmology. Brazil basked in the economic power it had attained, and no longer considered Angola to be the political core that it should celebrate. The pre-Durban Pan-African narrative was now understood to be obsolete across the diaspora, and the enterprise to find a new comprehension was launched.

Emerging from the ashes of the politically discredited twentieth-century Pan-Africanism is the "Global Africa" paradigm, a version of which Kenyan scholar Ali Mazrui had helped to popularise from 1986 through his book and nine-part documentary series, *The Africans* (see also Ndlovu-Gatshini in this volume).[14] In every way, this concept has sought to rescue Pan-Africanism from its internal contradictions that many had found suffocating and condescending. At the heart of this new idealism is a liberating horizontalism that is to be the twenty-first-century face of Pan-Africanism. The diaspora was freed by its rejection in Durban. As home to developing nations with their own internal concerns, they were encouraged to look inward for the first time.

"Global Africa", then, integrates dozens of black majority nations and communities on multiple continents, all seeking solidarity around a range of ideas and actions that facilitate their collective well-being. Political mutualism has replaced cultural hierarchy. African states could now be seen for what they had become – neo-colonies – and diasporas were no longer blinded by their romantic mysticism of the Motherland.

There is no longer an expectation of solidarity among black nations. Pragmatism is the principle that now propels the new political understanding. When francophone Africa, for example, aligns with France in the UN against the Caribbean quest for the independence of Martinique and Guadeloupe, there is no longer a reading of the vote as retrograde. When Angola minimises its commercial relations with Cuba – its revolutionary partner – and maximises investments with imperial Portugal, such expediency is likely to be understood as the new normal.

It was inevitable that twentieth century Pan-Africanism would shed its hegemonic political and military skins, thus enabling the framing of an evolved discourse. The new network of mutual cultural and commercial alliances will be devoid of a liberationist impulse and shaped by a more familiar focus on domestic nation-building imperatives. The conflation of parochialism and nationalism will seek to ground the legitimacy of the new diversity, thus challenging Pan-Africanists to choose between old skins and new wines. It will not be an easy task to imagine or embrace the positive in this postulation, and to contemplate its epistemic power.

Many Pan-Africanists will not agree that Durban was also the site of an ontological awakening. Fifty-five nation-states have been created in Africa out of the twentieth-century Pan-African paradigm. The diaspora has spawned dozens of its own states. While these nations have a common historical pedigree in Pan-Africanism, the degree to which they have diverged has to be recognised, and reasons for these divergences must be carefully analysed.

With the twentieth-century mission completed – and Du Bois's "colour line" struggles partly vanquished – a new perception of Pan-Africanism is now required. With eyes wide open to post-liberation national diversity, Pan-Africanists have the option of determining the degree to which twenty-first-century black internationalism can be understood as "Global Africa" in action. Furthermore, they have a golden opportunity to frame the narrative of Global Africa as an organising and operational discourse capable of sustaining Pan-Africanism as an effectively empowering philosophy for the future.

PART 2

THE PIONEERS

3

Edward Wilmot Blyden: Pan-African Pioneer

Gilbert M. Khadiagala

"Kwame Nkrumah – the first African nationalist to become president of an independent Ghana – hung a picture of [Edward] Blyden in his office. In this way, Nkrumah demonstrated who had inspired him and taught him the basic tenets of modern African nationalism. Blyden was the intellectual forefather and teacher of black and African nationalists as diverse as Du Bois and Garvey, Casely-Hayford and George Padmore, Azikiwe and Kenyatta, and finally Césaire and Senghor."[1]

This quote from Israeli scholar Benyamin Neuberger shows that, in the twenty-first century, Edward Wilmot Blyden remains one of the powerhouses of Pan-Africanism due to his unique and historical contributions to ideas around African unity, identity, dignity, sovereignty and prosperity. Blyden had a profound influence on the makers of modern Pan-Africanism; current generations unfamiliar with his ideas, therefore, need to revisit his perceptive reflections on African identity, self-determination, Africa's umbilical links with the diaspora and the meaning of territorial nationalism in colonial West Africa. Also important, Blyden's work speaks directly to contemporary debates about the decolonisation of education, the centrality of indigenous knowledge production to African liberation and the obstacles to realising these objectives. Revisiting Blyden's work is also essential in recreating the indivisible links between black nationalism and Pan-Africanism. Before Pan-Africanism, there was African nationalism, but nationalism was inconceivable without a sophisticated conception of racial pride, patriotism and consciousness that Blyden helped to articulate throughout his writings. In this regard, Blyden's erudite defence of black identity and self-respect forged the parameters of Pan-Africanism both as the universal idea uniting African people and the organisational impetus for continental emancipation and integration.

Born in St Thomas, a Danish-occupied Caribbean island, on 31 August 1832, Blyden spent his early years in Charlotte Amalie, the capital of St Thomas, and in Porto Bello, Venezuela. Some biographers, such as Tobagan-American scholar Hollis Lynch, have claimed that Blyden's father's family traced its ancestry directly to the Igbo of south-east Nigeria.[2] Although born in a family that was free and literate, Blyden was sensitive in childhood to the slavery that was all around him. After moving to the United States in 1845 to pursue further education, he was denied admission to three different theological colleges due to his race. In the US, he became acquainted with leading members of the American Colonization Society (ACS) who inspired him to emigrate to Liberia in 1850 at the age of 18, barely three years after Liberia had attained independent statehood in 1847 under an Americo-Liberian oligarchy.[3] In Liberia's capital of Monrovia, Blyden completed his high school education – the only formal education he obtained – before launching a long career as a clergyman, scholar, activist, educator and diplomat. In a distinguished career in Liberia, Sierra Leone and Nigeria, Blyden served in various positions, including: professor of Classics at Liberia College (1862–71); Liberia's secretary of state (1864–6); president of Liberia College (1880–4); Liberian educational commissioner to the United States and Britain (1861); Liberian ambassador to Britain (1877–8, 1892); and Sierra Leone's agent to the interior (1872–3).

As a citizen of West Africa until his death on 7 February 1912, Blyden witnessed momentous political transformations in the sub-region that shaped his thinking and writing. But, equally germane, through his activism and advocacy Blyden helped to shape the political and educational trajectories that unfolded in West Africa and beyond. As an immigrant from the Americas in West Africa in the nineteenth and twentieth centuries, Blyden acquired a unique vantage point to lend fresh perspectives to the formative ideas of racial consciousness and black nationalism, which laid solid foundations for subsequent ideas such as Négritude (see Irele in this volume) and the "African Personality" (see Biney in this volume). These concepts drove the movements for African self-determination, liberation and continental Pan-Africanism. Having lived through both slavery and colonialism, Blyden's entire life embodied the triumph over adversity and enormous intellectual resilience in the face of serious obstacles.

In this chapter, I focus on two related strands of Blyden's political thought: the first embraces the emancipatory ideas of dignity, self-respect and self-assertiveness that marked his reflections on the state of the black race and the meaning of Africa. These ideas were critical in lending sharpness to the notions of racial identity and pride which informed and suffused Pan-Africanism. Through vigorous articulation of black consciousness and efficacy, Blyden created a universal but essential ideational and cultural bridge between the diaspora and Africa, a bridge that was to infuse Pan-Africanism with energy and vitality. The second strand captures efforts to mobilise notions of racial identity and dignity into the spatial and territorial domains of West Africa. This phase of Blyden's career is important because he was then wrestling with how to use the experiments and experiences of Liberia and Sierra Leone as the pivot for an incipient political community in West Africa. Through this mobilisation, Blyden inspired the Pan-Africanist movement that propelled the project of decolonisation and continental integration in Africa.

Affirming Africa and Blackness

Even though he was born a free man, Blyden grew up before slavery was abolished in the Danish Caribbean (1848). This was years before the abolition of slavery in the United States (1865), Cuba (1886) and Brazil (1888). As a young man in the US, he was frequently afraid of being taken into slavery, particularly after the passage of the Slave Fugitive Act (1850), which mandated the forcible arrest of black people, even in the American North, where there were many freemen. The oppression and humiliation of slavery followed by colonial repression formed the backdrop to Blyden's life of activism. Alongside physical oppression were the powerful ideas of racial inferiority that he had to deal with. But these practices and ideas also forced his determination to reverse these notions and reclaim the humanity of black people.[4] Embracing and celebrating an African identity was Blyden's antidote to the ravages of slavery and colonial capitalism. In a famous letter to the British Liberal politician William Gladstone in 1862, Blyden observed:

> I belong to a race which, for centuries, has been despoiled by other races;
> we have been made to serve the commercial and agricultural interests of

the American continent, for no other reward than physical brutalization and mental deterioration. And I can conceive that every effort made in England – the commercial mistress and law giver of the world – to place commerce on a just and proper basis, will tend to loosen the bonds and hasten the disenthralment of my people. The gigantic evil by which a large portion of mankind is degraded, and made to labor without compensation for another portion, proves that there is derangement somewhere in the "economy" of leading statesmen, some "screw loose" in the commercial machinery of the world.[5]

Apart from collective humiliation and degradation, Blyden personally faced similar experiences to those of his fellow blacks, as vividly demonstrated in being rejected by theological colleges in the US in 1849. While on assignment as a Liberian commissioner to the United States responsible for recruiting returnees to Africa, Blyden confronted the face of American racism, as he recounted in his letter to William Gladstone in 1862: "Though Congress has acknowledged Liberian independence, I, as a citizen of Liberia, was not allowed to enter the House of Representatives during the session because I was a black man; and before I could leave that distinguished city I was obliged to get a white man to vouch that I was a free man."[6]

The systematic discrimination that Blyden lived through led to his conviction of the need to affirm his individual identity as a black man, and to use his intellectual acumen to champion blackness and the collective aspirations of black people. The affirmation of Africa was important to him because, contrary to the existing theories that posited the African as inferior – without culture or capacity for creative thought – Blyden started from the fundamental premise that all races were distinct but equal. By this logic, Africans had their own traditions and their history different from those of Europe. But this distinctiveness afforded Africans space to make a significant contribution to world civilisation. This theme of African capacity for enriching global knowledge systems and enterprises was to inform Blyden's life-long approach to education as the cultivation of African values. There was no stronger defence of African capacity and ingenuity than Blyden's conviction that the African was on a par with the European. Thus he asserted:

The mistake, which Europeans often make in considering questions of Negro improvement and the future of Africa, is in supposing that the

76

Negro is the European in embryo – in the undeveloped stage – and that when, by and by, he shall enjoy the advantages of civilization and culture, he will become like a European; in other words, that the Negro is on the same line of progress, in the same groove, with the European, but infinitely in the rear.[7]

In further debunking the myth of European superiority, Blyden railed against the beliefs of what he called "superficial observers" that the "Negro has not the mental or more susceptibilities of the European – that we have no eyes to see and no ears to hear, and no hearts to feel; but this is a serious mistake ... The African also has lessons of wisdom to impart to mankind. He can truly say to the European: 'I hear a voice thou cannot hear, I saw a hand that thou cannot see.'"[8] In refuting the basic premises of the prevailing racist thought of this epoch, Blyden had to resort to a counter-narrative that celebrated black pride and identity. Hence the underpinnings of black nationalism that he propounded were anchored solidly on blackness and cultural nationalism. As Neuberger notes:

Blyden's nationalism was not confined to the refutation of white beliefs in white supremacy. His cultural nationalism aimed to free blacks and Africans from internalized notions of cultural inferiority injected into them by racist ideology. In a sense, he called for psychological and cultural decolonization before the advent of colonialism. Blyden urged blacks to be proud of black achievements and contributions to world civilization, whether originating in "Mother Africa" .... or in the Diaspora.[9]

African-American sociologist Andrew Billingsley summarises Blyden's contribution to blackness:

Now there was a black man! Black in body, mind, and soul. He walked the earth for eighty years across three continents telling himself, his people, and the world, that unlike the teachings of the Christian Church that black is bad and inferior, black is beautiful and good, and strong and soft and prophetic, and makes a distinct contribution to civilization if the world would only listen; a world which did not listen in his time and does not listen in our time but which must be made to listen in the years ahead.[10]

Black nationalism in Blyden's thought is inextricably tied to the notion of the "African Personality", which captures a distinctive socio-cultural, spiritual, and ideological milieu in which Africans live. In contract to the "European Personality", which he saw as harsh, individualistic, materialistic, combative, and oriented to technology, Blyden depicted the African Personality as characterized by simplicity, natural spontaneity, emotion, connection to the soil, solidarity, communal harmony, and egalitarianism.[11] According to Nigerian academic Abiola Irele, the concept of the African Personality denoted "the unifying framework of ideas on African institutions and destiny".[12] These ideas sought the awakening of Africa and its people scattered across the globe, and, in Blyden's conviction, they would provide an alternative vista for their future in confidence and dignity. In his vociferous defence of black cultural distinctiveness, Blyden spoke of "spiritual decolonization", a process to reverse the contamination of black identity through Westernisation.[13] Most of Blyden's explorations in West Africa's hinterland focused on the search for the spirit and values that informed these institutions. Admiration for the African Personality and identity ultimately led the scholar-diplomat to an idealistic vision of Africa that contrasted sharply with the bondage and repression in the Americas. In his famous 1888 book, *Christianity, Islam and the Negro Race*, Blyden reflected on the significance of the black migration to Africa:

In Africa, he casts off his trammels, his wings develop, and he soars into an atmosphere of exhaustless truth for him. There he becomes a righteous man; he casts off his fears and his doubts. There for him is perpetual health; there he returns to reason and faith. There he feels that nothing can happen to the race. There he is surrounded by millions of men, as far as he can see or hear, just like himself, and he is delivered from the constant dread which harasses him in this country, as to what is to become of the Negro. There the solicitude is in the opposite direction. There he fears for the white man, living in a climate hostile, and often fatal to him.[14]

A similar optimism informs Blyden's vision of the contribution of returning exiles, alongside the indigenous Africans, to the regeneration of a bountiful continent:

In visions of the future, I behold those beautiful hills – the banks of those charming streams, the verdant plains and flowery fields, the salubrious highlands in primeval innocence and glory, and those fertile districts watered everywhere as the garden of the Lord. I see them all taken possession of by the returning exiles from the West, trained for the work of re-building waste places under severe discipline and hard bondage. I see too their brethren hastening to welcome them from the slopes of the Niger, and from its lovely valleys – from many a sequestered nook, and from many a palmy plain – Mohammedans and Pagans, chiefs and people, all coming to catch something of the inspirations the exiles have brought – to share in the borrowed jewels they have imported, and to march back hand-in-hand with their returned brethren towards the sunrise for the regeneration of a continent.[15]

The "Return to Africa" Movement

Impelled by this vision of Africa, Blyden participated actively in the movement to convince black Americans to return to their ancestral continent. As Liberia's commissioner responsible for the return of black people from the United States and Britain, Blyden was a fervent advocate of the return to give meaning and solidity to the idea of an independent black state in Africa, then epitomised by Liberia. Convinced that it was important for black people to migrate to Africa rather than live in servitude in the United States, Blyden led a movement for the resettlement in a number of visits to America before and during the Civil War (1861–65), which were unsuccessful. Billingsley attributes this failure to the conditions of life in the United States: "In the dark hours before the Civil War, the movement flourished; in the hope for freedom generated by the Civil War, it waned; in the disillusionment following Reconstruction it waxed again, only to trickle off in the years after."[16] Nonetheless, Billingsley concedes that Blyden's eloquence and persistence were significant in "holding high the concept of black identity, racial pride, and the idea of Pan-Africanism, which took root among black intellectuals".[17] While acknowledging the importance of the "Return to Africa" movement, Blyden conceded defeat but saw an opportunity for a renewed focus on advocacy and the building of African institutions. As he noted:

The Negro problem must be solved here [in America] or it will appear in Africa in a new form. The Negro must learn to respect himself here before he will be able to perform the functions of true manhood there [in Africa]. Should he leave this country now, harassed and cowed, broken in spirit and depressed, ashamed of his racial peculiarities and deprecating everything intended for racial preservation, he would be destitute of tenacity and force, the self-reliance and confidence, that faith in himself and destiny, which ... would guide him in the policy to be adopted toward the man like himself whom he would find in his ancestral home.[18]

Enhancing Black Rule through Education

After the failure to recruit more settlers from America, Blyden focused his energies on the popularisation of racial pride and blackness through education. His perspective on education proceeded from the powerful assumption that the "African must advance by methods of his own ... he must show that we are able to go it alone, to carve our own way of life."[19] In modern echoes of a decolonised education, Blyden was convinced that education that was adapted to African conditions was much more superior to that found abroad. To effect an enhancement of African life and customs, Blyden proposed an education system that was anchored on local conditions and circumstances: "The object of all education is to secure growth and efficiency; to make man all that his natural gifts would allow him to become; to produce self-respect, a proper appreciation of our powers and of those of other people to beget a fitness for one's sphere of life and action and an ability to discharge the duties imposed."[20] On this basis, therefore, Blyden decried foreign education, suggesting that it deprived the African of "race feelings":

> When a youth is sent for education from Africa to Europe, he must lose a great part of the very training for which he has been sent to school – viz, to prepare for the work of his life. The man who, in the process of his education, has not imbibed a large race feeling, in whom there is no developed pride of race, has failed in a great part of his education. And whatever else may be acquired in Europe, it is evident that, for the Negro, race feeling must be kept in abeyance.[21]

Furthermore, he castigated Western education in Africa for deepening the enslavement of Africa:

> In the case of the Negro, the truth is, that the despotic and overruling method which has been pursued in his education, by good-meaning but un-philosophical philanthropists has so entirely mastered and warped his mind that, in the whole civilized world, scarcely any important political or social issues can be witnessed as the result of the Negro training. All educated Negroes suffer from a kind of slavery in many ways far more subversive of the real welfare of the race than the amount of physical fetters. The slavery of the mind is far more destructive than that of the body.[22]

Consistent with his belief that nurturing African capacities was a collective undertaking between the diaspora and indigenous Africans, Blyden blamed foreign teachers for propagating fallacies and misapprehensions about the African Personality. More controversially, he claimed that foreign teachers from Europe were often prone to tropical diseases, and thus were unable to teach in Africa. Yet, in opposing the role of foreign teachers, Blyden did not reject the injection of foreign resources into educational infrastructure, particularly the African university:

> We cannot ignore the aid of foreigners. As a people not far removed from ancestral barbarism, we need their counsel and fostering care; but, after all, if we were to fulfill properly our destiny as a race; if we are to prove that we are not inherently an unprogressive race, we must strive to understand and grasp the conceptions which nature has given to us. We must crave the help of Europeans, not to Europeanize us, which must always be the labour of Sisyphus, but to help us to understand our own needs, to speak our own thoughts, to express our own feelings, and act ourselves out. Every state and nation and race must fight its own internal battles.[23]

Instead of looking at foreign aid as charity, Blyden, anticipating some of the current discussions on reparations, argued that Africa needed compensation for the egregious crimes committed over the many years of exploitation and oppression. In a December 1872 letter to the British governor of Sierra Leone,

John Pope-Hennessy, Blyden pleaded for resources to help educate a new crop of African leaders who would assume the mantle of leadership:

> Europeans owe us a great debt, not only for the unrequited physical labours we have performed in all parts of the world, but for the unnumbered miseries and untold demoralization they have brought upon Africa by the prosecution for centuries of the horrible traffic to promote their own selfish ends; and we feel that we do not simply ask it as a favour but claim it as a right when we entreat their aid as civilized and Christian Governments in the work of unfettering and enlightening the Negro mind, and placing him in a position to act well his part among the "productive agencies" of time.[24]

As with his views on an indigenous education that would reaffirm the African Personality and African values, Blyden had an optimistic view of the role of Islam in Africa. Although he was a Christian, his explorations in the African interior had convinced him that Islam accorded more closely with African cultures and that, unlike Christianity, the Muslim faith respected most of Africa's customs and institutions. In addition, within Islam Africans took leadership positions: "Mohammedanism in Africa has left the native mastery of himself and of his home; but wherever Christianity has been able to establish itself, with the exception of Liberia, foreigners have taken possession of the country, and in some places, rule the native with oppressive rigour."[25] Blyden also praised Muslim society for fostering scholarship, for encouraging urbanisation, and for creating an egalitarian spirit that "bound tribes together in one strong religious fraternity".[26] Throughout his life, the scholar-diplomat advocated cooperation between Muslims and Christians in realising the ideals of African traditions and customs. This cooperation would also be one of the foundations of the larger political community in West Africa that de-emphasised religious and sectarian differences.[27]

Blyden preferred Sierra Leone as the base for an African university that would impart and inculcate an ethos of racial consciousness and the moral development of Africans. This was primarily because of the country's rich history of racial and ethnic amalgamation and the colonial government's attempts to expand into the interior. More than Liberia, colonial authorities had played an "imperial" role in creating the basis for nationalism.[28] As he wrote to the British governor, Pope-Hennessy, in December 1872:

Sierra Leone is the only place in the world where there is so promising a basis for the erection of an educational institution adapted to our peculiar needs. This Colony, from its peculiar circumstances, the multiplicity of African tribes genuinely represented in it, and the facilities which it has of communication with all parts of the Negro-land, must, for the present, at least, be regarded as the centre of the race: here, therefore, the special educational work at which we are aiming should be begun.[29]

Blyden was also cognisant of Sierra Leone's role in promoting education in West Africa through the first modern university college in the region, Fourah Bay College, which had been established in 1827. He was further aware of the large numbers of West African students in Freetown. This was therefore the natural place to establish an African university that would complement and gradually supplant Fourah Bay. But Blyden was not successful in raising funds for his university. In responding to him, Hennessy noted: "To establish such a University in Africa must be the work of Africans themselves. There are so many monuments of benevolent failures in Sierra Leone, the Government would shrink from undertaking the initiative of such an Institution."[30] Blyden was again ahead of his time as the British colonial government created universities in Nigeria and Ghana only by 1948.

The reaffirmation of blackness coupled with the expression of a transnational black identity and belief in the liberating power of Pan-Africanism spurred Blyden's advocacy of a geographical and political community that would form the foundation of African self-determination in economic, cultural and political terms. But Blyden could not arrive at a territorialised Pan-Africanism without a strong vision of a universal and ideational Pan-Africanism. As British academic, Christopher Fyfe suggested:

Blyden saw the people of Africa not just as Africans, but as members of a dispersed Negro race inhabiting both sides of the Atlantic ... Hence he gave American Negroes a new vision of themselves in relation to their ancestral home. He preached an inner identity with the people of Africa – all members of one great Negro race ... Africans too were given a new vision of themselves as part of a wider identity than they had hitherto perceived. At a period when the educated inhabitants of the British West African colonies were becoming conscious of their own achievement and looking forward to self-government, he made them aware of their affinities not only with transatlantic Negroes but with the inhabitants of the vast continental inland. Thus Blyden can be seen as a forerunner of the Pan-Africanist movement.[31]

Actualising the Pan-Africanist Vision

The second strand of Blyden's thought converged on the transformation of the ideas of African self-consciousness and self-respect into the construction of territorial political and economic communities. As with his participation in the "Return to Africa" movement, Blyden confronted enormous obstacles in the search for this transformation. Despite these challenges, his vision of Pan-Africanism in wider territorial spaces was not diminished. A key part of this vision was Blyden's active engagement in founding newspapers that were aimed at forging a common bond among English-speaking West Africans, in particular in Liberia and Sierra Leone. Thus both the *Negro* and the *West African Reporter* newspapers, which Blyden helped to establish in Freetown in the 1870s, were vehicles for elite socialisation and consciousness-raising to build support for Pan-Africanism.[32]

Equally important, as a diplomat Blyden worked frantically from the mid-1860s to promote rapprochement between Liberia and Sierra Leone because of his belief that the two West African countries were central to the realisation of the dream of a larger political community. For example, at a bilateral event over which he presided in 1866, the two countries resolved that "the time had arrived when there ought to be a contribution of Negro talents and ability on the West Coast of Africa .... for the elevation of our race, morally, socially and politically".[33] Furthermore, in a landmark speech in Sierra Leone in 1884, Blyden maintained that the "two peoples are one in origin and one in destiny and, in spite of themselves, in spite of local prejudices, they must cooperate ... Sierra Leone is a Negro nationality under the British Protectorate, but sooner or later, the two countries would have to unite."[34] This idea anticipated, in a sense, the Mano River Union and the Economic Community of West African States (ECOWAS), which were created in 1973 and 1975 respectively (see Afeikhena in this volume).

Years before the "Scramble for Africa" in 1884–85, Blyden advocated West African unity as the foundation for nationalism beyond borders. This transnational vision of collective self-determination would, in turn, create a solid basis to consolidate the ideas of black consciousness, nationhood, identity and sovereignty. In this enterprise, Blyden consistently advocated the collective mobilisation of the energies of all Africans: indigenous and those in the diaspora. Just as he had stressed the centrality of Sierra Leone in the educational advancement of Africans, Blyden regarded Liberia as the nucleus of a West African political community, the crucible for the actualisation of his Pan-African ideas. Liberia was strategically located to expand its governing institutions into Africa's interior as the first step in the creation of a large territorial space in which the mission of black nationalism would be fulfilled. As Hollis Lynch noted, Blyden was "convinced that the only way of bringing respect and dignity to the Negro race was by building progressive new 'empires' in Africa whose civilization, while remaining basically African, would incorporate useful elements of Western culture, and this he envisaged as coming about through the large-scale New World Negro emigration to the 'fatherland'."[35]

Furthermore, as African-American scholar Judson Lyon observed: "In Blyden's vision, Americo–Liberians were to amalgamate with Africans, thus combining the best Western civilization had to offer the Africans with the essentials of African culture. The Americo–Liberians would then provide the leadership in an African renaissance that would help lead the whole continent to independence."[36]

But in Liberia, Blyden confronted a recalcitrant and obdurate Americo-Liberian settler group ensconced in socio-economic and political privileges and unable to countenance the integration of the Africans of the interior into a new political framework. Illustrating his frustration with the True Whig leaders in Monrovia, Blyden noted in a speech in February 1909:

A group of returned exiles, refugees from the house of bondage, settled along a few hundred miles of the coast of their Fatherland, attempting to rule millions of people, their own kith and kin, on a foreign system in which they themselves have been imperfectly trained, while knowing very little of the facts of the history of the people they assume to rule, either social, economic or religious, and taking for granted that the religious and social theories they have brought across the sea must be adapted to all the needs of the unexpatriated brethren. We are severed from the parent stock – the aborigines – who are the root, branch, and flower of Africa and of any Negro State in Africa.[37]

Frustrated by the unwillingness of the Americo-Liberian oligarchy to contribute to the realisation of his dream of a strong and functional black state, from 1871 Blyden tried to persuade the British colonial authorities in Sierra Leone to extend their jurisdiction in West Africa to Liberia, eventually to create an English-speaking West African state in which black people could assert their own identity and sovereignty.[38] In this regard, Blyden was prepared to sacrifice Liberia's independence for the long-term objective of a larger territorial space for Pan-Africanism.[39] He made similar appeals to the United States in the face of London's reluctance to take on such a responsibility. But here, too, he was unsuccessful. Although critics have harped on this point to castigate Blyden for his support of British imperial expansion, he was convinced that the British would do a better job in reaching out to the peoples of the interior than the Americo-Liberians. In addition, as Hollis Lynch observed:

> Blyden himself never doubted that the European political overlordship was a temporary one, and that independent West African nations would emerge from the former European colonies. This optimism was based on his oft-repeated conviction that, because the climate and diseases accounted for a high mortality rate among them, Europeans could never successfully colonize tropical Africa. But their imperialism would serve the purpose of preparing Africans for political independence.[40]

Concluding Reflections

Blyden's ideas and visions coincided with two momentous eras in black history. Firstly, he lived in the nineteenth century when slavery had devastated black people (see Introduction and Beckles in this volume). Although slavery was abolished during his era, its scars continued to plague the social psyche of black people. Secondly, Blyden was present in the early twentieth century as colonial regimes imposed their imprint on newly established territorial states. In both eras, Blyden sought to establish a cultural thread centred on black consciousness, highlighting the fact that African institutions and customs had their place in human history. With strong convictions about the necessity of a positive portrayal of the black race, Blyden sought to reclaim African humanity and dignity at a time when his was a lone voice in the world.

Even as Africa was transitioning into brutal and harsh colonial conditions, Blyden was optimistic that large territorial spaces would create the opportunities for continental regeneration and renaissance. In a much–cited work, Senegalese poet-president Léopold Senghor acknowledged Blyden's contribution to the ideas around Négritude and the African Personality, noting that, through "the stimulus of a 'revolution of mentalities'", Blyden tried to lead African Americans to cultivate what is "authentically theirs: their 'African Personality' ... and advocated already the method which is ours today: to find one's roots in the values of Négritude, while remaining open to those of non-African civilizations".[41] As Abiola Irele also concluded, Blyden was "in a full sense the originator of the forward movement of the African consciousness whose impulse continues today to sustain our sense of historical being".[42]

Blyden's incredible legacy can be seen in his influence on some of Africa's most important leaders: he helped to shape South Africans, Pixley Seme and Thabo Mbeki's "African Renaissance" (see the Ngqulunga and Adebajo chapters on Mbeki in this volume); Ghana's Kwame Nkrumah's "African Personality" (see Biney in this volume); and Kenyan Ali Mazrui's "Triple Heritage." (see Ndlovu-Gatsheni in this volume).

W.E.B. Du Bois: "The Father of Pan-Africanism"?

Aldon D. Morris

Numerous scholars and political activists view William Edward Burghardt Du Bois as the "father of Pan-Africanism". Du Bois was clearly one of the premier architects of the Pan-African perspective and the historic Pan-African movements. This claim can be sustained by analysing him as a path-breaking scholar and prodigious activist of the twentieth century. When placed within this context, it becomes undeniable that Du Bois was a pioneer of Pan-Africanism.

An African American born in 1868, just three years after the overthrow of American slavery, Du Bois grew up in an America that embraced white supremacy. Indeed, two and a half centuries of slavery had embedded racism deeply in the core of American culture and institutions. White Americans were projected as superior to black people. In fact, black Americans were thought not to be fully human; they were viewed as subhuman creatures with qualities more akin to chimpanzees than to human beings. It was in this milieu that Du Bois matured into a major twentieth-century sociologist, historian, novelist, poet, public intellectual, journalist, activist, leader and Pan-Africanist.

Personal Life in the American North and South

Du Bois's childhood was different from that of most other African Americans. Unlike most black people who grew up in the American South under the brutal oppression of Jim Crow racism, Du Bois was raised in the far-eastern region of the United States in Great Barrington, Massachusetts. Racism in this part of the country was subtle and genteel. As a youngster, Du Bois was spared the horrors of lynching and racial violence. He lived a life fairly typical of New England children, although he grew up in a relatively poor family headed by a single mother. His father deserted the family while William was still a toddler. Because racism was present in every part of the US, Du Bois first experienced discrimination while attending elementary school in Massachusetts. Yet it was a gentle discrimination that bruised his ego rather than the raw life-threatening racism which awaited him in the American South.

After completing high school in 1885, Du Bois headed south to Fisk, a black university in Nashville, Tennessee. There he entered the land of Jim Crow, a system that still bore striking resemblances to slavery, which had endured until just two decades before Du Bois arrived in the South. By then, Jim Crow racism produced the severely exploitative system of sharecropping which routinely involved black people in perennial peonage debt. Thus, Jim Crow constituted slavery by a new name. Lynching was so commonplace in the South that the great jazz artist Billie Holiday could sing,

"Southern trees bear a strange fruit,
Blood on the leaves and blood at the root,
Black bodies swinging in the southern breeze,
Strange fruit hanging from the poplar trees."

Black Americans were stripped of the vote, starved economically, and treated as subhumans with no rights that whites were bound to respect. These conditions caused former slaves to sing, "Nobody knows the trouble I have seen."[1] These troubles constituted a tripartite system of domination that oppressed blacks personally, politically and economically.[2] Jim Crow racism descended upon 17-year-old Du Bois as he set foot on Southern soil. It was a domination that demanded that blacks accept their fate as an "inferior" race.

Warrior against the Black Inferiority Thesis

Du Bois, even as a young boy, never thought he was inferior to white people. When he first discovered racism as a child in elementary school, he pledged he would outperform his white peers:

Then it dawned upon me with a certain suddenness that I was different from the others or like mayhap, in heart and life and longing, but shut from their world by a vast veil. I had thereafter no desire to tear down that veil, to creep through; I held all beyond it in common contempt, and lived above it in a region of blue sky and great wandering shadows. That sky was bluest when I could beat my mates at examination time, or beat them at a footrace, or even beat their stringy heads.[3]

This drive to excel motivated Du Bois throughout his life, especially during his years of schooling. At the age of 20, he earned a bachelor's degree from Fisk University; by 22, he had obtained a second bachelor's from Harvard University; at 23, he had been awarded a master's degree from Harvard; by 25, Du Bois had completed two years of advanced graduate studies at the University of Berlin; and by 27, he had become the first African American to earn a doctorate from Harvard University, in 1895. His doctoral dissertation, "The Suppression of the African Slave-Trade to the United States of America, 1638–1870", became the first volume published in Harvard's series of Historical Studies in 1896.

However, American education during the Jim Crow era taught blacks that they were inferior to whites. This doctrine of scientific racism was prevalent in university curricula. White scholars throughout academia, from the natural sciences to the humanities, from biology to literature, and from history to sociology, reached a solid consensus claiming that science proved that blacks were inferior to whites. Thus, in the twentieth century, white science and white supremacist ideology marched in lockstep in justifying racial oppression. Du Bois strongly opposed this ubiquitous scientific racism, noting:

When I entered college in 1885, I was supposed to learn there was a new reason for the degradation of the coloured people that was because they had inferior brains to whites. This I immediately challenged. I knew by experience that my own brains and body were not inferior to the average of my white fellow students. Moreover, I grew suspicious when it became clear that treating Negroes as inferior, whether they were or not, was profitable to the people who hired their labour. I early, therefore, started on a personal life crusade to prove Negro equality and to induce Negroes to demand it.[4]

Rather than accept scientific racism, Du Bois challenged this doctrine intellectually and politically. Civil rights leader and Nobel peace laureate Martin Luther King, Jr described Du Bois's reaction to the black inferiority thesis:

> One idea [Du Bois] insistently taught was that black people have been kept in oppression and deprivation by a poisonous fog of lies ... The twisted logic ran if the black man was inferior he was not oppressed – his place in society was appropriate to his meager talent and intellect. Dr. Du Bois recognized that the keystone in the arch of oppression was the myth of inferiority and he dedicated his brilliant talents to demolish it.[5]

In the South, Du Bois confronted routine racism which assaulted his sense of personhood and dignity. He was forced to obey the dictates of Jim Crow, which applied to all aspects of Southern life. Like all Southern blacks, Du Bois was segregated from white life. The laws and customs of racial segregation forced him to ride in the back of trains in filthy carriages full of tobacco smoke. He had to eat meals with blacks only, and relieve himself in segregated toilets. As a highly educated man, Du Bois was not accorded the status routinely conferred on educated whites. He never adjusted to the racist insults he endured. Rather, Du Bois recognised insults when they were directed at him, and they often infuriated him. Summing up the racist experiences that he encountered in the South, he simply declared, "I rode Jim Crow."

After his studies at Fisk, Harvard and Berlin, Du Bois became a sociologist. He chose sociology because he wanted to study the causes of race inequality that had relegated his people to the bottom of the racial hierarchy. But William became a social scientist not merely to understand racism, but also to acquire knowledge that would help him and his people to dismantle it. Early on, he developed an international perspective on the race oppression prevalent in Africa, Asia, the West Indies and the US. This perspective guided his dissertation on the African slave trade, in which he analysed the tangled racial ties between Europe, Africa and the Americas that had produced slavery and colonialism. Du Bois's international approach was strengthened during his graduate studies at the University of Berlin in 1892–4. Reflecting on his European educational experiences while in his early twenties, Du Bois said that he came to see as one America's race problem and those of the peoples in Africa and Asia, alongside Europe's political development.[6] Therefore, at the dawn of the twentieth century, Du Bois developed an internationalist view which stressed the interconnected and interactive nature of global racism. From this perspective, structural racism could only be understood if addressed locally and internationally.

New School for Sociological Thought on Race and Racism

Classical Western social scientists sought to identify the causes of modern capitalism. For example, German sociologist Karl Marx located capitalism's origins in a historical class struggle driven by the relations of social classes to the means of production. His compatriot, Max Weber, on the other hand, argued that capitalism grew out of a rationalism peculiar to the West that was anchored in the Protestant work ethic. As Asian-American scholar Julian Go argued in 2016, these explanations share fundamental claims. Both argued that the causes of capitalism lay exclusively in Western Europe. In this view, people of colour across the world had played no role in producing capitalism, but had only reacted to its global reshaping of human societies. Both perspectives thus failed to investigate how Western empire-building had been crucial to the evolution of modern capitalism. That is, neither argument took into account how European captains of empire had constructed exploitative relations between their nations and those of people of colour to amass great fortunes on which modern capitalism was built. For Marx and Weber, white Westerners provided the agency that had given rise to capitalism. Black people, in these perspectives, were too culturally and materially backward to have contributed to the development of this social formation.

Du Bois always surveyed the globe to analyse black agency and its impact on human history. He paid great attention to relations between empire and black populations because he felt that these exploitative relationships were the driving forces of capitalism. Indeed, Du Bois theorised that capitalism and modernity itself were products of centuries of the African slave trade and European colonialism. These oppressive systems made available to Western bourgeois societies the exploitable labour forces and raw materials that they then used to develop modern capitalist states. For Du Bois, racial inequality, manufactured by the white West, was a crucial determinant of capitalism.

Accompanying his analysis of capitalism, Du Bois interrogated the global "colour line", documenting how it had structured race stratification throughout the world. This was the colour line that Du Bois had famously predicted in 1900 would be *the* problem of the twentieth century. That colour line produced and structured "the relation of the darker to the lighter races of men in Asia and Africa, in America and the islands of the sea".[7] These concepts of the colour line and black agency contained the intellectual seeds that enabled Du Bois to develop a Pan-Africanist perspective. That is, shared oppression behind the veil of racism bound the darker races into a potentially unified force, making possible a collective struggle for freedom.

While Du Bois explored macro-structures of racial inequality, he explicated their relationship with micro-dynamics relating to personality and identity. In this respect, he formulated a theory of how the self evolves that stressed the tensions within the subjective lives of African Americans. Through his concept of "double consciousness", Du Bois explained how the self was socially constructed through social interactions and communication, especially through the use of language. Moreover, in Du Bois's formulation, the self was also shaped by race and power relations which inhibited full self-consciousness.[8] However, consistent with his Pan-Africanist thought, these subjective tensions in the black self were enabling agents, since they produced a second sight allowing black people to understand societies from fresh viewpoints.

Du Bois also analysed how racial systems of domination did not exist in isolation. Rather, race oppression interacted with oppressions along class, race and gender lines. By taking the matrix of oppression seriously, Du Bois was among the first scholars to theorise how people's views shaped their social realities. Thus, Du Bois's sociology developed analysis from the perspective of the oppressed. His sociology of black people proceeded from a profound question: "How does it feel to be a problem?"[9]

From this perspective, he made four observations. Firstly, African Americans were the equals of other races because racial oppression – rather than biological traits – relegated blacks to the bottom of the racial hierarchy. Races, therefore, were not strict biological populations but socially constructed through common experiences, language and custom. Secondly, there was no such thing as "black crime" because social conditions, and not racial characteristics, produced crime. Thirdly, the black community was heterogeneous, consisting of various social classes and diverse experiences. Fourthly, the black church was the central institution that served as the organisational umbrella for the social and cultural activities of the black community. Long before the modern civil rights movement, Du Bois had predicted that a black movement, situated in the mass-based black church, would arise to overthrow racial inequality.[10] Breaking radically from conventional wisdom, he predicted that the creative and organisational capacities of black people would change their history. Thus, Du Bois emerged as the first American sociologist to theorise the agency of the oppressed. What distinguished Du Bois's social thought from that of his white contemporaries was the idea that within black people there existed an agency capable of history-making.[11]

The Scholar as Activist

Du Bois was one of those rare scholars of the first rank who combined scholarship and activism. During the twentieth century, he was a prolific and profound scholar, as well as a prodigious activist of major consequence. Indeed, as Du Bois researched and wrote, he marched onto the battlefield, leading important movements for justice. He was the founder of the 1905 Niagara Movement, the 1909 National Association for the Advancement of Colored People (NAACP), and an architect and participant in five Pan-African Congresses. Du Bois engaged in activism throughout his career, participating in protests alongside such figures as the world-renowned singer and activist Paul Robeson. Recognising Du Bois's unique blend of scholarship and activism, Martin Luther King, Jr remarked: "It was never possible to know where the scholar Du Bois ended and the organizer Du Bois began. The two qualities in him were a single, unified force."[12]

Du Bois's scholarship informed his activism and assisted other activists in applying intellectual ideas to liberation struggles. Ruling ideologies are complex intellectual constructs that sustain systems of domination and constrain insurgency. Du Bois was a masterful analyst of ruling ideologies, and deconstructed them in ways that were useful to black liberation movements. Thus, slavery, colonialism, and the Jim Crow regime were all sustained by ideologies claiming that black people were inferior. These ideologies were elaborated in fine detail by white scientists, historians, and philosophers. These cultural workers developed what they claimed to be scientific proof that blacks were at the bottom of societies because of their own intellectual and cultural inferiority. Du Bois – highly trained as a social scientist and scholar – addressed scientific ideologues on their own turf, and painstakingly demolished their fatuous and racist intellectual justifications, brick by brick.

King also explained how Du Bois's intellectual work would enable activists to conduct struggles more effectively to overcome oppression: "The truths [Du Bois] revealed ... arm us for our contemporary battles."[13] Moreover, King amplified how crucial it was for Du Bois to have combined the plane of intellectual deconstruction with the combative grounds of collective struggle: "History had taught [Du Bois] it is not enough for people to be angry – the supreme task is to organize and unite people so that their anger becomes a transforming force."[14]

Du Bois was a scholar with big international ideas about how racial oppression operated across the globe. He transmitted these thoughts through scholarship and addresses in the public sphere. He also possessed fire in the belly which led him to utilise these ideas in collective struggles to liberate the black world from the tentacles of oppression wielded by white elites sitting atop Western ivory towers. A key weapon in Du Bois's arsenal was Pan-Africanist thought and the liberation movements that these ideas helped to propel.

Du Bois and Pan-Africanism

Du Bois is widely considered to have been "the father of Pan-Africanism" because he played key roles as a theoretician of Pan-African philosophy and as an organiser and leader of the first five Pan-African Congresses between 1919 and 1945. He also influenced second-generation Pan-Africanist leaders.

By the first decade of the twentieth century, most of the African continent had fallen under the control of Western European powers through colonisation. Indeed, major European powers, including Britain, France, Germany, Spain, Portugal, Belgium, and Italy, had carved up Africa among themselves for the exploitation of its land and natural resources, and to force its inhabitants to provide cheap labour upon which their empires could be erected and expanded.[15] This domination – made possible through colonisation and slavery – extended to Asia, South America, the West Indies and the United States. European domination of people of colour across the globe was achieved through violence, brute means of oppression, mass murder and theft (see Introduction and Beckles in this volume). Resistance to European control was weak initially because of various differences, including those of language, ideologies, customs, traditions, political rivalries, and village and ethnic formations among Africans. Europe exacerbated and hardened these differences in order to maintain its rule. Africa could offer little collective defence to European domination.

From the 1880s, black intellectuals and leaders throughout the diaspora began contemplating collective resistance to European dominance. They grappled with the need to overcome the numerous barriers preventing a unified assault on slavery, colonialism and racial discrimination. They reasoned that it was necessary for members of the black diaspora to meet, discuss common problems stemming from racial conquest and unify so as to organise collective efforts to defeat their oppressors. An effective response required a Pan-African challenge from insurgents throughout the black world. The initial Pan-African vision did not originate with Du Bois or other legendary Pan-African leaders, including Trinidad's George Padmore and Ghana's Kwame Nkrumah (see Duggan and Biney in this volume). Rather, following the groundbreaking work of the legendary nineteenth-century scholar-diplomat, St Thomas's Edward Blyden (see Khadiagala in this volume), Pan-Africanism was developed as a movement in 1897 by Henry Sylvester Williams, a London-based barrister from Trinidad. Williams "began thinking about a political movement organised around a series of conferences that would draw representatives of the 'African race from all the parts of the world'". His vision was intended to "encourage a feeling of unity [and] facilitate friendly intercourse among Africans" and to "promote and protect the interests of all subjects claiming African descent, wholly or in part, in British Colonies and other places, especially in Africa".[16] In 1897, Williams founded the African Association to give organisational expression to this Pan-Africanist perspective. To move the Association forward, a cluster of Pan-Africanists from throughout the African diaspora assisted him. The Reverend H. Mason Joseph of Antigua served as chair, T.J. Thompson of Sierra Leone was deputy chair, while a South African woman, Alice V. Kinloch, was treasurer. As honorary secretary, Williams quickly directed the African Association into political engagement.[17] He and his organisation published news items and studies, and appealed to local and imperial governments.

The Pan-African Proselytiser

Although Du Bois did not originate the idea of Pan-Africanism, his scholarship on global racism and his history of activism made him an ideal candidate to spread the ideology across the black world. He was well positioned to advance Pan-Africanism because he was admired throughout the diaspora as a great thinker, writer and uncompromising warrior for racial equality. He was a scholar with big ideas who possessed the ability to express them with power and eloquence. These were ideal qualities needed to lift the Pan-Africanist view to global prominence and spur collective action to overthrow European domination.

Du Bois brought to the Pan-Africanist struggle fresh conceptions of race, of the world-wide colour line, and the agency of the oppressed. As in Jim Crow America, European colonisers justified their oppression of black people by arguing that they were inherently inferior and incapable of acting on the global stage. By 1897 Du Bois had begun to re-theorise the nature of race. The accepted view claimed that races were unchanging biological groups endowed with fixed qualities and trajectories. Thus, if one race was inferior to another, such a race was locked into an eternal position at the bottom of the racial hierarchy. In this view, Europeans were inherently superior to blacks and destined to rule over them. In fact, European domination was viewed as good for blacks because it helped to civilise the dark-skinned "savages".

At the dawn of the twentieth century, Du Bois rejected this political claim by arguing that physical differences between races explained neither their social positions nor their potential for great achievements. From a scientific perspective, Du Bois argued:

> When we thus come to inquire into the essential difference of races we find it hard to come at once to any definite conclusion. Many criteria of race differences have in the past been proposed, as colour, hair, cranial measurements and language ... Unfortunately for scientists, however, these criteria of race are most exasperatingly intermingled ... the grosser physical differences of color, hair and bone go but a short way toward explaining the different roles which groups of men have played in Human Progress.[18]

Du Bois, therefore, rejected biological explanations of race while advancing a sociological interpretation: "But while race differences have followed mainly physical race lines, yet no mere physical distinctions would really define or explain the deeper differences – the cohesiveness and continuity of these groups. The deeper differences are spiritual, psychical, differences – undoubtedly based on the physical, but infinitely transcending them."[19]

Du Bois established the logic that races were not oppressed on the basis of biological criteria, but by human-constructed racial hierarchies established for purposes of human domination. In so doing, he dismantled a key intellectual justification enabling whites throughout the world to enslave, colonise and exploit black people. Thus, the system of white imperial capitalism was a brutish and uncivilised arrangement of domination, pure and simple.

The Concept of the Colour Line and Unmasking "the Veil of Racism"

Another pivotal idea that Du Bois contributed to Pan-Africanism was the concept of the global colour line and unmasking the "veil of racism". White oppressors across the globe constructed a colour line that pushed black people behind a veil of racism where they were exploited, disenfranchised and insulted. As with the concept of race, Du Bois maintained that the colour line had been socially constructed and, therefore, could be overthrown by deliberate collective action on the part of the oppressed. The global problem that the Pan-African movement faced was thus the dismantling of the colour line.

Another pivotal idea that Du Bois brought to the Pan-Africanist struggle was that the oppressed – black people behind the veil of racism – possessed the capacity and genius to engage in collective action capable of dismantling the colour line. Du Bois revealed the agency of the oppressed and their history-making capability when they acted collectively. In 1897, he wrote:

> Manifestly some of the great races of today – particularly the Negro race – have not as yet given to civilization the full spiritual message which they are capable of giving. For the development of Negro genius, of Negro literature and art, of Negro spirit, only Negroes bound and welded together, Negroes inspired by one vast ideal, can work out in its fullness that great message we have for humanity ... if the Negro is ever to be a factor in the world's history – if among the gaily-colored banners that deck the broad ramparts of civilizations is to hang one uncompromising black, then it must be placed there by black hands, fashioned by black heads and hallowed by the travail of 200,000,000 black hearts beating in one glad song of jubilee ... we are Negroes, members of a vast historic race that from the very dawn of creation has slept, but half awakening in the dark forests of its African fatherland.[20]

Although Du Bois argued that races were socially constructed, he did not mean races were inconsequential or lacked the agency to shape history. The agentic power of races derived from their shared history, especially a common history of oppression. For Du Bois: "The forces that bind together [races] are, then, first, their race identity and common blood; secondly, and more important, a common history, common laws and religion, similar habits of thought and a conscious striving together for certain ideals of life."[21]

Explicating the direct relationship between races and their propensity to act collectively, Du Bois noted:

> The actual ties of heritage between these individuals of this group vary with the ancestors they have in common with many others: Europeans and Semites, perhaps Mongolians, certainly American Indians. But the physical bond is least and the badge of color is relatively unimportant save as a badge; the real essence of this kinship is its social heritage of slavery; the discrimination and insult; and this heritage binds together not simply the children of Africa, but extends through yellow Asia and into the South Seas. It is this unity that draws me to Africa.[22]

Thus, Du Bois argued that, although black people were oppressed throughout Africa and the diaspora, there were historical and sociological factors capable of binding them into a unified force that might deliver a death blow to European domination. Pan-Africanism badly needed this message during the dark days of slavery, colonialism and Jim Crow. In order to succeed in the liberation struggle, movements require a sense of hope and not simply despair and resignation. Du Bois, who early on developed an international view of the race problem of the twentieth century, provided the emerging Pan-Africanist movement with an empowering view of race, an analysis of its major foe – the colour line – and insights into the agency that the dominated could utilise to overthrow their chains of oppression.

Du Bois was not the father of Pan-Africanism merely because he was an organiser, presiding figure, fundraiser and writer of many of the declarations of the first five Pan-African Congresses. Rather, he transmitted powerful ideas to the young movement which provided it with intellectual, moral and ideological clarity. Indeed, briefing the first Pan-African Conference in London in 1900, Du Bois interjected the importance of the colour line into the proceedings in a sharp rebuke of the enemy:

In the metropolis of the modern world, in this the closing year of the Nineteenth Century, there has been assembled a Congress of men and women of African blood, to deliberate solemnly upon the present situation and outlook of the darker races of mankind. The problem of the Twentieth Century is the problem of the color line, the question as to how far differences of race, which show themselves chiefly in the color of the skin and the texture of the hair, are going to be made, hereafter, the basis of denying to over half the world the right of sharing to their utmost ability the opportunities and privileges of modern civilization.[23]

During the Second Pan-African Congress in London in 1921, Du Bois wasted little time in declaring the principle of racial equality:

The absolute equality of races, physical, political and social, is the founding stone of world peace and human advancement. No one denies great differences of gift, capacity, and attainment among individuals of all races, but the voice of science, religion, and practical politics is one in denying the God-appointed existence of super-races, or of races naturally and inevitably and eternally inferior.[24]

Through his writings and exhortations, Du Bois attempted to empower colonial subjects and victims of Jim Crow to harness their agency to fight racism through the Pan-Africanist movement. Working with other Pan-Africanist leaders, he produced resolutions stating the goals of the movement, which included Africans having voice in their own government, native rights to the land and to natural resources, a modern education for all children, the development of Africa for the Africans and not merely for the profit of Europeans, the reorganisation of commerce and industry so as to make the main object of capital and labour the welfare of the many rather than the enriching of the few, and the treatment of "civilised" men as "civilised" despite differences of birth, race, and colour.[25]

Du Bois made available to the five Pan-African Congresses his scholarship and theoretical elaborations so that the movement could base its actions on solid principles, as they tried to free black humanity from the bondage of white oppressors. Speaking of Pan-Africanism in 1923, he argued: "We have kept an idea alive; we have held to a great ideal; we have established a continuity and some day, when unity and co-operation come, the importance of these early steps will be recognized."[26]

The idea of Du Bois as the "father of Pan-Africanism" can be misleading when it overlooks the crucial contributions that other important figures made to the movement. I have noted that the idea of Pan-Africanism and its first organisational expression came not from Du Bois, but from a group of activists and intellectuals in the late 1880s. Moreover, Du Bois's ideas about Pan-Africanism were developed in tandem with those of other scholars and activists. Indeed, Edward Blyden pioneered ideas of Pan-Africanism three decades before the first Pan-African Conference (see Khadiagala in this volume). Du Bois also worked directly with George Padmore and C.L.R. James in developing his Pan-Africanist perspectives (see Duggan and Cudjoe in this volume). Like Du Bois, Padmore and James both produced foundational scholarship on Africa and used it to inform their extensive activism in the Pan-Africanist movement. Marcus Garvey, another "father of Pan-Africanism", elaborated his own version of Pan-Africanism in the 1920s and developed a mass base of tens of thousands of adherents throughout the diaspora who propelled the Garveyist movement (see Grant in this volume). Du Bois's and Garvey's Pan-Africanism unfolded in a context of extreme conflict. Yet, while these battles may have impacted on the movement negatively, they also benefited it because each combatant was forced to sharpen and clarify his own perspective. In the process, new Pan-African energy was infused into the movement.

Another serious pitfall of the "father of Pan-Africanism" trope is that it ignores major contributions by black women. Amy Ashwood Garvey was a stalwart of Marcus Garvey's Pan-African activities (see Reddock in this volume). Women like Alice V. Kinloch were also among those who initiated the Pan-African concept in the late 1880s, and organised the African Association to achieve its goals. From the time of the first Pan-African Conference, women such as Ida Gibbs Hunt, Anna Julia Cooper, Anna H. Jones, Addie Waites Hunton, Helen Curtis, Jessie Fauset and Coralie Franklin Cook were actively involved in the movement. These women were Congress organisers, fundraisers and thinkers who in their own right provided critical intellectual contributions desperately needed by the movement. There would have been no Fourth Pan-African Congress in New York in 1927 if black women had not organised and funded it, thus enabling the movement itself to survive. Du Bois, who recognised the many contributions that these black women made to the black community and the Pan-Africanist movement, worked alongside them as they articulated and advanced the cause of Pan-Africanism. These were the "mothers of Pan-Africanism", without whom Blyden, Du Bois, and others could not have been its fathers.

Concluding Reflections: Du Bois, Nkrumah and the Liberation of Africa

W.E.B. Du Bois and Kwame Nkrumah were pivotal leaders of the Fifth Pan-African Congress in the English city of Manchester in 1945. The conference provided the blueprint for African independence movements that would sweep the continent in the second half of the twentieth century. The meeting assembled many of the future leaders of the movement, who debated strategies and developed bonds that emboldened them to return home to lead their countries to freedom. Moreover, in Manchester grassroots leaders of labour unions and student groups pledged to lead mass movements to overthrow European colonial rule in Africa.

The goals of the Fifth Pan-Africanist Congress were radical. Whereas the previous congresses had advocated peaceful means, the Fifth Congress advocated violent struggles, if necessary, to achieve Africa's liberation. Nkrumah emerged as the towering figure of the Fifth Congress, who, with George Padmore, organised the Congress and, with Du Bois, authored its resolutions. It was during this Congress that Nkrumah and Du Bois became close. Nkrumah later explained: "When George Padmore and I organised the Fifth Pan African Congress in 1945 at Manchester, we invited Dr. Du Bois, then already 78 years of age, to chair that Congress. I knew him in the United States and even spoke on the same platform with him. It was, however, at this Conference in Manchester that I was drawn closely to him."[27]

Du Bois and Nkrumah helped to determine the future of Africa. Du Bois became Nkrumah's adviser, instructing him on strategies and future directions. Following the Fifth Pan-African Congress, Nkrumah stated, "Since then, Du Bois has been personally a real friend and father to me."[28] But, even more important for the future of the Pan-African movement, Du Bois explicitly passed the torch of leadership to the next generation, especially to Nkrumah:

I hereby put into your hands, Mr. Prime Minister, my empty but still significant title of "President of the Pan-African Congress", to be bestowed on my duly elected successor who will preside over a Pan-African Congress due, I trust, to meet soon and for the first time on African soil, at the call of the independent state of Ghana. I am, Sir, your obedient servant.[29]

In response, Nkrumah asked "Dr. Du Bois to come to Ghana to pass the evening of his life with us ... I want my father to have easy, comfortable and beautiful days."[30] Having arrived in an independent Ghana in October 1961, Du Bois noted: "I have returned that my dust shall mingle with the dust of my forefathers. There is not much time left for me. But now my life will flow on in the vigorous young stream of Ghanaian life, which lifts the African personality to its proper place among men. And I shall not have lived in vain."[31]

In concert with many other Pan-Africanists, Du Bois and Nkrumah helped free Africa of colonialism. From a historical perspective, it is clear that the Pan-African movement instilled in Africans and their descendants a sense of self-determination that led to the overthrow of European colonialism. The removal of the shackles of colonialism was a major step in freeing Africa. But, alas, the continent is far from free today because of the legacies of colonialism and the failure of many independent African leaders to remain true to the goals of the Pan-Africanist movement. Hopefully, new winds will revive this historical movement to make Africa a shining light beckoning humanity to freedom.

Marcus Garvey: "Africa for the Africans"

Colin Grant

"A LITTLE SAWED-OFF, HAMMERED-DOWN black man with determination written all over his face," was how John E. Bruce remembered Marcus Garvey. Bruce succumbed to Garvey's "engaging smile that caught you and compelled you to listen to his story".[1] It took a while, though, for the fastidious African-American journalist, self-taught historian and scholar of black life to come round and see the virtues of Garvey. At first he was sceptical. Bruce, like many African Americans on their first encounter, believed he was something of a charlatan, full of "wild, chimerical [ideas] impossible of accomplishment".[2] The veteran journalist even ridiculed Garvey as being a "four-flusher" or "grafter".

But then one evening in October 1919 at Speakers' Corner on 135th Street in New York's Harlem neighbourhood, Bruce confessed that he "heard" Garvey as if for the first time. He listened to the singular clarity of Garvey's voice and to his earnest message. From then on, the 63-year-old was converted, and remained steadfastly loyal to Garvey and his cause. That story and, more important, its trajectory were repeated regularly throughout Garvey's ascent from a street orator (aka "Ebony Sage") to one of the most powerful political leaders and black nationalists of his generation. Many came to a Garvey speech expecting to jeer, and yet remained to cheer. The man was simply irresistible.

Marcus Mosiah Garvey was unheralded when he arrived in Harlem in the unusually warm spring of 1916. Though he was buoyed by a titanic certainty of his abilities and of his place in the destiny of black people, his early attempts to establish himself in the United States – specifically in Harlem, which was then considered to be the mecca of black life in America – were not so sure-footed. Hurrying to the offices of W.E.B. Du Bois to pay his respects to the great scholar (see Morris in this volume), Garvey was, as he later recalled, snubbed by the light-skinned staff there. And other witnesses of his first attempt at public speaking recounted that Garvey was so nervous that he allegedly fell off the stage. But within months of his arrival, Garvey was to prove repeatedly to be a great orator, a master of rhetoric, and a human barometer, registering the mood and aspirations of a down-trodden people. As a character in African-American writer Ralph Ellison's book *Invisible Man* (1952) notes, "Garvey must have had something. He must have had something to move those people. Our people are hell to move! He must have had plenty!"[3]

From the soapbox at Speakers' Corner, from the podium at Liberty Hall, or through the thundery editorials of the *Negro World*, Garvey articulated the dreams and aspirations of masses of black people, and, when he spoke, it was as if they were hearing their own words come back at them, just as John E. Bruce had intimated. Such was Garvey's sensibility. And yet the more his fame grew, it appeared that Garvey was built to transmit and not receive: he had an amazingly tin ear; and his unwillingness to listen to strong advisers who counselled caution was to prove to be the Jamaican-born activist's undoing. Early on, his public speeches served as recruitment drives for his fledgling organisation: the Universal Negro Improvement Association and African Communities League (UNIA-ACL). To the discerning, the alignment with Pan-Africanism and the scale of its ambition were announced in that title. In contrast to the National Association for the Advancement of Colored People (NAACP), which was an unashamedly top-down organisation run primarily by a tertiary-educated light-skinned elite (who in African-American scholar David Levering Lewis's words aimed to achieve "civil rights by copyright"[4]), the UNIA was a bottom-up organisation presided over by energetic activists and amateur scholars with an appeal to poor working-class black people, sometimes disparaged by critics as the "cow-tail and broom-handle brigade".[5]

The Black Moses

The word "improvement" in the name of Marcus Garvey's organisation was integral to his objective. Garvey's improvement started at home. Like many growing up on the island of Jamaica, Garvey believed that he was existentially an African in exile, one whose understanding of his ancestry had been denied to him by colonial authorities more determined to accentuate British imperial history. In Jamaica, his African education had been superficial, scraped together from limited resources. It was only through travelling and self-education that Garvey began to envisage the part that black people in the diaspora might play in an African Renaissance (see Ngqulunga in this volume). The UNIA's mission was boldly Pan-African. Its stated aim was to "establish a brotherhood among the black race, to promote a spirit of race pride, to reclaim the fallen and to assist in civilising the backward tribes of Africa".[6]

Marcus Garvey's understanding and framing of the history and politics of Africa began in earnest when he journeyed to England in 1912. He was an autodidact and, in support of his application for a reader's pass to the library of the British Museum, he cited a desire to explore the works of the Liberian scholar of St. Thomas descent, Edward Wilmot Blyden, in particular his 1887 *Christianity, Islam and the Negro Race* (see Khadiagala in this volume).[7] Blyden's writing was to serve as a life-long spiritual guide for Garvey on the issues that were most pressing to black people. On the question of religion, Blyden argued that Islam – with its lack of social and racial distinction – was a more attractive option than Christianity for black people. His modernist text – a hybrid of history, philosophy and personal reflections on the impoverished state of the black race gleaned from his travels – greatly influenced black scholars and educationists. Garvey proved receptive to Blyden's ideas about Ethiopianism and the redemptive role that it might play in Africa. Indeed, later in life, Garvey was fond of referring to Blyden as a fiercely black author who had "done so much to retrieve the lost prestige of the race"[8] in the face of the commonly advanced proposition in the West that nothing significant had ever come out of Africa.

Blyden also countered the negative propaganda of critical thinkers, even allegedly sympathetic figures such as the naval commander Andrew H. Foote, who argued that the obliteration of Negroes from the planet would not be detrimental as "the whole world would lose no great truth, no profitable arts, no exemplary form of life. The loss of all that is African would offer no memorable deduction from anything but the black catalogue of crime."[9] Such was the West's hubristic attitude, underscoring the pervasive racial theories which Garvey had to confront. This hubris only served to fuel his ambition to answer Blyden's assertion that "The Negro leader of the Exodus, who will succeed, will be a Negro of the Negroes, like Moses was a Hebrew of the Hebrews."[10]

Back in 1913, the black Moses-in-waiting was further deepening his African education at the *African Times* and *Orient Review*, where he graduated under the tutelage of the proprietor, Duse Mohamed Ali, from initially working as a handyman and messenger to penning his first significant scholastic and journalistic piece, "The Evolution of Latter Day Slaves: Jamaica, a Country of Black and White" in 1914.[11]

As well as literary clues to Africa, there were personal testimonies to consider. Garvey later recounted an epiphany when leaving Britain in 1914 to sail back to Jamaica. Falling into conversation with some other third-class passengers (a missionary returning from Basutoland with his Mosotho wife), Garvey was shocked to hear their descriptions of life there, especially to learn of the horrible and pitiful abuses of Africans. Each night in his tiny cabin Garvey had the same dream in which he asked himself: "Where is the black man's government? Where is his President, his country, his ambassador and his army ... I could not find them."[12] And on that long journey home, with the kind of arrogance that is the preserve of genius and of youth, Marcus determined to put together a plan for a movement that would bring together all black people from every corner of the world.

Jamaica was to prove too toxic an environment and too small a platform from which to launch such a huge endeavour. Garvey would find more favourable conditions in America. It might seem that he was fortunate in meeting so many like-minded Afrophiles in the US, but he actively sought out men and women who were similarly fired up with the conviction that the time was long overdue for the restoration of Africa, and with it the rebirth of a "new Negro" who need no longer feel subordinate to the white man.

Notwithstanding his chance meeting with Africans on ships or with students in London, the idea of Africa remained something of an abstraction for Garvey and many of his followers. As his movement grew, so too did Garvey increasingly solicit Africans to come and talk to his followers, and to help educate them about their motherland. It was often reported in the *Negro World* that the arrival of any bona fide African in the midst of Garveyites – who retained a romanticised notion of the continent – caused great excitement, and was felt with awe and wonder. But, equally, there were sections of black American society for whom Africa was a degraded embarrassment, a continent that they did not want to be reminded about or associated with. After three centuries of enforced separation, these African Americans felt ambivalent about their ancestry; they were likely to consider themselves as American as any other hyphenated group, and less likely to be persuaded by Garvey's increasing advocacy of "Africa for the Africans".

Vanquished in Versailles

Whether he was balancing on the running board of a vehicle with a megaphone to his lips, on the podium at UNIA headquarters at New York's Liberty Hall, or on the soapbox or stepladder at Speakers' Corner, "Africa for the Africans: those at home and those abroad" became Garvey's rallying cry. There had been rehearsals of this cry for Africa during the 1919 Versailles Peace Conference in France at the end of the First World War (1914–1918). For those unfamiliar with Garvey's intent in Versailles, British military intelligence offers a handy guide. In monitoring Garvey, the British spooks transcribed a speech in which Garvey attempted to rally his supporters during this psychological moment for the organisation. Garvey compared his own dream of Africa with that of Wilhelm II of Germany, who had fantasised about ruling the world from Potsdam or Berlin: "In his [Wilhelm's] dream he saw a great Central Empire ... But [as he] declared war, so did he lose the war; and as he lost the war, he lost the vision of a great Central Africa. In his defeat of 1918, the renewed Negro has caught the vision not only of a great Central Africa for the Africans, but a United Africa for the Africans of the World."[13]

Such a notion may have been heard by receptive ears at Liberty Hall, but prominent Africans in Paris such as Senegal's Blaise Diagne considered it preposterous: an *idée insensée*. For these francophone Africans, it was an outrage that Harlem presumed to speak for scattered "Ethiopia": a disconnected continent presently ruled by European imperial powers.

The UNIA sent a young Haitian high commissioner, the aptly named Elizier Cadet, to promote the claim of the world's black people at this "clearing house of Fates" in Versailles. This was, as the *New York Times* reported, only after the UNIA had passed resolutions which suggested that, in the settlement at Versailles, the confiscated German territories in Africa should not be divided up among the conquering allies, but rather "be turned over to Negroes under the rule of Negroes educated in this country and in Europe".[14]

But Cadet did not have accreditation to the Versailles Peace Conference and, despite his excited telegrams about his overtures to the great and the good at Versailles – eagerly read out to the faithful back at Liberty Hall – he remained largely, frustratingly, on the fringes of the conference, failing to capture much attention for the 400 million African souls he purported to represent in Versailles. W.E.B. Du Bois was also in Paris, and though he too made little inroad, he was at least granted permission to stage discreetly an African Congress to run alongside the important matters being debated at Versailles. Cadet complained in his dispatches back to UNIA headquarters that Du Bois, in disingenuous briefings about the insignificance of the UNIA, was further undermining his position. It was an assessment which provoked numerous denouncements of Du Bois back in Harlem at an emergency mass convention where three thousand people crowded into the Mother Zion AME Church to hear Du Bois's actions characterised as treacherous, and the NAACP's leading light and the editor of *Crisis* portrayed as "a reactionary under [the] pay of white men".[15]

But neither Garvey, the NAACP, nor the African Congress had an impact on Versailles that affected the fortunes of Africa. So much so that Garvey went on to dub the Peace Conference as the "Pieces Conference" when the annexed German territories in Africa were transferred under mandate to Berlin's European adversaries: Togoland and Cameroon (shared by France and Britain), Tanganyika (to Britain), Urundi-Burundi (to Belgium) and South West Africa (to South Africa).

Versailles was a profound set-back for the UNIA. But, pretty soon, Garvey was laying out plans to mitigate the damage done to black fortunes in Paris. A year later, the idea of an emancipated African continent, free of European powers, crested with Garvey's first International Conference of the Negro Peoples of the World.

The "President of Africa"

Sporting a feathered bicorn helmet and Victorian military uniform, Garvey led twenty-five thousand of his supporters from Harlem to Madison Square Garden to witness his "coronation" as the provisional "President of Africa" in August 1920.[16] In introducing the notion and desirability of a "provisional" president, Garvey had paid particular attention to the Irish struggle for independence and used Sinn Fein as a model. The highlights of the conference included an announcement of a declaration of rights for 400 million black people worldwide; and also an honours system modelled on the titles that Europe's monarchies bestowed on their worthy citizens. Garvey had consistently said that the problem that black people faced at the turn of the twentieth century was the problem of perception: both how they were perceived and how they perceived themselves. At that time, when black people were considered to be what Martinican intellectual Frantz Fanon referred to as the "wretched of the earth" (see Jinadu in this volume), Garvey introduced a notion of self-worth that would not rely on the white man for validation. Titles handed out at the conference included "Duke of the Nile" and "Baron of the Zambezi". John E. Bruce was knighted "Duke of Uganda". Garvey, of course, took the highest rank as provisional president.

Not all of the delegates in Madison Square Garden were in support of the new honours system. The Nigerian delegate, Prince Madarikan Deniyi, was appalled. When challenged as to the validity of his appointment as provisional president of Africa, Garvey pointed to the delegates (less than a hundred) who had elected him. But this only underscored, in the minds of critics, the fallacy and pomposity of the UNIA leader who had not taken it upon himself to find out whether anyone in Africa would support his elevation as the continent's titular head.

Garvey and his followers had long reserved a special place in their hearts for any visiting African nobility, but a conference proposal for the establishment of an African Redemption Fund caused Prince Deniyi (later denounced in the *Negro World* as an impostor) to vent his disapproval in the columns of the *New York Tribune*, where he fumed that "the so-called Negro Moses [Garvey] is using his fraudulent schemes to catch suckers as easily as molasses always catch[es] the flies without molestation".[17]

The "Back to Africa" Movement

In Garvey's estimation, the African Redemption Fund would serve as a down payment on black people's future development. But it would not be enough. To achieve the central plank of a new African dawn and empire, Garvey resurrected the old idea of a return to Africa – "Back to Africa" – of all the descendants of Africans in the diaspora. The establishment of a shipping line to be called the Black Star was announced at the conference in August 1920. And it was proposed that the Black Star Line would serve as a fleet to transport people en masse back to the mother continent. Its destination would initially be the Liberian capital of Monrovia. This news drew great guffaws from cynics but the purchase of a first ship, the *Yarmouth*, was a spectacular achievement which silenced Garvey's critics for a while. The morning after its maiden voyage, Garvey trumpeted in the pages of the *Negro World*: "The Eternal has happened ... For centuries the black man has been taught by his ancient overlords that he was 'nothing', is 'nothing' and never shall be 'anything'. Five years ago the Negro ... was sleeping on his bale of cotton in the South of America; he was steeped in mud in the banana fields of the West Indies and Central America, seeing no possible way of extricating himself from the environments; he smarted under the lash of the new taskmaster in Africa; but alas! Today he is a new man."[18]

Garvey the showman and promoter understood well the Pan-African propaganda potential of a black-run shipping line. Wherever that first ship sailed into port, it was met by ecstatic black people for whom it represented a long-awaited reversal of fortunes. Long before the first black US president, Barack Obama (2009–16), Marcus Garvey, with the Black Star Line, said, "Yes we can! You can accomplish what you will." But more than a tool of propaganda, Garvey conceived the fleet as a trading line that would trade and transport goods and people between Africa, the Caribbean, and the US, in an inversion of the Atlantic slave trade.

Paying five dollars per share, black people who financially contributed to the Black Star Line were not looking for a monetary return on their investment. Rather, they were underwriting a long-held dream of Exodus, with Garvey as their black Moses. Any black person could buy into the dream, and many did. Tens of thousands of small investors – not just in the US, but in every corner of the globe where black people were to be found – bought shares which, by the end, totalled close to $1 million in value.

But if the Black Star Line was the pinnacle of the UNIA's achievement to date, it also turned out to be a spectacular failure. The handful of ships purchased for this answer to the White Star Line and the Irish Green Star Line were incapable of ferrying large numbers of people back to Africa. They were barely able to transport goods. Purchased at exorbitant prices, even after expensive repairs had been done on them the fleet of ships was not fit for purpose. Joshua Cockburn, the Bahamian captain of the *Yarmouth*, had been employed as an expert who would broker its purchase. But Cockburn was also working for the vendor and determined to push up the sales price to reap greater financial reward for himself. Inexperience reverberated all down the line in the UNIA, from the purchase of ships to trade negotiations, insurance and maritime law. Within a couple of years, the *Yarmouth*, which had been launched with such great fanfare, was sold off as scrap. Garvey, an astute student of the psychology of black people, seems to have been caught unawares by human avarice and greed: "I gave everyone a chance, and the story is that very nearly everyone that I placed in a responsible position fleeced the Black Star Line."[19]

The debacle over the shipping line exposed the gullibility of Garvey and his team, as well as the dangers of over-expansion. The UNIA membership and businesses had not grown steadily and carefully; they had exploded with insufficient attention paid to the building of a solid infrastructure. Garvey had tried to run before he had learnt to walk.

This "Back to Africa" scheme was not the first, and would not be the last. It was the latest of perhaps half-a-dozen previous attempts by black people to carry out the mass migration of African Americans to Africa. They included pioneering voyages organised by Martin Delany and Paul Cuffe and, latterly, in 1913, by Chief Alfred Sam's emigration clubs. Sam was so persuasive that he inspired the establishment of more than two hundred clubs throughout Oklahoma with shareholders qualifying for free passage to the Gold Coast (now Ghana). Liberia had been the preferred destination of the American Colonization Society (ACS), which had aggressively promoted the voluntary repatriation of free African Americans since its formal beginnings in 1822. By the latter half of the nineteenth century, more than twenty thousand pilgrims had braved the passage to Monrovia. Although black Americans had continued to make the perilous journey – sometimes with disastrous results – the urgency for such a return had abated with the end of the American Civil War in 1865 and the consequent emancipation of black slaves. Garvey and "Back to Africa" advocates would argue, however, that slavery continued in the guise of Jim Crow and the myriad restrictions that still limited black lives in America (see Morris in this volume).

Labouring in Liberia

Initially Garvey sent a team of six emissaries and engineers to scout for land in Liberia and to secure the approval of local and national authorities. If successful, they would thereby set up a vital beachhead for the UNIA, which eventually intended to extend its ambitions across the whole of the African continent. Cyril A. Crichlow, fastidious accountant and stenographer, would be Garvey's point man, parlaying with the Liberians for 1,000 acres of arable land. The UNIA hoped the negotiations would be smoothed by the brokerage of the mayor of Monrovia, Gabriel Johnson, who was on the UNIA's payroll at $12,000 a year, and who had been proclaimed "Supreme Potentate" by Garvey at the international conference in Madison Square Garden.

But Garvey fully recognised that he could not expect the metropolitan black inhabitants of Harlem to pack up and relocate to Monrovia, unless and until the facilities and comforts of New York could be replicated in Liberia. Indeed, even as he was promoting the idea of voluntary repatriation to Africa, Garvey was simultaneously applying for an American passport. "The majority of us may remain here," Garvey argued, "but we must send our scientists, our mechanics and our artisans and let them build roads, let them build the great educational and other institutions necessary, and when they are constructed the time will come for the command to be given, 'Come home' to Lennox Avenue, to 7th Avenue."[20]

Garvey's team in Liberia seemed stuck in a permanent state of preparation mired in a useless embroidery of negotiations with the Americo–Liberian oligarchy. They generally did not reckon on the duplicity of President Charles D.B. King nor on W.E.B. Du Bois's antipathy and unrelenting counsel against Garvey's movement, which continued to alarm the British colonial authorities, especially in neighbouring Sierra Leone and Togo. Ultimately, the UNIA's Liberian project was strung along by Monrovia for a number of years. Eventually, it became clear that the negotiations had always been a charade. There could be no doubting that conclusion when President King wrote a final severance letter published in Du Bois's *Crisis* journal, publicly spelling out his disavowal of the UNIA project: "Under no circumstances will Liberia allow her territory to be made a centre of aggression or conspiracy against other sovereign states."[21] The Liberians had had no intention of ever granting Garvey land. Instead, the plots would later be leased to the Firestone Rubber Company at 50 cents an acre.

Garvey was left to rue his decision not to take a more direct role in the negotiations. His last-minute efforts to secure a passport so that he might rush to Monrovia to force the deal through came too late. It would be a source of great disappointment to the latest proponent of a "Back to Africa" movement that he would forever be denied an opportunity himself to travel back to the African motherland. It was not for want of trying. Deported to Jamaica on his release from the Atlanta Penitentiary in 1927, where he had spent two years for mail fraud, Garvey was kept by the British, according to local papers, virtually a prisoner on the island, refusing to issue him with travel documents. Although Garvey disputed the claim, it was certainly the case that every European power in Africa considered him a "Negro agitator", someone whose very presence in their territories would have posed a threat to their dominion and the status quo.

Saluting and Slagging Off Selassie

The UNIA mission was grievously damaged by the failure in Liberia, but Garvey's enthusiasm for Africa remained undiminished. This was never more evident than in his fervent championing of Ethiopian emperor Haile Selassie. Though the UNIA was a secular organisation, Garvey recognised that many of its potential members, especially in North America and the Caribbean, were Christian. Indeed, the churches were recruiting grounds which he could not afford to forgo. If Garvey was critical of the Christian church for its tacit acceptance of the status quo, for being prophets of the hereafter as opposed to prophets (such as Garvey) of the here and now, he was nonetheless prepared to draw on the language of the Bible to further his organisation's ambitions, to suggest that "better must come" for his supporters in the near future. Haile Selassie was a case in point.

Through much of the 1920s, Garvey, in speeches to the black faithful, had sought to play the role of John the Baptist to Haile Selassie's Jesus Christ. At a time of woe, he turned to Scripture and told his supporters to look to the east, for as the Bible foretold "Princes shall come out of Egypt; Ethiopia shall soon stretch her hands unto God".[22] And lo and behold, in 1930, with the coronation of Haile Selassie, that prophecy appeared to have come true. Like millions of other black people, Garvey was ecstatic. Alongside Liberia, at that time, Ethiopia was the only African country ruled independently of European powers. Garvey believed the coronation of the emperor of Ethiopia to be a racial sacrament, heralding a new order with better prospects for black people worldwide. Selassie was not only highly regarded by the imperial authorities, who sent emissaries to kneel at the emperor's feet in 1930, but he had somehow managed to maintain his country's independence in the face of creeping colonial encroachment. Five years later, that narrative would be challenged with the Italian invasion of Ethiopia.

Like almost all significant black leaders, Garvey was outraged by the Italian aggression. He was vociferous in his condemnation of fascist dictator Benito Mussolini. Countering apologist headlines like the one in England's *Saturday Review* whose photo caption of the *Duce* ran "Mussolini – the World's Most

Benevolent Ruler",[23] Garvey wrote: "the real facts reveal Mussolini as a barbarian compared to Haile Selassie, the Emperor of Abyssinia ... the one man is a tyrant, a bully, an irresponsible upstart, whilst the other is a sober, courteous and courageous gentleman."[24]

Later, though, the UNIA leader – now in self-imposed exile in London – was to call into question the courage of Haile Selassie. The humiliation of Ethiopia and, by extension, the black race had been brought about by Selassie's negligence and unpreparedness, suggested Garvey, which was "characteristic of the Negro, [and] contrary to the doctrine of the UNIA preached even from the housetops for the last twenty years".[25] In 1936, as the Ethiopian army dissolved into "nothingness", Selassie, with British assistance, managed to escape the advancing Italian forces, first fleeing to Djibouti, and then Jerusalem, before being brought to England. Arriving at London's Waterloo Station, Haile Selassie was greeted by two welcoming parties: an official British party of government officials and dignitaries, and a group of well-meaning friends of Ethiopia (a coalition of black delegates that included Marcus Garvey). As he proceeded down the platform onto the concourse, Selassie embraced the British and ignored Garvey's welcoming committee.

Garvey was outraged, believing that the snub by the emperor's entourage had been intentional. At first, Garvey suggested that he would not hold Selassie responsible for shunning his own people. But thereafter he took a much more critical view of the exiled emperor of Ethiopia. Garvey was wide awake now to his transgressions, and lambasted Selassie as a fool and puppet who had "surrounded himself with white advisers". There would be no pity from Garvey or quarter given to Selassie, "a great coward who ran away from his country to save his skin and left the millions of his countrymen to struggle through a terrible war".[26]

But Garvey had miscalculated. He had failed to take the temperature and the mood of black people – and, most importantly, black activists – who were even now rallying to support the exiled emperor. The Jamaican poet Claude McKay reported that Ethiopian supporters, who drew on the same pool of support that had sustained Garvey's organisation, were not swayed by the UNIA leader's denunciation. Garvey's intervention was considered divisive and dangerous. He had concluded that "the Emperor's term of usefulness is at an end", but there were many who now thought that such sentiments were better applied to the UNIA leader, whose movement had dwindled in the years since his deportation from the United States.

These events also brought Garvey into sharp and direct conflict with black intellectuals such as the Trinidadian Pan-Africanist George Padmore, who recalled that Garvey's stance "made him very unpopular among African university students, who attempted to break up his meetings".[27] (See Duggan in this volume.) In the eyes of numerous former admirers, Garvey could never recover or be forgiven for his transgression.

Concluding Reflections

Decades after Garvey's death in London in May 1940, the story of his rise and fall was largely written by critics who cast him in a poor light (at least relative to W.E.B. Du Bois) as a criminal and buffoon who had defrauded millions of his followers out of their meagre savings through the folly of investing in the Black Star Line. This negative narrative was offset by champions such as African-American congressman Charles Rangel, who urged several US presidents to pardon Garvey. And then there were the wives – Amy Ashwood (see Reddock in this volume) and Amy Jacques – old stalwarts of the UNIA, and the Rastafarians (see Hutton in this volume), who kept his name alive through their songs.

A new chapter in the narrative of Marcus Garvey opened up in the 1960s with the unwinding of colonial rule. For more than three hundred years, until 1962, Britain had ruled Jamaica, latterly by proxy through Afro-Saxons and an anglophile elite. In the crisis of identity that followed independence, Jamaica's fledgling government recognised the importance of establishing a new culture distinct from that which had gone before, a rebranding that was to be characterised by a turning away from Albion towards Africa. This would involve a reconfiguration of the country to reflect the African ancestry of the majority of its population. Politicians such as Edward Seaga saw clearly that there was an urgent need for some figure that could bind Jamaicans together. Marcus Garvey fulfilled this brief to perfection. His remains were disinterred from St Mary's Catholic Church in London for reburial in November 1964 in Kingston, Jamaica, where Garvey was proclaimed the island's first national hero (see also Knight in this volume).

Marcus Garvey's Pan-African efforts extend beyond the grave. His methods may have been flawed, but his intention was sincere. To his admirers, there was God and there was Garvey. Though Garvey's star faded and his message and achievements were eclipsed for decades, he has never gone away. He comes back to us again and again on the current of our times. Garvey's note from the Atlanta Penitentiary in 1925 seems ever more urgent and prescient. On that first night in jail he addressed his many loyal followers, writing to the present and the future: "Look for me in the whirlwind or the song of the storm. Look for me all around you, for with God's grace, I shall come and bring with me countless millions of black slaves who have died in America and the West Indies, and the millions in Africa to aid you in the fight for liberty, freedom and life."[28]

6

GEORGE PADMORE: THE PAN-AFRICAN SCHOLAR-ACTIVIST

Seamus Duggan

THIS ESSAY PROVIDES AN OVERVIEW of George Padmore's contributions to the development of Pan-Africanism as an intellectual tradition and political movement. Padmore, who was born in Trinidad and Tobago at the turn of the twentieth century, does not enjoy the same levels of popular recognition as W.E.B. Du Bois, Marcus Garvey and Kwame Nkrumah (see Morris, Grant, and Biney in this volume). And yet he was seminal in Pan-Africanism's evolution, and his impact on the movement continues to be felt to this day.

Padmore's most notable achievement was his instrumental role in organising the Fifth Pan-African Congress in Manchester in 1945. At the time of the Congress, Pan-Africanism was in a state of flux. The movement lacked ideological and organisational coherence. It had yet fully to cross the Atlantic, remaining in large part bound to ideas of Western civility and the emancipation of African Americans rather than of the African continent.

The Fifth Pan-African Congress helped fashion Pan-Africanism into something quite different. Indigenous Africans became both the leaders and principal constituents of Pan-Africanism in Manchester, as the movement's leaders started to call for unity among the diverse groups of African peoples, and moved away from the previous emphasis on solidarity among individuals of the same race. Pan-Africanism essentially evolved from a civil rights movement into one that was international and political. It further adopted a virulent anti-imperialist tone, vilifying external actors – largely European imperial powers – and casting suspicion on those who continued to cooperate with Western powers or to espouse their values and practices, as well as those who were seen to place their own interests ahead of those of the African collective.

Pan-Africanism became more coherent, more militant and more focused on African self-determination than at any prior point in its history. This, I argue, was in no small part thanks to Padmore. The qualities that would define Pan-Africanism after 1945 were evident early in his life and were actively instilled in the international movement through his ability to organise. Indeed, Padmore's life before the 1945 conference evolved in three distinct phases: his early years; the communist years; and the London years. Each had a unique influence on how Padmore thought about Pan-Africanism.

This chapter argues that Padmore's contributions to Pan-Africanism should be understood in three important ways. Firstly, the Trinidadian activist was able to bring intellectual and organisational coherence to an otherwise disjointed movement. Secondly, he helped to instil in Pan-Africanism a distinct ethic of African self-determination, separating the destiny of Africans from a reliance on powerful actors either in the East or the West. Thirdly, Padmore oversaw the transition of Pan-Africanism to a movement that was increasingly concerned with the question of unity among African states rather than the independence of individuals. Taken together, these interventions would help define the parameters of Pan-Africanism that emerged after the independence of African states – largely in the 1950s and 1960s – and that continue to dominate contemporary debates on Pan-Africanism.

A Brief Note on Pan-Africanism

Pan-Africanism is a broad intellectual tradition and diverse political movement whose adherents are united by their commitment to, or belief in, collective action. The ideology represents a shared belief system whose systematic doctrines reflect the aspiration of Africans for self-determination through unity. While the practice of Pan-Africanism has historically been characterised by shifting values and changing sets of rules for what constitutes a Pan-African identity, these have nevertheless been underwritten by three general principles that give the idea its distinct character. Firstly, the principle of African unity, which reflects the belief that Africans ought to act in unison as they strive towards a common destiny. Secondly, the principle of self-determination, which is the belief that Africans have a right to exercise their own agency and decide their own fate. Thirdly, the principle of equality, which applies to relations both between Africans and "non-Africans" and among Africans themselves.

However, the principles of Pan-Africanism are open to diverse interpretations.[1] What, for example, is meant by unity and what end does it serve? Is unity intended to preserve the integrity of the individual or to develop a sense of community and collective consciousness? Similarly, it is unclear from the principle of self-determination whether this "self" is defined as the individual or the collective, nor whether it is simply a right of action or includes jurisdiction over a particular geographical space. Finally, while equality between members of an identity may stand as a self-evident notion intended to prevent the formation of hierarchies, it is not evident how this can be reconciled with the necessity of, or desire for, leadership. Nor is it always clear to whom this equality applies. In short, while Pan-Africanism may be identified as a distinct idea, given its intellectual and practical histories there are a multitude of ways in which its core principles may be enacted, interpreted and understood.

The process of interpretation and enactment occurs through the actions of thinkers and actors who translate the ideology's fundamental principles into patterns of behaviour and sets of rules for what constitutes Pan-Africanism. This transition from principle to practice is, however, dependent on the a priori cognitive frameworks informing agent subjectivity at a particular moment in time, which make up their identities and interests. While these frameworks are informed by either the general principles of Pan-Africanism or by existing interpretations of how the idea ought to be enacted in practice, the relation of a particular agent to Pan-Africanism is also a product of other social influences making either competing or complementary claims on their identity and behaviour. Historically, these have included anti-imperialism, nationalism, socialism and liberal internationalism, as well as the various ideas linked to the assertion of developing world agency in international affairs, such as the "African Personality", non-alignment or the notion of a "global South".

This chapter uses this understanding of Pan-Africanism as an evolving body of thought subject to interventions by individuals and groups, to grasp the extent of George Padmore's contributions to the movement. I consider, for example, how the Pan-Africanism that Padmore helped define was given shape by his experiences with black nationalism, socialism and the international communist movement. I argue further that Padmore was able to influence Pan-Africanism to the extent that he did because of his intimate grasp of these shifting contours, and his ability to bring stability and clarity to the movement through concrete action and not just by theoretical ideas.

The Early Years

Goerge Padmore was born on 28 June 1903 in Arouca, at the time an agricultural hub to the east of the Trinidadian capital of Port of Spain. He moved to the capital, and attended school there until 1918. From an early age, Padmore evinced an interest in the black nationalism that emerged in the latter half of the 1800s and a particular concern for the position and treatment of Africans – whether based in America, the Caribbean or Africa – in social relations with the ruling elite. Indeed, his childhood friend and fellow Pan-Africanist luminary, C.L.R. James (see Cudjoe in this volume), once recounted how the two would, as young boys, steal copies of Marcus Garvey's paper the *Negro World*, and how they were both avid readers of W.E.B. Du Bois.

James's recollection of these early years is telling. At the time, Garvey and Du Bois were engaged in a well-publicised dispute and advocated contending ideas on how African Americans ought to confront their socio–economic and political marginalisation in the US. The longstanding dispute led to a fierce rivalry that divided their supporters, often along class lines. Where Garvey continued a call for emigration with his "Back to Africa" project (see Grant in this volume) – an echo of similar calls by Martin Delany and Edward Blyden – and even advocated racial segregation, Du Bois fought initially for equal rights and the complete legal integration of African Americans into American society (see Morris in this volume).

Despite these differences, the young Padmore is likely to have been attracted to their common thread: the plight of the marginalised black man and the necessity of overcoming this exclusion. Although Padmore would in future years, and only for a time, diverge from these men, his interest in both underlines the continuous theme throughout Padmore's life – his impatience of any form of oppression.

Garvey's and Du Bois's influence on Padmore would, however, prove more entrenched than this lowest common denominator, and the presence of both can be found in Padmore's later writings and political activism. In the case of Marcus Garvey, this was evidenced in a shared sense of distinct racial pride and, in comparison with other figures including James and Du Bois, a fervent militancy that could energise his supporters and fellow Pan-Africanists.

The impact of embracing these now seemingly fundamental aspects of post-independence Pan-Africanism should not be overlooked. Garvey was not the first Pan-Africanist to emphasise the importance of black self-esteem. This had been a cornerstone of work done by Africanus Horton in the late nineteenth century through his focus on the virtues of African society. Nonetheless, Garvey's popularity helped move this thinking to the centre of the Pan-Africanist movement, where it could reach and shape the thinking of young men, such as Padmore and James. This is not to say that Padmore was a Garveyite – he was clearly not. He vociferously disagreed with much of what Garvey advocated. The threads of racial miscegenation and the desire to "civilise" Africa, which were apparent in some of Garvey's rhetoric, were anathema to Padmore's own political beliefs throughout his life and writings.

Du Bois's influence on Padmore, meanwhile, was profound. Unlike Garvey and many of his predecessors – arguably including Blyden and Delany – Du Bois sought an Africa that was independent of both white and black colonial rule and free to associate on its own terms. His acknowledgement of, and emphasis on, the importance of self-determination for people of African descent around the globe continued Horton's tradition and was fundamental in shifting Pan-Africanism from a largely American phenomenon to an idea and movement that was relevant to all Africans. Certainly, this global focus and the striving for self-determination are perhaps the most distinctive elements of the Pan-Africanism that Padmore would later come to champion.

Padmore and Communism

In the first twenty years of Padmore's life, a global Pan-Africanist movement had begun to emerge. Du Bois sought to organise this movement following the First World War (1914–18) by rejuvenating Trinidadian lawyer Henry Sylvester Williams's idea of a Pan-African Conference, first held in 1900. Du Bois presided over four similar congresses between 1919 and 1927, and they were notable for attracting delegates from around the world and for placing African self-determination as the central theme of the Pan-Africanist campaign. Meanwhile, Garvey's Universal Negro Improvement Association (UNIA) boasted as many as four million members, and scholars like C.L.R. James were becoming prolific contributors to public opinion.

Yet both Pan-Africanism and the broader black nationalist movements found themselves only on the margins of the global stage. European empires were the principal organising units of international society, and global debates were largely defined by the imperial West and the increasingly communist East. As a classic example, African independence and black self-determination were not prominent items on the agenda of the 1919 Versailles Peace Conference, which followed the First World War and which sought to establish a new structure of international relations.

Padmore saw in communism – a movement with the backing of one of the world's most powerful states in the Soviet Union – a global platform to fight for the emancipation of Africa and its diaspora. His association with communism began at a relatively early age, and was evident while he attended college in the United States, initially at the Historically Black College, Fisk University in Nashville and New York University (NYU) before going on to the Historically Black College, Howard University, in Washington DC, where he joined the American Communist Party in 1927. The impact of the international communist movement on Padmore's political thought was clearly spelled out in his 1931 publication, *The Life and Struggles of Negro Toilers*.[2] Although Padmore would become disillusioned with communism two years after its publication, his activism and intellectual evolution in these years would have a lasting impact on his approach to Pan-Africanism.

Perhaps one of the less valued of Padmore's contributions to the Pan-Africanist movement was his ability to organise a mass movement. Although, as C.L.R. James and others have recounted, Padmore was always meticulously well organised and presentable, the communist movement gave him a platform for mobilising like-minded individuals. He did this largely through his work as the head of the Negro Bureau of the Red International of Labour Unions (Profintern), a body established by the Communist International (Comintern) to organise the workers' movement. It was here that Padmore agitated for emancipation, not only of Africans, but of all the working class around the globe. Arguably Padmore's greatest organisational feat during this time was a conference held in the German port city of Hamburg in July 1930, which saw the creation of the International Trade Union Committee for Black Workers (ITUCNW) and its monthly publication, the *Negro Worker*, both of which placed the issue of African independence at the centre of the global communist agenda.

However, it was also during the time of his affiliation with the international communist movement that another of Padmore's starker traits became evident. While the young Padmore appeared more open to different thinkers, *Negro*

Toilers was critical of several prominent black intellectuals. Interestingly, the magazine was particularly critical of Garvey and Du Bois, the former of whom Padmore at the time labelled as a demagogue and the latter a petty-bourgeois reformist and office-seeker.

These views are one example of Padmore's growing militancy between 1927 and 1933. This gave rise to an increasingly dichotomous worldview, a sense of "us versus them" that would remain present in his thinking for much of the remainder of his life. While this was evident initially in his writings on class, it would later shape how Padmore viewed race relations and the position of the African continent within the Western-dominated international system. Indeed, although calls for African independence and criticisms by African states of Western interference in African affairs became commonplace in contemporary discourse, they were not prominent features of Pan-Africanism when Padmore was in his twenties. The Du Bois inter-war Pan-African Congresses, for example, largely failed to call for an end to colonialism. Rather, they adopted a far more moderate position, calling, as Padmore would himself critique in his *History of the Pan-African Congress*, for "the recognition of *civilized* men as *civilized* despite their race or colour [emphasis added]".[3] Furthermore, at their most insistent, these conferences only went so far as to call for the right of native Africans to have "a voice in their own government",[4] and for "the development of Africa for the Africans and not merely for the profits of Europeans".[5] Thus, while the congresses made progress in demanding that Africans be treated as equals, they did not call for a rupturing of the links between Africa and Western colonialism in the same way that Padmore was advocating.

This difference between Padmore and the Pan-Africanism represented by its congresses would, somewhat ironically, become the same reason for Padmore's rupture with the Comintern. While Padmore had been able, through his work at the ITUCNW, to keep African self-determination on the communist agenda, the rise of Adolf Hitler in Germany and fascism in Italy and Eastern Europe forced a reorientation of the communist movement, which diluted its opposition to Western imperialism and thus the willingness of communist leaders to call for African independence. Disillusioned with communism's apparent embrace of imperialism amid the greater threat of fascism, Padmore broke from communism in 1933, the same year that Hitler came to power in Germany.

The rupture is likely to have been traumatic for Padmore. Ever loyal to the cause of African self-determination and independence, he had, by the mid-1930s, become disillusioned with both organised Pan-Africanism and communism.

Neither at that point appeared able to fulfil its promise and provide a platform on which Padmore could meaningfully achieve mass emancipation. That neither East nor West could be relied on to help the cause of Pan-African emancipation is likely to have reinforced Padmore's militancy and revitalised – if not given birth to – his belief that if Africans were to achieve self-determination, they would have to rely on themselves to accomplish it.

Padmore in London

Padmore arrived in London in 1934 – on C.L.R. James's doorstep – seized with the belief that self-reliance in an international system defined by realpolitik was the only means through which Africans would attain independence from foreign oppression. If his early years had nurtured an ability to rationalise the contending impulses of the likes of Garvey and Du Bois, and his association with the international communist movement had imbued Padmore with a sense of urgency and developed his organisational abilities, then his years in London were formative in the role that he played in shifting Pan-Africanism from a predominantly African-American movement to one that was simultaneously international and political.

Padmore had been a prolific writer in the years between his arrival in London in 1934 and the 1945 Pan-African Congress in Manchester. His publications during this period shifted their focus from the working-class issues of *Negro Toilers*, and became more explicitly concerned with Africa as a continent. This includes his 1936 *How Britain Rules Africa*;[6] the 1937 *Africa and World Peace*;[7] the 1942 *The White Man's Duty*;[8] and the 1942 collection of speeches and press statements entitled *The Voice of Coloured Labour*.[9] While Padmore's writing in these years continued to privilege socialist principles, he was scathing in his critique of the failures of international communism and Western imperialism in equal measure.

It was, however, through the individuals that Padmore befriended during his time in London that he was able to influence Pan-Africanism's post-war transition. Indeed, it was during this period that he became a close associate of Jomo Kenyatta, who served as Kenya's first post-independence president from 1964 to 1978, and later of Kwame Nkrumah, who served as independent Ghana's first leader from 1957 to 1966, and who would become one of the most fervent advocates of a united Africa before being deposed in a military *coup d'*état in February 1966. Both Kenyatta and Nkrumah have cited Padmore as a seminal influence on their own thinking not only about Pan-Africanism, but also on the future organisation of a united Africa.[10]

1945 and Beyond

By the time of the Manchester Congress in 1945, the three distinct phases of George Padmore's life had fashioned him into an agent of Pan-Africanism able to influence how the movement was thought of and practised. Indeed, it was during these years, as C.L.R. James would later recall, that Padmore started to become known as one of the most prominent advocates of African emancipation or, as has become more common, the "father of Pan-Africanism".

In addition to being an organiser of the 1945 Manchester Congress, the texts produced at the meeting were heavily influenced by Padmore's thinking. By that point, his view of relations between the black and white races, on the one hand, and Africa and the West, on the other, was heavily informed by his socialist worldview. To Padmore, the plight of native Africans was rooted in race and class, and this could only be remedied through challenging the structures of international capital. Indeed, Padmore conceptualised racial oppression as the same as the subjugation of the "black nation". In order for this nation to break free of the structures of international capital, it had to sever its reliance on, and tacit acceptance of, the practices of imperial Western nations. At the same time, Padmore's growing frustrations with international communism resulted in the determination that self-reliance was the only means of achieving true independence for Africa.

Thus, while Padmore followed in the steps of earlier thinkers such as Horton through his emphasis on self-determination, the Pan-Africanism he helped forge was stripped of many of its previous normative commitments, including those to Christianity and "Western civility". The 1945 Manchester Congress did not call for the recognition of "civilised" men as civilised. It did not call for Africans to have a voice in their own government, as the preceding congresses had done. The Manchester Congress made an unambiguous and unapologetic call for African independence.

The resolutions of the Fifth Pan-African Congress repeatedly noted the evils of the exploitative and "alien imperialist powers",[11] and stated that the presence of these Western powers in Africa had resulted in "regression instead of progress".[12] The language of the resolutions was a far cry from the *mission civilisatrice* of Blyden and Garvey, or even from the more conciliatory approaches adopted by such thinkers as Horton and Du Bois. Manchester thus removed any pretence of the benefits of foreign involvement in Africa, going to some lengths to portray the Western world as untrustworthy. Furthermore, in the most forceful statement on African independence up to that point, the conference resolved that "complete and absolute independence for the Peoples of West Africa is the only solution to the existing problems".[13]

But Manchester went further than this. Before Padmore's intervention, Pan-Africanism had been concerned, first and foremost, with the emancipation of individuals and, secondly, with the emancipation of African states. The Manchester Congress began to consider what self-determination should mean in a post-independence era. Here again, Padmore's influence can be felt. While notions of African solidarity were an integral part of both black nationalism and Pan-Africanism, Padmore, in close collaboration with Nkrumah, began to call for an understanding of solidarity or African unity bound to a single African state in the form, for example, of a "United States of Africa" – an idea that would form a central plank of debates on Pan-Africanism during Nkrumah's presidency, and continue into the twenty-first century through the rhetoric of leaders such as Libya's Muammar Qaddafi.

Thus, it was Padmore who, through organising the Fifth Pan-African Congress in Manchester in 1945, oversaw the final transformation of Pan-Africanism from an American-based racial movement into an African-based movement whose principal aim was to protect Africans from the abuses of foreign interference on their own continent. The shift in focus was heralded by a change in the attendees of the conference and the resulting change in the intellectual and political leadership of the movement. Indeed, W.E.B. Du Bois was the only prominent African-American Pan-African thinker present in Manchester. The conference was, however, partially organised and attended by both Nkrumah and Kenyatta, and received a letter of support from Nnamdi Azikiwe, who was unable to attend. These three men would go on to become the first leaders of Ghana, Kenya and Nigeria respectively, though Azikiwe was largely a ceremonial president. Whether intended to align with Du Bois's thinking or not, therefore, the Manchester Congress began the process whereby Pan-Africanism would become the preserve of Africa's ruling elite, moving it away from individuals and towards the level of states.

The period between the conference and Ghanaian independence in 1957 saw Padmore's understanding of what Pan-Africanism was and how it ought to be practised solidified as the movement's dominant intellectual thread. While Pan-Africanism struggled to implement Manchester's ambitions, in part due to their magnitude, Padmore and Nkrumah laid the foundations of both an important personal relationship and an understanding of Pan-Africanism that would dominate the movement for the remainder of the twentieth century. It was during this time that Nkrumah established a West African National Secretariat of the Pan-African Federation, which, while located in London, nevertheless attracted the support of a number of like-minded organisations operating in West Africa. The purpose of the secretariat was to collate and disseminate "information on matters affecting the destiny of West Africans"[14] and to "work for unity and harmony among all West Africans"[15] by formulating common African positions on African affairs.

Meanwhile, in 1954, Padmore published *Pan-Africanism or Communism? The Coming Struggle for Africa.*[16] The book was both a reflection on the evolution of the movement and an effort by Padmore to consolidate his own thoughts on how Pan-Africanism ought to be implemented in practice. While the volume was undoubtedly an attempt by Padmore to draw a clear distinction between the two international movements amid growing suspicion in the West that Pan-Africanism was an African expression of communism, the book was at the same time clear testimony of the extent to which Padmore's experiences in the Comintern had shaped his interventions in Pan-Africanism.

When Ghana did achieve its independence in March 1957, Pan-Africanism was almost immediately brought to the centre of African affairs, and Padmore was present in the country to witness the celebrations as Nkrumah's advisor on African affairs. The moment marked not only the partial achievement of the movement's driving objective, but also the inauguration of its most strident leader. As the first prime minster of the newly independent West African nation, Nkrumah was provided an opportunity to elevate Pan-Africanism from the level of infrequent and impotent conferences to that of African states and to inject the movement with a new lease of life. Furthermore, whereas the Manchester Congress had signalled the transition of Pan-Africanism from North America to Africa, so Ghanaian independence and Nkrumah's subsequent efforts to enact his vision of a united Africa heralded the beginning of an era in which Pan-

Africanism would become the preserve of Africa's ruling elite rather than the peoples that they represented (see Introduction and Biney in this volume).

Concluding Reflections: A Lasting Legacy?

The Pan-Africanism that Padmore helped to forge after 1945 shifted its gaze to the continent and was given both greater coherence and a singularity of purpose by the twin goals of African independence and unity. The emergent leadership was born on the continent, and now believed that it should serve as the organisational home of the movement, instead of North America or Europe. It argued that "henceforth, the struggle for the emancipation of people of African descent focused on the homeland".[17] Although it paid homage to Africa's unique cultural heritage and societal values, the Pan-Africanism of the post-1945 era was essentially a political movement with a particularly virulent stance against any form of Western colonialism or imperialism. Its immediate objectives were to ensure the attainment of independence for all African peoples, and to unite these people by freeing them from the artificial boundaries that had been imposed at the Berlin Conference of 1884–5.[18]

However, despite Padmore's influence, questions over the movement's ideological coherence once more arose as independent Africa began to consider the nature of its future relations. This was most evident in the question of African unity, and what this would mean to a post-independence Africa. This ambiguity was well captured through reference to the ideas of an "African Personality" and the ambition to establish a "United States of Africa". Whereas the former's purpose was to make clear that Africa could be distinguished from "the West" and championed unity in the form of a single African voice in international affairs, the unity implied in the latter was of a more formal arrangement in which the existing states would be federated or confederated under a single government.

Indeed, the trajectory of Pan-Africanism in the years following Ghana's political independence would, to a large extent, mirror Padmore's own fortunes. He died in a London hospital of complications from a liver condition in September 1959 at the age of 56. By all accounts, his time in Ghana was difficult due in part to his ill health. The Pan-African movement that Padmore left behind almost simultaneously fell back into the ideological and practical contradictions that had defined it before his incredible intellectual influence on the movement.

Although Africa's newly independent states achieved a remarkable feat with the creation of the Organisation of African Unity (OAU) in 1963, the body's founding Charter retreated from many of the principles that Padmore had attempted to instil into the movement. Pan-Africanism, once more, was demoted in the face of the interests of nation-states, and became more concerned with safeguarding their territorial sovereignty. This was a Pan-Africanism of leaders, rather than of citizens.

In the years following Padmore's death and in the absence of a leader with his particular vision for the movement, Pan-Africanism was once more sidelined as East and West entered the Cold War, with Africa's disparate states aligning themselves according to the interests of their economies and security. Padmore had intervened in a flailing movement and helped guide the emergence of Pan-Africanism as many understand it today. While his intellectual legacy remains self-evident, it was not until half a century later – under the guidance of South Africa's Thabo Mbeki and Nigeria's Olusegun Obasanjo – that Pan-Africanism would again see leaders with the ability meaningfully to translate thought into practice in the way that Padmore had done (see Adebajo on Mbeki in this volume).

7

AMY ASHWOOD GARVEY: GLOBAL PAN-AFRICAN FEMINIST

Rhoda Reddock

UNTIL THE TURN OF THE TWENTY-FIRST CENTURY, Amy Ashwood Garvey – the first wife of Marcus Garvey (see Grant in this volume) – was relatively unknown globally, and even locally in her native Jamaica. Much more known was Marcus's second wife, Amy Jacques Garvey, his biographer and the mother of his two sons. Amy Jacques Garvey was an outstanding thinker, writer and activist, and it is probably to his credit that both of Garvey's wives – the two Amys – were more than simply the helpmates of a great leader, as the practice of that time would have expected. Indeed, it has been argued by American scholar and historian Ula Taylor that the work of both women reflected "the unflinching determination … to make feminist issues fundamental to the global black intellectual enterprise".[1] In many ways, this has changed. A growing scholarship on the life and career of Amy Ashwood Garvey has emerged, shedding new light on her. The more recent biography by Marcus Garvey scholar Trinidad and Tobago's Tony Martin provides the most comprehensive and detailed record of her life and work; however, it is also the most unsympathetic.[2]

This essay focuses on Amy Ashwood Garvey as a life-long internationalist, Pan-Africanist and feminist, tracing the shifts in her intellectual and political development. Pan-Africanism cannot be understood as a monolithic paradigm. Rather, I argue that it represents a diverse solidarity of people of African heritage on the continent and globally, committed to the idea of Africa and the improvement in the lives of African peoples everywhere. Garveyism is one variant of this tradition. While the history of Pan-Africanism is often one of great men, it is also one of great women, who, like Amy Ashwood Garvey, shaped and were shaped by this intellectual and activist tradition (see also Morris in this volume).

Why Amy Ashwood Garvey?

Amy Ashwood Garvey was one of a number of Pan-Africanist women of the early twentieth century whose work was central to the emergence, spread and successes of Pan-Africanism.[3] Her contribution was remarkable in that it spanned several decades, extended to over four continents and regions, and involved collaboration with some of the most influential thinkers, political activists and Pan-Africanist and socialist leaders of the early to mid-twentieth century. What is often forgotten is that these often full-time activists survived primarily by their wits and the benevolence of well-wishers, eking out an existence for themselves and their cause. This was no easy task in the racist, colour-barred and anti-communist witch-hunt in the United States during the McCarthyite era in which they operated. This was true for both Amy Ashwood and Marcus Garvey. As full-time activists, their visions of racial upliftment and black business success were fuelled both by Amy Ashwood's family background in business and Marcus Garvey's attraction to Booker T. Washington's ideas of black self-reliance. The realities of day-to-day survival and the conflict between the business and political imperatives of their lives would, however, dog them for the entire period of their adult existence.

After a brief introduction to her early life and the formation of the Universal Negro Improvement Association (UNIA), this essay focuses primarily on three of the many locations of Amy Ashwood's internationalist journeys: New York's Harlem, London and continental Africa.

Amy Ashwood Garvey: Background and Early Life

Amy Ashwood Garvey was born on 10 January 1897[4] in Port Antonio in the parish of Portland, Jamaica, the last of three children born into a middle-class family. Her parents were Jamaican-born Maudriana Ashwood, whose mother was described as a "Haitian mixed-race (mulatto) woman", and Michael Ashwood whose enslaved grandmother reportedly had been born in Africa, being brought to Jamaica in captivity. Her father, a Port Antonio businessman, was primarily a baker, but also worked as a government-contracted undertaker for the indigent. During her early childhood, Amy lived in Panama, where her family relocated shortly after she was born. Her father ran a printing works in the Panamanian seaport city of Colón.[5] In 1904, Amy returned to Jamaica with her mother, and was subsequently enrolled at the Baptist Westwood High School for Girls at Stewart Town, Trelawny,[6] which had been founded by a Baptist minister specially for dark-complexioned girls who were not accepted into other secondary schools. This was a reflection of the structured "colourism" that affected Jamaica and other parts of the Caribbean at that time and continues, to a lesser extent, today.

From very early on, Amy showed tremendous intellect and an extraordinary inclination to articulate her opinions. By the time of her Westwood years, according to Amy's later recollection, she was already beginning to manifest the social consciousness and rebellion against the values of her class which were to characterise much of her life.[7] Her "sense of racial consciousness" was awakened at the tender age of 12 when she was informed about slavery and her African ancestry by a teacher at Westwood.[8] Until that time, Amy – like many Jamaicans – had been unaware of her African heritage.

As in other parts of the English-speaking Caribbean, literary and debating societies were part of the intellectual life of many Jamaicans, especially in urban areas. Amy aspired to a theatrical career, and had acquired excellent recitation and debating skills. This enabled her to assume public roles with confidence and skill.[9] In her teenage years, she attended weekly debates at the Baptist Church Hall in Kingston. In July 1914, at the age of 17, she met Marcus Garvey at one such event where she debated the topic "Morality Does Not Increase with the March of Civilization" under the auspices of the Kingston Literary and Debating Society. Marcus had supported her perspective. Ashwood later recounted how an elaborate exchange of ideas sparked a romantic relationship in which her connection with Garvey revolved around their similar passion for Africa and African peoples, and a strong belief in the need for urgent action to unite Africans.[10]

The Birth of the UNIA

In her account of "The Birth of the Universal Negro Improvement Association and African Communities League", Amy Ashwood claimed to have been its co-founder.[11] Garvey historian Tony Martin, however, disputes this claim, suggesting that she may have exaggerated her role in the formation of the UNIA.[12] He also suggested that such a role would have been impossible for a 17-year-old.[13] Nevertheless, Amy and Marcus – who was 26 at the time – were the earliest members of the UNIA-ACL. Ashwood would definitely have been one of its first members at its formation in 1914 and, although young, her devotion to the Association and her work in its promotion would have begun with the founding of the organisation. Amy was heavily involved in the planning of the inaugural meeting of the UNIA at Collegiate Hall in Kingston, as well as in weekly Tuesday night elocution meetings, musical and literary meetings and fundraising activities. She also served as the first general secretary and a member of the board of the Association's management. During this time, she started the Ladies' Division of the UNIA, which later became the Black Cross Nurses Arm,[14] and secured fixed positions for women on the UNIA branch executives. Ashwood was also heavily involved in early plans for an industrial school. It should be noted that the activities of the early UNIA were less ambitious than its published aims. Amy also helped to organise many UNIA humanitarian efforts such as dinners for the poor in Kingston, and visits to the sick in hospitals. She further participated in UNIA-sponsored debates such as one in 1914 on the question "Is the Intellect of a Woman as Highly Developed as That of a Man?", thus demonstrating her early feminist inclinations.

Despite their concerns about Amy's relationship with the older but not yet self-supporting Garvey, the Ashwood family appears to have been quite involved in the affairs of the early UNIA. For example, in 1915, the house rented for the UNIA headquarters was paid for by the Ashwood family, though initially they opposed the idea. Amy's younger brother was one of ten contestants at a musical and literary evening; her mother served on a committee; while her father is reported to have sat with Amy on the platform at one meeting, reciting a poem and offering the largest contribution of £1.1s towards the UNIA's fundraising appeal.[15]

But Jamaica proved to be a difficult ground for the growth of the organisation. While the class and colour hierarchies in the country should have provided the opportunities for such mobilisation, there was little support for their efforts at this time. Their appeal to the government for land to establish a school modelled on the Tuskegee Institute was rejected. So, like many other Jamaicans, Marcus Garvey sought his future elsewhere, travelling to Panama, London and Montreal before settling in New York's Harlem in 1916 (see Grant in this volume).[16] Meanwhile, Amy's parents' concerns about the relationship with Marcus grew, and in 1916 she was sent back to Panama.[17] She was, however, determined to continue her relationship with Garvey. They corresponded regularly, and after two years in Panama, Amy journeyed to New York where she was reunited with Garvey in September 1918.

Harlem, New York

Amy Ashwood's arrival in New York brought significant changes in the fortunes of the UNIA. Prior to her arrival, Marcus had already established himself as a powerful orator, completing speaking engagements throughout the US. These had been used as opportunities to raise funds and encourage membership of the organisation. Amy arrived just after Marcus's decision to incorporate the UNIA in the US, a process completed in July 1918. *The Afro-American* newspaper of December 1918, in an article headlined "A New Radical Organisation", reported that the UNIA's members included "all colored peoples, Americans, West Indians, Africans and Indians in its membership".[18]

By 1919, the organisation had acquired its headquarters at Liberty Hall in Harlem. Amy became general secretary and secretary of the Ladies' Division of New York Local, and, with Marcus, immediately embarked on a fundraising drive in Detroit and Virginia. That same year, she joined Garvey in the production and dissemination of the *Negro World*, the UNIA's weekly newspaper, which would become the most widely distributed Pan-African newspaper in the US. Nevertheless, "it was Amy's weekly chore to use tact and persuasion to get Mr Ragowski [the printer] to extend credit to the UNIA, and to get his promise to publish the next week's issue".[19] Then, together, it would be their job to distribute the free paper between midnight and 4 a.m.[20] In addition to political and historical entreaties, the *Negro World* reflected the integration of the arts and literature evident since the UNIA's inception in Kingston. This newspaper was something of a precursor to the "Harlem Renaissance" of the 1920s.

From 1919, Amy joined Marcus speaking and "street-strolling"[21] in Harlem. Ula Taylor has observed that street-strollers understood the importance of engaging with people on the streets: it was an opportunity to get the message of black empowerment directly to the grassroots. What was also important was Amy's use of poetry, in particular that of her favourite poet, African-American Paul Laurence Dunbar. In this way, Ashwood played a pivotal role in the development of the UNIA's membership base and securing financial support for the Association's activities. To promote the UNIA and persuade crowds on the sidewalk to attend meetings at Liberty Hall on Harlem's West 135th Street, she gave "speeches about the importance of the UNIA as a political organisation seeking to reconnect Blacks throughout the world to an imagined homeland in Africa for their economic, political, social, and cultural well-being".[22] These speeches by Amy and Marcus also promoted grassroots investment in their key business venture of the time – the Black Star Line, founded in 1919. This was an idea so big that it captured the imagination of African Americans across the US.

From early on, Amy and Marcus were under continuous surveillance by the US District Attorney, and Amy was summoned by the American Secret Service to their office up to 17 times. As she noted: "I was summoned to the same District Attorney's office and on each occasion, I had to go through the same wearisome procedure. Strange to relate, no other officer from the UNIA – not even Marcus Garvey – was questioned by the police at that time."[23] Years later, in 1944 when she wrote to the US Consulate in Kingston about jobs for Jamaican domestics as part of the US Emergency Farm Labour Scheme, which catered primarily for men, no less a personage than J. Edgar Hoover, director of the Federal Bureau of Investigation (FBI), would advise the US State Department not to approve the request because of Amy's links to Marcus Garvey and the UNIA, and the fear that her success could strengthen the Association's influence.[24]

In October 1919, Amy intervened in an attempted assassination of Garvey by George Tyler, described as a "discontented investor". After an initial shot which injured Garvey, Amy rushed at Tyler, throwing him to the floor,[25] and thus preventing further harm. This would be the subject of much debate, as Marcus and Amy Jacques would deny this incident occurred, providing different accounts.[26] While Amy Jacques dismissed Amy's role outright,[27] Tony Martin outlines three explanations provided by Marcus on different occasions. In the first two, Martin claimed that Amy was behind him, or was holding his hat and coat, crediting a certain May Clarke Roach with having moved in front of him to prevent the second shooting. Three years later, during legal proceedings for mail fraud, Garvey would credit both Amy Ashwood and Clarke Roach with getting in front of him and preventing the second shot.[28]

Amy and Africa: England and the "Motherland"

Amy Ashwood's divorce from Marcus in 1922 – six months after their elaborate wedding – marked the end of their collaboration and the end of an era for her. The break-up of her marriage remained a source of pain, sadness and regret, but it also opened new vistas for her. As her biographer notes, at 25 Amy had "youth, intelligence, self-confidence, vigour and experience".[29] After travels to Montreal, Jamaica, Trinidad and Tobago, London, and across Europe, and then back to New York, she settled in London in 1930, where her interests in Africa would move in new directions. Her Florence Mills Social Parlour and the International Afro Restaurant run with her partner, Trinidadian Calypso singer Sam Manning, became a key meeting point for Caribbean and African intellectuals. She came into contact with continental Africans and was influenced by the more socialist-oriented West Indians and Africans such as C.L.R James, George Padmore (see Cudjoe and Duggan in this volume), Una Marson, Ras Makonnen, Jomo Kenyatta, Kwame Nkrumah (see Biney in this volume) and others. This interaction would be different from the black nationalism of the Harlem period, and, most significantly, it allowed for the decolonising of the prejudiced views held by West Indians about continental Africans, the state of Africa, and the role of Caribbean citizens in the continent's future.[30] This resulted in a shift from Marcus's "Race First" ideology to a more anti-colonial, anti-imperialist Pan-Africanism.

The Negro Progress Union

One of Amy Ashwood's first projects would be her collaboration with Nigerian law student Ladipo Solanke in the formation of the Negro Progress Union (NPU) during her first period in London.[31] In July 1924, the NPU was created with 13 students. At the inaugural meeting, Amy Ashwood was given the Yoruba title of "Iyalode" (Mother has arrived) "in appreciation of her love, interest and services for the Union as its organiser and in view of her position and future activities on behalf of the Union".[32] From early on, Ashwood shared her vision for an educational policy for Nigeria which she felt was a necessary prerequisite for the country's political emancipation.[33] According to British historian of Nigerian descent Hakim Adi, the aims and objectives of the NPU reflected Garveyite ideas of self-reliance and self-help, which were popular across West

Africa.[34] The NPU's emphasis on the education of girls would have reflected Amy's feminist influences. This experience broadened her understanding of the African condition, causing her to question Garvey's vision of a single African nation. Writing in the *Jamaica Gleaner* in 1924, Amy observed: "Mr Garvey's idea of an African kingdom is a geographic blunder. There are too many tribes, each differing from the other in customs [so] that it is quite impossible to form them into a single people. What is more they want no Afro-Americans or West Indians as rulers over them."[35] The NPU would eventually develop into the West African Students' Union (WASU), an important organisation in the movement for the independence of the sub-region.[36]

The Abyssinian Invasion

The 1935 Italian invasion of Ethiopia attracted attention throughout the African diaspora. It was at Amy's restaurant that a solidarity organisation, the International African Friends of Ethiopia (IAFE), was formed, with the aim of assisting "by all means in their power, in the maintenance of the territorial integrity and the political independence of Abyssinia".[37] Members included Kenya's Jomo Kenyatta as honorary president, T.A. Marryshow of Grenada, J.B. Danquah of the Gold Coast (Ghana), George Padmore, C.L.R. James, Sam Manning and Mohammed Said of Somalia.

As with the UNIA, Amy was the honorary secretary and became the main spokesperson for the IAFE.[38] As American scholar Minkah Makalani noted: "Ashwood soon emerged as the organisation's central figure, speaking at London rallies of both the Labour Party and the Communist-controlled League against Imperialism and connecting the IAFE to various organisations. A tireless organiser, she assumed much of the responsibility for the group, and while [C.L.R.] James devoted his attention to struggles among British Socialists, she built the organisation into an international network."[39] This group was able to mobilise action across the world, for example in Trinidad and Tobago where there was wide grassroots and middle-class support for this campaign among the African-descended population,[40] and in South Africa, where dock workers refused to service Italian ships.[41]

In a move to broaden the group's focus to the entire African continent, and under the leadership of George Padmore (see Duggan in this volume), the International African Service Bureau (IASB) was established in 1937 as a successor body to the IAFE. This new group, which included Ashwood,

James and other future African leaders, such as Sierra Leonean I.T.A Wallace-Johnson and Nigerian L.N. Mbanefo, decided to adopt a "socialist programme and publish a journal to disseminate information on African problems and the problems of all black people".[42] The journal, *International African Opinion*, was edited by C.L.R. James.

Manchester: The Fifth Pan-African Congress

The Fifth Pan-African Congress held in the English city of Manchester in 1945 was undoubtedly the most important and influential of all the Pan-African congresses. It was, in many ways, a catalyst for the future independence of Africa. Manchester built on the work of British-based organisations and their connections to anti-colonial movements across Africa and its diaspora. Amy Ashwood was a member of the organising team along with C.L.R James, George Padmore and Kwame Nkrumah. Participants included activists and many of the future leaders of Africa, the Caribbean and the Americas, such as Kenya's Jomo Kenyatta, Nigeria's Samuel Akintola, South Africa's Peter Abrahams, Jamaica's Alma La Badie of the UNIA and the American, W.E.B. Du Bois.[43] Amy chaired the first session of the meeting, entitled "The Colour Problem in Britain". Ghanaian Frederick Robert Kankam-Boadu recollects:

> The Chairman for the occasion was Mrs. Amy Garvey, wife of Mr. Marcus Garvey of the Black Star fame … [she] opened the meeting with a very mature and balanced speech touching on freedom and humanity: soldiers of the Commonwealth and others had fought and sacrificed their lives to this end, and freedom and peace should be the prize to be won. She directed the audience's mind to democracy as opposed to dictatorship, which had caused wars and miseries, and appealed for peace and fraternity among nations. She asked for freedom and self-rule for the British colonies. She referred to racial discrimination and other prejudices and advised their liquidation.[44]

Of the three women who were recorded as having attended this conference, two were from Jamaica: Amy Ashwood and Alma La Badie, who was representing the Jamaica UNIA. Amy's opening statements at the 19 October Caribbean session were not surprising. As she noted: "Very much has been written and spoken of the Negro, but for some reason very little has been said about the black woman.

She has been shunted into the social background to be a child-bearer. This has been principally her lot."[45]

Ashwood then discussed the problems of women in Jamaica, highlighting the class divisions, distinguishing between the traditional upper class and the new middle classes of teachers, civil servants and store clerks. She criticised women of the wealthier classes for their lack of interest and political participation, noting that the ten thousand black women teachers were a potentially powerful new political force. Amy also drew attention to the working-class women of Jamaica, primarily domestic workers and labourers, and blamed black men for doing little to improve their lot, noting that the poor living and working conditions of women fuelled the drive for emigration, which was so prevalent.[46] Alma La Badie, for her part, stressed the problem of water supply, women's poverty, resultant child labour and the absence of juvenile courts or social systems to deal with the inevitable consequences. The Congress resolutions on the West Indies were the only ones to include women's issues such as equal pay for equal work. This conference was no doubt a high point in Amy Ashwood Garvey's career.

Travels through Africa

Ashwood's urge to travel to Africa was sparked at the age of 12 when her grandmother – Grannie Dabas – told her about being kidnapped and sold into slavery. This thirst for reconnection was stimulated further when Amy met Marcus Garvey and learnt about his passion for "returning" to Africa. Ashwood's tour of Africa was a fulfilment of their dream, and her wide connections with African leaders and intellectuals facilitated her journey. Unfortunately, Marcus was never able to visit the continent during his lifetime.

Amy's West African tour began in March 1946 at the age of 49. She spent three and a half years travelling throughout the sub-region, and was heavily involved in researching the status of women there. She travelled from Liverpool to Senegal, to Sierra Leone, then on to Liberia. She returned to Sierra Leone, then went on to Ghana, where she spent a significant amount of time. During her tour, she also made short visits to Chad, Togo, Cameroon, Nigeria, Gambia, Senegal and Dahomey (now Benin).[47] She further visited Spanish Guinea and sections of French Equatorial Africa. Ashwood identified as one of her main tasks "to investigate the conditions facing African women and, where possible, exert whatever influence she could to improve their lot".[48]

In Sierra Leone, she contacted women and women's groups, and embarked on a two-day journey to visit a woman chief, 150 miles away. Her "joy was complete," she said, "when the Queen of the Gallinas, Paramount Chief Madam Woki Massaquoi, embraced me, and said, 'Daughter of Africa welcome home.' To be able to see a woman of my race, the great grand-daughter of Siaka, one of the first known kings of Sierra Leone, holding the reins of power in her hands made me very proud."[49] On asking Chief Massaquoi for a message to the women of the Americas, she responded: "Tell them to keep up their courage. Africa will live again as a free Nation."[50]

Liberia

Liberia was another important destination for Ashwood in West Africa, as it was a point of connection for those who had left and returned to Africa. Amy was received with diplomatic honours in Liberia by President William Tubman,[51] who shared her enthusiasm for the political emancipation of women, extensive reforms in education and the extension of universal suffrage to the indigenous population. Tubman supported Ashwood's efforts to write the history of Liberia, providing her with transportation and an interpreter when she travelled to the interior of the country.[52] Ashwood visited rural areas and recorded local customs. She also spoke to women on female hygiene, home and family relationships, social living, education, the care of the young, and the history of African peoples in the diaspora.[53] Ashwood further engaged in a number of failed businesses relating to the emerging rubber and diamond industries in Liberia. One outcome of these efforts was the writing of the manuscript "Liberia, Land of Promise", which was taken to England to be edited and retyped but was never published. British feminist Sylvia Pankhurst wrote a preview, which summarised the contents of the manuscript. In her introduction, Ashwood gave as her reasons for having written the book:

> I felt very strongly that peoples of African descent should become alive to the experiment that has been going on amidst Africans and has been conducted by Africans, the experiment in the science of statesmanship and nationhood that has been undertaken within the Republic of Liberia. The fruits of the experiment will be of immense value to all Africans during this period of transition.[54]

Amy Ashwood applied for and was eventually granted a declaration of intent for Liberian citizenship in July 1946.[55] She was commissioned by the Liberian government as a special representative of the Liberian centennial to the Gold Coast and Nigeria in 1946. Her plan was to spend six months there, but her tour lasted instead for three and a half years.[56]

The Gold Coast

The Gold Coast (now Ghana) was the next significant stop on Amy's West African tour. This was the country of her ancestry. There, Ashwood was able to confirm the story of her grandmother's ancestral roots, traced to the Ashanti as far back as the seventeenth century. She met some of her relatives from the Juaben ethnic group, including the King of Darman (the Darmanhene). Her story was confirmed by the Asantehene, Agyeman Prempeh II, and she was officially welcomed as a long-lost daughter of the Ashanti.[57] Amy remained in Ghana for two years, enjoying the Asantehene's hospitality.[58] She also rekindled an old friendship with J.B. Danquah, founder of the Gold Coast Convention Party, which brought her into conflict with her long-time friend in London, Kwame Nkrumah, its former secretary. There was eventually a split between Nkrumah and Danquah, with Ashwood caught in the middle.[59]

From Ghana, Amy moved on to Nigeria, where she rekindled her NPU/WASU connections. By the time of her return to London in July 1949, she had visited almost every country in West Africa and organised 15 women's associations. Her reflections show a deep concern for the sub-region's poor and rural women, and a recognition that, in Africa, poverty existed in the midst of plenty.[60] After a tour of the Caribbean in the 1950s, Ashwood returned to Africa in the late 1950s and in 1960. In May 1969, she died in her native Jamaica, leaving behind three unpublished manuscripts.

Concluding Reflections

By all standards, Amy Ashwood Garvey was an outstanding woman. Her love and commitment to Africa and its diaspora were legendary, and her willingness to defy the US secret service was praiseworthy. Her commitment to women's liberation was a common thread running through all her activities and was a struggle with which she was never afraid to identify. This was remarkable for her epoch. Ashwood's life was, however, full of unfulfilled ambitions, failed business ventures and incomplete projects, including her many writings. It was apparently difficult for her to see projects through to completion. But there is no doubt that the insecurities of the activist life would have contributed to this failing. The inability to secure full-time work and regular income was the lot of most activists discussed in this essay. They often lived on the largesse of benefactors and supporters, as well as their own business ventures. Yet, Amy was able to travel widely and extensively in Africa, North America, the Caribbean,[61] Central America and Europe.

In 2005, the African Union adopted the African Protocol on Women and also designated the diaspora as its sixth sub-region. In many ways, the coming together of these two events can be seen as part of the combined legacy of Amy Ashwood Garvey. It is in this context, therefore, that we celebrate her achievements in the establishment of the early UNIA in Jamaica. Ashwood ensured a strong place for women in this organisation, energising and stabilising the UNIA in Harlem while her support for the anti-colonial and independence movements in Africa and the mobilisation efforts that took her through many countries on several continents, ensured that women were not forgotten in the movements for self-government and independence across Africa. As Trinidad and Tobagan-American scholar, Carole Boyce-Davies observed:

> Amy Ashwood ended up being present at most of the 20th Century's Pan-Africanist organising, ranging from the UNIA through the pre- and post-independence activities of African and Caribbean countries, early African Diaspora feminist activism ... coming up to and even touching the Black Power period when she was already ... on her last legs, still desiring to be buried like Du Bois in Africa.[62]

No doubt there is much more still to be written about this remarkable woman.

8

PIXLEY SEME: THE REGENERATION OF AFRICA

Bongani Ngqulunga

PIXLEY KA ISAKA SEME – the moving spirit behind the formation of South Africa's African National Congress (ANC) in 1912 – is also known as one of the pioneers of Pan-Africanism.[1] His association with Pan-Africanism originates from an address he gave to a student public-speaking competition at Columbia University in New York in April 1906. At the time that he gave the speech, Seme was about to graduate from Columbia College with a bachelor's degree. The address, titled "The Regeneration of Africa", earned him the first prize, the Curtis Medal in gold in the competition, and attracted wide media attention in the United States and back home in South Africa. Overnight, Seme's name became associated with a nascent Pan-Africanist movement, and the address itself became a touchstone and a source of inspiration for many generations of Pan-Africanists and nationalists on the African continent fighting for independence from colonial rule. No less a figure than the legendary Ghanaian leader, Kwame Nkrumah (see Biney in this volume) – an iconic figure in Africa's struggle for independence – found the speech so relevant fifty years after Seme had delivered it that when he addressed the first International Congress of Africanists held in the Ghanaian capital of Accra in December 1962, he read out Seme's speech in its entirety.

By invoking Seme at the first Congress of Africanists to be held on African soil, Nkrumah was linking the Pan-Africanist ideals of his time to the vision that Seme had espoused five decades earlier. What is remarkable about the speech is not only the oratorical acumen that was evidently deployed in its formulation, but also the depth of vision for, and pride in, the African continent and the black race. Alongside the creation of the African National Congress in 1912, "The Regeneration of Africa" speech is often regarded as one of Seme's enduring legacies.

"The Regeneration of Africa" is therefore critical in assessing Seme's contributions to Pan-Africanism. I begin this chapter by analysing the content of the speech, focusing on its key arguments as well as the context that had shaped it, before discussing Seme's public life after his return to South Africa from over a decade studying in the US and Britain. I suggest that although Seme completely disengaged from the Pan-Africanist movement when he returned to South Africa, severing contact with the key personalities who had led the movement, his many public endeavours on his return to South Africa can be considered as concrete attempts on his part to bring into being the new African modernity that he had espoused in his famous 1906 speech in New York. The most important of Seme's work, and indeed the embodiment of his vision for Pan-Africanism, was the forging of black political unity through founding the South African Native National Congress in 1912 (renamed the African National Congress in 1923).

The Regeneration of Africa

"I am African, and I set my pride in my race over against a hostile public opinion."[2] So Seme began his famous 1906 address. He argued that Africa should not be compared to Europe or any other continent. The basis of his plea was not that such a comparison would "bring humiliation upon Africa", but that there was no standard according to which each race could be compared. To prove that Africa was as great as any other continent, Seme listed a number of its achievements, starting with the ancient capital of Egypt, Thebes, "the city of one hundred gates" as he described it. Of the city, Seme noted, "The grandeur of its venerable ruins and the gigantic proportions of its architecture reduce to insignificance the boasted monuments of other nations." From Thebes, Seme moved to the Egyptian pyramids to which he argued the world could present nothing comparable. All the glory of the Egyptian monuments, noted Seme, belonged to Africa and her people, and they served as an indestructible memorial to the genius of Africans. He then moved on to the pyramids of Ethiopia, which he conceded were not as large as the Egyptian ones, but noted that they far surpassed them in architectural splendour. Perhaps moved by Africa's genius, which was demonstrated by the beauty of Egypt's creations, Seme uttered what have become the iconic words associated with his speech:

> Oh, for that historian who, with the open pen of truth will bring to Africa's claim the strength of written proof. He will tell of a race whose onward tide was often swelled with tears, but in whose heart bondage has not quenched the fire of former years. He will write that in these later days when Earth's noble ones are named, she has a roll of honor too of whom she is not ashamed. The giant is awakening! From the four corners of the Earth, Africa's sons who have been proved through fire and sword, are marching to the future's golden door bearing the records of deeds of valour done.[3]

Seme then proceeded to a subject that was closer to his current home. He directed his oratory at John Caldwell Calhoun, the seventh vice-president of the United States, whom he described as having been the most philosophical of slave-owners in the American South. He noted that Calhoun had said that, if he could be shown a black person who understood Greek syntax, he would change his mind and consider black people as being part of the human race. Seme expressed regret that Calhoun was not present to listen to him give a list of many black people who had accomplished great things, "black men of pure African blood" who could "repeat the Koran in memory, skilled in Latin, Greek and Hebrew – Arabic and Chaldaic".[4] Were Calhoun present, Seme added, he would have shown him men of African descent who possessed great wisdom and profound knowledge, such as a black professor of philosophy at a celebrated university in Germany.[5] Fired by a desire to defend the honour and dignity of his race that had been injured by statements such as Calhoun's, Seme declared that "there are many Africans who have shown marks of genius and high character sufficient to redeem their race from the charges which I am now considering".[6] For Seme, signs of genius of the African people were also evident beyond the Sahara Desert. In the Congo, he extolled the bravery of her people who, in his words, fought like men and died like martyrs. In Botswana, he praised the system of governance that valued the wisdom of ordinary people.

Turning to the subject of his address, "The Regeneration of Africa", Seme noted lyrically:

The brighter day is rising upon Africa. Already I seem to see her chains dissolved, her desert plains red with harvest, her Abyssinia and her Zululand the seats of science and religion, reflecting the glory of the rising sun from the spires of their churches and universities. Her Congo and her Gambia whitened with commerce, her crowded cities sending forth the hum of business and all her sons employed in advancing the victories of peace – greater and more abiding than the spoils of war.[7]

It is to this new and powerful period that the regeneration of Africa belongs. By the term "regeneration", Seme was referring to entry to a new life, embracing the diverse phases of a higher, complex existence. The basic factor which assures the regeneration resides in an awakened race-consciousness. This gives Africans a clear perception of their elemental needs and of their undeveloped powers. It therefore should lead them to the attainment of that higher and advanced standard of life.

A modern Africa in Seme's vision will contribute a "new and unique civilization" which "is soon to be added to the world". This is a civilization that will be "thoroughly spiritual and humanistic – indeed a regeneration moral and eternal".[8] The African of this modern continent is "not a proletarian in the world of science and art," but has "precious creations" of his own, "of ivory, of copper and of gold, fine, plated willow-ware and weapons of superior workmanship".[9]

The *Daily Spectator*, the university's student newspaper, reported Seme to have been inspired by his topic and animated in his delivery, which, together with the high quality of the content of the address, earned him the Curtis Medal. The address continues to inspire generations of Pan-Africanists. Its enduring appeal often obscures the fact that it was, in many respects, a product of its time. The turn of the nineteenth century and the beginning of the twentieth was a period of robust and lively political debate about the rights of black people and of political awakening in the African diaspora and on the African continent. That political awakening crystallised in the convening of the first Pan-African Conference by the Trinidadian lawyer Henry Sylvester Williams at Westminster Hall in London in July 1900 (see Introduction and Morris in this volume). Among the issues that participants at the conference discussed was the political condition of black people in South Africa.

The Heir of Crummell?

What appears to have greatly influenced Seme's "The Regeneration of Africa" speech was debates among African-American intellectuals about the status of black people in the United States and their relationship to the African continent. One of the leading protagonists in that debate was Alexander Crummell, an influential African-American leader, missionary and intellectual, who had spent 16 years living in Liberia. In 1861, Crummell delivered a speech on exactly the same subject as Seme's address in 1906 on the regeneration of Africa. The fact that Seme used the same topic and addressed the same issues that Crummell had touched upon, going so far as to mention the same names, suggests that Seme was fully aware of Crummell's speech.

The views of the two on the subject were, however, fundamentally different. In order fully to understand this divergence, it is useful to examine another address that Crummell delivered, also in 1861, titled "The Progress of Civilization along the West Coast of Africa", published in his book *The Future of Africa*. Crummell's view of Africa's past was diametrically opposed to Seme's. Whereas Seme saw in Africa's past grandeur, valour and accomplishment, Crummell saw their antithesis. Crummell's view of Africa's past history was bleak:

> Thrown thus back upon herself, unvisited by either the mission of letters or of grace, poor Africa, all the ages through, has been generating, and then reproducing, the whole brood and progeny of superstitions, idolatries, and paganisms through all her quarters. And hence the most pitiful, the most abject of all human conditions! And hence the most sorrowful of all histories! The most miserable, even now, of all spectacles![10]

Crummell also held a different view on the subject of Africa's regeneration. Like Seme five decades later, he believed that Africa was at the threshold of regeneration. In a sermon that Crummell delivered in 1853 titled "Hope for Africa", he argued that there was evidence that Africa had entered a period of regeneration. Speaking specifically of Africa's west coast, he observed – as a sign of progress and regeneration – that the slave trade had been entirely abolished and replaced by what he described as "legitimate trade". Crummell noted that "industrious communities [were] springing up, civilization introduced, and a trade commenced which already has swelled up, in exports alone to Europe and America to more than two million pounds per annum".[11] This apparent regeneration was also evident in the number of people of the black race who were distinguishing themselves in various fields of human endeavour. Some of the names that Crummell mentioned were exactly the same as those that Seme would include in his Columbia University speech in 1906. Crummell cited "philanthropists like Howard; scholars, classical and mental; scientific men – one, a Doctor of Philosophy in a German university; distinguished painters and artists; officers well known in Europe".[12] Among Crummell's signs of the black race's progress were the black government in Haiti, the black republic of Liberia, and the establishment of the colony of Sierra Leone.

According to Crummell, progress in Africa had been driven by forces external to the continent. Among these were the leading European powers at the time, which he described as having been merciful in "scattering darkness from her [Africa's] agonized brow, and her hastening the day of her final relief and regeneration." Another important force was Christian missionaries whose endeavours on the continent had "helped to change to hopefulness the condition of Africa".[13] Equally important was the introduction of commerce, which, together with Christianity, had brought about the development of the continent's resources, thereby conveying to "its rude inhabitants the aids and instruments to civilization, to active industry, to domestic comfort, and to a budding social refinement".[14] Crummell thus supported British explorer-missionary David Livingstone's three "Cs": Christianity, Commerce and Civilisation.

Seme's vision of the regeneration of Africa formed a counterpoint to Crummell's. While Crummell was extolling the virtues and benevolence of European expeditions in Africa, Seme was declaring that "the day of great exploring expeditions in Africa are over!"[15] Whereas Crummell considered missionaries as a force for good and civilisation in Africa, Seme, a product of missionary education, dismissed their contributions to the regeneration of Africa. This disdain was not accidental: it was a consequence of Seme's politicisation as a Pan-Africanist, which had evolved while he was a student at Columbia. His vision of Africans was hopeful and triumphant. For Seme, not only did Africans possess a proud history of accomplishment, they were also harbingers of a new human civilisation, and contributors to science and art.

Oxford: The Dreaming Spires

Seme carried this hopeful vision of a new African modernity when he entered Oxford University in October 1906 to study law. He was already considered to be one of the intellectual leaders of the nascent Pan-Africanist movement. Seme used his new-found fame to forge links with other like-minded individuals in England. This became evident when he, together with his African-American friend Alain Leroy Locke, a fellow student at Oxford, founded the Cosmopolitan Club. The purpose of the club was to foster mutual understanding among students from diverse nationalities. It met every Tuesday to debate speeches delivered by its members. Seme served as treasurer of the club, while Locke was its secretary. Its members were mostly students from British colonies who saw their education at Oxford as a preparation for future leadership on their return to their home countries. By 1908, the Cosmopolitan Club had established a journal called the *Oxford Cosmopolitan*, which was used as a forum to counter and overturn "many a narrow or racial prejudice by coming into contact with new ideas and ways of thought".[16]

While at Oxford, Seme met and developed friendships with several other major figures in the African diaspora. One of his acquaintances was Theophilus Edward Samuel Scholes, whom Seme described as "a great Negro scholar". Born in Jamaica in 1858, Scholes had made a name for himself as a medical doctor, missionary and political commentator. It was, however, his contributions as a critic of British imperialism, especially through his books, that Scholes became well known.[17] Although it is unclear how Seme came in contact with so revered a public figure, it is likely that his widely reported 1906 speech might have made him known to Scholes. In any event, their relationship was close enough for Seme to introduce Locke to Scholes.[18]

We Are One People

Seme went back to South Africa in October 1910. The South Africa to which he returned proved a fertile ground for him to put into practice his ideals for a new African modernity. And he was well equipped for such a role, having been admitted in December 1910 as only the second black South African to practise as an attorney, after Alfred Mangena, whom he admired. A few months after his return, Seme spearheaded a remarkable effort aimed at forging black political unity through the formation of a national political party, something that a generation of black political leaders had hitherto failed to do. Black political parties in South Africa, at the time, were principally splintered along provincial and even ethnic lines. The idea of one single political organisation that represented the political aspirations of all black people in South Africa, though gaining ground at the time, mostly through the efforts of eminent leaders such as Walter Rubusana and John Langalibalele Dube, had not yet borne fruit. It was a remarkable achievement that, in just over a year after Seme's return, the ANC came into being in January 1912.

Through helping to found the ANC, Seme was not only uniting regional political organisations. His ambition was much bolder and far-reaching: he sought to cajole black people in South Africa to reimagine themselves as political subjects by casting aside their ethnic identities which had hitherto divided them and embracing a more inclusive and broader political identity which was "African". He articulated this goal and ambition explicitly in a clarion call issued in October 1911. In an article published in all major black newspapers, such as *Ilanga lase Natal* and *Imvo Zabantsundu*, Seme called for black political unity and argued for the establishment of one national political organisation. In terms that were evidently meant to inspire a spirit of unity among black people and spur them into action, he noted:

> The demon of racialism, the aberrations of the Xosa-Fingo feud, the animosity that exists between the Zulus and the Tongaas, between the Basutos and every other native must be buried and forgotten; it has shed among us sufficient blood! We are one people. Those divisions, those jealousies are the cause of all our woes and of all our backwardness and ignorance today.[19]

Seme's leading role in the founding of the ANC was remarked upon by several black newspapers on the occasion of his death in June 1951. For example, *Bantu World*, a leading black newspaper at the time, captured the dominant sentiment: "if today, Basutos, Zulus, Xhosas, Shangaans, Bechuanas and Vendas know themselves as Africans, and that Africa is the land of their fathers, they owe this to the inspiring foundation of African nationalism laid by Pixley ka Izaka Seme."[20] In his tribute, Jordan Ngubane, a pre-eminent journalist, editor of *Inkundla ya*

Bantu newspaper and co-author of the ANC Youth League's 1944 Manifesto, suggested that Seme would go down in history as "the greatest African of the first fifty years of the twentieth century – if not of the century as a whole".[21] Alfred Bitini Xuma, the sixth president-general of the ANC, echoed the same sentiment at Seme's funeral in June 1951, when he called him an "architect of our people", who gave them the "inspiration of being a nation, he himself having laid the foundation of our freedom".[22]

Having succeeded in his mission of forging black political unity through the creation of the ANC, Seme took another step important in uniting black people on a national scale. He established the first black national newspaper, *Abantu-Batho*. This was a significant development because, although black newspapers existed at the time, they were primarily regional newspapers aligned to, and advancing the political causes and interests of, regional political elites. The name *Abantu-Batho*, which means "the people" in both the Nguni and Sotho languages, as well as its use of several languages in its columns, including English, Nguni and Sotho, underscored Seme's mission of uniting black people and forging a common identity among them. Using a newspaper to promote his message of unity highlighted the modernity of his political project.

Seme's Struggle for Land Ownership

Seme's vision of black economic emancipation was ambitious, bold and innovative. Here, he did not only lay out a vision and build institutions to buttress it, but he also embarked on a complete programme to bring it into fruition. In no area were Seme's ambitions clearer than in his initiative to purchase land from white farmers for the settlement of black people. He did this through a company, established in 1912, called the Native Farmers Association of Africa Limited. The company was owned and managed by black people; its shareholders and directors were all black. It is estimated that, at its founding, the Association had about 50 shareholders. Prior to, and in anticipation of, the establishment of the company, Seme bought three farms in the Wakkerstroom district of the Transvaal.

Although the Native Farmers Association ran into difficulties later, Seme's purpose in establishing it was to address the immediate challenge of a shortage of land that large numbers of black people experienced at the time. But it also reflected Seme's deep philosophical belief about the importance for black Africans of owning land. Seme outlined these beliefs in detail in an article published in several newspapers in 1929, noting: "I am one of those who often think that a man (unless he is a real Saint) cannot be really good to himself and his children unless he has a home." Employing his well-known poetic language, Seme further argued that home ownership "shapes the mind and character of every growing child and it is the dream of every maiden and a delightful heaven on earth to the sick and the aged". Not until Africans owned their own homes and their own land could they "hope to develop a civilisation which shall be our own, a civilisation which shall be more spiritual and humanistic".[23]

Seme's strong commitment to the cause of land ownership was further demonstrated through his involvement in attempts by the Swazi royal house to reclaim the land it had lost to white concessionaires. The case, which was waged through the courts in Swaziland and England, consumed much of Seme's time and attention, and, in a sense, became a defining moment of his political and legal career. As can be recalled, the Swazis had lost substantial hectares of land when the previous king, Mbandzeni, granted land and mineral concessions to white companies and individuals on a large scale. Although each concessionaire had to relinquish one-third of the land granted to him for allocation to the Swazis, the remainder of the land under concession would be held in freehold title. Native Swazis who resided on the land that had been made the private property of concession holders were given five years to live on the land without eviction.

The Swazi royal family enlisted the services of Seme to assist in claiming back its land. He represented King Sobhuza II when the matter was brought before a special court in Swaziland.[24] The Swazis lost the case, as well as a further appeal in 1926 in which Seme again served as the defence counsel for the Swazi royal family.[25]

Concluding Reflections

One of the striking threads that run through all Seme's public endeavours was his faith in, and reliance on, modern institutions to advance his many causes. When he saw a need to forge black political unity, he established a political party with a constitution and other modern accoutrements. Similarly, the cause of black land ownership was pursued through a registered company with articles of association and a board of directors after raising loans from banks to buy the land. Seme followed the same route when trying to regain Swazi land by working through British-established courts. He did more of the same in the 1930s when he was elected president of the ANC. With the exception of the ANC, which has survived for over a century, all of these experiments failed in one way or the other. Part of the explanation for their demise may lie in the mistakes that Seme made. The other explanation is that Seme's grand schemes of modernisation withered on a political system founded and anchored on racial discrimination and exclusion. His belief that he could change a political system so entrenched in racial inequality by working through the very institutions that buttressed them was perhaps the biggest strategic weakness of his approach to political struggle.

Seme is considered to be one of the pioneers of Pan-Africanism, despite the fact that upon his return to South Africa from his studies abroad in 1910, he disengaged from the broader Pan-Africanist movement and the personalities who led it. The exception was his African-American friend Alain Locke, with whom he continued a long friendship. Even when Seme encountered a political system in South Africa that excluded and discriminated against black people, he did not tap into his Pan-Africanist network for support and inspiration. This was despite the fact that some of his contemporaries in the leadership of the ANC, such as John Dube and Solomon Plaatje, were connected to the Pan-Africanist movement and some of its leading personalities such as W.E.B. Du Bois (see Morris in this volume). The reason for Seme's disengagement is difficult to explain. It may be that he was too consumed with personal and professional matters in South Africa and neighbouring territories such as Swaziland.

Seme's disengagement is also disappointing considering the impact that he had had in his early life with his famous 1906 Columbia University speech. One consolation we can draw is that his powerful vision of a rising Africa went on to inspire several generations of Pan-Africanists on the continent and in the diaspora such as Nigeria's Nnamdi Azikiwe, Senegal's Cheikh Anta Diop and South Africa's Thabo Mbeki. The organisation that Seme helped found in 1912, the African National Congress, over time embraced Pan-Africanism as one of its ideological pillars. When it was banned in South Africa in April 1960 and its leaders exiled, the ANC forged strong links with the African diaspora and became an active participant in the Pan-Africanist movement globally (see Adebajo on Mbeki in this volume). Seme's vision for the regeneration of Africa and his public endeavours in South Africa in forging a new African modernity should thus earn him a central place in the Pan-African pantheon.

PART 3

_____

THE POLITICIANS

Kwame Nkrumah: "A Great African, But Not a Great Ghanaian"?

Ama Biney

In a controversial essay published in 1966, "Nkrumah: The Leninist Czar",[1] Kenyan scholar Ali Mazrui (see Ndlovu-Gatsheni in this volume) provocatively characterised Kwame Nkrumah (1909–72), the first president of independent Ghana and key architect of African unity in the 1960s, as "a great Gold Coaster" who "fell short of becoming a great Ghanaian".[2] The aim of this chapter is to revisit the debate unleashed by Mazrui's strident allegations, and to contest the validity of his claims.

Mazrui argued in his 1966 essay that "while Nkrumah strove to be Africa's Lenin, he also sought to become Ghana's 'Czar' which was the 'worst side' of his personality and behaviour".[3] For Mazrui, "Nkrumah's tragedy was a tragedy of excess, rather than of contradiction".[4] The Kenyan scholar then drew parallels between Lenin and Nkrumah, noting that the two leaders believed in the necessity of mass organisation – or what Mazrui pejoratively characterised as "the cult of organisation".[5] Nkrumah also embraced "Lenin's economic interpretation of imperialism",[6] according to which the imperial powers had occupied the colonies for economic exploitation, a view which Nkrumah reflected in his small book *Towards Colonial Freedom* (1947).[7] Mazrui contended that, integral to "Nkrumah's secular radicalism", was a "royalist theme" which he referred to as "Czarism".[8] He considered this type of lifestyle typical of African leaders and their self-aggrandising pursuits, though conceding that "[Nkrumah] was almost less self-seeking than a large number of other leaders in Africa, Asia, and Latin America", despite his "flamboyance" and "monarchical tendencies".[9]

Mazrui's article aroused vociferous responses on the pages of the journal *Transition* between ardent champions of Nkrumah and his avid detractors and opponents.[10] It was widely read "by the global African literati",[11] so much so that the journal had to produce a second edition. As Michael West noted, Mazrui's article came swiftly in the wake of Nkrumah's overthrow by the Ghanaian military in February 1966.

From "Leninist Czar" to "the Villain of the Piece"

Thirty-six years after writing "Nkrumah: The Leninist Czar", Ali Mazrui delivered the Aggrey-Fraser-Guggisberg memorial lecture at the University of Ghana, Legon, in March 2002. The address was titled "Nkrumah's Legacy and Africa's Triple Heritage: The Shadows of Globalization and Counter Terrorism". In it, Mazrui reinforced his previous indictment of Nkrumah, declaring, "By a strange twist of destiny, Kwame Nkrumah of Ghana was both the hero, who carried the torch of Pan-Africanism, and the villain who started the whole legacy of the one-party state in Africa".[12] Furthermore, "Nkrumah started the whole tradition of Black authoritarianism in the post-colonial era. He was the villain of the piece."[13]

Mazrui contended that there were three factors which led Nkrumah to embrace a one-party state, introduced in Ghana in 1964. The first lay in Nkrumah's adoption of the 1957 Avoidance of Discrimination Bill, which banned the establishment of religious and ethnic parties. Mazrui asks: "Was the one-party state the antidote to political tribalism?"[14] He appears to answer this question in the affirmative. Yet, for Nkrumah and his contemporaries, in the aftermath of the formal hand-over of power, the various steps he and others took, including co-optation, intimidation and detention of political opponents, modification of the electoral system to reduce competition, interference in the independence of the judiciary, as well as the absorption of trade unions, women's organisations and youth groups into ruling parties, were justified as efforts to achieve national unity in Africa's newly independent states. This also meant the dismantling of political opposition in efforts to manufacture some sense of political order in which ruling parties controlled all aspects of the state including the media, the police and the army.

Secondly, Nkrumah denounced dissent, which Mazrui considered to be anathema to "free consent"[15] or pluralism. In the view of Nkrumah and the Convention People's Party (CPP), there was no room for divisions in a society that was viewed as inherently communal in nature. Third, for Mazrui, "the Leninism in Nkrumah outlasted the Garveyism" (see Grant in this volume): he embraced the one-party state in 1964, introduced detention without trial, and destroyed the independence of the judiciary.[16]

While Mazrui argued that "Nkrumah started the whole tradition of Black authoritarianism",[17] he also acknowledged that Kenya became "a *de jure* one-party state for the first time since independence"[18] in December 1963, before Nkrumah introduced the same in Ghana. It is surprising and peculiar that as an esteemed scholar of comparative political studies, Mazrui failed to consider that Nkrumah's contemporaries – Sékou Touré of Guinea, Julius Nyerere of Tanzania, Kenneth Kaunda of Zambia, Hastings Banda of Malawi, Jomo Kenyatta of Kenya, Félix Houphouet-Boigny of Côte d'Ivoire and Léopold Senghor of Senegal – all established their own forms of one-party state and did not need to look to Ghana as their template for doing so.

American scholar Aristide Zolberg contends that newly developing nations like Ghana confronted colossal burdens and expectations on the eve of independence that were not only psychological and sociological, but also cultural.[19] In the 1950s and 1960s, the majority of political parties in West Africa stressed unity as a precondition for economic and political development. The Parti de la Féderátion Africaine (PFA) of Senegal, the Parti Démocratique de Côte d'Ivoire (PDCI), the Parti Démocratique de Guinée (PDG) and Nkrumah's Convention People's Party all believed that a ruling party was the ultimate expression of the people: it was the party in power that welded the nation as one, directed the state and built the nation.[20] Characteristic of all these political parties was the belief that the state owed its legitimacy to the party, and the party owed its legitimacy to the leader. Hence, "the CPP is Ghana" and "Ghana is the CPP" was a common slogan in Nkrumah's Ghana.

Zolberg argues that Sékou Touré, who declared "*non!*" to membership in President Charles De Gaulle's French Community in 1958, had long before stressed the importance of unity to the people of Guinea as a means of defeating colonialism and achieving socio-economic progress.[21] Moreover, it appears that unity was a euphemism for intolerance of the existence of rival political parties and political dissent, and a preference for a single-party order.

In July 1959 Senegal's Léopold Senghor enunciated his own version of the one-party ideology which also appeared to be ambiguous.[22] Senghor stated that the "Opposition ... must pursue the same goal as the majority Party. It is to prevent the crystallisation of social groups into antagonistic classes.

Its function is, very precisely, to be the conscience of governments and of majority parties."[23] In effect, Senghor was giving the illusion that Senegal was a democracy when in effect he was denying the opposition the right to oppose the government based on the need for unity. Zolberg asked: "How, then, does Senghor's 'unified' party differ from the 'single party'?" For Zolberg, Senghor's rhetoric was also characteristic of the one-party ideology of Guinea. Likewise in Côte d'Ivoire, a concern with "conflict and cleavage" had also prevailed.[24] The unity of the nation was considered paramount, and was threatened by ethnic and other primordial inclinations. In short, the one-party ideology prevailed in many African countries after the formal attainment of political independence. Zolberg argues that the corollary of this was the planned economy, which eventually failed to raise the living standards of ordinary citizens.

Another criterion for assessing whether Nkrumah was what Mazrui referred to as "the villain of the piece" was the extent to which Ghana under Nkrumah and its West African neighbours employed capital punishment and deportations as instruments of one-party rule to eliminate opposition to their governments. In 1950 Nkrumah and Houphouet-Boigny wagered as to which country would be the economic star in West Africa over the next two decades. Ghana lost this famous "West African wager", while Côte d'Ivoire "won" on the political front by executing the highest number of political opponents. Therefore, as Zolberg notes, "If coercion can be evaluated in terms of the total number of death sentences imposed by a government on its opponents, the Ivory Coast is probably the harshest country in Africa."[25] In May 1963, Houphouet-Boigny sentenced 13 young members of the Rassemblement Démocratique Africain (RDA) to death for allegedly threatening the security of the state and the president's life.[26] The only state execution that took place in Nkrumah's Ghana, according to South African journalist H.M. Basner, was the execution of police sergeant Seth Ametwee, who shot and killed Nkrumah's bodyguard Salifu Dagarti in an abortive presidential assassination attempt of January 1964 in the grounds of Flagstaff House.[27]

Another yardstick for measuring the allegedly "villainous" record of Nkrumah and his contemporaries is the extent of their deportation of political opponents. Zolberg notes that formal and informal deportation of opponents was carried out by the governments of Côte d'Ivoire, Guinea, Ghana and Senegal. However, he remarks: "Although it is well known that an increasing number of persons have been detained, it is impossible to compare the records of different countries in this respect because some publicize their actions while others do not. Much more is known about Ghana in this as well as in other respects because in spite of all, Ghana, as we have already suggested, has retained a greater sense of rule of law."[28]

That Nkrumah's political adversaries whom he previously worked with in the United Gold Coast Convention (UGCC), such as Obetsebi Lamptey and J.B. Danquah, languished in prison while Nkrumah was in power is lamentable and iniquitous. However, Nkrumah was not exceptional in such malfeasance, as demonstrated by the record of Côte d'Ivoire and other West African countries during the 1960s.

Is Mazrui Fair to Nkrumah?

Ali Mazrui noted: "The question arises whether we should hold Kwame Nkrumah responsible for the origin of the one-party state in Black Africa. As the first Black African country to win independence, Ghana had immense responsibility. And poor Kwame Nkrumah was the beast of burden on whom Africa had piled her weighty hopes. The rest of Africa looked to Nkrumah for a sense of direction. Some of us looked to him for immortal precedents. Was it fair to Nkrumah?"[29]

Retrospectively, it was unfair to look to Nkrumah "for immortal precedents", for, like other African leaders, Nkrumah not only possessed considerable strengths, but he also made critical errors in his performance as leader of Ghana between 1957 and 1966. Among the latter was unquestionably his introduction of the one-party state, which fundamentally suppressed democratic values and hegemonised all institutions. However, it is my contention that Nkrumah was not the progenitor of black authoritarianism in Africa, for authoritarian rule characterises post-independence politics all over the continent and has been implemented in various forms by many African leaders as a consequence of failure to decolonise states inherited intact from their former colonial masters.

Nkrumah's famous mantra, "Seek ye first the political kingdom, and all other things shall be added unto you", was adopted by other African leaders. However, Africa's nationalist political leaders failed to transform the political kingdom that they had inherited. Colonial state structures remained unaltered and were simply "Africanised": that is, European officials were replaced by

Africans who in their mindsets and aspirations formed a comprador elite with an umbilical cord to Europe. This elite's concept of democracy asphyxiated the existence of civil society as trade unions, women's organisations and the youth were turned into appendages of ruling parties across Africa. In short, while the political ruling class talked democracy, they continued to strangle the people they claimed to be representing and, in so doing, denied the voiceless a voice.

Nkrumah's other shortcomings included the failure of his economic policies due to mismanagement, his own financial indiscipline and corrupt officials. However, there was also the fact beyond his control that in 1965 cocoa prices fell on the world market, to 276 cedis a tonne. Nkrumah's government had anticipated a price of 400 cedis. This created a huge budget deficit.[30]

In addition, Nkrumah entrusted authority to men who lacked integrity. For example, after the death of his Trinidadian mentor George Padmore (see Duggan in this volume), Ghana's minister of African affairs who had been in charge of the Bureau of African Affairs assisting freedom fighters in dependent territories to gain their independence, Nkrumah appointed Padmore's stenographer, A.K. Barden, to this position. The Ghanaian leader failed to heed criticisms of Barden by freedom fighters from South Africa, South West Africa and elsewhere, who severely criticised Barden's use of the Bureau as an instrument for personal patronage and loyalty.[31] There were many individuals whose loyalty to Nkrumah's socialist and Pan-Africanist convictions was also dubious, as was their efficiency in the tasks that were allocated to them.[32]

Nkrumah was also insufficiently sensitive to the challenges of newly independent African states. For example, while Nigeria was grappling with the attempt to build national unity among over 250 diverse ethnic groups, Nkrumah appeared to be dismissive of such problems. He may therefore have appeared to be a zealot who was unrealistic in his ambitions for immediate continental unity. In an interview, Ahmed Ben Bella, the former president of Algeria, who often spoke warmly about Nkrumah, noted that, at the time, Nkrumah's ideas of continental unity appeared to be "pie in the sky".[33]

For Nkrumah's ardent political opponents such as Ugandan journalist, Peter Omari, his Africa policies "sacrificed Ghana on the altar of Pan-Africanism".[34] Equally, when Nkrumah was overthrown, General A.K. Ocran noted that Africans on the continent lamented the fall of Nkrumah because with his demise "they have ceased to have free access to the Ghanaian taxpayer's money which Nkrumah dished out to them".[35]

According to Mazrui, Nkrumah was "a great African but not a great Ghanaian".[36] What "great" means can be very subjective. Yet, it is on account of Nkrumah's Pan-African policies that Ghana became what Malcolm X (see Daniels in this volume) characterised as the "the very fountainhead of Pan-Africanism".[37] During Nkrumah's 1951 visit to his alma mater, Lincoln University, in the United States, he warmly invited African Americans to come and help build Ghana. Many heeded his invitation.[38] Ghana became not only a tourist destination for many Africans of the diaspora – particularly African Americans and African-Caribbean individuals who sought to connect with Africa psychologically and physically (see Brown on Maya Angelou in this volume) – but a small but significant diaspora community currently still lives in Ghana, testimony to Nkrumah's Pan-Africanist beliefs and commitment. Even Nkrumah's vehement detractor Peter Omari wrote in 1970: "Nkrumah's fall has affected many things, most of all Ghana's image in the eyes of the world. His foreign policy was greatly admired throughout Africa and the world; and many Ghanaians are still proud of it. A future elected government will no doubt always be judged in its foreign policy against the background of Ghana's dynamic leadership in this field under Nkrumah."[39]

Nkrumah's Record Revisited

Nkrumah's political and economic record is on the whole a complex mixed bag of positives and negatives that Mazrui's simplistic characterisations obscure. On the domestic front and politically, Nkrumah and his Convention People's Party waged an often bitter anti-colonial struggle with the opposition, while winning three elections.

On gaining independence in 1957, Nkrumah's government attempted to construct a welfare state or "developmental state" in Ghana by building effective infrastructure. There was an expansion of school provision, especially for girls, the construction of two universities, a university college, technical schools and the extension of free education from kindergarten to university level.[40] A new hospital – Korle Bu – with medical and teaching facilities was set up in Accra, and regional and district health centres and clinics were established in remote parts of the country. Housing was constructed for ordinary Ghanaians. In addition, Nkrumah set up the Black Star Shipping Line in honour of Marcus Garvey, who had had a significant impact on Nkrumah (see Grant in this volume).

Nkrumah further initiated the Volta River Project in order to provide electricity, not only for Ghana, but for the entire West African sub-region.

Subsequent Ghanaian leaders – both military and civilian – in the five-and-a-half decades since Nkrumah was ousted from power have failed abysmally to build on the hydro-electric capacity of the dam to fulfil Nkrumah's vision not only for the sub-region, but some would argue, more importantly, for the benefit of Ghanaians. Since at least 2007, Ghanaians have experienced "*dim-su*" ("lights off", or power cuts) under successive governments.[41]

In the view of the Ghanaian scholar Takyiwaa Manuh, Nkrumah's government "catapulted women onto the political scene in a way that was new both in Ghana and Africa. For him, this was part of the attempt at projecting 'African Personality' and boosting the status of 'African Womanhood'".[42] It is rarely acknowledged in the narrative of Ghana's anti-colonial struggle – or, if it is, as a mere footnote – that both in the struggle for independence and in the post-independence era, women not only contributed to fundraising for the CPP, but were also propaganda secretaries and served on the party's Central Committee.[43] One of these stalwarts is Hannah Kudjoe, who requires rescuing from what American scholar Jean Allman characterised as "the cultural production of ignorance" or "agnotology".[44] Since the overthrow of the CPP, Kudjoe, who was "arguably *the* leading woman nationalist in post-Second World War Ghana, and certainly the first to assume a prominent and sustained public role in the struggle for independence, has now disappeared from the narrative of Ghana's struggle for independence."[45] Not only did Kudjoe lead a petition for the release of Nkrumah and his colleagues – referred to as the "Big Six" of the United Gold Coast Convention when they were arrested after a 1948 boycott of European stores and riots in the Gold Coast – but she was one of the signatories of the April 1949 document that initiated the split from the UGCC, thus helping to engineer the creation of the CPP two months later.[46]

Despite Kudjoe's considerable organisational skills and political commitment, the very politically orientated Ghana Women's League, which she led, was merged by Nkrumah with the apolitical National Federation of Gold Coast Women in September 1960.[47] The manner in which these two organisations were amalgamated, according to the description provided by Tawia Adamafio in his memoirs,[48] captures the top-down patriarchal and hegemonising mindset of Nkrumah and his CPP, despite the Ghanaian leader's promotion of a few capable women to positions of power.[49] This prevailing patriarchal mindset is illustrated in the views of John Tettegah, the leader of the Ghana Trades Union Congress, in expressing his fears of an independent National Council of Ghana Women (NCGW). Tettegah believed such an independent women's body "would be disastrous for Ghana, for [he] could see men being ridden like horses! A male tyrant could be twisted round a woman's little finger. An Amazonian tyrant could only probably be subdued by a battery of artillery!"[50]

Nkrumah's record as a political leader should also be compared with his contemporaries who faced comparable challenges in building new states into nations. Jomo Kenyatta, Sékou Touré, Hastings Banda, Félix Houphouet-Boigny, Léopold Senghor and Julius Nyerere – to name but a few – all grappled with the dilemmas of modernising and industrialising their societies while seeking to weld together disparate ethnic and social groups in efforts at nation-building. In various degrees, they embraced economic policies of "import substitution" and a pragmatic mixture of market incentives and state direction of the economy, with very little success. All were initially committed to meeting the economic aspirations of their citizens, after achieving the "political kingdom". In the immediate aftermath of the transfer of power, an economic paradise was still awaiting construction. However, on the political front, "Black authoritarianism" underpinned the economic policies of all these African leaders. For example, Tanzania's Julius Nyerere declared: "we must run while others walk."[51] Nyerere, too, like Nkrumah, was in a hurry to develop his country, believing that "we cannot afford liberal checks and balances."[52] In the preface to his 1957 autobiography, Nkrumah uncannily echoed Nyerere's thinking: "Capitalism is too complicated a system for a newly independent nation. Hence the need for a socialistic society. But even a system based on social justice and a democratic constitution may need backing up by measures of an emergency nature in the period which follows independence."[53]

Nkrumah's words appear to be contradictory, for social justice and democracy cannot be reconciled with "measures of an emergency nature". The latter remains vague, and yet suggested that harsh and draconian measures were likely to conflict with the pursuit of social justice and democracy. However, proponents of the one-party state, such as Nkrumah and his contemporaries, advocated the need for strong executive control against the enemies of "tribalism", neo-colonialism and the like. Nkrumah also believed that a disciplined mass party could effectively mobilise Ghana's resources to raise the living standards of its citizens.

Concluding Reflections

In his 2002 memorial lecture referred to earlier, Ali Mazrui referred to "positive Nkrumahism" and "negative Nkrumahism". The former are "those aspects of his legacy which are constructive and good for the future", while the latter are "those which are related to his legacy of authoritarianism".[54]

The damaging aspects of Nkrumah's legacy were, in Mazrui's view, his descent into authoritarianism, of which, as I have argued, Nkrumah was not the progenitor. The positive aspects of Nkrumah's legacy were said by Mazrui to lie in his Pan-Africanist vision and policies in which he assisted both ideologically and materially other liberation struggles across the African continent.[55] On the eve of Ghana's independence Nkrumah proclaimed, "The independence of Ghana is meaningless unless it is linked with the total liberation of the African continent."[56] Nkrumah's Pan-Africanist foreign policies were founded on the following eight principles:

(1) opposition to colonialism and neo-colonialism, (2) support for African freedom and unity, (3) the adoption of a common Pan-African foreign policy, (4) an overall economic planning on a united African basis including a more equitable system of international trade, (5) the creation of a joint African military command, (6) the establishment of a 'Third Force' – a grouping of non-aligned states independent of the East and West and capable of a concerted policy of its own, (7) the international legal equality of all independent states, and (8) cooperation between the industrialised states and the poor states which comprise the great bulk of mankind.[57]

These Pan-Africanist objectives remain valid for the African continent in the twenty-first century. As we revisit the political and social thoughts of Kwame Nkrumah, it is important to accept that his vision of a genuinely economically and politically united continent remains an unfinished project. The tentacles of neo-colonialism and new forms of coloniality have further entrapped African economies and, equally importantly, the minds of African people.

Nkrumah, like all political figures, was a flawed human being and made mistakes. However, the challenge for all Africans is to realise the positive aspects of his vision of a strong and self-reliant African continent no longer subjugated to external interests, but committed to genuine democracy and social justice for all continental Africans as well as Africans in the diaspora.

10

THABO MBEKI: THE PAN-AFRICAN PHILOSOPHER-KING[1]

Adekeye Adebajo

THE IDEA OF THE PHILOSOPHER-KING is derived from Plato's *Republic*, in which, as part of a vision of the just city, the best form of government is said to be one in which philosophers rule. The philosopher is the only person who can rule well, since they are intellectually and morally suited for this role, and are expected to employ their knowledge of goodness and virtue to assist their citizens to achieve these ends.[2] Plato's mentor, Socrates, famously remarked: "Until philosophers rule as kings in their cities, or those who are nowadays called kings and leading men become genuine and adequate philosophers … cities will have no rest from evils."[3] For Socrates, the philosopher was a lover of wisdom and a seer committed to a perennial quest for the truth.[4]

Thabo Mbeki was born in the rural Transkei (now the Eastern Cape province) on 18 June 1942. Like his father Govan – a leader of South Africa's liberation movement who spent two decades on Robben Island – the young Thabo was a voracious reader, consuming the books in the family home: James Aggrey, A.C. Jordan's famous Xhosa novel *Ingqumboyemi Nyanya* (The Wrath of the Ancestors), English poetry, Marxist literature, Dostoyevsky, and even his father's own volume of critical essays, *Transkei in the Making* (1939). At Lovedale College in the Eastern Cape, Thabo joined the African National Congress (ANC) Youth League at the age of 14, learning to sing struggle songs in honour of the ANC president, Albert Luthuli, and the Congolese liberation hero, Patrice Lumumba.

Later at Sussex University in England between 1962 and 1966, Mbeki imbibed the ideas of Aimé Césaire, Léopold Senghor (see Irele in this volume), W.E.B. Du Bois (see Morris in this volume) and Frantz Fanon (see Rabaka in this volume). He also greatly admired the African–American civil rights leader and Nobel laureate Martin Luther King Jr. His master's thesis focused on industrialisation in West Africa, and his studies helped develop a Pan-African awareness alongside a deepening of interest in the Western intellectual canon. It was at Sussex that Mbeki further engaged his passion for Shakespeare and W.B. Yeats, discovered the German playwright Bertolt Brecht, and began a lifelong interest in the African American poets of the Harlem Renaissance of the 1920s, led by Langston Hughes.

Thabo Mbeki was the most important African political figure of his generation. From June 1999 until September 2008, he was leader of Africa's most industrialised state, having succeeded the revered Nelson Mandela as president of post-apartheid South Africa. Even before then, Mbeki ran the country as *de facto* prime minister under President Mandela, who for the most part entrusted the reins of power to his heir apparent shortly after assuming the presidency in May 1994. As a key leader of the ANC in exile, Mbeki had, from the 1960s, played a significant role in the anti-apartheid struggle, under the mentorship of the ANC president Oliver Tambo, and then led secret talks to end apartheid with the white South African corporate sector, Afrikaner intellectuals and National Party politicians in the late 1980s. Between 1990 and 1994, during the negotiations for a political settlement, Mbeki played an important part in laying the foundations for a post-apartheid state and establishing what would become one of the most respected constitutional democracies in the world. He had thus dedicated 52 years of his life to the ANC and to the politics of his country by the time of his sudden ousting from power by his own party in September 2008.[5]

In understanding the importance of Mbeki as a political figure, I have compared him with Ghana's legendary first president, Kwame Nkrumah, who was in power between 1957 and 1966. Both were philosopher-kings who articulated bold Pan-African visions and generated ideas to which other leaders and civil society were compelled to respond. Both were political prophets whose compelling visions were, however, ultimately unfulfilled. Both also ruled in a monarchical fashion, imperiously dominating decision-making within their respective parties, though, Mbeki – unlike Nkrumah – remained a constitutional "monarch." Both men are likely to be remembered more for their Pan-African achievements in foreign policy than for their domestic policies.[6]

It is also important when placing Mbeki in an African leadership context of monarchical and prophetic rule to note some of the influences – conscious or unconscious – on his political leadership style derived from his two decades in African exile. Between 1971 and 1990, Mbeki lived in Botswana, Swaziland, Nigeria and Zambia. Two of the African leaders with whom he worked closest during these years – Zambia's Kenneth Kaunda and Tanzania's Julius Nyerere – were themselves philosopher-kings and political prophets who attempted to provide visionary leadership in their own countries. Their leadership styles would influence Mbeki when he came to power as president of South Africa, though he stuck closely in his own presidency to constitutional rules, never moving towards the one-party autocracy of his fellow African leaders.

The African Renaissance

Already as deputy president, Mbeki, the philosopher-king and prophetic leader, began calling for an African Renaissance. This vision had antecedents in the thoughts and writings of St Thomas's Edward Blyden (see Khadiagala in this volume), Nigeria's Nnamdi Azikiwe, Senegal's Cheikh Anta Diop and South Africa's Pixley Seme. Seme, one of the founding members of the ANC and its president-general between 1930 and 1936 (see Ngqulunga in this volume), gave a famous speech in 1906 at Columbia University in New York, where he was the first black South African graduate, aptly entitled "The Regeneration of Africa." Ghana's Kwame Nkrumah (see Biney in this volume) memorably quoted Seme's speech in its entirety at the Congress of Africanists in Accra in December 1962. Employing words that Mbeki would later use to title his most famous speech in 1996, Seme noted, "I am an African", before lyrically setting out his vision of a regenerated continent:

> The brighter day is rising upon Africa. Already I seem to see her chains dissolved, her desert plains red with harvest, her Abyssinia and her Zululand the seats of science and religion, reflecting the glory of the rising sun from the spires of their churches and universities. Her Congo and her Gambia whitened with commerce, her crowded cities sending forth the hum of business, and all her sons employed in advancing the victories of peace – greater and more abiding than the spoils of war … The regeneration of Africa means that a new and unique civilisation is soon to be added to the world.[7]

Mbeki's own vision of an African Renaissance was inspired by his shock at discovering what he regarded as the "slave mentality" of black South Africans after his return home from exile in April 1990. As he noted: "The beginning of our rebirth as a Continent must be our own rediscovery of our soul ... It was very clear that something had happened in South African society, something that didn't happen in any other African society. The repeated observation is that 'These South Africans are not quite African, they're European.'"[8] Mbeki also criticised the black intelligentsia, many of whose members he felt were timid and too deferential to their white colleagues. He was determined, through his African Renaissance vision, to reverse damaging stereotypes about the continent, remarking in September 1995: "Many in our society genuinely believe that as black people we have no capacity to govern successfully, much less manage a modern and sophisticated economy. These are very quick to repeat the nauseating refrain – look what has happened in the rest of Africa!"[9]

Mbeki also sought to use the Renaissance vision to persuade fellow South Africans to embrace not just a new South African identity, but a new African identity as well. As Mbeki said: "No longer capable of being falsely defined as a European outpost in Africa, we are an African nation in the complex process simultaneously of formation and renewal ... We will work to rediscover and claim the African heritage, for the benefit especially of our young generation."[10] In Mbeki's famous 1996 "I am an African" speech, he set out an inclusive definition of what it is to be an African that represented a stirring attempt to encourage his compatriots to embrace and celebrate the African identity they had long been denied by white rulers. As he lyrically noted:

I am an African. I owe my being to the hills and the valleys, the mountains and the glades, the rivers, the deserts, the trees, the flowers, the seas and the ever-changing seasons that define the face of our native land ... I am formed of the migrants who left Europe to find a new home on our native land. Whatever their actions, they remain part of me. In my veins courses the blood of the Malay slaves who came from the East ... I am the grandchild of the warrior men and women that Hintsa and Sekhukhune led, the patriots that Cetshwayo and Mphephu took to battle, the soldiers Moshoeshoe and Ngungunyane taught never to dishonour the cause of freedom.[11]

As well as being a doctrine to encourage South Africans to embrace an African identity, Mbeki's African Renaissance vision sought to promote the continent's political, economic and social renewal, and the reintegration of Africa into the global economy. He urged Africans to adapt democracy to fit their own specific conditions without compromising its principles of representation and accountability. The foot soldiers of Africa's Renaissance were urged to embrace the same revolutionary zeal that had freed the continent from the twin scourges of colonialism and apartheid. Mbeki further challenged Africans to discover a sense of their own self-confidence after centuries of slavery and colonialism, which had systematically denigrated their cultures and subjugated their institutions to alien rule.[12] The African Renaissance did not naively assume, as some critics asserted, that this renewal was already under way: it merely sought to set out an inspiring vision and prescribe the policy actions that could create the conditions for Africa's rebirth. Mbeki's African Renaissance had as its central goal the right of people to determine their own future. It called for a cancellation of Africa's foreign debt (about $290 billion at the time), an improvement in Africa's terms of trade, the expansion of development assistance, and better access to foreign markets for African goods. Mbeki also pragmatically urged African governments to embrace the positive aspects of globalisation by attracting capital and investment with which to develop their economies.

As an insightful analysis by South African scholars, Peter Vale and Sipho Maseko, noted: "South Africa's idea of an African Renaissance is abstruse, puzzling, even perhaps mysterious, more promise than policy."[13] With Mbeki as their chief architect, the drafting of the New Partnership for Africa's Development (NEPAD) in 2001 and the birth of the African Union (AU) in 2002 were clearly attempts to add policy flesh to the skeletal bones of his Renaissance vision. There was certainly some truth to the criticism that the Renaissance was devoid of substantive policy content. Seventeen African Renaissance festivals were held each May between 1999 and 2015 in different South African cities. They focused on such themes as conflict resolution, poverty, NEPAD, the Freedom Charter, the role of intellectuals, uniting the diaspora and connecting Africa. Mbeki delivered keynote addresses at some of these meetings. But they mostly involved South African government, business, civil society leaders and musicians, and thus tended to be parochially focused on South Africa rather than the broader continent and its diaspora. No grassroots Renaissance movement actually developed.

Despite his reputation as the prophet of Africa's Renaissance, the culturally polyglot and cosmopolitan Mbeki also had a complicated relationship with his ancestral continent. He clearly recognised, for instance, the huge importance of Nigeria for Africa, having headed the ANC office there from 1977 to 1978. As he later noted, "It's an extraordinary society, an African society. It doesn't have this big imprint of colonial oppression. It's something else. Very different from here [South Africa]. You get a sense that you are now really being exposed to the real Africa, not where *we* come from ... they do their own thing. [And] they are of such importance on the African continent that they could mislead lots of people."[14] South African writer, Mark Gevisser's depiction of Mbeki's reaction to Nigeria is particularly interesting: "Mbeki is not an 'outside observer': he has crossed over into the 'real Africa' as other South Africans have not. And yet his relationship to this 'real Africa,' of which he has been made a citizen, is fraught with ambivalence, for with every example he presents, it becomes clearer that even though he is attracted to it, it is antithetical to everything he stands for."[15]

This fascinating observation suggests that Mbeki was somewhat alienated from his African roots. Though an instinctive Pan-African intellectually, the Sussex-trained Mbeki is also an acculturated Englishman. When he came face to face with what he himself clumsily described as the "real Africa", he needed to make some adjustment to it, and did not seem totally comfortable with what he had encountered. These observations on his path to power are important to bear in mind, as Thabo would often borrow lessons from the West – for example, in his cabinet office and education system – as president rather than from Africa, based perhaps on failed economic policies in countries like Zambia, Tanzania and Nigeria. One also needs to remember that when he became deputy president and then president of South Africa, he was ruling a country from which he had been absent for three decades.

Engaging Africa

Mbeki's legacy will doubtless be in the area of foreign policy – including his engagement with Africa and its diaspora – rather than domestic policies. As a historical figure, it is important to place Mbeki within an African context. His sense of belonging to the wider African continent and his later vision of an African Renaissance were inspired by his upbringing, education and career in exile. He was critically shaped by the two decades he spent in exile in Swaziland, Botswana, Nigeria and Zambia between 1971 and 1990. His time in Nigeria as head of the ANC office there, between 1977 and 1978, was particularly significant. Africa's most populous country provided him with an example of black self-assertion and cultural authenticity. Mbeki's tenure in Lagos also helped him to forge an enduring relationship with the military head of state, Olusegun Obasanjo (1976–1979), which would later enable him to promote peacemaking in Africa and build Pan-African institutions like the African Union, the New Partnership for Africa's Development and the African Peer Review Mechanism (APRM) when both men were in power as elected heads of state between 1999 and 2007.

Leaders like Mbeki were profoundly aware of their debt of gratitude to the continent, which had made great sacrifices for South Africa's liberation. The ANC's presence in the Front Line States (FLS) was nevertheless not always assured during the years of exile. After Angola's independence in 1975 and its collapse into a 27-year civil war, Zambia's and Tanzania's support for a united front of liberation movements in Angola strained relations with the ANC, which strongly backed the ruling Popular Movement for the Liberation of Angola (MPLA). Zambia at one stage shut down the ANC's Radio Freedom broadcasts, while Tanzania became increasingly averse to hosting the ANC's military camps, which impelled its army to set up facilities in Angola.[16] Underground ANC operatives were jailed and tortured in Zimbabwe in 1982. These developments all shaped Mbeki's understanding of the potential ambivalence, shifting nature and even duplicity of Pan-African diplomacy. Though a pragmatic Marxist Pan-African at the time, Mbeki took to heart many of the lessons learnt from these African experiences. While African governments all pledged rhetorical support to South Africa's liberation struggle, many also promoted more parochial, short-term interests, while some – above all, Mozambique with the Nkomati Accord in 1984 – felt forced to bow to apartheid pressure. Mbeki therefore adopted an approach of diversifying the ANC's dependence without becoming over-reliant on any one African government. A similar pragmatism guided his foreign policy once he assumed office in 1999.

Mbeki hosted the launch of the African Union in Durban in July 2002, and was the organisation's first chair. In his opening address, he noted with gratitude that South Africa was "a country that owes its birth as a non-racial democracy to the great sacrifices that the peoples of Africa made to ensure that the continent is free." He paid tribute to leaders he described as African heroes: Abdel Gamal Nasser, Ahmed Ben Bella, Kwame Nkrumah, Sékou Touré, Eduardo Mondlane,

Patrice Lumumba, Julius Nyerere, Samora Machel and Modibo Keita. He called for African peoples and states to promote unity, solidarity, and cooperation, and to observe democratic principles and popular participation in governance, noting: "We must build all the institutions necessary to deepen political, economic and social integration on the African continent."[17] Interestingly, Mbeki did not once mention the African diaspora in this inaugural speech of the premier inter-governmental Pan-African body.

As president, Mbeki pursued an "African Agenda", consistently seeking multilateral solutions to regional conflicts, and pursued what Kenyan academic, Al Mazrui, defined as a *Pax Africana*: a peace created, cultivated and consolidated by Africans themselves (see Ndlovu-Gatsheni in this volume). He was more prepared than Mandela to send peacekeepers abroad, deploying about 3,000 troops to Burundi and the Democratic Republic of the Congo (DRC) as well as sending others to Sudan's Darfur region and Ethiopia–Eritrea with the goal of ending the conflicts there.[18] South Africa further contributed to peacemaking efforts in Zimbabwe and Côte d'Ivoire. In order to ensure effective implementation of the Arusha peace agreement for Burundi of August 2000, Tshwane (Pretoria) led the cash-strapped African Union Mission in Burundi (AMIB), involving 2,645 South African, Mozambican and Ethiopian peacekeepers, from February 2003. AMIB, however, struggled to keep peace in a decade-long civil war owing to a lack of financial and logistical support. In May 2004, the UN Security Council established the 5,650-strong UN Operation in Burundi (ONUB), subsuming AMIB's peacekeepers into the new mission under the leadership of South African force commander Derrick Mgwebi.[19]

Under Mbeki's presidency, South African diplomacy was also instrumental in securing a peace accord in the DRC by 2002, with the country sending 1,400 troops to a strengthened UN mission in the Congo (MONUC). By December 2002, Congolese parties meeting in Tshwane under the mediation of Thabo Mbeki signed the Global and Inclusive Agreement on Transition in the Democratic Republic of the Congo, calling for a two-year transition period with the establishment of a government of national unity. The accord led to the holding of the first national election in 40 years in July 2006 (supervised by the UN), and a more controversial disputed poll in November 2011 (run by the DRC's electoral commission). Despite continued instability in the former Orientale, North and South Kivu, and Kasai provinces, South Africa's role helped to promote stability in a conflict that has seen over three million deaths and six million displaced since 1996.[20]

Mbeki also skilfully used both strategic partnership with Nigeria and his chair of the African Union between 2002 and 2003 to pursue his foreign policy goals on the continent. South Africa's second post-apartheid leader served as the chief mediator in Côte d'Ivoire between 2004 and 2006 in a bid to resolve the conflict in that country. Tshwane was the host and chief architect of the African Peer Review Mechanism of 2003 – comprising 40 African states by September 2020 – which involved a peer review of governance and economic performance, including both government and civil society actors.[21] South Africa further hosted the AU's Pan-African Parliament (PAP) from March 2004. These were all examples of Pan-African solidarity.

Engaging the Diaspora

One of the most important aspects of Mbeki's foreign policy was its Pan-African outlook and diasporic reach. As South Africa's deputy president in April 1997, he sought to reverse deeply entrenched stereotypes about Africa by invoking his own country's transition to majority rule at a Council on Africa speech in the US state of Virginia: "As Africans, we are moved that the world concedes that miracles of this order can come out of Africa, an Africa which in the eyes of the same world is home to an unending spiral of anarchy and chaos, at whose unknown end is a dark pith of an utter, a complete and unfathomable human disaster."[22] Mbeki thus tried to replace an apocalyptic Afro-pessimism with an aspirational Afro-optimistic vision of an African Renaissance in which countries like Zaire (the DRC) "is not the heart of darkness, but the light of a new African star".[23] South Africa's deputy president consciously set out to counter Polish-British author Joseph Conrad's bleak, hopeless vision of Africa in his 1902 novella, *Heart of Darkness*, set on the Congo river.[24] Mbeki boldly declared in biblical tones: "Those who have eyes to see, let them see. The African Renaissance is upon us."[25]

In another speech to Partnership Africa in the Swedish capital of Stockholm in June 1997, Deputy President Thabo Mbeki invoked the African-American intellectual W.E.B. Du Bois's (see Morris in this volume) prophetic words at the first Pan-African Conference in London in 1900: "The problem of the twentieth century is the problem of the colour line, the question as to how far differences of race...are going to be made, hereafter, the basis of denying half the world the right of sharing to their utmost ability the opportunities and privileges of modern civilisation."[26] Mbeki then acknowledged the stubborn persistence of racism in updating Du Bois's famous prophecy to note that: "The problem of the twenty-first century is the problem of the colour line."[27]

In 2000, President Mbeki travelled to the Brazilian state of Bahia to receive an honorary doctorate from the University of the State of Bahia in a region whose population is largely descended from African slaves (see Introduction in this volume). Citing two of the country's prominent literary scholars, Silvio Romero and Joao Capistrano de Abreu, Mbeki berated the Eurocentrism of Brazilian culture. He echoed the same idea as his "African Renaissance" that Brazil must discover its own "national soul" and craft an identity from its specific environment and circumstances. He also praised Brazil's solidarity with South Africa during the anti-apartheid struggle: "...when our dungeons were dark and scary, you extended hands of solidarity to our cause, which you selflessly took upon your own, embraced our suffering and offered us hope."[28]

The South African president then read from a poignant poem, "The Slave Ship", by the nineteenth-century Brazilian poet Castro Alves:

It was a dantesque dream ... the deck
Great lights reddening its brilliance,
Bathing it in blood
Clang of irons ... snap of whip...
Legions of men black as the night
Horrible dancing
Black women, holding to their breasts
Scrawny infants whose black mouths
Are watered by the blood of their mothers...[29]

Mbeki called for the banishment forever of the nightmare of the slave ship, before telling his audience: "Only ourselves ... should marshal our energies, harness our resources and use our comparative advantage strategically for our own development. This is what the African Renaissance seeks to achieve."[30] South Africa's philosopher-king then noted Africa's progress in the areas of democratization and conflict resolution since the end of the Cold War. Mbeki returned to the theme of identity in observing: "Africa cannot achieve its Renaissance unless it celebrates its Africanness."[31] He then went on to tell his audience of the importance of using its own diverse cultural resources: "Brazil cannot achieve its full identity unless it celebrates, also, its historical and cultural connection with Africa", before calling for the nurturing of more Afro-Brazilian scientists, economists, and business people.[32] The South African president ended his lyrical address with a rousing call for solidarity across the global South: "Let us continue our solidarity and treat the artificial divide of the Atlantic ocean like that of the river across our common village."[33]

Mbeki visited the United States several times, notably addressing an African-American audience at Martin Luther King's famous Ebenezer Baptist church in Atlanta in May 2000 and delivering the inaugural Oliver Tambo lecture at Georgetown University in Washington DC in the same month. During the latter address, he demonstrated his identification with African Americans in noting: "I am convinced that you will find here [in Washington D.C.], also, the broken human beings, who are our brothers and sisters, whose lives have been devastated by poverty."[34]

Mbeki promoted his vision of an African Renaissance at the University of Havana, Cuba, in March 2001. He began by noting that similar racist stereotypes were applied to Latin American and Caribbean citizens, as applied to Africa: "dark-skinned, quick-tempered, emotional, unimaginative, unintelligent, dishonest and inefficient." He then went on to call for self-definition and autonomy, challenging his audience: "...we have a duty to define ourselves. We speak about the need for the African Renaissance in part so that we ourselves, and not another, determine who we are, what we stand for, what our vision and hopes are, how we do things, what programmes we adopt to make our lives worth living, who we relate to and how."[35]

Mbeki went on in the Havana speech to note the common bonds between Africa, Latin America and the Caribbean, singling out Cuba's special role in the liberation of Africa: "Cuba occupies a prominent place in the history of the struggle for, and achievement of, freedom on the African continent ... the Renaissance of our continent is inextricably interwoven with this country that has sacrificed so much so that Africans can stand tall as equals amongst fellow human beings."[36] He went on to praise Cuba's role in the historic 1988 battle of Cuito Cuanavale in Angola, supporting Cuban leader Fidel Castro's saying that Africa's future history would be divided into "before and after Cuito Cuanavale".[37]

Mbeki hosted the United Nations "World Conference against Racism, Racial Discrimination, Xenophobia and Related Intolerance" in Durban in August 2001. In a stirring opening speech, he championed cultural equality and unequivocally condemned racism in noting: "We meet here because we are determined to ensure that nobody anywhere should be subjected to the insult and offence of being despised by another or others because of his or her race, colour, nationality or origin ... there are many in our common world who suffer indignity and humiliation because they are not white. Their cultures and traditions are despised as savage and primitive and their identities denied."[38] He then went on to demonstrate diasporic solidarity in musical tones: "To those who have to bear the pain of this real world, it seems the Blues singers were right when they decried the world in which it was said – if you're white you're alright; if you are brown, stick around; if you are black, oh brother! Get back, get back, get back!"[39]

But, despite these stinging words, Caribbean delegates later criticised Mbeki and other African leaders such as Nigeria's Olusegun Obasanjo and Senegal's Abdoulaye Wade, for betraying the continent and the diaspora by allowing Western delegates to exclude strong clauses in the final conference resolution condemning slavery and colonialism, and for failing to hold these countries accountable for their crimes against humanity (see Beckles in this volume).

South Africa's philosopher-king further sought to play a role with regard to the small Caribbean island of Haiti. In January 2004, Mbeki was the only African head of state to attend the bicentenary celebrations of the country's slave revolt against France, following which Haiti had won its independence as the first black republic in the world. The South African president provided R10 million (about $1.4 million at the time) to support these celebrations. After Haitian president, Jean-Bertrand Aristide, was pressured to leave Haiti in 2004, reportedly by American and French diplomats, Mbeki offered him and his family political asylum in South Africa.

Concluding Reflections

Mbeki is a complex figure, full of contradictions and paradoxes: a rural child who became an urban sophisticate; a prophet of Africa's Renaissance who was also an anglophile; a committed young Marxist who, while in power, embraced conservative economic policies and protected white corporate interests; a rational and dispassionate thinker who was particularly sensitive to criticism and dissent; a champion of African self-reliance who relied excessively on foreign capital and promoted a continental economic plan – NEPAD – that was disproportionately dependent on foreign aid and investment; and a thoughtful intellectual who supported policies on HIV/AIDS that withheld antiretroviral drugs from infected people until the country's Constitutional Court forced the government to provide them in 2002.

Mbeki's legacy will inevitably be a mixed one. On the positive side, he led efforts to extend basic services and facilities to millions of poor and previously disregarded black citizens and, through a massive extension of social grants, helped lift many millions out of dire poverty and social misery. In foreign policy, he also provided a vision and energetically led the building of – admittedly fragile – African institutions like the AU, NEPAD and the APRM. One guiding theme of Mbeki's time as president was his consistent espousal of Pan-Africanism. Despite criticisms of his supposed "essentialism", "nativism" and "Afrocentrism" by South African critics like Daryl Glaser and Eusebius McKaiser,[40] Mbeki was absolutely correct to put race at the centre of debates on transformation in South Africa. Apartheid and its social divisions had, after all, determined privilege and poverty entirely on the basis of race.

Mbeki's Pan-African credentials may, however, have been somewhat tarnished by an incident in March 2017 when he delivered the keynote address on the occasion of the African Peer Review Mechanism's 13th year anniversary in Midrand, South Africa. During the discussion, Mbeki was asked whether he regretted that his own government had failed to act on the 2007 APRM report about impending xenophobic violence in South Africa. In response, the former South African leader launched into an extraordinary tirade that effectively amounted to "xenophobia denialism". His government had denied the warnings of the APRM report – led by the respected Nigerian economist Adebayo Adedeji – as "simply not true". Mbeki's attack on the APRM report was seen by many, at the time, as an act of infanticide by one of the "Founding Fathers" of the mechanism, one that had damaged the institution's credibility.

A year after the 2007 report's warnings were ignored, 62 foreigners in Gauteng – mostly from Zimbabwe, Mozambique and Malawi – were killed in xenophobic acts of horrendous brutality. As a result, about 100,000 African nationals were forced to seek refuge in camps set up in Johannesburg. At the APRM anniversary meeting in March 2017, Mbeki warned, "To attach this label 'xenophobic' results in many instances of us not understanding … what is the source of this issue." He rightly noted that one needs to examine the root causes of xenophobic attacks such as "township thuggery", poverty, more efficient foreign traders outcompeting locals, and police unresponsiveness to crime. But despite Mbeki's words, there is simply no contradiction between simultaneously calling attacks "xenophobic" and "criminal", which is the false distinction that he and many South African leaders continue to insist on. The frequent attacks on gays and lesbians in South Africa – including "corrective rape" and murders – are, after all, examples of both homophobia and criminality. One can surely recognise and condemn both at the same time. Xenophobic attacks resulted in an estimated 350 deaths of foreigners in South Africa between 2008 and 2015.

After Mbeki spoke at the APRM meeting in March 2017, the Zambian high commissioner to South Africa, Emmanuel Mwamba, offered a stinging rebuke to the former president's "xenophobia denialism". Mwamba started by observing that Mbeki had lived in Lusaka during his exile and that Zambian leaders had not spoken in the way he had just spoken. The high commissioner went on to reject Mbeki's denials and justifications as effectively condoning unacceptable behaviour, arguing that both xenophobia and Afrophobia needed to be strongly condemned. He highlighted the venal brutality visited on African nationals and their frequent harassment by the South African police; observed that foreign nationals in schools were now required to produce permits; and noted that rather than focusing on petty Nigerian drug dealers, Mbeki should instead assess the more complex structural supply chain of drug trafficking, which involves nationals from other countries. Nigerian scholar-diplomat Ibrahim Gambari, Mbeki's fellow panellist, also noted the widespread involvement of South African nationals in crime, and called for a more effective response by the South African police in protecting foreign nationals.

More positively, Mbeki was an active peacemaker, and his peacemaking ventures across Africa were noteworthy at the time and will remain among his most impressive successes. He devoted much effort, time, patience and intelligence to efforts that brought greater stability to these countries and saved tens of thousands of lives. Mbeki was also responsible for providing the vision for, and helping establish, a number of AU institutions. The 15-member AU Peace and Security Council has played a significant role in efforts to manage African conflicts, but other institutions remain fledgling and the AU remains dependent on external donors to provide much of its resources. NEPAD, the APRM and the Pan-African Parliament are all based in South Africa, but all three appeared to be cash-strapped and increasingly moribund by 2020.

Both Mbeki and Kwame Nkrumah were Africa's most prominent philosopher-kings of their respective generations. Both leaders attempted to carry out a socio-economic revolution without genuine revolutionaries. Both lacked competent cadres and administrators in the numbers needed to ensure the success of their revolutions. But, while Nkrumah led a poor country that punched above its weight in global politics, Mbeki was the head of Africa's richest and most industrialised state, and there were thus greater expectations that his African Renaissance vision would succeed. However, South Africa's deep socio-economic inequalities and injustices remain stubbornly untransformed. Having worked so tenaciously to secure the political kingdom, both leaders discovered that all other things were not added unto it. Failure to deliver the economic kingdom in the end led to the political crucifixion of both prophets.

Ali Mazrui famously argued in 1966 that Nkrumah was a great Pan-African, but not a great Ghanaian (see Biney in this volume). Five and a half decades later, we ask: Will Mbeki come to be viewed in a similar vein as a great Pan-African, but not a great South African? When Nkrumah was ousted from power, angry protesters destroyed his statue, and streets named after him were changed. Within 26 years, Nkrumah's successors had so mismanaged the country that nostalgia for his memory returned. A new statue and memorial park were built in his honour in Accra in 1992 in an impressive act of national restitution. Will South Africans also come to view Mbeki – Africa's Renaissance man – more favourably, with the passage of time?

11

DUDLEY THOMPSON: PAN-AFRICAN POLITICIAN AND DIPLOMAT

W. Andy Knight

DUDLEY THOMPSON WAS AN ACTIVIST LAWYER, advocate, intellectual, a Rhodes Scholar at Oxford University, educator, politician, war hero, statesman, diplomat and raconteur of the highest order. Born in Panama on 19 January 1917 to Jamaican parents, Thompson was raised mostly in Westmoreland, the westernmost province of Jamaica. This part of Jamaica was inhabited by Arawak and Ciboney Indians who had lived in the labyrinth of caves along the cliffs of Negril before Christopher Columbus and the first Spanish settlers arrived in the late 1400s. Britain took over Jamaica from Spain in 1665; and in 1703 they named the area where Thompson eventually grew up as "Westmoreland".

It is interesting that much of Westmoreland's population is made up of a mix of ethnic East Indians, descendants of indentured servants who came to work in Jamaica after the British abolished slavery in that country in 1833, as well as people of African descent who were captured on Africa's west coast and forced into slavery in Jamaica where they later regained their freedom. Over the years, many East Indians in Westmoreland have intermarried with Africans, and their offspring are generally referred to in Jamaica as "half-Indian". Dudley Thompson grew up in this ethnically mixed cultural environment. He was baptised as a Catholic, and remained a practising Catholic all of his life. His well-educated parents, Daniel and Ruby Thompson, taught him from an early age that all races were equal and that no race was superior to any other.

Thompson's Formative Years

While he remained an adherent of his religious faith, education, more than religion, seems to have propelled Thompson into political activism. His parents were highly literate school teachers who ensured that he had a solid educational foundation. He attended "the Mico", a higher education institution for boys and girls founded in 1835. After completing his schooling in Jamaica and having taken on the duties of headmaster in a rural school, the Retreat Elementary School in Western St Mary, in 1937, before his 21st birthday,[1] Thompson went on to become a member of the British Royal Air Force, seeing action during the Second World War (1939–45). He was one of the first black pilots in the British air force, becoming a second flight lieutenant and navigator of bombers during the war. When the war ended in 1945, Thompson was awarded a Rhodes scholarship and studied law at Oxford University. He distinguished himself as an outstanding and articulate scholar, serving as president of the West Indian Students' Union at Oxford. Upon graduation, he was called to the bar at Gray's Inn in London in 1950. Instead of joining a reputable and lucrative British law firm as he had the opportunity to do, Thompson chose instead to practise law in the town of Moshi, Tanganyika, and is still remembered, to this day, in Tanzania as one of the founders of the Tanganyika African National Union (TANU).

Thompson had migrated to East Africa with his family, on the advice of that great Pan-Africanist George Padmore (see Duggan in this volume), who felt that the young man could use his legal expertise to assist the movement for independence that was sweeping across the East African sub-region. He used his legal knowledge, British training and advocacy skills to assist East African nationalists in drafting legal challenges to British control and, in so doing, helped to establish Moshi as a major hub for the coordination of the work of freedom fighters not only in Tanganyika, but also in neighbouring Kenya. Thompson thus became a major contributor to the liberation movements in East Africa and to the process which eventually led to decolonisation across the African continent. Indeed, it is well known that he helped to prepare TANU's legal presentations to the United Nations Decolonisation Committee.[2]

As detailed in his 1993 book, *From Kingston to Kenya: The Making of a Pan-Africanist Lawyer*, Thompson's British legal training came in handy, while living in Moshi, during his anti-colonialist struggle for the rights of Africans. His focus was particularly on individuals across Africa who had suffered indignities and exploitation at the hands of the European colonial powers. Some of those individuals included young leaders such as Kenya's Jomo Kenyatta, a Kikuyu whom Thompson had met in London during his university days and Tanzania's Julius Nyerere, whom he had met during his early days in Moshi. Both men went on to confront the British authorities in their fight for the liberation and self-determination of their respective countries. Both became the first post-independence leaders of Kenya and Tanganyika. Thompson played an instrumental role in the successful elevation of these individuals to leadership positions as East Africa was decolonising. The young Jamaican lawyer selflessly assisted Nyerere in drafting the constitution for what was later to become Tanzania (after Tanganyika had forcibly merged with Zanzibar in 1964). It is no exaggeration to state that Thompson played a key role in saving Kenyatta's life, after the Kenyan was abducted by the British and charged with treason during the Mau Mau uprising against colonial rule in the 1950s.[3]

In 1947 Jomo Kenyatta had been elected president of the Kenya African Union (KAU), which later became the Kenya African National Union (KANU), following a merger with Tom Mboya's Kenya Independence Movement in 1960. Having embraced anti-colonial ideas, he used that position to lobby for Kenya's independence from British colonial rule. The British considered Kenyatta – a prominent and charismatic Kikuyu intellectual – an agitator and probable leader of the Mau Mau rebellion, which was intent on reclaiming land from the British. As a result, the colonial power unleashed a brutal counter-insurgency campaign against the Mau Mau in which about 100,000 Kikuyu were incarcerated in detention camps.[4] In 1952 Kenyatta was among the "Kapenguria Six" who were arrested and charged with having masterminded the Mau Mau insurrection. Thompson came to Kenyatta's defence, putting together an international legal team to challenge the British action. His role in Kenyatta's trial was not only legal but also political. As Jamaican scholar Horace Campbell put it, during this trial Thompson laid bare "the criminality of British colonialism in East Africa and its attempt to destroy the African liberation movement using British military counter-insurgency tactics, and he exposed the British tactics of sowing the seeds of the tribal division that continues to plague African societies today".[5]

Despite Thompson's vigorous legal defence of his client, Kenyatta was summarily thrown into prison by the British in Lokitaung until 1959, and stayed there until he was exiled to Lodwar in 1961. Upon his release, Kenyatta was appointed president of KANU and led the party to victory in the 1963 general election. Owing in no small part to the legal assistance provided by his friend Dudley Thompson, Kenyatta went on to play a significant role in the transformation of Kenya from colony to independent republic. As prime minister, Kenyatta oversaw this transition, and went on to become Kenya's first post-independence president from 1964 until his death in 1978, being widely known by the honorific title of "Mzee" (Father of the Nation).

Thompson used his experience at the heart of African decolonisation to drive his life-long political advocacy against European colonialism and imperialism. This advocacy began during an era of militant activism that characterised the decolonisation process in both Africa and the Caribbean. Thompson understood, as did Guyanese scholar Walter Rodney (see Montoute in this volume), the links between the domination of Africa by colonial powers and the underdevelopment of the continent. He also recognised the devastating impact that slavery had had on Africa's socio-economic development. The euphemistically labelled "slave trade" was, according to Rodney, not trade at all, but rather a combination of "warfare, trickery, banditry and kidnapping".[6] Anti-imperialism and African liberation therefore undergirded much of Thompson's philosophy, strategy and political activism.

It was the Atlantic "slave trade" that had resulted in the uprooting of 15.4 million Africans from the continent and their shipment to other parts of the world between the fifteenth and nineteenth centuries.[7] When the African "slave trade" reached its apogee in the nineteenth century, Pan-Africanism as an ideology and strategy began to take root, particularly in America.[8] Despite having grown up in Jamaica at the height of militant Garveyism, there is little indication that Dudley Thompson fully embraced these militant ideas in his youth. While he was a student at Oxford, Thompson was very much aware of anti-colonial activity in Britain. He became a student leader in the West Indian Students' Union (WISU) – a parallel organisation to the West African Students' Union (WASU). But despite his sustained commitment to the Pan-Africanist ethos, Thompson never really seemed to hitch his wagon to the militant strand of Pan-Africanism. His brand of Pan-Africanism was definitely more moderate and pragmatic than that of Garvey, and yet Thompson played a major role in rehabilitating Garvey in Jamaican society whose ruling elite had become nervous of the strident black self-pride which Garvey championed.

The Pragmatist Politician, Lawyer and Diplomat

Thompson lost two elections to Edward Seaga (a future prime minister) in parliamentary polls in Jamaica. But he did not let those defeats define or derail him. Despite the dissolution of the West Indies Federation in 1962, Thompson never succumbed to narrow nationalist nativism, but rather believed in many of the ideals of the West Indian integration movement: its promises of a customs union, the free movement of West Indian people between various islands, as well as economic and functional cooperation. Beginning in 1962, Thompson served as president of the Jamaican Bar Association (before the Association was actually incorporated in January 1973),[9] and used his regional network and connections to practise law in many of the Caribbean islands: the Bahamas, Barbados, Dominica, Grenada, St Kitts and Nevis, and Trinidad and Tobago. In that sense, Thompson did not let the physical and mental insularity of the countries in the region act as a barrier to the pursuit of his own concept of Pan-Caribbeanism. Indeed, he was integrally involved, both politically and legally, in the independence movements of both the Bahamas and Belize.

In Jamaica, politics remained a central preoccupation of Thompson's. He became vice-president of the People's National Party (PNP), and was appointed to the Senate, where he served as a non-elected member from 1964 to 1978. In 1972 his mentor and friend Michael Manley won the national election and became prime minister of Jamaica. He appointed Thompson as foreign minister three years later. In that position, Thompson strongly supported Cuba's right to domestic and foreign policy independence. In the mid-1970s, he travelled with Manley to Cuba for a secret meeting with Fidel Castro. Castro convinced both men of the need for Jamaica to rally around Cuba's support of armed liberation struggles in southern Africa. Thompson worked closely with members of the Non-Aligned Movement (NAM) in defence of their right to be treated justly and fairly within the international system. He became a strong advocate for a New International Economic Order (NIEO) from the 1970s, and was a primary driver of the renegotiation of contracts with bauxite and aluminium multinational companies operating in Jamaica. These foreign firms were siphoning off much of the country's natural resource wealth to the metropole. Thompson played a major role in the creation of the International Bauxite Association, which was viewed as a new cartel similar to the Organisation of the Petroleum Exporting Countries (OPEC).[10] He was also appointed to serve as his country's representative at the United Nations Conference on the Law of the Sea (UNCLOS). Indeed, Thompson played a significant role in securing Jamaica as the permanent headquarters of the International Seabed Authority (ISA). Thus, his politics were not limited to Jamaica. Thompson demonstrated a keen understanding of the common struggles of African and Caribbean citizens, who had been shackled by the colonial chains of dependency, and pushed for them to become fully independent of their European "mother countries".

Apart from serving as Jamaica's foreign minister between 1975 and 1977, Thompson was appointed as the minister responsible for mining and natural resources (1977–8), and the minister of national security (1978–80), two key posts that helped the country affirm its sovereign independence. Just before and during his tenure in the national security portfolio, the fledgling Jamaican state experienced intensified political violence.

In 1976 the famous reggae superstar Bob Marley was shot in the middle of a parliamentary election campaign (see Hutton in this volume). Michael Manley was seen at the time by Washington as having moved Jamaica too far to the left. As a result, the Central Intelligence Agency (CIA) tried to destabilise the Jamaican government. Thompson found himself, as minister of national security, in the vortex of this politico–military instability. Five young men, who were apparent supporters of the Jamaican Labour Party (JLP), were shot dead at a military range in Green Bay, St Catherine, Jamaica, by government soldiers. Ten government soldiers faced charges ranging from murder to conspiracy to commit murder. However, they were all freed in February 1982, four years after this incident.[11]

This created a scandal for the ruling People's National Party led by Manley. Thompson, as his national security minister, made an intemperate remark about the shooting when he said that "no angels died at Green Bay".[12] This was a comment that he would regret uttering for the rest of his life, and for which he later apologised profusely. But, in some respects, it tainted his otherwise stellar reputation.

Jamaican scholar Horace Campbell wrote a critical review of Thompson's autobiography precisely because of the ill-advised comment that Thompson had made about the extra-judicial killing of those five young men in Green Bay. Campbell could not reconcile the actions of a man who had stridently and consistently supported liberation struggles in Africa with that of a minister who was part of a government that was seemingly repressing its poor and its youth.

Campbell later came to believe that this one indiscretion should not be allowed to overshadow the overall legacy of Dudley Thompson.

From 1990 to 1995, Thompson was appointed Jamaica's high commissioner to Nigeria, with accreditation to Ghana, Sierra Leone, Cameroon and Namibia.[13] His fight for social justice and human rights had already earned him the nickname "Burning Spear", a sobriquet given to him by Kenya's Jomo Kenyatta. But as his diplomatic career blossomed, Thompson became an advocate for reparations for slavery, and cemented his place at the centre of the Pan-African movement. As the editor-at-large of the *Jamaica Observer*, H.G. Helps, put it, Thompson's dream was to see "a federation or confederation of Africa". Thompson himself expressed this hope, suggesting that there should be one government for the whole of Africa – "a federal government, which would include the diaspora as the sixth district, by which I mean a jurisdiction of a central Africa over North Africa, South Africa, East Africa, West Africa, Central Africa and the diaspora as an integral part of the African scenario. That is our aim, and once we do that we would place Africa, us, as a major player in global affairs."[14]

Thompson became the president of the World African Diaspora Union (WADU), a body whose idealistic mission it was to liberate and unify people of African origin under one central government in Africa. Examining the main goals of this organisation can help in understanding some of the fundamental philosophical ideas which underpinned Thompson's career. WADU aimed to unify the various associations, groups and individuals in the African diaspora through the utopian Afrocentrism that coalesced around radical Pan-Africanist philosophy. That philosophy called for the establishment of a new global order of justice and equality for all Africans through the empowerment strategies of what was later called the "African Renaissance" (see Khadiagala on Edward Blyden, and Adebajo on Mbeki in this volume). Members of WADU were expected to work towards the unification of Africa, with one central government under the "African Union"; the official acceptance of the diaspora as the sixth region of a united Africa; opposition to and the eradication of "racism, imperialism and neo-colonialism and its vestiges in all forms everywhere"; the promulgation and recognition of "the full dignity and equality of women in all aspects of life, globally"; the recognition and emulation of the philosophies and teachings of African history, culture and sciences, as well as the perpetuation of these values "in the education of our children"; the promotion of economically sustainable development in "business, trade and commerce among African people and the world"; the promotion of humanitarian assistance, peace support, reconciliation and security "for the African people and its most vulnerable, our children"; acknowledgement of, and support for, the Abuja Declaration of November 1989 calling for reparations for slavery; the acceptance of the findings of the Durban Conference of 2001 on racism, xenophobia, and other such matters, as well as support for an action plan to address these issues (see Beckles in this volume); and, cooperation with "all individuals, groups, and associations which adopt these tenets and principles".[15]

The Reparations Advocate

It is on the issue of reparations that Dudley Thompson was perhaps at his most articulate. At the peak of his career as a diplomat, Thompson had come to the conclusion that the West owed a perennial debt to black people for the years of enslavement and degradation (see Introduction and Robinson in this volume). One can get a sense of his fervent advocacy of reparations by reviewing some of his speeches and writings. Essentially, Thompson was convinced that the mass kidnapping and enslavement of Africans formed one of the most egregious crimes against humanity in recorded history. Yet, this crime had not been properly acknowledged by the European imperial powers, and to date no compensation had been paid to those who have suffered nor to their descendants. The consequences of slavery are still being felt by the descendants of the victims of slavery, even to this day.

Thompson made the point that, in some other cases of crimes against humanity, there has been a legal precedent in the demand for reparations (see Beckles in this volume). For example, in the case of the Nazi genocide and extermination of approximately six million Jews during the European Holocaust between 1933–45, about $60 billion of reparations had been paid out by 2014 to survivors and descendants of those who had suffered from these atrocities.[16] During the Second World War, many Japanese Americans were interned in concentration camps on the US west coast on the orders of President Franklin D. Roosevelt. When Japanese Americans challenged the American government in court after the war, the latter paid out $1.2 million as reparation for the 120,000 Japanese-Americans who had been unjustly interned.[17] Native American Indians have received $1.3 billion in reparations and large areas of land from the American government.[18] Poland received $440 million, in addition to land and concessions, from Germany for using Poles as slave labour during the Second World War (1939–45).[19] The Nunavut Inuit initially requested $1 billion as compensation for the Canadian government's failure to fulfil its obligations as laid out in the Nunavut Land Claims Agreement. While the Inuit were unsuccessful in obtaining the full amount, the roughly 19,000 Eskimos who inhabit Canada's eastern Arctic signed an agreement with the Canadian government in 1989 which gave them legal title to 136,000 square miles of Arctic land, limited rights over a further 1.5 million square miles, and roughly $700 million for the next 15 years.[20] Ottawa also formally apologised to 1.3 million indigenous people for 150 years of paternalistic assistance programmes and racist schools that devastated their communities.[21]

Dudley Thompson consistently made the case that slavery is one of the most serious international crimes.[22] As he put it, when the Europeans forced Africans to become slaves, "they cut off not only a person's language, religion, family support and everything else that used to mean anything to him, and put him away in a foreign land – the land of Babylon".[23] For this abominable crime, no amends have ever been made, and no apology ever issued. Indeed, it was only the British slave-owners who received compensation for the loss of their "property".[24] Thompson understood well the legal claim that can be made for reparations for slavery. The uprooting of Africans from their homes, their mass capture, the horror of the "Middle Passage" –in which an estimated 1.8 million people perished while crossing the Atlantic[25] – the chattelisation of Africans in the Americas, and the extermination of their languages and cultures can all be considered as crimes against humanity. These are, according to international law, defined as "murder, extermination, enslavement, deportation, and other inhumane acts committed against any civilian population".[26]

According to international law, those who commit crimes against humanity must make reparations. And those reparations can be paid to descendants of the victims of the crimes. In addition, governments can lay claim to reparations on behalf of their populations. And those claims can be brought against governments of countries that promoted slavery or benefited in some way from the slave trade and the institutionalisation of slavery. It should be noted, as well, that slavery has had a long-term impact on Africa and its citizens. British human rights lawyer Anthony Gifford has remarked that, as a result of slavery, flourishing civilisations on the African continent were destroyed; ordered systems of government were brought down; and millions of the strongest and most productive African citizens were forcibly removed from the continent.

In the Americas, the system of slavery gave rise to "poverty, landlessness, underdevelopment, the crushing of culture and language, loss of identity, inculcation of inferiority among black people; and the indoctrination of whites into a racist mindset".[27] Gifford argues that all of these factors "continue to this day to affect the prospects and quality of black people's lives".[28]

It is hard to dispute this proposition. Scientists are beginning to realise the inter-generational impact of slavery on the health of the descendants of slaves. Non-communicable diseases are more common among African Americans and populations in the Caribbean, for example.[29] They are devastating individuals and communities in the Caribbean, threatening their quality of life and contributing to the further underdevelopment of the islands. According to the Pan American Health Organisation (PAHO), the Caribbean has "the highest death rates from heart disease and the top five countries for diabetes in the Americas".[30] Poor diets of salted fatty pork, corn, rice, and sugary drinks from the days of slavery resulted in an inter-generational case of undernourishment and poor health outcomes for millions of people in this region.[31]

And then there is the psycho-social and psychological impact of the institution of slavery on the descendant of slaves; the continuation of racist and xenophobic attitudes; and the dehumanising of people on the grounds of their race or skin colour. America – the so-called "land of the free and home of the brave" – leads the world in incarcerations, and the vast majority of those imprisoned are of African descent (see Daniels in this volume). The institutional system of control that African-American scholar-activist Angela Davis described as the US "prison-industrial complex" is a direct legacy of slavery.[32] It is clear that Dudley Thompson was well aware of the lasting impacts of slavery in the areas mentioned above, and that this drove his desire to seek reparations from European colonial powers on behalf of citizens of African descent.

The Organisation of African Unity (OAU), during its 1992 Dakar summit, appointed an Eminent Persons Group (EPG) to pursue the issue of the effects of slavery and its consequences on Africa and its descendants, and to investigate the modalities by which this problem could be addressed. The Group later held a conference to adopt the Abuja Declaration on reparations in 1993. The EPG consisted of prominent individuals such as the late Nigerian business tycoon Moshood Abiola, Kenyan academic Ali Mazrui (see Ndlovu-Gatsheni in this volume) and Nigerian historian Jacob Ade Ajayi. Dudley Thompson was given the responsibility of acting as the rapporteur for this summit.

At annual meetings of the African Studies Association (ASA) of the US, Dudley Thompson, Ali Mazrui and Ade Ajayi would regularly convene sessions on reparations for scholars from Africa and its diaspora.

The 1993 Abuja Declaration made calls for the international community to recognise the "unique and unprecedented moral debt owed to the African peoples" – the "most humiliated and exploited people of the last four centuries of modern history".[33] That debt is yet to be paid. The Declaration further called on African heads of state and government, and those in the diaspora, to establish national committees to study the damage of slavery and colonialism on the continent and to disseminate information and encourage the creation of educational courses that would address the impact of enslavement, colonisation and neo-colonialism on contemporary Africa and its diaspora. The document further urged the OAU to grant observer status to "select organisations from the African Disapora in order to facilitate consultations between Africa and its Diaspora on reparations and related issues". It requested the continental body to demand "full monetary compensation" through "capital transfer and debt cancellation".[34] Furthermore, the Declaration noted that artefacts, goods and traditional treasures stolen from Africa by individuals and countries in the West must be returned to their rightful owners, the African people. Abuja further called on the OAU to set up a legal committee on the issue of reparations. One of the more interesting statements in the Declaration, which indicates that reparations are not only about monetary compensation, is its request to the OAU – now the African Union – to "intensify its efforts in restructuring the international system in pursuit of justice by insisting that a permanent seat on the UN Security Council be given to an African nation".[35] These are all goals which Dudley Thompson pursued doggedly, and would have wanted the Pan-African movement to achieve in his lifetime.

Concluding Reflections

While Thompson did not follow the same radical path of Marcus Garvey, in many of his speeches he preached the philosophy of Garvey. In one of his keynote addresses on "Pan-African History and Garvey", which Thompson delivered at the University of the West Indies (UWI), on Jamaica's Mona campus, at the Pan-African summit in July 2007, he bemoaned the fact that Jamaica's leaders seemed ashamed to acknowledge their African heritage. He told the story of his efforts in the Jamaican Senate to have the life and philosophy of Marcus Garvey taught in every school in Jamaica – from kindergarten to university. Thompson had moved a motion in the Jamaican House of Assembly which took 12 months before it came up for debate. Despite his own reluctance to embrace the more utopian radical vision espoused by Garvey, Thompson considered Garvey to have been the greatest Jamaican that ever lived because he provided the country with a philosophy based on black pride. Thompson noted that Jamaicans were suffering from "negrophobia": one of the legacies of slavery, which made people of African heritage feel inferior to whites. He affirmed that Garvey "taught us that you can be equal to anybody in the world if you believe in yourself. That is the direction that we ought to go and the direction that we will go."[36]

Working alongside Barbadian political activist David Comissiong and Barbadian historian and Vice-Chancellor of the University of the West Indies, Hilary Beckles, Thompson helped to advance the Caribbean Reparations Movement and to strengthen the African diaspora platform for the UN World Conference Against Racism held in Durban, South Africa, in September 2001. Clearly, Thompson and the Caribbean delegation were extremely disappointed with the failure of continental African governments to support the demand for an apology from European imperialist nations for the crime of slavery. African states – led by South Africa, Nigeria and Senegal – also backed down from supporting countries in the African diaspora that were calling for reparations for transatlantic slavery. European governments had threatened to end their attendance at the Durban conference if such demands were included in the final agreement. The accord eventually avoided any direct references to European culpability for these glaring crimes against humanity (see Beckles in this volume). The final wording of the conference declaration, in reference to this issue, reads: "We acknowledge that slavery and the slave trade, including the trans-Atlantic slave trade, were appalling tragedies in the history of humanity, not only because of their abhorrent barbarism, but also in terms of their magnitude, organised nature and especially their negation of the essence of victims."[37]

While this could be considered an apology of sorts by European imperialists, it did not go far enough for Thompson and other participants from the African diasporic states who wanted the term "crimes against humanity" included in the draft and for direct culpability for the crimes to be acknowledged.[38] Nevertheless, Thompson's notion that reparative justice is inevitable has started to take hold, not only in Jamaica, but also in Brazil and the US. Closer to the end of his life,

Thompson's moderate Pan-Africanist philosophy seemed to be merging with the more radical thought of Marcus Garvey. He was envisioning a shift to socialism for Africa and the African diaspora, while simultaneously advocating the unity of Africa.

When he died in New York City at the ripe old age of 95 on 20 January 2012 (a day after his birthday), Dudley Thompson was widely praised in Africa and its diaspora as a Jamaican Pan-African politician and lawyer who had made significant contributions to the jurisprudence and politics of Jamaica, the Caribbean, Africa and internationally.[39] He served his country at many levels, and yet had a vision that went beyond the narrow nationalist goals of his adopted nation. Former Jamaican prime minister P.J. Patterson eulogised Thompson after his passing: "His contribution to the building of Jamaica as a nation – to its constitution, its jurisprudence, its diplomacy, its political system, global reputation and its international standing – is unparalleled."[40] The Jamaican media recalled that in 2011 the African Union had declared Thompson to be the "first citizen" of the continent of Africa – so great was his influence on the continent, and so profound were his contributions internationally on behalf of the African motherland.

The legacy of Dudley Thompson is one which carries the right blend of moderate pragmatism in the concrete steps he took as a committed Pan-Africanist and a more radical utopian vision of the direction in which Pan-Africanism ought to go in future. Thompson did not get ahead of himself in his quest for "the holy grail" of the Pan-African ideal. He worked methodically in the trenches to build the intellectual pillars upon which this Pan-African ideal can be constructed.

Boutros Boutros-Ghali: The Afro-Arab Peacemaker

Adekeye Adebajo

Boutros Boutros-Ghali, the sixth United Nations (UN) secretary-general (1992–6) – the first African and the first Arab in the world body's history since its founding in 1945 – died in a Cairo hospital at the age of 93 in February 2016.[1] This essay highlights the Egyptian scholar-diplomat's strong Pan-African diplomatic background and fierce pro-African battles to promote what Kenyan scholar Ali Mazrui described as Pax Africana (see Gatsheni-Ndlovu in this volume). I assess Boutros-Ghali's election as UN secretary-general in 1991 and examine his personality, before analysing the constraints of the international context within which he had to operate. The chapter further examines the relationship between Boutros-Ghali and the 15-member Security Council.[2] The central relationship between the UN secretary-general and the most powerful Council member –the United States (US) – is a major focus of this essay, as it effectively determined the Egyptian's relationship with the Council as a whole. I then assess the peace and security challenges encountered by the UN during Boutros-Ghali's tenure, with most of these conflicts located in Africa. Some of the innovative ideas and concepts promoted by Boutros-Ghali are then analysed, before I conclude by assessing his legacy.

Boutros Boutros-Ghali's Election and Personality

At an Organisation of African Unity (OAU) closed summit in the Nigerian capital of Abuja in June 1991, African leaders met to discuss candidates for the position of UN secretary-general. The Non-Aligned Movement's 106 members argued forcefully that it was "Africa's turn" to occupy the post, as the only major region in the world that had not produced a secretary-general. Boutros-Ghali, as Egypt's deputy prime minister since May 1991 and its minister of state for foreign affairs for 14 years, was present at the meeting. At that summit, it was Gabonese autocrat Omar Bongo who suggested that, since there were no French-speaking candidates being proposed and a preponderance of West Africans, Boutros-Ghali's name should be put forward as a fluent speaker of French, Arabic and English. The OAU eventually proposed six official candidates: Boutros-Ghali; Zimbabwean finance minister Bernard Chidzero; former Nigerian military leader Olusegun Obasanjo; Ghana's Kenneth Dadzie, the secretary-general of the UN Conference on Trade and Development (UNCTAD); Sierra Leone's UN assistant secretary-general for Special Political Questions, James Jonah; and former Gabonese culture minister Nguema François Owono.

In the voting for the secretary-generalship, which took place in the Security Council by the end of October 1991, Boutros-Ghali and Chidzero each had nine votes, while Obasanjo had seven votes.[3] The 69-year-old Boutros-Ghali would eventually pull away from the field by November 1991, overcoming American and British opposition to his age, in part by promising to serve only one term. France had strongly backed Boutros-Ghali from the start, with Russia also pledging support, while China insisted on an African candidate for the position. In the final voting, Boutros-Ghali secured 11 positive votes, while Washington – along with three other Council members – abstained. Boutros-Ghali thus became the first African and first Arab UN secretary-general in November 1991.

Boutros-Ghali obtained a doctorate in international law from the Sorbonne in Paris in 1949, taught at Cairo University for 28 years, and published widely in law and politics journals. He also wrote the first book on the UN to appear in Arabic. The Egyptian was thus the most intellectually accomplished secretary-general in the history of the post. He was arrogant (as he himself acknowledged) and cerebral. Even his worst enemies, however, conceded that Boutros-Ghali was a genuine intellectual. The introverted and workaholic Egyptian avoided the social limelight and bright lights of New York once settled in the job on "Turtle Bay". In many ways, he lived up to the appellation "the Pope on the East River".

A Coptic Christian from a rich and politically connected family, Boutros-Ghali acquired a deep sense of *noblesse oblige* and a commitment to public service. His grandfather Boutros Ghali Pasha had served as prime minister of Egypt under the British protectorate before being assassinated. His father, Yusuf, had served as finance minister, while two uncles had both served as foreign minister. Boutros-Ghali was aloof and often impatient with people who were less intelligent. UN staff came to refer to their boss as "the Pharaoh", because of his authoritarian leadership style. Boutros-Ghali did not endear himself to staff by publicly criticising his own secretariat, and for tactlessly telling the *New York Times* that the only way to run a bureaucracy was the way he had treated the Egyptian civil service: "by stealth and sudden violence".[4] As Marrack Goulding, an insightful British diplomat who served as Boutros-Ghali's undersecretary-general for peacekeeping and, later, political affairs between 1992 and 1997, noted: "Boutros-Ghali has charm, gracious manners, and an agreeable wit, but he can become assertive in argument, speaking directly and not always resisting the temptation of the *bon mot* that will raise a laugh but may also cause offence."[5]

Boutros-Ghali was steeped in the intricacies of Third World diplomacy, having served as Egypt's minister of state for foreign affairs between 1977 and 1991, under the autocratic regimes of Anwar Sadat and Hosni Mubarak. He had a profound and intuitive grasp of the global South, and was deeply involved in both the Arab–Israeli dispute and the politics of the Organisation of African Unity.[6] As UN secretary-general, Boutros-Ghali often expressed the Southern criticism that the rich North was too focused on peace and security issues, and did not pay enough attention to the socio–economic development concerns of the global South.[7] He often decried the lack of democratisation in the decision-making structures of the World Bank and the International Monetary Fund (IMF). He frequently voiced the Southern concern that the anachronistic UN Security Council was in urgent need of reform to ensure the presence of permanent members from other regions of the world in a body that did not have any such membership from Africa and South America. But he was astute enough, most of the time, to understand the UN's power dynamics.

The pompous Boutros-Ghali often annoyed permanent representatives during meetings with him by cutting them off in mid-sentence to inform them that he had previously talked to their foreign ministers or presidents.[8] He also frequently scolded African ambassadors in New York for not keeping properly abreast of matters concerning their continent.[9] He often noted that he was more of a politician than a diplomat. American journalist Stanley Meisler described Boutros-Ghali as "the most stubbornly independent Secretary-General in the half-century history of the United Nations".[10]

As Chinmaya Gharekhan, the former permanent representative of India to the United Nations between 1986 and 1992, noted: "Boutros-Ghali is an intellectual giant … He provoked us into thinking along new, creative lines. He frequently liked to act as the devil's advocate. His own contributions were original and unorthodox."[11] David Hannay, Britain's permanent representative to the UN between 1990 and 1995, who regarded the Egyptian scholar-diplomat as the most assertive holder of the post since the Swedish secretary-general, Dag Hammarskjöld (1953–61),[12] similarly noted: "Boutros-Ghali … was a man of charm and erudition. He had an encyclopaedic knowledge of international, and in particular of African, affairs … He was forceful and decisive, perhaps sometimes too much so for his own good."[13]

International Contexts and Constraints

It is significant to note that Boutros-Ghali was elected as the first secretary-general after the end of the Cold War by 1990 and the "unipolar moment" that ensued. This period witnessed the reunification of Germany and the dissolution of the Soviet Union, leaving the United States as the world's sole superpower. In ending the five-decade East–West rivalry that had made decision-making difficult in the UN Security Council, the new international context increased cooperation among the five veto-wielding permanent members (P5) on the UN Security Council (the US, Russia, China, France and Britain), making deployment of peacekeeping missions and ending long-running proxy wars between the American and Soviet blocs easier to resolve.[14] At the tail end of his administration, George H.W. Bush sent American troops to Somalia in December 1992 to assist a humanitarian mission. President Bill Clinton (1993–2000) came into office a month later, championing "assertive multilateralism". Such euphoria would, however, soon be dissipated by failure and withdrawal from Somalia a year later, and the continuing weak American response to the slaughter in Bosnia.[15]

Boutros-Ghali's failure to manage effectively the crucial relationship with the most powerful member of the Security Council – the United States – eventually led to his ousting from office in 1996. After Washington denied him a second term in office, Boutros-Ghali published an embittered memoir of his tenure as UN secretary-general in 1999, which he significantly subtitled "A US-UN Saga". He would later bemoan the limits of his power, noting:

As Secretary-General I was duty-bound to carry out the resolutions of the Security Council to the letter. But as a lifelong student of international law, I lamented this situation, which both disparaged international law and displayed the United Nations not as an organisation of sovereign states equal under the Charter but as a political tool of the major powers.[16]

Further complicating his interaction with the powerful members of the Security Council, the Egyptian played the role of stubborn Pharaoh, arguing that "Article 100 of the Charter is 'the one-hundredth Psalm' of the Secretary-General. The Secretary-General must be prepared to stand up to any pressure, any criticism, and any opposition."[17] Boutros-Ghali bluntly condemned the double standards of powerful Western powers on the Council in selectively authorising UN interventions in "rich men's wars" in the Balkans, while ignoring Africa's "orphan conflicts". He believed that one of the major goals of the UN was to prevent the marginalisation of the Third World. But he was also a pragmatist who recognised the limits of his power in a system dominated by the Council's P5. As he eloquently put it: "I do not claim to elevate the vision of the Utopian city called for by the Islamic thinker Al-Farabi to that of a Utopian world, for I cannot promise to go beyond what is feasible and what is possible. Despite the close ties that bind me to optimism, my ties to realism are even closer."[18]

He chastised his political masters on the Council for turning the UN into an instrument for parochial national interest over Libya and Iraq (sanctioning Muammar Qaddafi and Saddam Hussein), and he berated them for their lack of political will in dumping impossible tasks in Rwanda and Bosnia on the UN without providing the organisation with the resources to do the job.

Boutros-Ghali was often seen as a pompous Pharaoh who made some ultimately fatal errors of political judgement. He broke tradition by appointing Chinmaya Gharekhan as his "personal representative" to the Security Council, thus failing himself to attend the informal meetings of the UN's most powerful body, which he found tedious and some of whose permanent representatives he considered mediocre. The appointment of Gharekhan also alienated officials in Ghanaian, Kofi Annan's Department of Peacekeeping Operations (DPKO), who thus tried to undermine him, contributing to the debacle in Rwanda in 1994.

The US soon turned against Boutros-Ghali. Senior American political figures Jeane Kirkpatrick and Richard Armitage accused him of trying to become "chief executive officer of the world" and "the world's commander-in-chief".[19] These attacks were ironic considering that Boutros-Ghali was, at first, regarded as pro-

American by a sceptical Third World at the UN when he was first appointed. Irresponsible US politicians eventually turned him into a bogeyman, blaming Boutros-Ghali for everything from the death of 18 US soldiers in Somalia in October 1993, to the failure to protect "safe havens" in Bosnia between 1992 and 1995, and obstruction of reform within his own bureaucracy.

Boutros-Ghali was particularly scapegoated for the Somali debacle in 1993, a fiasco that had been entirely planned and directed from the Pentagon. Bosnia's failures were largely due to European realpolitik and American policy vacillations.[20] But the pugnacious US permanent representative to the UN, Madeleine Albright, accused the United Nations of "betrayal", and when Boutros-Ghali complained about the "vulgarity" of the language of the US delegation, it was clear that relations between these two strong personalities had reached a head: the time was fast approaching when an irresistible force would confront an immovable object.

Boutros-Ghali also appointed more American nationals to top positions than any of his predecessors. But the Bill Clinton administration – notorious for a reactive foreign policy and led by a president obsessed with short-term polls – failed to defend the United Nations, and instead joined the criticisms of alleged UN profligacy. Boutros-Ghali's undisguised disdain for Madeleine Albright's diplomatic skills – he felt she was a hectoring novice – would prove fatal. He complained that she was trying to instruct him on which countries to visit (for example, he was discouraged from visiting Somalia in October 1993, but went nonetheless); which special representatives and envoys to appoint; what to say or avoid saying in speeches; and the importance of keeping a distance from the hostile US Congress.

In 1996 Boutros-Ghali complained prophetically that he felt like a man condemned to execution.[21] Madeleine Albright boosted her own chances of winning bipartisan support for her successful bid to become the first female American secretary of state by acting as Clinton's willing executioner: she personally put Boutros-Ghali's head on the guillotine and administered the fatal blow. She then presented the bodiless head to a bloodthirsty US Congress in a modern version of King Herod's gift of John the Baptist's head to his sanguinary wife's daughter, Salome.

In his bitter 1999 memoir, *Unvanquished*, Boutros-Ghali's indictment of Washington in blocking UN action to halt the genocide in Rwanda in 1994 and its vacillations in acting to end the slaughter in Bosnia was devastating.[22] However, though he focused much of his venom on the US, he often failed to point out in similar detail some of the shortcomings of other powerful members of the United Nations. For example, France, the closest ally of this Sorbonne-educated intellectual, who became the first secretary-general of the French-led Organisation Internationale de la Francophonie between 1997 and 2002, got off particularly lightly for its training and arming of Hutu death squads before Rwanda's 1994 genocide.[23]

The Challenges of Pax Africana and Global Peace

Boutros-Ghali's tenure in office witnessed the rise and fall of the practice of UN peacekeeping in Rwanda, Somalia, Haiti, Bosnia and Cambodia. At its peak in 1994, the United Nations deployed 75,000 peacekeepers to 17 trouble spots at an annual cost of $3.6 billion. During the previous four decades, the UN had deployed just 13 peacekeeping missions.[24] There were successes in Mozambique, Cambodia and El Salvador, but also spectacular failures in Rwanda, Bosnia, Angola and Somalia.

The UN mission in Mozambique between 1992 and 1994 helped end a two-decade civil war, overseeing disarmament and demobilisation, and helping to organise elections before leaving the country. The world body was determined to avoid a repeat of the debacle in Angola when both sides had kept soldiers in reserve for the post-election phase. Beyond Africa, Boutros-Ghali steered the UN mission in Cambodia between 1992 and 1993 to halt a two-decade civil war, and to organise successful elections.

Rwanda, however, proved to be the biggest disaster during Boutros-Ghali's tenure. About three months before the start of the country's genocide in 1994, in which about 800,000 people were killed,[25] the UN mission's Canadian force commander in Kigali, General Roméo Dallaire, had asked for authorisation to take military action to forestall the impending genocide. Dallaire had received instructions from the Department of Peacekeeping Operations to avoid a Somalia-like fiasco and to abstain from the use of force at all costs. A subsequent UN inquiry report published in December 1999 criticised UN undersecretary-general for peacekeeping, Kofi Annan, and his Pakistani deputy, Iqbal Riza, for this shortcoming.[26] Boutros-Ghali was also criticised for consistently portraying the crisis in Rwanda as a civil war rather than an evolving genocide until after the Security Council decided to withdraw most of its 2,500 peacekeepers in April 1994.[27] As the genocide began, Boutros-Ghali was on a tour of Europe. Not only was he slow in returning to New York, he also dithered before belatedly calling for a stronger UN force.

Boutros-Ghali later admitted that he felt personally responsible not for his failure to respond timeously to the massacre, but for failing to convince the Great Powers to do so,[28] describing Rwanda, in 2005, as "my worst failure at the United Nations".[29] Most of the blame for UN non-intervention, however, lay with powerful Western powers. At the start of the genocide, African governments and their allies at the UN urged the Council to strengthen and reinforce the UN force to enable it to protect civilians. Nigeria's permanent representative to the UN, Ibrahim Gambari, wondered aloud whether Africa had fallen off the map of the world's concerns.[30] But led by strong American, Belgian and British demands, the Security Council withdrew most of its peacekeepers from Rwanda, leaving a token force of 270 by the end of April 1994.[31]

In his 2012 memoirs, Kofi Annan appeared to place more blame for UN failures in Somalia, Rwanda and Bosnia on what he saw as "Boutros-Ghali's autocratic and secretive style, which had long caused difficulties within the UN, alienating large numbers of staff and diplomats".[32] Annan accused Boutros-Ghali of seeking to control information to and from the UN Security Council. The Ghanaian also claimed that Boutros-Ghali kept the leadership of Annan's own Department of Peacekeeping Operations out of the loop on Somalia, and negotiated directly with troop contributors.[33] These criticisms, however, scarcely suggest that a different leadership style could have masked the far more serious charges made against Annan in Rwanda and Bosnia.

In Angola, the UN's peacekeeping tasks were complicated by the warlord Jonas Savimbi's refusal to conclude the electoral process and to disarm his fighters. Despite pleas from Boutros-Ghali not to abandon the process, the truculent rebel leader withdrew all his men from the national army in October 1992, and fighting resumed.[34] The conflict continued for another decade at the cost of tens of thousands of lives, and would end only with Savimbi's assassination in February 2002.[35] In the Caribbean nation of Haiti, much to Washington's irritation, Boutros-Ghali refused to approve a UN deployment in 1994 until troop contributions and time frames had been properly resolved.[36] As in Somalia, the UN took over from a US-led multinational force in Haiti in March 1995 and helped to stabilise the country, enabling elections to be held nine months later. In both Somalia and Moroccan-occupied Western Sahara, the Pharaoh was, however, regarded as less than impartial, having previously supported regimes in Mogadishu and Rabat while serving as Egypt's minister of state for foreign affairs.

Intellectual Contributions

Boutros-Ghali's enduring legacy to the United Nations will be *An Agenda for Peace*, a landmark 1992 document on the tools and techniques of peacemaking, peacekeeping and peacebuilding for a post–Cold War era. The Security Council had asked him to present it with such a text in January 1992. In true professorial style, Boutros-Ghali spent 40 hours meticulously polishing countless drafts of the text. His *Agenda* called for "preventive deployment"; a rapid reaction UN force to enable action without the need to seek new troops for each mission; heavily armed peace enforcers for dangerous missions; and the strengthening of regional peacekeeping bodies to lighten the burden on the United Nations. It also outlined a continuum from conflict prevention, to peacemaking, peacekeeping, and peacebuilding.[37]

Boutros-Ghali further argued forcefully in his *Agenda* for "humanitarian intervention" in Somalia, Liberia and Burundi, noting that "human rights are, by definition, the ultimate norm of all politics".[38] He regarded what was later enshrined by the UN in 2005 as the emerging norm of the "responsibility to protect" in universal terms. He also strongly advocated the use of regional security arrangements to lighten the UN's heavy peacekeeping burden.[39] The concept of "peacebuilding" that he elaborated in *Agenda* is now associated with multi-dimensional missions in places like Angola, Mozambique, Somalia, Haiti and Cambodia, where efforts were made to adopt a holistic approach to peace. Disarmament, demobilisation and reintegration (DDR) of fighters; security sector reform (SSR); repatriating refugees; monitoring human rights; and organising elections are some of the tasks linked to this concept. Not only are diplomatic and military tools employed in building peace, but peacebuilders also focus on the political, social, and economic root causes of conflicts in societies emerging from civil war.[40]

Finally, in his Oxford University Cyril Foster lecture in January 1996, Boutros-Ghali called for UN member states to accept the jurisdiction of the

International Court of Justice (ICJ) without reservation. Just as with his idea of promoting democratisation within and between states, he called for the creation of both a local and a global "rule of law".[41] Two international criminal tribunals on Rwanda and Yugoslavia were created under Boutros-Ghali's watch, and these innovations would eventually culminate in the establishment of the International Criminal Court (ICC), with the signing of the Rome Statute in July 1998.

Concluding Reflections

Boutros-Ghali was removed from office in November 1996 under controversial circumstances. His undersecretary-general for peacekeeping, Kofi Annan, and some of Annan's key officials within the UN secretly worked with the US as it plotted the removal of the first African secretary-general. Annan – a supposedly apolitical international civil servant – candidly admitted in his 2012 memoirs that he met with Madeleine Albright in mid-1996 to discuss removing his boss and replacing him.[42] Boutros-Ghali later talked of betrayal by his "closest collaborator", and some of the American officials involved in ousting Boutros-Ghali, such as Bob Orr and Michael Sheehan, later joined Annan's UN.[43] The United States stood alone among the 15 Security Council members in vetoing Boutros-Ghali's reappointment in 1996. Washington and London then launched a manipulative campaign on behalf of Annan, arguing that continued support for Boutros-Ghali suggested to the world that there was no qualified black African candidate. Paris assumed a typically Gallic cultural arrogance, posturing about Annan's lack of fluency in French. Eventually everyone agreed to Boutros-Ghali's departure, and Annan became the first UN secretary-general from sub-Saharan Africa.[44] He died in August 2018, having served two terms, and won the Nobel Peace Prize, in conjunction with the UN, in 2001.

Despite his arrogance and tactlessness (not uncommon among many senior Western officials in similar positions at this level of responsibility), some of the visceral, and often prejudiced, reactions to Boutros-Ghali were reminiscent of the treatment of another outspoken senior African at the UN, Amadou-Mahtar M'Bow. The Senegalese served as the director-general of the UN Educational, Scientific and Cultural Organisation (UNESCO) between 1974 and 1987, and was eventually hounded out of office following a sustained disinformation campaign orchestrated by Western governments and media organs.[45] Like the Shakespearean Iago's hatred for the black Othello, the venom of the attacks on both African officials was often irrational and incomprehensible. Though Boutros-Ghali often "spoke truth to power", his utterances were sometimes treated as those of an "uppity native": the Egyptian himself complained that the British media were unhappy with him over the Bosnian crisis "because I am a wog".[46] The American stereotype of the "angry black man" appeared to be revived in some of the dismissive outbursts against him. Many Western governments and scholars reacted strongly against an intelligent, articulate, outspoken African who did not look like nor sound like them, and who dared to act as their equal or even superior.

American analyst Michael Barnett described Boutros-Ghali as "a leader who placed his ego above the needs of the organisation".[47] Another American scholar, Edward Luck, criticised him for self-servingly framing "subjective political judgments" as "moral obligations" and for representing his own preferences as those of the world's values.[48] Norwegian scholar Mats Berdal argued that "Boutros-Ghali lacked the key qualities of political judgment and tact", noting further that temperament was more important to the job of UN secretary-general than intellect.[49]

While one can agree about Boutros-Ghali's personal tactlessness, his political judgement was almost always correct. Indeed, as Marrack Goulding noted about his former boss: "he knew where power lay and he knew that power could not be ignored, even if what the powerful demanded was sometimes unpleasant or unfair."[50] The fact that, in the first vote for Boutros-Ghali's re-election in 1996, 14 out of 15 members of the Security Council agreed to keeping the secretary-general (leaving the US diplomatically isolated as the sole dissenting voice) suggests that the vast majority of governments were angrier at the tactlessness of America's heavy-handed efforts to remove Boutros-Ghali than they were about the undoubted arrogance of "the Pharaoh". As for Berdal's idea of temperament trumping intellect in this job, this is of course more sound-bite than solid social science. The better temperament of Kofi Annan and predecessors such as U Thant did not make them any more successful in the job once they had incurred the wrath of Washington. This suggests that understanding the rather limited powers of this office is more important for sound analysis than the temperament or intelligence of office-holders.

Despite these criticisms, Boutros-Ghali's tenure was not devoid of real achievements. He oversaw some reform of the UN bureaucracy. The American Joseph Connor, the undersecretary-general for management, cut the UN bureaucracy from 12,000 to 9,000 while freezing the UN budget, saving $100 million a year. Departments were also slashed by a third, while increased computerisation cut down on the organisation's notorious paper-load.[51]

UN peacekeeping successes were achieved under Boutros-Ghali's watch, while peacebuilding missions were largely initiated during his tenure. He led innovative cooperation between the UN and regional bodies in Africa and Europe. His landmark 1992 report, *An Agenda for Peace*, remains – three decades later – an indispensable guide to the tools and techniques employed by the United Nations. Boutros-Ghali further led mega-conferences, between 1992 and 1995, to focus global attention on the environment (Rio), human rights (Vienna), population (Cairo), social development (Copenhagen) and women (Beijing). The Egyptian forcefully and consistently defended the world body against its critics.

However, Boutros-Ghali's bruising confrontations with Madeleine Albright were, in retrospect, a costly error, and he misread the mood of an unforgiving American political establishment. For all his undoubted achievements, the pompous Pharaoh eventually earned himself the unenviable distinction of being the only UN secretary-general to have been denied a second term in office.

PART 4

———

THE ACTIVISTS

Malcolm X: Pan-African Crusader for Social Justice

Lee A. Daniels

We know who Malcolm X was: the young black American who rose out of a life of poverty and crime to extraordinary international fame in the late 1950s and early 1960s as the fiery, charismatic spokesman of the black American separatist organization, the Nation of Islam. But who was El Hajj Malik El-Shabazz, the man who had been Malcolm X, but who discarded that name and left the Nation of Islam after journeying to Mecca and seeing the true face of Islam and the true faces of the world's Muslims? And why is it that the world almost universally still speaks the name "Malcolm X" and almost never speaks the name that man called himself in the last year of his life, El Hajj Malik El-Shabazz?

From Malcolm X to El Hajj Malik El-Shabazz

In one sense, it is astonishing that Malcolm X continues to fascinate the world, so that his autobiography – as "told to Alex Haley"[1] – is still widely considered to be one of the most important books of the post-Second World War (1939–45) era.[2] The 1992 Spike Lee film biopic, *Malcolm X*, continues to have iconic status, while the late black American scholar Manning Marable's 2011 biography, *Malcolm X: A Life of Reinvention*,[3] immediately provoked and continues to provoke furious controversy.[4]

After all, Malcolm X was literally just all talk. He led no true organised national or local community movement. He was responsible for nothing that tangibly improved the situation of black Americans in the 1950s and 1960s: no broad national legislation advancing their interests; no assistance to blacks in a small Southern city or town in their quest for basic human rights; no broad or small-scale economic development programme. Not even the building of one housing project for poor people, nor a single free-breakfast community programme of the type that the Black Panthers operated in several American cities from the late 1960s to the early 1970s.[5] The man who took the name Malcolm X, and then El Hajj Malik El-Shabazz, flashed across the political landscape spectacularly, but briefly, from the mid-1950s to the mid-1960s, and then was gone, assassinated not by the "white devils" he had so often railed against – at least not directly – but by adherents – *black men* – of the Nation of Islam itself.

But *which* black men had really pulled the triggers of the guns used to kill Malcolm X before a shocked and panicked throng at Harlem's Audubon ballroom that 21 February 1965? Fifty-five years later, in February 2020, a six-part Netflix documentary, "Who Killed Malcolm X?" asserted that two of the three men convicted of the crime in March 1966 were innocent – a claim the convicted men themselves and numerous supporters of Malcolm X had made since their arrest. The renewed controversy led New York's Manhattan District Attorney's Office to announce a "preliminary review" of the case file to determine whether a full reinvestigation was warranted.

Both the 2020 documentary and the decision of the District Attorney's Office underscore the fact that many black and other Americans continue to consider Malcolm X a hero. Yet, since that shocking moment in February 1965, Malcolm has been, for many black Americans, for the broader American society, and for the global community in general, a figure of continuing fascination and controversy. One reason for this, of course, is that, for many, the man who called himself Malcolm X was then and remains the counterpoint to – in historical terms even, the sceptic of – the non-violent, integrationist ethos of the civil rights movement of those decades. As the Nation of Islam's chief spokesman, Malcolm X scathingly denounced the Martin Luther King, Jr-led civil rights movement's Christian and Gandhian stance of black Americans "turning the other cheek" to white racist violence, and "pleading" with white Americans to let blacks integrate into a society which, throughout the three and a half centuries of black presence on American soil, had made it clear that they were there only to be unfairly used and degraded.[6]

Tall, handsome – his ramrod-straight posture seemingly the physical manifestation of a profound personal asceticism and an unbending, energetic defiance of white racists – Malcolm X was the very epitome of a fierce, unyielding black American race warrior. An integral part of that allure was his aggressive promotion of a militant black pride through praising black Americans' rootedness in, and contemporary connection to, Africa and to people of African descent wherever they lived across the globe. Malcolm's promotion of the idea of Pan-Africanism – the notion that the common genealogical root of people of African descent provided a commonality of purpose in fighting white oppression – struck a resonant chord among many black Americans[7] at that historic moment when the non-violent, "mass action" phase of the US civil rights movement was sweeping across the American landscape, and black peoples in sub-Saharan Africa and the Caribbean (and other people of colour in Asia and Latin America) were using violence and threats of violence in a bid to break the chains of European colonialism.[8]

None were more committed to that ideal nor more admiring of Malcolm X than the small number of black Americans who in the early 1960s had left the United States to plant themselves in the land of their African ancestors. Ghana was a particular magnet for these black expatriates, not only for its history and potential but also because its president, Kwame Nkrumah, had attended college in America, at Lincoln University, the first college established for blacks before the American Civil War (1861–65). Maya Angelou's memoir of her three years in Accra from 1962 to 1965, *All God's Children Need Traveling Shoes*, provides a keenly observed portrait of Malcolm's April 1964 visit to Ghana – and his first post-Mecca discussion with a sizable group of black Americans.[9]

Ghana's 200-strong black American expatriate community included W.E.B. Du Bois, the great scholar-activist. He died the night before the August 1963 March on Washington, but his widow, the scholar Shirley Graham Du Bois, remained in Accra, and was revered by Nkrumah. It was she who arranged for Malcolm, whose fame had preceded him everywhere he went, to have a 45-minute meeting with Nkrumah the morning he was to leave the country.[10] What the two paladins of the Pan-African ideal discussed has never come to light. But several nights before at an informal reception for Malcolm, the black rights activist made it clear he was more committed than ever to using Pan-Africanism as a force to fight white racism in America and across the world.

"I am still a Muslim," Malcolm declared to his enthralled audience, who were fully aware of his split with the Nation of Islam and of his remarks repudiating his past blanket condemnation of all white people. "I am still a minister, and I am still Black."[11] Malcolm pledged a renewed focus on mobilising the support of African governments like Ghana to take the case of blacks in America to the United Nations because "If our cause was debated by all the world's nations, it would mean that ... America would be forced to face up to its discriminatory policies ... If South African blacks can petition the UN against their country's policy of apartheid, then America should be shown on the world's stage as a repressionist and bestial racist nation."[12]

Malcolm X as a Pan-African Prophet

Until the early 1960s, discussions in the United States about Africa and Pan-Africanism had overwhelmingly been the province of a small number of black (and some white) leftists, activists, intellectuals and veterans of the Garvey movement of the 1920s (see Grant, Hutton and Reddock in this volume). The mainstream civil rights organisations had largely kept silent about the African and Caribbean anti-colonial movements, and publicly avoided any discussion of Pan-Africanism.

Their reticence was pragmatic and understandable, given that America's white racists had, since the Russian Revolution of 1917, denigrated the black freedom struggle as "un-American", a communist, socialist, or some other kind of foreign plot.[13] That American society in the late 1950s was just recovering from its vicious bout of witch-hunting for communists and other radicals – known as McCarthyism[14] – made the mainstream civil rights movement's posture the right one for the moment.

But by the early 1960s, one did not need to be a committed activist or possess a college degree in the US to understand that, across the globe, people of colour were challenging white supremacy. The news headlines alone – of this or that African or Caribbean nation gaining independence; of Fidel Castro and the Cuban Revolution (1953–9); of South Africa's Sharpeville massacre of 1960 and Nelson Mandela's liberation struggle; of Patrice Lumumba's CIA-assisted assassination in 1961; and of the faint sounds of war coming from a far-away place called Vietnam – made that clear. For growing numbers of black Americans, who as late as the early 1960s were still being bombarded with Tarzan "King of the Jungle"-type depictions of black Africa in Hollywood,[15] and in European movies and the news media, Malcolm's repeated enthusiastic embrace of connections between Africa and its diaspora – along with the civil rights demonstrations in the American South – helped jump-start the "Black is Beautiful" cultural and political movement that would sweep black America later in the decade.[16]

From its shadowy founding in the 1930s by Elijah Muhammad, the Nation of Islam[17] had seemingly taken up the mantle of Pan-Africanism and the stance of antagonism towards whites, which had been the foundation of Marcus Garvey's "Back to Africa" movement in the wake of the First World War (1914–18) (see Grant in this volume).[18] Both Garvey and Elijah Muhammad had built their organisations on two of the fundamental responses of black Americans to their oppression in American society – race pride, on the one hand, and, on the other, anger towards whites. The stark symbol of the Nation of Islam – the "X" designation to replace its members' "American" family name, symbolising that black Americans were an African people who had been robbed of their true African names and, thus, their true heritage – was the brilliant idea of Elijah Muhammad, the leader of the Nation of Islam and Malcolm X's mentor.[19] But it was the charismatic Malcolm himself, not the decidedly uncharismatic Muhammad, who, during the post-Second World War years of worldwide ferment for liberation, made the black Muslims' fierce indictment of America's flawed democracy enormously appealing, even to many black Americans who otherwise wanted nothing to do with what they considered to be a black Muslim sect. No figure in American history so effectively embodied and so fiercely and openly articulated the qualities of a militant race pride and anger as Malcolm X.

In other words, Malcolm's forging of a place for Pan-Africanism on the roster of public discourse among black Americans during these years – while expanding his indictment of America's white power structure to include its policies and actions abroad, and denouncing the pernicious impact of European colonialism[20] – led the way in helping many black Americans to intensify their pride in being black and to consider their predicament within a global context. Furthermore, the fame that Malcolm's fierce criticism of the American government and fervent embrace of the Pan-Africanist cause brought him in black Africa, the Middle East, and even in China undoubtedly led many abroad to jettison or at least modify the stereotypes that they had about black Americans, too. These developments are likely Malcolm's greatest contribution to the black American liberation struggle.

Nonetheless, the black nationalist stance of the Nation of Islam and the engagement of the post-Nation of Islam Malcolm X/El Hajj Malik El-Shabazz with Pan-Africanism are far more complex than is usually acknowledged. Both postures represented the twentieth-century culmination of one side of the long-standing intra-group debate among black Americans about the two major responses to their struggle in the US. The other side of that debate – whose chief spokesman was Martin Luther King, Jr[21] – declared an unabashed allegiance to the non-violent pursuit of democratic political reform.

The outcome of this contest had, and has, enormous consequences and implications. On the one hand, the ultimate victory of King's viewpoint over that of the Malcolm X of the Nation of Islam was not only underscored by black America's reaffirmation of regarding itself as an American as well as an African people. It was most strikingly reflected by the transformation of Malcolm X himself, a change – only partially completed at the time of his murder – that resulted from his discovering through his hajj to Mecca the simultaneously simple and complex qualities of two other elements of black Americans' fundamental group make-up: faith and its offspring, hope.

That discovery is why the man, who had become globally famous as Malcolm X, would leave the Nation of Islam, begin to reconceive his views of white people as individuals and as part of the American and European political systems, and change his name to El Hajj Malik El-Shabazz. But the complexity does not end there: the efforts of El Hajj Malik El-Shabazz to connect the American black freedom struggle to the Pan-Africanist idea not only illuminated Pan-Africanism's positive impact among African peoples but also exposed its limitations.

Malcolm X and the "Northern Context"

What Malcolm X represented cannot be understood without considering the specific black environment into which he was born and the specific cohort of black Americans he most directly spoke to and for. The bite of his rhetoric was all the sharper because he was speaking not just about the racism of the slave era or of the apartheid of America's Jim Crow South, where civil rights activists and ordinary blacks seeking fundamental civil rights were right then being beaten, lynched and murdered by the legal and de facto agents of the white power structure.

Rather, the appeal of Malcolm X was most directly rooted in the twentieth-century experience of black Americans outside the South, those who lived in the urban centres of the North and West. Born Malcolm Little in Omaha, Nebraska, on 19 May 1925, the fourth of seven children, he would grow up there, and then in Detroit, Michigan, and thereafter in Boston, Massachusetts, in communities peopled by those who had made up the "Great Migration" out of the South of nearly six million black Americans during the first six decades of the twentieth century.[22] These migrants were both fleeing that region's increasingly rigid, violence-filled racial apartheid and pursuing the jobs and greater sense of freedom that the country's industrialising regions offered. In 1900, roughly 90 per cent of the country's 8.8 million black Americans (compared to a total of 66.3 million whites) lived in the South, most still in the isolated towns and hamlets of the rural South.[23] By 1960, 48 per cent of America's 19 million blacks lived in its northern-western regions.

True, their critical massing outside the South, and especially the suffocating isolation of the rural South, gave black Americans access to the income that a far more variegated job structure provided; to elementary, secondary and college- and university-level education, as well as to training and credentials; to participation in politics – albeit largely minimal – and, thus, to developing a certain level of political influence; to stimulating news and information about the larger American society and the world; and, in individual and mass terms, to acquiring a level of cultural sophistication that was absolutely crucial to making black Americans, as a whole, a modern people.

Furthermore, the Great Migration was the vital component in the psychological recovery of blacks, over time, from the devastating impact of the US Supreme Court's 1896 *Plessy vs. Ferguson* decision legalising racism, and in enabling them to develop the resources for an all-out assault on America's legal structure of apartheid.[24] Among other things, these struggles made possible the creation of a broadly educated black middle class and a stable working class whom Southern racists could not reach physically or economically to intimidate into surrendering their civil rights activism.

This development created, and then continually nourished, family, professional and institutional links between Northern and Southern blacks that ensured Northern blacks would remain committed to considering the civil rights struggle in the South as the front line of the overall black freedom struggle and thus, worthy of having "first call" on their attention, psychic energy, and resources. The critical mass of black people resulted in city after city producing civil rights and other civic organisations of a strength that would likely have been quickly destroyed by the Southern racist power structure. And the mass movement of blacks out of the South gave them access to Northern white-liberal money and expertise that helped in funding numerous black civil rights and communal activities locally as well as in the South.

Yet, what the black newcomers to the North also immediately discovered was what the relatively small number of blacks living outside the South before the twentieth century had always known: the North was no racial Promised Land. Most Northern whites considered black Americans as, at best, interlopers or, more often, invaders who refused to stay confined to the ghettos which public agencies and private institutions had created to cage them in. Blacks in the North and West endured sustained, pervasive levels of discrimination in every sector of American life: in job opportunities in both the private and public sectors; in housing and public schools; in shopping and restaurants; in access to communal recreational and cultural offerings; in access to public and private colleges and universities; and in their treatment by the white-run criminal justice system – from policemen to prosecutors, prison guards, judges and wardens.

The corrosive attitudes that this process of inclusion based on white supremacist notions bred in many blacks was perfectly captured in an incident recounted by Malcolm X's African-American biographer Alex Haley. Noting that on one occasion Malcolm had driven to the airport to pick him up, Haley writes, "I remember one incident within the airport that showed me how Malcolm X never lost his racial perspective. Waiting for my baggage, we witnessed a touching family reunion scene as part of which several cherubic little (white) children romped and played, exclaiming in another language." It was apparently a family coming to visit relatives or to stay in the US. Malcolm drew a bitter conclusion from the scene. He told Haley, "By tomorrow night, they'll know how to say their first English word – *nigger*."[25]

The anger of blacks at their experience in the North comes through repeatedly in the speeches of Malcolm X, especially in his conflating, to negative effect, all Northern whites with "white liberals" as a group. His speeches rarely focus on the injustices of a region hundreds of miles distant from his base in New York; and he actually spent very little time in the South. Instead, his words often concentrated on his audiences' often bitter, maddening lived experiences of "Northern-style racism".

And black Americans understood who Malcolm X was and who were the specific cohort of black Americans he most directly spoke to and for. Like all black achievers, he embodied the powerful human capital of black Americans that white America, as a whole, had forever sought not just to ignore, but to suppress. But Malcolm also most directly represented the potential of the most disrespected, the most crisis-ridden of black Americans: the poor and those ensnared, as he himself had been, in a debilitating spiral of criminality. There he stood, an ex-convict with little formal education – as were a significant number of the men in the Nation of Islam – but who had shown himself to be a brilliant, charismatic orator and debater who could more than hold his own in a university forum or on a street-corner soapbox. In that regard, Malcolm X was both the complement of and the contrast to the backgrounds and lives of Martin Luther King, Jr and the rest of the civil rights movement's leadership, many of whom were highly formally educated and often led conventionally respectable lives.

This difference between Martin and Malcolm, however, was not a function of social class, as Malcolm often claimed it to be. White America's post-civil war commitment to white supremacy meant that most black Americans were born into poor families and that all black Americans were born into, and lived in, an environment of civic danger. Despite that burden, many millions of them, whether born poor or not, had been able to forge lives of relative comfort, stability and achievement. A significant number of others, however, had not escaped the consequences of the broken family and community environments that America's structure of apartheid still promoted. Some of them – women as well as men – found relief in the Nation of Islam, whose rigid ideological and behavioural framework explained and sheltered them from the dangerous past life they had endured and the pervasive and vicious psychological dynamics of white racism. Indeed, the rules of membership in the Nation required them to, in most respects, lead clean-living, conventionally bourgeois lives that not only isolated them from white American society, but also banned them from participating in significant measure in the civic life of black communities.

For many blacks, however, that latter fact, and the Nation of Islam's bizarre assertions about the origins of black and white people – which declared that whites, thousands and thousands of years ago, were created by an evil scientist as genetic mutations of blacks, "the Original People", and were devils who had taken over the world[26] – were overshadowed by the major contribution that Malcolm X made to the black freedom struggle during these years: he provided black Americans with a psychic safety valve for their anger.

By the early 1960s, that well of anger was deep, fed not just by the remembrance of the slave era or the late-nineteenth-century *Plessy* ruling. White America's betrayals during the decades from the First World War (1914–18), when the migration of blacks out of the South first swelled to flood-like proportions, to that very moment were becoming increasingly difficult to bear.

After all, black Americans were Americans, too. Like their white counterparts, they had entered the post-1945 era ready to enjoy the prosperity that America's new-found global dominance promised. Furthermore, bolstered by a keen sense of their own contributions and sacrifices – military and civilian – to the war effort, they were determined finally to secure the "inalienable rights" that the US Constitution had promised to all American citizens. That "challenge-demeanor",[27] as African-American Harvard scholar Martin Kilson put it, led to the civil rights movement's pitting its commitment to non-violent democratic reform against the white South's determination to using physical violence and economic intimidation to stop them. The set-pieces of these battles would quickly capture the attention and imagination of the world.

Elijah Muhammad's Nation of Islam stood aloof from the battle – or, rather, it said it did. In fact, led by Malcolm X, it constantly sniped at the civil rights movement from the sidelines, declaring through Malcolm's fiery rhetoric and the Nation of Islam's unbending hyper-masculine culture that non-violence was for cowards and people who had no pride in themselves. Blacks who supported and joined the movement were fools, dupes of a corrupt black leadership that had been bought and paid for by hypocritical white liberals and the administrations of presidents John F. Kennedy and Lyndon B. Johnson. Malcolm's rhetoric, by turns satirical, bluntly comedic, or coldly scathing, appealed to many blacks of all classes because he seemingly held nothing back. He "told it like it is", as a popular phrase of that time put it.

Of course, the Nation of Islam, especially during Malcolm X's years, considered itself in competition with the mainstream civil rights groups for the allegiance of black Americans. That was not actually true; the competition was completely lopsided, even as Malcolm's flash and fervour steadily increased the Nation of Islam's membership from the 1950s into the 1960s, pushing its enrolment to above the 60,000 mark,[28] and drawing significant attention from the white media. Indeed, Malcolm never quite understood a striking fact: that most black Americans – even many of the non-Nation of Islam blacks who cheered his harsh anti-white rhetoric – considered his role as a black leader in quite limited terms.

As a psychic safety valve, Malcolm X was for many blacks a surrogate who could powerfully express their justifiable anger at having continually to struggle against the second-class status to which white America had consigned them – "the denial of the right to simply be – the perpetual state of otherness".[29] Malcolm was a magnificent, magnetic symbol of black Americans' will to resist, to persevere. But he was not the only such symbol. He was not the only conduit through which black anger was being expressed. In fact, the civil rights movement itself was also a psychic safety valve for the release of black anger about white racism. Try as he might, Malcolm X could not obscure the fact that the civil rights movement was a mass movement, dwarfing in numbers and support the Nation of Islam and other "militant" black groups. Nor could he deny with any effect that the adherence of the movement's activists to non-violence in the face of white racist brutality was not cowardice or foolishness. On the contrary, it expressed an extraordinary courage and sense of purpose: the individual and group discipline required was itself a means of channelling individual and group anger to a positive purpose and, in so doing, asserting the true worth of black Americans.[30]

In other words, Malcolm never understood the singular force from within black America that he was up against. That force was black American patriotism. Black American patriotism was not like the often superficial, flag-waving patriotism of white Americans, which depended on obscuring the many wrongs of the American past and present. On the contrary, black American patriotism pledged – in full awareness of America's flaws – allegiance to America as it could be in the future. It pledged allegiance not to a feckless integration that was merely a cover for white hegemony, but rather to the idea of true equality of opportunity and tolerance among American citizens. Black American patriotism both sprang from and nourished the faith and the hope that were the true foundations of the existence of black Americans.

That equanimity and optimism were the polar opposite of the Nation of Islam's reliance on anger, a rigid patriarchy that falsely exalted men and suppressed women, and a bitter isolation from mainstream white and black American societies. The former is the attitude that black Americans had continually had to reconsider and re-adopt all through their long sojourn in America and through the debates among them, from the American War of Independence in 1776 down to the present, about whether they should emigrate or stay in America. The debate that took shape in the 1950s and 1960s – best represented by such words as "integration", "black nationalism", and "Pan-Africanism", and by Malcolm X and Martin Luther King, Jr – would settle the issue conclusively.

Ironically, neither man would live to see black Americans do to the black nationalist and Pan-Africanist sentiment that Malcolm X/El Hajj Malik El-Shabazz had expressed so powerfully, what they had done to Garveyism – and to white Christianity. African Americans incorporated these ideas as a means of spiritual sustenance and cultural expression into their struggle to gain their full rights as American citizens. There would be no significant support among black Americans for pleading their case to the United Nations, as Malcolm had consistently urged. They rightly considered that approach wildly impractical: why would the governments of Africa and Arab nations – necessarily consumed with their own pressing post-independence challenges of nation-building and the enormously complicated process of jockeying for position and advantage in international affairs – spend their political capital taking on the rich and powerful Uncle Sam over an "internal" American matter? Furthermore, black Americans understood all too well that asking foreign governments to help them plead their case in an international – rather than American – forum would undermine the very thing that they had always been insistent on: their gaining the full rights of their American citizenship. Malcolm, along with other American black nationalists and Pan-Africanists of the 1960s and early 1970s, loved to declare: We are an African people! But, in fact, the political and cultural actions of the mass of black Americans then, and over the ensuing half-century, show conclusively that black Americans themselves modified that statement to declare: We are an American people of African descent!

Concluding Reflections

Malcolm X was destined to break with Elijah Muhammad and the Nation of Islam, after discovering the falsehood of the man and his jerry-rigged ideology. Even a cursory reading of the arc of Malcolm's life and thought during his last half-decade makes that clear. His restless intellect and curiosity, and the tumult of the moment, drove him to it. And the great result of his hajj to Mecca in March 1964 – his discovery that faith in humanity and hope for humanity were as essential as racial pride and racial anger in the fight for social justice – intensified his determination to aid the black freedom struggle in the US, as well as the global freedom struggle.

But Malcolm X – now largely consumed with dodging the numerous assassination plots that the Nation of Islam had launched against him, and simply trying to earn enough money to provide for his family – had too little time left to develop a coherent body of thought or an organisational framework to carry on his life work. Moreover, his post-Mecca rejection of the anti-white rhetoric which, frankly, had been so integral to his rise to public prominence; his advocacy of blacks becoming involved in politics; his assertion that orthodox Islam could become a powerful force in resolving America's racial problems; and his urging that black Americans, with the help of African and Arab nations, take their case for human rights to the United Nations, were all wildly disorienting to many of his long-time supporters. After his assassination in February 1965, the organisations that Malcolm had established after his break from the Nation of Islam – Muslim Mosque Inc. and the Organisation of Afro-American Unity – were soon reduced to complete irrelevance.

Nonetheless, consider this: Malcolm X/El Hajj Malik El-Shabazz was a man in the process of becoming. His twisting and turning this way and that – that, too, is part of the "tradition" of the black American freedom struggle's continual confrontation with the shape-shifting nature of anti-black racism in America. If his public search for a solution was more dramatic than, say, that of W.E.B. Du Bois (see Morris in this volume) or, yes, of Martin Luther King, Jr, it is because it was compressed into a tragically short few months. That certainly does not detract from the stature that Malcolm X well deserves: as an enduring Pan-African symbol of the necessity of resistance to injustice.

14

MAYA ANGELOU: PAN-AFRICANISM WITHIN A POLITICS OF RESPECTABILITY

Alease Brown

MAYA ANGELOU'S AWARD-WINNING WORK as a novelist and poet, her decades-long sisterhood with African-American media mogul Oprah Winfrey, and the consistent accolades bestowed upon her – not least those from American presidents – have resulted in her veneration as the most American of icons. She is revered as a champion of the human spirit, and as one who embodies the potential and promise of the American ideals of opportunity and equality for all, regardless of race or gender. A somewhat different portrait emerges from her biographies, however.

Relying primarily on the *The Heart of a Woman*[1] (1981) and *All God's Children Need Traveling Shoes*[2] (1986)[3], this essay will argue that Maya Angelou's years of civil rights activism – both in the US and on the African continent – demonstrate a deep commitment to an ethics of globalised black nationalism, rather than an ethics of quintessential American patriotism. I will also argue that Angelou's global black nationalist activism was constrained by her identity as a black woman. Angelou attempted to negotiate the boundaries of her identity as an African-American woman during the liberation struggle of the 1960s. However, her activist career ultimately appears to have been stymied by the social politics of her era which she absorbed.

New York and New Maya

Maya Angelou's political activism progressed rapidly during the early 1960s along a trajectory of conscientisation, participation and leadership. In 1960, she moved from California to New York with the intention of developing her craft as a writer by joining the Harlem Writers Guild. After living in New York for a short time, the struggle for liberation energising the black community in America drew Angelou away from the world of the arts and into the world of political activism. She made the decision to leave the literary and performing world permanently.

Initially, her involvement in political activism included passive support of "Fair Play for Cuba", an organisation supporting Fidel Castro's revolutionary efforts in the 1950s. Angelou's passive support (through membership and donations) turned into active support when she took to campaigning in the streets of Harlem in support of Castro. Her activism then shifted further, from rallying to organising. After hearing Nobel Peace laureate Martin Luther King, Jr deliver a sermon at a church in Harlem, Maya and African-American friend Godfrey Cambridge[4] felt compelled to participate in the burgeoning civil rights movement. Sitting together after the church service, they decided that they would get their artist friends together and produce a show to benefit King's main funding organisation, the Southern Christian Leadership Conference (SCLC).

Angelou took the lead in bringing this idea to fruition. She immediately met with Bayard Rustin, Stanley Levinson and Jack Murray at the northern headquarters of the SCLC in Harlem, to seek permission to fundraise in their name. After securing their approval, Angelou spearheaded the production of the *Cabaret for Freedom*, as the show was called. It opened with celebrities such as Oscar-winning actor Sidney Poitier, Ossie Davis, Ruby Dee and celebrated playwright Lorraine Hansberry in attendance. *Cabaret* became an immediate sensation. The proprietor of the Village Gate theatre – the show's venue – offered the use of the theatre free of charge for five weeks. By the end of the show's run, actors and musicians had been employed and paid, a marketing campaign designed and executed, and funds had been raised for the SCLC and the work of the civil rights struggle. This had all been driven by Maya Angelou. Her work managing the performers, overseeing administrative functions, coordinating logistics, gaining the support of the public, generating excitement and positive energy for the civil rights cause, and successfully raising funds confirmed her new role as civil rights organiser.

As a direct result of Angelou's work with *Cabaret for Freedom*, Bayard Rustin, who led the SCLC's Harlem office, chose Angelou as his replacement when he left the organisation in June 1960.[5] During the time that she headed the office of the SCLC between June 1960 and January 1961, Martin Luther King, Jr came to know and value Angelou for her work on behalf of the organisation and the movement.

These were the experiences that shaped Angelou's development as a black activist. Her support of the Cuban freedom struggle, as well as her activism on behalf of the civil rights movement, whose leaders were regularly involved in controversially breaking the law through civil disobedience and protest, reflected Angelou's bent towards a globalist and black nationalist agenda rather than mainstream American establishment politics. Her roles during this period – signing petitions, donating money, appearing in the streets, fundraising and organising events – were not uncommon for black women at the time. Angelou could undertake these roles as a woman in 1960 without contestation, and was able to thrive as an activist.

Resistance and Respectability

Though Angelou was professionally engaged in combating a structural politics that denied freedom to black people, at the same time she was inextricably entangled in a personal politics of black womanhood that placed constraints upon her life and self-actualisation. The latter has been described by African-American historian Evelyn Brooks Higginbotham as a "politics of respectability",[6] which was characterised by adherence to a set of social mores that generally mirrored the Victorian moralism of white middle-class America. Sexual propriety, behavioural decorum, neatness and comportment were seen as outward, visible markers signifying an inward sense of one's worth. Adherence to such mores was also seen as both uplifting of the African-American community and as demonstrating to white Americans that blacks could be respectable and should be respected. Throughout the first half of the twentieth century, it was respectable character – not wealth, education or social standing – that endowed black women such as African-American civil rights icon Rosa Parks, with dignity and lent their deeds far-reaching impact. The politics of respectability employed by blacks was deemed necessary for gaining moral authority in the face of racism and the legalised contempt shown to them by white society. What it meant for the individual has been expressed by the African–American journalist Kimberly Foster as follows: "I am worthy of respect … You don't treat me like an equal person, but I know that I am an equal person, and because I am an equal person, I'm going to fight for my rights. I'm going to demand equality. I'm not going to let you treat me like a second-class citizen."[7]

The politics of respectability extended to behaviour within personal relationships. Black women had historically been captive to a racist system that allowed them to be sexually assaulted by white men at will. This sexual exposure made them vulnerable to being perceived by the white majority as unchaste and impure, and consequently as unworthy of respect. Thus, the conventional morality of the marriage relationship became a powerful symbol of respectability for black women. Though Harlem's artists and performers in Angelou's milieu had adopted far less rigid sexual standards since the time of the "Harlem Renaissance" of the 1920s,[8] the institution of marriage remained, in 1960, the centre of a raced and gendered moral order that established a code of acceptable sexual conduct.[9]

Personal relationships and marriage – under the logic of respectability politics – were subject to standards prescribed by the dominant culture. As Angelou describes it, this meant, for men, "property control and economic provision", and for women, "[receiving] economic support and [providing] sexual and domestic service".[10] The politics of respectability accommodated the fact that, unlike their white counterparts, black women engaged in various work roles outside the home and contributed economically to the support of the household. Despite male control and female domestic and sexual service in the home, interpersonal relationship standards of respectability remained intact.

It is telling that at the point in her published account when Angelou became the head of the Northern regional office of the nation's most visible civil rights organisation in 1960, she turns away from telling the story of her involvement in activist circles, to recounting the developments under way in her personal life. The level of responsibility that Angelou achieved less than a year after entering the life of social activism was as much as she might ever expect to accomplish within the structures of the civil rights movement as a woman organiser. Professionally, Angelou had peaked at the age of 32. Since she was no longer a performer, but now a "bright young woman executive",[11] her commitment to liberation and achieving full citizenship for African Americans demanded an embrace of the traditional, respectable family structure. Her political commitments necessitated her making a personal commitment to marriage. Though as a performer she could have a lover, as a leader within the civil rights movement it was essential for her to have a husband.

Angelou described in her narrative the sustained tension entailed by her black womanhood during her time at the SCLC, as she negotiated the world of public politics and her own personal politics. She was an organiser and an executive "dedicated to justice, Fair Play for Cuba, and a member of the Harlem Writers Guild, but also an unmarried woman with rent to pay and a fifteen-year-old son" to look after.[12]

She described her first visit to a favourite local pub, where the bartender enquired whether she was a "working girl" or if she had a job. She "knew better than to act offended",[13] and simply told the barman that she had a job and lived alone with her son nearby. "Appearances to the contrary," Angelou wrote, "there is a code of social behaviour among Southern blacks (and almost all of us fall into that category, willingly or not) which is as severe and distinct as a seventeenth-century minuet or an African initiation ritual."[14] There was a protocol for a single woman in a new social situation: "She should be sensual, caring for her appearance, but taking special care to minimise her sexuality."[15]

Angelou met Thomas Allen at the pub, and dated him. Allen was a man who did not engage in conversation, was not interested in politics or social justice, and did not regard Angelou's work with the SCLC as anything more than a job. Angelou was not in love with him. Despite these things, because Allen was a strong provider and a satisfying lover, Angelou proposed to him.[16] Allen then took charge of deciding when, where and how they would be married without consulting Angelou. She noted, "The decision to marry me automatically gave him authority to plan all our lives [his, hers and her son's]. I ignored the twinge which tried to warn me that I should stop and do some serious thinking."[17]

Angelou's marriage to Allen never happened, however. Before it could, she met and fell in love with a more promising candidate to confer upon her the requisite respectability. Vusumzi Make was a South African freedom fighter whose oratorical skills were described by Angelou as having the force of those of Martin Luther King, Jr. Make was in New York with other South Africans seeking an audience at the United Nations. His eloquence and passionate involvement in the apartheid struggle in South Africa captivated Angelou. Make was equally captivated by her. Days after their first meeting, Make proposed. On the verge of a final rejection of his proposal, Angelou reconsidered "the facts":[18] that ending her engagement with Allen and marrying Make would grant her "a life of beckoning adventure and Africa."[19] That "Make needed [her]" and that "[she] would be a help to him".[20] That if she let Make go, and he became involved with white women in Europe on his forthcoming visit there, "[she] might be betraying the entire struggle."[21]

Within one week of meeting Make in January 1961, Angelou broke off her engagement to Allen and became engaged to "Vus". Weeks later, Angelou and Make were husband and wife, though, interestingly, the marriage was never legally formalised. Within months, Angelou, her son Guy, and Make were settling themselves into their home in the Egyptian capital of Cairo, where the politically exiled Make would be based while working for the Pan Africanist Congress of South Africa (PAC).

Marriage represented for Angelou the next step in her career as a social activist. She had married Make for socially approved reasons. She loved him, he needed her, and she would be a great help to him and his work. At the same time, along with respectability, marriage to a prominent liberation fighter advanced Angelou's standing as a social activist. She had secured the respectability that was requisite for black women in the civil rights movement. Furthermore, though she may have peaked professionally as a single-woman activist, as a wife alongside her freedom-fighting husband there was no limit to the work of justice that might come to include her, nor to the places to which the struggle for justice might take her. There would be adventure, and even Africa! The fact that Angelou's marriage to Make was not legally formalised due to Maya's demurral is framed in her narrative as a mark of romantic sincerity. Another reading might be that the successful and fiercely independent Angelou was not as interested in the formal commitment of marriage to Make as she was in the privileges that she gained from the appearance of being married to him.

Radicalisation

Angelou implies in her narrative that Stanley Levinson and Jack Murray at the SCLC had difficulty accepting her as an activist equal. Rather, regarding her as an entertainer, they installed men in the office who undermined Maya's authority there.[22] Thus, after becoming engaged to Make, Angelou resigned from the SCLC and ceased to work outside the home. She worked tirelessly in the home "trying to be a good housewife".[23] Angelou prepared gourmet meals, cleaned exhaustively to satisfy Vus's stringent standards, and eagerly joined him in the marital bed. But it was not a satisfying life. Maya noted: "I wanted to be a wife and to create a beautiful home to make my man happy, but there was more to life than being a diligent maid with a permanent pussy."[24] In a short span, she refocused her energy on activism.

Angelou and friends Abbey Lincoln and Rosa Guy, who were experienced in supporting various civil rights groups, decided that what was needed was one more organisation. They planned that their Cultural Association for Women of African Heritage (CAWAH) would be "on call to perform, give fashion shows, read poetry, sing, [or] write for any organisation ... that wanted to put on a fund-raising affair".[25] Their "group of talented black women ... would make themselves available to all the other groups".[26]

CAWAH's mandate almost immediately changed, however. When Patrice Lumumba, the first prime minister of the Democratic Republic of the Congo, was assassinated on 17 January 1961, Angelou and Rosa Guy agreed that it was necessary to show solidarity with those on the African continent. "We've got to let the Congolese ... know that we are with them."[27] Angelou convened a meeting of CAWAH. The decision to pursue a Pan-Africanist agenda split the fledgling organisation. The six Pan-African members who remained set about organising a demonstration at the United Nations secretariat in New York to protest against the assassination.

After determining their planned course of action, Angelou and Abbey Lincoln went to Harlem to address a gathering at the local black nationalist centre in order to gain the community's support for the demonstration. On 15 February 1961 hundreds of people marched in protest,[28] including those from other black nationalist organisations.[29] The streets leading to the UN building in Manhattan were filled with angry black marchers. A small group of between 25 and 75 people[30] went into the gallery of the UN General Assembly. Instead of the silent symbolic demonstration that had been planned, a raucous melee ensued among the protesters. The violent group was ejected from the UN building, whereupon they rejoined the crowd outside. Hordes of marchers, who chanted and threw rocks and snow at guards and police, continued on from the UN to the Belgian permanent mission to the UN, before police dispersed them. "The day had proven that Harlem was in commotion and the rage was beyond the control of the [middle-class] NAACP [National Association for the Advancement of Colored People], the SCLC or the Urban League."[31]

The UN protest further revealed the ways in which Angelou's identity as an organiser coexisted in tension with her identity as a black woman. At the time of the creation of the CAWAH, numerous organisations in New York were being established to fight for justice for black people. CAWAH was distinct in that its membership and leadership were composed exclusively of black women, and was not religious. Its founders made clear that they had no ambitions to provide direct leadership on any civil rights issue. Though the women wished to participate meaningfully in the struggle, they sought to observe the cultural dictate that leadership and control – particularly in the public sphere – were largely the preserve of men.

Nonetheless, when an international calamity involving African people arose, the dynamic female founders of CAWAH unhesitatingly led the public in responding to the Congo crisis. Even their planned response, though, firmly adhered to the politics of respectability: demonstrators wore symbolic mourning attire, and were asked simply to stand silently (and respectfully) together in the official halls of power. The women's attempts to defer to respectable notions of public leadership and protest protocol left them astonished at the show of support that they received from Harlem's black community. The black residents of Harlem deemed their gender irrelevant, and embraced the eruption of aggressive tactics during the demonstration. Having witnessed the protest turn into an uprising, the women of CAWAH acknowledged that what they had accomplished was the inaugural act of an irrepressible, working-class mass movement. It was a movement of impassioned and willing people desperately in need of leadership and organisation.

We must pause here briefly, and take a broader view of this historic moment. The background of Martin Luther King, Jr – he was a Baptist preacher, born into a long line of Baptist preachers, groomed to lead impassioned ideologues, and bred on the American South's dehumanising treatment of black people – could be viewed as having prepared him for a moment of destiny in 1955 following the arrest of Rosa Parks. King was new to Montgomery, Alabama, having arrived from Atlanta, and was relatively unknown. He was 26 years old, was well educated with a doctorate from Boston University, and had a stable and attractive family. The local civil rights leadership believed that he would be a good face of the movement. But King stepped into the role with unique gifts and abilities, and with a sense of his own significance as a leader. By his handling of the issue of bus transportation in Alabama, he would influence the laws of the nation, and acquire international influence, winning the Nobel Peace Prize in 1964 at the age of 35, the youngest recipient of the award until then.[32]

Just as it might be said that King met with a moment of destiny in Alabama, which changed his life and, to some extent, changed the world, it might also be said that Maya Angelou encountered such a moment in the wake of the UN protest against Lumumba's assassination in 1961.

Angelou was a six-foot-tall performer, with charisma and magnetism. She was an autodidact, and spoke multiple languages. Her impressive intellect was often demonstrated by her memorisation of every single line of every part in the productions in which she appeared. She was a woman who was well travelled, and who had awareness and knowledge of the universal plight of African people. She had been raised in rural Stamps in Arkansas, but was at home in several global cities. She knew what it meant to struggle to pay the rent, but easily associated with the wealthy. She was a Pan-African black nationalist, but befriended non-racists of every colour. Her name came to be recognised from the east to the west coast of the United States. She was a mother, a doer, a prolific writer and energetic activist, made brilliant rhetorical use of language, and she was one of "the people" of the working class, not having been born into the black middle class.

After organising the UN protest in 1961, Angelou was perfectly positioned, with respect to time, place, interest, temperament and talent, to organise and lead the masses of black working-class people in their strident demand for liberation. Remarkably, she did not. It was 1961, and Angelou was constrained by her personal politics which dictated that black women did not do such things.

Returning to Maya's narrative, instead of her taking the lead in organising, we see a disavowal of that responsibility. Angelou and Rosa Guy approached Malcolm X – "the most radical leader in the country"[33] (see Daniels in this volume) – to "lay the situation in his lap ... it would be a relief to shift the responsibility",[34] Maya later wrote. The women told Malcolm X that they had organised the UN protest, and that it was much larger and more volatile than they had anticipated. He, and the Nation of Islam, they urged, should step into the leadership void and organise the long-suffering black masses who were now ready and willing to be led.[35] Malcolm X declined to help them to organise protests, saying, "Muslims do not demonstrate."[36] He reprimanded them, and advised them that protests at "the United Nations ... will not win freedom for anyone", before giving them alternative counsel and solid encouragement.[37]

Subsequently, conservative mainstream black leaders publicly decried the UN protest as irresponsible and disrespectful.[38] The "unknown"[39] male leader of a different group claimed responsibility for organising the UN protest. Angelou went back to the stage to perform for a brief period. Thereafter, she followed her husband, Make, to Africa.

One wonders, by way of comparison, what the world might have looked like today if Martin Luther King, Jr had been unconvinced of his power and significance, and had declined to go against the grain of his culture when a moment of destiny presented itself to him.

Mrs Make in Egypt

Make took Angelou to Africa, who was then exposed to the world of the African liberation struggle. She met freedom fighters from Uganda, Kenya, Tanganyika (now Tanzania), Northern and Southern Rhodesia (now Zambia and Zimbabwe), Basutoland (now Lesotho) and Swaziland. Yet, the confines of the role of dutiful wife were even more pronounced for her living as an African liberation fighter in Cairo than they had been in the US.

Make's work required him to make contacts, which meant entertaining guests frequently in their home. These occasions were elaborate and managed by Angelou. Make's work required formal appearances as well. She befriended other wives at formal occasions, and while their African husbands made allies or enemies in other nations, the wives were tangential, like "foot soldiers, bringing up the rear in a war whose declaration we had not known, left on the battlefield after a peace was achieved, in which we had not participated".[40]

Angelou's inner struggle, between being an engaged activist and a dutiful wife, continued. Since she had been shaped in the belief that respectability was the handmaiden of moral authority, and that this dual force was key to black liberation, she remained submissive to Make. Commitment to the struggle, more than love of the man, kept Angelou's resolve firm to inhabit the role of servile wife. Her husband, however, was not possessed of so firm a resolve to live out his assigned role of head of the home and financial provider. Make's moral authority was undercut by his infidelities during his travels. His leadership of the home was compromised by his running up debt and exposing the family to the risk of financial embarrassment. The framework of the marriage began to disintegrate, providing Angelou with a suitable justification for recasting her identity in Cairo from Mrs Make, wife of the freedom fighter, to Maya Angelou Make, the black American.

Without consulting her husband, and despite his anticipated objection, Angelou secured a job, becoming the associate editor for African affairs at a new English-language weekly, the *Arab Observer*. She had no background in journalism, or in African affairs, so Angelou studied newspapers, journals and essays. She supplemented this with information provided by Make, who had direct knowledge of the intricacies of African history and politics. Angelou's articles were authoritative and insightful. She gained the respect of her office colleagues and of the broader press corps in Cairo. Before long, Angelou had embraced the additional opportunity to write commentary for Radio Egypt. She was the only woman journalist in Cairo and possibly in all Egypt. Despite the gender, language, cultural and religious barriers that she encountered, Maya succeeded in delivering news and commentary, and in becoming an authority on African affairs.

Angelou did not succeed, however, in performing the role of African and American wife. When her relationships at the *Arab Observer* became strained around US entanglements with Russia over Cuba, Angelou determined that it was time to leave both Vusumzi Make and Egypt. Her work in Cairo had created an opportunity for her in Liberia's Department of Information. Angelou would pursue her Pan-African ambitions on her own, without a husband.

En route to Liberia, Angelou's son, Guy, was involved in a serious car accident after the two arrived in Ghana to enrol him in university. His recuperation period altered Angelou's plans to travel to Liberia. She took up residence in Accra during Guy's convalescence, and her short stay became a three-year sojourn in the country then led by Kwame Nkrumah (see Biney in this volume).

Returning Home – to Herself – in Ghana

In 1957 Ghana became the first black African nation to achieve its formal independence from colonial rule. Ghana became an inspiration to oppressed people throughout the world. It beckoned as a place of enticing possibility, for African Americans in particular. Many black Americans made the trip to the West African country; some were drawn to Ghana with the hope of permanently building a life there. Thus, when Maya arrived in Accra, she found an existing, small, yet tightly woven network of black American émigrés.

Angelou worked with the Institute of African Studies at the University of Accra, and taught in the music and drama department there.[41] She also freelanced for the *Ghanaian Times*. She embraced her life in Ghana. She braided her hair, wore customary African attire and acquired fluency in the Fanti language. Her life in Accra was the embodiment of the ideals of Pan-Africanism.

Life in Ghana resurrected Angelou's organising impulse. When Martin Luther King, Jr rallied black Americans to join a "March on Washington" for jobs and freedom in the US in August 1963, Angelou helped organise a concurrent Ghanaian "March of Solidarity" on the US embassy in Accra. In an extraordinary coincidence, during the early morning hours, as the march was set to begin, word came to the assembled group that fellow émigré W.E.B. Du Bois, aged 95, had died. Du Bois and his wife, Shirley Graham Du Bois, had exiled themselves to Accra in October 1961, and planned to spend the remainder of their lives there. Angelou was among those leading the march for justice in Accra which also honoured the life of a towering intellectual champion of racial equality.

In Accra, Angelou's path again crossed that of Malcolm X, who was on a post-hajj tour of several African nations in April 1964. In the Accra living room of another African-American exile, Julian Mayfield, Malcolm revealed that he planned to bring the status of black Americans before the UN General Assembly. He said, "If our cause was debated by all the world's nations ... America would be forced to face up to its discriminatory policies ... If South African blacks can petition the UN against their country's policy of apartheid, then America should be shown on the world's stage as a repressionist and bestial racist nation."[42]

Malcolm X told the group of black exiles, who knew of his expulsion from the Nation of Islam, that he would be founding a new organisation to pursue his announced agenda. Inspired by Africa's Organisation of African Unity (OAU), which had been created on the continent in May 1963, his new endeavour would be called the Organisation of Afro-American Unity (OAAU). Malcolm requested that Angelou help him with this new project.[43] The former Nation of Islam preacher was travelling through Africa to confer with African leaders and to gain their support for the OAAU and his UN strategy. Angelou and her small but influential circle of exiles used every political contact in their network to ensure the success of Malcolm's visit to Ghana. As a result of their efforts, Malcolm X was able to meet with cabinet ministers, members of the diplomatic corps, and, finally, President Kwame Nkrumah himself.

The reunion between Maya Angelou and Malcolm X in Ghana can be viewed as a kind of centripetal force, turning both of them around, and incorporating the two activists into the work of liberating black people globally. Their Accra meeting was an almost complete reversal of their previous encounter in New

York. During their first meeting, Maya's identity had been precariously balanced between performing as an activist leader while simultaneously performing as a submissive wife. During their second meeting, Maya's identity was firmly grounded. She was a woman living a politics of Pan-Africanism in place of a rejected politics of respectability. Malcolm's identity had moved in the opposite direction. During their first meeting, he had been rooted in his membership of the Nation of Islam and his status as favourite son of the Nation's patriarch, Elijah Muhammad. Malcolm was a black man who did not associate with "white devils". By the time of their second meeting in Accra, Malcolm X had been rejected by the Nation of Islam and Elijah Muhammad, and he had subsequently renounced the anti-white teachings of his former organisation as false. He was now a Muslim, not a black Muslim, open to partnership with whites, with whom he had had positive interactions in Mecca during his transformational hajj (see Daniels in this volume).

Maya and Malcolm's strategies had also reversed. During their first meeting in New York, it was Maya who had wrestled with the issue of how best to serve the interests of black people, and who had requested Malcolm's help in view of her own limitations. During their second meeting in Accra, it was Malcolm X, wrestling with the issue of how best to serve the interests of black people, who requested Maya's help as an organiser, in view of his own limitations.

Their stance on the UN had also been reversed. During their first meeting, Malcolm X had told Maya, with reference to protest action, that "going to the United Nations ... will not win freedom for anyone".[44] During their second meeting, Malcolm's entire organisational strategy was now based on UN intervention, while Maya had abandoned this strategy.

These coincidental encounters, with Du Bois and Malcolm X, as well as the echoing methodologies, underscore the ways in which Maya Angelou's life and outlook were interconnected with black radical thought, with the liberation struggle, and with the most influential leaders of the civil rights movement. These encounters again raise the question: What if Maya Angelou had not felt confined to a customary gender role?

Returning Home – to the Struggle – in America

After Malcolm X left Accra, Angelou began considering her own return to the US. "I had begun to feel that I was not in my right place [in Ghana]."[45] Also, the political climate in the country was shifting. "It was a known fact that anti-government forces were aligning themselves ... to bring down the regime of Kwame Nkrumah."[46] Added to this, Angelou's son was anxious to gain distance from her close mothering. The coalescence of her inner stirrings, Ghana's political instability and Guy's rejection of her mothering determined Maya to make the decision to leave Accra and return to the US. She would continue with her political activism, she decided, working with Malcolm X and the Organisation of Afro-American Unity.

Angelou flew back to the US from Ghana in February 1965. She landed in New York en route to San Francisco, where she had plans to visit her family before returning to New York. She called Malcolm X during her New York lay-over. Malcolm offered to pick her up from the airport. She told him there was no need; she was continuing on to California and would return to New York in one month. She would call him in the next week. Two days after their telephone conversation, while Angelou was in San Francisco, Malcolm X was assassinated.[47] Maya was shattered. And her career as a Pan-Africanist social activist was never resumed.

Concluding Reflections

Maya Angelou's significance as a Pan-Africanist lies primarily in her being one of the few black women leaders in the US whose convictions culminated in her migration to Africa, albeit temporarily. Though her radical politics were hampered in large degree by her personal politics, which limited black women from full participation in leadership positions in the public sphere, Angelou nonetheless seized the opportunity to exercise the methods of leadership available to her in this historical epoch. She used these methods skilfully to accomplish her vocation of working for the cause of freedom. Maya's social activism – her support of radical positions, her organisation of a protest march on the streets of New York, and her work in Egypt and Ghana – undoubtedly influenced the more radical generation of women activists who followed in her footsteps from the late 1960s.

It is both notable and lamentable that though Maya Angelou ardently believed in, and campaigned for, both the black nationalist and Pan-African agendas, both failed to serve her as a woman during her own era. The demand for respect for people of African descent stopped short of recognising that equal levels of respect were due to black women in their roles other than that of wife. Maya – the brilliant activist – was never affirmed by her peers as a leader of the people.

Angelou's activism provides a millennial generation with a threefold lesson. Firstly, she made herself available to do the work that needed to be done: from organising a show, to running a non-profit organisation, to reporting on African affairs. Though she may not have had prior experience, she possessed a willingness and determination to make her activism real in whatever ways that her involvement could be beneficial. Secondly, Angelou's activism maintained a Pan-African ethic. Her involvement consistently reflected a consciousness of the link between African-American liberation and the freedom of Cuban, Congolese, Ghanaian and other peoples of African descent across the globe. Finally, in the current moment in Africa in which several leaders of nations are septuagenarians, the importance of giving way to successors of transition must be acknowledged. Where an individual has the talent and ability to enter into a leadership role, she or he would serve the community and the world well by daring to assume that role, whether or not custom and tradition deems the individual suitable to lead.

15

WALTER RODNEY: PAN-AFRICAN MARTYR

Annita Montoute

WALTER RODNEY WAS BORN IN GEORGETOWN, Guyana, on 23 March 1942 to working-class parents. His mother, Pauline Rodney, was a seamstress and housewife, while his father, Percival Rodney, was a self-employed tailor who worked part-time for a tailoring firm to supplement the family income.[1] Walter attended Queen's College, Guyana, and graduated in 1960 at the top of his class, winning an open scholarship to attend the University of the West Indies (UWI), Mona Campus, in Jamaica. He graduated from the UWI with a first-class honours degree in history in 1963. That same year, Rodney went on to pursue a doctorate in African history at the School of Oriental and African Studies (SOAS) at the University of London, graduating in 1966. He was only 24.[2] Walter thereafter took up a lectureship at the University of Dar es Salaam in Tanzania the following year. In January 1968, he returned to the Caribbean to work as a lecturer in African history at the UWI in Mona.

His tenure proved to be short-lived: he was banned from Jamaica by the administration of Hugh Shearer upon returning from a writers' conference in Montreal in October 1968. Rodney went back to the University of Dar es Salaam in 1969, this time in the position of senior lecturer. He returned to Georgetown in 1974 and applied for the post of professor of history at the University of Guyana. This post, and the head of the History department, were granted by the academic appointments committee, but blocked by the university's board of governors, which was influenced by the Forbes Burnham administration in an attempt to stop revolutionary and progressive elements "infiltrating" the university. From then on, until his assassination in 1980, Walter did not have a regular job or consistent source of income.[3]

Rodney seamlessly merged his academic pursuits and the struggle for a just society. Guyanese historian Winston McGowan, citing the International

Scientific Committee of the UNESCO *General History of Africa* noted that Rodney "was a scholar who recognised no distinction between academic concerns and service to society, between science and social commitment. He was concerned about people as well as archives, about the workplace as well as the classroom. He found time to be both a historian and a sensitive social reformer."[4] Jamaican scholar Ajamu Nangwaya shared similar sentiments when he said, "Rodney was not an arm-chair revolutionary who sequestered himself on the academic plantation theorising on what must be done to transform society. He waded into the messy, complicated and threatening world of practice to facilitate resistance to the violent forces of oppression."[5]

The early seeds of Rodney's progressive political ideas and activism had been planted by his father, when Walter distributed the material of the People's Progressive Party (PPP), a Marxist and multiracial grassroots organisation in Guyana, of which his father was an active member.[6] The PPP's aim was to mobilise both Indian and African Guyanese citizens against colonial rule.[7] As Nangwaya noted, this experience ensured that Rodney's political activism would be inclusive of the diverse races among the working class.[8]

The Historian

Rodney's career as a historian was shaped by his history teachers at the secondary and university levels. The young Walter found history to be among the most exciting and engaging subjects when he was taught by Guyanese teacher Robert Moore during his secondary school years at Queen's College. His career as a historian was later moulded by the outstanding Guyanese historian Elsa Goveia, who was the first female professor at the University of the West Indies. Goveia had been Rodney's teacher during his undergraduate years in Jamaica between 1960 and 1963.[9]

Walter acquired a reputation as an outstanding historian. McGowan posits that his main achievements were as a historian, researcher, writer and teacher of African and Caribbean history,[10] describing Rodney as one of the Caribbean's most "outstanding historians" and "one of the most renowned and international Guyanese scholars of all time".[11] Rodney's reputation as a distinguished scholar and historian stemmed from "the nature, quality and quantity of his historical writing".[12] His works can be grouped into four main categories: academic writing on African history; popular articles on African history and culture; lectures on Black Power; and his work on the Tanzanian Revolution.[13] Only 14 years after having completed his doctorate, Rodney had written three major books and published more than 70 journal articles, as well as dozens of pamphlets and booklets.[14]

The 1969 book *Groundings with My Brothers* was his first major publication. This was a collection of speeches and statements that Rodney had made while interacting with the poor on the streets of Kingston. *The History of the Upper Guinea Coast, 1545–1800* (1970), based on Rodney's doctoral thesis from the University of London, was his first major academic work.[15] This publication earned him the reputation of being "one of the leading authorities on the Trans-Atlantic slave trade from Africa to the Americas".[16] His 1973 book *How Europe Underdeveloped Africa* was Rodney's third major work[17] and his best-known. It was also, as the Walter Rodney Foundation noted, the "first major historical study of African development, in which Rodney challenged the prevailing assumptions about African history and put forth his own ideas and models for analyzing the history of oppressed peoples".[18] Other publications by Rodney included a 1976 monograph, *World War II and the Tanzanian Economy*;[19] *A History of the Guyanese Working People: 1881–1905*, (published posthumously in 1981); and the 1979 book *Guyanese Sugar Plantations in the Late Nineteenth Century: A Contemporary Description from the "Argosy"*.[20]

Rodney has been described as a "revisionist" historian, as he endeavoured to correct and rewrite history when he felt it had been misrepresented or misinterpreted.[21] As he noted, "The white man has already implanted numerous historical myths in the minds of black people; and those have to be uprooted, since they can act as a drag on revolutionary action in the present epoch."[22] Rodney adopted a multidisciplinary approach to the study of history, and his writings drew from the approaches and insights of the social sciences, particularly economics and political science. He also felt that the study of history was essential to understanding and solving current challenges. For example, he argued that the contemporary socio-economic problems plaguing Africa in his day, such as poverty and dependency, were a consequence of the transatlantic slave trade and European colonialism.[23]

But what took Rodney in the direction of African history? He had earlier said of his preoccupations as a scholar that he sought to advance the study of Caribbean history, and "to deepen my own understanding and our collective understanding of Caribbean history".[24]

Pan-Africanist Influences

Walter Rodney was influenced by the legacy of Pan-Africanism, but he also had an influence on Pan-Africanism in the Caribbean. Jamaican scholar Horace Campbell described him as an outstanding "scholar-activist in the tradition of W.E.B. Dubois, C.L.R. James, Marcus Garvey, or George Padmore" (see Morris, Cudjoe, Grant and Duggan in this volume) and as one of the Caribbean's most significant contributors to Pan-Africanism.[25] Similarly, Jamaican scholar Robert A. Hill described Rodney as:

> a Pan-African thinker and political activist in the fullest sense [who] stands out as a unique symbol and embodiment of a Pan-African revolutionary consciousness from the Caribbean. Whereas his own life was significantly shaped by the revival of Pan-African nationalism after 1957, it is equally true that his contribution ... was no less than the regeneration of the theory and practice of Pan-Africanism within the operational sphere of the Caribbean.[26]

Many scholars have justified the Pan-Africanist label conferred on Rodney. According to American academic Jeffrey Howison, Rodney "saw an inherent connection between the peoples of African descent, a connection that was not based upon a fixed geography or even on skin tone, but upon a collective history and consciousness rooted in experiences of slavery, colonisation, and oppression".[27] Belizean-American scholar Kurt Young maintained that "Rodney was foremost a Pan-Africanist [because] the essential thread throughout his lifework was his commitment to the eradication of political exploitation and economic underdevelopment in the African world ... African people in the Diaspora, and indeed ... all exploited people".[28]

Rodney's life and work found inspiration in the tenacity and resilience of enslaved black people, who resisted and mounted a struggle against slavery and subsequently established "free villages and emancipated spaces" away from the "racialized" spaces on the plantations (see Introduction and Beckles in this volume).[29] This influence is reflected in his monograph, *Guyanese Sugar Plantations in the Late Nineteenth Century.*[30] The origin of the word "grounding" used in the title *Groundings with My Brothers* lies in the quest of slaves to gain their freedom from various types of oppression. The term therefore connotes a space of self-determination.[31]

Rodney's contributions to Pan-Africanism were therefore shaped by intellectuals who "brought together the history of the black world and Pan-African agency with larger ideas about world-historical change".[32] Among these was C.L.R. James, who lauded the Haitian Revolution (1791–1804) and the black pioneer revolutionary, Toussaint L'Ouverture. James believed that Haitian slaves had actively taken their destiny into their own hands and, in a sense, he saw them as a "conscious 'proletariat'".[33] As Howison noted: "From James, Rodney also acquired a respect for the historical agency and the role of the masses during the transformative processes of social revolution."[34] Rodney was particularly influenced by James, when he informally became the latter's mentee while he was a student at SOAS (see Cudjoe in this volume).[35] Rodney's scholarship was also shaped by W.E.B. Du Bois, whose work also stressed the "agency" of black people. In the book *Black Reconstruction in America, 1860–1880*, first published in 1935,[36] Du Bois had portrayed black slaves as having influenced the course of history during the American Civil War (1861–65). He also felt that African slavery had been a key contributor to the development of the US and Europe, as well as to global capitalism in general (see Morris in this volume). Trinidadian scholar-statesman Eric Williams's 1944 *Capitalism and Slavery* further had a great impact on Walter.[37]

Rodney's Pan-African consciousness was fuelled, too, by the merging of the inspiration he received from black agency and broader historical circumstances and national developments. He saw these as a key part of the struggle against, and the dismantling of, European colonialism as well as of the economic injustices which remained in "neo-colonial" states after independence. As Hill noted: "The consciousness of the overlapping domains of popular struggle in Africa, America, and the Caribbean formed the basis of Rodney's essential political mission that guided his career as a revolutionary and scholar."[38] The immediate triggers for the Guyanese scholar-activist's Pan-Africanism were the events which followed the end of the Second World War in 1945: the struggle for self-determination in Africa, which inspired the same battles in the African diaspora. At the Fifth Pan-African Congress in Manchester in 1945, the mostly African delegates tabled a resolution which demanded an end to European colonialism in Africa.[39] This subsequently galvanised liberation struggles across Africa and led to political independence from European colonial rule for many African countries.

This new thrust was further driven by the renewal of the post-Marcus Garvey black nationalism emerging under the umbrella of the Black Power movement throughout the African diaspora. Additionally, black radical intellectuals and activists such as Frantz Fanon (see Jinadu in this volume), and C.L.R. James launched a "socialist critique" of imperialism and neo-colonialism. This context of the emergence of Western neo-colonialism and a class of African compradors provided ideal conditions for mounting a sustained assault on racial oppression.[40] The American civil rights movement also provided additional impetus for the development of black and Pan-African consciousness (see Daniels and Brown in this volume).[41]

The Theory and Praxis of Pan-Africanism

Rodney's Pan-Africanism must also be located in the context of circumstances in the Caribbean itself. The African experience of decolonisation and renewed racial pride provided inspiration for the Caribbean. The region at the same time also sought alternative paths to the neo-colonial order,[42] after the West Indies Federation lasted a mere four years (1958–62), and Guyana's experiment with socialism and Trinidad's people's movements were crushed in the 1960s. One of the issues which persistently preoccupied Rodney was that, although political independence had been achieved, the newly independent nations remained economically colonised.[43]

In the Caribbean, Rodney's Pan-African intellectual ancestors of the nineteenth century included John B. Russwurm, Edward Wilmot Blyden (see Khadiagala in this volume), Theophilus E.S. Scholes, John Jacob Thomas, Samuel Celestine-Edwards and John Albert Thorne. In the twentieth century, these figures included Marcus Garvey, Cyril Valentine Briggs, Antenor Firmin, Jean Price-Mars, C.L.R. James, Richard B. Moore, George Padmore, Aimé Césaire (see Irele in this volume) and Frantz Fanon; and in Guyana, Norman Eustace Cameron and Eusi Kwayana.[44]

Rodney's ideas about Pan-Africanism can be found across his work. According to Jamaican scholar, Horace Campbell, one of Rodney's most significant writings on Pan-Africanism can be found in an essay he wrote for the Sixth Pan-African Congress in Tanzania in June 1974, titled "Toward the Sixth Pan-African Congress: Aspects of the International Class Struggles in Africa, the Caribbean and America".[45] In *Groundings with My Brothers*, Rodney had provided a clear statement of Pan-Africanism, in particular in the chapter

"African History in Service of Black Revolution".[46] Here, Rodney stressed the importance of African history, life and culture, noting that they can be seen as a valuable source of pride for all Africans. In an interview following the Sixth Pan-African Congress published in the journal *Black Scholar* in November 1974, Rodney suggested that although efforts to advance the cause of black people on the African continent was, compared to the Americas, more important, they were essential for the struggle simultaneously being waged in the diaspora.[47] His seminal book *How Europe Underdeveloped Africa* illuminated the relationships of exploitation and racism between Europe and Africa, and further "popularised a new brand of committed Pan African scholarship".[48]

So how did Rodney conceptualise Pan-Africanism? He noted: "Any 'Pan' concept is an exercise in self-definition by the people, aimed at establishing a broader redefinition of themselves than that which has so far been permitted by those in power."[49] According to Rodney, the idea of Pan-Africanism and international solidarity carry certain responsibilities:

> One of the most important of our responsibilities is to define our own situation. A second responsibility is to present that definition to other parts of the black world, indeed to the whole progressive world. A third responsibility, and I think this is in order of priority, is to help others in a different section of the black world to reflect upon their own specific experience. The first priority is that we address ourselves to our own people – this is how we analyze where we're at. Secondly, we can say to other participants in a Third World struggle, here is the analysis, as we see it, of how we are going. Those people will take it and they will do with it as they see fit. But if they have a certain sense of internationalism, they will treat it very seriously. They will say, this is how a people see themselves. And only thirdly then am I in a position to say, from our particular standpoint, your struggle is moving in this direction, or this is how your analysis seems to be working, or in light of our experience here or there, we might want to question this or that aspect.[50]

Rodney felt that Africa was crucial in advancing the struggle against colonialism and neo-colonialism in the Caribbean and the United States. As he noted:

> I feel that to the extent that the African struggle advances and that continent is freed from the web of capitalism and imperialism, to that

extent the impact on the Caribbean and, particularly, the United States, the black population here is likely to be decisive ... I believe it is an important historical dimension and, therefore, success of the struggle in Africa is likely to be critical with regard to creating new conditions and new avenues for struggle in what we call the New World.[51]

Rodney felt that Pan-Africanism should take a bottom-up and class-based approach, and should be pursued along a socialist, Marxist path. He saw Pan-Africanism as representing a solidarity in which links were forged with social groups "between the Caribbean peoples and the African peoples", rather than "developing solidarity between African states and the Caribbean states".[52] Rodney believed that it was important to liaise with governments to reach citizens effectively in order to forge these links. However, he argued that one needed to be "more selective in insuring that ... relations are nurtured with particular progressive governments, with particular liberation movements and particular social organisations ... that develop a perspective on African struggle".[53]

In this regard, as Hill has noted,

Pan-Africanism ... was a critical tool for analyzing revolutionary new forms of genuine African liberation [and] an essential component [for] recapturing popular initiative against imperialism and challenging the decaying neo-colonial regimes of the African and Caribbean state petty bourgeoisie which, for him, represented the negation of Pan-Africanism: all it meant in their hands was interstate collaboration for the advancement of the petty bourgeoisie.[54]

Broadly, Rodney suggested that "Pan" movements are essentially a class struggle – a struggle by the representatives of the population against those who hold the reins of power. As he argued:

Invariably, however, the exercise [of self-definition] is undertaken by a specific social group or class which speaks on behalf of the population as a whole ... Consequently, certain questions must be placed on the agenda ...: Which class leads the national movement? How capable is this class of carrying out the historical tasks of national liberation? Which are the silent classes on whose behalf "national" claims are being articulated?[55]

Rodney argued that in the post-independence era, while Pan-Africanism was internationalist, it also had a nationalist character. He felt that nationalism did not reflect the interests of the masses but rather those of their bourgeois leaderships. According to Rodney, pro-independence nationalist movements in Africa were essentially political fronts or class alliances in which the grievances of all social groups were expressed as "national" grievances against the colonizers. However, while the workers and peasants formed the overwhelming numerical majority, the leadership was almost exclusively petty bourgeois. Understandably, this leadership placed to the fore those "national" aims which contributed most directly to the promotion of their own class interests; but they voiced sentiments which were historically progressive, partly because of their own confrontation with the colonialists and partly because of pressure from the masses.[56]

In a *Black Scholar* interview of 1976, Rodney noted that,

> the class which governs Africa is prepared to ally with the class which governs the Caribbean ... the same class is operating in both societies, irrespective of the fact that in some African countries that class may be behaving in a more responsive manner to the interests of the mass of peasants and proletariat ... But still it is the same class that we are dealing with, and people in the Caribbean – so-called radicals and progressives in the Caribbean – have had to learn that hard lesson – that we are dealing with state power and that we must examine the class nature of that power.[57]

Rodney thus felt that Pan-Africanism had been weakened because class considerations in this discourse had been diluted in Africa's post-independence era. This had rendered Pan-Africanism "a toothless slogan" in relation to imperialism, to the extent that it was embraced by "African chauvinists and reactionaries, marking a distinct departure from the earlier years of this century when the proponents of Pan-Africanism stood on the left flank of their respective national movements on both sides of the Atlantic".[58]

Rodney therefore felt that it was important to consider "state power ... and the class nature of that power".[59] This was necessary in understanding that not all African governments – or those in the Caribbean, for that matter – in the post-independence era were necessarily in support of revolutionary change. For this reason, he argued that it was vital to "draw distinctions [and ask]: Who is who in Africa? What are the state structures? What are the classes?"[60]

Rodney felt that the holistic transformation of Africa could only happen by traversing a socialist path led by the masses. As he argued:

> The transformation of the African environment, the transformation of social and productive relations, the break with imperialism, and the forging of African political and economic unity are all dialectically interrelated. This complex [of historical tasks] can be carried out only under the banner of Socialism and through the leadership of the working classes.[61]

Pan-Africanism in the post-independence era had international elements on two levels. Rodney noted that "Pan-Africanism in the post-independence era is internationalist in so far as it seeks the unity of peoples living in a large number of juridically independent states".[62] But the aim of Pan-Africanism also provides it with another international dimension: "to develop a perspective that is anti-capitalist, anti-imperialist, that speaks to the exploitation and oppression of all people."[63] In this way Pan-Africanism acquired a global reach far beyond Africa, the Caribbean, and the US.

What impact did Rodney's work have on African peoples and the understanding of their societies? He elevated African culture and society in the minds of blacks in the Caribbean and America to the same level as that of Europe, and sought to correct misconceptions in comparisons made between Africa and Europe. Rodney further argued that black people needed to "base [themselves] solidly within the culture of Africa"[64] in order to correct the myths and negative impressions about the continent and the inferiority complex that many blacks harboured in their interactions with white Europeans. He contended that Western Sudan (a geographical area stretching from Senegal to Chad) between the fifth and fifteenth century was comparable to Europe in the Dark and Middle Ages, with Africa having the edge. He further argued that, not only was Europe's advancement directly correlated to the Third World's stagnation, but that Europe's political organisation had been projected as the only way to organise every society. Yet, Rodney felt that some African patterns of social relations were superior to those of Europe.[65] He thus asserted that "an overall view of ancient African civilization and ancient African cultures is required to expunge the myths about the African past which linger in the minds of black people everywhere. This is the main revolutionary function of African history in our hemisphere."[66]

How Europe Underdeveloped Africa and the Caribbean

Rodney explained the underdevelopment of colonised and exploited societies in his 1973 classic, *How Europe Underdeveloped Africa*. He demonstrated that the root causes of underdevelopment could be found in unequal patterns of relations and structural considerations which explained development and underdevelopment. He highlighted the outstanding achievements of many African states before contact with Europe, arguing that Africa was not underdeveloped because of the inability and shortcomings of Africans, but mainly because of the European exploitation of the continent. For over four and a half centuries of regular contact between Europe and Africa, "Africa helped to develop Western Europe in the same proportion as Western Europe helped to underdevelop Africa".[67] This was done primarily through the trade in 12 to 15 million African slaves by Europeans, which caused the loss of African labour and devastation to Africa's economic activities, agriculture in particular, by depriving the continent of its agents of innovation – its human resources, particularly its young minds.[68] Since Europe's imperialist, capitalist and exploitative relationship with Africa was similar to its colonial relationship with the Caribbean, Rodney provided a rationale and a platform for uniting blacks in their common struggle for emancipation from the legacy of these relations.

Another important intellectual contribution that Rodney made to theory was his challenge to modernisation theories. *A History of the Guyanese Working People* showed that a capitalist system was incapable of developing "free labour" in a colonised environment. This view differed from previous scholarship, which subscribed to the perspective that the road to development had to follow the path of European industrialisation.[69] Rodney therefore contributed to developing the indigenous knowledge of Africa and its diaspora. *How Europe Underdeveloped Africa*, in particular, made a significant contribution to our understanding of the development of post-colonial societies, as well as to broader theoretical issues related to development. According to Howison, "Rodney contributed to the development of dependency theory, building upon theorists such as Andre Gunder Frank, but also to the rise of world systems analysis, whose origins can be traced to the publication of the first volume of Immanuel Wallerstein's monumental project two years after the appearance of HEUA [*How Europe Underdeveloped Africa*]."[70]

The Dar es Salaam School of Political Economy

Furthermore, at the University of Dar es Salaam, Rodney contributed to creating an intellectual tradition which came to be known as the "Dar es Salaam School of Political Economy" in the early 1970s. The novel perspectives that Rodney brought to the study of socio-economic development, slavery and the emancipation of the oppressed set the University of Dar es Salaam apart from other institutions on the continent. The university sought to foster an interdisciplinary approach to studying social processes in the humanities and social sciences.[71] More substantively, Rodney's intellectual contribution "on class formation, on disengagement, on underdevelopment, slavery and the emancipation of the oppressed" also distinguished the University of Dar es Salaam from teaching traditions elsewhere on the continent, which still taught anthropology as well as modernisation theory.[72] Among the criticisms levelled at the Dar es Salaam school was that its focus on class as a lens for understanding African history was limiting, and that Marxist versions of class were not directly applicable to Africa.[73]

Apart from his own research and writing, Rodney helped to train the first set of history graduates at the University of Dar es Salaam, in the process developing a new generation of progressive intellectuals. Of significance was the new course he established at Dar, called "History of the Black People in the Americas", in which students were exposed to the similarities in the struggles in Africa and the Americas against colonialism and neo-colonialism.[74]

Concluding Reflections

Rodney's work as a historian and Pan-Africanist cannot be separated from his political activism, grassroots engagements and role as a public intellectual.[75] In Jamaica, he came to identify with the struggle to attain social and economic justice for the dispossessed and the marginalised.[76] Rodney reached out to them primarily by establishing links with poor urban youth, Rastafarians, and middle-class students and intellectuals who had come to embrace radical ideas.[77] His knowledge of Africa and his skills at applying this knowledge to the legacy of black resistance were part of the appeal he would later have for Jamaican youth.[78] Rodney was also similarly engaged in his native Guyana. Following his disappointment with the Sixth Pan-African Congress in 1974, he helped to organise the Working People's Alliance in Guyana – which became a political party in 1979 – a grassroots multi-racial group to oppose the exploitation of working people and to advance their interests.[79]

What broad lessons can be drawn from Rodney's work for Pan-Africanism and beyond? Two are particularly important. The first is the question of agency in Africa's development and future. Rodney fervently believed in individuals and their potential to effect change. The belief that Africa's masses had the power to change their circumstances had major implications for how they thought about themselves and their future. Although Rodney blamed African underdevelopment on European colonialism, this did not stop him from working with people on the ground to empower the masses to try to change the course of their history and to chart their own independent future.

In this regard, Rodney's work points to the need for considering multiple levels of analyses, and the need to embrace both agent- and structure- informed epistemologies for understanding and finding solutions to the development challenges of Africa and the Caribbean. This is particularly critical considering the macro-discourses of globalisation and the supranational character of global governance, which seem to disempower ordinary people and strip them of their agency. There are strategies which can be used to leverage and negotiate this new global environment successfully. Pan-Africanism is one of these, but other forms of broad-based collaboration are also available.

The structural and external obstacles to development make it important to embrace the responsibilities that Rodney has placed on Africans and Caribbeans: that they first have to define what they want, rather than allow someone else to define it for them. This approach must be based on the specific needs of Africans and Caribbeans, as well as their unique circumstances. This means that Pan-Africanism should not be subordinated or sacrificed to artificial constructs of regional integration which have been forced upon Africa and the Caribbean, such as the African, Caribbean and Pacific (ACP) – European Union (EU) Economic Partnership Agreements.[80]

Rodney's second and final lesson relates to the importance of bottom-up approaches to solidarity and collective action. In the Caribbean and Africa, one of the reasons for the continuing difficulties in achieving effective regional integration is that a top-down approach has traditionally been adopted rather than allowing for a people-driven process. Rodney felt that Pan-Africanism should be driven by civil society and mass movements, and not by governments. Genuine and sustainable Pan-Africanism will thus flourish only if it is owned by ordinary citizens in Africa and its diaspora.

RUTH FIRST: PAN-AFRICAN REVOLUTIONARY

Maureen Isaacson

"There's Ruth First, a white woman whose name is not evoked nearly enough."

– ANGELA DAVIS[1]

THIS ESSAY FOCUSES ON RUTH FIRST'S commitment to Pan-African activism. The first section broadly introduces the South African journalist, writer, scholar and activist, setting out the defining themes of her life's work as a revolutionary and her "courage of principle".[2] As a Pan-Africanist in her intellectual pursuits and in her martyrdom and burial in Mozambique, First was ahead of her time in the South African context. Her role as a tireless fighter for liberation extended to the entire continent. Her dedication and determination to see social transformation in her lifetime made her life a political act,[3] and led to her tragic death in August 1982. The second section examines her daughter Gillian Slovo's attempts to rescue her mother from the canonisation often conflated with political martyrdom, illustrating her many dimensions and contradictions, far removed from the figure of the cardboard cut-out revolutionary.[4] Ruth First herself was acutely aware of the contradictions of her white privilege in a black working-class movement, the African National Congress (ANC).[5] The third section focuses on First's published books, *South West Africa* (1963), *The Barrel of a Gun: Political Power in Africa and the Coup d'État* (1970) and *Libya: the Elusive Revolution* (1974). The fourth and final section deals briefly with First's role as director of research at the Centre for African Studies at Eduardo Mondlane University in Maputo, where she spent the last five years of her life.

"I am an African"

Ruth First's grave in Maputo's Lhanguene cemetery stands as a defiant reproach. When the letter bomb that stilled the force of nature that was Ruth First in 1982 – in what her publisher Ronald Segal described as an "ultimate act of censorship"[6] – she was 57 years old and in her political and intellectual prime. In 1998 First's killers, Craig Williamson and his subordinate Roger Raven, justified her killing before the amnesty committee of the South African Truth and Reconciliation Commission (TRC). Amnesty, for deeds committed within a given period, was conditional on political motivation and full disclosure. The two men walked free, despite testimony that at the time of her death First was working as an academic and not as a foot soldier of the African National Congress[7] or the South African Communist Party (SACP), of which organisations she was a member.[8] In her role as head of research at the Centre for African Studies at Eduardo Mondlane University, she supported the ruling Mozambique Liberation Front (Frelimo) in its urgent efforts at achieving socio-economic transformation.

First's remains lie some 550 kilometres from her birthplace in Johannesburg, close to the 17 soldiers massacred by the apartheid South African Defence Force's raid in Matola, Mozambique, a year prior to her murder. Her daughters' decision not to rebury her remains in South Africa pays tribute to First's commitment to Pan-African liberation and to her expressed identity.[9] In the sense that First had fought against colonialism, confronted racism and struggled against apartheid, she was a Pan-African,[10] who said, "I count myself as an African and there is no cause I hold dearer."[11]

Going Down Fighting

Ruth First was born in Johannesburg on 5 May 1925 to a life of political struggle. Her image is painted on a mural in the giant black township of Soweto; her name is laid into the asphalt of numerous roads and freeways across South Africa; several memorial lectures, trusts and fellowships are stamped with her name. Ruth First House, with a museum, was established in Johannesburg's Saxonwold suburb in September 2013. Her biography reads like a citation for the Nobel Peace Prize.

Awareness of discrimination, persecution and displacement was the consequence of First's parents' own journey. Julius First and Matilda ("Tilly") Leveton came to South Africa in the early twentieth century as part of the mass migration of Jews from the Pale of Settlement in Russia; both were active in the Communist Party[12] of South Africa (CPSA).

In 1949 Ruth married Joe Slovo, who was to become a member of the South African Communist Party's central committee, later the party's general secretary, as well as chief of staff of the ANC's armed wing, Umkhonto we Sizwe (MK), or "Spear of the Nation". Slovo had arrived in South Africa from Russia at the age of nine in 1935 and, like First's parents, had lost his fluency in his mother tongue, Yiddish, by the time of their marriage.[13] They had three daughters: Shawn, Gillian and Robyn. Ruth had, by this time, earned a social science degree from Johannesburg's University of the Witwatersrand, where she met Ismail Meer, a lawyer whose Indian descent meant that their subsequent love affair was in breach of "the colour line". First met ANC leader Nelson Mandela, as well as Mozambican leader Eduardo Mondlane, the future founder of Frelimo who would also be assassinated by a parcel bomb, in September 1969. Ruth had launched a career as a radical journalist-activist, reporting on human rights violations, and focusing on labour abuse on farms and mines. *Sechaba*, the journal of the ANC, later eulogised First as the "raising agent" of the masses; her political mobilisation, investigation, writing, reporting and teaching had fuelled a "two-way exchange" with mass organisations outside the country, including Frelimo.[14]

A committed Marxist, whose goal was to see radical social change through socialism, in all of her work, First reported in *The Guardian*, a radical opposition newspaper and CPSA mouthpiece (and its several reincarnations, despite gagging and banning).[15] As editor of *Fighting Talk*, a radical political and literary journal, facing its closure in 1962, she declared, "at least we will go down as we have lived, fighting."[16] First was named under the Suppression of Communism Act of 1950, and later charged, with Joe Slovo, and stood trial in the 1956 Treason Trial as a consequence of her participation in the 1952 Defiance Campaign, her founding membership of the Congress of Democrats, and her election to the drafting committee of the Freedom Charter, which was ratified at the Congress of the People in Kliptown in 1955.[17]

"Prison is the Hardest Place"

First was the first white woman to be detained under solitary confinement in terms of apartheid's 90-day detention law, for 117 days in 1963. Angela Davis, writing the introduction to the 2008 edition of Ruth's prison memoir, *117 Days: An Account of Confinement and Interrogation under the South African 90-Day Detention Law*, noted First's successful assertion of her identity as part of a radical community of resistance, despite observing that "prison is the hardest place to fight a battle".[18] The memoir provided an intimate insight into First's experience of psychological torture. Her interrogator referred to her as "a fighter"[19] but nonetheless succeeded in taking her to the brink of suicide. Afterwards she left South Africa to join Joe Slovo, with her three daughters, in exile in Britain in March 1964. She left on an exit permit, which did not allow for her return, although she had applied for a passport.[20]

Her fight for social justice continued. She wrote for the United Nations Commission for Human Rights, and with Jonathan Steele and Christabel Gurney she published *The South African Connection: Western Investment in Apartheid* in 1972. First engaged with the ideas of the "New Left" at the London School of Economics and Political Science (LSE). As a research fellow at Manchester University, she taught sociology and met Gavin Williams,[21] a South African sociologist. From Durham University, she was seconded to Tanzania's University of Dar es Salaam for one semester in August 1975.[22]

In addition to her earlier publications, *South West Africa* (1963) and *117 Days* (1965), First also produced *The Barrel of a Gun: Political Power in Africa and the Coup d'État* (1970) and *Portugal's Wars in Africa* (1971). Her co-authored books include *Olive Schreiner* (1980) with Ann Scott, and the posthumous *Black Gold* (1983). First assisted in editing Nelson Mandela's essays collected in *No Easy Walk to Freedom* (1967), Govan Mbeki's *The Peasants' Revolt* (1967) and Kenyan politician Oginga Odinga's autobiography, *Not Yet Uhuru* (1968). With Ronald Segal, she edited *South West Africa: Travesty of Trust* (1967).[23]

Several Ruth Firsts, One Principle

Writing about her mother's funeral, Gillian Slovo noted that the revolutionary who was buried with fervour was but one of "several Ruths".[24] This understanding is key to grasping First's complexity, including the contradictions and incongruities implicit in all struggles for liberation, both internal and external. Such a quality is commonplace in someone so consistently willing to accept the consequences of the risk integral to what Dikgang Moseneke, South Africa's former deputy chief justice, described as the "courage of principle".[25]

It is necessary to deal briefly with First's sartorial style and personality, for these have been subjected to the intense scrutiny that is the lot of women in political life. Such scrutiny also serves as a distraction from her accomplishments. A taste for Italian shoes, cosmetics and perfume was apparently inconsistent with the representation of other women in the liberation movement. The American academic Barbara Harlow cited Ambalavaner Sivanandan, director of the Institute of Race Relations in London, who coined the catch-phrase "looked class" and "talked red" for First. Harlow noted that the scholar-activist had not been known to wear either diamonds or gold.[26] An attractive woman – by all accounts elegant and articulate – First had an imposing personality and her energy was formidable. Described by those who knew her as scathing, relentless, harsh and intimidating – as well as generous, uncertain and even insecure – former South African Constitutional Court Judge Albie Sachs, who was a close friend, noted the obvious contradictions of First's position as a white person in a black political environment; a middle-class activist in a working-class movement; and a woman operating in a man's world.[27]

The irony of such incongruity did not escape First, who in *117 Days* reported that while even behind bars she retained her status as a "white South African madam".[28] She and her fellow white revolutionaries were considered "darkly dangerous to the survival of the state".[29] The British sociologist Ralph Miliband famously described Ruth as the least utopian of revolutionaries, but not the least disappointed. He also drew attention to a lesser known aspect of her persona: her sense of the ridiculous.[30] This is apparent in her memoirs and in a great deal of her writing. Nelson Mandela once told Ruth during a heated argument to "go to hell", but he was quick to restore their friendship. He would later note that First was among the brightest stars, "nothing but brilliant", fearless, direct.[31]

In a memorial lecture for Ruth First given in August 2000, ANC policy intellectual Pallo Jordan, noted that her solidarity with socialist countries was always critical, and that this made her a true revolutionary. First, who adhered to Marx's favourite adage, "Doubt and question everything", considered it her revolutionary duty to be critical, pointing to anomalies implicit in both Soviet and Chinese communism, and challenging the official SACP line in arguing for the independence of Eritrea from Ethiopia.[32] Joe Slovo admitted after Ruth's death that she might have been expelled from the SACP had she not been married to him.[33] First was among the few SACP members who were prepared to admit that her party's appreciation of the dialectics of race, class and gender was sometimes inadequate.[34] She confessed to being "a late bloomer" as a feminist. Co-authoring a book on Olive Schreiner and teaching a course on the sociology of sex and gender relations at Durham University helped to make up for this.[35]

Travelling in post-independence Africa, First balked at the professed concern of Africans for the "unliberated South" that was bolstered by only "a ricocheting knowledge".[36] She was undoubtedly aware of the echoes of such parochialism in the attitudes of some of her "comrades" at home and those exiled in Lusaka, who, like Joe Slovo, often failed to understand the reason for her focus on the continent outside South Africa.[37] Her independence and refusal to accept the constraints of ignorance which would have hindered her research on Africa were, in fact, Ruth's essence. Everything that she wrote, co-authored and edited was aimed at facilitating the liberation of Africa.[38] That is what made her a revolutionary Pan-Africanist.

South West Africa

Under close surveillance in Windhoek when researching her book on South West Africa, published in 1963, First was placed under house arrest on her return to Johannesburg. Namibia – then South West Africa – was under South African rule, although the League of Nations, responsible for handing the mandate to South Africa after the First World War (1914–18), had been replaced by the United Nations in 1945. The case was, at the time of her writing, before the International Court of Justice in the Hague.

This first work on Namibia's history from an anti-colonial perspective was well received.[39] Here were "two South West Africas": the one, a white South West Africa, was mired in privilege and fear; the other, a black majority country, wearied by deprivation, was non-cooperative with the racist white rulers in Pretoria.[40] First described "a unique form of colonialism",[41] defending itself by force from an independence revolution within, but also fearing the very real possibility that a revolution in South West Africa could topple the apartheid edifice in South Africa.[42]

The power of this work lies in the stories of black Namibians, including workers, activists and members of independence movements, whom First interviewed in bus shelters and under trees, and in South West Africa's Ovambo and Herero "reserves", constructed under apartheid for the provision of exploited labour to the apartheid colonial state. What was the United Nations doing to stop apartheid's ravages? Always dramatic in her expression, First wrote, "This is the hour before the battle. Must the blood flow before the world body will act?"[43] However, liberation could not stand or fall by the debates or resolutions or even actions at the UN, noted First. She stressed, as always, the need for solidarity between Africa's independence movements, and wrote with prescience about the new pressure gathering from two sides: a changing and newly articulate South West Africa, and a newly liberated and increasingly confident Africa. It was only in 1966 that the UN General Assembly ended Pretoria's mandate, and five years later that the International Court of Justice declared the South African presence in Namibia to be illegal. Only in March 1990 was Sam Nujoma formally sworn in as independent Namibia's first president.

The Barrel of a Gun: The Military in Africa

First's declared intention in the introduction to her 1970 book about military coups in Africa, *The Barrel of a Gun*, was that it would contribute to "at least tentatively a general theory of power for newly independent states in Africa, which explains why they are so vulnerable to army interventions in politics".[44] She begins with a foregone conclusion: "The guns mediate shifts in the balance of internal power but they do not in themselves alter social structures. In the end coups change nothing."[45] As First illustrates, power begins with those who control the means of violence. It lies in the barrel of the gun, fired or silent.[46] The signals of vulnerability to coups are clear: the cumulative economic crises caused by an inability to break through economic dependence; power contests within independence movements; the role of external forces; external hostility and coup-making; the often poor conditions of the military.[47]

First's conclusion was that in order for an army to achieve radical change, it would have to have links to radical forces, connected to a popular base with popular support. The idea took its impetus from the ANC's own armed struggle, its armed wing, Umkhonto we Sizwe, was launched in December 1961. In seeking a strategy of social revolution, First asked whether this would be possible in countries other than Guinea-Bissau and the embattled South consisting of Angola, Mozambique, Rhodesia and South Africa.[48]

She suggested that Africa's "omnibus political parties" could be radicalised from within, thereby linking army officers with revolutionary intellectuals and a popular front as in Sudan, where the Free Officers campaign in 1969 joined and defended the cause of change by building a civilian government, although this was not sustained.[49] Algeria's liberation by armed struggle in a gruelling and brutal eight-year war with France (1954–62) set a record for decolonisation without parallel in Africa. However, no unified guerrilla base of leadership in post-independence Algeria was built, and the army became a competitor for power in a military bureaucracy.[50]

Egypt's was the only *coup d'état* in Africa – in 1952 – that led to major social change, even if this was not its initial intention. But this was also a seminal case of an army in danger of destroying the very transformations that it had initiated.[51] The Free Officers, led by Gamal Abdel Nasser, who brought down a corrupt British-backed monarchy, found themselves having to institute land reform and nationalisation, alongside a desire to build a popular political base. Egypt's military elite was, however, not prepared for war, and instead engaged in conspiracy to defend its privilege, and was even prepared to topple Nasser, as the 1967 Six-Day War with Israel revealed. This incident again demonstrated the intrinsic limitations of professional armies in politics and government.[52]

First asserted repeatedly that there could be no liberation in Africa without mass-based, grassroots, bottom-up uprisings, like those in Cuba, China and Guinea-Bissau, and cited country after country which had failed to make the essential change to end external dependence. The *coup d'état* that toppled Kwame Nkrumah in February 1966 (see Biney in this volume) signalled a tragic failure not only for the West African country, but for a Pan-African unity of radical social transformation and commitment to socialism. Although this Pan-African vision had been Nkrumah's, First blamed Ghana's failure on his limitations as a theoretician and revolutionary leader. Nkrumah saw socialism and economic development as a process to be promoted by edict from the pinnacle of government, by himself.[53] First noted that the Ghanaian leader's attempts to extricate himself from his self-inflicted isolation by creating "a private army" became the very justification for the 1966 coup by Ghana's soldiers and police.[54] Despite his denunciation of foreign capital, Nkrumah's Seven-Year Development Plan (1964–70) was entirely dependent on external resources, and he refused to recognise the economic crisis in his country. Although Ruth noted Nkrumah's claim that the US, British and West German embassies had been implicated in a plot to overthrow his government, he was not too distracted by what she considered to be "conspiracy theories".[55]

Outside forces were ubiquitous in post-independence Africa, and when the political system in Nigeria collapsed from a fierce struggle over the spoils of power in January 1966, the ensuing conflict took violent communal forms, ultimately expressed in civil war between 1967 and 1970. Nigeria's First Republic (1960–6) was "an orgy of power being turned to profit … Political party, public and private financial interests fed greedily upon one another. The men who controlled the parties used them to commandeer business, and the business, in turn, to buy party support."[56] In describing "the new shape of Africa's dependence" – increasingly the product of huge American financial and industrial concerns – First observed that while the US State Department was officially neutral in the Nigerian civil war (1967–70), its corporations were expanding their influence in the spirit of "reconstruction".[57]

Ruth First's efforts to extricate herself from harsh judgements of African leadership, assuring readers that there was no cause that she held dearer than the liberation of Africa, failed to prevent Afro-pessimists from seizing the book to justify their cause, as South African academic Shula Marks noted.[58] Some of First's research also did not do justice to her erudition. A possible explanation could be the dearth of facts at her disposal, for she informed readers that while case studies of the coups on which she wrote were derived largely from official sources as well as empirical research, in the case of Nigeria, for example, the stories narrated were based largely on rumour and gossip.

Libya's Perverse Revolution

Ruth First visited Muammar Qaddafi's Libya four times after the 1969 military coup in search of the causes and achievements of what she considered a "contradictory" and "perverse" revolution. In a book written against a backdrop of detailed history, about the country's idiosyncratic leader who admitted that he had not succeeded in breaking the "cult of the leader", his regime provided much fodder for parody. Qaddafi's version of the "revolution" had seen King Idris deposed in an act of regicide, involving two soldiers, in 1969. This was the only permitted official version of the event. First's criticisms of the regime in Tripoli are insightful, if harsh. She attempted, as she did in *The Barrel of a Gun*, to exonerate herself from blame in her research. She claimed to have seen Libya in its own context, away from the European gaze.

Yet, her pronouncement on Qaddafi's revival of Islamic fundamentalism and his "government by demagogy"[59] contradicted this claim. For First, Qaddafi's fusion of religion and politics was "peculiar":[60] surely, Islam could not be expected to supply the indissoluble core of identity and communal heritage that ignored the diversity and differentiation of the Arab world?[61] Although the revolution paid lip service to a "people's revolution", engagement in party politics was banned, and Qaddafi's vision of a Libyan Arab Socialist Union – involving development, transformation and religion to regenerate the Arab world – had no place for theories of class struggle.[62] Noting the Libyan autocrat's mistrust of the masses, First's prediction that Libya could be an ideal breeding ground for the Muslim Brotherhood, and a source of inspiration for their counterparts in Egypt,[63] proved to be correct. Her prediction that Libya would be subject to a coup syndrome rather than civilian challenges to the army regime was, however, wrong.[64] In February 2011, Western-backed rebels in Libya rose up against Qaddafi in the wake of the Afro–Arab uprisings that had begun in Tunisia the previous year, which also spread to Egypt and Yemen.

"It's Exciting Working in Mozambique"

Aquino de Bragança, director of the Centre for African Studies at Mozambique's Eduardo Mondlane University, recruited First as he considered her the ideal candidate to organise research on the southern African sub-region. First had told him that she wanted to get back into the front line of the revolution.[65] From 1977 she led a research project on the export of Mozambican migrant labour to the South African mines, and, from 1979 until her death in August 1982, she served as research director in charge of setting up and running the Centre's research-based development course.[66]

A special issue of the *Review of African Political Economy*, "Não vamos esquecer (We will not forget)", published in 2014, is instructive about First's work and her sometimes tense personal relationships with colleagues. Dan O'Meara, a South African researcher at the Centre for African Studies, described

First's "confrontational political style" as "frequently bullying and sometimes hectoring".[67] Yet Ruth was known as "a peasant lover" for her empirical research methods. She was also forced to fight for space within the university to conduct research, as well as for the autonomy of other researchers. Colin Darch, a British researcher at the Centre, noted that First's and de Bragança's broadly supportive approach to research was incorrectly interpreted as being simply determined by Frelimo.[68] However, as the South African sociologist Harold Wolpe argued, while the research priorities of the Centre were defined at the political level, they also became the priorities of social research, not as conclusions, but as starting points for investigation.[69] The "activist conception of research" did not mean that this work was not independent.[70]

Thus, while First's research for *The Mozambican Miner* (1977) – a collective study on migrant labour from Mozambique – addressed Frelimo's repeated commitment to ending migrant labour, it also warned that such a move would have to appeal to "the political commitment of the migrant" and, if migrant labour was to end, all its implications would have to be analysed.[71] *The Miner* was published posthumously as *Black Gold: The Mozambican Miner, Proletarian and Peasant* in 1983.[72] It dealt with the lives of migrants on mines, and the impact of the labour system on their livelihoods. It returned to the themes of First's 1961 paper – "The Gold of Migrant Labour" – which tackled the export of labour, miners and mine labour, peasant society and the interactions between these issues.

Ruth's *pièce de résistance* was her development course at Mondlane University. The experimental interdisciplinary course taught research by doing collective work. Uniquely, First insisted that the course be taught at the postgraduate level to students who had no formal university education. Its purpose was clear: to provide revolutionary cadres with scientific training that would assist them in their work. Students had to know what they were fighting for: the radical transformation of the organisation of production through socialist development.[73] The questions kept coming, and a few days before her death in August 1982, while addressing a social science conference in Maputo, Ruth admitted that she was faced with many challenges. "It is exciting working in Mozambique … because the work is exciting … but as a social scientist in struggle, you have no choice but to work in institutions that are creating change."[74]

Thus ended First's five years of struggle in Mozambique, which were the happiest and most productive years of her life.[75]

Concluding Reflections

Ruth First was a standard-bearer of Pan-African liberation. Her inspirational legacy lies not only in her outrage, her bravery and her determination to fight for liberation and an equitable world. It lies too in her essential revolutionary commitment, her insistence on asking questions, noting the failures within independence movements, and her willingness to experiment with methods that would achieve her overriding goal of a socialist reality.

That the issues with which First wrestled remain unresolved four decades after her tragic martyrdom provides an impetus for those ready to take up her tasks. In Africa, continued dependencies and reliance on outside sources, the failure of commitment to radical economic transformation, and erratic policy implementation and a widespread lack of foresight on the part of leaders, all render what First referred to as "constitutional niceties" virtually irrelevant.

The radical transformation for which Ruth fought extends to curricula for African scholars in universities as well as faculties, and her work has at least set a precedent. Tebello Letsekha, a South African researcher, noted in 2014 that First's work was representative of the ways in which African scholars have combined advocacy with scholarship in looking for new approaches to the study of the continent. As a young African scholar, Letsekha learnt through First the meaning of community research that can make a difference in the real world.[76]

Wangari Maathai: Pan-African Peacebuilder

Janice Golding

Wangari Muta Maathai (1940–2011) – "the "Earth Mother" – loved the power of community activism expressed in the conservation of nature, and abhorred the oppression of vulnerable members of society. This love evolved in the course of her becoming an ardent environmental activist, women's rights supporter and pro-democracy advocate.[1]

Born near Nyeri in Kenya's Central Highlands, Maathai was the first individual to win the Nobel Peace Prize – awarded in 2004 – for a life's work of steadfast protection of the natural environment, and for her "contribution to sustainable development that embraces democracy, human rights and women's rights".[2] She was also the first woman from Africa to be honoured with the prize. Of the 97 individuals awarded the Nobel Peace Prize before Maathai, only 12 had been women.[3]

As one of Africa's most charismatic leaders, Wangari taught and inspired hundreds of thousands of people to improve their quality of life by protecting the natural environment. In drawing inspiration from nature and dedicating her life to helping the poorest of the poor, she was the world's first icon of sustainable development.

The presentation speech by Ole Danbolt Mjøs, the Norwegian chair of the Nobel Committee, summarised the fruits of Maathai's life efforts in a particularly poignant manner:

Peace on earth depends on our ability to secure our living environment. Maathai stands at the front of the fight to promote ecologically viable social, economic and cultural development in Kenya and in Africa. She has taken a holistic approach to sustainable development that embraces democracy, human rights and women's rights in particular. She thinks globally and acts locally.[4]

Twenty years before being awarded the Nobel Peace Prize, Maathai had been honoured with the Right Livelihood Award in 1984 for "converting the Kenyan ecological debate into mass action for reforestation".[5] This award – founded by Swedish parliamentarian and writer Jacob von Uexküll and often referred to as the "alternative Nobel Peace Prize" – was visionary in its recognition of the relationship between peace, environmental protection and human rights. Wangari was thus a pioneer of the environmental movement at a time when there was little global awareness about the post-colonial "state of the land" plight besetting Kenya and indeed, more widely, Africa and beyond.

The tapestry of Maathai's life was rich and productive. Her sense of self-embodied elements of the Greek concept of Gaia: her worldview was that humankind had lost its integrated relationship with nature, and the remnants of the relationship were threatening and corrupt.[6] With energy and vision over more than 40 years, she demonstrated that fighting environmental injustices was the very essence of democratic struggles.[7]

Maathai's focus was on transforming degraded landscapes into productive ones by promoting tree-planting and implementing traditional land-management practices at the community level. By working to protect the environment and by planting trees, she provided opportunities for rural women to claim their dignity by becoming self-reliant. Wangari understood that the divide between rich "haves" and poor "have-nots" could not be reduced unless people's relationship with the state was changed. She recognised that restoring and affirming self-worth – which is typically negated by abject poverty – was necessary for improving people's lives. Her approach was to advocate that poor people be recognised as under-engaged citizens who possess untapped reservoirs of innovation from which society can draw, and for them not be seen as powerless subjects without "know-how" and at the mercy of the patronage and patriarchy of the powerful.

Even today, Africa's post-colonial context remains one in which traditional land management and land rights are frequently poorly implemented, and women are often marginalised. Maathai worked to include the excluded in social and political life, and inspired people to become self-sufficient in order to reap the rewards of hard work and commitment. Most importantly, she recognised the immense power of African women as agents of change, and she enabled many

– with skills and confidence – to tap into their personal power and take control of their livelihoods. By mobilising activism against domination and dispossession of natural resources, Wangari became a bold and independent voice for peace and justice.[8]

Perhaps Maathai should have received the Nobel Peace Prize for gender activism and social mobilisation in strengthening women's access to, and control over, natural resources. However, at the time of her award in 2004, the global gender agenda was still evolving. Had Wangari been alive today, I have no doubt that over and above her contribution to the environment, she would have received additional recognition for her efforts at gender empowerment.

At a philosophical level, Maathai believed that sustainable development and protection of the environment could only be achieved if women had access to the necessary assets and resources for promoting their livelihoods, and if they possessed a stronger voice in decision-making in planning and managing community development. Women were – and still are – under-represented at all levels of government and other decision-making arenas, whether at work or, for many, in rural households. Such lack of power was linked to the higher levels of poverty that women endured, most acutely in rural areas where women were responsible for 70–80% of food production, as well as energy and water provision. Yet, they had little access or control over natural assets such as land, water and ecological conditions that often create opportunities for a better livelihood.[9]

Cultural norms tended to be rooted in patriarchy, with high levels of child marriages and illiteracy among women; lack of land rights (including land ownership); and lack of access to justice or protection against sexual and gender-based violence. In many rural communities, women were the decision-makers as heads of households, particularly in homes where men were absent for long periods of time. Even Maathai's early personal life had been affected by these issues. She and her husband, Mwangi Maathai, a former member of Kenya's parliament, divorced in 1977 because of her activism. In her 2006 biography, *Unbowed*, Wangari noted that her husband called her "too educated, too strong, too successful, too stubborn and too hard to control".[10] Divorced with three young children at the age of 37, Maathai returned to her rural homestead where she sought nurturing from women, acceptance and an opportunity to rebuild her life.

African women today still remain under-educated and subject to patriarchal norms that limit them from reaching their full potential. Unpaid labour, unequal access to resources such as loans or micro-finance, and limited networks continue to impose critical constraints on the economic empowerment of women. As the first African woman to be awarded the Nobel Peace Prize, Maathai inspired Africans – especially its young women – to liberate themselves from fear and silence. Like the two other female African Nobel Peace laureates (Liberia's Ellen Johnson Sirleaf[11] and Leymah Gbowee,[12] who were jointly awarded the prize in 2011), Wangari, through her social activism, provoked significant changes to entrenched social inequalities and injustices.

Germination of the Seed: The Early Years

Wangari Maathai first worked as a director of the Kenya Red Cross Society in 1972, but essentially started her career as a scientist. As one of about 300 Africans selected in 1959 for scholarships from the Joseph P. Kennedy Jr Foundation, through the efforts of Kenyan politician and Pan-Africanist Tom Mboya, she rode this wave of academic opportunity which had initiated the "Kennedy Airlift" (or "Airlift Africa"). Incidentally, Barack Obama Sr (the father of Barack Obama, the first president of the United States (US) of African descent (between 2009–16) was one of the first students to have been airlifted to America. Wangari obtained a Bachelor's degree in biological sciences from Mount St Scholastica College in Kansas in 1964; a Master of Science degree from the University of Pittsburgh in 1966; and a PhD from the University of Nairobi in 1971, where she also taught veterinary anatomy. She was appointed associate professor and, from 1977, chaired the Department of Veterinary Anatomy at the University of Nairobi. At the age of only 37, she was the first woman in Central and East Africa to have occupied these prominent positions.

Maathai became active in the National Council of Women of Kenya (NCWK) between 1976 and 1987, a busy period that shaped the course of her life's work. The organisation had been founded in 1964, after Kenya's independence the previous year, and was affiliated to the International Council of Women. Its mission was to unify common concerns and objectives concerning the role and promotion of mainly rural women who were often impoverished and had no political voice. At the time, malnutrition and food insecurity in Kenya's rural households were a grave concern. The decline in soil productivity, lack of clean water, depletion of tree and firewood stocks, and the drying up of rivers had resulted in insufficient food production and impoverishment. Maathai's empathy was the catalyst for a new NCWK environmental programme called Save the Land Harambee. Her commitment to the environmental cause had been ignited by empowering women to become financially self-sufficient in an inexpensive manner. Wangari's inspiration was deeply embedded in her memories of pre-independence Kenya, and in the landscape surrounding her childhood home near the central town of Nyeri overlooking the scenic slopes of Mount Kilimanjaro.

In 1976 Maathai applied her academic knowledge of biology in transforming the Save the Land Harambee project, and founding the community-based tree-planting organisation, the Green Belt Movement. This organisation, which worked with women's groups in rural Kenya, became the mother body for Wangari's environmental peacebuilding efforts.[13]

By 1980 – just four years after the Green Belt Movement had been founded – almost 600 tree nurseries, involving as many as 3,000 women, had been built. By this time, about 2,000 green public areas with about 1,000 seedlings each had also been established, and more than 15,000 farmers had planted woodlots on their land. By 2004, over 30 million trees had been planted across Africa through the Green Belt Movement's influence.[14] Through its modus operandi of simplicity and old-fashioned naturalism, the movement developed a Pan-African mandate which became widely adopted in several African countries, spreading to countries bordering Kenya by the late 1980s. In the process, farming techniques and traditional knowledge systems about land management were also transferred to local communities. By 2011, the Green Belt Movement had planted over 51 million trees across the continent.[15]

Over the years of work by the Green Belt Movement, the result was a more stable natural environment enhanced by tree-planting. Women were able to grow and sell crops, support the needs of their families, and release themselves from the enslavement of poverty. Maathai is warmly remembered for the Kiswahili slogan that she used to mobilise the hearts and minds of the Green Belt Movement's women, "Harambee" – let us all pull together! The movement's members were requested to reaffirm their commitment at every tree-planting ceremony, reciting the following pledge:

Being aware that Kenya is being threatened by the expansion of desert-like conditions; that desertification comes as a result of misuse of the land and by consequent soil erosion by the elements; and that these actions result in drought, malnutrition, famine and death; we resolve to save our land by averting this same desertification through the planting of trees wherever possible. In pronouncing these words, we each make a personal commitment to save our country from actions and elements which would deprive present and future generations from reaping the bounty of resources which is the birthright and property of all.

Maathai actively lobbied to protect the environment, human rights and democracy, stridently fighting government corruption. Her persistent agitation for environmental justice and social equality was driven by illegal developments on public land or in ecologically fragile territories on which people depended for their well-being and incomes. She also fought against the frenzy of post-colonial "big men": powerful elites and office-holders who forcibly displaced poor communities from public land. Between 1978 and 2002 – during the tumultuous years of Daniel arap Moi's dictatorship in Kenya – the Green Belt Movement led campaigns that aimed to narrow power divides. These ranged from excursions to tree nurseries and tree-planting ceremonies to mass rallies. The campaigns sometimes ended up with the protesters being beaten up, and even killed, by the police. Moi labelled Maathai "a mad woman" and declared her a serious threat to the stability of Kenya. He suggested that she should behave like an obedient African woman and do as she was told.[16] Throughout these years, Wangari endured repressive patriarchy, jail sentences, police brutality and living in hiding. Essentially, hers was a life of sedition and struggle for the greater good.

Maathai was fortunate to witness a dynamic epoch of environmental governance. A series of global events – led primarily by the United Nations – gradually created an ideological platform for her rise to global environmental peacebuilding. The most notable was the UN Conference on Human Environment – also known as the Stockholm Conference – hosted in 1972 by the UN General Assembly.[17] In recognising the ecological importance of forests, the Stockholm Conference made recommendations to monitor, protect, and manage forest ecosystems as natural assets.

A more pronounced and strategic approach to environmental governance came about after 1983 as a result of the UN Brundtland Commission, named after its chair, Gro Harlem Brundtland, a doctor and diplomat who had served three terms as prime minister of Norway (1981, 1986–9 and 1990–6). The commission discussed the social, economic and political dimensions of environmental management and governance, introducing a shift from narrow species-based concerns for nature ("saving" species and ecosystems) to broader but still well-defined objectives and solutions for protecting the environment.[18]

The Brundtland Commission's 1987 report, *Our Common Future*, was ground-breaking in introducing the concept of sustainable development, redefining it as "development that meets the needs of the present without compromising the ability of future generations to meet their own needs".[19] This idea became the engine of the environmental movement in subsequent years. It heralded the emergence of a concerted global response, in particular an increasingly sophisticated governance response to the requirements for, and expectations of, sustainable development.

Noteworthy was the Stockholm Conference's agreement to establish a new UN agency with a specialised mandate to coordinate environmental activities and policy development in developing countries. This became known as the United Nations Environment Programme (UNEP), and its new headquarters were located in Wangari's home city of Nairobi in 1972. In order to support the UNEP's establishment, the newly formed non-governmental membership Environmental Liaison Centre International (ELCI) provided an oversight, consultation, and monitoring role of the UNEP. In 1974, Maathai became a board member of the ELCI (and later chair of the board), and she was intimately involved in the creation of the UNEP. However, for many years after its establishment, the UN agency struggled to gain acceptance and traction in the very countries that it was meant to serve. The prevailing paradigm was essentially neo-liberal, arguing that environmentalism was an elitist obsession among the privileged and educated classes of the rich North, and that other priorities such as education, public health and literacy were more important in the global South. The notion that environmentalism and poverty eradication were somehow in opposition to each other was comprehensively debunked by Wangari, who demonstrated throughout her life's work that poverty and environmental degradation were not mutually independent phenomena, but that each drives the other. Maathai insisted that the cycle of poverty – from unemployment and hopelessness, to illness and malnutrition – could only be broken when the natural environment was managed in a responsible manner. A widespread belief among many environmentalists from developing countries, like Wangari, was the idea that the protection of nature requires an overall recasting of society's norms and values, as well as effective economic structures.

Winning a Nobel Peace Prize that honoured the environmental activism of an African female scientist could not have come at a better time for Maathai. Furthermore, the appointment of a new UNEP executive director in 2006, the Brazilian–German environmentalist Achim Steiner, provided the ideal opportunity for the agency to fortify its credibility in the global South and embed the sustainable development agenda firmly in the multilateral system. Maathai was one of the first people from the developing world adopted into the UNEP family, which resulted in her exposure to environmental governance, global politics in the multilateral system and the work of the UN in this critical area. This politically mutual relationship between individual and institution was productive and highly transformative. As Steiner said of Maathai:

> I am pleased that in some of the dark days of her campaigning, when not everyone welcomed her stance and commitment, Wangari was able to turn to UNEP for safety and sanctuary. She returned that support in so many ways by backing and batting for UNEP at home and abroad. For UNEP, she was an excellent partner who never tired of supporting the organisation's ideals, and represented it well whenever requested.[20]

Putting Down Roots: Working Widely

Maathai entered the political arena in Kenya by unsuccessfully running for parliament and for the presidency in 1997. She again campaigned for parliament in the 2002 Kenyan elections. A year later, after Moi had stepped down following 24 years in office, she won a parliamentary seat by a 98 per cent margin in her rural constituency of Tetu, and was appointed assistant minister in Kenya's Ministry for Environment and Natural Resources in the government of President Mwai Kibaki.

Maathai was neither a strategist nor a politician, perhaps lacking the hard skills and temperament to navigate the halls of power. Her association with the UN (primarily through the UNEP) had provided her with political safety nets and diplomatic leverage, but she was ostensibly stripped of this armour when she served in government. As a politician, she was exposed to the realities of the day-to-day machinations of national politics, and the vagaries and intrigues of the system. This change came with as many restrictions as opportunities, and was a challenging context in which to balance her diverse responsibilities and commitments. The prestige associated with the Nobel Peace Prize attracted envy and disfavour among fellow parliamentarians and politicians. Amid much controversy, she was voted out of national office in the 2007 elections.

The years after Maathai's Nobel award in 2004 were spent largely in airport lounges for long-haul flights, on podiums, behind lecterns and in conference halls. She had become everything to everyone, and a memory and inspiration to the rural women she had once served. Some argued that Wangari was more needed in the developing South, as an activist and local critic of recalcitrant governments and corporates, as well as to inspire social movements. No longer a people-centred environmental activist, she became an environmental campaigner and climate change lobbyist, working around the globe, principally through the UN, the African Union (AU), and their agencies.

Apocalyptic fears fuelled by climate change, particularly concerning food and water security, and by the race for technological intelligence appear to have shaped Maathai's post-Nobel work. Her intention was to help reduce greenhouse gas emissions by actively promoting forest protection and tree-planting, as well as by lobbying governments to undertake concerted efforts to combat the effects of climate change.

Maathai was appointed by the African Development Bank (AfDB) as the "Goodwill Ambassador of the Congo Forest Basin" in 2005.[21] She noted that "the Congo rainforest should not be seen just as a national or regional resource, but rather as a global treasure that acts as the Earth's lung and one of its greatest hopes for the mitigation of global warming and climate change".[22] From 2006, Wangari was an active patron of the UNEP's "Plant for the Planet: Billion Tree Campaign", launched in 2006.[23] With the campaign fully mature and having exceeded its tree-planting targets, more than 12.6 billion trees had been planted by 2012 through this global UN programme and its large number of partners.[24] Numerous complementary campaigns with even more ambitious targets have since replaced it, such as the Trillion Trees Campaign spearheaded by prominent international NGOs such as Birdlife International, World Wildlife Fund and Wildlife Conservation Society.[25] In 2005 Maathai was elected as the first president of the African Union's Economic, Social and Cultural Council (ECOSOCC), which was charged with promoting interaction between AU leaders and civil society.[26] She sought to place climate change on the AU agenda, and called on African heads of state to reduce the vulnerability of their countries to this phenomenon by equipping them with knowledge, skills, and jobs to adopt sustainable technologies. She argued that climate change presented a serious threat to Africa, with the poorest people likely to be hardest hit.[27] As Maathai noted on the eve of the AU Summit in Malabo, Equatorial Guinea, in June 2011:

Many of our countries have experienced decades of environmental mismanagement or outright neglect. Indeed, some governments – including my own – have facilitated the plunder of the forests, the degradation of the land and unsustainable agricultural practices. Many communities in Africa are already threatened by the negative impacts of climate change. Children in Africa are dying from malnutrition as women struggle to farm on land that is less and less productive. People on coastlines are losing their homes as the seas consume the coastlines.[28]

Maathai's activism on behalf of the UN climate change process was launched when she was inaugurated as a UN "Messenger of Peace" in 2009. At the 15th Conference of Parties convened by the UN Framework Convention on Climate Change (UNFCCC) – also known as COP15 – which was hosted in the Danish capital of Copenhagen in 2009, the Kenyan environmentalist called on world leaders to commit resources to support African countries in addressing the destructive impacts of climate change. Thereafter, Wangari put shoulder to the wheel on behalf of the UN's calls to action, including becoming an advocate of its Reducing Emissions from Deforestation and Degradation in Developing Countries Programme (UN-REDD).

Maathai also sought to elevate the influence of female leadership and to garner support for women's rights, first through the Green Belt Movement, and later through various international platforms. She was a founding member of the Nobel Women's Initiative, along with other female Nobel Peace laureates: Iran's Shirin Ebadi, American Jody Williams, Guatemala's Rigoberta Menchú Tum, and Northern Ireland's Betty Williams and Mairead Corrigan Maguire.[29] Wangari was the recipient of numerous awards from governments and international institutions. She received France's Légion d'honneur (2006), the Nelson Mandela Award for Health and Human Rights (2007) and Japan's Order of the Rising Sun (2009), among others.

Growing Branches and New Leaves: Maathai's Essential Contribution

In Western countries, many environmental "radicals" and protesters from the 1970s and 1980s became hardened professionals, entering political office or influential NGOs. Unlike Maathai, most lost touch with the needs and aspirations of local communities with whom they had worked during their formative years. She remained one of a handful of seasoned activists who continued to work "in the trenches" and to get soil under her nails for most of her life. She rose to fame and started a massive movement by planting tree after tree. Her achievements were not what she had aspired to, but she won victories by virtue of her leadership and courage.

Maathai worked locally, at the grassroots level, by harnessing people power, and using traditional knowledge systems instead of Western science. By planting one tree at a time in degraded landscapes to form rows of "green belts", she grew a movement. In so doing, she dedicated her life to improving women's livelihoods by empowering them to lead the restoration of degraded ecosystems across Africa.

Her contributions to the environmental and peace movement were especially significant in the decade following the tragic and brutal execution of Ken Saro-Wiwa and eight of his fellow environmental activists by General Sani Abacha's military dictatorship in Nigeria in November 1995. As the founder of the Movement for the Survival of Ogoni People (MOSOP), Saro-Wiwa had fought against Anglo-Dutch company Shell's exploitation of oil, which had turned Nigeria's Niger Delta region into an environmental wasteland and impoverished the Ogoni people.[30]

Critical of the international community's apathy towards Africa, Maathai was a much-needed voice of hope for the continent.[31] She was listened to by the UN and other influential global institutions long before she received the Nobel Peace Prize in 2004, a recognition all the more important because Africa has had so few female icons and role models.

Maathai had several significant interactions with other Nobel Peace laureates, the most notable being with former American vice-president Al Gore, who was awarded the Nobel Peace Prize in 2007, jointly with the UN Intergovernmental Panel on Climate Change (IPCC). Wangari met Gore (then still an American senator and an ardent green campaigner) when he visited the Green Belt Movement's headquarters and field sites in Kenya in 1990. Together, they planted a *Podocarpus* tree (African yellowwood). Gore subsequently recounted his positive impressions about the Green Belt Movement in his 1992 bestseller, *Earth in the Balance*.[32]

In 1992, two years after their meeting in Kenya and the year that Gore became US vice-president in the Bill Clinton administration (1993–2000),

Maathai called on the US Senate Foreign Relations Committee to intervene in respect of the criminal charges by the Kenyan government that prevented her from travelling to the Earth Summit in Rio de Janeiro that year. Eight senators, including Gore, asked the Moi regime to substantiate the charges against her. By then, Wangari was already well known internationally for her pro-democracy campaigns. The charges were subsequently dropped, and she was able to attend the Earth Summit where she held a much-publicised press conference with Gore and the Tibetan spiritual leader, the Dalai Lama.

Maathai continued to work tirelessly with Gore in lobbying powerful grant-makers to protect the world's forest expanses in order to reverse the damaging effects of climate change. They campaigned for the US Senate, as well as the UN General Assembly, NGOs and others, to invest in forest conservation projects that could significantly reduce deforestation and mitigate the negative effects of climate change.

Maathai's meeting with US president and fellow Nobel Peace laureate, Barack Obama, was much like that with Gore. In 2006, Obama – then a senator – paid his first official visit to Kenya. Maathai and Obama held a public tree-planting ceremony at Uhuru Park in the Kenyan capital of Nairobi, the same site where Maathai had held a successful mass protest rally 15 years earlier against a proposed Kenya Times Media Trust complex development on public land. Uhuru Park's Freedom Corner became synonymous with Maathai's struggle for democracy and environmental conservation in Kenya. It was in this same park that hunger strikes, violent skirmishes and unlawful arrests involving security forces armed with live ammunition had occurred on several occasions.

During her brief parliamentary tenure, Maathai worked with fellow Nobel Peace laureate and former UN secretary-general, Ghana's Kofi Annan, who died in August 2018. Years earlier, she had served on Annan's advisory board on disarmament, which condemned the 1998 violence at Karura Forest, an ecologically spectacular area just 20 kilometres from the centre of Nairobi. The upheaval, in which more than 200 people were killed, was the result of opposition to the juggernaut of proposed luxury developments in which government officials reportedly held personal business interests. Large groups of concerned citizens, members of UNEP, and the Kenya Human Rights Commission, as well as parliamentarians, journalists and affiliates of the Green Belt Movement, confronted thugs hired by the developers. Maathai was severely beaten until she lost consciousness. When Annan was appointed by the AU as its chief mediator to facilitate a power-sharing election deal in Kenya between Raila Odinga and

Mwai Kibaki in 2007, Maathai worked with the former UN secretary-general on national pro-democracy efforts. Brutal clashes had erupted throughout Kenya in the aftermath of the 2007 polls, resulting in 30 days of violence during which an estimated 1,000 people were killed.

Concluding Reflections: The Tallest Tree in the Forest

Maathai was not without international controversy. The weeks preceding her Nobel Peace Prize award were marred by reports in Kenya's national press about her comments that HIV/AIDS had been created by evil scientists in Western laboratories to "decimate the African population". She provided clumsy clarifications, defending her comments in an interview with *Time* magazine in October 2004:

> I have no idea who created AIDS and whether it is a biological agent or not. But I do know things like that don't come from the moon. I have always thought that it is important to tell people the truth, but I guess there is some truth that must not be too exposed. I'm referring to AIDS. I am sure people know where it came from. And I'm quite sure it did not come from the monkeys.[33]

Over and above Maathai's achievements, perhaps her most formidable quality was her simplicity. She was personable and approachable by nature. Fondly remembered by many as a "village girl" – always resplendent in African traditional clothing – she was a warm and genuine person, with a rare grace who could disarm officials in black suits. Most who knew her recall her as humble and compassionate with the determination of a lion.

The excessive burdens on Maathai's shoulders eventually took their toll on her health when she was just 71, losing her battle with ovarian cancer. Until her death in September 2011, Wangari continued to be active in Kenya and on the world stage – particularly through the UN – and she was still being honoured with awards of lifetime achievements and honorary doctorates from universities across the globe.

As one of Africa's most powerful female leaders and ambassadors, Maathai remains unrivalled. She took up the monumental challenge of changing history and socio-political culture. Today, Pan-African land and gender struggles continue in ever-changing forms and guises. For Maathai's tireless efforts, the world has many reasons to be thankful to Africa's "Earth Mother".

18

RANDALL ROBINSON: PAN-AFRICAN FOREIGN POLICY VIRTUOSO

Pearl T. Robinson

"For centuries, Africa has been painted in lurid pictures. Its culture
has been covered with stupid machinations. Its conditions have been
represented as sardonic, its future, gloomy, and so we see the African
from the Nordic's perspective. This is but Caucasian propaganda to
keep the Negro American in ignorance and apparent disinterestedness,
on matters African."
– BEN NNAMDI AZIKIWE, *THE HILLTOP,* 1928[1]

"In public life, you are only who you appear to be."
– RANDALL ROBINSON, *DEFENDING THE SPIRIT:*
A BLACK LIFE IN AMERICA, 1998[2]

ON 7 NOVEMBER 1928, A LETTER PENNED by the young Nnamdi Azikiwe appeared
in Howard University's campus newspaper, *The Hilltop.* "Zik", a brilliant
but penniless student from colonial West Africa, titled his message "Africa
Speaks". He challenged the student body of the pre-eminent black university in
Washington DC to move beyond the white man's depictions of Africa as a land
held back by the relics of "primitive barbarism." In pursuit of this goal, Azikiwe
sought to engage his fellow students in a Pan-African dialogue:

It is highly essential that the African speak and open his mind to his
Afro-American brother ... We do not hold you guilty for your notions ...

277

We realise the effects of your history. We understand fully the situation which necessitated your psychologic and philosophic concept of the average African. Nevertheless, as representatives of a new Africa, we deem it wise to correct your notions and submit to you the thoughts of a modern and progressive Africa.[3]

This future Nigerian president was already thinking about "a revolutionary advance" for his homeland, and considered it important to cultivate relationships rooted in knowledge and respect with Howard's black, cosmopolitan student body. After all, they shared "the same ethnic origin". Simply put, the young Azikiwe was a Pan-Africanist who believed that "establishing understanding and mutuality between the Afro-American and his international brothers" might just be the best strategy for achieving "the ultimate amelioration of the Motherland". His political ideas were far from fully formed at the time, yet "Zik" envisaged a role for this historically black college as "a centre for the diffusion of knowledge among Negroes the world over".[4]

Randall Robinson began his Pan-African career on a trajectory that mirrored Zik's Howard blueprint. This Harvard-trained African-American lawyer served for 25 years as executive director of TransAfrica, the United States-based political lobby for Africa and the Caribbean. Robinson is best known for his progressive activism, edgy style and a readiness to speak truth to power. In the view of former American congressman Howard Wolpe, who chaired the US House of Representatives' subcommittee on Africa for nearly a decade, Randall was "the best ever witness to testify at a subcommittee hearing".[5] Above and beyond his acumen as a foreign policy virtuoso, Robinson, like Tanzanian president Julius Nyerere, relished the role of the *Mwalimu* (teacher).[6] Whether galvanising the crowd at a divestment rally, delivering the keynote address at a Cleveland City Club luncheon, or presenting testimony at a Congressional hearing, Robinson never neglected the teaching dimension of his work. Long after stepping down as executive director of TransAfrica, he continued to teach, touting the need for sustained efforts to correct "the sand of ignorance" in America about African issues.[7]

Discovering Africa

A proud black man – some would say, arrogant – Robinson was not shy about acknowledging his own early misconceptions about Africa, developed while growing up during the 1950s and 1960s in racially segregated Virginia. Recalling his early avoidance of all things African, he explained: "Africa, when mentioned at all during my childhood, was invariably in a humiliating context."[8] References to the continent in newspapers and books, images of Africans in movies and on television, were always negative. Randall learnt nothing about colonialism in school, and slavery was mentioned only briefly – as a cause of the American Civil War (1861–5). It was this kind of education that kept him ignorant about, and reluctant to engage with Africa, its people, its cultures and its contemporary problems.

Randall connected with Africa while a student at Harvard Law School, initially through the printed word, which soon triggered an affinity for activism. A voracious reader, he introduced himself to the classics of black world liberation literature: Frantz Fanon's *The Wretched of the Earth*,[9] C.L.R. James's *The Black Jacobins*[10] and W.E.B. Du Bois's *The Souls of Black Folk*.[11] By his own account, the more Robinson read, the angrier he became. Instinctively, he recognised the African condition as a version of his own encounters with Jim Crow racism in the US. As Randall noted:

> I could see no real substantive distinction between my American experience and the painful lot of the Haitians, South Africans, Mozambicans, Angolans, Zairians, Afro-Brazilians, and other blacks in other places about whom I was reading. The American official hand was everywhere, and invariably on the wrong side.[12]

For a news source, Robinson turned to the New York-based American Committee on Africa, a clearing house that disseminated information about African wars of liberation from Portuguese colonialism in Angola, Mozambique and Guinea-Bissau. Accounts of US military support for Portugal through the North Atlantic Treaty Organisation (NATO), the presence of American multinational Gulf Oil in Angola, and the US Polaroid Corporation's sale of photographic equipment that enabled apartheid South Africa to restrict the movement of blacks in that country stoked Randall's political awakening. This young law student from Virginia also drew inspiration from reports of armed local resistance in southern Africa, and stories about grassroots communities establishing schools, hospitals and co-operatives in liberated zones. In short, Robinson felt a connection to the ancestral continent.

Critical of the traditional news media's neglect of these developments, Randall and his wife, Brenda Robinson (now Randolph), decided they could support African liberation movements by launching an informal information campaign.[13] Brenda, a librarian and civil rights activist from Virginia, developed a slide show on imperialism and apartheid for presentations at local schools, community organisations and regional events.[14] Randall proved particularly adept as a speaker, and became a popular guest on the local Boston public television programme "Say Brother". Together, the Robinsons became part of a politically conscious Pan-Africanist circle of Kenyans, Tanzanians, Liberians and African Americans animated by Chris Nteta, a South African exile studying at Harvard Divinity School. Informational exchanges in their living rooms coalesced around an anti-imperialist ideology supportive of liberation movements in southern Africa, and a belief that African strategies of resistance and resilience could be successfully replicated in the US. These activists believed that problems in Africa and American inner cities were interconnected. It was in this setting that the Southern African Relief Fund (SARF) had its earliest beginnings.[15]

Randall pushed for the establishment of SARF in 1969 as a fundraising vehicle for the humanitarian support of southern African freedom fighters, and to advocate US disengagement from supporting Africa's white minority regimes. The campaign to provide food, clothing and other forms of material assistance doubled as a means to establish a relationship between local activism and global issues. As Robinson put it, "We must provide our people with informational materials demonstrating the relationship of our oppression to that of our brothers living in the homeland."[16] SARF's ideology rested on a critique of capitalism as an economic system that promoted race branding.

By the end of his third year at Harvard, the seasoned law student knew that he had no interest in a career as a practising lawyer, and wanted instead to become involved with African liberation struggles on a long-term basis. In order to finance a trip to the continent, Robinson successfully applied for a Ford Foundation Middle East and Africa Field Research Fellowship for African Americans. This grant to study "The Africanization of European Law and its Social Impact in Tanzania" opened the door to a life-long Pan-African journey. The year was 1970. The choice of Tanzania was strategic.

A Ford Foundation Fellow in Tanzania

The Organisation of African Unity (OAU) located its Liberation Committee in the Tanzanian capital of Dar es Salaam at the invitation of Julius Nyerere. The committee provided publicity for all liberation movements officially recognised by the OAU – including armed movements fighting against Portuguese colonial rule in Mozambique, Angola and Guinea-Bissau, as well as resistance movements in South Africa, Namibia and Southern Rhodesia. The body also served as a conduit for funding, logistical support and training. As a result, Dar became a home for refugees and liberation fighters from across Africa.[17] Upon arrival in Tanzania, Randall and Brenda Robinson personally delivered the sum of $4,000 to the OAU's Liberation Committee on behalf of SARF. While largely symbolic, this contribution was material affirmation of the "mutuality of interests and shared commitment" required for the global Pan-Africanism envisaged by the young Nnamdi Azikiwe.

Spending time with some of the leaders and foot soldiers of southern Africa's liberation struggles sharpened Robinson's understanding of their goals and methods, and he internalised their aspirations.[18] The future lobbyist was also able to observe the efficacy in the fight against colonial racist domination of a media strategy developed from a global rather than a local level. The Liberation Committee organised much of its diplomatic work through conferences, visits, press campaigns and radio broadcasts aimed at drawing resources into the struggle. In an international context dominated by intense East–West Cold War rivalry, media outreach helped to build a broad front of solidarity and support from Africa, Asia, the Nordic countries, the Soviet Union and China. The opportunity to watch this process unfold also schooled Robinson in the intricacies of Great Power games in the Third World. These lessons were carried forward to the next phase of his career.

Tanzania deepened Randall's political connections with the continent, and exposed the "made in America" configuration of his identity as an individual of African descent. The anti-black racism of Southeast Asians transported to colonial Africa by the imperial British was a constant irritant to this American native son. He was never comfortable with the practical politics of Nyerere's non-racialism, which prioritised nation-building over ethnic or racial solidarity. Indeed, with time came the recognition that many of the lessons learnt from dealing with racism in the US were out of sync with Tanzanian attitudes towards British colonial racism. What Randall would learn much later was that, even when problems in Africa and America's inner cities were interconnected, they were not necessarily viewed through the same prism.

The complexities of Pan-African identity were revealed in the full glare of the Tanzanian sun. Nyerere – like Ghana's Kwame Nkrumah from the 1950s (see Brown in this volume) – encouraged African Americans to live and work in his country. But for Randall, something was missing. Reflecting back on this period of his life, he would later recall the disappointment of feeling culturally stateless and emotionally binational: "I would always be a guest at an ancestral family table ... a long-gone son involuntarily re-acculturated in a far-off land. I could never be Tanzanian for the simple reason that I had not been born there, socialized into its mores ... into the rich mosaic of its culture."[19]

By the end of his Ford Foundation fellowship, this "guest at an ancestral table" had consolidated his personal relationship with Africa through the bonds of a shared political struggle. Believing that "America had become a substantial contributor to Africa's problems", Robinson reasoned that he could best serve the continent by returning to the home of his birth. Tanzania was a transformative experience. Yet Randall left East Africa without fully understanding the pitfalls and constraints of the post-colonial political economy.

Serving Africa by Returning to America

In the 1970s, the political landscape for America's black population was in flux, domestically and internationally. The passage of the 1965 Voting Rights Act by the US Congress outlawed racial barriers to the ballot box. A year later Edward Brooke, a Republican from Massachusetts, became the first black to serve in the US Senate since the era of Reconstruction (1863–77). Blacks in the US House of Representatives increased in number from three to thirteen between 1955 and 1971, when congressman Charles Diggs, a Democrat from Michigan and a Pan-Africanist, took the lead in organising the Congressional Black Caucus (CBC) into a formal legislative network. Some members of the CBC broke with tradition, and pledged to act as Representatives-at-large for black citizens nation-wide, in addition to representing their own districts. This convergence of new forms of political mobilisation and Black Power politics resulted in a push for collective political action in policy-making arenas. The field of US policy towards Africa was a logical next step.

Diggs used his role as chair of the House subcommittee on Africa to stir the waters. Following a 1972 fact-finding mission to Africa, he issued an Action Manifesto and audaciously endorsed violence as a legitimate means of liberation "so long as the recalcitrance of the South African government continues".[20]

This was rousing rhetoric. Liberation strategists understood that precision tools would be needed to affect desired outcomes.

Randall Robinson returned to the US from Tanzania in 1972 to a position as community development director for the Roxbury Multi-Service Centre. Juggling the daily routines of a legal aid lawyer in inner-city Boston, he re-engaged with the southern African liberation struggle as a local community activist. Under his energised leadership, the Pan-African Liberation Committee (PALC) attracted about a hundred local activists, and championed divestment protests targeting shareholder support for white minority rule. But it was a sit-in organised by black students at Harvard that brought Randall back to his former campus, and opened the door to national media exposure.

The revelation that Harvard's endowment included Gulf Oil stocks valued at $21 million in 1971 became a rallying cry for campus protests in April 1972.[21] After the Corporation voted to retain its portfolio and abstained on a shareholder resolution calling on Gulf to detail its operations in Angola, some two dozen black students seized and occupied Harvard president, Derek Bok's office, demanding the divestiture of the university's funds from the oil giant. The PALC joined the protest, and Randall worked with members of Harvard-Radcliffe Association of African and Afro-American Students and the PALC to coordinate an information campaign that reached out to Diggs and the CBC, bringing national attention to the complicity of Gulf and Harvard in Africa's colonial wars. President Bok ended the take-over by pledging to send an envoy to southern Africa to investigate the protesters' claims, but the university ultimately declined to divest.[22] Still, the divestment movement had scored a partial victory: the five-day occupation drew national press coverage, and demonstrated the power of a compelling message to move the needle of public opinion on an African policy issue.[23] This media victory also propelled Robinson onto the national stage.

Three years later, in 1975, a move to Washington as a staff assistant to Representative William Clay, a Democrat from Missouri, placed Randall at the heart of the US legislature on Capitol Hill. Clay's activist background as a union organiser, civil rights advocate and member of the CBC was a good match for Robinson's activist experiences in Boston. Clay's legislative priorities were largely domestic. His emphasis on labour relations, inner-city poverty and matters directly affecting his local constituencies was a good Congressional assignment for Robinson in learning the ropes and getting noticed. In 1976, four years after returning from Tanzania, Randall landed the plum post of administrative assistant to Charles Diggs, whose political goal was to raise the prioritisation of Africa in US foreign policy. Staff work for the House's Africa subcommittee and its parent body, the Committee on Foreign Affairs, would put the final touches to the training of an African foreign policy virtuoso. The moment was pregnant with possibilities for the simple fact that Randall Robinson was not alone.

The mid-to-late 1970s was an extraordinary period on Capitol Hill for African Americans with an interest in government policy. Career opportunities opened up, and increasing numbers of young black activists were being hired as Congressional staffers. Among them was a new generation of black internationalists, many of whom identified politically as Pan-Africanists or anti-imperialists, while rejecting the notion that working inside the political establishment was tantamount to co-optation. Their interest in Africa policy typically grew out of experiences garnered during study-abroad programmes, Crossroads Africa, the Peace Corps, Pan-African conferences or overseas research fellowships.[24] These thirty-somethings sought to develop policy-relevant expertise in areas that would enable them to contribute to political change and socio-economic development in Africa. In a highly insightful commentary, African-American scholar-activist Sylvia Hill concluded that these youthful civil society actors were not necessarily careerists in the traditional sense of the word. Rather, "They wanted to influence US foreign policy, and so they used their time ... on [the] Hill to understand how Congress worked and how they could influence change by knowing how it works."[25]

From this cohort of Congressional staffers came the foot soldiers who helped the CBC convene an action-oriented Leadership Conference on Southern Africa. Meeting in Washington DC in September 1976, 120 black leaders drawn from labour, business, civil rights, churches, government and other organisations called for a progressive US policy towards Africa, adopting an African–American Manifesto on Southern Africa, with an 11-point programme.[26] These conferees affirmed the need for a national organisation to express their views on African and Caribbean issues to the US administration of Gerald Ford and to the American Congress. This call for action led to the founding of TransAfrica in 1977, with Randall Robinson as its first executive director.

A Black Political Lobby for Africa
and the Caribbean

The launch of TransAfrica was a collaborative effort. Established in July 1977 as a non-profit, non-partisan foreign policy lobby, it began as a gutsy start-up. Its co-founders sought to create a distinctive African-American voice to address US policies affecting the black world – defined as continental Africa and the Caribbean. Herschelle Challenor of the US Committee for UNESCO, MIT political science professor Willard Johnson, and Randall Robinson are credited with fashioning the lobby's institutional design. In addition to the Washington DC headquarters, local chapters expanded TransAfrica's reach to activist constituencies in Washington, Boston and Cleveland. More would follow.

Within a decade, a mix of foundation support, celebrity fundraisers, individual donations and an annual dinner seemed to put the new foreign policy lobby on track for a sustainable future with solid financial backing. Robinson symbolised the organisation's brand. His media savviness provided a unique Pan-African patina of professional authenticity to a new generation of black foreign policy specialists.

Under Randall's leadership, TransAfrica developed a two-level media strategy, making subtle distinctions between messages targeted to the elite news media and those directed to black niche markets. An innovative feature of the mainstream outreach was Robinson's use of C-Span[27] to establish visibility and credibility in Washington's foreign policy landscape, and to become a reliable source of information on African and Caribbean issues. The TransAfrica director's frequent appearances at press conferences, Congressional hearings and protest demonstrations captured the attention of journalists in America's national media as well as in the black press. Stories citing TransAfrica's Randall Robinson eventually became staples in the *Washington Post*, the *New York Times* and affiliates of the Associated Press news agency.

Two Black Power-era magazines further anchored TransAfrica's niche media presence: *Black Enterprise* and *Essence*. The former, published by Earl Graves, is the leading business magazine for African-American entrepreneurs, professionals and corporate executives. The latter, founded by Ed Lewis, is a lifestyle magazine directed at "upscale African-American women" who "cultivate a Black identity".[28] Both monthlies began in 1970. Both covered TransAfrica's action agenda by profiling Randall Robinson as a successful black foreign policy professional, a role model for black youth, and a champion for racial justice.[29] Graves joined TransAfrica's national board in 1992, while Lewis spent two decades as board chair of the TransAfrica Forum think tank. According to Graves, they considered themselves "brothers-in-arms in the publishing industry who [took] strides to stamp a positive African identity into the larger culture".[30] Their media support for TransAfrica, coupled with their coverage of Randall Robinson as a foreign policy guru, was central to the lobby group's efforts.

This two-level media strategy converged to place Robinson's public persona at the nexus of social justice, foreign policy and black self-esteem. It also linked the political lobby to a larger narrative of black global empowerment and Pan-African solidarity. In Randall's hands, the media became effective tools for education and the mobilisation of support for his cause. As the chapter structure gave way to an emphasis on amorphous affiliate groups, appearances on popular talk shows filled many more gaps. An hour of radio time on the Larry King Show guaranteed an audience of at least two million listeners. A skilled communicator with a compelling message such as Robinson could do a lot with that level of outreach.[31]

The establishment of the TransAfrica Forum in 1981 signalled an effort to institutionalise Robinson's charisma. Conceived as the lobby's education and research arm, the Forum convened an annual foreign policy conference in Washington DC. Its quarterly journal, *TransAfrica Forum*, appeared the following year in 1982. Featuring content garnered from scholars, policy-makers, activists and politicians based in Africa, the Caribbean and the United States, it brought voices seldom heard in official Washington circles into the American foreign policy arena. African-American political scientist, Edmond Keller – then director of the University of California Los Angeles's (UCLA) African Studies Centre – edited the journal during its heyday.[32]

The Forum's energetic young staff operated out of modest offices in south-east Washington DC. Harvard Law School fellowships in human rights and public interest law sponsored legal interns such as African-American Hope Lewis, Kenyan Makau wa Mutua and Sierra Leone's Ibrahim Gassama, who brought their own Pan-African networks and cutting-edge research to the new think tank. These future law professors contributed technical expertise, policy knowledge and analytical skills that helped establish the Forum's bona fides as a legitimate research institute.[33]

Robinson's steady dedication to the mundane tasks of public interest lobbying produced impressive results. In little more than five years, he had delivered on the Leadership Council's call for a national organisation to express the American black community's views on foreign policy issues. Still, much of the work was reactive – critiquing ill-conceived policies or trying to rectify harmful outcomes. TransAfrica had yet to position itself in front of the policy process with proposals originated by black constituency groups or crafted in-house by its own expert staff.

The Free South Africa Movement: A Legislative Triumph

In November 1984, Robinson, together with three fellow African Americans – congressman Walter Fauntroy, civil rights commissioner Mary Frances Berry and Georgetown law professor Eleanor Holmes Norton – went to the South African embassy to talk to Ambassador Brand Fourie about the recent arrests of 13 black trade union leaders in the country. When they asked that African National Congress (ANC) leader, Nelson Mandela, be released from 21 years in jail, the ambassador abruptly ended the meeting. Robinson, Fauntroy and Berry refused to leave the embassy, and were arrested. Holmes Norton contacted the American media.

This act of civil disobedience triggered a series of cascading events. The protest leaders held a press conference in the US Congress's House office building, where they introduced the Free South Africa Movement (FSAM) as a TransAfrica project focused on the goal of passing comprehensive sanctions legislation that would end US complicity with the apartheid regime.[34] Returning to the embassy, the activists chained themselves to the entrance, and invited arrest. This was the trigger action. Waves of demonstrators across the country targeted South African consulates and US companies involved in South Africa. A steady stream of volunteers calling for economic sanctions joined daily marches and sit-ins. Made-for-media events included the arrest of celebrities who travelled to the nation's capital to be handcuffed in front of the South African embassy. Randall worked closely with the Congressional Black Caucus, helping to focus the movement's energy on specific legislative objectives. Protests and advocacy continued for two years, during which more than 4,500 people were arrested.

The atmospherics of passionate debate over policy issues played to Randall's strengths. He brought years of experience to the struggle, and could communicate across a wide range of platforms. By all accounts, he was "a master at unifying the radically and ideologically diverse groups" that coalesced under the FSAM umbrella.[35] Most significantly, Robinson helped many African Americans to forge a new sense of personal solidarity with the struggles of black South Africans, bringing momentum and a sense of urgency to the long-standing undercurrent of anti-apartheid activities in the US.[36] His movement's perseverance eventually delivered. Seventeen years after Representative Diggs introduced his first sanctions bills in 1969, the US Congress ended the Ronald Reagan administration's apartheid-coddling policy of "Constructive Engagement" by legislative fiat.

The Comprehensive Anti-Apartheid Act (CAAA) of 1986 directed the release of Nelson Mandela, established a timetable for the elimination of apartheid laws, and outlined a sanctions regime that prohibited investments, bank loans and certain forms of trade with South Africa until the required changes had been accomplished. The law passed both Houses of Congress with bipartisan support over President's Ronald Reagan's veto, which two-thirds of the legislature overrode.[37] It was a stunning victory – one that added new lustre to Robinson's reputation as a visionary Pan-Africanist and a champion of justice.

On 11 February 1990, South Africa's last white president, F.W. de Klerk, ordered the release of Nelson Mandela after 27 years in detention. The process of ending apartheid and creating a non-racial democracy had been formally launched with help from the black African diaspora.

A New Headquarters Building along Embassy Row

TransAfrica's growth continued under Robinson's stewardship. In 1992, the non-profit lobby reported an annual budget of $800,000, with a headquarters staff of 12, seven local chapters and a research institute that published issue briefs, news highlights and a journal. Despite these impressive assets, black America's premier foreign policy lobby was losing ground as a proliferation of think tanks transformed official Washington's landscape.[38] Major Washington-based institutes such as the Brookings Institution, the Council on Foreign Relations and the Centre for Strategic and International Studies (CSIS) were positioned to challenge TransAfrica's claim to be the only source of reliable analysis of US policy towards Africa. Randall took note of these developments and determined that TransAfrica must move to the next level. As he explained in a June 1993 interview with the *New York Times*: "This town produces policy as a result of the competition of policy ideas ... We have never competed evenly institutionally in the arena of foreign affairs. That's why we [want] a fully fleshed out think tank to grind out the analysis that represents the interests of our community."[39]

When an opportunity to acquire prime real estate at recession-era prices surfaced, the executive director acted. With help from an eclectic group of sports and celebrity supporters, Robinson worked out a deal to acquire a historic Washington DC property that once housed the German embassy. Contributions from tennis superstar Arthur Ashe, former boxing champion "Sugar" Ray Leonard and Reebok International covered the down payment. Celebrity-hosted fundraising galas and a steady stream of small donations bought time for a longer-term business model to kick in.

As renovations to the five-storey headquarters building advanced, it fell to Robinson to explain why TransAfrica, at the height of its lobbying success, was transitioning to a foreign policy think tank. An interview with *Black Enterprise*'s Frank McCoy in August 1992 sought to clarify the matter: "Our tactics range from training black students to pass the foreign service examination to demonstrating outside the South African embassy. We need to be able to apply pressure outside the system. The National Rifle Association is a role model for effective lobbying. It is well funded and can push against the grain for its own interests."[40]

A year later, in 1993, on the eve of the dedication of the building, Robinson gave *New York Times* reporter Karen DeWitt a tour of the renovated facility. They visited the computer centre, the public reading room, various meeting spaces and the area slated to house a 6,000-volume library. Robinson explained the rationale for establishing a think tank. DeWitt was briefed on the planned Scholars Council and a possible foreign service training programme for students at historically black colleges. Her reporting surmised that the TransAfrica Forum would provide a counterpoint to official Washington's analysis of US policy towards Africa and the Caribbean. She concluded: "There is no precise way to gauge whether its policy positions on Africa and the Caribbean reflect the views of most black Americans."[41] When reported by an icon of the mainstream media, appearances matter. DeWitt's story raised doubts.

C-Span featured the dedication reception for TransAfrica Forum's Arthur Ashe Foreign Policy Library on its 6 June 1993 *Sunday Journal*. This black-tie event, co-hosted by Randall Robinson and the NBC "Today" Show's Bryant Gumbel, attracted about 500 guests – including US cabinet secretaries, members of Congress, members of the African diplomatic corps, two Caribbean political leaders, Foundation officials, media personalities, aid officials, academics and a number of celebrities.[42] Views of the building's facade and interior decor conveyed a sense of the excitement and anticipation that animated the occasion. Billed as the dedication of a foreign policy library destined to become "the nation's primary repository of US foreign policy material on Africa and the Caribbean", the affair showcased Robinson in the role of a seasoned foreign policy virtuoso.

Politics, Polls and Triangulation

Bill Clinton's January 1993 inauguration brought a new generation of political leadership to Washington. He won the presidency with 43 per cent of the popular vote, garnering 83 per cent of the black vote, with only 39 per cent of whites casting their ballot for him.[43] Clinton repaid his political debt by making more black appointments than any previous US president. Ron Brown became commerce secretary, Mike Espy became agriculture secretary, Hazel O'Leary energy secretary and Jesse Brown the secretary of veterans affairs. Among other appointments were two high-level advisers with overlapping responsibilities for African affairs: career diplomat George Moose became the first African American to serve as assistant secretary of state for African affairs,[44] while Clinton's fellow Rhodes Scholar at Oxford University, Susan Rice, a 29-year-old Africanist, joined the National Security Council staff as director for international organisations and peacekeeping.[45] The combined foreign policy expertise of Moose and Rice carried considerably more insider gravitas on Africa than TransAfrica Forum's nascent think tank could muster.

TransAfrica timed the dedication of its Arthur Ashe Library to coincide with its annual foreign policy weekend. Held four months into the Clinton presidency in May 1993, these back-to-back events were promoted as an African World Together homecoming. The coordination of an international careers fair, a Smithsonian cultural exhibit and the annual membership meeting to coincide with the foreign policy conference underscored Randall's commitment to constituency-broadening. The TransAfrica Scholars Council marked the occasion by releasing a special policy brief titled "Rethinking US Foreign

Assistance".[46] This proposed "rethinking" called for American aid policy to encourage equitable economic growth in developing countries by promoting poverty eradication, gender equity, environmental sustainability and long-term food security – with broad-based participation in decision-making and governance as basic human rights. Funding these initiatives would necessitate increases in the US aid budget, and debt relief for Africa and the Caribbean, along with efforts to increase private investment.

It is, however, unclear whether the State Department's Africa Bureau was aware of these proposals, as Moose's remarks to TransAfrica's national conference were tone-deaf. He told the audience that President Clinton's pledge to reduce the US budget deficit made discussions about debt relief for poor African countries "especially difficult".[47] Unable to promise an increase in aid, Moose instead pledged to fight for Africa getting "its fair share" of resources available to support business development, democracy promotion and human rights. In closing, Moose invited support for the administration with assurances that a sustainable and progressive US policy towards Africa would depend on the efforts of Randall Robinson and organisations like TransAfrica.

After thanking Moose for his remarks, Robinson invited questions from the floor. First to speak was a TransAfrica supporter who objected to the focus on democracy promotion and human rights for Africa, when blacks "don't have human rights and democracy in America". The aggrieved speaker noted that she had expected to hear the views of her community advanced in Moose's speech. Instead, the African-American diplomat had simply reiterated Clinton's agenda. Her retort to Moose was unforgiving: "You are not representing us! You are representing the other side!" This outburst was an open condemnation of the TransAfrica director's inability to curtail the effects of Clinton's triangulation between Democrats and Republicans – taking issue-based positions on matters designed to please Republicans, reassuring white Americans, and attracting private investors, while making no explicit commitment to pursue TransAfrica's foreign policy agenda.

Following heavy losses to the Republicans in the US Senate and House of Representatives in the 1994 mid-term elections, Clinton doubled down. Triangulation as a political strategy provided the wily politician with a hedging strategy. He would discard the extremes of the left and the right; take the best from each position; and move up to a third way.[48] Clinton worked this strategy in the domestic arena with programmes favouring the cutting of social benefits and promoting welfare reform. He also pursued the mass incarceration of mostly African-American and Latino youths – often for petty crimes – instead of pushing for genuine criminal justice reform. Triangulation in the foreign policy arena was evident in the forced repatriation of refugees fleeing Haiti, the dismissal of Robinson's call for nation-building in Somalia, and the ban against American participation in UN peacekeeping missions, many of which were deployed in Africa.[49] This resulted in Clinton's preventing any international action to stop the genocide that killed about 800,000 in Rwanda in 1994.

Consistently working to retain overwhelming support among African Americans, Clinton simultaneously manoeuvred to increase his popularity with whites. The strategy eventually worked. Despite impeachment by the House of Representatives, the president left office in 2001 with approval ratings of 89 per cent among blacks and 59 per cent among white Americans.[50] During this same period, Robinson's influence in official Washington steadily declined.

Towards a Repertoire of Pan-African Dialogues

African-American Black Power theorist Ron Walters explained that in order to wield power effectively, black people in America must own their institutions.[51] Randall Robinson broached the subject in his 1998 memoir, *Defending the Spirit*, by outing himself as a jaded fundraiser. Observing that almost no African-American organisations are owned by those whose messages they are perceived to convey, he conceded that TransAfrica was no exception.[52] For years, reliance on media and communications strategies to mobilise support around social justice campaigns had attracted sufficient funding to advance TransAfrica's work. But the ground had shifted considerably during the Clinton administration (1993–2000). As the post-apartheid era imposed the logic of private sector investment to finance South Africa's deracialisation process, TransAfrica's ability to fund its core mission in a sustained way had badly eroded. The lack of institutional ownership had become a clear and present danger.

The young Azikiwe's prescient insights on self-determination in the 1920s – quoted at the beginning of this essay – had anticipated the problem of resource constraints, and proposed a black world solution. While insisting on the importance of sharing his aspirations for Africa's future with Howard's student body, Zik had also recognised the need for broader Pan-African dialogues to cultivate mutuality of respect and understanding. Decades later, when Randall looked back with disappointment at the fracturing of his relationship with South Africa's first black president, Nelson Mandela, he reached the lamentable conclusion that the anti-apartheid cause had "obscured their underlying ignorance about each other".[53]

How could this be? When the two men met in Cape Town in February 1990, Randall was part of the NBC news team that covered Mandela's iconic walk to freedom. Four months later, they travelled together, criss-crossing the US on a historic 12-day, eight-city "Freedom Tour". Their joint public appearances were regarded as Pan-African celebrations. Mandela symbolised what black Americans had endured: state-sanctioned segregation, denial of human rights, police brutality; in short, the lived experiences of a white supremacist regime. Randall proudly touted a narrative of their shared worldview: "He [Mandela] had an impact on me as a child of the South because I grew up under similar conditions ... And here was a figure who stood against it all with enormous courage, and completely unbowed."[54]

In reality, TransAfrica's leader and South Africa's future president had divergent views on the relevance of the racial order for strategies of economic renewal. Mandela – even more than Tanzania's Julius Nyerere – faced the challenges of governing an economy owned largely by whites and heavily reliant on foreign investment, to improve the conditions for the country's 90 per cent black majority. The 1990 Freedom Tour of the US had been a carefully scripted roadshow that enabled Mandela to thank his supporters, raise funds for his ANC party, and urge foreign governments to maintain sanctions on South Africa until a multiracial democracy had replaced white minority rule. The two leaders did not seek to cultivate mutual understanding. Instead, they kept their sights on the political and strategic demands of ending American foreign policy support for the apartheid regime.[55]

Mandela returned home from the Freedom Tour with millions of dollars for his party's electoral campaign war-chest. Although Randall's facilitation contributed significantly to this success, neither man raised a flag of caution about the financial vulnerability of TransAfrica or South Africa's networks of anti-apartheid NGOs. Within a few short years, this missed opportunity to establish understanding and mutuality between African Americans and their Pan-African kin would have serious repercussions for the institutional architecture of foreign policy lobbying in the US, and related grassroots mobilisation in the new South Africa.

Interestingly, the predicate for launching a Pan-African dialogue around the importance of institutional ownership already existed. Randall's involvement in the US Congressional negotiations that resulted in the passage of the 1986 Anti-Apartheid Act had leveraged financial support for the victims of apartheid by earmarking millions of dollars for scholarships, refugee assistance and community development projects.[56] This infusion of cash into South Africa's NGO sector helped sustain militant activism at a critical time when Mandela was still in jail, and the internal resistance to apartheid was at its most imperilled. Although the Congressional funding ended after Mandela's release from prison in 1990, generous private foundations and bilateral donors took up the slack until South Africa's first universal election in 1994 resulted in a Government of National Unity (GNU) headed by Mandela. At that point, the World Bank, the International Monetary Fund (IMF) and key bilateral donors joined forces to marshal their funding instruments to try to reverse the effects of the boycotts and to attract foreign investment into South Africa. Private American philanthropic bodies such as the Ford Foundation and the Carnegie Corporation followed suit.

Within a few years, the vitality of South Africa's NGO sector had eroded, with serious consequences for poor and disadvantaged South Africans.[57] Bewildered by these developments, Moeletsi Mbeki, brother of South Africa's deputy president Thabo Mbeki, complained that the West was selectively "manipulating official development assistance to NGOs to bring South Africa under its wing".[58] Robinson took careful note of this statement. By 1997, TransAfrica was a shell of its former self, and in no position to re-engage with the African development debate with vigour.

As early as 1994, the African-American lobby was experiencing a loss of corporate and foundation support, just as the business plan devised for its think tank fell short of vital backers needed to host celebrity fundraisers.[59] Word that President Nelson Mandela would attend a two-hour fundraising brunch at TransAfrica's headquarters in Washington DC in October 1994 while on his first state visit to the US thus came as welcome news. The $5,000-a-person price tag signalled that new money should soon be available to support some of the organisation's key programmes. But shortly after Mandela's plane landed in New York, the South Africans called to inform TransAfrica that his schedule had had to be adjusted: "Madiba" (Mandela's clan name) would not attend the fundraiser.

Mandela's withdrawal from the dinner was a devastating blow. Neither the staff nor board members could figure out why a modest fundraiser for the pre-eminent black foreign policy lobby would be so casually dismissed by an African liberation hero. Had the new South Africa turned a blind eye to generations of Pan-African struggles? Though desperately in need of Mandela's patronage, Robinson refused to beg. He instead cancelled the fundraiser, returned the cheques in hand, and declined President Clinton's invitation to attend the state dinner for Mandela. Two and a half years passed before the two men were reconciled with the help of African-American comedian Bill Cosby.[60]

In December 2001 *Black Enterprise* publisher Earl Graves served as chief moderator for TransAfrica's tribute to Randall Robinson. Graves recognised Randall as a historic figure, crediting his leadership for the institution's global stature, as well as its considerable influence on US policy and public opinion. The praise was hard earned and well deserved. Yet the founding director was stepping down after publicly stating that "African Americans have virtually no power or influence".[61] Contriteness was a mismatch for his old job, but a good fit for his new calling. It enabled Robinson to convince considerably more black people that they were indeed owed a debt for the cumulative emotional and institutional damages attributable to the Atlantic slave trade (see Introduction and Beckles in this volume).

As Randall stood in front of the TransAfrica building's large fireplace at the December 2001 tribute, surrounded by his wife Hazel and two of his children and a grandchild, two giant carved African ancestor figures hovered in the background. One tribute followed another in a flood. Then, it was Robinson's turn to take the microphone. Speaking with a quiet eloquence in modulated tones, Randall claimed credit for helping to build the groundwork for an institution that would survive. After expressing pride in TransAfrica's accomplishments, he bemoaned the crippling cruelty of resource constraints: "Every position that we took cost us money. And [no] corporation would embrace us after we finished standing for what we thought was important to stand for."[62]

Ending on a note of humility mixed with self-deprecating humour, Randall reminded his audience of admiring friends and supporters: "We are less important than the institution itself."[63]

Concluding Reflections: Quitting America to Write *The Debt*

Robinson embarked on a new journey to make sense of his own life by trying to understand and explain "the inner psyche of Africans and African descent peoples".[64] To begin this journey, he let go of America as the place called "home".

His destination was the small Caribbean island of St Kitts and Nevis, the home of his second wife, Hazel Ross Robinson. Here, Randall was able to plant new roots. He began to talk about the issue of reparations as his next great crusade. The titles of four books memorialise this remarkable metamorphosis: *Defending the Spirit: A Black Life in America* (1999); *Quitting America: The Departure of a Black Man from his Native Land* (2000);[65] *The Debt: What America Owes to Blacks* (2001);[66] and *The Reckoning: What Blacks Owe to Each Other* (2002).[67]

After quitting America for a welcome home, Randall became a teacher of diasporic histories and basic human rights. He would later find his twenty-first-century voice as a professor of law at Penn State Law School, and by rendering a rationale for *The Debt* in compelling narratives. He insisted that a monetary debt was owed to diasporic and continental Africans in payment for uncompensated labour, as well as for the psychic damage caused by the impact of slavery and its associated ills. This debt, he argued, was owed in order to repair the myriad human consequences of slavery which he characterised as a human rights crime against African and African-descended people. He noted that the legacy was institutional; the damage intergenerational; and, hence, the debt must be paid forward.

PART 5

THE SOCIAL SCIENTISTS

C.L.R. James: With Africa on His Mind

Selwyn R. Cudjoe

No account of Western civilization could leave out the names of
Toussaint L'Ouverture, Alexander Hamilton, Alexandre Dumas (the
father), Leconte Delisle, José Maria de Heredia, Marcus Garvey, René
Maran, Saint-John Perse, Aimé Césaire, George Padmore, Frantz
Fanon, and allow me to include one contemporary, a Cuban writer,
Alejo Carpentier. I do not mention the remarkable novelists whom we
of the British Caribbean have produced during the last twenty years.
– C.L.R. James, "The Making of a Caribbean People", 1966[1]

If one were to leave Port of Spain – the capital of the island of Trinidad and Tobago – and travel east along the Eastern Main Road (formerly the Royal Road) for twelve miles, one would come across a site where a charming house with two sloping sides attached to an extended roof – reminiscent of the charming Victorian houses of the nineteenth century – once existed at the corner of Lopinot Road and the Priority Bus Route. Both Henry Sylvester Williams and George Padmore (see Duggan in this volume) lived in that house. In May 2017, the government of Trinidad and Tobago demolished that house in what it described as a "clean-up campaign". Apparently, the building had become an eye-sore to the government, and thus had to be destroyed. Presumably, many of the residents of Arouca were unaware of its importance.

Destroying History

Lopinot Junction – the site of the house in which both Williams and Padmore once resided – was named after Charles Joseph Comte de Loppinot, a powerful Haitian planter who fled the island when the Haitians revolted against their hated French oppressors in 1792. When he left Haiti, Loppinot took some enslaved Africans with him. He settled first in Jamaica before travelling to Trinidad where he purchased a plantation and settled at Arouca. Count Loppinot's home is still intact, having been spared destruction by the government of Trinidad and Tobago. The count's residence, like that of Williams and Padmore, has all the architectural charms of early nineteenth-century Trinidadian buildings. Louis B. Homer, a Trinidadian researcher, noted: "Legend has it that his [Count Loppinot's] demise came about while returning from Arouca, in a landslide that carried him down a cliff and half-buried him. He died in 1819 and was interred next to his wife, Marie Cecile Dannoy, who died before him."[2]

However, if one were to retrace the count's steps along the Eastern Main Road and travel four miles west of Arouca, one would wind up in Tunapuna, the village in which C.L.R. James was born. Tunapuna – located in the quarter of St Joseph – first entered into the island's topographical lexicon in the Slave Register of 1813 as a provision plantation that was owned by Antonia Delaone.[3] In 2016, one would have encountered the house from which James watched the exploits of Matthew Bondman and of which he wrote so lovingly and with such great nostalgia in his 1963 book *Beyond a Boundary*. As James noted:

> Our house was superbly situated, exactly behind the wicket. A huge tree on one side and another house on the other limited the view of the ground, but an umpire could have stood at the bedroom window. By standing on a chair a small boy of six could watch practice every afternoon and matches on Saturdays – with matting one pitch could and often did serve for both practice and matches. From the chair also he could mount on to the windowsill and so stretch a groping hand for the books on the top of the wardrobe. Thus early the pattern of my life was set.[4]

Hands eager to make more money destroyed this house in 2016. As with the former residence in which Williams and James had lived, few citizens protested the destruction of these homes. It hardly registered with the residents of the island that in one short year the Trinidadian government had destroyed two monuments that signified Pan-African wisdom and intellectual excellence, without even giving it a second thought.

It is this shameful neglect of our intellectual legacy and the lackadaisical manner in which we research our intellectual heroes that is, in part, the subject of this essay. For too long, scholars of C.L.R. James's work have failed to examine the intellectual milieu from which James came, which has led to a certain paucity – or should I say misinterpretation – of his work. After all, is it for nothing that James spent the first 31 years of his life in Trinidad and Tobago?

In *Beyond a Boundary*, his semi-biographical work of 1963, James wrote that he had mastered cricket and English literature virtually on his own. That is only half of the truth. Language and literature were vibrant aspects of the life of nineteenth-century Trinidad. This cosmopolitan society included a great diversity of people, cultures and languages. It was a society in which the literary – oral and written – and the cultural, were valued, and appreciated. In September 1840, two years after the post-slavery apprenticeship system ended, the Port of Spain Literary Society was created. George Scotland, chief justice of the island, was elected as its first president; George Cowen, a member of the Anti-Slavery Society, was named as treasurer; while Charles Warner, the attorney-general, was elected as a member of the committee.[5]

Warner was one of the most distinguished scholars of his day. L.B. Tronchin, another outstanding black Trinidadian scholar, described him as "a man who had become conspicuous in the annals of the colony by his eloquence as a lawyer, his ability as a legislator and his profundity as a scholar".[6] In 1877, James Anthony Froude, an English historian at Oxford, met Warner on the island, one month before Warner died. Froude, "one of the greatest intellectuals of his time",[7] according to James, said of Warner: "To have seen and spoken with such a man was worth a voyage round the globe."[8]

James also admired Warner's intellectual brilliance, which he believed was matched equally by Michel Maxwell Philip, another distinguished black Trinidadian thinker of the era. Philip – James wrote – "was definitely of the same stamp intellectually [as Warner], recognised as such by those of his fellows best qualified to judge".[9] Philip had studied at the Jesuit College of St Mary's, Blairs, in Scotland, and had written *Emmanuel Appadocca* in 1854, the first novel of the English-speaking Caribbean.

In 1865 William Hamilton Gamble, a Trinidadian who studied at Oxford University, described the diversified manners and customs of Trinidadians. He noted that several African, Indian and European languages were spoken on the island: a Babel of voices. In his 1866 work, *Trinidad: Historical and Descriptive*, Gamble described John Jacob Thomas – "a jet-black man" who was born in 1836 during slavery – as "one of the most intelligent and learned of the Trinidadians" who was in the process of writing a grammar and dictionary of Creole, a medium through which "the African and the Creole, and the stranger in general, learn first, and of course, for the simple reason that he hears it most frequently spoken".[10] Four years later, after much intensive work, Thomas produced *The Theory and Practice of Creole Grammar*, an important linguistic breakthrough of its time.

Thomas was in Grenada when he read Froude's *The English in the West Indies*. Froude asserted his belief in the "natural superiority" of whites and their God-given right to rule over Africans. He claimed that West Indian blacks needed a religion to keep them from "falling back into devil worship", arguing that "If left entirely to themselves, they would in a generation or two relapse into savages; there were but two alternatives before not Grenada only, but all the English West Indies – either an English administration pure and simple like the East Indian, or a falling eventually into a state like that of Hayti [Haiti], where they eat the babies, and no white man can own a yard of land."[11] Trinidad, he claimed, was the island "from which the cannibal savages came".[12]

Caribbean scholars and European administrators in the Caribbean rebutted Froude's deeply prejudiced work. Thomas's 1889 reply, *Froudacity: West Indian Fables by James Anthony Froude*,[13] was the most forceful of these. Froude had written for the English public; Thomas had written for the edification of his fellow Caribbean people. James claimed that, in his rejoinder, Thomas "showed in every possible way … the attitude of a person with a mind and mentality, a social conception and a historical method, which was vastly superior to that of the highly educated and famous English historian and writer".[14]

Thomas defined his response as a task of "self-vindication" and characterised it as a "patriotic duty" against what he called the "bastard philosophy" of Froude.[15] While Froude concluded that West Indians were not capable of self-government, Thomas made it clear that the whole population – white, black, mulatto and the other inhabitants – were an integral part of the movement towards self-government. He argued that colonialism and "race madness" were the real enemy of the people, and took strong objection to Anglo-Saxons who believed that they had a seemingly divine right to dominate in any land in which they found themselves.

Thomas had mingled and conversed with the Mandingoes, Foulahs, Hausas, Calvers, Gullahs and Congoes who had inhabited the island. He affirmed that not "even three in ten of the whole number [of African ethnoi in Trinidad] were slaves in their own country, in the sense of having been born under any organised system of servitude".[16] As to the good breeding that slavery was supposed to have imposed upon Africans, Thomas reminded Froude that "African explorers, from Mungo Park to [David] Livingstone and [Henry Morton] Stanley, have all borne sufficient testimony to the world regarding the natural friendliness of the Negro in his ancestral home, when not under the influence of suspicion, anger, or dread". [17]

The same social and economic forces that shaped Thomas, the Barbadian lawyer Conrad Reeves, and the great African-American freedom fighter Frederick Douglass, made James into the writer and personality that he would become. Elsewhere, I have described the particular forces that shaped James's life and work.[18] He did not go to England empty-handed or empty-minded. In 1967 he said to Robert Hill, his literary executor, that "I want to say, without having any national pride or national faith or anything of the kind, that a great deal of the West Indies is in every book that I have written, although I have written as widely as a history of the Communist International, a book on cricket, a novel, and so forth. But I left the West Indies late. I was already thirty-one years old and everything that I write has its origin in the West Indies."[19]

The Black Jacobins

In 1934 James wrote *Toussaint L'Ouverture: The Story of the Only Successful Slave Revolt in History*, a play about the leader of the Haitian Revolution that was produced in London. The talented African-American scholar-artist Paul Robeson, who would become a good friend of James, took the lead role. In 1938 James wrote *The Black Jacobins*,[20] which can be seen as an extension of the work he had begun in the West Indies. He noted that *The Black Jacobins* "was written in the company of George Padmore, Jomo Kenyatta, and those of us who were concerned with African emancipation at the time ... [It] was written about the West Indies but with the idea of African emancipation in mind and the slaves of San Domingo and their struggle for freedom as a kind of model, and even a moral incitement to the Africans to do the same."[21]

James has said that, while he was in Trinidad, his thoughts were not very ordered. London helped him to straighten them out: "It was after reading Marx and Lenin and studying Trotsky's polemics against Stalin that I began to develop a coherent view of the world."[22] James, however, was not completely oblivious of socialism and Marxism while he was in Trinidad. In an interview granted to Al Richardson, Clarence Chrysostom and Anna Grimshaw in 1986, he spoke about his relationship with George Padmore:

> I knew Padmore in Trinidad. As boys we used to live in Arima and go and bathe in the river there. When we grew up, he was far more of a leftist than I was. I was a historian, whilst George had joined the labour movement, and became a Trotskyist. Then he went to America [in 1924 and in 1928 changed his name to Padmore], and I lost him. Then I came to England and joined the labour movement, and became a Trotskyist. Then the news came that George Padmore had been expelled from the United States and had come to England."[23]

They met in London under fortuitous circumstances. Padmore had become a high official in the Communist Party of Russia and had lived in Moscow for several years. When Padmore left the Communist Party, he and James reignited their friendship and formed the International African Friends of Ethiopia (IAFE) (see Reddock in this volume). This organisation later became the International African Service Bureau. James noted that he had started the black movement in England, and Padmore later joined. Padmore informed James that he was a Marxist. James asked him about the colonial question and African liberation. Thereafter, as James explained, "the movement became an African movement, a Marxist movement. Padmore did that. He educated me and I carried it on. After he died, people began to think that I had brought Marxism to the African movement. It wasn't so."[24]

Padmore had become a big political leader in Moscow. On Labour Day on 1 May, he joined Joseph Stalin, Vyacheslav Molotov, the long-serving foreign minister of the Soviet Union, and other Russian dignitaries as they reviewed the armed forces of the Union of Soviet Socialist Republics (USSR). But then Lenin died in January 1924 and Moscow changed its position on the "Negro Question" in the Caribbean and the United States. These blacks were no longer to be considered revolutionary forces in and of themselves. Padmore refused to go along with such a position (see Duggan in this volume). He told James that he had denounced "democratic capitalists" for a long time previously, and asked: "How do you expect me to go there [the US and the Caribbean] and write and say that this is democratic capitalism?" The Communists said to him, "Well, George, sometimes you have to change the line", to which Padmore responded, "Well, boys, this is one line I can't change." James said: "[He] broke with them and went to England and we joined together and re-formed the Pan-African movement. This was a movement of strength."[25]

This remarkable story tells of two men who had come from small villages in Trinidad and had been forged in the crucible of Pan-Africanism. They were two intellectuals who perennially had Africa on their mind, and were determined to continue a struggle which their forebears in the Caribbean had commenced. Although they had not visited Africa yet, James and Padmore were imbued with certain customs and practices that had resonances in their African past. This is why James said of African and Caribbean social forces that had shaped him and other Caribbean intellectuals and activists:

> All these questions that are being discussed will not be understood unless we have a profound historical conception of where the African people are going and where they have come from. That is the ocean of thought and feeling from which emerge historical manifestations as Marcus Garvey, Aimé Césaire, George Padmore, Frantz Fanon ... That is exactly the driving force of those Caribbean politicians (and writers) who have distinguished themselves in their impact on Western civilization ... I have long believed that there is something in the West Indian past, something in the West Indian environment, something in the West Indian historical development, which compels the West Indian intellectual, when he gets involved with subjects of the kind, to deal with them from a fundamental point of view, *to place ourselves in history*.[26]

Living in America

James went to the United States in 1938 after having spent six years in Britain. While living in England, he travelled to France to research and write *The Black Jacobins*, which meant that he did not even spend a full six years there. James participated in the black struggle in the United States, where he spent the next 17 years of his life. In 1955 he was deported for having overstayed his visa.

While he was in America, James travelled to Mexico to meet with Leon Trotsky, and they discussed "in some detail, plans to help create an independent black organisation in the United States".[27] As a Marxist, James always stressed that African Americans had a right to self-determination, that is, the right to decide in which direction they wanted to go. After speaking with Trotsky, he made the fascinating observation that "I am now certain that no one in America, none in the party, has ever seen the Negro question for the gigantic thing it is, and will increasingly be. L.T. [Leon Trotsky] sees it. I was groping towards it. I begin to see it now, every day more clearly."[28] This was an important insight. It explained the energy that James and his colleagues devoted to the emancipation of American workers, particularly in places such as Detroit.

Ten years after he arrived in the United States, James wrote *Notes on Dialectics* with Grace Lee Boggs and Raya Dunayevskaya in which he sought to "develop a philosophic cognition about ... international labour". The authors believed that "Labour acts empirically and then its innumerable acts crystallise in a formed movement, an organisation, a category. One such category is a revolutionary international."[29] Later in his life, James observed that "most of the African leaders of the independence movement, who were in Europe, oriented naturally towards the Marxist movement which said we are for freedom in the colonies".[30] James could have written this book with African leaders in mind. When national independence arrived in Africa during the 1950s and 1960s, many African leaders needed a scientific way to deal with the challenges thrown up by working-class movements in their own countries. James's *Notes on the Dialectics* was surely a useful guide to this challenge.

After leaving the US and spending three years in England, in 1958 James returned to Trinidad to work with Eric Williams and the nationalist movement there. James had known Williams from his student days in Trinidad – he had taught him at Queen's Royal College, the island's major high school while Williams was a student there from 1922 to 1930. He had also worked closely with Williams when the latter wrote his doctoral dissertation at Oxford University on capitalism and slavery in the West Indies. James had further corresponded with Williams while they both lived in the United States.[31] James left Trinidad in 1962 after a spat with Williams and the People's National Movement, issuing the following warning:

> People of the West Indies, you do not know your own power. No one dares to tell you. You are a strange, a unique combination of the greatest

driving force in the world today, the underdeveloped formerly colonial coloured people; and more than any of them, by education, way of life and language, you are completely a part of Western civilization. Alone of all people in the world you began your historical existence in a highly developed modern industry – the sugar plantation.[32]

Beyond a Boundary: Locating James in His Caribbean Homeland

After James left the West Indies, he travelled to Spain to complete *Beyond a Boundary*, another of his masterpieces which he had begun in Trinidad. He noted: "I had written a book on cricket and the philosophy around the game of cricket. I said cricket was not a game alone, it was an art."[33] I do not think it is an exaggeration to say that, in that book, James reiterated all of the claims I have consistently made about his rootedness in the Caribbean soil and the way the social, historical and political environment made him what and who he was. This time, I suspect that James added a much more philosophical base to his ideas.

I have discussed this point in detail in "C.L.R. James: Plumbing His Caribbean Roots".[34] I will repeat two points here. First, at the end of *Beyond a Boundary*, James confessed: "We have traveled, but only the outlines of character are changed. I have changed little. I know that more than ever now."[35] Second, James reiterated this position when he sought to explain George Padmore's origins to an English audience: "I am going to begin with the material circumstances in which he grew up and the social relations that shaped him: the longer I live the more I see that people are shaped to a degree that they do not yet understand by the social relations and family and other groups in the society."[36]

Apart from being made by the West Indies, James was more aware of Trinidadian and Caribbean history than any other writer of his epoch. This emerges clearly in his preface to *Beyond a Boundary*, in which he argues: "This book is neither cricket reminiscences nor autobiography. It poses the question: What do they know of cricket who only cricket know? The answer involves ideas as well as facts."[37] For many years, scholars of his work thought this was one of James's original ideas. James, in fact, borrowed this epigram from Trinidadian Aucher Warner's *Sir Thomas Warner: Pioneer of the West Indies*,[38] and amended it to fit his own purposes. He admired Charles and Pelham Warner. He devoted a chapter – entitled "Three Generations" – of *Beyond a Boundary* to the Warner family. It did not hurt that Pelham Warner, the son of Charles Warner who was born in Port of Spain, became "the Grand Old Man of English Cricket" who "played for England in 15 test matches, with a top score of 132".[39] James had written about the Warner family as early as 1931.

It may come as a surprise that a book of such scholarly charm and attraction as *Beyond a Boundary* should emanate from so remote a corner of Empire, and from one who, save for occasional visits to England, spent his life far away from the "centres of literary thought".[40] After James posed the question "What do they know of cricket who only cricket know?" he went on to argue: "The autobiographical framework shows the ideas more or less in the sequence that they developed in relation to the events, the facts and the personalities which prompted them. If the ideas originated in the West Indies it was only in England and in English life and history that I was able to track them down and test them. To establish his own identity, Caliban, after three centuries, must himself pioneer into regions Caesar never knew."[41]

It seems that when James decided to talk about Caliban's task – that of pioneering regions that Caesar never knew – he could do no better than point to the opposite role that Prospero – in the form of the Warners – had taken in this drama. After all, the Warners had resided in the West Indies since the seventeenth century. Theirs was one of the oldest families who had peopled the West Indies and who, in the process, had made innumerable contributions to the Caribbean. Suffice it to say that James knew Caribbean history intimately, and used it to demonstrate how it had shaped the unique West Indian identity.

I therefore want to use this essay to express my strong disapproval at the widespread Western notion that James was "made in England", an idea that so many scholars insist on making and repeating. British academic Christian Høgsbjerg – in an otherwise fine book – insisted that James was made or influenced by "the profound, early intellectual inspiration provided by the Victorian cultural critic [Matthew Arnold]", and that the Trinidadian writer "actively and creatively shaped Arnold's tenets so they could serve his own purposes as he orientated toward West Indian nationalism during the 1920s".[42] Such a statement cavalierly mistakes the seminal influence of Caribbean history, and particularly its intellectual history, on the making of James. While Arnold undoubtedly had an influence on James, I would not look in that direction to answer the question "where him [James] come from?" as posed by the Jamaican dub poet and musician Linton Kwesi Johnson.[43] I suggest that Høgsbjerg take a closer look at *Beyond Boundaries: The Intellectual Tradition of Trinidad and Tobago in the Nineteenth Century* to get a better understanding of the intellectual culture that had shaped James.[44]

James has said that, while he was writing *The Black Jacobins* (published in 1938), Aimé Césaire was writing *Notebook of a Return to the Native Land*, which was published a year later (see Irele in this volume). French writer André Breton has described Césaire's book as "nothing less than the greatest lyrical monument of our times".[45] James has also said that it was very strange that both he and Césaire were "writing with the West Indies in mind, but with Africa as a kind of immediate and historical perspective".[46] In paying tribute to the Mighty Sparrow, a popular Trinidadian calypsonian, and drawing on the works of Césaire, the Haitian sociologist Price Mars, Marcus Garvey and George Padmore, James noted:

> What emerges from all that is this, a profoundly remarkable historical fact. The recognition of Africanism, the agitation for recognition of Africa, the literary creation of an African ideology, one powerful sphere of African independence, all were directly the creation of West Indians. The exact proportion of their contribution need not be estimated. The indisputable fact is that able and powerful West Indians concentrated their exceptional familiarity with Western thought, expression and organisation on Africa and Africans when these qualities were urgently needed both in Africa and elsewhere. This is part of the history of the West Indies, a very important part. But West Indians do not study it.[47]

Concluding Reflections

James is indisputably part and parcel of an extraordinary Pan-African past from which we can draw so much intellectual strength and courage to help us fulfil the social, cultural, economic and political tasks that await us as a people. It is a past and a way of looking at the world that we do not study and – in many instances – that we cannot be bothered with. I hope this essay on James can be helpful in our thrust to rehabilitate the black race in a way that Haitian intellectual Hannibal Prince tried to bring to our attention in 1900, the year of the first Pan-African conference – led by Trinidadian lawyer Henry Sylvester Williams – when Prince wrote:

I am a man of Haiti, the Mecca, the Judea of the black race, the country where are to be found the sacred fields of Vertieres, la Crete a Pierrot, la Ravine aux Couleuvres, le Tombeau des Indigenes [scenes of battles in the Haitian War of Independence], and a hundred others where every man with African blood in his veins should go on a pilgrimage at least once in his life, for it was there that the Negro became a man: it was there that, breaking his chains, he condemned slavery in the New World for ever.[48]

James ought to be placed at the centre of any serious African imaginary. We cannot speak of him without thinking of his Caribbean roots, and the history that made him what he was: an African patriot par excellence. He is the centre of our strivings. We must honour him, and pay tribute to his rich legacy.

ARTHUR LEWIS: NOBEL ACTOR ON A PAN-AFRICAN STAGE

Alison E. Stone Roofe

ARTHUR LEWIS – BORN ON 23 JANUARY 1915 – was awarded the Nobel Prize for Economics in 1979, the only person of African descent to have been so honoured by 2020. Along with another famous St Lucian, the Nobel Literature laureate Derek Walcott (see Lucien in this volume), he helped to make this small island in the Caribbean famous. The Arthur Lewis Institute for Social and Economic Studies was established at the Mona Campus of the University of the West Indies (UWI) in Jamaica in August 1999, and similar institutes have been established on UWI campuses in Trinidad and Tobago, and Barbados. Lewis is very much a Caribbean treasure, valued in both regional and global history.

A Drama in Four Acts

This essay is a drama in four acts. First, I aim to set out the elements in the development of the angst that drove Arthur Lewis to seek to intervene at a global level in the politics of transition in the throes of the African struggle against colonial dominance and the complex construction of independent nation-states. Second, I seek to analyse the nature of the plot that characterised the era, in particular from the early 1940s to the late 1960s, with the years between 1952 and 1957 being particularly significant. Specifically, I seek to explain the elements around which blacks – particularly intellectuals – chose to cohere and frame an alternative vision rooted in new understandings of African culture, politics, economics and society. Third, the essay examines in detail the idea that Lewis was an important contributor to the unfolding of a global drama of a certain and unique kind. Finally, I assess Lewis's legacy, and seek to answer two key questions: What has been the St Lucian scholar-activist's contributions to economics and society? And which of his ideas can be passed on to the current generation of scholars and activists?

I do not wish to be accused of intellectual revisionism or of what Lewis once described as a phenomenon in which analysts, needing solutions, tended to read them into a text and to attribute to the writer positions which he did not hold.[1] American professor Gerald Meier delivered a lecture on "Sir Arthur Lewis and Development Economics, 50 Years On" in November 2002. In it, Meier identified Lewis as the leading pioneer in development economics, and as the first economist to "establish the subject on a worldwide basis through his large ideas and policy insights".[2] Against Meier's comment, I would place Guyanese scholar-activist Walter Rodney's observation that "the major and first responsibility of the intellectual is to struggle over ideas" (see Montoute in this volume).[3]

I begin with Arthur Lewis's battle of ideas and practical contributions to Pan-Africanism. As a result of an angst in Lewis's consciousness awakened by his exposure to anti-imperialism at an early age in St Lucia,[4] then moving to the English "mother country" for his further education at the London School of Economics and Political Science (LSE) where he met and interacted with other anti-imperialists,[5] he became perhaps what the Trinidadian author and Nobel Literature laureate, V.S. Naipaul, would have called a "Mimic Man of the New World". His was an experience similar to that of Jamaican sociologist Stuart Hall (see Magubane in this volume).

Lewis's professional engagements with Africa in the pre-independence era were noteworthy. From 1951 to 1953, he served as a member of the Colonial Economic Advisory Committee (CEAC), the organisation that gave birth to the Colonial Development Corporation (CDC), of which Lewis was a member until the end of its term in 1953. He served as an economic adviser to Kwame Nkrumah's government in Ghana. Lewis's 1953 report, "International Development and the Gold Coast", became the blue-print for the £100 million Volta River Project, which accelerated Ghana's industrial development. He was also an adviser to the government of Nigeria on international banking issues. Finally, he served as a member of a United Nations Group of Experts providing advice to the world body on developing countries.

The Nobel laureate's affinity with Africa grew when he provided technical assistance, through the UN, on a two-year assignment as economic adviser to the government of Ghana between 1957 and 1959. A fast-moving career and even more prolific writings emerged over the next two decades from 1960 to 1980, with over 75 publications, many dealing with Africa's economic and political development. This post-independence era moulded a peculiar set of leaders, and gave birth to a unique type of conversation and an "angst" which Lewis – an economist bred intellectually in white Britain – was driven to confront.

England became the launch pad for Lewis's early engagement with pre-independence Africa, as the search for an alternative post-colonial government and society became central to Pan-African thought and praxis. London proved to be a melting pot for a diverse mix of scholars and change-makers driven by a unique energy, an incubator of revolutionary thought.

In summing up the scope of the ideas with which Lewis grappled, the late Jamaican scholar Norman Girvan suggested that the Nobel laureate can be identified with three main areas in his research: first, industrial economics, which was the subject of his doctoral thesis and the least well-known and "probably the least interesting branches of his work"; second, the history of the global economy since the middle of the nineteenth century; and third, the problems of economic development, to which Lewis made the "most significant contributions to scholarship".[6]

In making his mark as a black Caribbean man stepping onto the world stage as a young academic, Arthur Lewis was confronted with new areas of research. Needing to find a voice in the larger political and economic arena, he focused on the end of colonialism in the African "Motherland". His primary objective, at that time in the mid-1940s and 1950s, was to contribute to the end of the imperial era and to build up the practice of Fabian and democratic socialism – theories to which he aligned himself ideologically.

Lewis provided intellectual clarity to the conundrum that was unfolding in the new states of Africa from the 1950s, and in so doing wielded influence from the front line. This revealed his commitment to the African continent, which never wavered, built as it was on a longing to put right what he saw as historical colonial wrongs.

Mark Figueroa, a Jamaican academic, who has written on Lewis for over two decades, examined his academic and professional publications specifically on Africa, ethnicity and race. Figueroa noted that Lewis's work on Africa included two single-authored books; one jointly authored book; and more than 15 other works including short monographs, journal articles and book chapters – not counting shorter items appearing mainly in more popular publications. Figueroa suggested that "perhaps [Lewis] could have qualified for a chair in Africana studies on these alone and [in fact] in the late 1970s, Lewis was appointed as a Distinguished Visiting Professor in Social Sciences and Afro-American Studies at Yale University in the United States".[7]

Further examination of Lewis's works shows that each period had a distinct characteristic. For example, his scholarship between 1935 and 1939 was characterised by his challenging of white Eurocentric hegemony. This focus continued into the early 1950s but was mostly visible in his unpublished works. The thrust of his writing in the 1940s and 1950s not only presented arguments against the predominant norms of the day, but also offered alternatives to colonial policy. Had these policy alternatives been adopted and implemented, they would have had a tremendous impact in improving the lives of people of African descent. Throughout his career, Lewis continued to push for these ideas in his writing. In the 1960s, he was heavily involved in the examination of the economics and politics of post-colonial West Africa, which transitioned into a broader exploration of the political economy of race, especially in the US.[8]

In short, what were Lewis's principal views on Africa and Pan-Africanism, and how were these manifested? In a 2006 journal article, Japanese scholar Yoichi Mine traced Lewis's career from what he described as a "Black Advisor to the White Empire",[9] and concluded by suggesting that, in assessing the Nobel laureate's commitment to Africa's democratic rebirth, "[it] would be justified for us to locate the political writings of Arthur Lewis somewhere in the diverse works left by the African Diaspora intellectuals like Eric Williams, George Padmore, C.L.R James, Frantz Fanon and Aimé Césaire".[10]

Mine focused specifically on Lewis's 1954 model of economic development with unlimited supplies of labour. He brought a fresh perspective to the St Lucian scholar-administrator's work on Africa. Mine recalled that in Lewis's 1965 *Politics of West Africa*,[11] the Nobel laureate clearly identified himself as a Pan-Africanist, stating that he had "known the chief Pan-African leaders personally for 30 years, sharing their anti-imperialism, and their goal of an Africa united in stages".[12]

Indeed, we can look further back historically to Lewis's early days when he worked for the British Colonial Office in the 1940s. He was often the "token black" in the room. As a young lecturer at the LSE between 1938 and 1948 who was also part of the Colonial Economic Advisory Committee, his early thinking on what changes might be needed to shape policy prescriptions, and the leadership required to bring about these developmental goals, was influenced by the socio-economic conditions of both the Caribbean, which Lewis had left behind, and of Africa, which he was then discovering.

Mine further suggested that "so many of the elements of Lewis' development theory had already taken shape in embryonic form in his days in the Colonial Office: agricultural revolution as a precondition of industrialization, advancement of agricultural productivity based on scale economy as well as mass education, and the desideratum of economic planning to name but a few".[13] Having examined some of the key elements in the early ideas about what might constitute a "new" Africa, let us now look at the context and the larger plot of Lewis's policy development efforts.

The Plot

The post-war climate in Britain, after the July 1945 electoral victory of the Labour Party under Clement Attlee, brought its own set of questions and expectations of change both in the British colonies and globally. In 1945, nearly a hundred nationalists, journeying from Africa and the Caribbean, organised the Fifth Pan-African Congress in the English city of Manchester. The Congress featured prominently Ghana's Kwame Nkrumah, the foremost and most vocal defender of Pan-Africanism at that time (see Introduction and Biney in this volume). It was after this Congress that Lewis attempted to pursue open, critical dialogue with Africa's colonial elite, including Nkrumah. His engagement with the Ghanaian leader was marked by what Mine described as "the politics of colonial ambiguity".[14] This relationship was complex, turbulent, and ultimately ended in frustration.

While teaching at the University of Manchester between 1948 and 1957, Lewis co-authored an article "Attitude to Africa" (1951) in which he set out a "Policy for Colonial Agriculture" which called for a massive financial transfer from Britain to Africa, the proposed amount annually being £100 million.[15] This veritable "Marshall Plan" for Africa was an ambitious bid to secure Britain's commitment to developing its tropical colonies and ex-colonies, as the empire unravelled. Indeed, Lewis thought and dreamt big, and this ambition was matched by his detailed technical and carefully researched advice to African governments. Interestingly, when one examines the historical contexts and imperatives that characterised this period in the Caribbean and Africa, there were parallels between West Indian economic integration and Africa's goal of consolidating an economic Pan-African project (see Introduction in this volume). K. Dwight Venner, a Vincentian citizen and former governor of the Eastern Caribbean Central Bank, argued that "the trick [was] to get the right balance between sovereignty and efficiency which can [still] be considered to be a work in progress".[16]

Figueroa suggested that Lewis's tenure in Ghana from October 1957 to December 1958,[17] as well as his earlier service in Ghana and Nigeria, was motivated, in part, by issues of race. This is evident by the fact that in 1955, two years before going to Ghana, Lewis declined a request to serve as an economic adviser to the recently elected Labour Front government in Singapore, despite pressure from the secretary of the Fabian Colonial Bureau, Hilda Selwyn-Clarke.[18] Perhaps his earlier frustrations working with officials at the British Colonial Office had left a bitter taste in his mouth. The goal of removing the imperialist hold on British colonies in Africa and the Caribbean was very dear to Lewis's heart. Clearly, he viewed the independence and economic development of Ghana as a major catalyst in the global anti-imperialist movement. However, Lewis was not prepared for the complexities he would encounter in Ghana.[19]

It is well known that the relationship between Nkrumah and Lewis was turbulent. Lewis was convinced that Nkrumah, like many other African nationalists, had a myopic view of how Africa should be developed. The St Lucian scholar indicated as much in his 1946 speech to a conference organised by the Fabian Colonial Bureau.[20] Mine illustrates the divergent views of Nkrumah and Lewis on the matter of budgetary allocation. He noted that Nkrumah presented a budget which disproportionately allocated more funds to the development of the capital city, Accra, than to the rest of the country. This, in Lewis's view, was a colonial approach. He instead proposed a more egalitarian mode of development in which there would be more focus on developing the rural agricultural sector inhabited by most of the population. Lewis also preferred focusing on adult education as opposed to youth education, which, in his opinion, only resulted in a "brain drain" from rural areas and in large-scale urbanisation.

American historian Robert Tignor suggests that Lewis's time in Ghana was a drama intensified by differing expectations. On the one hand, the St Lucian economist was expected to give advice that would further Nkrumah's famous injunction, "Seek ye first the political kingdom, and all other things will be added unto it". This saying was indicative of Nkrumah's ideal that African states should be developed according to their own customs and beliefs. This led the

Ghanaian leader to offer financial assistance to other African states. Lewis, on the other hand, believed that it was his duty as an economist to offer objective advice to African political officials in a way that would strongly impact on their continued economic growth. He believed that the professional economist should have free rein in matters of economic development. However, Nkrumah did not agree with this approach, as he believed that Lewis did not fully understand the intricacies of African politics. Accordingly, the Ghanaian leader welcomed Lewis's advice only to the extent that it furthered his own political ambitions.

Lewis and Nkrumah's disagreements may have been caused by much more than their differing points of view. Tignor suggests that there were external factors that may have contributed to these disputes. Powerful international actors such as the United States, Britain and the United Nations may have added to these problems. Since Lewis's tenure in Ghana had been funded by the UN, policy-makers in Accra expected him to act as a sort of mediator and champion in protecting Ghanaian interests within the international system. Some of Ghana's politicians, such as Kwesi Amoako-Atta, John Tettegah and J.B. Danquah, instead viewed Lewis as an "agent" of the colonial West.[21]

Despite these challenges, Mark Figueroa noted: "Even when convinced that Nkrumah was totally off track, Lewis was careful to avoid an acrimonious break as he did not wish the enemies of Africa to make capital of this."[22] Furthermore, "referring to the Pan-African group of thinkers," Lewis explained: "I also share their goal of a free Africa, and it is only the defection of some from this goal that has wrung this pamphlet [*Politics in West Africa*][23] from me."[24]

Although Lewis's tenure as economic adviser to Nkrumah was short – 14 months – his work on economic development in Africa continued. He produced two publications, "Some Aspects of Economic Development"[25] and *Politics in West Africa*.[26] Both works were aimed at addressing the political complexity of newly independent states. Lewis drew from his time in Ghana. He identified African societies as "pluralistic" with multiple ethnicities that all have unique cultures. Hence, he argued that any effective political system would need to be open enough to represent the interests of these diverse groups. Such a system would also provide assurance that all citizens would be included and their needs met. Lewis's views were opposed by many African politicians and Western theorists who argued that a single-party system such as the one Nkrumah had established in Ghana would work best in quelling ethnic tensions. However, Lewis insightfully noted that such a system would only provide an avenue for *coups d'état* and disastrous internal power struggles. He believed that such an unstable political environment would ultimately pose a threat to socio-economic development efforts in Africa.[27]

As a direct solution to this political dilemma, Lewis suggested that a pluralistic democratic system be established. He suggested three methods for achieving this goal: first, by using the system of proportional representation. Lewis noted that "National loyalty cannot immediately supplant tribal loyalty; it has to be built on top of tribal loyalty by creating a system in which all tribes feel there is room for self-expression."[28] His second proposal was to establish a coalition in which the rule of law was respected and freedom to criticise was allowed, so that people could freely express their wishes. Lewis's third idea was to establish genuinely federal systems which would also help enhance tax collection. His ideas received a mixed reception within and across West Africa.

The Drama

The global stage which Arthur Lewis bestrode for three decades had its own drama of a unique kind, within which the Pan-African conversation – pro, cons and rebuttals – unfolded. In addition to his famous "empirical recommendations made in the classical tradition", Lewis himself noted:

> Particularly, if you want to be a revolutionary in science, achieving some great breakthrough, you have to understand the existing system which you wish to overthrow better than it is understood by its supporters, not less so. [John Maynard] Keynes was able to invent a new economics because he thoroughly understood the old. If any new physics or sociology is going to come out of the West Indies it will be from people who have mastered the old physics or sociology and not just from people who have rejected the old without really coming to grips with it.[29]

Lewis was often asked to reflect on his research and opinions in the many lectures that he gave. In his Schumpeter memorial lectures at Princeton University in 1977, he argued:

> The development of the LDCs [Least Developed Countries] does not, in the long run, depend on the developed countries; their potential for growth would be unaffected if all the developed countries were to sink

under the sea. The LDCs have within themselves all that is required for growth. They should not have to be producing primarily for developed country markets. International trade cannot substitute for technical change, so those who depend on it as their major hope are doomed to frustration. The most important item on the agenda of developing countries is to transform the food sector, create agricultural surpluses to feed the urban population, and thereby create the domestic basis for industry and modern services. If we can make this domestic change we shall automatically have a new international order.[30] (See also Montoute on Walter Rodney; and Afeikhena on Adedeji in this volume.)

Perhaps the more interesting point here – as Lewis wrote widely as a development economist – is the importance of building sound theory and encouraging "home-grown" advice. The lessons from this son of the diaspora for the African continent were offered as transformative, carefully researched, technical expertise: a global vision which transcended his humble and seemingly unremarkable beginnings in St Lucia. The former governor of the Eastern Caribbean Central Bank, Dwight Venner, suggests that Lewis's lectures were remarkable for the way in which they reflected the ethos of his approach to development and the utility of economics as a problem-solving discipline.[31]

By the time that Lewis won the Nobel Prize in Economics in 1979, he had already long left Africa, but his ideas were no less influential for the continent. Canadian economist Kari Polanyi Levitt recalled that Lewis won the Nobel Prize in recognition of his contributions to development economics. His seminal 1954 article on "Economic Development with Unlimited Supplies of Labour" grounded development economics in a model that assisted in establishing the subject as a distinct area of economics. The open version of the Lewis model provided the theoretical foundation for the radical conclusions that he drew from a lifetime of research and from his intimate familiarity with the economics of peripheral, tropical developing countries.[32]

What, at its core, did Lewis say about the drama that was unfolding in global economics? He noted: "Genuine social scientists, gathered together from all parts of the world, have no difficulty in understanding each other's concepts, and in my profession of economics we have found that any tool which is illuminating in one part of the world – like monetary theory or linear programming or the discounting of future return – is equally illuminating everywhere, whether in the Soviet Union, or the USA or Tanzania."[33] Indeed, Lewis had a global approach to finding answers to the problems of individual nation-states. It is true to say that any list of change-makers that characterised this global drama over three decades must include Arthur Lewis. He remains a towering figure in our understanding of what unfolded in economic history in the post-colonial era.

Lewis's experiences on the African continent added a peculiarly rich intellectual context which fuelled his ideas and research. Even on his return to the West Indies in 1959, after 27 years abroad, he remained vocal in his views on Africa.

Promoting Regional Integration in the Caribbean

In 1959, the 44-year-old Lewis was appointed as the principal of the University College of the West Indies. Norman Girvan compared public reaction to this appointment as being similar – in the Caribbean – to the euphoria that greeted the announcement of Barack Obama as the first African-American president of the United States in 2008.[34] As principal of the institution, Lewis was instrumental in establishing the St Augustine campus in Trinidad in 1960. It was also under his watch that the university was renamed the University of the West Indies, at which point he was appointed vice-chancellor in 1962.[35]

What appealed even more to Lewis was the idea of the "West Indies Federation" involving Antigua and Barbuda, Barbados, Dominica, Grenada, Jamaica, Montserrat, St Kitts-Nevis-Anguilla, St Lucia, St Vincent, and Trinidad and Tobago. Figueroa surmises that "it was the formation of the Federation [in 1958] of which he was a supporter since his early teens that spurred him [Lewis] to return to the region. He saw it as a decisive step towards his long-held vision that, 'Out of a mosaic of complexions a new nation is beginning to arise which is neither European nor African nor Indian; it is the West Indian nation of the future'".[36]

According to Girvan, Lewis viewed the West Indies Federation as having more than economic and political benefits. He also believed that the new entity would promote democratic governance across the region. The federation would provide a structure to safeguard citizens against corruption and political manipulation. In addition, Lewis believed that this bloc would provide access to a supply of labour for national public services and greater leverage when accessing international financial aid. In many ways, this model had some resemblance to the federal arrangement that Lewis had proposed for West Africa in the 1950s. However, in 1961 Jamaica held a referendum in which the majority voted against remaining in the West Indies Federation. This was the beginning of the demise of the federation, which lasted only from 1958 to 1962 (see Introduction in this volume).[37]

Unsurprisingly, Lewis was disappointed and frustrated with the failure of the federation. He had worked tirelessly to preserve the bloc both before and after Jamaica's withdrawal from it. He tried to convince the leaders of the region that a federation could work and would be the best approach for achieving mutually beneficial regional integration. Despite his personal appeals, as well as numerous technical papers and budgets presented to the various national leaders, the West Indies Federation did not survive, much to Lewis's distress. This led the Nobel laureate to pen a 39-page analysis of the failure of the federal efforts titled "The Agony of the Eight" in 1965.[38] Once again, as with West African integration, Lewis's aspirations for an economically independent and thriving post-colonial region had been thwarted by the parochial machinations of its leaders.

Although disappointed, Lewis did not lose hope for regional integration and development in the Caribbean. He later returned as the founding president of the Caribbean Development Bank (CDB) from 1970 to 1973. A key establishing feature of this bank was the separation of its operations from political influence.[39] Neville Nicholls, a former president of the bank from 1988 to 2001, noted that Lewis set as the condition for his acceptance of the bank's presidency that "the CDB should be fully insulated and isolated from political interference".[40] Doubtless, this insistence was a direct result of Lewis's long experiences in the Fabian Colonial Bureau, in Ghana with Nkrumah, and in the Caribbean with failure of the West Indies Federation.

Concluding Reflections

In concluding this essay, I pose two key questions: What were the key concerns of Arthur Lewis as he entered on the world stage as a young academic? And what was the central thread running through all of his work?

Norman Girvan provides his own answers to these questions in characterising Lewis as "a man of his time in his anti-imperialism, his nationalism, his regionalism ... his conviction that what matters is to make the best use of one's own resources, and his theories of economic development for poor countries.

He was a 'head' [*sic*] of his time in his formidable professional accomplishments. And he was ahead of his time in maintaining the necessity for an agricultural revolution and insisting that trade should be at the service of development."[41]

So much has been written about Arthur Lewis, particularly as an economist. However, there are other areas of his work that need greater attention, and his writings on post-colonial Africa still need to be thoroughly researched. One area that calls out for more research is Lewis's early work as a colonial administrator. Not much work has been published on his views on pre-independence and post-independence Africa, and perhaps his more mature, considered pieces need to be matched against the early Arthur Lewis.

In view of Lewis's relative proximity to the African continent during the critical period of the unfolding of Pan-African thought, his reflections may have been less refined, less reflective, less pointed than if he had had the benefit of reflecting on the Africa that we see as citizens of the wider world today. If he were alive today, would Lewis's views on contemporary Africa be positive? Would he have felt the journey to have been worth it? Would the economics of growth and development and the politics of change have found favour with his critical eye as a researcher, with this proud, black man who had worked hard to have his voice heard and respected on the global stage?

We have more questions than answers, and currently Africa is an even greater conundrum than it was in the 1980s. The tools we need as researchers, advocates and practitioners have to be built on new expressions of the vibrant, colourful, resourceful activism which characterises urban and rural cultures in both Africa and its diaspora.

I end this chapter by borrowing a conclusion from the late Jamaican scholar Norman Girvan, who knew Lewis well. Girvan, in a lecture on Lewis in February 2008, said: "For me the enduring part of his legacy is that he took it for granted that the purpose of scholarship is public service to community; and his belief that the West Indian people have it within themselves to bring about their own advancement."[42] Girvan recalled one of Lewis's concluding statements, written in 1950, when the Nobel laureate would also have been thinking about the challenges of economic growth and African renewal: "A visit to the British West Indian islands at the present moment is a depressing experience ... The British West Indians can solve their problems if they set to them with a will. But first they must find the secret that will put hope, initiative, direction, and an unconquerable will into management of their affairs. And this is the hardest task of all."[43]

As we continue to honour Arthur Lewis and the ideational legacy that he left behind, let us push past the mistakes of history and find instead a renewed will to unite strategically with a common goal of sustainable, sound economic and political development in Africa and its wider diaspora.

Ali Mazrui: African Identity and the African Condition

Sabelo J. Ndlovu-Gatsheni

Ali A. Mazrui's intellectual and academic work, like all products of great minds, escapes precise analysis and is not reproducible.[1] The sheer expansiveness and diversity of his archive, as well as his encyclopedic knowledge, continue to make it difficult to subject his intellectual and academic work to any precise perspective. Mazrui's concerns touched on almost every aspect of human life: colonialism, education, nationalism, conflict, identity, culture, power, ideology, economy, religion, politics, the state, governance, gender, nuclear weapons, leadership, race, the role of intellectuals and international relations.

The ease with which Mazrui crossed disciplinary boundaries and the versatility of his mind compound the difficulties of precise analysis. Basically, Mazrui was many things at once: an African, a global citizen, a liberal nationalist, a pan-Africanist, a Muslim, a leading and controversial political scientist, a historian, an international relations student, a global cultural studies scholar, and a post-colonial theorist. This chapter is, therefore, focused on one of the key debates in Mazrui's encyclopedic archive: African identity and the related question of what he called the "African condition".[2] This is a theme that has preoccupied many Pan-Africanists, Africanists and nationalists for decades.

Mazrui's "Triple Heritage"

Mazrui was a walking embodiment of the "triple heritage". He was a descendant of Arab Muslims, an African and a respected intellectual product of "Westernised"

324

institutions of higher learning: Manchester, Columbia and Oxford universities. Perhaps Mazrui's academic interest in the question of African identity arose from his own personal complex identity. But the subject of African identity preoccupied many other African intellectuals, who had a different genealogy from Mazrui's. For example, the earliest advocate of the "African Personality" was Edward Wilmot Blyden (see Khadiagala in this volume) who grappled with the question of a common African destiny, the distinctiveness of African mentality, the role of religion in African life, the inherent socialist orientation of African society, and the notion of the separation of races.[3] It was Blyden who first posited that the "African Personality" would develop organically, embracing the best attributes from indigenous African, Arabic/Islamic and Euro-Christian traditions.

Some of Blyden's ideas re-emerged within the Négritude Movement as its advocates such as Aimé Césaire and Léopold Sédar Senghor engaged pertinent questions of universality, particularity European rationality, reason, time, emotion, materiality, morality, and nature as resources that shaped humanity and the future of the world (see Irele in this volume).[4] In the 1960s the leading Pan-Africanist, Kwame Nkrumah, also contributed to the debate on African identity, centred on its rootedness in African, Arab-Islamic and Western Christian traditions. The Ghanaian leader introduced the concept of "consciencism" to contrast the cultural, historical and cognitive convergence of Africa's communal and humanistic ethos with the Western capitalist, acquisitive, individualistic, scientific and Christian redemptive logic, as well as the secular, holistic and spiritual precepts of the Arabic-Islamic heritage.[5] Nkrumah was optimistic that from this synthesis, there would emerge a "post-colonial", liberated, modern and confident African subjectivity capable of creating a future on the continent (see Biney in this volume).

In the 1990s the Congolese scholar Valentin-Yves Mudimbe published two books: the first entitled *The Invention of Africa: Gnosis, Philosophy and the Order of Knowledge* in 1998, and the second *The Idea of Africa* in 1994 (see Thiam and Opoku-Agyemang in this volume). Both books dealt extensively with the invention of Africa and the idea of Africa as articulated mainly by Europeans, beginning with Greek stories about Africa, missionaries, anthropologists and, subsequently, philosophers. Concerned with the workings of discursive processes and the orders of knowledge, Mudimbe demonstrated how African intellectuals have consistently failed to liberate knowledge from the skein of colonialism, coloniality, and the colonial library.[6] Kenyan scholar Ngũgĩ wa Thiong'o had a different take from Mudimbe:

V.Y. Mudimbe describes the idea of Africa as a product of the West's system of self-representation, which included creation of an otherness conceived and conveyed through conflicting systems of knowledge. But I prefer to think of the idea of Africa – or, more appropriately, the "African idea," as African self-representation. To distinguish it from the Mudimbeist formula according to which Europe is finding itself through its invention of Africa, I see the African idea as that which was forged in the diaspora and travelled back to the continent.[7]

Ngũgĩ introduced the "African idea" which speaks to how Africans invented themselves and how, through ideas of Pan-Africanism, they forged a common Pan-African identity. But the interventions of Kwame Anthony Appiah in his book *In My Father's House: Africa in the Philosophy of Culture* (1992) challenged the use of "race" to describe African people as a common "black race" (see Ampiah in this volume). Appiah was extremely critical of what he regarded as essentialist ideas of Africa, arguing that African identity has never been a primordial racial fixture. To him, Africans were not common people as they were moulded from different racial and cultural "clays" – to borrow a term from Malawian scholar Paul Tiyambe Zeleza.[8] Appiah's critique thus challenged narratives of nationalism and Pan-Africanism that later became important resources in the formulation of an "African idea", as opposed to Mudimbe's "idea of Africa".

On the Concept "We Are All Africans"

Even former South African president Thabo Mbeki's widely quoted 1996 "I am an African" speech spoke to the complexity and contingent nature of African identity, articulating it as hybrid and open, born out of human encounters, some tragic and others heroic (see Adebajo on Mbeki in this volume). The significance of the question emanated partly from the reality that anthropologists, such as American, Melville Herskovits, doubted the substance and essence of Africa, arguing that the idea was a mere "geographical fiction" which only existed as a product of "the tyranny of the mapmaker".[9] Some African intellectuals challenged this denial of Africa's existence, while others sought to make sense of the existence of a geographical fiction. Ali Mazrui actively engaged with this question of the invention of Africa from as early as 1963.

The Kenyan was one of the pioneers of this debate on African identity among the first generation of post-independence African scholars. In a 1963 journal article, "On the Concept of 'We Are All Africans'", Mazrui examined how African identity emerged as a complex product of "double invention" by colonial and African imperatives.[10] The colonial imperatives included map-making, the partition of Africa, European colonial domination, and the promotion of a singular idea of an African people who were collectively thought of as inferior, backward and primitive. Mazrui interrogated African ideas of the continent as represented by such nationalists as Ghana's Kwame Nkrumah and Tanzania's Julius Nyerere. It was Nyerere who introduced the concept of "African sentiment" as a form of consciousness born out of the colonial racial humiliation of black people. Mazrui also demonstrated empirically how African nationalist figures like Ghana's Nkrumah, Egypt's Gamal Abdel Nasser and Senegal's Léopold Senghor played an active role in the invention of an African identity, using such means as the First All-African People's Conference held in Accra, Ghana, in December 1958 to "re-member" Africa after its "dismemberment" at the Berlin Conference of 1884–5.[11] African nationalism and Pan-Africanism thus provided the discursive framework for Africans on the continent and in its diaspora to invent themselves as one people.

African Identity and the "Triple Heritage"

But to Ethiopian scholar Seifudein Adem, Mazrui's "theory" of the "triple heritage" was his "most innovative, and possibly, most enduring contribution to scholarship".[12] However, as demonstrated above, the triple heritage thesis was not Mazrui's origination. It had a long genealogy dating back to Blyden and the Négritude movements. Paul Zeleza articulated the triple heritage thesis as the "Blyden-Nkrumah-Mazrui cultural typology" in his attempt to explain its genealogy.[13] What is innovative about the triple heritage thesis is that it attempted to take into account the historical realities that have shaped ideas of Africanity, particularly how the indigenous African ethos intersected with the Arabic-Islamic and Western Christian traditions. But Mazrui was heavily criticised by Nigerian Nobel Literature laureate Wole Soyinka[14] (see Osha in this volume) for allegedly denigrating indigenous African religions and cultures and for privileging Arabic-Islamic ones. In the midst of what Zeleza[15] described as "the clash of gigantic intellectual egos" which resulted in the "Mazrui-Soyinka debate", Soyinka dismissed the triple heritage thesis as nothing more than "triple tropes of trickery".[16]

Broadly speaking, one can argue that the complex themes of African identity and the African condition to which Mazrui actively contributed were framed by two broad strands: a post-Enlightenment Eurocentric view, and an anti-colonial and decolonial perspective which is itself constituted by a diverse family of ideological and intellectual streams.[17] Framed in this way, these debates can be flashed back to "colonial imaginists" such as Rudyard Kipling, Frederick Lugard and Cecil John Rhodes, as well as forward to the anti-colonial and "decolonial imaginists" such as Marcus Garvey, W.E.B. Du Bois, Aimé Césaire, Léopold Senghor, Cheikh Anta Diop, Frantz Fanon, Kwame Nkrumah, Nelson Mandela and many others (see Grant, Morris, Irele, Jinadu and Biney in this volume). In Mazrui, this idea is as much accentuated as it is politicised.

Mazrui emphasised the fragmentary nature of African identity in his 1963 article, "On the Concept 'We Are All Africans'", elaborated further in *The African Condition* (1980). The triple heritage that he stressed in the 1980s was founded on a "double invention" of Africa, highlighted by Jamaican-American scholar Lewis R. Gordon: "It is in this sense that Africa is 'invented'. It is invented by systems of knowledge constituted by the processes of conquest and colonization, which always erupted with discovery, on the one hand, and it is also constituted by the processes of resistance borne out of those events the consequence of which is an effect of both on each other."[18] Gordon noted that "Africa is not, in other words, simply invented but continues to be invented and reinvented, both inside and outside the terms of African peoples".[19] Unlike Mazrui and Appiah, for example, Wole Soyinka seemed to highlight the primordiality of Africa, and was critical of the "discovery" paradigm, which is used widely with reference to Latin America:

> The African continent appears to possess one distinction that is largely unremarked. Unlike the Americas or Australasia, for instance, no one actually claims to have "discovered" Africa. Neither the continent as an entity nor indeed any of her later offspring – the modern states – celebrates the equivalent of America's Columbus Day. This gives it a self-constitutive identity, an unstated autochthony that is denied other continents and subcontinents.[20]

Can we speak of a pre-colonial African "authentic" identity and "authentic" being? Mazrui's concept of the "triple heritage" problematises the ideas of a primordial and "authentic" African identity without discarding the importance of "African" as an enduring pre-colonial culture in the invention of Africa and in shaping notions of Africanity. But we need to take note of what Soyinka understood to be "the crisis of African emergence into modernity",[21] which had profound effects on the development and fossilisation of Africanity as an identity. We must understand the logic of imperial reason and the operations of the "paradigm of difference". It is in this Eurocentric discourse that the racial paradigm of difference and the politics of alterity are rooted. This is why Mudimbe argued: "As a conceptuality, Africa has been presumed a transparent concept in most politics of alterity and by almost everyone as a key to the assurance of a difference."[22]

In imperial reason, human species re-emerge as socially classified and racially hierarchised in accordance with assumed differential ontological densities. In this paradigm, at the apex is the white race and at the bottom is the black race. Here was born what Du Bois termed the "colour line", Puerto Rican decolonial theorist Nelson Maldonado-Torres[23] described as "imperial Manichean misanthropic skepticism",[24] while Portuguese sociologist and decolonial theorist Boaventura de Sousa Santos, dubbed it as "abyssal thinking".[25]

At another level, the Eurocentric discourse's presentation of Africa as a "Dark Continent" inhabited by a deficient human subject locked horns with a decolonial perspective that was articulated in various ideological terms, including Ethiopianism, Garveyism, Négritude, the African Personality, Pan-Africanism, African Socialism, African Humanism, the Black Consciousness Movement and the African Renaissance.[26] The logic informing the decolonial perspective is provided by Nigerian novelist Chinua Achebe:

> You have all heard of African personality; of African democracy; of the African way to socialism, of négritude, and so on. They are all props we have fashioned at different times to help us get on our feet again. Once we are up we shall not need any of them anymore. But for the moment it is in the nature of things that we may need to counter racism with what Jean-Paul Sartre called an anti-racist racism, to announce not just that we are as good as the next man but that we are better.[27]

The decolonial perspective is informed by the spirit that asserts African being: sovereign African subjectivity. It is largely a response to imperial and colonial discourses on African subjectivity. It was imposed on Africans as an agenda by a history of domination, racial discrimination, and exploitation. This reality was well captured by South African academic Archie Mafeje:

> We would not talk of freedom, if there was no prior condition in which this was denied; we would not be anti-racist if we had not been its victims; we would not proclaim Africanity, if it had not been denied or degraded; and we would not insist on Afrocentrism, if it had not been for Eurocentric negations ... Of necessity, under the determinate global condition an African renaissance must entail a rebellion – a conscious rejection of past transgressions, a determined negation of negations.[28]

The inscription of Islamic and Western cultures was also accompanied by epistemicides, that is, attempts to eradicate indigenous histories, cultures, religions and traditions. Generally speaking, the spread of Islam and Christianity was underpinned by violent jihads and crusades. Christian missionaries often worked closely with colonialists in their project of "pacification of barbarous tribes". We can, therefore, speak of "colonially imposed heritages" with reference to Islamic and Western civilisation. African culture predated Islamic and Western cultures.[29]

Thus, Mazrui's reintroduction of the "triple heritage" thesis must be taken as both a recognition of complex histories from which Africanity emerged, and also a search for the creation of a new African humanism. The Kenyan intellectual was not "opening a closed file", as the Palestinian-American intellectual Edward Said wanted us to believe.[30] The file had remained open since the time of colonial encounters and the decolonisation process had failed to close it. The decolonisation and deracialisation projects of the twentieth century had only partially closed the chapter.

The Epic and Episodic Schools of Colonialism

What is also enlightening about Mazrui's interventions in respect of African identity is that he directly confronted the impact of colonialism and engaged with the "epic" and "episodic" schools of colonialism. Mazrui belonged to the "epic school", which emphasised the radical interventions of colonialism on African identity and on the mindset of Africans. This school highlighted the violent incorporation of Africa into the global economy through "the slave trade, which dragged African labour itself into the emerging international capitalist system".[31] This was followed by what Mazrui termed the "territorial imperative": the conquest of African space as well as the appropriation and physical occupation of its territory. The third element was the refusal to admit Africa into the state system of the world that emanated from the European Peace of Westphalia of 1648.[32] The fourth element was "Africa's incorporation into world culture", which included the imposition of European colonial languages on the continent. The fifth element was "Africa's incorporation into the world of international law, which is again heavily Eurocentric in origin".[33] Finally, Africa was "incorporated into the modern technological age". Colonialism even introduced a particular "moral order" that was Western-centric.[34] Thus, if one takes into account all of these interventions and their implications for the invention of Africa, the conclusion is that there was a deliberate "dis-Africanisation" and "Westernisation" of Africa to the extent that, as Mazrui noted, "What Africa knows about itself, what different parts of Africa know about each other, have been profoundly influenced by the West."[35] Such colonially imposed identities as anglophone, francophone and lusophone are good examples that indicate the influence of the enduring legacy of colonial encounters.

Then the "episodic school of history" emerged as a counter to the "epic school of history" and became informed by nationalist historiography, which developed in particular at Nigeria's University of Ibadan. It was Nigerian historian J.F. Ade Ajayi who depicted colonialism as an "episode" in African history. Nationalist historiography was ranged against imperial historiography, which had denied the existence of African history prior to the colonial encounter.[36] The important point of the "episodic school" is that the European impact on Africa was not as profound as generally depicted: it was brief, shallow, transitional and not long-lasting. Capitalism as an economic system was shallow. Consequently, there was a continuity of African history from the pre-colonial period to the post-colonial era, with colonialism having been a brief disruption to the continuity of African history. The implication of this interpretation of the impact of colonialism is that Africans have continued to make their own history, and to invent themselves as a people with agency. In the face of these two schools, Mazrui's conclusion was that "European colonial rule in Africa was more effective in destroying indigenous African structures than in destroying African culture. The tension between new imported structures and old resilient cultures is part of the post-colonial war of cultures in the African continent. The question has therefore arisen as to whether Africa is reclaiming its own."[37]

Mazrui has a point in that post-colonial Africa has been haunted by "a war of cultures". However, whether this cultural crisis is responsible for "inefficiency, mismanagement, corruption and decay of the infrastructure" is highly debatable.[38] Is post-colonial Africa suffering from what Mazrui rendered as the "failure of transplanted organs of the state and the economy"?[39] Is the decay of infrastructure in post-colonial Africa to be celebrated as a form of African resistance to imposed Western "civilisation"? Mazrui noted that, "Before a seed germinates it must first decay. A mango tree grows out of a decaying mango seed. A new Africa may germinate in the decay of the present one – and the ancestors are presiding over the process."[40]

It was Mazrui who remarked that what Africa knows about itself is informed by colonial thought. This has massive implications for understanding the "African condition", which is an encapsulation of Africa's post-colonial predicaments.[41]

Mazrui and the Post-Colonial African Condition

For Mazrui, the post-colonial predicaments and instabilities haunting Africa were a "symptom of cultures at war", with Africans fighting "to avert the demise of Africanity".[42] At the centre of these "culture wars" is what Mazrui described as "Africa's triple heritage of indigenous, Islamic and Western forces – fusing and recoiling, at once competitive and complementary".[43] Therefore, the redemption of Africa, according to Mazrui, lies in two options: "the imperative of looking inwards towards Africa's ancestors" and "the imperative of looking outward towards the wider world".[44] Indigenous African culture is the basis of the inward-looking option, but is "not identical with looking inward at yesterday's Africa". Instead, it must gesture towards "a special transition from the tribe to the human race, from the village to the world".[45]

But this option needs to take into account what Mazrui described as the "six paradoxes" of the post-colonial African condition.[46] The first is the "paradox of habitation", which speaks to how a continent that has been identified as the "cradle of mankind" is, at the same time, the least hospitable today. The second is the "paradox of humiliation", which highlights how Africa is a product of a humiliating history of enslavement, colonialism, and racial discrimination. The third is the "paradox of acculturation" cascading from the imposition of foreign cultural, political, economic and social forms that disturbed and reproduced Africanity as a nest of conflicting identities.[47]

The fourth is the "paradox of fragmentation", rooted in a capitalist economic system of exploitation which reproduced Africa as a site of underdevelopment, maldistribution of income and resources, and economic disarticulation. The fifth is the "paradox of retardation", manifesting itself in the form of Africa's failure to act in unison due to internal weaknesses resulting from national, ethnic, ideological and religious cleavages. The sixth is the "paradox of location", which speaks to how a continent which is centrally located is simultaneously the most marginal in global power politics.[48]

How does Africa extricate itself from these six paralysing paradoxes? Mazrui offered seven solutions. The first is that Africa must indigenise its governance personnel and avoid relying on non–Africans for advice on these issues. The second is that Africa should domesticate foreign resources, making them relevant and appropriate to the continent's needs. The third is that Africa must diversify its products, trading partners, investors, sources of aid and foreign cultural relationships. The fourth solution is that Africa should pursue a strategy of "horizontal inter-penetration" in its economic relations. This strategy would rely on pooling together resources in an effort to subvert external domination. The fifth is that Africa must pursue "vertical counter-penetration". This is predicated on African self-assertion and the projection of its identity in world affairs. The sixth is that Africa should work hard to narrow the gap between elites and ordinary citizens. The final solution is that Africa must "encourage northern extravagance, particularly in the form of oil consumption", so as to get resources in the short term to finance its own development.[49]

These post-colonial predicaments are compounded by a leadership crisis. For Mazrui, post-colonial Africa produced four types of leadership: the "elder tradition" whose symbol was Kenya's Jomo Kenyatta; "warrior leadership" represented by Uganda's Idi Amin; the "sage tradition" typified by Tanzania's Julius Nyerere; and the "monarchical tradition" embodied by Ghana's Kwame Nkrumah. These four typologies of leadership in turn produced five styles of leadership: intimidatory, patriarchal, reconciliatory, bureaucratic and mobilisational.[50] As Mazrui noted, these styles of leadership had the following outcomes:

Almost every other African country which attained liberation from European colonial rule in the 20th century was unable to maintain its democratic order beyond its first decade of independence. Within the first decade either the military captured power or the elected president became a dictator, or a civil war broke out, or the ruling party outlawed any rival political party and turned the country into a single-party state.[51]

Building on Mazrui's work, it becomes clear that the continuing struggle for democracy in Africa is intrinsically related to the struggle for a democratic tradition of leadership and a democratic style of governance. South Africa, which Mazrui celebrated in 2011 as "truly democratized", as a country that "has not outlawed opposition parties"; has not "experienced a military coup" and has not "permitted the head of state to govern" as a dictator; is facing its own challenges (such as deepening inequalities, corruption and poor "service delivery") that question the quality of its democracy and the prospects for its sustainability.

Concluding Reflections

There is no doubt that Ali Mazrui was an engaged Pan-African who fully embraced his African identity even within a context in which others like Wole Soyinka wanted to deny him this identity by reminding him of his Arab genealogy. It is also clear that Mazrui deployed his vast intellect and knowledge in explaining the post-colonial "African condition". Interestingly, towards the end of his academic career, Mazrui – who died in October 2014 at the age of 81 – increasingly focused on the equally topical and important question of Islamophobia. He justified this shift by arguing that, with the election of Barack Obama as the first black president of the United States, there were signs that 'negro-phobia' had de-escalated, while "Islamophobia" had increased, with the "culture line" superseding the "colour line".[52]

Stuart Hall: The Making of a "Post-Colonial" Sociologist

Zine Magubane

"The distinction between my life and my ideas really has no hold."[1]

STUART HALL, *FAMILIAR STRANGER*, 2017

DESPITE BEING WIDELY RECOGNISED as one of the most important cultural sociologists of the modern era, and one of the founders of the discipline of "Cultural Studies", Stuart Hall (1932–2014) embraced both titles reluctantly. "People say I'm a cultural theorist," he wrote. "Although I believe in theory as an indispensable critical tool, I have never been interested in 'producing theory' and, in any case, I am not a theorist of any rank in this age of theory, so I regard the designation of cultural theorist more as a polite, convenient postponement, a holding operation, than a well-understood resolution."[2]

The Reluctant Pan-Africanist and Cultural Theorist

By his own admission, Stuart Hall came somewhat late to Pan-Africanism. Although he had the "melanin coursing through [his] veins" and the "skin colour to prove [his] African origins", for much of his life he did not identify himself as "African in any meaningful, contemporary sense of the word".[3] Hall maintained that his homeland of Jamaica did not even begin to really think of itself as a "black" society until the 1960s (see also Knight in this volume), and described himself as a child who, despite being the darkest in his family, "was not yet black in my head".[4] As he explained in his posthumously published 2017 autobiography, *Familiar Stranger: A Life between Two Islands*:

> I became vaguely aware of Garveyism, although I didn't know much about Garvey himself and it was a long time before I came to appreciate his influence. I knew of Edelweiss Park, where Garvey's UNIA (Universal Negro Improvement Association) had established itself. I'd occasionally encountered Garveyite publications. I came to understand that Garveyism had connections with larger Pan-African aspirations, and a philosophy of black independence, pride and self-improvement.[5]

Hall did not see any value in theoretical posturing for its own sake. He also resisted the "burden of representation" that he bore as a "black" theorist. Speaking at the University of Illinois Urbana-Champaign in 1990 on the topic "Cultural Studies and Its Theoretical Legacies", Hall resolved to "speak autobiographically" to absolve himself of the "burdens of representation" which he felt that all black intellectuals bore: the expectation to speak for an entire race on all questions, theoretical, critical, political and cultural. As he noted: "In order to be authoritative, I've got to speak autobiographically. I'm going to tell you about my own take on certain theoretical legacies and moments in cultural studies, not because it is the truth or the only way of telling the history. I myself have told it many other ways before; and I intend to tell it in a different way later."[6]

Hall's theoretical engagements arose from his experience as "the last colonial".[7] A crucial link between his theoretical innovation and his lived experience lay in his attempts first to achieve and then to describe his process of "dis-identification" or "unlearning the norms" in which he had been born and brought up.[8] This "dis-identification" was enormously productive for thinking through the ways in which self-understandings are open to change over time but can also harden and congeal. Hall took on the questions of what it meant to be "West Indian", "black" and ultimately "Pan-African" at first personally, then politically, and finally theoretically. In so doing, he wrestled artfully with the duality of identity, seeking to understand when, how, and why it at times appeared to be, and was experienced as, something constructed and, hence, embraced willingly and at other times appeared to be forcefully and, thus, coercively imposed.

Hall's many intellectual achievements will be explored below, with particular attention to his engagements with the possibilities of living a "Pan-Africanist" identity personally; engaging with Pan-Africanism politically; and rewriting sociology from a Pan-African perspective. Like all theorists, however, Hall had his limitations, particularly when it came to his engagement with Marxism. In his own estimation, Marxism was something he approached "as a problem, as trouble, as danger, not as a solution".[9] This was completely understandable given his location as a displaced colonial subject bearing witness to the "articulation of decolonization with the darker geopolitics of the global Cold War".[10] For Hall, the 1956 Soviet invasion of Hungary and the Soviet leader Nikita Khrushchev's condemnation of Joseph Stalin, were game-changers. It was a "curious time for a colonial to be experiencing life in the metropole", and Hall came to question profoundly whether class struggle alone was enough to undo racism and colonialism.[11] His ambivalent stance towards Marxism stamped itself on the work that he did at the Centre for Contemporary Cultural Studies (CCCS) at the University of Birmingham in England, which was founded by Richard Hoggart, a British professor of English, in 1964. Hall took over directorship of the Centre in 1968 and remained there until 1979, when he left to take up a professorship in sociology at the Open University. The Centre was unusual at the time in that it steadfastly avoided doing work on "high" culture, preferring to produce scholarly treatises on popular music, television shows and advertising. The aim was to show that popular culture had profound political implications and was thus worthy of serious study. During his tenure at CCCS, path-breaking books such as *The Empire Writes Back*, which is widely considered to be a foundational text in the field of post-colonial studies, were published.[12]

Hall often noted that he "came into Marxism backwards".[13] By that, he meant that as the "other" in relation to the West, he entered Marxism and Left politics as a "born revisionist".[14] The lack of attention that the British Labour Party paid to issues of racism and colonialism made it clear to Hall that the "old practices of the Left could no longer be viable" and impressed on him that the need to fashion a new politics was urgent – in fact, a matter of cultural survival.[15] Hall thus concluded that "the fundamental relations of class, decisive as they were, couldn't tell us politically what we needed to know".[16] Neither could they tell him, theoretically, what he needed to know. Much of Hall's work on culture and identity sought to engage "the things that Marx did not talk about or seem to understand", as well as Marx's Eurocentrism. I will address whether, and to what extent, Hall was correct in his evaluation of Marx's "profound

Eurocentrism" and the ways in which this point of view informed the work that came out of the Centre for Contemporary Cultural Studies, in the final section of this chapter.[17]

The Evolution of Stuart Hall's Pan-Africanist Sensibility

Hall explained his distance from Pan-Africanism as having arisen, in no small part, from his class background. His father and mother were, as he explained to Kuan-hsing Chen, an academic based at the Centre for Cultural Studies at National Tsing Hua University in Taiwan, "both middle class but from very different class formations".[18] His family, which self-identified as "coloured", occupied an intermediary position between the wealthy white elite and the mass of poor and unemployed black Jamaicans. They felt, however, no affinity for, or with, the mass of poor Jamaicans. Stuart's father came from a "modest but respectable lower-middle class family" and was the first "coloured" chief accountant for United Fruit Company, an American multinational which dominated the banana trade in the Caribbean and Central America.[19] The annual visits of the United Fruit Company's accountants from Boston were the "high point" of his parents' social calendar.[20] His mother was "born to light-skinned but not well-off parents".[21] In the distant past, his mother's family had been slave-owners. Hall recalled, with some trepidation, how his mother had never repudiated this legacy. Rather, plantation life became the "aspirational model of her hopes and fears" for Stuart, his brother and his older sister.[22] When she learnt of his anti-colonial activism in England, his mother admonished him to stay away – not to come back and "make trouble for [the family] with those funny ideas".[23] Despite being born and bred in Jamaica, Stuart's mother so identified with her colonisers that, until the day she died, she thought of England as her "real home".[24]

Although Hall came eventually to find his parents' worldview "negative and regressive",[25] he understood it as reflecting the general tenor of the times. It was thus that he came to know, on a deep existential level, that "questions of race and ethnicity are never far removed from social class".[26] As he noted:

[Pan-Africanism] wasn't part of my family's world because they in no sense identified themselves with the black masses or with an African Diaspora. Indeed, "Back to Africa" was a source of ridicule around Kingston middle-class dinner tables. It took me some time to understand the "Back to Africa" message and its considerable resonance, not only among the urban poor and the unemployed, who were at the forefront of the industrial struggles of the late 1930s, but also among sections of the colour-conscious nationalist lower middle classes as well.[27]

Like many people of African descent on the continent and in the diaspora, Hall only began to develop a Pan-African consciousness when he migrated from colony to metropole. He spoke and wrote often about the fact that he had "no West Indian consciousness to speak of" when he arrived in England to study at Oxford University as a Rhodes Scholar in 1951.[28] Indeed, the process of becoming both West Indian and "black" developed not only as a result of his migration to Britain, but also from his exposure to the connected, yet by no means identical, dynamics of racism and resistance to racism that occurred in different national contexts. As Hall explained, although the evolution of "voter-registration categories" like "Black Caribbean" or "Afro-Caribbean" emerged in the wake of the post-Second World War Caribbean migration to Britain, they only became part of Hall's self-understanding – or what he termed "black as a personal identity" – when Hall became involved with black diasporic politics, much of which were centered around Notting Hill, a neighbourhood in London that was the site of a great deal of racist violence and anti-racist organising. Hall described Notting Hill as a neighborhood with an "underground, Diasporic, cultural colony life" that "reconnected people to the Caribbean".[29]

This was the setting in which he learnt the most about "decolonization, the Alabama bus boycott, the Notting Hill riots, US Civil Rights, Martin Luther King's 'I Have a Dream', Sharpeville, Malcolm X, Stokely Carmichael, Angela Davis, and then later, in the 1970s, black resistance politics in Britain, Rock Against Racism, roots music, reggae and Bob Marley".[30] West Indians in Britain "knew the US first hand" and thus acted as "bridgeheads between black Britain and black America".[31] As bridgeheads, they introduced Martin Luther King and Malcolm X (see Daniels in this volume) to their British counterparts. Hall acknowledges, however, that even though decolonisation was occurring rapidly across the continent, and Tom Mboya, the Kenyan trade unionist and later cabinet minister, played an active role in the Socialist Club – a moribund organisation originally founded in the 1930s which Hall helped to revive – the Jamaican emigré was not particularly knowledgeable about African politics. As he noted:

> Notwithstanding the pace of decolonization in Africa, African politics didn't at this time possess me with the same intensity as the new race politics emerging from the US. Nor did it, really, until the politicized Africanization of the Caribbean during the Black Power years. Of course we were excited by the winning of independence by the African nations. The revival of older Pan-African traditions, particularly evident in the Independence of Ghana in 1957, was a moment of historic optimism. But we were only too aware of the extent of problems unresolved across the continent, and unnerved by the resurgence of white ascendency, both in apartheid South Africa and in the not-quite-apartheid Southern Rhodesia.[32]

The experience of coming to know and understand himself first as "West Indian" and eventually as a member of the African diaspora and, thus, in some sense "Pan-African" was formative in Hall's evolution as a sociologist. He was best known for his work on culture and power, as well as race and identity. The great strides that Hall made in fleshing out what, sociologically, it meant for identity to function as an analytical category, ultimately can be traced back to his having been the "product of *two* Diasporas".[33] As he explained, although his migration from Jamaica to Britain marked a journey into the diaspora, as an origin point Jamaica, too, must be thought of "diasporically". None of the major groups which constitute Jamaican society, Hall noted, originated there. As such, "every Jamaican is the product of migration, forced or free. Everyone is originally from somewhere else."[34]

Hall became obsessed with knowing more about how slavery had transformed inherited African cultures into a syncretic or creolised Jamaican folk culture. In a 1992 article, "Cultural Studies and Its Theoretical Legacies", he described how he "entered cultural studies from the New Left" by way of the African diaspora.[35] The origins of Cultural Studies, Hall maintained, could be traced back to what he believed, at the time, would be a brief exploration of the history of slavery, with a particular focus on African "survivals" in Caribbean culture. This intellectual excursion – which the Jamaican intellectual later described as a "diversion in [Oxford's] Rhodes House library"[36] – took him away from the abstract questions of culture, power and ideology that had animated the New Left, and into the specificities of how migration had brought to the fore the "most pressing" questions about self-identification. Hall became determined to apply the "practical skills of cultural reading" developed by British scholars Richard Hoggart and Raymond Williams "consciously and explicitly" to the Caribbean world and the "peculiar nature of its intimate subordinations, and how it had been shaped by, and in relation to, the colonial metropole".[37] This deep dive into slavery marked, for Hall, "the origins of Cultural Studies".[38]

"A Diversion in the Rhodes House Library": The Roots and Routes of Cultural Studies

Hall felt that fully understanding the "cultural formation of the post-colonial nation" was an urgent problem. For him, it brought into focus the political possibilities and prospects of the "new black Diaspora in Britain" and how it might construct its "'negotiated relationship' to the colonised culture at home".[39] It also held possibilities for understanding how a "black" – but not necessarily "Pan-African" – identity became "hegemonic over other ethnic/racial identities" that were available to people of African descent, providing an avenue for understanding how blackness "came to provide the organising category of a new politics of resistance".[40] Coming to think of himself in diasporic terms offered Hall "not a solution but some distance from the raw emotional impact of the renunciation of [his] colonial family formation [and] the inevitable sense of rupture, refusal and loss it entailed".[41]

The diasporic perspective also proved to be intellectually fertile. Hall explained that "It provided what new problem spaces always do: an opportunity to change not the answers but the questions … It provided not only a home from home, but a new site of knowledge."[42] The Jamaican intellectual built his sociology around the premise that diaspora was "a space in which to think".[43] In an interview with Kuan-hsing Chen, he explained: "I did have a Diasporic 'take' on my position in the New Left. Even if I was not then writing about the Diaspora, or writing about black politics (there weren't yet many black settlers in Britain), I looked at the British political scene very much as somebody who had a different formation. I was always aware of that difference. I was aware that I'd come from the periphery of this process, that I was looking at it from a different vantage point."[44] This "diasporic take" also provided Hall with a unique avenue into sociological theory – a way of disrupting and decentring mainstream Eurocentric sociology. His life story, with its multiple instances of displacement and marginalisation existing alongside newly forged connections and different conceptions of community, needed to be made "visible" in not just personal, but also theoretical, terms. As he noted:

> I identified with the aspirations of black Jamaicans and the emergent indigenous culture which, I believed, only the end of colonialism could fully erase. But I had been formed in a distanced and troubled relationship to my own nation. I was also shaped in relation to the culture of the colonizer "elsewhere" but, for very different reasons, I found it impossible to identify with *that*. This seemed to leave me with only a binary choice between impossible alternatives. Then, unexpectedly, a "third space" opened up ... This, I realized subsequently, was the space of the Diasporic.[45]

American sociologist C. Wright Mills maintains that "neither the life of an individual nor the history of a society can be understood without understanding both".[46] The sociological imagination, he reminds us, "enables us to grasp history and biography and the relations between the two within society".[47] Mills's notion of the sociological imagination is clearly evident in Hall's trajectory towards becoming a theorist of culture. As the Jamaican intellectual noted:

> Contrary to common sense understanding, the transformations of self-identity are not just a personal matter. Historical shifts *out there* provide the social conditions of existence of personal and psychic change *in here*. What mattered was how I positioned myself on the other side. Or positioned myself to catch the other side. How I was involuntarily hailed by and interpellated into a broader social discourse. Only by discovering this did I begin to understand that what black identity involved was a social, political, historical, and symbolic event, not just a personal and certainly not simply a genetic one.[48]

The "diasporic" became, over time, a matter for "analysis, investigation, and interpretation", and thus theoretically, and not simply personally, pertinent.[49] As Hall explained in his 1987 address on "Postmodernism and the Question of

Identity", when viewed from the perspective of the diasporic, sociology – the discipline that takes "the modern" as its central theoretical concern – suddenly must face the fact that "margin" and "centre" have traded places. As Hall observed: "My own sense of identity has always depended on the fact of being a migrant ... [now] I find myself centred at last. Now that, in the postmodern age, you all feel so dispersed, I become centred: what I've thought of as dispersed and fragmented comes, paradoxically, to be *the* modern experience."[50]

In a 1992 interview, he reiterated the point, and further elaborated on its implications for what has now come to be called "post-colonial sociology".[51]

So, you have what German sociologist Georg Simmel talked about: the experience of being inside an outsider, the "familiar stranger". We used to call that "alienation" or "deracination". But nowadays it's come to be the archetypal later-modern condition. Increasingly, it's what everybody's life is like. So that's how I think about the articulation of the postmodern and the postcolonial. Post-coloniality, in a curious way, prepared one to live in a "postmodern" or Diasporic relationship to identity. Paradigmatically, it's a Diasporic experience. Since migration has turned out to be *the* world historical event of late modernity, the classic postmodern experience turns out to be the Diasporic experience.[52]

In Hall's quest to challenge not only the historical and empirical questions at the heart of sociology, but also the concepts through which they are approached, he set about the task with the mindset that struggle was productive rather than disabling. In his words, Hall took on the task of "wrestling with the angels [because] the only theory worth having is that which you have to fight off, not that which you speak with profound fluency".[53]

Wrestling with Angels: The Birmingham School of Cultural Studies

Hall's evolution from thinking of "West Indian" as a "geographical term" to thinking of it as a term bearing immense cultural significance deeply informed how he approached culture as an object of empirical and theoretical inquiry.[54] As a son of the diaspora, he often remarked that the interrelationship between class and race was the "most difficult theoretical problem" facing modern intellectuals.[55] Marxism, because of its Eurocentrism and its privileging of the working-class European male as the main agent of history, was not up to the task. As Hall explained in his 1996 essay "Gramsci's Relevance for the Study of Race and Ethnicity": "There is the question of the non-homogenous character of the 'class subject'. Approaches which privilege the class, as opposed to the racial, structuring of working classes or peasantries are often predicated on the assumption that, because the mode of exploitation *vis-à-vis* capital is the same, the 'class subject' of any such exploitative mode must be not only economically but politically and ideologically unified."[56]

Hall felt that the phenomenon of "working-class racism" had been so "resistant to analysis" because of the limitations of Marxism in understanding ideology and culture.[57] He also found fault with what he saw as Marxism's tendency to seek "guarantees". By this, he meant its impulse to fix the correspondence between dominance in the socio-economic sphere and dominance in the ideological sphere. This was the notion that there was a "guaranteed" correspondence between class position and ideas.[58]

Hall postulated instead that Marxism's quest for theoretical guarantees was inextricably bound up with its Eurocentrism. Had Marxism been able to see, engage with, and theorise from the point of view of Europe's "others", the notion that theory could in any way secure guarantees would have been more quickly exposed for what it was: the Western "will" to dominance. The idea that the European working man was the privileged subject of history would also have been cast into radical doubt. As would have been the idea that particular forms of consciousness are class-specific. Hall noted that, in Jamaica, political arrangements were "cross-cut" by profound differences – certainly of class, but also of colour, race and education. What Hall described as "vernacular lived cultures" came to speak more powerfully than – and substitute for – formal politics. They became "symbolic resources" which allowed the dispossessed to express their dissatisfaction. "Class interests, racialized divisions and political differences" found expression in, and through, "the subterranean emergence of a black, Afrocentric consciousness, of the Rastafarians, of Black Power, and of reggae".[59]

This critical posture towards Marxism critically informed the work produced by the Birmingham Centre for Contemporary Cultural Studies – dubbed the "Birmingham School of Cultural Studies". We cannot understand the posture that the CCCS took without understanding how disillusioned Hall and other progressives at the time were as they witnessed the rise of Britain's future conservative prime minister, Margaret Thatcher, between 1975 and 1979, and the ways in which she was able to mobilise white Britons of all classes around regressive and racist rhetoric. Given the wide reach of Thatcherism and the decline of the Labour Party, it did indeed seem that class politics were "dead" in some sense. The fact that the "New Social Movements" mobilised people around "extra-economic" identities such as gender, race and sexuality, and that the British working and middle classes saw themselves first and foremost as consumers, led to the Birmingham School's focus on what the academy traditionally considered "low" forms of culture like pop music and advertising. As Hall explained:

> The purpose of a great deal of advertising, for example, is to condition the worker to the new possibilities for consumption, to break down the resistances to consumer purchase, which became part of working class consciousness at an earlier period ... Through the purchase and display of certain kinds of consumer goods, which have gathered from themselves status value, a working class family can define its social standing ... they can even – so the advertisers suggest – raise their class position by buying the right kinds of goods.[60]

The Birmingham School thus sought to produce work that took seriously how cultural identities, particularly consumer identities, became salient in politics. One of the most well-known and widely cited texts produced during Hall's tenure, the 1978 *Policing the Crisis*, examined how Thatcher created a sense of moral panic around "mugging" and street crime, which constructed white Britons as "law-abiding tax payers, citizens, and consumers" under siege by black criminals with no respect for law and order.[61] Sally Davidson, David Featherstone and Bill Schwarz capture how innovative and important the analysis presented in *Policing the Crisis* was at the time of its publication. "What remains remarkable about this text is the degree to which 'race' works as the decisive explanatory concept that gives form and meaning to Hall's reading of authoritarian populism and the exceptional state ... There was virtually no other figure at the time who was centrally reading the crisis of the British state, in its most general manifestations, through the lens of 'race'."[62]

Thus, Hall and the Birmingham School deliberately and self-consciously rejected any Marxian notion of an ideological "superstructure" being determined by a material base. When he took up the directorship of the Birmingham Centre in 1968, Hall deliberately pursued a research plan that centred on race and gender, seeking to expand the focus of the Birmingham School to take seriously how societies were "structured in dominance". At his Centre, Hall introduced a decidedly sociological and Pan-Africanist perspective. The American sociological tradition of symbolic interactionism, which stressed the idea that societies were constituted by the meanings assigned to them by individuals and groups, was an important intellectual resource. Hall and his colleagues examined how racially structured social formations could be rendered as autonomous objects of inquiry. The purpose of examining racial formations was not, however, simply theoretical. Its ultimate purpose was to develop strategic political interventions. The Birmingham School's political commitments were reflected in the Centre's structure. Unlike many university research units which adopted a "top-down" approach, the CCCS was committed to producing collaborative work, much of it with students. The traditional Birmingham School student was not traditional at all. Many of these students came from under-represented or marginalised backgrounds. The Birmingham School thus deliberately sought to break down the hierarchical structures that characterised academic life. The traditional boundaries between teachers and students were continually and deliberately transgressed. Thus, the commitment of the Birmingham School to breaking down the "high culture vs low culture" distinction mirrored its commitment to challenging the binary opposition of "expert" and "student".

It was within this practical activity that Hall also developed the notion of culture as a site for negotiation – a place of "give and take" where new meanings emerged in the course of cultural contestation. It was, for example, in the course of contestation (oftentimes violent) that racialised ideas about "deviancy" and "criminality" were produced and reproduced. It was also, however, in the responses of marginalised persons and communities that new popular cultural objects and forms of communication were born. Since culture was produced in the contest between the powerful and the powerless, the notion of cultural reception also became central to the Birmingham School's theoretical project. Hall maintained that all subjects – but raced subjects in particular – were always decoding the meanings that were being transmitted through mass culture. Hence, mass culture emerged for him as a key site for identity formation.

Refining Hall's Critique of Marx

Indeed, many of the insights that Hall developed as to how consumer cultures would not only become racialised but would also come to reign supreme were issues that Marx had been ill equipped to foresee. Nevertheless, recent work that seeks to "decolonise" Marx argues that the German sociologist did recognise and provide helpful ground for theorising how integral colonialism has been to the making of modernity, and also suggests that Marx was well aware that radical class struggle might diffuse from the "outside in" – from the colonies to the metropole – rather than from the inside out. American historian Kevin B. Anderson's 2010 book, *Marx at the Margins*, is a fascinating and rigorous exploration of Marx's work on Algeria, Ireland and slavery in the American South. By focusing on articles that Marx had written about the American Civil War (1861–65), labour, racism, and slavery while he was chief European correspondent for the *New York Tribune*, as well as on his extensive (yet not widely known) notebooks on Algeria, India, Russia and China, Anderson demonstrated that Marx actually had quite well-developed ideas, which changed significantly over time, about colonialism, capitalism and racism.

Marx was aware that these societies possessed social structures that differed markedly from those found in the metropole. He was also deeply interested in exploring their prospects for revolution and their deep potential for becoming alternative sites for resistance to capital. The German sociologist's proletariat – as Anderson demonstrated – was not only white and European, but also African American, Arab and Berber. Furthermore, Marx's observation of the colonisation of Algeria, India and Ireland challenged his Eurocentrism early on and showed him that new possibilities for revolutionary change would most likely emerge from those locations.[63] Anderson's deep dive into Marx's writings on the American Civil War conclusively demonstrated that Marx was well aware of, and sought to amend, his perspective to accommodate the fact that "labor movements in core capitalist countries that failed to support adequately progressive nationalist movements on the part of those affected by their governments, or failed to combat racism ... within their own societies, ran the danger of retarding or even cutting short their own development".[64]

This line of argument is echoed by, and elaborated in, African-American historian August H. Nimtz's 2003 book *Marx, Tocqueville and Race in America*. Nimtz provides an in-depth exploration of Marx's writings on the American

Civil War, which drew empirically from the historically accurate appendices to French intellectual Gustave de Beaumont's book, *Marie: Or Slavery in the United States* (1835),[65] and Marx's correspondence with Friedrich Engels on slave resistance. Nimtz analyses how and why Marx concluded that slave rebellions were among the most important political advances in the nineteenth century. He also shed new light on Marx's analysis of the imperialism of the American slave-holding class in its attempt to extend the frontiers of the American slaveocracy to Cuba and Nicaragua. Marx further connected this imperialism with the co-opting of poor whites in America. The plantocracy's quest to conquer Cuba and Nicaragua must also be understood – Marx wrote – as part of an effort to "square the interests of the poor whites with the slaveholders ... to tame them with the prospect of one day becoming slaveholders themselves".[66]

The existence of these writings does not so much prove Hall "wrong" as suggest productive and fruitful new directions in which to take his theory. Hall called for an end to what he termed "the innocent notion of the essential Black subject".[67] By this, he meant that academics, activists, lay persons, and government officials would eventually be forced to reckon with the "extraordinary diversity of subject positions, social experiences, and cultural identities which compose the category 'black'".[68] The most difficult part of that reckoning would come when the political stakes of that recognition became clear. It might be one thing to *say* that "black" is a politically and culturally constructed category which "cannot be grounded in a set of fixed trans-cultural transcendental racial categories" and thus has "no guarantees in nature", but it is quite another to wrestle with what this means for political and social praxis.[69]

Concluding Reflections: "Without Guarantees"

Stuart Hall provides an invaluable resource for thinking about the possibilities of, and for, a post-colonial, Pan-African sociology that is – to borrow one of Hall's most iconic phrases – "without guarantees". To give oneself the freedom to theorise without guarantees is both dangerous and necessary. Dangerous because what *is* theory without guarantees? Is it a theory at all? To commit to theorising without guarantees as a stated goal – rather than as an unfortunate outcome – is, however, absolutely necessary when the object of that theorising is the "post-colonial" or "Pan-African" condition. An essential condition shared by the concepts "post-colonial" and "Pan-African" is that they do not exist as conditions "out there" in the world that one can simply theorise about. As Hall eloquently put it: "Nothing would be more mistaken than to imagine that, because black people in the New World are overwhelmingly of African origin and because there are many connections to African cultures, something called Africa – an imaginary construct, in any event – has been frozen in time since its inhabitants were forced into servitude, waiting for us to rediscover it. This is not so."[70]

"Pan-African" is a concept that was brought into being in, and through, political imagination and action followed by theorisation. In many instances, these acts of theorisation have not only – or even primarily – taken place in the academy. Nevertheless, they have taken place and, in so doing, have called the "post-colonial" and "Pan-African" into existence. As we go forward and build on Hall's legacy, we would do well to seek to live and work as he did. As the Jamaican sociologist movingly wrote in the final pages of his autobiography:

> I had to find a modus vivendi with the world I had entered and indeed with myself. Surprisingly, this turned out to be partly through politics ... I wanted to change British society, not adopt it. This commitment enabled me not to have to live my life as a disappointed suitor, or as a disgruntled stranger. I found an outlet for my energies, commitments, and interests without giving my soul away.[71]

23

ADEBAYO ADEDEJI: PROPHET OF PAN-AFRICAN INTEGRATION

Afeikhena Jerome

"Indeed, there are hardly any innovative economic ideas and programmes for Africa that do not bear Adedeji's indelible finger-print."[1]
– JAMES O. C. JONAH, FORMER UNITED NATIONS UNDERSECRETARY-GENERAL FOR POLITICAL AFFAIRS AND FORMER MINISTER OF FINANCE, SIERRA LEONE.

NIGERIAN ACADEMIC, ECONOMIST and international civil servant Adebayo Adedeji, who died in April 2018, headed the United Nations (UN) Economic Commission for Africa (ECA) between 1975 and 1991. UNECA is one of the five UN regional commissions established by the UN General Assembly's Economic and Social Council (ECOSOC) in 1958 to promote the economic and social development of its member states, foster intra-regional integration and promote international cooperation for Africa's development. Adedeji was undoubtedly one of Africa's most visionary proponents of economic integration. He guided the creation of several regional integration schemes in Africa. This essay appraises his contributions to development economics.

Fifty Years of Toil: From Rebuilding Post-Civil War Nigeria to the AU Summit in Kampala

Adebayo Adedeji was born in Ijebu-Ode in the present Ogun State in Nigeria on 21 December 1930. He had his elementary education at St Saviour's School, Ijebu-Ode, from 1940 to 1943, and thereafter attended Ijebu-Ode Grammar School for his secondary education from 1943 to 1949. Adedeji began his tertiary education at the University College Ibadan in 1954, where he took a diploma course in local government administration. He proceeded to University College Leicester in England in 1955 on a government scholarship, and received a BSc degree in economics in 1958. Adedeji subsequently obtained a master's degree in public administration (MPA) in 1961 from Harvard University on a Ford Foundation fellowship, and a doctorate in economics from the University of London in 1967.

On graduating from Leicester in 1958, Adedeji returned to Nigeria and was employed as assistant secretary for planning in the newly established Ministry of Planning of the country's Western region. On returning from Harvard in 1961, Adedeji had a short spell in his old ministry, before being transferred to the Ministry of Finance in 1962 as senior assistant secretary.

He joined the University of Ife (now Obafemi Awolowo University, Ile-Ife) in 1963, becoming Nigeria's first professor of public administration in October 1968. He also, concurrently, became director of the Institute of Administration where he transformed the nascent institute into one of the most effective training grounds not just for Nigerian but for all African public servants.

Between 1971 and 1975 Adedeji served as Nigeria's post-civil war federal commissioner (minister) for economic reconstruction and development. Apart from overseeing the reconstruction efforts after the devastating Nigerian civil war (1967–70), his achievements as minister included the inauguration of the mandatory one-year National Youth Service Corps introduced for all university graduates in 1973; the preparation and launch of the Third National Development Plan (1975–80); and intense negotiations through "shuttle diplomacy" across the West African sub-region with 15 countries that led to the establishment of the Economic Community of West African States (ECOWAS) in May 1975. Adedeji joined the United Nations, and became the third executive secretary of the UN Economic Commission for Africa in June 1975.

Adedeji resigned from the ECA in 1991, and returned to Nigeria where he unsuccessfully bid for his country's presidency. He established the African Centre for Development and Strategic Studies (ACDESS) in his hometown of Ijebu-Ode, as an independent think tank, to propagate his scholarship, including some path-breaking studies on conflicts in Africa. ACDESS, unfortunately, by 2017 had become moribund because of the illness of its founder.

Adedeji, however, continued to serve Africa in various capacities after his retirement. He was a member of the South African-based African Peer Review Mechanism (APRM) Panel of Eminent Persons from 2003 to 2010 (where I worked under his leadership), and its chair from July 2007 to July 2010. He also led the 13-member high-level panel tasked to carry out an audit of the African Union (AU) in 2007[2] for purposes of facilitating the political integration of the continent. Adedeji retired from public service at the APRM summit held on the margins of the AU summit in the Ugandan capital of Kampala in July 2010 after five decades of service to Africa's development. He gave his valedictory remarks in an emotional event chaired by the late Meles Zenawi, erstwhile prime minister of Ethiopia, and then chair of the African Peer Review Forum.

Contextualising Adebayo Adedeji's Economic Ideas

In order to situate Adedeji's contributions appropriately, we first need to appraise leading paradigms in development economics, whose emergence as a sub-discipline of economics is fairly recent. The study of "development" only became an institutionalised and professionalised area of study in the period after the Second World War (1939–45). Its specific purpose was to study the economies of developing countries in Latin America, the Caribbean, and Africa, most of which were, at that time, just emerging from colonial rule.

On the theoretical front, the intellectual underpinnings of development have grown and evolved over six decades into a daunting and formidable array of ideas, concepts, theories, empirical studies and distinct schools of thought, consequently leading to a fundamental change in development thinking. As Irma Adelman,[3] the Romanian-born American economist, rightly observed, no area of economics has experienced as many abrupt changes in its leading paradigms since the Second World War as development economics. At the heart of these transformation is the role of the state in accelerating development. Since the rejection of British political economist, Adam Smith's "invisible hand" and the "laissez-faire" doctrine prominent during the Great Depression of the 1930s, the pendulum has oscillated from one extreme to another, reigniting fierce debate about the roles of the market and the state, particularly in the developing world.[4]

After the Second World War, there was a great distrust of the market following the experiences of the Great Depression of the 1930s, and implicit confidence began to grow in the ability of the state to play an active and productive role in directing investment. At the beginning of the 1950s, development economists formulated grand models of development strategies that involved structural transformation and extensive government involvement in development programming or planning to correct pervasive market failures. The central focus of these models was on capital accumulation.[5]

In the 1970s, concerns about poverty became more prominent, notably as a result of World Bank president Robert McNamara's celebrated speech to the World Bank Board of Governors in Nairobi in 1973, and the subsequent publication of *Redistribution with Growth*[6] in 1979. The definition of poverty, beginning with a focus on income, expanded to embrace other dimensions of living standards such as longevity, literacy, mortality, potable water, sanitation and health. All these derived from a concern about, and sense of solidarity with, the vulnerable in society: the risks they are exposed to, their powerlessness and their lack of voice.

A new body of knowledge also emerged emphasising the power of ideas. The new endogenous growth theory brought about marked changes in the analysis of the aggregate production function.[7] Instead of the earlier exogenous growth model expounded by the American professor of economics Robert Solow, the new theory stressed investment in human capital, innovation and knowledge as significant contributors to economic growth.

With the end of the golden age of global economic expansion in the mid-1970s, a range of economic, social, political and technological tensions surfaced, including oil shocks and debt crises. These tensions characterised what Adedeji famously referred to as the "lost decade" of the 1980s, and presaged the turbulent post–Cold War decade of the 1990s.

Against the backdrop of widespread unemployment, inflation and a rapid process of economic globalisation, there was a resurgence of neoclassical economics in the early 1980s, which placed great emphasis on "getting prices right" and sought to move away from distortions in wages, interest rates and exchange rates.[8] The new orthodoxy was firmly skewed towards economic liberalisation, deregulation, privatisation and the free play of market forces, as opposed to state interventions. It emerged in the mid-1980s as the dominant mode of development thinking and practice. This orthodoxy, which dominated mainstream economics during the late 1980s and the 1990s, became known as the "Washington Consensus". The weakness of these ideas, which were paraded as the intellectual showpiece of the so-called reform movement, is that they have not lived up to expectations, not only in Africa, but across the world. As a package, these polices were neither necessary nor sufficient for growth; and too often, even when they brought a modicum of growth, such growth was not inclusive, with the benefits going to relatively few people.[9]

Paradoxically, the decade of the 2010s became a period of great intellectual ferment after the global economic crisis of 2008–9, which laid bare the continuing fragility of the economic systems of Western societies and the unpredictable and sometimes shaky capacity of their governments to manage them. At the same time, the world witnessed the rise of new global actors such as China, India and Brazil. The previous near-consensus on the wisdom of deregulating markets eroded quickly. Yet, it was not obvious what should take its place. New approaches to development thinking and practice are being encouraged, and several developing countries are already looking east, especially to China.

As a result of the current mutability in the field, profound stocktaking continues and there is intense scrutiny and re-evaluation of the lessons of the "Washington Consensus". The challenges of the past fifty years[10] indicate that development can no longer be seen purely in terms of economics and economic growth. It can also no longer be seen as dependent either solely on state direction or on the free play of markets. Development "wisdom" no longer emanated solely from the rich countries of the North. There has not been a greater example of poverty reduction in history than that of China in the quarter-century since the 1970s, during which an estimated half a billion people were lifted out of poverty, according to World Bank sources.[11] Yet, not a single Western economist or Western researcher played an instrumental role in China's economic reforms.[12]

The objectives of development have broadened, from a narrow focus on per capita income growth, to include political empowerment, capabilities in the broadest sense, and even "happiness". The actors in the development discourse have changed too. Civil society organisations and other non-state actors are increasingly partnering with the state on poverty reduction, as developing countries claim ownership of their own development. Political economy frameworks are becoming more prominent in development studies. Economics – though, still dominant in the development discourse – has increasingly been challenged, complemented and supplemented by other disciplines such as sociology, political science, philosophy, history and the natural sciences. There is an emerging consensus that successful development depends on the state playing an active role, and governments need to be empowered to provide a framework of law and order, the enforcement of contracts and other basic institutions underpinning the market, while at the same time the state executive has to be constrained so as not to interfere with the security of property rights and avoid "elite capture".[13] Beyond being a "nightwatchman" of property rights and markets – as postulated by the orthodox reform package – the state also needs to be a guide, coordinator, stimulator and catalytic agent for economic activities in situations where – for various historical and structural reasons – the development process has become atrophied, and the path forward is darkened by all kinds of missing information and market failures.[14]

Adedeji's Alternative Development Paradigms

When Adedeji took over at UNECA in 1975, the commission was essentially a "technical" body and its mandate limited it to research and advisory functions. Unlike the UN Economic Commission for Latin America and the Caribbean (UNECLAC) and the UN Conference on Trade and Development (UNCTAD), which had carved out niches for themselves in development, UNECA had never managed to create an original approach to development to suit the African context. Rather, the commission championed the development orthodoxies of the era.

Adedeji made several landmark contributions to economic development. He used his pivotal position as executive secretary of the ECA to build a distinctive African voice on developmental issues of great significance to the continent by strengthening the research capability, policy advocacy and human capacity of the institution; and by serving as a trusted adviser to African leaders on economic issues.

The search for an indigenous development strategy has been identified as one of the most enduring legacies of the UN Economic Commission for Africa[15] under Adedeji's stewardship.[16] He became the executive secretary of UNECA at a very challenging time for the organisation and the continent.

With the founding of the Organisation of African Unity (OAU) in 1963, UNECA had lost its status as the sole continent-wide international organisation. Intense rivalry between the two Addis Ababa-based UNECA and the OAU emerged almost from the founding of the continental body, and this was not helped by the tense relationship between Robert Gardiner, the Ghanaian technocrat who was Adedeji's predecessor at UNECA, and Diallo Telli, the Guinean diplomat and politician who served as the first secretary-general of the OAU from July 1964 until June 1972.

Only 43 of the 54 African countries at the time were independent,[17] and the world was starkly divided between North and South as a result of the Cold War. Africa was only nominally in charge of its own socio-economic development. African economies were in free fall, and in 1975 the regional gross national product (GNP) per capita of sub-Saharan Africa stood at 17.6% of global per capita GNP, as the quadrupling of oil prices during 1973–4 badly affected oil-importing African nations.

A staunch believer that self-sufficiency was Africa's escape from repressive colonial regimes which constrained the continent in archaic structures of production, Adedeji pushed the boundaries of intellectual theory on economic self-sufficiency and decolonisation, using some of the finest ECA brains and policy strategists from across the continent.

Five landmark strategies, which together outlined the continent's preferred development agenda, emerged in the 1980s and early 1990s. Unfortunately, all these economic proposals for Africa's development remained mere statements of intent, as the dominant forces in the global economy – particularly the Bretton Woods institutions of the World Bank and the International Monetary Fund (IMF) – were either opposed to them or gave them a cold reception. Powerful external actors – largely in the West – sought to deploy their political and economic leverage on African countries to sway them away from blueprints such as Adedeji's.

Leaders from developing countries in all parts of the world were at this time agitating for a New International Economic Order (NIEO). In 1976 the ECA's secretariat in Addis Ababa, Ethiopia, produced the "Revised Framework of Principles for the Implementation of the New International Economic Order in Africa". This national and regional development strategy framework was built on three pillars:[18] the promotion of an increasing measure of self-reliance; an acceleration of growth and diversification, linked to geography and local capacity; and a progressive reduction of unemployment and mass poverty, including a fairer distribution of the benefits of economic development and income. This strategy implied driving growth and self-reliance domestically, looking inwards rather than outwards, and promoting regional development by African, and not foreign, interests.

Ideas from this document constituted the basis for the "Strategy for the Development of Africa in the Third United Nations Decade",[19] formulated and adopted by the African ministers of finance and development planning at their meeting in Rabat, Morocco, in March 2009, and subsequently approved and renamed as the "Monrovia Strategy for the Development of Africa" by the Assembly of AU Heads of State and Government at its meeting in the Liberian capital of Monrovia in July 1979.

At the beginning of the 1980s African leaders came together to consider the OAU's approach to the issue of social and economic development. From these deliberations emerged "The Lagos Plan of Action for the Economic Development of Africa, 1980–2000", prepared for the ECA Conference of Ministers and later endorsed by OAU leaders in Lagos in July 1980. The Lagos Plan of Action (LPA), written in the tradition of the first generation of development economists of the 1940s and 1950s, comprised five action areas: (1) the environment, (2) the Least Developed Countries (LDCs), (3) energy, (4) women, and (5) planning, statistics and population. The LPA enunciated the goals of collective self-reliance. It sought to adopt a new development strategy of an inward–looking, rather than the colonially inherited, externally oriented, pattern. The LPA emphasised, among other things, the development of domestic markets in Africa rather than reliance on external markets; the control of natural resources by African countries; the role and importance of domestic factor inputs in development; the imperative of self-sufficiency in food production; the development of human capital; and the provision of social infrastructure for Africa's citizens. Clearly, by concentrating on sectoral programmes, the LPA – like the previous import–substitution industrialisation strategy – envisaged the structural transformation of African economies. The plan repudiated the whole logic of the dominant neoliberal development thinking of the time. Not surprisingly, the LPA did not elicit the necessary support from the international financial institutions (IFIs) and Western powers. In spite of its clear vision for sustainable, equitable and poverty-reducing growth accompanied by structural transformation, the LPA achieved very little, as the World Bank used its leverage on many African governments to persuade them to jettison the home-grown plan.

Perhaps Adedeji's most significant contribution was the presentation of a development strategy for Africa as an alternative to the orthodox World Bank-

and IMF-sponsored structural adjustment programmes (SAP), which he strongly and consistently criticised. Within a year after the LPA was adopted, the World Bank launched a report entitled *Accelerated Development in Sub-Saharan Africa: An Agenda for Action* in 1981.[20] Otherwise known as the Berg Report – having been named after its principal American author, Elliot Berg – the report was a scathing criticism of the LPA,[21] praising the role of the market and external trade in economic development, with a spirited attack on the African state. The path to economic development in Africa, the report concluded, was for the continent to liberalise its economy, reduce the role of the state and privatise public enterprises. It is now firmly established in the literature that the Berg Report provided the theoretical justification and formed the basis for the imposition of SAPs on Africa from the mid-1980s.

By the mid-1990s, over thirty African countries had implemented structural adjustment programmes. These did not serve their declared objectives, and left in their wake a serious deterioration in human welfare. An authoritative evaluation of the SAPs using several case studies came to the grim conclusion that there was an increasing convergence of views that SAPs had not worked and that, as designed, they were grossly defective in addressing Africa's endemic poverty and pervasive underdevelopment.[22] Even the World Bank, in its evaluation, has admitted that there were several challenges in the implementation of SAPs.[23]

Throughout the adjustment years, the Bretton Woods institutions seized much of the initiative, foreclosing the debate by insisting that there was no alternative to SAPs. African scholars and policy-makers were largely relegated to reactive protest. With the shift of emphasis from human development to macroeconomic stability – as recommended by numerous IMF and World Bank reports – African ministries in charge of local government, rural development, education, health, employment and infrastructural development were downgraded. In several African countries, finance and economic planning ministries were stripped of their economic planning functions in order to focus on financial issues – mainly inflation and exchange rate management.

While the LPA could not be achieved, Africa continued to tinker with alternative development strategies separate from the neoliberal doctrine of structural adjustment, which had brought such immeasurable pain. These strategies, among others, included Africa's Priority Programme for Economic Recovery (APPER) (1986–90), which was presented to the UN General Assembly as a blueprint for Africa's development, and subsequently modified and adopted by the UN General Assembly as the UN Programme of Action for Africa's Economic Recovery and Development (UN–PAAERD) (1986–90), though it has remained unimplemented.

In response to the challenge of the UN General Assembly that Africans should not content themselves with criticising SAPs, but should instead come up with an alternative to the programmes, the ECA unveiled the "Alternative Framework to Structural Adjustment Programme for Socio-Economic Recovery and Transformation" (AAF-SAP) in 1989, which was prepared under Adedeji's leadership, and approved by the UNECA Council of Ministers and the OAU in 1989.

The thrust of the AAF-SAP was that adjustment should be an integral process of socio-economic transformation, based on the principles of self-reliance and self-sustainability, which had been advocated by the LPA. This was a direct critique of the debilitating IMF policies that had operated in Africa since the early 1980s, and had greatly disadvantaged Africa through a system of export-led integration into the world economy. AAF-SAP draws its substantive thrust from the Lagos Plan of Action and the Final Act of Lagos of 1980. The direct relationship emanates from the plan's emphasis on the alleviation of mass poverty through broadening the production base, self-reliance, and self-sustained development within a context of regional integration, and on correcting the continent's standing in the global order. The major thrust of AAF-SAP, therefore, was that, though desirable and even inevitable, structural adjustment must be accompanied by policies and programmes that could ensure structural transformation which would help overcome the deficiencies and peculiarities of African economies.

The last of these documents was the "African Charter for Popular Participation in Development and Transformation", which was adopted by the participants of the International Conference on Popular Participation in the Recovery and Development Process in Africa, held in February 1990 in the Tanzanian city of Arusha. The conference was organised out of concern for the serious deterioration in the human and economic conditions in Africa in the decade of the 1980s, in recognition of the lack of progress in achieving popular participation, and in belief that popular participation ought to play a role in the process of recovery and development. The unanimous adoption of the African Charter stemmed from a frustration with the failure of traditional development paradigms to appreciate the role of "popular participation". Consequently, the Charter called for the encouragement of increased participation by governments, community groups, individuals and the international sector in the design and evaluation of development projects.

359

Regional Integration

Adebayo Adedeji has been one of Africa's foremost advocates of regional integration to overcome the challenges of small markets and land-locked countries as well as to create economies of scale in order to accelerate the continent's economic development. His vision for African integration was initially outlined in a 1970 article titled "Prospects for Regional Economic Integration in West Africa", published in the *Journal of Modern African Studies*. Adedeji championed regional integration as a means to promote peace and development in Africa. Indeed, he has been likened by Nigerian scholar Adekeye Adebajo to the French political visionary Jean Monnet,[24] who was instrumental in the establishment in 1951 of the European Coal and Steel Community (ECSC), precursor to the present European Union (EU).

In the early 1970s, as Nigeria's federal commissioner for economic reconstruction and development, Adedeji took a leading part in the negotiations that brought about the establishment of the Economic Community of West African States. Then, as executive secretary of the ECA from 1975, he actively promoted the creation of other regional groupings such as the Preferential Trade Agreement (PTA) in 1981, which subsequently became the Common Market for Eastern and Southern Africa (COMESA). Adedeji was also instrumental in the establishment of the Economic Community of Central African States (ECCAS), in 1983.

While regional integration has an enduring appeal for Africa as an appropriate strategy for overcoming the constraints of high fragmentation, small domestic markets, and growing transnational threats, these arrangements have been ineffective, and have so far failed to propel the continent's economic transformation. The multiplicity of constraints, which include inadequate political will and commitment to the development process; poor design and sequencing of processes, coupled with slow implementation; inadequate funding; the exclusion of key stakeholders and overlapping membership, have all led to development failures. Of the AU's 54 members in 2017, only five belonged to just one sub-regional body, while three belonged to four. Deeper integration could improve Africa's regional cooperation efforts by tackling structural economic shortcomings such as lack of infrastructure, institutional frameworks, skills, and economic diversification.[25]

Institution-Building

Under Adedeji's watch, institution-building was given a boost in order to promote self-reliant socio-economic development and to build indigenous capacity. This enabled otherwise weak and minuscule African economies to cooperate and jointly provide for themselves technical services which individually they would otherwise have been unable to do.

In its first decade of existence, UNECA established two institutions: the African Institute for Economic Development and Planning (IDEP) in 1962 to fill the critical capacity gap in the area of training and research in economic planning, management and implementation; and the African Development Bank (AfDB) in 1963 as Africa's premier financing institution. Building on this foundation, Adedeji championed the establishment of a UNECA-sponsored institution specialising in development and integration in various areas such as development planning, cartography, solar energy, social development, demography, aerospace surveys, engineering design, manufacturing, standardisation, and finance. Some of these institutions include the Dakar-based Association of African Central Banks (AACB) for coordination of monetary and financial policies; the Addis Ababa-based Association of African Tax Administration (AATA) for coordination of tax policies and legislation; and the Dakar-based African Regional Centre for Technology (ARCT) for the development and use of technology within African states. In all, 25 such institutions were established during Adedeji's tenure.

Concluding Reflections

In recognition of his meritorious service to Africa, Adebayo Adedeji has received numerous awards and commendations. He received the International Gold Mercury Award in 1982, the Arthur Houghton Star Crystal Award of the African-American Institute in 1991 and the Gordon Draper Award instituted by the Commonwealth Association for Public Administration and Management in 2008. In further recognition of his service to Africa, Adedeji was made an honorary citizen of Namibia in March 1997, bringing to eight the national honours that he had received from various African countries. In addition, Adedeji was awarded eight honorary degrees from various academic institutions,[26] the last of which was from the University of Johannesburg in 2008.

He is listed in a 2006 book on *Fifty Key Thinkers on Development*,[27] a guide to the world's most influential development thinkers. He was also identified as one of the 71 personalities who had influenced policy formulation and development paradigms in the United Nations system.

The diverse contributions of Adedeji as a scholar, practitioner and international civil servant to Africa's development perspectives and processes are the subject of a 2014 book[28] with contributions from mostly African scholars, policy-makers, former and current senior UN officials, as well as leaders of civil society and think tanks. Joaquim Chissano, the former president of Mozambique, in the foreword to the book, referred to Adedeji as "the intellectual leader of Africa's quest for home-grown approaches to development and good governance", adding that "Adedeji has been a brilliant, confident and tenacious proponent of African development".[29]

The UN Economic Commission for Africa inaugurated the annual Adebayo Adedeji lecture series during the seventh joint annual meeting of the AU Conference of Ministers of Economy and Finance and the ECA Conference of African Ministers of Finance, Planning and Economic Development in Abuja, Nigeria, in 2013. The lecture series honours and recognises Adedeji's intellectual contributions to development in Africa.

Adedeji died at the age of 87 in April 2018 after a protracted illness. He was buried in his hometown of Ijebu-Ode, Nigeria, on 6 July 2018. A memorial symposium in his honour was held in Lagos the next day by the Economic Commission for Africa. Adedeji will be remembered as an extraordinary public servant, academic giant and visionary of regional integration in Africa. He will also be remembered for his substantive contributions to the discourse on people-centred development in Africa.

PART 6

THE PHILOSOPHERS

24

FRANTZ FANON: PAN-AFRICAN PHILOSOPHER OF DEMOCRACY AND DEVELOPMENT

L. Adele Jinadu

So comrades, let us not pay tribute to Europe by creating states, institutions, and societies which draw their inspirations from her ... If we wish to live up to our people's expectations, we must seek the response elsewhere than in Europe.[1]

– FRANTZ FANON

To put Africa in motion, to cooperate in its organisation, in its regrouping behind revolutionary principles. To participate in the ordered movement of a continent – this was really the work I had chosen.[2]

– FRANTZ FANON

FRANTZ FANON WAS BORN into an upper-middle-class family on 20 July 1925 in Fort-de-France, capital of Martinique, which became a French overseas department from 1946. He rose to become a major Pan-African philosopher, revolutionary and diplomat whose short intellectual and political career (he died at the age of 36 on 6 December 1961) is remarkable for the insights it throws on the complex historical-material and psycho-cultural connections between racism, colonialism, post-colonialism and globalisation. Frantz attended the private Lycée Victor Schoelcher from 1939 to 1943. In 1944, he enlisted in the Free French Forces, the resistance organisation formed by General Charles de Gaulle in 1943 to liberate France from German occupation. Fanon saw active duty in North Africa (in Casablanca, Morocco, and Oran, Algeria), and in France and Germany, and was decorated with the Croix de Guerre for gallantry in military operations in Besançon in eastern France. He returned to Fort-de-France in 1945, and received his baccalaureate in the same year. Winning a university scholarship, he left Fort-de-France in 1947 to study dentistry in Paris, but ended up with a degree in psychiatry from the University of Lyon in November 1951. Thereafter, he married Marie-Josèphe (Josie) Dublé, with whom he had a son, Olivier.

Fanon worked briefly at the Hospital of Saint-Ylié near Lyon, and returned to Fort-de-France in 1952 to set up a private practice. Later in 1952 he left Fort-de-France to take up an appointment at the Saint-Alban Hospital in Lyon. In July 1953, he passed the *Medicat*, a rigorous professional qualifying examination for French psychiatrists. During his stay in France, Fanon moved in liberal and leftist-leaning, anti-colonial intellectual circles, also contributing articles to *Esprit*, the journal of the French Catholic left. He later developed close relationships with leading French intellectuals and activists such as Jean-Paul Sartre, Simone de Beauvoir, Jean-Marie Domenach, and Francis Jeanson. He also cultivated the burgeoning black and African intellectual networks in France, taking part in discussions that led to the establishment of the journal *Présence Africaine* in 1947 as "an African presence within French culture";[3] and he was active in the Federation des etudiants d'Afrique noire. After trying unsuccessfully to secure employment in Senegal, he took up appointment as *chef de service* at a psychiatric hospital in Pontorson, on the French Atlantic coast, which he left in December 1953 to take up appointment as head of the Psychiatry Department at the Blida-Joinville hospital in Algeria.

Fanon arrived in Algeria at a time when the Algerian War of Independence, led by the Front for National Liberation (FLN), was becoming intensely radicalised, internationalised, and popularised as part of the worldwide resistance against racism, imperialism, and colonial domination. His stay and experience in Algeria provided a major point of convergence in his evolution and development as a revolutionary thinker and political activist, who weaved into a bold, variegated, and compelling tapestry his experiences with racism and imperialism in the French Antilles (including Martinique), Europe and North Africa. As British historian David Caute noted, Fanon was, before taking up the appointment at Blida-Joinville, committed to assimilation and was still "refining and polishing the bright jewel of universal reasoning which alone could release both oppressors and oppressed from their mutual mystification".[4]

The critical milestone in this respect, underscoring his transition from political to revolutionary consciousness and action, was Fanon's resignation as *chef de service* of the Blida-Joinville Hospital in December 1956 after three years. His resignation letter was not so much a shift from the emphasis in his 1952 book *Black Skin, White Masks* on individual action, as it was an extension of the logic of that book's analysis to embrace and expound revolutionary action for group emancipation and the structural-material reconstruction of social relations in the state, expressed more fully in his 1961 book, *The Wretched of the Earth*. This also represented a reflection and expression of Fanon's disappointment with the tepid response of the French intellectual and political left to the iniquities and racism of French colonialism in Algeria. As he noted in the resignation letter,

> If psychiatry is the medical technique that aims to enable man no longer to be stranger to his environment, I owe it to myself to affirm that the Arab, permanently an alien in his own country, lives in a state of absolute depersonalization ... The social structure existing in Algeria was hostile to any attempt to put the individual back where he belonged ... There comes a time when silence becomes dishonesty ... For many months my conscience has been the seat of unpardonable debates ... The decision I have reached is that I cannot bear a responsibility at no matter what cost, on the false pretext that there is nothing else to be done.[5]

From December 1956 to December 1961, when he died, Fanon immersed himself passionately in the Algerian War of Independence. He became one of the major spokespersons and emissaries of the FLN and its government-in-exile, the Provisional Government of the Algerian Republic (GPRA), which was formed in September 1958. He worked for the FLN, under the pseudonym Dr Fares, as director of the FLN Press Service in Tunisia, and served between 1957 and 1960 as editor of the FLN newspaper, *El Moudjahid*. Fanon was appointed the ambassador of the GPRA to Ghana in 1960, in acknowledgement of his efforts to build bridges between the FLN – and indeed other nationalist movements in North Africa – and other nationalist movements in the rest of Africa. A theoretician of the FLN, he was the arrowhead of the diplomatic offensive to drum up support for, and recognition of, the GPRA across Africa.

Fanon attended the Inter-African Congress in Bamako, Mali (1957), and Cotonou in Dahomey (now Benin) in 1958; the Conference of All Independent African States and the All African People's Conference, both convened in

Accra in 1958; the Conference of Independent African States, in Addis Ababa, Ethiopia, in 1959; the Afro-Asiatic Solidarity Conference, in Conakry, Guinea, in 1960; and the Pan-African Congress in Leopoldville (now Kinshasa) in 1960.

The significance of Fanon's attendance at these meetings as representative of the GPRA and his tenure as ambassador of the GPRA to Ghana was threefold. First, these interactions placed the Martinican philosopher at the centre of the unfolding network of national liberation movements and efforts at achieving African continental unity and integration, which sought a convergence between Pan-Africanism and Arab nationalism in North Africa. Fanon's role enabled him to establish contacts with African heads of state and leaders of nationalist movements such as Roberto Holden (Angola), Félix-Roland Moumié (Cameroon), Patrice Lumumba (Congo), Sékou Touré (Guinea), Tom Mboya (Kenya), Modibo Keita (Mali), Félix Houphouet-Boigny (Côte d'Ivoire) and Léopold Sédar Senghor (Senegal).

Second, an important project that Fanon conceived and pursued as GPRA representative to these meetings was the establishment of an African Legion consisting of "troops based south of the Sahara [that] could be used to open up a second front within Algeria itself", to support the FLN's military effort.[6] The third important aspect of Fanon's diplomatic role was that, although his field experiences were limited to the Maghreb (Algeria, Libya, Morocco and Tunisia) and West Africa (Ghana, Guinea and Mali), he offered a reinterpretation of the roots of African nationalism beyond the conventional focus on Western-educated nationalist leaders, to focus on local revolts and uprisings – "incipient nationalisms".[7] At the same time his experiences were critical to his characterisation and analysis of emergent contradictions within the African state, within the nationalist movements, and within the African political class and African political parties, and in his prescriptions for moving beyond these contradictions, as I shall argue in this chapter.

Set against this biographical sketch, I advance three propositions in arguing for the contemporary, even lasting, relevance of Frantz Fanon as a political theorist of democracy and a political sociologist of development, who brought a modified Marxist political-economy approach to the analysis of politics and development in Africa. These propositions provide a framework of political analysis that remains Fanon's enduring legacy for exploring the challenges of democracy and development in Africa. They illustrate how the unfolding constitutional and political architecture of governance in the African state since the 1980s – envisioned and outlined in various African and extra-

African international standards and codes, and especially in the 2003 African Peer Review Mechanism (APRM) – bears an affinity in its design outline with Fanon's emphasis on political decentralisation and the democratic management of diversity.

The three propositions – which will be elaborated in more detail later – are these. Firstly, Fanon viewed and utilised political philosophy or theory as an ethical and culturally grounded policy-oriented activity. Secondly, Fanon's analysis of the relationship between racism and imperialism, and the asymmetrical structure of global power relations in the division between rich ("bourgeois") nations and poor ("proletarian") countries, provides rich insights into the structure of contemporary global politics.[8] Thirdly, Fanon's revisionist Marxist theoretical framework foreshadowed the application of "Marxisant" class analysis and underdevelopment theory to African politics.

The Broader Intellectual Context of Fanon's Political Theory

My introductory remarks provide the broader intellectual context within which I shall proceed to argue and illustrate these three propositions. What anchors Fanon's political theory and political activities is a humanistic concern with the use of political power in national and international society to create a "new man", and to build institutions driven by bonds of mutuality, reciprocity and solidarity. This is done to promote human security, broadly defined, as the collective development and welfare of African citizens. Thus, Fanon's political theory and sociology of development demand the imperative of building and strengthening state and cultural institutions that are informed by "the basic values that constitute a human world",[9] notably accountability, equality, freedom, social justice, recognition, reciprocity, and solidarity.

Flowing from this imperative, the core intellectual question that frames Fanon's humanism is woven around intersecting concerns about citizenship, political obligation and political legitimacy. These concerns involve the nature of access to, and the ownership of, the state. This question has historically provided the defining core or substantive subject-matter of political theory and sociological thought: "Who owns the state? Whose interest does the state serve?" The long history, since time immemorial, of the struggle for democracy and development worldwide, sometimes assuming the form of revolutionary warfare, within, across and between countries, reflects an attempt to resolve these core questions.

For Fanon, confronting the "perpetual crises" of democracy requires focusing on, and analysing, the character of the state, especially its material base and the social relations of power that it spawns. For the Martinican philosopher, the material base matters and makes all the difference not only to the enjoyment of citizenship rights, but also to the possibilities of advancing democracy and development. This perspective underscores the symbiosis of theory and praxis in Fanon's political, intellectual and professional life. It defines his concern with the morality of politics and with solidarity as a categorical imperative, which he expresses thus: "I cannot dissociate myself from the future that is proposed for my brother. Every one of my acts commits me as a man. Every one of my silences, every one of my cowardices, reveals me as a man."[10] This concern informed Fanon's formulation of the existential, action-oriented and normative-cultural concept of commitment and the social responsibility of the intellectual vocation in politics, reflected in his contention that "to educate man to be *actional*, preserving in all his relations his respect for the basic values that constitute a human world, is the prime task of him who, having taken thought, prepares to act".[11]

In the same vein, Fanon's much criticised moral justification of revolutionary praxis is anchored on his assumptions about not only its possibilities, but also its limitations for creating a "new man" and redefining citizenship in an inclusive way. This bears affinity with Italian scholar-diplomat Niccolò Machiavelli's thesis about the economy of violence, the view that "it is the man who uses violence to spoil things, not the man who uses it to mend them, that is blameworthy".[12] This also has parallels with some variations of liberation theology in Latin America, North America and South Africa.[13]

For this reason, Fanon's views on revolutionary praxis must be set against his triadic concept of violence as physical, psychological and structural, as well as against the sociology of wars of national liberation, the politics of decolonisation and his reinterpretation of the Hegelian master–slave paradigm applied to the pathologies of race and power relations in a globalised colonial and post-colonial world.

The Essential Fanon: Fragments of a Sociology of African Development

It is Fanon's concern with the citizenship question in national and global politics – framed around issues of freedom, inclusion, participation, justice and human security as imperatives of democracy and development – that explains the continuing interest in his political and social thought. A collection of his unpublished papers, including his correspondence, psychiatric notes and articles on the Algerian War of Independence (1954–62) and national liberation wars in the Third World more broadly, appeared in English in 2018, translated from the original French publication.[14]

Yet, there is still a tendency to talk today, as was the case when Fanon's *The Wretched of the Earth* first appeared in English in 1968, about the "utopian dimensions" of his political philosophy, and to argue that the "tragedy of his impossible life" is that "his vision of freedom and solidarity lost out to the narrower affiliations of nation, tribe and sect".[15] Or that "the uniformity of Fanonism's portrayal of the NLMs [national liberation movements] in power minimises important realities: the existence within them of continuing factionalism, of discussion between nationalist and socialist tendencies, between populists and political progressives, and contested as well as collaborative relationships with foreign and domestic capital".[16]

But this misses the point of Fanon's sociological analysis, which is anchored on certain normative conceptions about man, state and society that entail certain conditions – not any conditions – for their attainment. This is why Fanon's *Studies in a Dying Colonialism* (1965), *Toward the African Revolution* (1964) and *The Wretched of the Earth*[17] are essays, combining pessimism and optimism, in which Fanon the political sociologist analyses contradictions in state and society that are still relevant today, as they were when the essays were first published. These contradictions constitute impediments to democracy and development in Africa. For Fanon, this is why these obstacles must be removed, if what he, the political theorist and moralist, prescribes as the nature of man and the ideal society are to be created and realised, as they ultimately must be, in view of the transformative power of ideas.

Fanon offered, in this respect, a prolegomenon of the sociology of African development. These fragments provide perspectives on how to analyse and understand trends and tendencies in not only the politics of the immediate post-independence years of the 1960s, but also recent democratic transitions in Africa. They also indicate pathways to pursue today, as they did in the 1960s, to diminish the prospects of another "revolution of rising expectations" in Africa, in view of the dismal human security situation in many contemporary African countries. This is evidenced by the poor performance of African countries in the United Nations Development Programme (UNDP) human development index and related measures, and their failure to meet a number of targets set in the UN Millennium Development Goals (MDGs) of 2000–15.

Tentative and sketchy as Fanon's fragments are, there is a sense in which they have been refined, developed and elaborated in the writings and political activities of a number of radical and progressive African intellectuals such as Claude Ake (Nigeria), Samir Amin (Egypt), Peter Ayang' Nyong'o (Kenya), Abdoulaye Bathily (Senegal), Emmanuel Hansen (Ghana), Archie Mafeje (South Africa), Mahmood Mamdani (Uganda), Dani Nabudere (Uganda), Okwudiba Nnoli (Nigeria), Georges Nzongola-Ntalaja (The Democratic Republic of the Congo [DRC]), Issa Shivji (Tanzania) and Yash Tandon (Uganda). The intellectual and political activities of these scholars were radical and progressive because they brought an Afrocentric perspective – as opposed to expatriate mainstream neoliberal ones – to bear on the analysis and, more critically, on the reinterpretation of the emergent problems of democracy and development in Africa and elsewhere in the Third World, and on the prescriptions for addressing these challenges.[18] Like Fanon, these radical African scholars held firmly to the view that the feasibility of democracy and development required as an antecedent condition the redesign of the post-colonial African state and the reform of the international system, both of which they characterised as constituting instruments of imperialist domination.

It is in this sense that there is a strong affinity between the scholarship, political activism, support of and involvement in, national liberation and pro-democracy movements of these radical scholars and Fanon's. They created and nurtured intellectual networks between the 1970s and 1990s in multidisciplinary intellectual sites such as those provided by the University of Dar es Salaam, the Addis Ababa-based United Nations (UN) Economic Commission for Africa (ECA), the Dakar-based Council for the Development of Social Science Research in Africa (CODESRIA), and by professional associations such as the Harare-, and later Tshwane-based, African Association of Political Science (AAPS). These paralleled earlier intellectual networks of Afrocentric historians at the universities of Ibadan, Ghana, Dakar, Nairobi, Dar es Salaam and Makerere

University, which sought from the 1960s to decolonise teaching and research in, and about, Africa.[19]

Challenging the notion of African societies as follower societies, and raising the issue of African ownership of the political architecture of the African state and the development process – as Fanon did – these Afro-centric intellectuals stressed the importance of African culture, metaphysics, epistemology, and history as critical elements in moving beyond liberal-capitalist, Marxist, social democratic, and related Eurocentric and other expatriate perspectives on democracy and development, especially in their application to Africa.[20]

For these intellectuals, as for Fanon, the reconstitution of the post-colonial state required the redesigning of the African state into a participatory, inclusive, income-redistributive and popular democratic one, anchored on the principles of political devolution, and defined and underscored by mutuality and reciprocity between African governments and citizens. Indeed, these are anchoring principles of the African Charter for Popular Participation in Development and Transformation, adopted at the 1990 Arusha Conference on Popular Participation in the Recovery and Development Process in Africa, organised by the UN Economic Commission for Africa, under the leadership of Nigerian scholar-administrator Adebayo Adedeji (see Afeikhena in this volume), as well as of the emerging African post-Cold War governance architecture of accountability at the national, regional and continental levels.

Beyond its seeming cultural relativism or "parochialism", Fanon's Afrocentric perspective envisions and demands the merging of "particularisms" to define and become the building blocks of the universal. The Martinican scholar-activist gave expression to this dialectical relationship when he asserted that he had "one duty alone: that of not renouncing my freedom through my choices. I have no wish to be the victim of the *Fraud* of a black world." [21] In a similar vein, the Afrocentric Nigerian intellectual Claude Ake, setting out the *raison d'être* of the *African Journal of Political Economy* in 1986, contended that

unless we strive for endogenous development of science and knowledge we cannot fully emancipate ourselves. Why this development must be endogenous should be clear for it is not a question of parochialism or nationalism. The point is that even though the principles of science are universal, its growth points and the particular problems which it solves are contingent on the historical circumstances of the society in which the Science is produced.[22]

The sustainability of an Afrocentric intellectual vocation in the service of African democracy and development, expounded vigorously by Fanon and these intellectuals, remains an enduring challenge. This serves to underscore the lasting relevance of Fanon at a time when serious and troubling questions have been raised about the future of higher education in Africa, including the substantive and pedagogic content of teaching and research in African universities.[23]

The Three Propositions about the Essential Fanon

Framing the Three Propositions

As noted earlier, the three propositions that now follow provide a framework of political analysis that remains Fanon's enduring legacy for exploring the challenges of democracy and development in Africa. The first proposition is that Fanon viewed and used political and social theory as an ethical and culturally grounded policy-oriented activity, which must inform the design of African economic, political, and social institutions and their governance processes. For him, political theory should draw on and reflect the lived experiences, shared cultural values and common interests of black and African peoples. In this respect, Fanon reflected a common theme in radical and progressive Pan-African thought about the social responsibility of black and African intellectuals as a social force for the emancipation of the black race, such as expressed in W.E.B. Du Bois's notion of the "Talented Tenth" (see Morris in this volume); Kwame Nkrumah's thesis about the "*social contention* in philosophical systems" (see Biney in this volume); Amílcar Cabral's notion of "return to the source" (see Rabaka in this volume);[24] the more recent debate on the African Renaissance led by South Africa's Thabo Mbeki (see Adebajo chapter on Mbeki in this volume); and continuing efforts to establish an African Union government; and the African Union's *Agenda 2063*.

But there is now a concern that the promise of an Afrocentric perspective on African governance, as expounded by Fanon, has waned, if it is not virtually dead. As the Ugandan political economist Dani Nabudere rightly observed,

> although the President [of the African Association of Political Science] referred to [our] commitment [to] Afro-centered scholarship, our lack of

resolve on this matter continues to be one of our main areas of weakness. Most of our analytical tools continue to be informed by a dominant Eurocentric epistemological paradigm. We still lack a social science that is structured to answer to the methodological needs and tools that can help generate new knowledge. Such new knowledge must be designed to describe, analyse and empower the African people and Africans of African descent to change the negative social forces into positive social forces as they impact on the life chances of African peoples all over the world.[25]

Fanon's second proposition is that the analysis of the relationship between racism and imperialism, and the asymmetrical structure of global power relations in the division between rich and poor nations, should provide insights into the structure of contemporary global politics and the residual racist and "imperial reflexes" that continue to manifest in relations between the great powers and multilateral organisations such as the World Bank and the International Monetary Fund (IMF), and Africa.[26] As he put it,

> the question which is looming on the horizon is the need for a redistribution of wealth. Humanity must reply to this question or be shaken to pieces by it ... We are not blinded by the moral reparation of national independence, nor are we fed by it. The wealth of the imperial countries is our wealth too. For in a very concrete way Europe has stuffed herself inordinately with the gold and raw materials of the colonial countries.[27]

Focused on rethinking and reinventing governance in Africa to address the challenges of globalisation more effectively, Fanon's political sociology brings out clearly the need for paradigm shifts to turn the searchlight on public interest politics and policy issues anchored on the redistribution of wealth, equitable development, justice, human security, and solidarity in domestic, regional, continental, and global politics.

These paradigm shifts informed the UN Economic Commission for Africa's Africa's Priority Programme for Economic Recovery, 1986–1990 (APPER); the African Charter for Popular Participation in Development and Transformation, 1990; the Organisation of African Unity's Declaration on the Political and Socio-Economic Situation in Africa and the Fundamental Changes Taking Place in the World, 1990; the Cairo Agenda for Action, 1995; the OAU's Sirte Declaration,

1999; and the New Partnership for Africa's Development (NEPAD), 2001 (see also Afeikhena in this volume).[28]

The third proposition is that Fanon's revisionist Marxist theoretical framework foreshadowed the application of "Marxisant" class analysis and underdevelopment theory to African politics. In this respect, Fanon belongs to a pantheon of revolutionary thinkers, such as Amílcar Cabral (see Rabaka in this volume), Regis Debray, Che Guevara and Mao Tse-tung, in modifying the Leninist reinterpretation of Marxism, and applying it to the analysis of the politics of non-industrial, non-Western societies.[29]

Elaborating the Three Propositions

Driven by the humanistic moral impulses of a committed intellectual who combines theory with revolutionary action, Fanon pioneered a reinterpretation of the problem of democracy and development in Africa away from the prevalent mainstream structural-functionalist and pluralist orthodoxies in their application to African politics in the 1960s.[30] In a broad, iconoclastic sweep, the Martinican philosopher situated Africa's political economy and the feasibility of democracy and development on the continent within the broader context of the limitations and constraints posed by the continent's "colonial inheritance", and by the hegemonising structural and social-psychological processes of globalisation.

This enabled Fanon to turn the attention of his analysis to the contradictions of African politics in order to demonstrate the historical-materialist structure and dialectics of class political behaviour within and between various social classes: the "petit bourgeoisie", the "proletariat", the "lumpen proletariat" and the "peasantry". His particular focus was on the emergent African political-bureaucratic-business class – "the national petit bourgeoisie" or "comprador bourgeoisie" – who, as proxies for international finance capital, used political power to accumulate economic power. Fanon portrayed the African petit bourgeois class as "that company of profiteers impatient for their returns",[31] castigating them as lacking "the dynamic, pioneer aspect, the characteristic of the inventor and of the discoverer of new worlds which are found in all national bourgeoisies".[32]

But Fanon modified his class analysis by also focusing on the salience of ethnicity, religion, race and the political party, among other elements of the cultural institutions of the African state, as intervening and explanatory variables, spewing out contradictions such as political centralisation, authoritarian rule, oligarchic tendencies in the African party, "tribal dictatorships" and narrow or micro-nationalism, which, in some cases, assumed the form of xenophobia.[33] This explains the apparent qualifications that Fanon made to the distinction he drew between "true decolonisation" and "false decolonisation",[34] and to his position on the two-stage strategy for a socialist revolution.[35] He drew back from making absolute claims and dogmatic statements, despite the broad generalisations he often produced for effect. He realised that politics was too complex and too much of an unfinished project to admit to such claims. This is why he rejected dogma, asserting that "My final prayer. O my body, make of me always a man who questions."[36]

Fanon's aversion to dogma explains why he raised serious concerns about authoritarian and fractious trends and tendencies in independent Algeria, such as those between the military and political wings of the ruling FLN, as well as racism, all of which made him warn of their dire and unwholesome implications and consequences for the democratic management of diversity in the emergent Algerian state.[37]

The APRM and the Essential Fanon

The unfolding constitutional and political architecture of governance in Africa – envisioned and outlined in various African and extra-African international standards and codes, and in the 2003 African Peer Review Mechanism[38] – bears significant similarities with Fanon's approach towards democratic governance and development in Africa. His approach and prescriptions both stress political decentralisation, the democratic management of diversity, human security, and the ownership of the development process by African citizens.[39]

The core principle of ownership, together with the inclusive and participatory formulation of the relationship between citizenship, the state and public policy – which is central to Fanon's approach – also anchors the principles that inform the APRM's four interlocking thematic areas: democracy and political governance; economic management and governance; corporate governance; and socio-economic development.

The APRM conceptualises the relationship between democracy and development as seamless, combining democratic political processes – governance or "soft infrastructures" – with socio-economic arrangements, including "social and physical infrastructures". These processes and arrangements are designed to protect and promote the freedoms and rights of citizens, as well as advance human development and security through broad-based, state-led allocation and distribution of social surpluses. While the thematic focus on economic governance and management, corporate governance, and socio-economic development outlines the policy framework and environment for achieving human security, the thematic focus on democracy and political governance elaborates the judicial, legislative and political environments to facilitate the pursuit of socio-economic policies in order to achieve and sustain human security and development in the 40 APRM member states.[40]

APRM Member States: Distribution by Regions (28 February 2020)

Region	Member states	Number
Central Africa	Cameroon; Chad; Equatorial Guinea; Gabon; Republic of Congo; São Tomé and Príncipe	6
East Africa	Djibouti; Ethiopia; Kenya; Rwanda; Seychelles; Tanzania; Uganda	7
North Africa	Algeria; Egypt; Sudan; Tunisia	4
Southern Africa	Angola; Botswana; Lesotho; Malawi; Mauritius; Mozambique; Namibia; South Africa; Zambia; Zimbabwe	10
West Africa	Benin; Burkina Faso; Côte d'Ivoire; Gambia; Ghana; Liberia; Mali; Mauritania; Niger; Nigeria; Senegal; Sierra Leone; Togo	13
	TOTAL	40

Source: Desk research by the author, 28 February 2020

The value addition that Fanon and the APRM bring to the democracy and development debate in Africa, in this respect, is broadly threefold. Firstly, the two approaches are framed within the challenges of contemporary globalisation as an unfolding historical process for Africa; secondly, they focus on the link between sustainable development and human security to enhance state capacity in Africa; and thirdly, in pointing to "the perpetual crises of democracy" and the need to engage them, Fanon's invocation "O my body, make of me always a man who questions"[41] and the APRM approach both help focus on the joint, seamless responsibility of state and non-state actors to routinise public debates on, and expand the "horizon" of, the possibilities offered by democracy and development in Africa.

Concluding Reflections

The essential Fanon provides theoretical navigational aids and a policy framework for charting the path towards people-centred democracy and development in Africa. These aids and frameworks are directed towards reinventing the core ethical and humanistic vocation of politics as a public trust; and rehabilitating democracy and development in Africa so as to achieve and sustain human security anchored on justice, freedom, equality, inclusion, respect for human dignity, and solidarity.

Achieving this requires structural and institutional reforms at the national, regional, continental and global levels in order to impose a social obligation on the state as the prime allocator of social surpluses to pursue income-redistributive objectives. It also imposes on the committed intellectual the obligation to provide theoretical and policy direction to actualise and sustain democratic politics as a humanistic vocation in national and global society. These reforms further demand the reconfiguring of the African state by creating many layers of decentralised and autonomous public authorities, affording local communities the opportunity for self-government, removed from the centralised and overbearing control of central governments. This process, finally, necessitates looking beyond the political class in Africa to create cultural, political and social institutional networks or subsidiary associations, consisting of professional and non-governmental organisations and community groups, to assert and defend people's power which can mobilise mass political action to resist anti-people policies pursued by autocratic administrative and political authorities.

In the final analysis, the enduring and contemporary relevance of Fanon is this: the historic role of the committed African intellectual is to use the symbiosis of science and policy to advance – in an Afrocentric or Pan-African manner – the development of black and African communities, as a way of reinventing democracy and development in Africa and its diaspora, and, in so doing so, reforming a hostile and Eurocentric world into a truly global one. As Fanon himself put it:

Come, then, comrades; it would be as well to change our ways. We must shake off the heavy darkness in which we were plunged, and leave it behind.[42]

For Europe, for ourselves, and for humanity, comrades, we must turn over a new leaf, we must work out new concepts, and try to set afoot a new man.[43]

25

AMÍLCAR CABRAL: CRITICAL THEORIST OF REVOLUTIONARY DECOLONISATION

Reiland Rabaka

THE CAPE VERDEAN AND BISSAU-GUINEAN revolutionary Amílcar Lopes da Costa Cabral was born on 12 September 1924 in Bafatá, Guinea-Bissau, and assassinated (by disgruntled, fellow Partido Africano da Independência da Guiné e Cabo Verde [PAIGC] leader, Inocêncio Kani) at the age of 48 on 20 January 1973. Cabral, a trained agricultural engineer, connects with, and contributes to, the Africana tradition of critical theory in several poignant, provocative and extremely profound ways. First, it should be mentioned that "although he did not start out or train as a philosopher," Cabral – according to the Nigerian philosopher Olufemi Taiwo – "bequeathed to us a body of writings containing his reflections on such issues as the nature and course of social transformation, human nature, history, violence, oppression and liberation".[1] Second, and as eloquently argued by the Eritrean philosopher Tsenay Serequeberhan, Cabral's ideas led to action: actual historical, cultural, social and political transformation, and ultimately revolutionary decolonisation, revolutionary re-Africanisation and national liberation.

Consequently, in many ways, Cabral represents "the zenith" of twentieth-century Pan-African revolutionary theory and praxis.[2] Third, and finally, Cabral's writings and reflections provide us with a series of unique contributions to radical politics and critical social theory, which – with those of W.E.B. Du Bois, C.L.R. James (see Morris and Cudjoe in this volume), Claudia Jones, George Padmore (see Duggan in this volume), Aimé Césaire, Léopold Senghor (see Irele on Césaire and Senghor in this volume), Louise Thompson Patterson, Frantz Fanon (see Jinadu in this volume), Malcolm X (see Daniels in this volume), Stokely Carmichael, Angela Davis, Walter Rodney (see Montoute in this volume), the Black Panther Party and the Combahee River Collective, among others – seeks simultaneously to critique the incessantly overlapping, interlocking and intersecting nature of racism, sexism, capitalism and colonialism in contemporary society.[3]

Cabralism: The Dialectic of Revolutionary Decolonisation and Revolutionary Re-Africanisation

One of the major dialectical dimensions of Cabral's concept of "return to the source" hinges on his contention that one of the strengths of a revolutionary nationalist movement, such as the PAIGC, is that it preserves pre-colonial traditions and values but, at the same time, these traditions and values are radically transformed through the dialectical process of revolutionary decolonisation and revolutionary re-Africanisation.[4] In other words, pre-colonial traditions and values are altered by the protracted struggle against the superimposition of foreign imperialist cultures and values and by the reconstitution and synthesis of progressive pre-colonial and recently created revolutionary anti-colonial African traditions and values. Therefore, according to Cabral: "The armed struggle for liberation, launched in response to aggression by the colonialist oppressor, turns out to be a painful but effective instrument for developing the cultural level both for the leadership strata of the liberation movement and for the various social categories who take part in the struggle."[5] Anticipating that many might misunderstand him, as they historically have misunderstood and misinterpreted Frantz Fanon's concepts of revolutionary decolonisation and revolutionary self-defensive violence, and continue to do so (see Jinadu in this volume), Cabral further explained his conception of the national liberation struggle as a "painful but effective instrument":

> As we know, the armed liberation struggle demands the mobilisation and organisation of a significant majority of the population, the political and moral unity of the various social categories, the efficient use of modern weapons and other means of warfare, the gradual elimination of the remnants of tribal mentality, and the rejection of social and religious rules and taboos contrary to the development of the struggle (i.e., gerontocracy, nepotism, social inferiority of women, rites and practices

which are incompatible with the rational and national character of the struggle, etc.). The struggle brings about many other profound changes in the life of the populations. The armed liberation struggle implies, therefore, a veritable forced march along the road to cultural progress.[6]

Cabral's concept of "return to the source", therefore, is not only, as shall soon be demonstrated, a "return to the upwards paths of [Africans'] own culture[s]" but also "a veritable forced march along the road to cultural progress".[7] This "return", similar to that of Aimé Césaire (see Irele in this volume), is a critical "return" that "is not and cannot in itself be an *act of struggle* against domination (colonialist and racist) and it no longer necessarily means a return to traditions".[8] Rather, the "return to the source", which is at the core of Cabral's critical theory, is a conscious anti-colonial and revolutionary step, however inchoate and anxiety-filled. Cabral asserted that this approach was the "only possible reply to the demand of concrete need, historically determined, and enforced by the inescapable contradiction between the colonised society and the colonial power, the mass of the people exploited and the foreign exploitive class, a contradiction in the light of which each social stratum or indigenous class must define its position".[9]

In defining their position in relation to or, better yet, against the colonial and imperialist powers, each member of the colonised society – individually and collectively – chooses and must – as a matter of life or death – will themselves into becoming revolutionary praxis-oriented participants, active anti-colonial agents in the dialectical process of revolutionary decolonisation and revolutionary re-Africanisation, that protracted process of rescuing, reclaiming and reconstructing their own sacred humanity, history and heritage.[10] In Cabral's candid words:

When the "return to the source" goes beyond the individual and is expressed through "groups" or "movements", the contradiction is transformed into struggle (secret or overt), and is a prelude to the pre-independence movement or of the struggle for liberation from foreign yoke. So, the "return to the source" is of no historical importance unless it brings not only real involvement in the struggle for independence, but also complete and absolute identification with the hopes of the mass of the people, who contest not only the foreign culture but also the foreign domination as a whole. Otherwise, the "return to the source" is nothing more than an attempt to find short-term benefits – knowingly or unknowingly a kind of political opportunism.[11]

The "return to the source" may be said to translate into Africana critical theory of contemporary society as the much-touted "cultural revolution" that many have often argued precedes and must continue throughout the national liberation struggle.[12] Culture, when approached from a dialectical perspective, can be reactionary or revolutionary, traditional or transformative, decadent or dynamic, and Cabral's "return" must thus be critical if it is to transcend and transgress futile attempts, as the Eritrean philosopher Tsenay Serequeberhan cautioned, to "dig out a purely African past and return to a dead tradition".[13] Cabral's "return", therefore, is only partially aimed at historical recovery, socio-political transformation and revolutionary reorganisation. There is another, often over-looked aspect of Cabral's concept that simultaneously and dialectically stresses revolutionary cultural restoration and revolutionary cultural transformation.[14]

Cabral further argued that it was prudent for Africans to develop critical dialogues and "real" relationships with pre-colonial and traditional African histories and cultures. But he also cautioned Africans to keep in mind the ways in which colonialism and Eurocentrism, and the struggles *against* racial colonialism and *for* revolutionary re-Africanisation, impacted on and affected modern African histories and cultures, consequently creating whole new notions of "Africa" and African cultures and traditions. What is more, and what is not always readily apparent, the dialectical process of revolutionary decolonisation and revolutionary re-Africanisation calls into question the very definition of what it means – ontologically, existentially, and phenomenologically – to *be* "African" – that is to say, "African" in a world dominated by European imperialism. To put it another way, Cabral's dialectic of revolutionary decolonisation and revolutionary re-Africanisation calls into question what it means to be "black" in a white-supremacist colonial capitalist world. The dialectical process of revolutionary decolonisation and revolutionary re-Africanisation at its core, then, redefines "Africanité" or "blackness."[15] It finds sustenance in Fanon's faithful words in his 1961 classic, *The Wretched of the Earth*, where he declared: "Decolonization is the veritable creation of new men", of a "new humanity", and the "'thing' which has been colonized becomes man".[16]

There is a deep, critical, self-reflexive dimension to Cabral's concept of "return to the source", one which – similar to Fanon's theory of revolutionary decolonisation – openly acknowledges that the colonised transform not simply the colonisers, but also themselves through the dialectical process of revolutionary decolonisation and revolutionary re-Africanisation. Their theory and praxis, situated in a specific historical moment, emerge from the lived experiences of their actually endured struggles; this in one way connects them to the past but, in another, to the post-colonial and post-imperial future.[17] The "return to the source", then, should not under any circumstances be a return to tradition in its stasis or freeze-framed form.[18]

The "return", simply put, is not to the past, but to the "source" – or, as I am wont to say, sources. The sources of a people's identity and dignity are, according to Cabral, contained in their history and culture: "A struggle, which while being the organised political expression of a *culture* is also and necessarily a proof not only of *identity* but also of *dignity*."[19] A people's history and culture (and, following Fanon, we may add language) contain and convey their thought traditions, belief systems and value systems.[20] These traditions and systems are – under "normal" circumstances – ever-evolving, always contradicting, countering and overturning, as well as building on and going beyond, the ideologies and theories, and the views and values of the past. This is why the "return" is not, and should not be, to the past or any "dead" traditions, but to those things – spiritual and material – from the African past (for example, ideologies, theories, views and values), which will enable them to construct a present and future that is, or would be, consistently conducive to the highest, healthiest and most humane modes of human existence and experience.[21]

The Weapons of Theory and Culture: Cabral's Critical Theory of Culture

Cabral's concept of "return to the source" is doubly distinguished in its contributions to the Africana tradition of critical theory in that it enables us to critique two dominant tendencies in Africana liberation theory and praxis. The first tendency is that of the vulgar and narrow-minded post-independence nationalists who seek to expunge every aspect of European culture, collapsing it almost completely into European colonisation, without coming to the critical realisation that "A people who free themselves from foreign domination will not be culturally free unless, without underestimating the importance of positive contributions from the oppressor's culture and other cultures, they return to the upward paths of their own culture."[22] To "return" to the "upward paths of [Africans'] own culture" means side-stepping the narrow-minded nationalists' knee-jerk reaction to everything European or non-African, and it also means making a critical and, even more so, a dialectical distinction between white supremacy, anti-black racism and Eurocentrism, on the one hand, and the authentic contributions of Europe and other cultures to human culture and civilisation that have benefited, or could potentially benefit, the whole of humanity, on the other.[23]

The second tendency that Cabral's concept of "return to source" strongly condemns is the usually Europeanised, petit bourgeois, alienated Africans living in colonial metropoles, who uncritically praise Africa's pre-colonial histories and cultures without coming to terms with the fact that

> Without any doubt, underestimation of the cultural values of African peoples, based upon racist feelings and the intention of perpetuating exploitation by the foreigner, has done much harm to Africa. But in the face of the vital need for progress, the following factors or behavior would be no less harmful to her: unselective praise; systematic exaltation of virtues without condemning defects; blind acceptance of the values of the culture without considering what is actually or potentially negative, reactionary or regressive; confusion between what is the expression of an objective and historical material reality and what appears to be a spiritual creation as the result of a special nature; absurd connection of artistic creations, whether valid or not, to supposed racial characteristics; and, finally, non-scientific or ascientific critical appreciation of the cultural phenomenon.[24]

Cabral advocated instead a "critical analysis of African cultures" and, in so doing, he developed a distinct dialectical approach to Africa's wide-ranging histories, cultures and struggles. This is extremely important to emphasise because, too often, Africa has historically been, and currently continues to be, engaged as if its histories, cultures and peoples are either completely homogeneous or completely heterogeneous: as if it were impossible for the diverse and dynamic cultures of Africa's one billion people simultaneously to possess commonalities and distinct differences. Cabral's critical theory of culture also includes a unique comparative dimension that recommends placing what Africans consider to be the "best" of their culture into critical dialogue with the contributions and advances of other non-African cultures. This, he argued, was important in order to get a real sense of what the continent has contributed to global culture and civilisation, and to discover what world culture and civilisation have historically also contributed to, and currently offer, Africa.

For Cabral, it is important to understand both the particularities and universalities of African culture within the specific context in which the war for national liberation is being waged. Therefore, an Africana critical theorist must not be conversant simply with, for example, Marxism, Leninism, Maoism, Gramscism, Fanonism, Guevarism and the Frankfurt School, among many others, but also, and more importantly according to Cabral, the cultural groups, political parties, social organisations and religious affiliations in the milieu that one is seeking to radically transform.

In Cabral's critical theory of national liberation, in order for the movement to succeed, its leaders must base their actions on "thorough knowledge of the culture of the people".[25] He believed that culture must be politically analysed in the new nation that is being forged on the battlefields of the national liberation struggle, where the ghosts of "tribalism" are eventually exorcised and the sectarianism of the past gives way to the principled Pan-Africanism, democratic socialism and revolutionary humanism of the nation's foreseeable future. This new humanity and new identity are a consequence of the armed struggle and the spirit of comradeship it cultivated among the people-in-arms.[26]

Recalling Fanon's contention in *The Wretched of the Earth* that "decolonisation is the veritable creation of new men", of a "new humanity", Cabral declared that the national liberation struggle is "not only a product of culture but also a *determinant of culture*".[27] In his critical theory, it is not simply theory that can be used as a weapon, but also the new culture that grows out of the overarching processes and dialectics of decolonisation, re-Africanisation and national liberation. In other words, Cabral's critical theory is not only distinguished by its emphasis on the weapon of theory, but also the weapon of culture. He argued that when and where culture is used as an effective weapon against colonial, neo-colonial and imperial forces, the people struggling for justice and freedom are able to nurture the development of not only a new national culture, but also a new ethical culture, political culture, popular culture and scientific culture, while simultaneously contributing to universal and international human culture and civilisation.[28]

Cabral contended that both a new humanity and a new culture grow out of the national liberation movement, which, in one way, is a conceptual continuation of Fanon's thought in *The Wretched of the Earth*.[29] However, in another way, Cabral's critical theory breaks new ground with its emphasis on disparate cultures converging through revolution to create a new humanity and a new national culture. In Cabral's critical theory, colonialism and other forms of imperialism were the greatest obstacles to social transformation and authentic human liberation in Cape Verde and Guinea-Bissau.[30] Hence, his work stresses that it is the solemn duty of each and every Cape Verdean and Bissau-Guinean citizen to participate actively in the national revolution. However, part of what Cabral meant by active participation entailed developing an openness to, and learning more about, African cultures other than one's own. Coupled with his emphasis on cultural openness is an emphasis on historical grounding.

History and culture, as we see here, play a special role in Cabral's critical theory of national liberation. He argued that careful and critical analysis of the specificities of African poets, histories, cultures and ethnicities is equally important in national liberation struggles as in broad-based theories touting everything from a distinct "black soul" and "African Personality" to a collective African mind and "African communalism" – if not more important.[31] Not only were many of these theories for Cabral historically, culturally and sociologically inaccurate, they were also extremely detrimental since they often glossed over important differences and precluded historical materialist and dialectical materialist interpretations of culture in the development of particular African societies. Moreover, from his African historical materialist perspective, catch-all concepts and umbrella theories about Africa had a tendency consistently to downplay the many ways in which ethnicity, occupation, class and religion often influenced participation, or non-participation, in revolutionary decolonisation, revolutionary re-Africanisation, and national liberation efforts.[32]

However, Cabral also did not believe that endless hours should be spent searching for minute details in efforts to distinguish one African cultural or ethnic group from another. What was, and remains, most important is that Africans critically analyse and assess their own histories, cultures and struggles, and develop a deeper comparative dimension in terms of placing their cultures into critical dialogue, not only with each other, but also with other non-African cultures, especially those involved in anti-racist, anti-colonialist and anti-imperialist struggles.[33] A strong humanist strain runs through Cabral's contributions to critical theory, and here we may observe, again, his principled stand against imperialism and in favour of revolutionary humanism. Even more, we can see that in promoting a critical comparative dimension to the national liberation struggle, Cabral was also connecting Cape Verde and Guinea-Bissau's national cultures with global cultures, their national history with world history and, most significantly, their national struggles with international struggles.[34]

Cabral's conceptions of national history and national culture indelibly informed his notion of the national liberation struggle. Fanon's concept of national culture connects with Cabral's critical theory in so far as both thinkers suggest a reliance on (or "return" to) those elements which the subjugated population have employed, and may continue to employ, to "describe, justify, and praise the action[s] through which that people has created itself and keeps itself in existence".[35] This means nothing less than the oppressed undergoing a "revolution in values" that totally contradicts and overturns imperialist values that are obstructions to the veritable creation of new human beings who envision, and seek to bring into being, a new humanity and a new society.[36] Cabral's critical return, understood as a "cultural revolution", at its core calls for – to borrow Herbert Marcuse's phrase – a "transvaluation of values".[37]

In summary, Cabral's critical "return to the source", which unequivocally advocates cultural revolution, is a rejection of "traditional", "conventional", "established" or "accepted" imperialist values, as well as retrogressive pre-colonial or traditional African values. His "return to the source", in this sense, is more of a kind of historical and cultural critical consciousness-raising, a form of radical political education, social (re-)organisation and revolutionary praxis that requests or, rather, challenges the "wretched of the earth" to remain cognisant at all times of "our own situation" and "be aware of our things".[38]

Concluding Reflections: Cabral's Pan-African Pragmatism

Unlike many other revolutionary leaders, Amílcar Cabral genuinely valued culture – specifically, the weapon of culture – as an asset in, and integral part of, the national liberation struggle. This was despite the fact that the heterogeneity of Cape Verdean and Bissau-Guinean culture, in many instances, limited the rapid development of the national revolution.[39] Instead of viewing both countries' poor as a *tabula rasa*, Cabral argued that their respective cultures actually provided important elements of the foundation on which the new decolonised, re-Africanised, and revolutionised Cape Verde and Guinea-Bissau must be built.[40] "Whatever may be the ideological or idealistic characteristics of cultural expression," declared Cabral, "culture is an essential element of the history of a people. Culture is, perhaps, the product of this history just as the flower is the product of a plant."[41]

Perhaps the most remarkable aspect of Cabral's contributions to radical politics and critical social theory in general, as well as black radical politics and Africana critical theory in particular, is his high level of conceptual consistency and pragmatism from the mid-1950s through to the mid-1970s. As his body of work in *Revolution in Guinea, Return to the Source, Unity and Struggle* and, more recently in 2016, *Resistance and Decolonization* all deftly demonstrate, although the words that Cabral employed to express certain theories and praxes differed from time to time, he was in fact articulating the same fundamental philosophy and core principles, whether addressing the All-African People's Conference in Cairo, the United Nations in New York, the Frantz Fanon Centre in Milan, the Conference of Nationalist Organisations of the Portuguese Colonies in Dar es Salaam, the Tricontinental Conference in Havana, Lincoln University in Pennsylvania, PAIGC leaders and comrades in Bissau or Praia, or Cape Verdean and Bissau-Guinean peasants in local villages. He did not alter the core concerns of his politics and critical social theory to suit his audience.[42]

Amílcar Cabral was a committed revolutionary who was grounded in the history, culture and struggles of the people of Cape Verde and Guinea-Bissau, but who had a deep and abiding respect for the histories, cultures and struggles of the "wretched of the earth" globally. He was a revolutionary who was disinclined to engage in verbose theoretical speculation and mealy-mouthed discursive excess. He privileged concrete philosophy and critical theory over racial, political or religious ideology. He also "valued independence of thought more than adherence to [widely] accepted political doctrine[s]".[43] Cabral's broader legacy is the critical theory and revolutionary praxes he created to describe, alter and inspire the Cape Verdean and Bissau-Guinean revolutions.[44]

Cabral's contributions to critical theory offer contemporary critical theorists alternatives not only to imperialism, but also to the Eurocentrism of much of what currently passes for "critical theory". Furthermore, his contributions do so without disavowing the crucial contributions that European and other non-African traditions of philosophy and critical theory provide for the Africana tradition of critical theory. When all is said and done, for Cabral the "return to the source" is not only about the dialectical process of revolutionary decolonisation and revolutionary re-Africanisation, but also about revolutionary humanism and the promise of a liberated future where the "new humanity" that Fanon envisioned, and the "transvaluation of values" that Marcuse described, form a concrete, actually existing, ever-evolving reality: a post-imperialist world.

STEVE BIKO: PHILOSOPHER OF BLACK CONSCIOUSNESS

N. Barney Pityana

> Let a new earth arise.
> Let another world be born.
> Let a bloody peace be written in the sky.
> Let a second generation full of courage issue forth,
> Let a people loving freedom come to growth,
> Let a beauty full of healing and a strength of final clenching be the
> pulsing in our spirits and our blood.
> Let the martial songs be written,
> Let the dirges disappear.
> Let a race of men rise and take control.
> — MARGARET WALKER, "FOR MY PEOPLE"

I HAVE INTRODUCED THIS CHAPTER with an extract from Margaret Walker's poem "For My People".[1] It is a verse from the African-American experience of slavery and dehumanisation. The poem was first published in 1942, and could be viewed as a precursor to the civil rights movement. It ends with a "call to arms", but it is also an affirmation of the struggle for social justice. This poem resonated with Steve Biko and Black Consciousness activists because the call for a "new earth" to arise, the appeal to courage, freedom and healing, constituted the precise meaning and intent of the gospel of Black Consciousness.

Margaret Walker does not so much dwell on the pain of the past or of lost hopes. She recognised the mood of confusion and fallacy that propelled the foundation of the Black Consciousness Movement so many years later on another continent and under different circumstances. The poem is confident and positive in asserting the humanity of black people and of their capacity to become agents of their own liberation.

The poem ends with the flourish: "Let a race of men arise and take control". That, in my view, was the attraction of Black Consciousness and Steve Biko's articulation of it to the young people of South Africa in 1968 when the voice of Black Consciousness was first heard. This philosophy brought into being a new generation of black freedom fighters, and added substance to an intellectual engagement with blackness and freedom. Walker's poem powerfully expresses what Black Consciousness did for black South Africa in the 1970s and the 1980s. South Africa has never been the same again.

There is evidence of a revival of the ideas of Bantu Stephen Biko (1946–77) in post-apartheid South Africa, especially among student and youth activists at universities. This interest has been fuelled by the disappointment and anger that many feel towards the unfinished business of South Africa's liberation project: freedom, equality and economic opportunity.

The student movement of twenty-first-century South Africa has drawn inspiration from the generation of student activists in the 1970s who rallied around the philosophy and ideology of Black Consciousness. They have done so as a means of addressing the contemporary challenges that they face as young people and students. The call is for the decolonisation of the university, the assertion of an African identity and for "radical economic transformation". Steve Biko has become somewhat of a poster boy for this movement. His name and the ideas around Black Consciousness have been popularised by a new generation of student activists. His writings are being read and reread, debated and interpreted. A great amount of Biko memorabilia – posters, films and videos – are to be found in bookshops and at Student Union cafés across South Africa. Discussion groups, radio talk shows and television programmes serve to inspire many young South Africans. It is fair to say that the resurgence of the cult of Biko is accounted for by the paucity of intellectual thought in South Africa's prevailing social and political climate. Furthermore, to many young South African students and intellectuals, Biko's ideas have a timeless quality about them and are applicable in a variety of contexts across different generations.

In large measure, this resurgence has been aided by the work of the Steve Biko Foundation, which was established in September 1997 to preserve and advance the legacy of the late Black Consciousness leader. The Foundation has set itself the task of making his ideas accessible to South Africans. It hosts an annual Steve Biko Lecture,[2] and has brought eminent scholars and practitioners, such as Kenya's Ngũgĩ wa Thiong'o, Nigeria's Ben Okri and former South African presidents Nelson Mandela and Thabo Mbeki, to South African university campuses to deliver the annual lecture since 2002. The resurgence of Bikoism can also be attested to by the fact that studies on this subject are being undertaken at universities across the world, while researchers increasingly make the academic pilgrimage to South Africa to conduct interviews and assess the relevance of Steve Biko to the contemporary society. In the process, scholarship on Biko has emerged at both South African and foreign universities.

Perhaps, among the more serious works that have been produced, one may cite the books of two South African scholars. Xolela Mangcu, a sociologist, published the 2013 biography, *Biko: A Life*,[3] as the first in-depth study of the Biko phenomenon and of the Black Consciousness Movement that he founded and led. The other South African intellectual who has published on Steve Biko is Mobogo Percy More, a philosopher who is also a product of the Black Consciousness era. His essays on Biko have engaged with the political and philosophical debates about the ideas and the man, rooted in a philosophical reading of Steve Biko and his socio-political context. More published a book in 2017 titled *Biko: Philosophy, Identity and Liberation*.[4] I cite only those two as they present different dimensions of their subject: one is a socio-biographical, historical study, while the other is an avowedly philosophical treatise. Both have strengths and limitations. Much of the scholarly opinion about Biko must address the current malaise in the politics of post-apartheid South Africa, which causes so many to reach out to Biko for answers and for inspiration.

This essay, then, is an interpretative appraisal of Steve Biko, his life and ideas, his key intellectual influences – from Hegel to Gramsci, Fanon and Du Bois (see Jinadu and Morris on Fanon and Du Bois in this volume) – and the power of his ideas to shape the future of South Africa. I conclude with reflections on the place of Steve Biko and Black Consciousness in contemporary South African politics. The essay also attempts to dig deeper than the Biko phenomenon, to try to find the roots and meaning that give value to the democratic and constitutional dispensation that South African society espouses. The abiding value of Steve Biko in the development of political consciousness and intellectual activism in South Africa is that his theorising draws from the lived experiences of black South Africans, and is informed by these experiences, developing lessons from them. In Biko's philosophy of Black Consciousness, we find the intricate interrelationship and interdependence of thought and activism, a critical insight into the human condition, and the courage to learn lessons, however uncomfortable. It is for these reasons that Biko has an intergenerational appeal, and his theory is not culture- or class-bound.

From Ginsberg to Natal: The Making of a Revolutionary Philosopher

The township of Ginsberg in the Eastern Cape is set atop a hill facing eastwards towards the coastline of South Africa. Below the simple dwellings lies the colonially named King William's Town on the banks of the Buffalo River, once the capital of the province of British Kaffraria. This was part of the British colonial scheme of land dispossession and occupation in the nineteenth century. There is a curious blend and atmosphere in the place evidenced in the street names and architecture of the buildings that still reflect its colonial past. To this day this small town oozes the irrepressible spirit of rebellion, history and the cultures of the Xhosa people who inhabited it long before the colonialists set foot in it.

As one approaches Ginsberg these days, one passes the Biko Centre, established in 2012 with the financial support of donors and the South African government. It is a community centre, with activities in the creative arts and education. The Centre has also developed a community library and has spaces for exhibitions, performing arts and dance. It hosts lectures and debates, workshops and conferences. It is a place of meeting and training for young and old, and represents a worthy tribute to one of the most prominent sons of Ginsberg. All manner of Biko memorabilia and Black Consciousness and struggle artefacts can be found in the Centre.

Ginsberg is where Steve Biko was born on 18 December 1946 at his home – 698 Leightonville, Ginsberg Location – the third of four children of Alice and Mzingaye Biko. His father was a clerk in the local courts. In those days, Mzingaye was among the *izifundiswa* – the educated people of the community – and a respected local figure. He was studying law by distance learning with the University of South Africa (Unisa) when he died in 1950. Steve was four years old at the time. His mother Alice ("Ma Mcete") took on the responsibility of raising their four children on her own: Steve, a brother and two sisters. Steve was very close to his mother, while in his later years his father was something of a distant memory.

After Biko completed his early schooling at Forbes Grant Secondary School in Ginsberg, he went to Lovedale High School in the little educational town of Alice. Lovedale was a missionary station established by the Scottish Glasgow Missionary Society in 1828 and set along the Tyhume River in what in colonial times was the Victoria East region. It was at Lovedale that Steve and I met. We shared a desk in class, and became firm friends. I remember being struck by this friendly and lively boy who was easy to get along with. We lived in the same boys' hostel, and played sports together. He was also incredibly intelligent. It was clear that Steve was destined to score high grades, had it not been for the fact that there was a strike at school and, in August 1963, we were among those expelled and sent home. Steve and I never returned to Lovedale. Instead, he went to St Francis College in Mariannhill, Natal, a Catholic boarding school and a more liberal educational environment than Lovedale. It is fair to say that Steve thrived in this setting. He made enduring friendships with fellow students, and studies under teachers whom he greatly admired. His religious tolerance was tested, and his rebellious streak was often driven close to breaking point.

Steve did well enough at St Francis to gain admission to the University of Natal Medical School, the only one in South Africa that was devoted solely to training black students as medical doctors. It was at Mariannhill that Steve read widely and developed his skills as a debater. His knowledge of literature and politics was expanded. He had fond memories of the nuns who had taught him in school, and who encouraged him to express himself. Steve was always conscious that, as a child of a single mother who had struggled to make ends meet and to bring up a family of four, he had a responsibility to apply himself to his studies. He was fortunate as a good student to have won bursaries. But, by this time, his eldest sister had qualified as a nurse, and she could help his mother to bear the burden. Steve was the first and only one of his siblings to attend university.

Even as a junior medical student, Biko established a reputation as being sociable, affable and intelligent, as well as being a good orator. His critical eye could sense that the environment of a segregated medical school, with teaching staff drawn wholly from white academics (with some Indian lecturers within a supposedly multiracial university), left much to be desired. He examined the prevailing student organisations and engaged with them, without joining any of them.

Biko soon became one of the leaders of the Alan Taylor Medical Residence. It was during his time that the Natal Medical School changed from being called the "Non-European" section to the "Black Section" of the university. It was also during his time that the University of Natal Black Section (UNB) sought and received its own representation on the National Union of South Africa Students (NUSAS), rather than remaining an appendage of the "white" University of Natal. Finally, it was during Biko's time that the political identity of the campus also changed. And yet Steve was never isolationist, nor was he a loner. He confronted the lily-white leadership of NUSAS on campus. He was friends with many of them, and was good at socialising with all and sundry. He held his own in debates, challenging hidden prejudices and helping whites to examine their own thinking. He made friends with many of the student activists and liberal academics. He became part of a group of younger or more junior medical students who brought an atmosphere of intellectual and political engagement into the medical school campus.

In 1967 I reconnected with Steve when I was then a law student at the University College of Fort Hare in Alice. He had a political interest in all student formations, and I had a spiritual or religious interest. That year, we attended various conferences together, including the inaugural conference of the University Christian Movement in Johannesburg, and later the Anglican Students' Federation held at Michaelhouse college in Howick, Natal. I was aware that Steve was also drawn, understandably, to the Catholic Society and their National Catholic Federation of Students (NCFS). What occupied us most was the superficial relations among students – black and white – including the unease that many of the young white students felt when they were in the company of black students. We were also determined to take a stand on the politics of church and country. On both counts, we were never disappointed. These gatherings became a meeting point for black students across all the segregated and isolated black campuses in the country. Bridge-building was an essential ethos of Christian student life.

The Origins of Black Consciousness

July 1967 marked the stirring of the rebel in Biko. At Rhodes University in Grahamstown (now Makhanda), NUSAS held its annual conference. Steve was a delegate from the University of Natal's Black Section. As was the custom, the university forbade black delegates from staying in the student residences where all other delegates were housed. The organisers had, as usual, made arrangements for the black delegates to be accommodated at church halls in the nearby African township of Joza (or Fingo Village). This was to avoid falling foul of the apartheid-era 1950 Group Areas Act separating the two races. For the first time in the history of NUSAS, Steve was the one who raised strong objections to this arrangement.[5] He insisted that black students were not to be accommodated anywhere else but at the venue where the conference was to be held. This stand elicited a stirring debate at the conference, and divided black and white groups. It was the turning point in South African student politics that was to shape the politics of South Africa for many years to come.

It was following this Rhodes University NUSAS conference that Steve and I met at my home in Port Elizabeth in July 1967 to start charting a new politics for student life in South Africa. Five months later, a small group met at Mariannhill under Biko's leadership. It adopted a concept statement, and planned for a larger gathering in 1968. The University Christian Movement (UCM) held a conference at Stutterheim in the Eastern Cape in July 1968. These were the best places for large numbers of representatives from black campuses to meet. Even there, too, blacks were required to contrive a way to avoid contravention of the segregationist Group Areas Act, as well as the influx control laws meant to restrict the movement of black South Africans beyond their residential magisterial districts. Once again, a stand was taken, challenging the whole conference to defy restrictive apartheid laws. A protest march was also organised.

It was at this conference in Stutterheim that Steve called a blacks-only caucus of conference participants. This caucus resolved to continue engagement across all black campuses, and to meet later that year. The inaugural meeting of what later became known as the South African Students' Organisation (SASO) was held in Durban in July 1969. At this conference, Biko was elected its first president.

It thus fell to Steve and his collective of fellow medical students at the University of Natal to bring this nascent organisation into life. This meant that SASO had to have an organising principle beyond mere opposition to racism and racial discrimination. This required an understanding of, and a critique of, the politics of liberation in South Africa, as well as knowledge about contemporary developments and events in Africa and the world. It also meant drawing from the reservoir of knowledge and theory that would serve as the fulcrum and anchor for the passion and enthusiasm that black students were then displaying. There had to be a strategy not merely in regard to the existence and sustainability of the organisation, but also in terms of the means for political education, human and leadership development, the astuteness required to manage the difficult situation on university campuses, and the expected barrage of attacks from the apartheid security establishment as well as from the white liberal controllers of black thought.

All this required extensive self-education. At a time when liberation organisations were not visible – being underground or in exile – black students needed to refresh their political focus. At a time when the security and political environment within South Africa spelt defeat for the forces of liberation, repression of all kinds was rife; the repressive state was at its most powerful; white liberal voices were muted; and those groups that could operate were advancing solutions whose effect was merely to mitigate the worst effects of apartheid. All the while, the apartheid government was advancing its grand plan of Bantustanisation and forced removals. In the face of these developments, the general black populace was cowed by fear, bannings and actual forms of repression. There was, in fact, no resistance possible under these circumstances.

It is fair to say that any attempt at resistance was considered futile or foolish or both. The conclusion of both the instruments of apartheid and the white liberal opponents of apartheid was that black people had been defeated. The African National Congress (ANC), in particular, was influenced by white liberal ideology, and the communist Left was also considered to be a dominant force within the movement, which could thus not be trusted. The ANC and the Pan Africanist Congress (PAC) were banned organisations; and an era of intense repression ensued in the wake of the Rivonia Trial in 1964. The result was that many ANC and PAC activists were banned, imprisoned or went into exile. Various proposals were then being bandied about. The Bantustanisation of South Africa was becoming entrenched, the voice of the white opposition was becoming increasingly muted, and the apartheid government was gaining support among the white electorate. The white liberal newspapers were toying with ideas of collaboration. None of these took the voice of the oppressed black majority seriously enough.

Black Consciousness, therefore, became an ideology driven from, and authenticated by, black students on segregated university campuses across South Africa. This meant that black students took ownership of articulating the lived experience and frustrated aspirations of black people in four key ways. Firstly, SASO aggressively asserted that black South Africans had to speak in their own voices, and that their voices were not to be mediated by any other interests, however well-meaning. Secondly, Black Consciousness was to become the voice of the oppressed seeking solutions *by* black people. Thirdly, SASO asserted that liberation must begin with human conduct, a behaviour that is free, assertive and courageous. Black people had to understand themselves and to cast aside their fears in order to challenge the systemic oppressive apparatus of the state. Fourthly, SASO defined blackness in such a way as to undermine the very essence of apartheid. "Black" in the language of Black Consciousness was a state of mind, an awareness of the condition of oppression, and a determination to challenge, resist, rebel and overturn the system – in effect, to break the chains of oppression. Black Consciousness was thus a philosophy of life, as much as of survival.

It was Biko who spent much time spreading the gospel of Black Consciousness: visiting many black campuses, addressing mass meetings and talking to student leaders. It was he who designed and articulated the theory, principles and ideology that were to form the bedrock of this new movement. It fell on Steve to lead the charge in training, education and research, and in communicating these ideas. It was he who became the principal strategist of this new movement. This was the context within which all of Biko's papers, addresses, speeches and articles were crafted. They were first compiled by the South African journalist Donald Woods. Following the murder of Steve Biko at the hands of South Africa's apartheid security police in September 1977, a book of the collected works of Biko edited by Father Aelred Stubbs was published in London in 1978 under the title *I Write What I Like*. Stubbs included in this first volume an epilogue essay with the title "Steve Biko: A Martyr of Hope".

Biko did not theorise in the abstract. All of his writing was done in the course of advancing a vision that was widely shared: that South Africa would never be liberated by the goodwill of others – whether it be the liberal do-gooders, or by armed forces from sympathetic states, or through the agency of the United Nations – but by our generation. All of this took its toll, and Biko just could not continue with his medical studies. He did not write a theoretical or academic treatise, nor did he write for social edification. He wrote solely to advance the cause of Black Consciousness.

Steve dropped out of medical school in 1970. It took him a long time to reach this monumental decision. He was aware of how much he owed to his mother and his siblings, and aware too of the burden of expectations that lay on his young shoulders. His marriage to Nontsikelelo Mashalaba in December 1970 also brought with it additional family responsibilities that would soon become overwhelming.

From Hegel to Fanon

Besides his medical studies, Biko was well read, in literature, both English classics and literature by African writers, such as novels by Chinua Achebe, as well as African-American writers. He was well versed in many of the standard works of philosophy, and Pan-African political writings by Ghana's Kwame Nkrumah (see Biney in this volume) and Tanzania's Julius Nyerere, as well as the struggles of African people in the diaspora, particularly American writers such as Malcolm X (see Daniels in this volume) and Martin Luther King Jr. Biko thus loved literature, poetry and philosophy. He wrote fluently. His was a critical engagement with history, culture, religion and the customs of the diverse people of South Africa. This expansive knowledge was supplemented by Steve's ease of articulation of ideas, his easy-going style of conversation, and his power of listening and understanding. I do not recall Biko ever raising his voice in anger, even where circumstances may have justified it. He had a commanding presence and leadership style that coaxed people to listen to him.

The idea of Black Consciousness therefore arose from all of these sources. This philosophy definitely had a South African pedigree: from the history of resistance to colonial subjugation and dispossession; to the ideas nurtured in various phases of, and from, all of the various elements of the liberation struggle since 1912; from theories and insights from philosophy, and a reading of the struggles of the people of Africa, to the American civil rights movement and its key proponents such as Malcolm X and Martin Luther King Jr, as well as the black church, artists, poets and cultures. Even theories of Pan-Africanism and Négritude (see Irele in this volume) had a lasting value in the ideas immortalised by Biko. He was the undisputed ideologue, theoretician and strategist of the Black Consciousness Movement during his epoch.

Hegel also became a very influential philosopher and sparring partner for those of us like Biko and me who were seeking answers to our many questions, despite Hegel's own racist opinions about Africa and African people. The very idea of consciousness is Hegelian. It suggests not just a psychological state of mind, but an inner being, a personality who thinks and acts. In other words, Hegel offered a ringing denunciation of the apartheid philosophy, designed as it was on separation and on the superficial characteristics of race.

In 1978 the London-based South African historian Baruch Hirson published his most strident attack on Steve Biko and Black Consciousness in the book

Year of Fire, Year of Ash.[6] Having emigrated from South Africa in 1974 after spending nine years in jail, Hirson had clearly never observed or understood the thinking and strategies behind Black Consciousness. He did not know Biko personally. In London, he made no effort to engage with the many of us Black Consciousness adherents who were there at the time to test his thinking, his reading and his ideas about the philosophy. In fact, his entire book was drawn from journalistic pieces that merely served to confirm his jaundiced mind.

For Hirson, the idea of "consciousness" as an organising principle for political action was not just counterproductive, but counter-revolutionary. He considered "consciousness" to be a "mysterious ingredient" in Black Consciousness philosophy. Without going into more detail about Hirson's misguided intellectual attack, we should note that the lived experience of black folk in South Africa was such that they lived apartheid oppression daily. This was not a theoretical construct. Biko knew that apartheid was wrong, and sought by various means to abate the worst effects of this dehumanising policy. Consciousness was not so much about educating people about their situation, of which they were well aware. Consciousness was about developing tools to overcome this condition, to begin with, by addressing the psychological state of being a "defeated" people and distrusting one's collective power. Black South Africans no longer believed in their capacity to overcome white oppression. This was quite understandable, given the many military battles that had been waged against colonial oppressors without much success, and the many casualties of wars against white oppression that littered the historical landscape of the Black Consciousness struggle.

Frankly, white people had come to be viewed by blacks as invincible. Consciousness was empowerment in the language of Black Consciousness. The mind of the oppressed need not simply be available for appropriation for the purposes of the oppressor. Rather, the mind of the black person should become the means of resistance for overcoming oppression. The apartheid state knew that Black Consciousness marked a silent revolution. It was no longer a question of educating people about their oppression but, rather, about equipping people with the tools for overcoming this condition. Biko defined his credo succinctly: "There is no freedom in silence."[7] Consciousness, as Mabogo More noted, cannot be understood outside its authenticity. "To exist authentically", states More, "is to exist in full consciousness of one's freedom and to choose one's self within the conditions of this freedom and one's situation."[8]

Freedom is neither given, nor does it exist as an internalised condition. Freedom exists in assertion and as a lived experience. In other words, to be free is to resist all that seeks to limit one's freedom. Intellectual life was therefore about the search for the truth and a challenge to some of the putative truth claims that were meant to restrict this freedom. Steve Biko was fascinated by this idea of acknowledging difference. And, yet, differences were being fused into a new kind of Hegelian syllogism, "an undivided unity of differences, which is enriched rather than dissipated by the multitude of its manifestations".[9] This is sometimes referred to as the principle of the identity of opposites: of knowing and being, a synthesis of opposites.[10]

The Italian philosopher Antonio Gramsci was also influential for the Black Consciousness movement, and so was Herbert Marcuse's seminal work *One-Dimensional Man* (1964).[11] Marcuse was a German philosopher and sociologist exiled in the United States. His work influenced the theorising of the 1968 student uprisings and the New Left movement. Through Marcuse, we became aware of the pressures in society exerted through vested interests who controlled the media, the church and the education sector; who viewed society through their own lenses of privilege and power; and whose messages reinforced the ideology of privilege and the justifications of the status quo.[12]

To criticise societal systems of authentication and to resist their capturing inertia was to claim one's freedom. The task of Black Consciousness was thus principally to provide a counter-education that would encourage black people to reject or resist the machinations of control put in place by the apartheid system.

Many of the studies of Black Consciousness I have come across tend to miss these influences that gave power and resilience to Black Consciousness. Engagement with philosophy brought into sharp relief the depravity of the South African environment that was being challenged. Those who felt threatened by Black Consciousness in the political contestations of the 1970s delighted in presenting it as lacking in revolutionary intent and confining the idea of consciousness to a psychological aberration. Indeed, consciousness had a revolutionary appeal in the conditions then prevailing in apartheid South Africa. It was a necessary prelude to preparing the oppressed to liberate themselves. As for critics like Baruch Hirson, we can only assume a misreading of Steve Biko and a misunderstanding of Hegel. Consciousness is both about the truth and about reality. It is concrete and material. It is the ultimate Being.

But this intellectual environment did not begin and end with Hegel. It was taken up in the studies of Frantz Fanon's book *The Wretched of the Earth* (first published in English in 1968).[13] As with Steve Biko and Black Consciousness, there is a resurgence of interest in Fanon in contemporary South Africa.[14] It is also heartening that there is a recognition that Fanon, during Biko's era, offered a stinging critique of the post-liberation practices in Algeria and elsewhere in Africa (see Jinadu in this volume). The Martinican who had studied and worked in France as a psychiatrist later became a naturalised Algerian and was much engrossed in the freedom struggle of the Algerian people as a diplomat across Africa. Fanon warned against practices that would undermine the value of the struggle and consign newly independent Africa to forms of subjugation not much different from those under colonial rule. He was important in our time because he offered a theory of liberation that affirmed its core values, and then provided the analytical tools of understanding when that vision faced betrayal. The important intellectual tools were both suspicion and distance: to learn to live by distrust, and to demand accountability and justification for actions by those in authority.

In his *Black Skin, White Masks* (1952),[15] he was a pioneer in his analyses of racism and dehumanisation as a post-colonial legacy. Fanon provided the theoretical and analytical tools to define the racism of apartheid. These two books by Fanon together present not just the theory, but also the means of resistance to apartheid that Biko developed in his own writing.

Fanon, who had participated in the freedom struggle of Algeria from a brutal French colonialism between 1956 and 1962, and later committed his life to the people of Africa, was not just a Che Guevera – a roving professional revolutionary – but an intellectual idealist who believed passionately that revolution would have no meaning if it did not have an abiding value for the people who had been liberated. He thus provided Biko with the analytical tools to critique the various manifestations of apartheid's social control and collaboration. This helped Steve to understand the mind of the oppressed, and the various stratagems of social control employed by the oppressive classes.

Fanon also inspired Biko in his analysis of the "cult of fear" among the oppressed, and in discovering the truth about black people participating in their own oppression. He further shaped Biko's thinking in exposing the role of white South African liberals in denying the oppressed the duty to be their own liberators. Nobody had ever done such an analysis of the South African condition before Biko in the various phases of the liberation process. With every push, there was defeat, and the ideal of freedom was expressed as a rallying call to action. There was an appeal to universal principles of humanity as well as of religious – mainly Christian – anthropology. Biko skilfully demonstrated how to address the reasons for the failure to succeed in our collective efforts. That was because we might not have paid sufficient attention to the psychology of oppression.[16]

Black Consciousness as Liberation Theology

In summary, then, Steve Biko and Black Consciousness began from a curiosity about human experience that raised questions which had no answers, and which perhaps would never have satisfactory, finite answers. Furthermore, these musings had a theoretical framework for their intellectual quest and, finally, they sought a liberatory praxis that gave effect to these ideals. What is clear is that Black Consciousness drew ideas from a wide spectrum of thought and practice: from African culture and traditions to European philosophy and Caribbean-inspired modern revolutionary practice. The radical effect of drawing on the language of consciousness can easily be lost sight of. This approach was radical in that none of South Africa's liberation movements had used this language before, even though the idea of Black Consciousness can be traced back to the 1930s. The ideology was also radical in that it sought to find explanations for the pathetic state of resignation of conquered black South Africans that was evident in the early 1960s. The philosophy thus sought to give new life to the quest for black liberation.

The late Nigerian philosopher Emmanuel Chukwudi Eze, in his book *Reason, Memory and Politics* (2008),[17] provided an insightful explanation of W.E.B. Du Bois's idea of "double consciousness"[18] (see Morris in this volume). Du Bois was referring to the split personality of the racially oppressed who have to live their life and identity as both American and African, have to seek freedom as human beings yet contend with their paralysing pathological fear and self-doubt. But Du Bois went further. He also believed that redemption and integrity were to be found in the pursuit of a higher self, and that this quest could start only when the injustices of slavery and colonialism as well as the ideologies of racial supremacy and their legacies had been recognised and dismantled.[19] In that sense, the Negro, rather than becoming a mere victim, becomes a revolutionary subject: a person with second sight, endowed with the fruits of wisdom, survival and hope. It is through self-actualisation and struggle through this double consciousness that black people achieve an original, universal compact with providence.[20]

Biko's liberatory scheme therefore allowed no room for moral or psychological resignation, since the conditions of existence of black people provided them with the tools for their own liberation. He understood well both the power of the forces of oppression and the transformatory power of resistance. The key strategy was for oppressed people to be empowered to overcome or to sense the possibility of the imagination that conquers. Black Consciousness gave South Africa's majority the confidence and courage to know that the apartheid system of oppression could be overcome, and that they were themselves the agents of their own liberation.

That is what Biko achieved in his lifetime and through his martyrdom: a life of sacrifice that today shapes the thinking of many for a better world. At the pinnacle of his thinking was the idea that liberation was the essence of being human. Two essays with which I conclude this chapter define the totality of Biko's ideas from which all else flows. His 1970 essay, "We Blacks", published in a column that Biko wrote in the *SASO Newsletter*,[21] provides an introspective gaze into the inner life and being of South Africa's long-suffering black community. It is a candid critique of the black experience. But it adopts this blunt approach in order to raise awareness about the debilitating effect of the psychosis of black subjugation. One of the most seminal principles of Black Consciousness is never to make the oppressed subject people: neither in conversation, nor in our consciousness. For Biko, black people were not destined to be subject people and supplicants to the white god, but people with the fullest humanity endowed by the Creator. Black people could spend much time preoccupied with the white oppressor to the point of paralysis, and overlook – even if unconsciously – the fact that the power of liberation was in their own hands. Steve believed that the material want of black people should not be taken for granted but instead had to be transcended.

The important point for Biko was for black people themselves to address their wants, desires and possibilities. The first thing, he argued, was that, to some extent, the black person was the author of her or his own condition; not that they were the cause of it. However, he noted that by resignation or by not doing enough to resist, they allowed the state of dehumanisation to prevail. Black people who succumbed to oppression had thus internalised the designs of the oppressor. They had become a "hollow shell, a shadow of a man, completely defeated, drowning in his own misery, a slave, an ox bearing the yoke of oppression with sheepish timidity".[22] This was a painful truth told to, and acknowledged by, black people themselves. Biko argued that to be free was to recover and exercise one's own personality: "to pump life back into his empty shell; to infuse him with pride and dignity".[23] "We Blacks" was therefore a rousing call from black people to themselves about themselves.

In his second critical and much-acclaimed 1975 essay, "Black Consciousness and the Quest for True Humanity", Biko made this emphasis clear: "While it may be relevant now to talk about blacks in relation to whites we must not make this a preoccupation, for it can be a negative exercise. As we proceed further towards the achievement of our goals let us talk more about ourselves and our struggle, and less about whites."[24] Biko thus infuses blackness with both the positive and the acknowledgement of what is possible – potentiality.

The second essay is Steve's most popular work. No doubt it was speaking to the state of not just non-humanity, but of active inhumanity and dehumanisation. To the extent that to be unfree is to be less than human, an acknowledgement and assertion of one's humanity is the very essence of liberation. Biko asserted that being human was to give positive quality to human relationships in order to negotiate a meaningful relationship with one's environment. In that regard, poverty was evil, and national resources had to be shared equitably. Steve provided a trenchant critique of apartheid and the laws by which it was enforced. For him, the racist ideology sought to undermine the human quest for "abundant life".

Concluding Reflections: Biko's Relevance to Contemporary South Africa

With these two seminal essays in mind we can next undertake, in concluding this chapter, a brief appraisal of contemporary Black Consciousness. South Africa is now a constitutional democracy, founded on the values of "human dignity, the achievement of equality, and the advancement of human rights and freedoms".[25] And, yet, this is an epoch in which the people of South Africa have been paralysed by all forms of violence, by brazen corruption and unaccountable government, of poverty and inequality, by an administration under Jacob Zuma (2009–18), who was forced to resign by the ruling ANC after nearly a decade of poor leadership and rampant corruption.

This raises two further issues. First, why in such a climate did Steve Biko's ideas become hollow and meaningless? The intellectual climate under Zuma was one of protest, as if the popular will existed outside, and in contradistinction to, the power of the state. Political parties that espouse the Black Consciousness philosophy have been obliterated in South Africa's parliament, unable to generate support among voters. Although among intellectuals and university students Biko and his Black Consciousness philosophy appear to have enjoyed a resurgence, the reality is that exponents of Black Consciousness are very confusing, from Andile Mngxitama of the Black First, Land First (BLF) Movement, which claims to espouse Black Consciousness, even as he supported a Zuma government enmeshed in corruption and state capture; to Itumeleng Mosala, erstwhile president of the Azanian People's Organisation (AZAPO), which was never clear as to whether its was a socialist ideology or a nationalist Pan-African accompaniment to the South African struggle for liberation. No wonder Black Consciousness has failed to gain traction among the rank and file of the electorate.

A more trenchant critique of Biko and Black Consciousness was undertaken by South African academic M. John Lamola in his essay "Biko, Hegel and the End of Black Consciousness: A Historico-Philosophical Discourse on South African Racism" (2008).[26] Lamola's criticisms are focused on the alleged philosophical incoherence of the dialectical reasoning of Biko and his application of the Hegelian triad.[27] The author argues that Biko's socio-philosophical analysis was deficient, and was thus bound to produce a result contrary to what he might have intended. Lamola argued, for example, that Biko's approach produced the unintended consequence not of the full humanity he envisaged, but instead of locking blackness into self-isolating and self-negating essentialism.[28] He concluded that "to lump these racially damaged senses of selfhood hastily and prematurely but without the necessity of liberation of one by the other, will lead to the perpetuation of false consciousness: a false humanity".[29]

How did Lamola arrive at this conclusion? He believed that Biko's fundamental analytical error was in positing black solidarity as an antithesis to white racist apartheid. This meant that black solidarity appeared to be similar to that which it sought to overcome, and the synthesis accordingly is what lacks a viable antithesis. This may well be one explanation in the new democratic order that has caused Black Consciousness to struggle to reach followers or to become viable in the changed environment of South African racism. The dialectical method, in Lamola's words, "inexorably exposes the theoretical inconsistences and practical contradictions of Black Consciousness as a political philosophy".[30]

Thus expressed, I believe, Lamola himself fails to understand holistically the Black Consciousness philosophy. For one thing, the Hegelian triad is a notional conceptual analytical device. The theory does not stand or fall by it. It remains true that the thesis as stated was a racist white apartheid system that needed to be overthrown. The only possible challenge to it was black solidarity, not black racism. But it had to be a black solidarity that was itself liberated, and this is not defined by the limits of its adversarial "other". This solidarity needed to transcend that which it objectified if it was to break out of the stranglehold of the vicious circle in which it found itself.

There does remain a problem, though, about the reception and interpretation of Black Consciousness in the changed circumstances of a post-1994 democratic South Africa. Black Consciousness, as defined by Biko, remains relevant today. To understand it more clearly, though, I believe that one needs both to take account of the context in which the ideas were first developed and to apply it meaningfully to the changed environment of post-apartheid South Africa. One must then readily admit that the Hegelian triad as a fulcrum of Black Consciousness theory will need to be redefined or reinterpreted if it is to result in the new consciousness of the new democratic humanity that Biko envisaged.

Among South Africa's contemporary student formations, Black Consciousness and Biko are often expressed with insensitivity to the rights of women, or as a black essentialism and without regard for the ethical implications of political activism. In other words, intellectual activism has substance to the extent that it advances a just and moral governance system of ideas. And then, of course, one is left with another dilemma: how to position Biko and Black Consciousness at the cutting edge of the transformation of society and of the ivory tower. This requires truly transformative thinking. Failure to provide such thinking over time meant that it was easy for the ruling ANC in ascendancy to incorporate much of Black Consciousness thinking, especially during the eras of presidents Nelson Mandela and Thabo Mbeki (1994–2008). The demise of Black Consciousness movements was thus, to some extent, inevitable.

I end with the reflections of African-American intellectual, Cornel West, who suggested that nihilism in the black experience can only be defeated and subverted through leadership that "exemplifies moral character, integrity and democratic statesmanship within itself and its organisations".[31] West termed this phenomenon the "politics of conversion", which "stays on the ground among the toiling everyday people, ushering forth humble freedom fighters – both followers and leaders – who have the audacity to take the nihilistic threat by the neck and turn back its deadly assaults".[32] West is referring here to the persistent problem of racism in the United States. This could equally apply to the condition of the people of South Africa: not just the prevalent forms of racism, but also the totality of corruption on the part of those within the political and economic elite entrusted with the well-being and the wealth of South Africans. It is because we live in a society so wedded to materialism, glitz and glamour that Biko's values of caring, sacrifice, courage and truth have only been honoured in the breach. With Steve's martyrdom has gone the entire project of human worth and the spirit of *Ubuntu*: the gift of discovering our shared humanity.

27

PAULIN J. HOUNTONDJI: AFRICA'S QUEST FOR AUTHENTIC KNOWLEDGE

M. John Lamola

BENINOIS PHILOSOPHER-POLITICIAN Paulin J. Hountondji, born on 11 April 1942 in Treichville, Côte d'Ivoire, is arguably Africa's most influential philosopher, with an impact that spans Africa's francophone–anglophone divide. Hountondji stands out as the most consistent and eloquent advocate for the scientific integrity and political efficacy of knowledge production in post-colonial Africa.[1] Beyond this, he belongs to a rare breed of African academics who have been able to combine their intellectual pursuits with political activism and public service.

Schooled at the École Normale Supérieure in Paris in the philosophical works of Karl Marx and Edmund Husserl in the early 1960s by Louis Althusser, Jacques Derrida, and Paul Ricoeur (his doctoral supervisor at the University of Paris), Hountondji devoted himself to the contextualisation and application of this European intellectual heritage to the African *problematique*, and attained the status of one of the most rigorous proponents of African philosophy. He is renowned for his critique of the mode of thought that he identified as "ethnophilosophy"[2] in his seminal 1983 work,[3] *African Philosophy: Myth and Reality*. However, as this essay will demonstrate, Hountondji's life and mission extend beyond the domain of the discipline of philosophy. His fundamental concern is how research and education in Africa, and on Africa, can be of such quality that it will enable and sustain the structural transformation of social life on the continent. Within his working *problematique l'Afrique*, Hountondji posed practical questions such as: "How can the state be transformed ... How can fear be overcome, and [how can] it be ensured that in this small corner of the globe ... dictatorship and arbitrary rule become things of the past for ever?"[4]

Hountondji is emeritus professor at the National University of Bénin, an institution to which he has been devoted since 1975. Between 1991 and 1995, he held various government positions as minister of culture and communication, minister of education and *Chargé de Mission du Président de la République* in Benin. This experience of a scholar-practitioner informs Hountondji's life project, expressed in a 2009 lamentation: "Despite all progress … we are still a long way from what should be perceived as our final goal: an autonomous, self-reliant process of knowledge production and capitalisation that enables us to answer our own questions and meet both the intellectual and the material needs of African societies."[5] In this vein, the Kenyan professor of African philosophy Frederick Ochieng'-Odhiambo has discussed Hountondji as an archetype of the revolutionary African academic within the tradition of Antonio Gramsci.[6] Hountondji is a crusader for the ontology[7] of African intellection as a mode of knowledge that is self-dependent, scientifically rigorous, and emancipated from genitive entanglements with the colonial metropole. The examples of the titles of his research output bear this out: "Scientific Dependence: Its Nature and the Ways to Overcome It",[8] and "Knowledge as a Development Issue".[9] Hountondji's theoretical concern is not what is being said by Africans and about Africa, but how it is being said, and whether whoever is saying it is the legitimate party to say it. Thus, the Beninois is a towering figure in contemporary debates on the decolonisation of knowledge and academic institutions in Africa.[10] In recognition of his achievements, he was elected vice-president of the Dakar-based Council for the Development of Social Science Research in Africa (CODESRIA) in 2002.

Hountondji's work resonates, augments and illuminates the epistemological revolution that South Africa's Archie Mafeje[11] initiated within African social anthropology and that Kenya's Ngũgĩ wa Thiong'o initiated in African literary theory.[12] The publication, in 1977, of *Sur la philosophie africaine: Critique de l'ethnophilosophie*[13] and its eventual publication in English six years later, as *African Philosophy: Myth and Reality*, established Hountondji not only as an innovative contributor to the field of philosophy, but as a significant African scholar in the politics of knowledge production. This book, according to Ghanaian-British philosopher, Kwame Anthony Appiah (see Ampiah in this volume), is "arguably the most influential work of African Philosophy in the French language".[14] The volume won the United States African Studies Association's (ASA) Herskovits Prize for the best book on Africa in 1984. The success of this publication, which is actually an elaboration of a selection of Hountondji's main essays, is a mark of the impact of his work beyond the academic confines of the area of philosophy.

In addition to providing a cursory account of the formative influences on Hountondji's thought and work, this essay will examine criticisms of his claim about the imperative conditionality of the feature of "science" in any African mode of knowledge production. I will thus also engage with Canadian Bruce Janz's critique of Hontoundji's "scientificism".

Around and Beyond Ethnophilosophy

Hountondji is generally caricatured as the *enfant terrible* of African philosophy[15] owing to his characterisation of the discipline as an ideologically vulnerable ethnology instead of a scientifically discursive philosophical enterprise: that is, an ethnophilosophy.[16] But, as he later clarified in the 1996 introduction to the second edition of *Myth and Reality*, this opposition to what he described as an uncritical celebration of African traditional knowledge systems and the presentation of products of indigenous African languages as philosophy was but a reflex of a much more agonised mental disposition and the groundwork for a broader mission. As the Beninois scholar put it:

> this criticism of ethnophilosophy broadened into a critique of intellectual self-imprisonment in general, a critique of the scientific and technological relations of production on a world scale, and finally a sociology of knowledge in the countries of the periphery, entailing an increasing interest in the anthropology of knowledge and issues in the politics of science.[17]

Behind and beneath this critical outlook lies Hountondji's sophisticated appropriation of a number of intellectual currents: the inspirational re-reading of the works and lives of Martinique's Frantz Fanon and Ghana's Kwame Nkrumah (see Jinadu and Biney in this volume); the influence of studying the German phenomologist, Edmund Husserl, and the French Marxist, Louis Althusser; as well as French philosopher, Jacques Derrida's *le langage*,[18] the post-structuralist interpretative system of signification that fed Hountondji's opposition to the way that African myths were treated in ethnological philosophy. In an enlightening response to the widespread charge of the "Eurocentric" nature of his demand for a scientific methodology for the validation of African philosophy, and African intellection in general, in the wake of the publication of the first edition of *Myth and Reality*, the Beninois scholar promised to explain his motivations and reveal "what idea of Africa and her destiny, what ambition, what vision of the continent's future, led me to reject the theoretical model of ethnophilosophy as a facile and unacceptable solution".[19] He further promised to explain "the role played by the works of [Aimé] Césaire and Fanon, by a certain understanding of Marx (highly influenced, it is true by Althusser's approach) and by the militant commitment within the democratic movement in Dahomey [now Benin]"[20] to his philosophical outlook. Hountondji undertook this comprehensive response in the autobiographical engagement of his critics, *The Struggle for Meaning: Reflections on Philosophy, Culture and Democracy in Africa* (2002), originally published in 1997 as *Combats pour le sens: Un itinéraire africain.*[21]

It was during his tenure in Zaïre – now the Democratic Republic of the Congo (DRC) – between 1970 and 1972, where Hountondji had just started his teaching career at the Université Lovanium in Kinshasa (1970–1) and the Université Nationale du Zaïre in Lubumbashi (1971–2), that his critique of ethnophilosophy emerged onto the anglophone scene, and his critical appraisal began to shake up the epistemological status quo. In his *Struggle for Meaning*, Hountondji noted that this agitation started around a project of *Présence Africaine* in 1969 that necessitated his interaction with Kenyan philosophers Dismas Masolo and Henry Odera Oruka, who had initiated a multilingual academic forum with philosophers in francophone Zaïre.[22]

In 1974 the Nairobi-based journal *Thought and Practice* published Hountondji's article "African Philosophy, Myth and Reality". In the same year, his "Le Mythe de la philosophie spontanée"[23] – with an argument framed along the lines of Louis Althusser's *Philosophy and the Spontaneous Philosophy of the Scientists*[24] – was translated and published in English as "The Myth of Spontaneous Philosophy".[25] The publication of these two articles would change the course of African philosophy. Through them, Hountondji established a standard for the Africanity and philosophicality of African philosophy. To borrow a typology from Bruce Janz,[26] Hountondji established a framework of discrimination and classification for non-African philosophy and African non-philosophy.

Hountondji's University of Paris doctoral thesis on Husserl under the tutelage of Derrida and Ricoeur had been defended under the title "L'Idée de science dans les 'prolégomènes' et la première 'recherche logique' de Husserl" in 1970. Besides an interest in Husserl, Hountondji's admiration for Althusser is ubiquitous

413

throughout his philosophical outlook and commitments. Although the subject and context of Husserl's and Althusser's corpus are much separated by time, linguistic-nationality, and ideological orientation – the former being a German who worked on the phenomenology of individuated consciousness around 1900, while the latter was a French philosopher and communist activist of the 1960s. An obsession with the methodological sanctity of philosophy relative to science informed the structure of Hountondji's thought. Husserl had set out in search of a "pure" philosophy: a scientifically cogent way of philosophising akin to what he observed in psychology. Althusser had railed against a reading of Marx's works that treated the German sociologist's writings as gospel, and failed to appreciate the "epistemological break" with contemplative epistemology that Marx had experienced in his discovery of the scientific way of thinking about socialism.[27]

With this educational background, Hountondji rejected an approach to African philosophy focusing on "the saying of ancestors" and "folk *Weltanschauung* (worldview)", and philosophers acting as "praise singers" of their cultures for a European audience.[28] There had to be a political value-system and a methodological system that could ground this discipline in a scientific context. Claiming to be philosophy, it had to differentiate itself from mere ethnology, and be able to address Africa's contemporaneous dilemmas. Hountondji thus explained in 2009:

> In my view African philosophy should not be conceived as an implicit worldview unconsciously shared by Africans … I could not admit that the first duty, let alone the only duty of African philosophers, was to describe or reconstruct the worldview of their ancestors or the collective assumptions of their communities. I contended therefore that most of these scholars were not really doing philosophy but ethno-philosophy: they were writing a special chapter of ethnology.[29]

Hountondji argued that this ethnophilosophy was demeaning to Africans, as it cohered with the assumptions of the European colonial tradition of anthropology in its implied suggestion that Africans could not engage in any enterprise that demanded a rigorous exertion of reason. He therefore argued that "African Philosophy, like any other philosophy, cannot possibly be a collective worldview. It can exist as a philosophy only in the form of a confrontation between individuals' thoughts, a discussion, a debate."[30] He dramatically concluded that until this standard was demonstrated, "Our philosophy is yet to come."[31]

Hountondji therefore felt that African philosophy would be only a "set of texts, specifically the set of texts written by Africans and described as philosophical by their authors themselves."[32] This assertion was particularly directed at the school which argued that African traditional thought and indigenous knowledge systems were either a philosophy or were imbued with a philosophical dimension. Ghanaian scholar Kwame Gyekye's *An Essay on African Philosophical Thought: The Akan Conceptual Scheme*[33] was, for Hountondji, the principal apologia for this school of thought. Even Kenya's Odera Oruka's *Sage Philosophy: Indigenous Thinkers and Modern Debate on African Philosophy*[34] was deemed problematic by him. Rwandan Alexis Kagame's argument that Kinyarwanda, like all human language, had an inherent philosophical structure – as presented in *La Philosophie bantou-rwandaise de l'être* (1956) and *La Philosophie bantu comparée* (1976) – symbolised the type of philosophical-linguistic studies that became the *bête noire* of Hountondji's critique.[35]

As a collective genre, the Beninois scholar judged the ethnophilosophical practice to be plagued with three major deficiencies: first, it was not constructed around nor did it honour the principle of critical engagement through tangible outputs of research and debate, as required by authentic philosophy. Instead, this work promoted what Hountondji described as "unanimism", described as "lacking structures of argument and debate without which science is impossible".[36] Second, Hountondji described ethnophilosophy as an ideology in the sense that it diverted attention away from, and ignored, socio-material experiences as lived African experiences on the continent.[37] African philosophy was thus, for the Beninois philosopher, a mythological mode of thought that was negligent of reality, hence Hountondji's decision to write *African Philosophy: Myth and Reality*. His third and principal critique was that ethnophilosophy itself was a symptom of these methodological pitfalls. It was an ethnological display, written and developed for the benefit of external readers in an idiom and inventory directed at facilitating the understanding of largely European outsiders as proof to them that Africans had some modicum of rationative capacity. Hountondji thus regarded ethnophilosophy as an epistemological extraversion.

In one of his later reflections, he critically observed: "We [African thinkers] tend to investigate subjects which are of interest first and foremost to a Western audience."[38] He noted that the small minority in African communities who understand the foreign languages and media employed by academics "know, however, that they are not the first addressees but only, if anything, occasional witnesses of a scientific discourse meant primarily for others".[39] Hountondji further observed:

> Most of our articles are published in journals located outside Africa and are meant therefore for a non-African readership. Even when we happen to publish in Africa, the fact is that African scholarly journals themselves are read much more outside Africa than in Africa. In this sense, our scientific activity is extraverted, i.e. externally oriented, intended to meet the theoretical needs of our Western counterparts and answer the questions they pose.[40]

Hountondji's quarrel was, therefore, not about philosophy per se. It was about African knowledge production and purpose, as well as its intended application and consumption. Philosophy, in any case, is a discipline whose ideal form and task are widely contested among philosophers. For Hountondji – greatly influenced by Husserl and Althusser – philosophy offered a means of tackling much broader and more pertinent questions about how African intellectuals themselves articulate the continent.

Engaging Althusser and Nkrumah

Integrated into the intellectual history mentioned earlier – or, rather, as a result of it – Hountondji did not see any contradiction between his profession as an intellectual and his active public service for Africa's development. For him, philosophy and learning in general could not be about just interpreting the world or understanding it for the sake of comprehension: it was about changing the world. *Mutatis mutandis*, as their results were directed at the management of human affairs, the methods of thinking characteristic of systems of knowledge about the world, about Africa, had – for Hountondji – to be precise, clinical, and systematic. In the Althusserian sense, these results had to be scientific; that is, grounded on the material factors that influenced them, so as to remain "non-ideological".[41] This Hountondji sought to demonstrate when in 2000 he edited *Economie et société au Bénin*, with a preface by the eminent Egyptian-French Marxist scholar Samir Amin.[42]

As a scholar of African philosophy and president of post-colonial Ghana, Kwame Nkrumah was, for Hountondji, an apposite case study of the fusion of methodical philosophical erudition with a practical political programme. But as an Althusserian, Hountondji had first to confront the conundrum of Nkrumah's notion of "philosophy as ideology" as presented in his book *Consciencism: Philosophy and Ideology for Decolonization* (1964).[43] Hountondji grappled with this issue in two of the ten essays that compose *Myth and Reality*: "The Birth of Nkrumaism and the (Re)Birth of Nkrumah",[44] and "The Idea of Philosophy in Nkrumah's Consciencism".[45]

Even though Hountondji's seamless engagement between philoso-phising and practical social policy-making bore some similarities to Nkrumah's experience, it is the Ghanaian leader's detection of "unscientific" political philosophising that most intrigued Hountondji. In his 1967 Cairo Peace Lecture, "African Socialism Revisited", Nkrumah protested that "some African leaders have made 'African socialism' meaningless and irrelevant. It appears to be much more closely associated with anthropology than with political economy."[46] Hountondji's dismissive critique of ethnophilosophical thought-patterns was reminiscent of, and consistent with, Nkrumah's rebuke of Senegal's Léopold Senghor (see Irele in this volume) and Tanzania's Julius Nyerere's versions of the spontaneous nature of African socialism, viewed as naturally deriving from African traditional communalism.

Although current usage of the term "ethnophilosophy" is closely associated with Hountondji, at the height of the debate about its meanings and efficacy the Beninois explicitly credited Nkrumah with having coined the concept:

As is well known, the word "ethno-philosophy" was used in the early seventies almost at the same time by my colleague Marcien Towa from Cameroon and myself in a derogatory and polemical sense … But the word itself was older. It dates back at least to the early forties when Nkrumah used it in a quite positive sense to describe a discipline to which he himself wanted to contribute. As mentioned in his autobiography, Nkrumah got his MA in philosophy in 1943 at the University of Pennsylvania, Philadelphia, and registered soon after for a PhD in "ethno-philosophy". He actually wrote the thesis but could not defend it before leaving in 1945 to Britain, where he served as secretary to the fifth Pan-African Congress. I am indebted to William Abraham for providing me with a copy of the typewritten manuscript. The word "ethno-philosophy" already appears in the title: *Mind and Thought in Primitive Society: A Study in Ethno-Philosophy with Special Reference to the Akan Peoples of the Gold Coast, West Africa.*[47]

Hountondji investigates and reviews Nkrumah's undefended doctoral thesis in the 1998 research paper "From the Ethnosciences to Ethnophilosophy: The Thesis Project of Kwame Nkrumah".[48] He is intrigued by the fact that Nkrumah recognised a priori that his reflective investigation of the rationative tradition and practices of the Akan was an ethnophilosophical and not a purely philosophical study.

While Husserl and Althusser are the lenses for his critical assessment of knowledge practices in Africa, it was Kwame Nkrumah's work that energised Hountondji's thinking and work on this topic.

Appraisal of a Critique

In exasperation, Alexis Kagame responded to Hountondji's strident refutation of his linguistic philosophising as not being theoretically scientific by exclaiming "but Hountondji, he is white!"[49] Indeed, in the foreword to *Struggle for Meaning*, Kwame Anthony Appiah observes that the Beninois author is "identified in many minds with a sort of eurocentrism".[50]

Kenyan philosopher Dismas Masolo's *Self and Community in a Changing World* (2010)[51] remains the most elaborate and engaging appraisal of Hountondji in anglophone African philosophy. We will here, however, only focus on the controversy around the demand for the scientificity of African philosophy, as typified by Bruce Janz's 2010 critique of Hountondji.[52] Both Janz's and Masolo's critiques are pertinent, as they appeared eight years after the publication of Hountondji's *Struggle for Meaning.* Janz accuses Hountondji of "imposing a linearity and an almost Cartesian [French sixteenth-century intellectual, Réne Descartes] foundation on African philosophy"[53] because of "his reliance on a particular, outdated form of science".[54]

Janz, in our assessment, totally misconstrued the meaning and use of "science" in Hountondji's work. The Canadian critic talks of a "positivistic science"[55] and rails against a "positivist such as Hountondji",[56] then concludes *ex cathedra*: "Philosophy's task is not to be the mirror of nature (or culture), nor is it to provide a reliable path to knowledge using the model of the sciences. It is to produce concepts that are adequate to the places from which their questions arise."[57]

This is an unfortunate critique, as it ignores Hountondji's elaborate self-clarifications in *The Struggle for Meaning*. Janz – like those who typically criticise Hountondji's scientificism – misses the fundamental point that "*la science*" in Hountondji's French tradition has a semiotic range that extends beyond the natural and social sciences. Hountondji's approach is about the systematisation and epistemic ontology of knowledge, in which the quality of the procedures of science used to achieve conceptual clarity is alluded to.[58] There are no traces of the influence of the French positivism of Auguste Comte in Hountondji's thought, nor is there an obsession with the linearity of the development of science that views ethnophilosophy as some early stage of a hierarchical evolution of philosophical thought or philosophies, as Janz charges.

Owing to Althusser's influence, the philosophy of science emerging in Hountondji's work bears no reference to Thomas Kuhn's 1962 *The Structure of Scientific Revolutions*, which postulates a decomposition of successive paradigms, as Janz alleges.[59] Instead, what Hountondji relies on is a theory of French philosopher of science Gaston Bachelard, whose work shaped Althusser's disquisition. This is about knowledge systems developing through "epistemological ruptures" which randomly inaugurate new theoretical insights within the knowledge system itself.[60] *La coupure épistémologique* does not entail the simple addition of new knowledge, but the "reorganisation of the very possibility of knowledge. It changes (re-territorialises) the conditions of what is and can be known."[61] Hountondji uniquely discerned a similarity between this French philosophy of science and Husserl's efforts at developing a philosophical method that could limit "surprises of history … and the unpredictable development of knowledge".[62] Arising from this background – in direct repudiation of Janz's allegation of linearity – Hountondji argued that the history of philosophy, in general, "does not move forward by continuous evolution but by leaps and bounds, by successive revolutions, and consequently follows not a linear path but what one might call a dialectical one – in other words, that its profile is not continuous but discontinuous."[63]

Hountondji's philosophy of science or development of human knowledge is Althusserian and, therefore, implicitly Marxian. It is derived from the hypothesis of German philosopher, Georg Hegel's dialectic, as historico-materialised in Marx as a theory, holding that one moment of consensus induces a new stage in a debate, which in turn also negates itself into a fresh consensus. Hence Hountondji's insistence that the modicum of a tangible discourse ("texts", in Derrida's phraseology) be upheld in African philosophy, so that this can enable critical reviews and progressive debate.

Hountondji's passionate demand for the scientificity of African philosophical discourse emanated from his appreciation of Althusser's deployment of the same methodological demands in his appraisal of a tendency – then in vogue – to impose humanistic-spiritualist interpretations on Marx's work. Althusser remonstrated that instead of being a dogma or an ahistorical meditation, Marxism had to be conceived of as a self-critical theory, as demonstrated in the "scientific" quality of *Das Kapital*,[64] as opposed to Marx's earlier writings, which show him under the spell of the Hegelian German theologian-philosopher, Ludwig Feuerbach.[65]

For African philosophy, this translates into an injunction to realise philosophy as a guide of life that is critical of the guide itself. This is philosophy, according to Hountondji, conceived of as a *Wissenschaftslehre*: "a theory of science necessarily called upon by the very movement of science as realization, or at least the condition of realization of this need for integral intelligibility that permeates science."[66]

Concluding Reflections

In the end, we can note that Hountondji is not primarily looking for a new "paradigm" for practising philosophy in Africa. He is rather advocating a mental disposition that could make African intellectuals across disciplines conscious of the dynamics of "historical" developments on a changing continent. He thus demands that "We [Africans] must *relearn* how to think",[67] noting that "African philosophy, like African science or African culture in general, is before us, not behind us, and must be created today by decisive action."[68] Hountondji is therefore proposing a change in the conditions of knowing, reconfiguring the terrain of intellection towards being future-oriented, as opposed to the past of uncritical and static "African tradition".

Hountondji is working for an epistemological tradition that is "living, uncomplacent and self-questioning".[69] Underpinning this perspective is "a political concern: political in the strictest sense of the term".[70] This concern is expressed in the preface to *Myth and Reality*: that "philosophy should,

420

directly or indirectly, enable its practitioners to understand better the issues at stake on the political, economic and social battlefields, and thereby contribute to changing the world."[71] The changing world will, in turn, change philosophy itself, eventually making the debate about ethnophilosophy obsolete.

28

V.Y. MUDIMBE: THE PHILOSOPHER-POET

Kwabena Opoku-Agyemang and Cheikh Thiam

THE RELATIONSHIP BETWEEN PREFACES and the literary works they precede has largely been under-explored in African studies. One noteworthy exception is that made by Kenyan scholar Evan Mwangi, who finds that the preface of the Gikuyu translation of Kenyan author Ngũgĩ wa Thiongo's *Devil on the Cross* (1980) pressures the narrator of the main text to reveal patriarchal structures that contextualise the relationship between gender and narratology in ways that would not be seen without this untranslated preface.[1] There is rich potential, in other words, in associating para-text with text to illuminate textual features of the latter. In this essay, we go further to connect preface not only to text but to author as well, in order better to place the work of Valentin-Yves (V.Y.) Mudimbe, a citizen of the Democratic Republic of the Congo (DRC), in a wider context.

Apart from his accomplishments as a philosopher, Mudimbe is also known and honoured as a literary artist, historian and scholar, among many other distinguished roles. These roles are not isolated but overlap in complex ways, as scholarship on Mudimbe has often highlighted. In a similar vein, this essay highlights his work as a literary artist by exploring the ways in which the preface to an example of his creative work provides insights into his profile as a philosopher. This exercise is carried out through a textual analysis of specific portions of the preface to Mudimbe's *Déchirures*, which was written in French and which has no known official English translation. As the first creative work to be published by Mudimbe, *Déchirures* holds an important place in his literary corpus in terms of chronologically fashioning his agenda as a literary artist, and also influencing his work as a philosopher.

Opening an Opus with Déchirures

Déchirures is a collection of poems published in 1971, and contains 15 "stations" of poetry with corresponding roman numerals. These sections are rendered in different styles and lengths with varying themes. Some of them are broken down further into subsections, which are either numbered in Arabic numerals or separated into distinct stanzas. Mudimbe ends a short preface to the collection by claiming that these constitutive stations are – in the banality of their variations and repetitions – the expression of an obsession that had consumed him for a decade. Despite this declaration, one could argue that the stations are not temporally, thematically or even structurally aggregated to present *Déchirures* as a united whole, not least because excerpts had previously appeared as slightly different and independent forms in the journal *Présence Universitaire*. Mudimbe reveals this fact at the end of the preface.

Apart from offering authorial intention and explication, this short preface also serves as an opening to approach the poetry. To buy into Mudimbe's metaphor, if the poems are stations, then the preface serves as the initial point of embarkation. Beyond setting the tone for the poems, the preface also functions as a connection between Mudimbe's creative opus and his body of philosophical work. While some research has been done on the nature and content of this preface, it is important to situate it within the context of Mudimbe's building his persona as a creative artist in tandem with his more renowned profile as a philosopher. The question that animates this essay, then, is: what is the importance of the preface to understanding and appreciating the Congolese academic's philosophy? This question is informed, as the title of his work suggests, by the "tears" in the preface which signal Mudimbe in different ways. Through a detailed analysis of the preface, we argue that these tears are positioned as ruptures to throw light on the persona of Mudimbe as a philosopher. It is important to appreciate these tears as indicators and not as the destination, because as a condensed text the preface does not contain expatiated nodes of his philosophy.

V.Y. Mudimbe's Philosophy

Through close reading, we assess the preface of Mudimbe's first work of poetry in order to explore the tears that gesture to his larger body of work. From the analysis, we contend that Mudimbe reclaims a hybrid intellectual identity that takes into consideration Africa's recent colonial, post-colonial and decolonial intellectual traditions. As Nigerian academic, E. Chukwudi Eze contends, Mudimbe provides an understanding of the historical scope of "Africa" as espoused in a long-standing Eurocentric imaginary which freezes Africa in a frame of primitivity.[2] Understanding the logic that informed this categorisation points to hybridity as a key concept in responding to the repercussions of floundering in this racist European imaginary.

In the same vein as Léopold Senghor's theory of the cultural half-caste (see Irele in this volume), Mudimbe's call for a recolonisation of the colonial past places him at the intersection of the post-colonial, decolonial and post-structuralist traditions (even though he rejects these labels). He reclaims the miraculous weapons that were imposed on colonised subjects, while still demanding mental emancipation and intellectual delinking from the West. It is precisely for this reason that, read in the prism of the "Africa-centred" tradition, his philosophy can be presented as, primarily, a call to question the limits of the coloniality of knowledge and a critique of the Afrocentric tradition and all discourses constricted in, and by, the colonial library.[3]

Mudimbe's intellectual stand is also inseparable from the discourses of the intellectual milieu of 1960s Paris in which he participated. Read in light of French theories of that time – especially Paul Ricoeur's deconstruction and Michel Foucault's genealogy – Mudimbe's philosophy appears more clearly to be less interested in defining Africa than in tracing the conditions that led to the "invention" of Africa. Such an epistemic stand creates the condition for emancipation rather than a focus on the effects of the very problem: the invention of Africa itself. In fact, one of the two most important of Mudimbe's contributions to the discipline of Africana studies is his theory that "Africa" – which we often assume to be an ontological reality – is an invented category, the result of discourses, practices and political postures that have, since the fourteenth century, led to the invention of the continent. It is therefore at the level of the meta-discourse that one can find the conditions for a better understanding of Mudimbe's work, and his strong critique of the historiography of both modern Western discourses on Africa developed since the fourteenth century and the reaction of African scholars to these discourses since the nineteenth century.

Thinking about Africa thus starts with a genealogy of Western anthropological discourses on Africa, which, the Congolese philosopher argues, have historically functioned as the conditions for the marginality of Africa. These discourses, based on a set of ordering principles determined by a European locus of enunciation, imagined Africa and Africans to be the "other" of the subliminal white self. Mudimbe claims that these views can be traced back to the imagination of the African body, the primitivisation of African cultural items, and the invention of African art. These three instances illustrate the processes that have led to the pervasiveness of the colonial library and the primitivisation of Africans. If Mudimbe insists throughout his texts on the pervasiveness of the colonial library, it is because the idea of Africa that it postulates, the seemingly logical discourses it produces, and the practices it legitimises seem to be insurmountable even in instances when Africanists from the continent attempt to question the very history of the dehumanisation of Africans. For Mudimbe, African scholars have not – given the ubiquity of the colonial library – escaped the Eurocentric invention of Africa in their different attempts to question this very invention. Despite the aims of African studies to reclaim the voice that was taken away from African subjects, there has been a general tendency to maintain the West as the subject of history and Western discourses as the essential matrix for the production of truth. Mudimbe's call to go beyond the colonial library which has led to the essentialisation of Africa, and its corollary, his hybrid and fluid relation to the idea of Africa, are clearly demonstrated in diverse ways throughout the preface to his first creative work, which is approached through the relationship between literature and philosophy in the context of representation.

The Power of a Preface

The Antillean scholar Bernadette Cailler states right at the beginning of "The Impossible Ecstasy: An Analysis of V.Y. Mudimbe's *Déchirures*" (1993) that the critical explication of a given poem is "shackled" by its meaning being rendered in prose; and that similar impediments are present when rendering the feeling of ecstasy into poetry. She further notes that the "gap" between language and the reality it seeks to capture is "paramount".[4] In other words, it is rare – if not impossible – for two different modes of representation to map neatly onto each other. The absence of a perfect overlap when depicting one concept through a different notion thereby leaves space not only for interpretation but perhaps, more obviously, for misinterpretation.

While Cailler admits that her contention is simple or even hackneyed, this point holds true for most creative expressions and translations, as well as for emotions and general communication, irrespective of culture, time or place. It is no surprise, then, that the relationship between genres has been an issue about which scholarship has consistently theorised. As a result, one can consider Mudimbe's literature and philosophy as different modes of representation that are separated by a gap. In this light, and by extension, we argue that the presence of the preface in *Déchirures* speaks to the gap between Mudimbe's creative expression and philosophical work.

In other words, we see a cognate relationship between philosophy and literature in the work of Mudimbe which is made filial through the preface to his first collection of poetry. While this perspective does not mean that the two hats that Mudimbe wears as philosopher and poet are identical, there exist points of affinity that afford the opportunity to process the ways in which his poetry extends into his philosophy, and vice versa.

American philosopher, Barry Hallen, rightly suggests that owing to Mudimbe's approach to philosophy "as an historian of ideas and literature", he "would justifiably protest at being typed simply a 'philosopher'".[5] This ability to write "from 'outside' [the] confines [of philosophy] more than ... from within" makes Mudimbe an interdisciplinarian.[6] In other words, and at the risk of straying into artistic intention, Mudimbe sees himself as not being confined to a single discipline. Much research confirms that his impressive body of literary work attests to this contention, and we take the opportunity afforded by this interdisciplinary approach to examine Mudimbe's philosophy through the preface to his poetry collection, with a few references to some of the poems themselves. For the purposes of this argument, and in order to delineate the scope of this essay, we focus less on his profile as a historian than we do on his literary and philosophical profiles.

It is important to premise this essay on the notion that the preface of *Déchirures* straddles a milieu between poetry and philosophy. This is because, on the one hand, the preface is not an organic part of the main work itself. Mudimbe goes so far as using a different font for both: while the preface is written in a roman font, the poetry is written in italics. This physical marker prevents the reader from transitioning smoothly from the preface to the poetry, and from treating them as if they were the same. Moreover, the numbering of the poems starts after the preface, meaning that the preface and the poems are intended to be digested differently. The creative style of writing – coupled with the mixing of verse and prose – makes Mudimbe's preface different from the conventional philosophical discourse associated with his work. This is obvious from even the most cursory comparative analysis of the preface and any or all of his scholarship. These assumptions enable us to process the poetic licence employed in both the preface and, to a lesser extent, in the poetry. This allows Mudimbe to engage with his audience through tears that lay the foundation for the dissemination of his philosophy.

Mudimbe's preface is authored by a narrator cast as a young man who presents the work as the culmination of a ten-year struggle. Accordingly, it is not controversial to argue that the constitutive poems were written at different times and took different time periods to be completed during the ten-year span. As a result, context, purpose and audience would radically shift, depending on each poem. That the preface is dated January 1971 means that in terms of chronology, the preface was actually the last piece of *Déchirures* to have been written. Looking back to look forward thus allows the narrator to present the preface as a reflection of what has been written before, while using it to prepare the reader for the poems that will appear after turning the pages of the preface. We argue that the preface goes beyond the poetry to Mudimbe's philosophy. This temporal paradox recalls a philosophical notion of the paradox of the preface.

As Australian scholar D.C. Makinson argues in his seminal essay "The Paradox of the Preface" (1965), the preface of a work is bound to reveal logically incompatible beliefs, if an author moves beyond the social ritual of accepting potential flaws within the text to hold a set of viewpoints that are meant to map onto the work itself.[7] While this argument refers to scholarly work, we transpose it here to creative work to find that the message in the preface relates to the poetry in complex ways. We also suggest that ideas present in the preface to Mudimbe's creative work transfer to his large body of philosophical work. In *Déchirures*, the preface is important because it conditions the reader to approach the rest of the poems. In other words, it exhibits a heightened sense of audience awareness.

Tears in the Preface

The narrator opens the preface with the following stanza:

Aujourd'hui
Je t'offre la nourriture que tu m'as donnée

427

Toi,
Ma termitière,
Sur qui je m'appuie et qui me procure
les termites dont je me nourris.

[Today
I offer you the food that you have given me
You,
My termite nest,
On whom I rely and who provides me with
the termites I feed on][8]

This opening stanza serves multiple functions that largely reflect the nature of the rest of the preface, and signals the forthcoming poetry and, by extension, the philosophy of Mudimbe. By starting the preface in verse form, on a basic stylistic level Mudimbe gestures to the fact that he is taking his reader on a poetic journey. The latter sections of the preface are, however, written in prose. This move could be interpreted as indicative or deliberately misleading, but it is ultimately reflective: the shifting genres are indicative of the verse and prosaic forms of the collection, as well as the versatile nature of Mudimbe's philosophical work. The sudden changes in genre could disorient a reader who expects a uniform mode of writing. Regardless of the reaction to this style, Mudimbe's choices imply that the concepts and ideas that constitute *Déchirures* – similar to his body of philosophy – do not appear as a monotonous argument, but rather reflect his work as functioning in a complex hybrid circulation of thoughts that defy monolithic categorisation.

The first two lines of the preface are of particular interest: the act of breaking a sentence into two lines implies that, on a structural level, the narrator is focusing on a different idea in each line. By starting with and isolating "aujourd'hui", Mudimbe imbues his contemporaneous present with immense value while temporally circumscribing his work by underlining its immediacy. Deciding to displace the verbs as well as the subject and object into the succeeding sentence thus subordinates the actors and action to the time in which the author intends to accomplish his task. It is safe to contend, then, that the act of exchange is not as important as the time in which the act occurs. This contention has strong implications for the ways in which we read Mudimbe's philosophy, and is discussed in the conclusion of this essay.

On a metaphorical level, Mudimbe uses these initial two lines to attempt an intimate bond with his audience by comparing the knowledge that is about to be circulated to nourishment. Like his philosophy, his poetry is solid food that is presented with the purpose of feeding the minds of those who engage with it. This intention means that his work is not, in the words of Ghanaian writer Ama Ata Aidoo, "fluff and treacle" or even art for art's sake.[9] This argument recalls the admonishment by Nigerian novelist, Chinua Achebe, to African writers who embrace the luxury of writing without a political purpose.[10]

Mudimbe's poet–audience relationship can thus be understood as a politically structured affiliation that takes into cognisance the politically charged context of the late 1960s and early 1970s when African countries were either battling to gain political independence from colonial powers (as was the case with Mozambique and Zimbabwe) or were grappling with the socio-economic and cultural difficulties associated with being newly independent (as was the case with Ghana and Senegal). The well-known situation in Mudimbe's home country of Zaïre (now the Democratic Republic of the Congo) at the time *Déchirures* was published, reinforces the impression that the food metaphor was meant to equate knowledge with power. His poetry and work are thus set up as a tool to resist oppressors such as Zaïrean dictator Mobutu Sese Seko.[11] And if Mudimbe is offering what he has been given, then the knowledge does not remain static, but is constantly circulating among relevant stakeholders. In other words, the narrator–audience relationship is reciprocal, because the food that Mudimbe presents has already been given to him by his audience. Away from the vertical relationship that Achebe calls for, the author mainly speaks to or "teaches" the reader.

Mudimbe seeks a more horizontal rapport where he can learn from his audience as he simultaneously educates them. His audience, in this sense, comprises the society from whom he has learnt, and whom he will teach. His cosmopolitan background characterises his education as formal and non-formal, as well as transnational, moving from his domestic setting of Likasi (formerly known as Jadotville in the present-day Haut-Katanga province) all the way to the Lovanium University in Kinshasa, through to communities and universities in France. Similar to the complex relationship between audience and narrator in oral literature settings which are common across Africa, Mudimbe appears repeatedly to interchange roles with the audience through this reciprocal sharing of food.[12]

This act of sharing, although reciprocal, is not identical. By using the synonyms *offrir* and *donner* to signify sharing, Mudimbe positions the former action as being more of a service: to "offer" food is to present the gift in a subservient manner. By extension, Mudimbe hopes to offer knowledge to his audience in a manner akin to presenting a sacrifice. If we consider the Congolese philosopher-poet's well-known religious background as a Catholic, then he is offering the knowledge as an act of worship to his audience.[13] This increases the sacredness of the bond that Mudimbe fashioned throughout his career as a public intellectual and creative artist between himself and his audience. The act of giving assumes more agency and control on the part of the giver. Even though Mudimbe is the speaker, he paradoxically deflects agency from himself to his audience in order to position the audience as an active partaker in his work.

Mudimbe is careful to present the relationship between his narrator self and audience as complemented by knowledge as another active participant. After acknowledging his audience, he recognises the source of his food through an apostrophe which addresses knowledge. By shifting his attention from audience to this direct address to knowledge, Mudimbe then personalises knowledge and further underlines its importance by isolating "*toi*" ("you") in a single line. Unlike the first act of isolation, where "*aujourd'hui*" embodies a stand-alone function, the effect of "*toi*" on a single line is complicated by the presence of a comma, which signals the fact that the information that follows ("*ma termitière*") is parenthetical to the subsequent lines which serve as a grammatical, semantic and adjectival complement to "*toi*". His description of knowledge as a termite nest also has important implications for understanding the relationship between himself, his audience, and the knowledge that is disseminated.

The end of the first stanza expands on the symbiotic relationship that Mudimbe seeks to build with his audience through the sharing of knowledge. Termites are a staple food in the Congo, and if in equating knowledge to a termite nest Mudimbe perpetuates the food metaphor in the context of abundance, then he is also teasing out traditional African notions of identity – which include the importance of community and hospitality – through the image of sharing precious food. It follows therefore that the next stand-alone line – "*Offrande congolaise des prémices*" ("Congolese offering of first fruits")[14] – both localises the relationship to his home country, and reinforces the positive nature of the poet–audience relationship which Mudimbe deems to be crucial to engaging with his collection of poems. Furthermore, using *prémices* reveals a keen awareness of the inchoate stage of his poetry project and of his incipient career. This intertwines with the obvious hint of self-promotion to reinforce his self-belief.

The subsequent section of the preface switches from verse to a more prosaic form, with conventional sentences that are demarcated by periods, thus implying a more conventional mode of address. Nevertheless, the idea from the first part is carried over. As Mudimbe theorises on the idea of sharing, he plays on words to expand on his food metaphor. Even though "*plat*" here is translated as "flat", it is also a pun on "plate". Thus, when he states that "*Le partage est un mot, plat, face aux habitudes, surtout, lorsque celles-ci sont coupes chargées de fleurs et de santé*", he could be defining the concept of sharing as "a word, flat, facing those accustomed to it, especially when they are cut, laden with flowers and health". Alternatively, Mudimbe could be positioning "sharing" as not just a word but, more crucially, a plate laden with flowers and health and placed in front of familiar faces. Flatness recalls the democratically horizontal relationship that Mudimbe seeks to build with his audience in which no stakeholder holds an inordinate amount of power. In another sense, a plate – itself also flat in nature – is not only meant to contain food, but in this line it also bears flowers which signify beauty and health. The preface therefore starts on a strikingly optimistic note in which Mudimbe invites the audience and knowledge into a complex but positive relationship of exchange.

An analysis of these initial portions of the preface thus calls into question the argument of Bernadette Cailler that as the subject in this preface, Mudimbe seeks to undermine his enterprise in the eventual poetry as "excessively painful, or drastically useless".[15] It is instructive to note that Cailler ignores these opening lines of the preface to arrive at her conclusion. Even though this oversight is probably due to her focus on the latter part of the preface, as well on the poems themselves more than on the preface, examining the beginning of the preface suggests a willingness to engage with the creative process that follows in the poetry. With this in mind, it is important to let the beginning of the preface direct an understanding of the rest of this para-text before any analysis of the poems themselves can be done.

As was previously mentioned, the structure of the preface mirrors the structure of the poems, which are not easily connected by a thematic or structural concern. The independence of the various parts of the preface thereby allows for a radical change in tone and direction. This could have informed Cailler's decision to focus on the negativity that is apparent in other portions of the preface. When Mudimbe expresses his desire to shout at poems in order for the "indiscreet insistence of ecstasy" to surge ("*J'aimerais crier contre les poèmes pour que surgisse l'indiscrete insistance de l'extase*"), Mudimbe seems to suggest, according to Cailler, that it is only by tearing off his tongue that ecstasy can have a chance.[16] The strong desire for ecstasy in this line, as juxtaposed with an antagonism to poetry, reorients the persona's attitude to the creative process, and questions the utility of aesthetic modes of expression. The subsequent allusion to St John of the Cross reorients the direction of the preface, and beyond textual analysis – most of which has been done by Cailler – post-colonial layers are thereafter introduced into the preface.

The immediately obvious layer is geographical, as John of the Cross becomes the embodiment of Europe, introduced to a preface that has hitherto been grounded in Africa through Mudimbe's reference to the Congo. Uprooting the setting from Africa to Europe suggests a complex engagement with hybridity that is the reverse of the journey of intellectuals such as Mudimbe himself who – like Pan-African contemporaries such as Ghana's Ayi Kwei Armah and Nigeria's Wole Soyinka – travelled to the West for educational purposes. If the reference to Africa is couched in pleasant hospitality, then the presence of John of the Cross is the antithesis of this positivity if we consider South African academic, Neil Lazarus's critique of Mudimbe as an essentialist.[17] This act of introducing John of the Cross therefore speaks to the binary between Africa and Europe, which has a long history and which has been examined by Mudimbe on many occasions.[18]

Mudimbe's choice of John of the Cross – a sixteenth-century Spanish mystic – appears deliberate and, if it is examined through another post-colonial layer, a question can be asked in the context of selection and suppression: What makes John of the Cross unique (or at least relevant) out of all the Western figures available to Mudimbe? Cailler provides clues through her strong contextual information about allusions to John of the Cross, suggesting cynicism, an obsession with ecstasy, and through the poetry "a miraculous moment in which the 'human' (imperfect, mortal) and the 'divine' (perfect, eternal) meet, though they may actually blend together".[19] And yet it appears also that Mudimbe has a more political rather than aesthetic, or even emotional, agenda in employing these religious tropes.

The choice of a religious figure recalls Mudimbe's background in priesthood, which he famously abandoned for secular monkhood in academia. In this light, Mudimbe positions John of the Cross as a peripheral figure who symbolises his own break with European religion. As Mudimbe notes in his work *The Invention of Africa* (1988), colonialism involved an intertwining of religious and political imperialism, as the missionaries used the presence of God as justification for violence.[20] This explanation resonates in Chinua Achebe's 1958 classic *Things*

Fall Apart, where towards the end of the novel, missionaries arrive in pre-colonial Nigeria to disrupt entrenched ways of life and cultures by upending established worldviews among the Igbo.[21] Mudimbe's disavowal of a position in authority relative to religion allows him to overturn the power of religion through the mere use of John of the Cross in his preface. This dismantling of religion as a political force runs through his literary and philosophical work in different ways as evidenced in his novel *Shaba deux* (1989), and his article "African Gnosis: Philosophy and the Order of Knowledge" (1985).[22]

Concluding Reflections: The Hybridity of an Intellectual Identity

Despite the extreme brevity of the preface to Mudimbe's *Déchirures*, this analysis has afforded us the opportunity to explore patterns of hybridity that are expressed in structural, thematic, stylistic and cultural modes. These modes are signalled by tears that suggest that approaching the question of Africa involves a complex composition of *conflicting* and sometimes *complementing* knowledge systems. One of the problems that Mudimbe tackles is that African discourses have been radically silenced or, in most cases, converted by conquering Western discourses. These both involved Western and African interpreters of Africa using categories and conceptual systems that depend on a Western epistemological order. While this issue is reflected in the use of the African languages debate between Ngũgĩ wa Thiong'o and Chinua Achebe that was triggered in the 1960s, Mudimbe is concerned in *The Idea of Africa* about the European conceptualisation of Africa, and examines the impact of how Greeks, Romans and modern Europeans have constructed the continent through their own prisms.[23]

In the preface, however, Mudimbe stops at the different tears which do not contain explicit responses to dealing with a system that is the symptom of centuries of epistemological violence. Such a question is large and unwieldy, and is perhaps reserved for the totality of the impressive body of work that Mudimbe has authored over his five-decade-long career. Nevertheless, the signal points in *Déchirures* served as a launch pad to catapult his inspiring career, which ultimately reimagined Africa as a hybrid entity that requires sustained and respectful engagement.

29

KWAME ANTHONY APPIAH: THE COSMOPOLITAN PAN-AFRICANIST

Kweku Ampiah

THIS ESSAY SEEKS TO ASCERTAIN the key attributes of a Pan-Africanist, and consequently poses the question, Who is a Pan-Africanist?, the opposite of which is, Who is not a Pan-Africanist? The mainstream discourse suggests that a Pan-Africanist is a person of African ancestry who aspires to address issues concerning the identity and dignity of people of African origin through the medium of emancipatory politics or intellectual discourse involving abstract thinking and reasoning.

Perhaps no one fits the latter role better than the Ghanaian-British philosopher Kwame Anthony Appiah, whose insights into Pan-Africanism are evocatively articulated in his monograph, *In My Father's House: Africa in the Philosophy of Culture* (1992),[1] in which he bears witness to the genealogy of, and the discourse regarding, Pan-Africanism. In his book, Appiah opens up a particularly local dialogue and narrative by engaging with African cultures and identities through a discussion of universal concerns about human associations. He simultaneously contends with a grand question germane to the Pan-African tradition: What is Africa? This further brings into perspective the even more imposing *problématique* raised by Appiah: "What, given all the diversity of the pre-colonial histories of the peoples of Africa, and all the complexes of colonial experiences, does it mean to say that someone is African?"[2] Despite their universal resonance, these four key questions are of particular personal importance to Appiah, as the title of his book demonstrates.

In this essay I essentially highlight some of Appiah's core ideas about Pan-Africanism, while interrogating his popular views about the movement. In so doing, the analysis also explores the core tenets of the Pan-African tradition and its ideals as well as its inherent inadequacies.

A few biographical comments about Appiah are appropriate at the start. His mother was English of aristocratic stock. Appiah thus grew up in Britain, where he was educated at Bryanston School in Dorset, and completed his undergraduate education and doctorate at Cambridge University. He derives his first name – Kwame – an Akan name given to boys born on Saturday, as well as his surname, from his father, Joseph Appiah, a former Ghanaian parliamentarian and barrister, and a member of the first generation of post-colonial African politicians. Joseph Appiah was also a member of the Ashanti royal family. With such pedigree, it could be said that the question of who is a Pan-Africanist is one that Kwame Appiah – a professor of philosophy at New York University, with a deep interest in cultural studies – might want to delve into and address, not least because of the implications of race and national identity that such a question immediately suggests. It is also worth noting that the conception of Pan-Africanism articulated by the movement's pioneers was predicated – as Appiah argues – on race.

However, Appiah appears to be uncomfortable with the racial implications of the Pan-Africanist discourse, and the binary opposition it projects – black versus white – in its politics of emancipation. Consequently, his passion seems to include an eagerness to redefine and recalibrate Pan-Africanism away from what he sees as its nationalist essence, on the grounds that a more inclusive approach – a progressive alliance with like-minded groups and peoples, irrespective of skin colour – would be more advantageous to the cause of Africans and people of African origin everywhere. In this regard, Appiah's book *In My Father's House* affirms his desire to inject elasticity into the Pan-African ideal, and to stretch the range of its discourses well beyond what he sees as its concentration on the parochial concept of race and its ideological implications. He therefore seeks to include in Pan-Africanism the diversity of human concern, at the heart of which, he seems to argue, is dignity. Thus, as a leading proponent of the idea of "Cosmopolitanism",[3] Appiah is inspired by the idea of "human variety", which entitles people to "the options they need to shape their lives in partnership with others".[4] Devoid of this, and with its concentration on a collective racial identity – which is an illusion – Appiah might argue that Pan-Africanism is enacting its own futility. In essence, he wants to diversify the conversations that Pan-Africanists have. Their rightful concerns about the dignity of black people should not end there. The conversation should also include – from a liberalist perspective – the dignity of women, homosexuals and the disabled in contemporary Africa.

Appiah's assessment of the Pan-African movement and the discourse surrounding it seems to pursue an argument along the following lines: since the essence and objectives of a social movement or political idea are not static – because they are mediated by evolving socio-political factors – the concept of Pan-Africanism demands revitalisation through change to its constituent parts and ideals. In other words, it does not serve the interests of Pan-Africanism for the ideology to be seen as unchanging, homogeneous, and with a unified essence: a position that is consistent with Appiah's cosmopolitan ideals. As he succinctly put it, "We do not need, have never needed, settled community, a homogeneous system of values, in order to have a home."[5] More importantly, Appiah holds the position that race, which suggests homogeneity, has no meaning or value – even in a utilitarian sense – in relation to the ideals being pursued through Pan-Africanism. This is because, as he notes, "there are no races", but even more significantly, from a utilitarian perspective, "there is nothing in the world that can do all we ask race to do for us".[6] What may be gleaned from this approach is that, since black people as a whole negotiate from a position of weakness in the global political economy, they would do well, in regard to the ambitions of Pan-Africanism, to win the support of relevant partners and powers in their struggles.

Race and Homogeneity in the Pan-African Ethos

Appiah is profoundly concerned with the emphasis on race as a premise of Pan-Africanism because he believes this approach panders to, and affirms, a kind of African nationalism that is potent with racism. He argues, "If we are to escape from racism fully, and from the racialism it presupposes, we must seek other bases for Pan-African solidarity."[7] From that perspective, he suggests that our shared humanity is a more reliable basis for common action, evoking a vision of the African Union without a negro race. Appiah provocatively pronounces that the "Organisation of African Unity can survive the demise of the negro race".[8] This is undoubtedly influenced by his belief that "Cultures are made of continuities and changes, and the identity of a society can survive through these changes".[9] More importantly, Appiah counteracts the notion of African cultural unity. Indeed, the concept of "Africa" as a collective identity – what the

Canadian philosopher Ian Hacking might refer to as a "dynamic nominalism" – was imposed on a disparate group of nations: Akan, Amhara, Ewe, Igbo, Kikuyu, Tswana, Welayta, Yoruba, Zulu, to name a few. This common identity has been embraced and politicised by many African nations in response to a seemingly collective historical colonial experience.[10] Thus, as Appiah affirms, "Once labels are applied to people, ideas about people who fit the label come to have social and psychological [and political] effects." While "these ideas [may] shape the ways people conceive of themselves and their projects", as with Pan-Africanism,[11] despite the common things Africans share "we do not have a common traditional culture", nor do "we … belong to a common race".[12] But then, of course, according to Appiah, there are no races.

It is also worth noting that no matter how different people on a sinking boat may be from one another, they are more likely to bond together and reconcile their differences to fend off the shark that is trying to sink the boat: an intuitive yet rational political decision, if nothing else. They may also continue to emphasise their common attributes in order to keep themselves safe. What matters, then, is the aspirations of the people and how they go about achieving them, a process that is often determined through political negotiations, decisions and articulation.

Appiah proposes an understanding of Africa that is not predicated on a vision of race. His core conceptual formulation is that Pan-Africanism is derived from, and expressed through, the language of "intrinsic racism", which amounts to making moral distinctions between people of different races. This is because "*intrinsic racists* … believe that each race has a different moral status, quite independent of the moral characteristics entailed by its racial essence".[13] Just as many people assume that "the bare fact that they are biologically related to another person – a brother, an aunt, a cousin – gives them a moral interest in the person … an intrinsic racist holds that the bare fact of being of the same race is a reason for preferring one person over another".[14] No amount of evidence would make an intrinsic racist alter his or her position in favour of an "outsider".

While acknowledging that the pioneers of Pan-Africanism had been infected by European and North American theories of racism, Appiah argues that Alexander Crummell, the African-American pioneer of Pan-Africanism, was a racist because he bought into the science of racial difference propagated in the nineteenth century.[15] But, as Appiah further states, "it was not always clear whether his racism was extrinsic or intrinsic". Appiah "suspect[s] that the racism that underlay [Crummell's] Pan-Africanism would, if articulated, have been fundamentally intrinsic".[16] In contrast, extrinsic racists inherently "make moral distinctions between members of different races because they believe that the racial essence entails certain morally relevant qualities" which legitimise a "belief that members of different races differ in respects that warrant ... differential treatment".[17] It is tempting to ask, "Who was not a racist in nineteenth century America?" if we accept Appiah's definition. In other words, the definition of racism that he proposes muddles the debate.

What is worth clarifying, in my estimation, is the difference between, on the one hand, a wealthy slave master who is at once a hero, because of his wealth, and a doyen of the community and church, even while treating human beings, his slaves, as animals, and, on the other hand, a slave who considers a white person as morally mysterious and unethical, because his wealth depends on his treatment of human beings as animals. There we have it: two racists, conceivably both intrinsic and extrinsic racists, and therefore both victims of racism. It gives us no comfort to compare such cases, as there is no indication of a level playing field in this situation. I would suggest that, if Crummell were a racist – as Appiah argues – his racism must be seen as qualitatively different from that of the slave master, although how to measure that empirically presents us with a conundrum. This is a puzzle that I would rather leave to Appiah to unravel, as he appears to be sufficiently "intellectually perverse"[18] to be able to assess the qualitative difference between such opposites. Simply saying Crummell was not a brutal racist,[19] as Appiah does, is inadequate. Suffice it to say, the racist tendencies of the slave were grounded in, and essentialised by, the fact that he was a victim of a system of capital accumulation in the US that was underpinned by the private ownership of slaves, an economy that was the domain of whites and supported by institutions – the government, the legal system, the banking sector, and so on – controlled by white people. Finally, the economic system was sanctioned and sanctified by the church and was also controlled by people who looked markedly different from the victims of that economy.

Indeed, as with the other progenitors of Pan-Africanism, Crummell's commitment to the emancipation of people of African origin was predicated on the sense of victimhood endured by the negro race, of which he was a part. In other words, Crummell's Pan-Africanism – whether derived from extrinsic or intrinsic racism – was as much a product of his sense of victimhood as the social and institutional racism that he and people like him suffered from. We should thus ask: In the absence of nineteenth-century European and North American theories of race, how would Crummell and his compatriots have intellectually, and in the vernacular, challenged the institution of slavery and the oppression of Africans and people of African origin?

Bearing in mind that Crummell and his friend Edward Wilmot Blyden (see Khadiagala in this volume) were ministers of the church, it would be fair to assume that they would have evoked biblical narratives about the Exodus – the suffering endured by the children of God in Egypt and their subsequent freedom – as the basis of their struggle for the freedom of black people in America. Moreover, Crummell would have seen himself as leading the "folk" – the nation, the people who physically looked like him, and with whom he shared socio-cultural attributes, including ignominy and oppression – out of the proverbial Egypt to the promised land of freedom and the "imagined" continent of Africa. However, in the context of contemporary discourse, Crummell, like Blyden and W.E.B. Du Bois (see Morris in this volume), could not have processed and articulated the suffering of people of African origin in the Americas without embracing the hegemonic theories about race on which slavery was essentially based. Thus, the early pioneers of Pan-Africanism used a combination of race theory and biblical narratives, in direct dialogue with each other, to reinforce their case and vision.

Appiah thinks it is "strange that it should be the whiteness of the oppressors – 'the whiteman' – as opposed, say, to their *imperialism*, that should stand out".[20] In the same vein, it is peculiar that the emancipation discourse among blacks was transfixed by the Exodus story and the traditions behind it, not least because the villain of the piece is Egypt rather than the economic and political system of the Pharaohs. The eager acceptance by black congregations on Sundays in Baptist churches across America of the fairy-tale of the Exodus is more *strange* – to borrow Appiah's expression – than the Pan-Africanists' concern with race.

The nineteenth century ushered in what Du Bois referred to as "the first century of human sympathy – the age when half wonderingly we began to descry in others that transfigured spark of divinity which we call Myself; when ... all helplessly we peered into those Other-worlds, and wailed, 'O World of Worlds, how shall man make you one?'"[21] Ironically, it was also the era when race theory was reasserted, as if to temper the rising human sympathy of which Du Bois speaks. His primary concern was "how, into the inevitable and logical democracy which was spreading over the world, could black folk in America and particularly in the South be openly and effectively admitted; and the coloured people of the world allowed their own self-government?"[22] It seems that Du Bois was more motivated by the values and logistics of social democracy and its universal relevance, although, in Appiah's estimation, Du Bois would have been both an extrinsic and an intrinsic racist.[23]

Appiah is right that the Pan-Africanists' concern should be with the system instead of with race. Indeed, the Atlantic slave trade and the expansive economies that emanated from it were a function and agent of capitalism, which subsequently made possible European and American imperialism. Du Bois and, later, George Padmore (see Duggan in this volume) understood this, and clearly identified capitalism as the main culprit. Ghana's Kwame Nkrumah (see Biney in this volume), among many African intellectuals, also articulated the role of capitalism and imperialism in the exploitation and oppression of Africans and descendants of Africans in the diaspora. Thus, both Du Bois and Padmore, and indeed Nkrumah, were drawn to a prevailing popular discourse, grounded in Marxism, perhaps in the same way that Crummell and Blyden were drawn to the prevailing theories about race in their own era.

Appiah argues that race is an irrelevance to addressing and remedying wrongs against humanity, including historical ones, and upholding human rights. After all, abuses against human dignity are not the preserve of any particular culture or homogeneous group of people, if ever there was such a group. Nor are such abuses a tool reserved for one group of people to use against another.[24] We have seen in recent history how Europeans have massacred other non-European peoples with reckless abandon, not unlike Africans slaughtering other Africans in the 1994 Rwandan genocide, for example. Thus, what Appiah might want to know is how Pan-Africanism, as a nationalist ideal that promises to defend the rights and dignity of Africans and people of African origin, can ensure that the genocide in Rwanda in which an estimated 800,000 people were killed, is not replicated anywhere else in Africa. How, indeed, does Pan-Africanism contend with the xenophobia in South Africa that killed over 350 people between 2008 and 2015? And how are the rights of minorities – for example, homosexuals – protected and safeguarded in Africa and among peoples of African origin in the diaspora? Appiah's primary concern, informed by his liberalist ideology, is with human dignity: the state or quality of being worthy of honour or respect.

Taking his cue from the English liberal philosopher John Stuart Mill, Appiah argues that while "identity matters ... it is not the only thing that matters".[25] In that context, he notes that "slavery is not the only obstacle to dignity".[26] Nevertheless, race and slavery are the two primary factors that inform Du Bois's conception of Pan-Africanism, which Appiah suggests was a product of extrinsic racism,[27] conceivably a result of the fact that, as with Crummell, Du Bois also bought into the science of racial difference. Thus Appiah further argues that Du Bois's claim that "Africa is of course my fatherland" was the feeling of an intrinsic racist,[28] because "[Du Bois] wanted desperately to find in Africa and with Africans a home, a place where he could feel, as he never felt in America, that he belonged".[29]

By identifying with Africa in this way, Du Bois helped to form the basis of the "Back to Africa" movement in the Pan-Africanist tradition of Marcus Garvey (see Grant in this volume). Appiah is right to ask how the "Back to Africa" movement – and indeed Pan-Africanism, with its emphasis on race – reconciles with the fact that "Africa" colluded in, and was complicit in, the sale and enslavement of its own "children" to the New World. Moreover, why would these "children" want to go back to a place that symbolically disinherited them, and even continued to feed the frenzy of slavery with more of its children century after century? Times, however, change. What is not in doubt is that the post-colonial generation of African intellectuals and politicians have different values from the earlier generation of African chiefs and brokers who were complicit in the slave trade. In other words, the historical circumstances were different. As such, it might be argued that diasporic Pan-Africanists like Du Bois and Trinidadian, George Padmore saw independent Africa – disinherited, as it were, of the racist colonial governments and institutions – as a metaphor for their freedom from racism, and relocation to Africa as a realisation of that long-cherished dream.

When Pan-Africanism "Came Home"

As late as 1965, Malcolm X (see Daniels in this volume) felt that while fighting for their constitutional rights in America, "philosophically and culturally ... Afro-Americans badly needed to return to Africa – and to develop a working unity in the framework of Pan-Africanism".[30] The idea of "working unity" of which Malcolm X spoke was conceived much earlier in terms of a vision of Africa as a "nation" by leaders, including Marcus Garvey[31] and Du Bois, who wanted to build an identity with a place to which they had no legal claim, nor to which they could "trace their particular roots",[32] but which was beset with socio-economic and political problems they believed were best dealt with through the diversity of African people. It was in that spirit that the presiding genius of Pan-

Africanism, Du Bois, moved to Ghana in October 1961 and eventually became a Ghanaian citizen in February 1963, six months before his death at the age of 95 (see Morris in this volume). Du Bois proclaimed, as he reaffirmed his new identity: "I have returned so that my remains may mingle with the dust of the forefathers. Now my life will flow on in the vigorous young stream of Ghanaian life which lifts the African personality to its proper place among men. And I shall not have lived in vain."[33] Much earlier, the restless "black activist" George Padmore, who would also join Kwame Nkrumah in Ghana, had become drawn to Du Bois and Pan-Africanism. At the risk of overstating the point, this idea of creating unity among negroes is a bone of contention for Appiah, who criticises the Pan-Africanists for putting race at the centre of their discourse.[34] This assessment that race persisted in post-colonial Pan-Africanism in Africa should, however, be qualified.

Post-colonial Africa's leading Pan-Africanist Kwame Nkrumah was indeed inspired by the idea of the unity of Africa and the liberation of Africans from Western domination. In the spirit of the liberation movement, he invoked the Pan-African tradition and proverbially reinforced it with the biblical narrative of the Exodus, as demonstrated in his speech in Liberia in January 1952:

> it was providence that had preserved the Negroes during their years of trial in exile in the United States of America and the West Indies; that it was the same providence which took care of Moses and the Israelites in Egypt centuries before. 'A greater exodus is coming in Africa to-day' ... and that exodus will be established when there is a united, free and independent West Africa. [35]

This Pan-African pronouncement – with its evocation of the plight of negroes in the Americas – has to be seen in its proper context. Nkrumah was speaking in Liberia, a country created for the homecoming of freed and free-born blacks from America and the Caribbean, to an audience that might have been made up largely of descendants of these returnees. The passage was therefore rhetorically apt, and Appiah rightly quotes it in his book, noting that Nkrumah had indeed proclaimed, "Africa for the Africans!" However, as Nkrumah further emphasised to his Liberian audience: "Africa for the Africans!, but not the kind of philosophy that Marcus Garvey preached. No! We are bringing into being another Africa for the Africans with a different concept ... A free and independent state in Africa. We want to be able to govern ourselves in this country of ours without outside interference."[36]

How and what we select or de-select from the information available to us is inherently political. While Appiah quotes from the above passage,[37] for some reason he does not include the passage concerning Nkrumah's thoughts about Garvey's philosophy, which Nkrumah had studied in *The Philosophy and Opinions of Marcus Garvey*.[38] Nor does Appiah comment on further parts of the speech in which Nkrumah proclaimed:

> We believe in the equality of races. We believe in the freedom of the peoples of all races. We believe in cooperation. In fact it has been one of my theses that in this struggle of ours, in this struggle to redeem Africa, we are fighting not against race and colour and creed. We are fighting against a system, a system which degrades and exploits, and wherever we find the system, the system must be abolished.[39]

This system of Nkrumah's focus, which the first generation of post-colonial African political leaders abhorred, was "colonialism and imperialism".[40] Nkrumah's admiration for the Ghanaian Kwegyir Aggrey is relevant to our analysis. In his autobiography *Ghana* (1957), Nkrumah reminisces about Aggrey, the Gold Coast missionary and teacher. According to Nkrumah, Aggrey was strongly opposed to racial segregation in any form, and he further noted that, although Aggrey understood Marcus Garvey's principle of "Africa for the Africans", he never hesitated to attack the precept because "he did not much appreciate the isolationist content of the principle". More importantly, Aggrey "believed conditions should be such that the black and white races should work together".[41] In essence, it is important to note that in its evolution, Pan-Africanist thought has been a broad church, not a homogeneous one, as is evident in Du Bois's critique of Garvey's tone and style of Pan-Africanism.[42] Indeed, African-American leaders, Crummell and Fredrick Douglass held contrasting views on the issue of race and black progress. If Crummell's plan for black progress "always included the ingredients of ethnic pride and collective effort", these two ingredients were apparently "Douglass's pet peeves".[43] The views of individual Pan-Africanists also naturally evolved. Malcolm X, for example, recalibrated his revolutionary perspective to "accept the idea that the struggle for the liberation of black people could not be racially defined ... to exclude true revolutionaries" as a result of a discussion he had in Accra in May 1964 with Tahar Gaid, the Algerian ambassador to Ghana.[44]

Appiah is thus wrong when he says that "Pan Africanism inherited Crummell's intrinsic racism".[45] He knows he is wrong because he further qualifies this statement by submitting, "We cannot say it [Pan-Africanism] inherited it from Crummell, since in his day it was the common intellectual property of the West."[46] He is also wrong to suggest that the movement inherited the racism of the West. Even accepting that Crummell and Blyden were racists according to Appiah's definition, that in itself does not make Pan-Africanism a racist movement, even if we agree that it was nationalist in its orientation.

Du Bois informs us that "At the London meeting of the third Pan-African Congress, Harold Laski, H.G. Wells, and Lord Olivier spoke, and Ramsay MacDonald" [47] had also been expected to speak. The Congress further held meetings with leading Labour Party members during which "the importance of labour solidarity between white and black labour in England, America, and elsewhere"[48] was emphasised. Du Bois further planned for what he referred to as "broader co-operation with white rulers of the world, and a chance for peaceful and accelerated development of black folk",[49] all of which suggests that the Pan-Africanist movement, at least in the 1920s, was determined to collaborate with its relevant compatriots, irrespective of skin colour. Suffice it to say, the nationalist aspirations of people of African origin in the New World were simply premised on the principle of freedom: freedom from slavery and racial discrimination.

Appiah's remark that "We can see Crummell as emblematic of the influence of this racism on black intellectuals, an influence that is profoundly etched in the rhetoric of post-war African nationalism"[50] is even more curious when one considers Nkrumah's views on Garvey's political thoughts. There is no doubt that Africa's post-colonial political leaders were nationalists who wanted political and economic independence for their countries. They were nationalists in the same way that Alex Salmond or Nicola Sturgeon – leaders of the Scottish National Party (SNP) – are nationalists fighting for the independence of Scotland from the Union. They are not racists, nor is the SNP considered a racist political party in popular British political discourse.

More importantly, the correlation that Appiah attempts to build between Crummell and the rhetoric of post-war African nationalism is asserted rather than proved. To use Nkrumah as an example, parts of the speech he made in Liberia in 1952 may evoke sentiments that Crummell might well have expressed. On the other hand, like Crummell, Nkrumah was simply taking his cue from biblical passages on the Exodus out of Egypt. It is fair to argue that, given the mission education that Nkrumah had received in the colonial Gold Coast, he would have come across the narrative about the Exodus well before he heard about Crummell. And for an aspiring preacher with a degree in theology, God's "Word" would have taken precedence over anything else. Basically, the source of Nkrumah's inspiration, in this particular case, might have been the Bible or, better still, the sermons he delivered and heard at the Baptist churches he attended while a student at Lincoln College in Philadelphia between 1935 and 1942. The Ghanaian leader did not need guidance from either Crummell or Blyden. Thus, Appiah's point that "It is striking how much of Crummell or Blyden we can hear in Nkrumah's speech in Liberia in 1952"[51] is grossly unfounded. Nkrumah does not even once mention Crummell in his autobiography.

Liberalism, Human Dignity and the Pan-African Discourse

I agree, however, with the implications of Appiah's argument that Pan-Africanism has been parochial in its ambitions and in the way it has attempted to operationalise those ambitions. Given its concern with human dignity, in particular with "cases where it is lacking",[52] Appiah notes that while "a slave … cannot lead a dignified existence … slavery is not the only obstacle to dignity".[53] From this, we can easily deduce that racism is not the only obstacle to dignity. Appiah notes, as an example, that a "life of hand-outs is not dignified; the dignity of people with severe physical disability is often challenged, denying women equal rights with men undermines their dignity, and forcing gay people and lesbians to deny their sexuality is undignifying to them".[54]

By invoking the issue of human dignity in this fashion, Appiah automatically challenges the Pan-Africanist tradition, impressing on the movement the need to broaden its remit and ambitions beyond what he sees as its primary focus on race and race-related issues. This is abundantly evident in the point that Appiah makes in his essay "Liberalism, Individuality and Identity" (2001): "liberalism is the articulation of the value of a life of dignity: a life as free and equal people, sharing a social world".[55] In that sense, how, as Appiah might ask, is the free will of gays and lesbians articulated in the Pan-Africanist discourse? Indeed, how are the identities of such a group protected and encouraged to flourish in contemporary African countries, and how is their right to dignity ensured? He posits that "dignity cannot come to those who are forced to leave what matters most to them about themselves locked away in a private realm".[56]

Appiah is thus making a point about sexual identity and how homosexuals are made to feel not only in most African societies, but also in black communities in the diaspora. And what about the rights of women and children in Africa? Appiah's critique of the overemphasis on race in the Pan-African tradition is an implicit recommendation for a post-racial approach to the socio-economic problems of Africans and of peoples of African origin in the diaspora. In other words, the processes for the execution of the movement's aspirations and ambitions would also have to be further diversified to include whoever and whatever is a potential solution to these problems. The obsession with race, as Appiah seems to argue, has prevented the mainstream proponents of Pan-Africanism from facing the "in-house" demons that need tackling in the struggle for the dignity of those it is concerned about.

Additional biographical information about Appiah might add further insight to our discussion. At an event in May 2014 in which he participated as one of three speakers, Appiah remarked that "In my mind I've had very little problem with racism in my life ... I was protected in England by going to private schools and Cambridge and on the whole having people around who were moderately civilized, and also being raised to think that there wasn't a problem, and not noticing other people who thought there was a problem except as thinking they had a problem." He further noted that although he has "had occasional problems with people because I'm gay", he had "not often thought [he] was having a problem because [he] was not white".[57]

These revelations about problems that Appiah has encountered with his identity are qualified in places with obfuscations, but the indications are that, despite his privileged upbringing, racism is not foreign to Appiah. Indeed, he admits to having had problems with racism – albeit, in his mind, very few. Thus, he is not oblivious to it. In any case, Appiah is aware that he was "protected" from a certain kind of threat, and he seems to have had the awareness and alertness to superimpose the problem on the racists he encountered. However, there is no doubt that Appiah has been the victim of homophobia, and he is possibly more likely to suffer homophobic abuse and intimidation in Africa than in Europe or the US. He could be arrested and prosecuted in Uganda for example, if he does not leave his sexuality "locked away in a private realm".[58] Thus, I suggest that there is also a "queer" sensibility to Appiah's discussions about the dignity of Africans and people of African origin in the diaspora, and to his perspectives on Pan-Africanism.

Concluding Reflections

In the traditional conception, a Pan-Africanist would be an African or a person of African origin committed to the advancement of the life chances of black people collectively across the globe. In essence, the starting point of the Pan-Africanist is race, reinforced by the victim narrative that is core to the discourse of Pan-Africanism. This serves as a basis for solidarity, thereby helping to essentialise Africa as a "haven" (in the "Back to Africa" movement) in the early nineteenth century. Appiah finds this approach problematic, and seems to lament that "Pan-Africanists responded to their experience of racial discrimination by accepting the racialism it presupposed".[59] Thus, although he identifies a contrast between the first generation of Pan-Africanists such as Crummell and Blyden and the movement's subsequent pioneers such as Nkrumah in terms of how they separately treated and responded to Africa's cultural traditions – with the former denigrating African cultures as "fetish" and uncivilised – Appiah argues that the category of race has persisted in the discourse of Pan-Africanism across generations.

As I have noted, Appiah's point that "Pan Africanism inherited Crummell's intrinsic racism"[60] is unconvincing. If the movement is guilty of racism, the source of that guilt is not Crummell, but the progenitors and propagators of race theories in Europe and North America. Given the potency of the race theories of the early twentieth century, even without Crummell the Pan-Africanists of that era would also have been conceivably infected by the same Western racist discourse. Appiah's discussion of the movement also wrongly creates the impression that Pan-Africanism in the New World is a homogeneous entity. As I have suggested, the movement was instead a broad church involving people such as Frederick Douglass, who was opposed to the idea of racial harmony as a means for black progress. Appiah also erroneously construes the rhetoric of nationalism in post-colonial African politics as a product of Crummell's views on race.

Appiah's insights are very much about modernisation, but, crucially, he seems to be mainly interested – in contrast to post-colonial African leaders and mainstream Pan-Africanists – in the role of Western liberal political thought and institutions in the political processes of the development of African countries.[61] He believes that contemporary Pan-Africanism is limited by its emphasis on race, and that the movement would do better to embrace all the options that black people need to shape their lives in partnership with others.[62]

There is no doubt about the insightfulness of Appiah's interrogation of race as the basis of a collective identity for the regeneration of the life of Africans and people of African descent in the diaspora. After all, his mother – Peggy Appiah, an Englishwoman – was possibly a more valiant Pan-Africanist than his father, Ghanaian politician Joe Appiah. The deeper truth, however, is that racial essentialism – as a by-product of race theory, but an illusion, nonetheless – is part of the fabric of political discourses in the West. At the very least, it is a weapon that people, organisations and institutions wield to assert a hierarchy in economic and political value systems and outcomes. Du Bois reminds us that during the First World War, "American white officers fought more valiantly against Negroes than they did against the Germans",[63] who were their enemy. The uses of race, "the oneiric exaltation of blood ... [and] skin" – as the Indo-British scholar Homi Bhabha[64] put it – dictates people's life across the Western hemisphere including Brazil, Haiti, Jamaica and beyond.

There are, of course, different ways of processing reality: race is a reality because it is part of the vernacular of hundreds of millions of people who use the ideology that it embodies to inform themselves when and where necessary. Race also influences national policy. Indeed, it impacts on the lives of tens of millions of people daily, even though Appiah correctly identifies it as an oxymoron.

PART 7

THE LITERATI

30

LÉOPOLD SENGHOR: POET-PRESIDENT OF NÉGRITUDE

Abiola Irele

LÉOPOLD SÉDAR SENGHOR, the poet-president of Senegal between 1960 and 1980, was born on 9 October 1906 and died on 20 December 2001. In any consideration of Senghor's life and career and his role in the evolution of contemporary thought in Africa, the starting point has to be the concept of Négritude with which his name has become closely associated. This was a concept that not only generated a literary and ideological movement aimed at the promotion of a renovated image of the black race, but was also, for a while, the subject of a vigorous controversy which has not altogether subsided.

We need to recall, at this time, the context which provoked the reaction registered by Négritude – the objective reality of the black experience – slavery and colonial domination, with the stresses that both introduced into the lives of black communities all over the world. We should also recall especially the discourse through which this domination was justified and rationalised: a discourse aimed at the global devaluation of the black race in its historical and existential constitution. It is this *problématique* of black existence that Senghor's Négritude seeks to address, and it is in this context that his role in the formulation and dissemination of the concept has to be examined and evaluated.

We must first recall the origins and development of the movement, for Négritude has a history.[1] Its point of departure can be placed in Haiti, which evolved from the slave colony of Saint-Domingue and, after a war of independence, emerged as the independent Republic of Haiti in 1804. A substantial body of literature clustered around the notion of *noirisme* developed among the country's educated class in a movement that culminated in what has been called the "Haitian Renaissance" in the early years of the twentieth century.[2] Beyond the Haitians, we are obliged to acknowledge the accomplishment of the francophone black writers and intellectuals in their movement of cultural reclamation heralded by Martinican writer René Maran's forceful novel, *Batouala*, which was published in 1921 and won the Prix Goncourt – France's pre-eminent literary prize – that year. For all its ambiguity, Maran's work bears a special historic significance, anticipating Nigeria's Chinua Achebe by nearly four decades in the major areas of fictional reference and expressive modes that we have come to consider as distinctive of the African novel.

It bears stressing that Maran's literary achievement was in both cases linked to the repudiation of the colonial ideology, an effort carried on the stream of a reinvented narrative idiom, expressive of a black African sensibility and grounded in a celebration of the African culture and environment.

The term Négritude was later invented – as Senghor himself acknowledged – by the Martinican poet Aimé Césaire to designate the further reaches of these developments. In this respect, it is indeed curious that, though he did not invent the term, the concept of Négritude has come to be so closely associated with Léopold Senghor. It is instructive as a matter of historical record to recall the friendship between Senghor and Césaire, which began in the 1930s while they were both students at the Lycée Louis le Grand in Paris. This friendship led to a fruitful and sustained collaboration over five decades. Césaire employed the term Négritude in the early editions of *L'Etudiant Noir*, the student journal that he founded in Paris in the years between the two World Wars (1919–39) as a forum of reflection for the group of French-speaking black students and intellectuals – African and Caribbean – living in Paris at the time. For Césaire, Négritude served to designate a common sentiment of racial belonging, as a term of self- affirmation, a response made imperative by their condition as members of a humiliated race within the universe of life and experience imposed by French colonialism. Césaire went on, in his famous poem "Cahier d'un retour au pays natal ("Journal of a Homecoming", the first version of which appeared in 1939) to endow the term with a deeper meaning, to denote a collective racial endowment derived from an organic bond with the earth:

My Négritude is not a stone, its deafness thrown against the
Clamour of the day
My Négritude is not a film of dead water on the dead eye of
the day...

It thrusts into the red flesh of the soil
It thrusts into the warm flesh of the sky
It digs under the opaque dejection of its rightful patience.[3]

The broader significance of Négritude as a collective condition and a mode of experience was further elaborated by French Nobel laureate Jean-Paul Sartre in his celebrated essay "Orphée noir" (Black Orpheus), which he wrote as a preface to Senghor's 1948 anthology of francophone black poets.[4] Sartre's essay defined Négritude in the terms of his existentialist philosophy as "the-being-in-the-world" of the black subject (*"l'être-dans-le-monde du noir"*). For him, the body of poetry on which he was commenting provided testimony of an awakening of consciousness to an objective collective situation and its inward resonances – a situation to which each poet in the anthology responded according to his own disposition and in an individual key of expression, but which brought them together in a shared relationship to history and, ultimately, to the universe.

In this perspective, we might distinguish the varied import of the term for the poets represented in the anthology. Thus, for Césaire, as a black person from the diaspora whose sense of history was centred on the ordeal of slavery and separation from his African homeland and inheritance, Négritude signified – as a function of his particular situation – an anguished quest for belonging, for an identity grounded in the collective historical and spiritual estate of the race. For Senghor, Négritude had an even more specific meaning, as a term connoting the project of dis-alienation of the assimilated African, of a self-definition, in relation to an immediate African background, a gesture that implied the moral obligation to assume his African identity in all of its implications. Here, we touch on the fundamental theme of all of Senghor's writing – of his poetry, as of his cultural and ideological writings.

The Poetry

It is no platitude to observe that Senghor's poetry is deeply marked by the colonial experience. This is not merely a statement of fact, a banal observation, but one that goes to the very roots of his inspiration in its dual manifestation – as poetic expression and as ideological construction. In their contextual references, his poems reflect a response to the objective circumstances of the colonial situation, understood in the first place in its global manifestation as the imposition of alien, white rule on the black world. The generative principle of Senghor's poetry – as indeed of his writing in general – derives from the dissident stance he assumes towards the colonial principle and the framework of life and awareness it stipulates for the black race. This aspect of Senghor's poetry emerges clearly in his poems, which, in their subjective import, are proof of the tensions involved in his ambiguous situation as a man of two worlds, astride two cultures, both sharply differentiated, and yet each with a claim on his allegiance and, ultimately, on his deepest responses. Senghor's poetry can be read as an extended meditation in varied registers on his burden of what African-American intellectual, W.E.B. Du Bois, famously called "double consciousness" (see Morris in this volume): in effect, as a narrative of this condition as a lived dilemma of existence and the adventure of will occasioned by this drama. In other words, Senghor's is a poetry of a reconversion of consciousness that is the necessary condition for the attainment of a full sense of self. In a profound sense, the poetry represents the record of a spiritual adventure inherent in situations and the existential project it becomes an obligation to assume.

We begin to take a measure of Senghor's predicament in the poems that constitute his first volume of the 1956 collection *Chants d'ombre* ("Shadow Poems"), poems which fully enact his crisis of identity.[5]

In *"Lettre à un poète"* ("Letter to a Poet") , we have both an encomium addressed to Césaire and a definition of the black poet's mission. In the declamatory character of the verse, we can discern a heroic tone which serves to recall the poet's antecedents. In the allusion to *"les princes légitimes"* ("the legitimate princes") we recognise a note of dissidence, a rejection of French colonial imposition and a statement of the Senegalese poet's fidelity to his origins.

This background lends force to Senghor's evocation in "Nuit de Sine" of the Sine-Saloum valley: the homeland of the Serer, his Senegalese ethnic group. The recalling of the familiar environment of his childhood is tinged with nostalgia. The poem presents a vision of a lost inheritance – the ideal home that he was later to name "the kingdom of childhood". Beyond the physical nature of darkness that night embodies, it is evoked here as conducive to an atmosphere of peace and reflection, associated with an environment endowed with mystic significance. Night serves as a natural figure of blackness, evoked here in its positive significance, revalued in its association with the black race. Night becomes the very expression of Négritude. Years later, this theme was to be given further elaboration in the volume *Nocturnes*.[6]

The idea of "return to origins" emerges as the organising theme of Senghor's poetry as dictated by his situation. This theme is given an unequivocal statement in *"Porte dorée"* ("The Golden Gate"). The lines are worth quoting:

I have chosen to live next to the rebuilt wall of my memory
And from the top of the high ramparts
I remember Joal-of-the-Shades
The face of the land of my blood.[7]

Beyond childhood and origins, Senghor's poetry also recalls the peripeteia of his life adventure. A prominent feature is his direct experience of the Second World War. The 1948 volume *Hosties noires* ("Black Hosts") is a recollection.[8] Senghor fought for the French army between 1939 and 1942, narrowly escaping death in a German prisoner-of-war camp. *Hosties noires* is dominated by the tragic memory of war and desolation, hence its elegiac tone. But it also takes on the character of homage to his black comrades, as an expression of a solidarity announced in the "Liminary Poem":

Who can praise you, if not your brother-in-arms
your brother in blood
You, Senegalese soldiers, my brothers with warm hands ... Lying under
ice and death.[9]

In "Taga for Mbaye Diop", as in other poems on this theme, notably *"Retour de l'enfant prodigue"* ("Return of the Prodigal Son"), poetry becomes a celebration of the nobility of the soul of the black soldiers. *Hosties noires* develops further as a volume that gives vent to Senghor's feelings of resentment as a colonial subject in the service of France. This tone is sustained by the expression of his disillusionment with France and the white world, whose negative aspects he has witnessed first-hand.

As against the theme of disillusionment with France and the white world, the poems build up a panoply of an authentic African culture. This is not a simple or naive exoticism, but a poetry of rediscovery. A whole series of poems turn on this theme, which finds its culmination in "Black Woman", presented as a primordial figure, the embodiment of the race, and the Muse. The feminine principle that the black woman represents is evoked in the concluding lines as a universal reference:

Naked woman, black woman

I sing your passing beauty and fix it for all Eternity

Before jealous Fate reduces you to ashes to nourish the roots of life.[10]

This vision of the black woman inspires the affirmative tone of this declaration:

They call us men of cotton, coffee, and oil

They call us men of death

But we are men of dance, whose feet draw strength

As we pound upon firm ground.[11]

The tellurism here goes with a strongly articulated historical consciousness: given expression in other poems such as "Chaka" in which the vicissitudes of a life of action and the South African warrior-hero's web of emotions are given dramatic representation. This accounts for the epic tone of the poem, in which some of the lines are governed by the aesthetic of the praise poem – *izibongo*.[12] There seems indeed to be an element of the identification of the poet with his subject, so that it is possible to read the poem as an externalisation of his own experience of dual status as political leader and creative artist. Indeed, Chaka emerges from Senghor's poem as a romantic hero: warrior and lover, an individual in whom contradictory impulses are at play.

Senghor's poetry exhibits a broad range of themes and dispositions, but their essential focus remains the black experience. The examples cited may serve to illustrate his preoccupations and his varied tones of address. They point especially to the fact that, in his poetry, the concept of Négritude assumed both a dramatic and an introspective significance.

An important dimension of this is that poetry came to represent an aesthetic reflection of human experience. Thus, beyond the reference to the black experience and the polemical significance of his poetry, a vivid sense of poetry in relation to the universe permeates Senghor's expression. This is an approach Senghor derived from his acquaintance with modern post-Romantic literature already intimated in French writer, Victor Hugo, and given full development in the Symbolism of Gallic poets Charles Pierre Baudelaire, Paul Verlaine, and especially Stéphane Mallarmé, leading to the discovery of the concept of Surrealism.

The African references in Senghor's poetry lend credence to the new orientation of French poetry. From the African point of view, we are dealing here not with a form of exoticism, much less of primitivism, but a mode of reconnection – a recuperation of the spiritual resources of African societies and cultures, as a foundation for an envisaged future of fulfilment. Senghor's works of prose represent the elaboration, in practical terms, of this project.

The Cultural and Ideological Writings

If in his poetry Senghor proceeds to a celebration of Africa in the evocative terms of imaginative expression, his works of prose constitute a demonstration in the idiom of debate and argument of Africa's cultural resources.

A polemical strain runs through his writing: the staunch defence and illustration of Africa as a realm of thought and culture. Négritude thus represents a new humanism: the title of Senghor's first prose collection, *Négritude et humanisme* ("Négritude and Humanism") (1964).[13]

For Senghor, the elaboration and justification of an African system of thought was central to his vocation. This project was elaborated and sustained over a long writing career, demonstrated by the multiple array of topics and the ample scope of his essays. These have been collected in five volumes, each highlighting the poet-president's interests, over time, as intellectual figure and political leader: *Négritude et humanisme*; *Nation et voie africaine du socialisme* ("Nationhood and the African Road to Socialism"); *Négritude et civilisation de universel* ("Négritude and Civilization of the Universal"); *Socialisme et planification* ("Socialism and Planning"); and *Le Dialogue des cultures* ("The Dialogue of Cultures").[14]

These titles indicate the multiple perspectives of Senghor's thought, as a function of an active involvement in the cultural and intellectual life of the race. We could also cite other incidental or occasional texts, such as his long essay on the French Jesuit philosopher Pierre Teilhard de Chardin, which was warmly received at the time of its publication in 1962.[15] This represents, by all accounts, a considerable output. Senghor was an active creator of a modern current of African thought and expression. Two further aspects of this literature deserve comment. On humanism, what is proposed in Senghor's essays is not merely a rehabilitation but a revaluation of Africa as a cultural area, a universe of values. This required a redefinition of the universal canons of thought in the light of developments within Western philosophy and scholarship.

The second aspect is the dominant idea and leitmotif of the "African Personality". A whole background of scholarship and learning has gone into the development of Senghor's thought. These are more than incidental influences, and are key elements in the construction of his thought. We can cite here the influence of German philosopher, Friedrich Nietzsche, French philosopher, Henri Bergson, and German ethnologist, Leo Frobenius: their inauguration of a mode of thought animated by a vitalist outlook on the world.

Senghor's formulation of Négritude was enabled by his efforts to open Western thought to alternatives to pure rationalism. His language adapted to this mode of thought, and was removed from rhetorical and expository methods of classical models. There was no longer a distinction of sharp categories but the language was evocative and intuitive, springing from a deep layer of affectivity. This explains what Senghor intended when he spoke of the role of emotion in cognition. Hence, his famous dichotomy, his differentiation: "L'emotion est nègre comme la raison hellène"[16] ("Emotion is Black; reason is Hellenic").

Perhaps a reconciliation of both is necessary. But seeking recognition for African modes of thought, Senghor's approach consists in a strategy of differentiation: the elaboration of a metaphysics of difference. Senghor also promoted a socialism derived from "Humanism". This expression was of a communal ethos, and was a common thread in African discourse. Communalism represented a free adherence to a social programme informed by a moral ideal.

The Négritude Debate

Senghor often highlighted the dual character of African nationalism: not only protest and political activity as a challenge to colonial institutions and a claim to legitimacy, but the cultural propositions of nationalism. This is the framework of the African Renaissance: a movement of reconstruction.

From this point of view, the literature of African nationalism within which Négritude is embedded represents a dissident discourse, a counter-discourse. As we have seen, this impulse predates Senghor and the Négritude movement. We have to go back to the eighteenth century and the body of literature now known as "slave narratives" by writers like the Nigerian Olaudah Equiano.[17]

For the intellectual formulation, the pioneer figure is the nineteenth-century black cultural leader Edward Wilmot Blyden (see Introduction and Khadiagala in this volume) and his concept of the African Personality.[18] Blyden has been called "the Father of Pan-Africanism". His cultural vision recognises three dimensions – black, Arab/Islamic and Western – resonating with the ideas of Nigeria's

Nnamdi Azikiwe (see Robinson in this volume), Ghana's Kwame Nkrumah (see Biney in this volume), and Kenya's Ali Mazrui (see Ndlovu-Gatsheni in this volume). Senghor recognises Blyden as an ancestral intellectual forerunner when he describes Négritude as the francophone equivalent of Blyden's notion of the African Personality. A distinctive feature of Blyden's scheme is the reclamation of the Arab/Islamic heritage as a component of the African heritage of values. Senghor was to integrate this aspect into his own system of thought, which is now generally accepted.[19]

This brings us to the case of South Africa. We might locate the beginnings of the "African Renaissance" in Pixley Seme's 1906 Columbia University speech, "The Regeneration of Africa"[20] (see Ngqulunga in this volume) and the work of writers such as Tiyo Soga, Benedict Vilakazi and Sol Plaatje, whose 1913 novel, *Mhudi*, builds on an ancestral myth to recount the fortunes of a primordial couple as symbolic of the very genesis of African self-awareness.[21] This narrative strategy has been reprised by the contemporary South African writer Zakes Mda in his historical novel, *The Heart of Redness* (2000).[22] The force of statement in Plaatje's work and much of this early literature in South Africa determined the character of an African awakening in what may be considered the first Renaissance, anticipating developments that were to follow on a broader front in later years.

Senegal's Cheikh Anta Diop also focused on the theme of the African Renaissance and its Egyptian origins, ascribing ancient Egyptian civilisation to Africa.[23] While acknowledging these developments, we must also note objections which have fuelled a controversy around the concept of Négritude. Two prominent figures in the controversy around the concept have been South Africa's Ezekiel Mphahlele and Nigerian Nobel laureate Wole Soyinka (see Osha in this volume).

Mphahlele his 1974 book, *The African Image*, dismissed Négritude as a "cult".[24] I believe he was put off by the extreme intellectualism of Senghor – a legacy of French education – and his francophone collaborators. Soyinka made a similar observation, describing Négritude in 1966 as "this magnitude of unfelt abstractions".[25] The Nigerian Nobel laureate proposed his own system of abstractions in his 1993 essay "The Fourth Stage", in which he developed an elaborate construction of a mythical structure of thought around the figure of Ogun, the Yoruba god of iron.[26]

South African philosopher-activist Steve Biko also developed the idea of Black Consciousness in the 1970s, which has affinities and parallels with Négritude in the specific context of apartheid (see Pityana in this volume). In his posthumous 1978 collection of essays, *I Write What I Like*, Biko pays attention as much to political issues as to cultural ones. He defines "Black Consciousness" as a reversal of the feeling of inferiority inculcated by apartheid, an ideology calculated to induce a feeling of "incompleteness" in black people. Biko summarised his ideology in his response to the judge at his May 1976 trial:

> I think basically Black Consciousness refers itself to the black man and to his situation, and I think the black man is subjected to two forces in this country. He is first of all oppressed by an external world through institutionalized machinery, through laws that restrict him from doing certain things, through heavy work conditions, through poor pay, through very difficult living conditions, through poor education, these are all external to him, and secondly, and this we regard as the most important, the black man in himself has developed a certain state of alienation, he rejects himself, precisely because he attaches the meaning white to all that is good, in other words he associates good and he equates good with white.[27]

Biko further speaks of the self-negation of the black subject, so that, as he notes, "you tend to begin to feel that there is something incomplete in your humanity".[28] As we know, Biko paid with his life for his defence of the humanity of black South Africans.

Finally, with South African president Thabo Mbeki (1999–2008), the notion of an African Renaissance assumed a new and urgent connotation. Mbeki focused on modernisation, continental rebirth and cultural equality, calling for new institutions and new attitudes. His modernisation was a collective project that was both technological and moral. It was, in essence, a project of African reconstruction. For Mbeki, the African Renaissance was essentially pragmatic: he felt that governance was a technical vocation requiring knowledge and skills (see also Adebajo on Mbeki in this volume).[29]

Concluding Reflections: The Legacy

In concluding this essay, it is important to note that African-American scholar Reiland Rabaka described Négritude as "an insurgent idea".[30] In both his poetry and ideological writings, Léopold Senghor's innovative work represents an extended rebuttal of the colonial ideology. His work was monumental in two senses: first, it was both abundant and comprehensive. Secondly, Senghor's oeuvre represented an enduring testimony to African intellectual capacities.

In his ideological writings, Senghor provided a systematic defence of the African inheritance. Its recreation exists in the very process of formulation, in the sense of Congolese philosopher V.Y. Mudimbe's use of *inventio* as a creative process.[31] (See Opoku-Agyemang and Thiam in this volume.) Ultimately, Négritude represented Senghor's worldview. The Senegalese poet joined the ancestors in 2001, and became one of their company. As we are encouraged to think in our traditional systems of thought, we must imagine him watching over us with benevolence.

31

WOLE SOYINKA: OGUN'S BARD

Sanya Osha

BORN ON 13 JULY 1934 in the historic Yoruba town of Abeokuta in south-western Nigeria, Wole Soyinka was described by his equally great compatriot, the novelist Chinua Achebe, as being gifted with "stupendous energy".[1] Achebe was right. Soyinka is, indeed, a man of many parts, activities and endowments: dramatist, poet, novelist, social activist, connoisseur of fine wines, hunter of wild game, raconteur extraordinaire, film producer, winner of the Nobel Prize for Literature in 1986, and composer of caustic political songs.

The Post-Colonial Renaissance Temper

Soyinka is simultaneously a biographer's delight and discomfort. The diffused nature of his interests and talents, on the one hand, makes him an exceedingly engaging subject. On the other hand, it could end up frustrating and exhausting even the most indefatigable admirer on account of his sheer prodigiousness. Arguably, he can be described as the ultimate "Renaissance man" of the post-colonial era in an age marked by an increasingly delimiting ethos of disciplinary specialisation and neoliberal downsizing and deregulation. Soyinka readily resists the imposition of easy or facile categorisations in a constant bid to attain and master ever more epistemologically challenging horizons. This factor alone makes him perhaps Africa's most engrossing literary personality.

Soyinka's main literary genre is drama. He has published 30 works of drama, including full-length plays, radio drama pieces and skits. In addition, he has published two highly experimental novels, *The Interpreters* (1965) and

Season of Anomie (1973), as well as eight volumes of poetry and five works of autobiographical writing in which he explores various aspects of his native Yoruba culture. He received early dramatic training in England, which he first visited in 1954 after a brief stint at the University College Ibadan (UCI, now the University of Ibadan). At the University of Leeds, he studied English literature and mingled with various artistic collectives, exploring and honing his craft as a young playwright. He then returned to Nigeria at the dawn of independence in 1960 thanks to a Rockefeller Foundation fellowship, which allowed him to conduct research across the West African coast.

Personal Cost of a Civil War

It was the best of times and the worst of times for post-independence Nigeria. Independence generated a tremendous amount of optimism, but there were also already signs of impending misrule, graft and venality among the ruling elite. Soyinka, characteristically, very quickly read these discouraging premonitions.

In January 1966, the first military *coup d'état* occurred in the country. This marked the beginning of a disconcerting series of coups and counter-coups that would irreparably impair the political development of the nation. Eventually, the first set of coups led to the Nigerian civil war (1967–70) and provided the first major opportunity for Soyinka to intervene in the Nigerian public sphere. Perhaps this view ought to be modified. During the political turmoil that followed the removal of Obafemi Awolowo as premier of the Western Region and his replacement by the voluble Samuel Ladoke Akintola, Soyinka is reputed to have held up a radio station at gun point on 15 October 1965 during an undoubtedly brash effort to change the political status quo. Needless to say, this was just the commencement of a phase of his creative life in which he always sought to combine the roles and responsibilities of a man of letters with those of a man of action.

Before the onset of the civil war, Soyinka had embarked on a desperate trip to the secessionist enclave of Biafra in order to avert a national catastrophe. His efforts did not yield the expected results. Instead, for his troubles, the federal side, led by General Yakubu Gowon, imprisoned the playwright for 22 months, most of which time he spent in solitary confinement. The experience did not dull, in the least, Soyinka's creative sensibilities and efforts, which had been in full flow before his imprisonment.

Before confinement, Soyinka had written several well-regarded plays such as *The Lion and the Jewel* (1959). He had also published his landmark novel, *The Interpreters* (1965), whose experimental and transgressive elements have continued to awe both critics and admirers. *The Interpreters*, for many, might be a difficult read, but it never fails to provide a rewarding account of an odd assortment of young idealists engaged in a variety of social experiments.[2] In other words, the book can be construed as an irreverent paean to youth with principles of idealism and courage. The novel also displayed the unusually eclectic turn of Soyinka's mind, which, over the course of several decades, has remained unfailingly inquisitive and sharp.

While in prison, Soyinka wrote another significant work, *The Man Died* (1972), which immediately became a classic of prison literature. In the book, he advanced his famous axiom, "justice constitutes the first condition of humanity".[3] The memoir – the first in a series analysing the intractable Nigerian condition and Soyinka's own personal involvement in it – often reads like a complex concatenation of intellectual exercises devised to ward off mental atrophy, and an elaborate ploy of self-preservation.[4] Indeed, the book can be regarded as a deft intellectual strategy for maintaining self-dignity in the face of enforced humiliation and psychological abjection.

Once released from jail at the end of the civil war in 1970, Soyinka ventured into self-exile in Ghana (where he had a spell editing *Transition*, the landmark Pan-African cultural journal), undoubtedly to create some distance between himself and the traumatic experiences of incarceration. Shortly after, he was offered a fellowship at the University of Cambridge between 1973 and 1974, which served as the beginning of another fertile period for him. Several major literary works such as *The Bacchae of Euripides* (1973), *Camwood on the Leaves* (1973), *Jero's Metamorphosis* (1973) and *Death and the King's Horseman* (1975) were completed during this time. He also began a fruitful relationship with the youthful duo of Henry Louis Gates Jr and Kwame Anthony Appiah (see Ampiah in this volume), who both subsequently became major scholars of African-American studies at Yale, Duke, and Harvard universities.

Man of Letters, Man of Action

At Cambridge, Soyinka worked on his book of literary criticism, *Myth, Literature and the African World* (1976). As with other works of his, this book of essays polarised critics and admirers, with prominent Nigerian literary scholar Isidore Okpewho dismissing it as "a learned waste of time".[5] Opting to eschew recognised protocols of literary criticism and theory, Soyinka advanced an alternative conception of Africanity, the African imagination and cosmogony.[6] As usual, there is a blurring of genres, discourses and preoccupations that can be by turns frustrating, overwhelming or exhilarating, depending on the reader's tastes.

However, less controversial works such as the widely acclaimed *Death and the King's Horseman* also emerged during this period. With this play, Soyinka proved himself to be an unquestioned master of the dramatic arts, in which his diverse knowledge of several cultures and literary traditions (ancient Greek, contemporary Western and Yoruba culture) was successfully demonstrated. He had spent many years studying ancient Greek dramaturgy, knowledge of which often informs his plays. Soyinka also has a fascination and relationship with literary language similar to that of the Irish novelist James Joyce. Least of all, he immersed himself deeply in Yoruba culture, language and traditions, as is evident in his translations of the works of D.O. Fagunwa, the foremost master of the early Yoruba novel. The Nobel laureate assembled these various backgrounds, traditions and influences in fashioning his distinctive artistic identity. Thus Soyinka's artistic profile is about the endless working and reworking of this disparate array of elements which have ultimately gifted the world of culture with a unique body of dramatic literature, and also secured his position as Africa's leading and most inventive playwright.

However, this is merely one aspect of Soyinka's exemplary dramaturgy. Another significant facet is the satirical nature of many of his plays in which African despots such as Uganda's Idi Amin, Equatorial Guinea's Macías Nguema, the Central African Republic's (CAR) Jean-Bédel Bokassa and Nigeria's Sani Abacha are viciously lampooned for their autocracy and governance failures. Along with Kenya's Ngũgĩ wa Thiong'o and fellow South African Nobel laureate Nadine Gordimer, Soyinka strongly believes that the literary arts need to be put in the service of worthy socio–political causes. In other words, literature has to act as bullets, relentlessly inflicting damage upon the bombastic facade of tyrannical power.

Of course, the belief in the social responsibility of literature – an activist literature – has often landed Soyinka in political trouble. One notable case was during the regime of the nefarious General Sani Abacha (1993–8) when Soyinka had to flee Nigeria on a motorcycle, disguised as a woman, to neighbouring

Benin. The Nobel laureate had raised Abacha's ire by his stance on the annulled presidential election of 12 June 1993, widely believed to have been won by Moshood Abiola. Once in exile, Soyinka promptly launched a wide range of pro-democracy movements to ensure that Nigeria returned to popular government. One such notable initiative was the pirate radio station Radio Kudirat, which was established as a pro-democracy platform in honour of the slain wife of Abiola. She had been murdered in June 1996 in broad daylight on the streets of Lagos, reportedly by the treacherous goons of Sani Abacha at the height of the struggle for democracy.

Even before this important attempt at relaunching Nigerian democracy, Soyinka had been critical of the criminal profligacy of the civilian administration of Shehu Shagari (1979–83) during which he released *Unlimited Liability Company* (1983), an album of songs satirising the corrupt civilian government. Beginning from the 1980s, Soyinka's dramatic output decreased, and he started to focus more on writing memoirs such as *Aké: The Years of Childhood* (1982), which signalled yet another aspect of his multivalent writing and talents. His earlier recondite writing often alienated popular readers, whereas in *Aké*, Soyinka is lucid, unfailingly engaging, and unusually willing to communicate directly with the reader without recourse to his usual eclecticism, pedantry and excessive verbal pyrotechnics.[7] Earlier in his career, critics such as Nigeria's Chinweizu Ibekwe had consistently labelled Soyinka as obscurantist, and a lackey of Western literary traditions.[8] These were invectives that Soyinka successfully managed to evade in the endearing offering of *Aké*, which explored his childhood, the world of his parents, and the south-western Yoruba town in which he had spent his formative years.

A few years later, in 1986, Soyinka was honoured with the award of the Nobel Prize for Literature. Unlike many globally acclaimed literary figures who retreat from the public domain once honoured, Soyinka's public-spirited engagements and other genres of writing markedly intensified after the award of the prize. For example, more memoirs followed such as *Isara: A Voyage around Essay* (1989), written as a homage to his father's homestead; and *Ibadan: The Penkelemes Years – A Memoir, 1945–1965* (1994), penned as a paean to the historic Yoruba city where Soyinka enjoyed immensely stimulating stints as a pupil of the renowned Government College Ibadan, and the University College Ibadan, as well as working as a research fellow and lecturer at the university.[9]

In Ibadan, Soyinka met Nigeria's greatest poet, Christopher Okigbo. He also met and interacted with other notable pillars of African literature and culture such as John Pepper Clark, Chinua Achebe, Duro Ladipo, Tunji Oyelana, Jimi Solanke, the German scholar and cultural activist Ulli Beier, Austrian artist Susanne Wenger, and many other formidable individuals working in drama, poetry and visual culture who clustered around the famous Mbari artistic collective. Ibadan is often touted as the birthplace of modern Nigerian letters owing to the sheer number of major African writers who sought refuge in the city at this time.

Even before independence, Ibadan had gained prominence as a veritable hub of culture in Nigeria and perhaps the entire West African sub-region. Soyinka had been present during the height of the city's historical glory. This was a time of great ferment, experimentation, daring and adventure, with the future Nobel laureate at the centre of a wide range of cultural and political activities. This was also an epoch of tremendous promise, which propelled various categories of artists to explore and transcend different kinds of limits. The pace was intense, and this aligned with Soyinka's impatient and exploratory temperament. He hardly slowed down, even in his mid-eighties when most of his contemporaries such as Nadine Gordimer, Alex La Guma, Dennis Brutus, Lewis Nkosi, Chinua Achebe, André Brink and Abiola Irele had departed from the global stage.

Custodian and Innovator

Soyinka's literary, cultural and political concerns have hardly changed since the beginning of his career when he was regarded as an *enfant terrible* in many quarters.

In his memorable book *The Burden of Memory, the Muse of Forgiveness* (1999), many of Soyinka's concerns about culture and politics are addressed. He focuses on the imperatives of truth and reconciliation in South Africa, which he calls a "zone of state engendered anomie", that apply just as much to Argentina, Chile, Sierra Leone, Rwanda, Somalia, Liberia and, in his own country, Nigeria. Soyinka's thesis is that "one of the pillars on which a durable society must be founded [is] – Responsibility – and ultimately – Justice".[10] It is also noteworthy that he reiterates his famous maxim from *The Man Died*, "justice constitutes the first condition of humanity".[11]

History remains central to Soyinka's concerns. On the historic importance of the Atlantic slave trade, he argues:

The Atlantic slave trade remains an inescapable critique of European humanism. In a different context, I have railed against the thesis that it was the Jewish Holocaust that placed the first question mark on all claims of European humanism – from the Renaissance through the Enlightenment to the present-day multicultural orientation. Insistence on that thesis, we must continue to maintain, merely provides further proof that the European mind has yet to come into full cognition of the African world as an equal sector of a universal humanity, for, if it had, its historic recollection would have placed the failure of European humanism centuries earlier – and that would be at the very inception of the Atlantic slave trade.[12]

Soyinka critically reminds us that "much of the division of Africa owed much more to a case of brandy and a box of cigars than to any intrinsic claims of what the boundaries enclosed".[13] But the Nobel laureate is not merely being dismissive here. Instead he is drawing attention to colonial forms of arbitrary territoriality and the destructiveness they have caused in the post-colonial era. The Organisation of African Unity (OAU) is also blamed for this balkanisation as it "formally consecrated this act of arrogant aggression".[14]

Undoubtedly, the Atlantic slave trade and the subsequent colonisation of Africa further entrenched the master–slave relationship between the continent and the West. In formulating a conception of humanism, Soyinka evokes the trauma caused by this relationship. However, he constantly draws attention to the generalised mismanagement of the continent by despots of all shades. In identifying the origins of the Atlantic slave trade and the dialectic of enslavement that transcends the moment of political liberation, he writes:

There are slaves in gilded cages and the world knows of others dangling on the gibbet, rotting on the magnolia tree. There are slaves as studs and slaves as victims of castration. There are married slaves and merely breeding slaves. And there are trusted slaves, keepers of the master's purse, commercial representatives who travel long distances on their master's business and return to give dutiful account. There are the virtual spouses, the *signares* of Senegal, whose status was no less than that of the mattress of the house. We have known slaves who, after manumission, aspire to inherit the kingdom of their erstwhile masters, sometimes even acquiring slaves in turn. But they have never been masters of their own existence, nor have they plotted their own destiny.[15]

Similarly, in the book *Harmattan Haze on an African Spring* (2012), Soyinka notes that the height of the genocidal campaign by the brutal Sudanese government-armed militia, the Janjaweed, against black-skinned Africans in the country's Darfur region was largely unnoticed by the global media, which preferred to focus on the inordinate furore caused by the cartoons of the Prophet Muhammad published in *Jyllands-Posten*, an obscure Danish newspaper. In Soyinka's view, "it is shortchanging the power of history to pretend that the events of the Sudan are not based on a perception that dates back to a relationship rooted in the history of slavery."[16]

Soyinka also alludes to similar massacres in Mauritania that reveal the prevalence of a master–slave relationship, which he considers to be the major cause of genocidal onslaughts. However, his claim does not reveal much about how the identities of master and slave came to be so immutably deadly. Rather than reading the ossification of native and settler identities through the prism of a colonial policy of "tribalisation" as the root cause of intolerance and the will to exterminate, Soyinka reduces the problem to one of slavery: "to slave master in the American Deep South and West Indies, including General Omar Bashir of Sudan, sections of humanity remain property, and ownership confers authority to dispose of one's items as wished – brand, amputate, castrate, rape, hang or eat them."[17]

Nigerian Battles: Between Defective Memory and the Public Lie

In 2015, Soyinka released yet another work of social criticism which caused considerable controversy in Nigeria and beyond. *Between Defective Memory and the Public Lie: A Personal Odyssey in the Republic of Liars* triggered great consternation, even among staunch Soyinka acolytes. The Nobel laureate employed the book to castigate detractors of all stripes. For example, his depiction of the former Nigerian president Olusegun Obasanjo was widely regarded as uncharitable. He also directs vicious attacks against Major R.O.A. Salawu, who was evidently a thorn in Soyinka's flesh.

To many, *Between Defective Memory and the Public Lie* appeared to be a gratuitous piece of self-indulgence directed mainly at Soyinka's real or perceived detractors and critics. As a piece of edifying writing, where does the book stand?

One is forced to say quite low on the level of art. The essays do not seek to soothe frayed nerves or draw upon the finer emotions, as is expected from much great writing. This is a book prompted by and written in anger, as Soyinka himself clearly revealed in press interviews. Even before its release, headlines screamed about Soyinka's intention to draw blood from those perceived to have wronged him in the past. So what is there to gain from the literary outburst of a man whom we have grown accustomed to displaying periodic public tantrums? One would have to admit: not much.

As with many other autobiographical offerings, Soyinka is more or less the sole protagonist in his own perennially interesting story. If he had chosen the path of Nobel respectability, a progressively empty and meaningless future might have been his, and then he would gradually have lost political relevance and probably become a less valued cultural icon. So, rather let him be the recalcitrant thorn in the side of all, forever irreverent, and ready to cause havoc like his Yoruba patron-god, Ogun.

Soyinka is still raging in his final days with an attitude that boldly declares: "I shall entertain you, I shall infuriate you, and by Jove, you shan't be bored!" It seems as if he is laughing to himself, and is not concerned with methodically demolishing the accusations of his critics, while creating delightful but intermittent bursts of scribal efflorescence. One could vaguely picture him: a grand old man of 81 at the time, gleefully giggling to himself and saying, "I'll get those bastards with yet another one of my poisoned darts." But too much vitriol might become too much of a demonstration of excessive mean-spiritedness, which trumps, or at least undermines, Soyinka's early espousals of supposedly basic, good-natured humanism.

It is not unusual that the Nobel laureate would court such considerable antagonism and dispute. He revels in strutting his stuff in the public realm, which in Nigeria, as elsewhere in Africa, is often a domain of amorality and impunity. Soyinka would have us believe that his interventions in that conflicted realm are informed by honour and good ethics. How successful has he been in transforming that fractious sphere? Certainly not very successful, judging from the list of personages who have managed to provoke his ire and others who will end up doing so when they have read this ill-tempered book.

Virtually no forensic evidence is presented to substantiate Soyinka's positions and views. It may well be that such evidence – even for reasons beyond his control – does not exist. The questions may thus be legitimately asked: Why go through the trouble of branding people liars, especially if the bulk of them are unsavoury attention-seekers? How edifying is this, and what are the literary merits involved? As earlier noted, perhaps the greatest merit of Soyinka's book is the fiery refusal – like Shakespeare's King Lear – to decline into grey, old and bored respectability. Indeed, old men should rage as much as possible against the dying of the light.

Soyinka's main grouse against former Nigerian head of state Olusegun Obasanjo (1999–2007), with whom he had often verbally sparred in the past, is that he had been judged by Obasanjo to be an inept political analyst, even though the politician noted he might be a skilled hunter of wild game and connoisseur of fine wines. Soyinka in turn described Obasanjo as "economically illiterate" in press interviews preceding the release of *Between Defective Memory and the Public Lie.*

The Nobel laureate is further able to demonstrate in his short book how the pathologies of power in Nigeria attract and nurture unsavoury characters, such as Salawu, Abiola Ogundokun and Godwin Daboh. According to Soyinka, these offensive characters surface each time there is a change of government. They offer their services to anyone interested in their penchant for slander, blackmail and all kinds of subversive activities usually committed on behalf of feckless public functionaries.[18]

Major Salawu is depicted by Soyinka as being thoroughly corrupt. Ogundokun built a professional career as a "smut disseminator". Obasanjo is dismissed as a "seasoned predator" who seems to have a seemingly inexhaustible capacity for "infantile mischief and for mind-boggling provocations", as described in a brief chapter satirically entitled "The Philosopher-King". Not all of Soyinka's adversaries are political figures. Chinweizu – an author of mixed Afrocentric credentials with a reputation for critiquing Soyinka at every opportunity for his perceived Eurocentric orientation – is a target of brutal excoriation, and is labelled a plagiarist to boot. Chinweizu is also branded a "Chichidodo", whose major characteristic as a bird is "a love of human excrement – but with a difference! As it dines on this human emission, it apparently makes a sound akin to *chichidodo* – to express how much the stuff disgusts it, thereafter resuming his feast with gusto."[19] Peter Enahoro – nicknamed "Peter Pan", an author and journalist – courts Soyinka's vexatious mood by suggesting that he was a common lackey of the brutal General Ibrahim Babangida. And for that criticism, Soyinka refused to shake hands with Enahoro when they met in public.

Often, the Nobel laureate's caustic attacks are not without wit. His writing continually straddles common Nigerian idiomatic expressions and standard

471

English to create an impact and ambience unique for native users of the English language. For example, a former governor of Ogun State, Gbenga Daniel, is given the moniker DaaniElebo. *Elebo* is a pun for both party animal and fetish lover, and can be employed interchangeably to devastating effect.

By all accounts, the Nobel laureate has always been close to those in the corridors of power or, at least, has often had direct access to them. According to his revelations, he has mostly been burnt by his close associations. It is often a wonder how he has remained productive in spite of the upheavals caused by his chosen public path. The Nobel laureate readily admits to have had dealings with "the poet Léopold Sédar Senghor (himself once a conscript and prisoner-of-war); traditional rulers like King Gbadebo II, Alake of Abeokuta, who would be chased off his throne by women; the revolutionary and fiery orator Fidel Castro; the urbane egg-head Bill Clinton; the reformist Paul Kagame; the take-no-prisoners Indira Gandhi; the universal avatar Nelson Mandela; the botanist Goodluck Jonathan; or the donnish Yar'Adua; not forgetting the know-all Olusegun Obasanjo".[20]

After all these years, Soyinka's passionate involvement in the Nigerian public sphere remains undiminished. It is indeed a boon that he has not suffered the fate of many gallant Nigerian public figures and intellectuals who exercised their obligations to intervene in the public domain and consequently suffered for it, sometimes at the cost of their lives. Christopher Okigbo, Ken Saro-Wiwa, Dele Giwa, Alfred Rewane, Kudirat Abiola and Bola Ige all come readily to mind in this regard. It is difficult to imagine any other author in the world with the ability to get away with many of the things that Soyinka says and does. Such fame is very likely to make him one of the few public intellectuals worthy of attention.

In many quarters, Soyinka's *Between Defective Memory and the Public Lie* fuelled apprehensions about the deteriorating quality of his work and the considerable tarnishing of his reputation. Some also felt that he appeared to be deliberately rubbishing the veneer of respectability expected of his age and status. But if respectability demands unnatural restraint and bourgeois complacency, then it definitely is not meant for Soyinka. Where other distinguished authors would rather fade into the mists of oblivion, Soyinka's rage and intractableness are what will continue to ensure that he is not forgotten in the Nigerian public sphere.

In addition, other critics have correctly observed that power is perhaps Soyinka's overriding concern. Power features prominently in the Nobel laureate's public life and creative work. Soyinka was a formidable adversary of the dictatorship of General Sani Abacha (1993–8), about whom he wrote the biting satirical play *King Baabu* (2002).[21] However, the Nobel laureate managed to maintain an unusually cozy relationship with the preceding regime of General Ibrahim Babangida (1985–93). On the face of it, it is easy to separate both regimes. However, on closer examination, the two are linked by the same dialectic of terror, chicanery and despotism. Abacha was Babangida's *de facto* number two. When Babangida was forced from power in August 1993, Abacha was left to shield the preceding administration and to establish its continuity after its apparent formal demise. Babangida remained untouched by Abacha, which further reinforces the line of continuity. Soyinka's analysis of both regimes would have us believe that there was a rupture between the two, when, in reality, both were effectively two sides of the same coin. Soyinka's fascination with, and closeness to, power sometimes besmirches the moral lens through which he observes and assesses its often devastating impacts.

In his writing, Soyinka is also weighed down by his inability to make himself vulnerable or, in a similar manner, cast himself in the role of the uncomplicated anti-hero. Vulnerability may not always mean unattractive weakness, as Soyinka might perhaps think. Indeed, it could mean an empathetic demonstration of humaneness, and a voice seeking a larger context of fellowship and community through innocent disclosure. However, Soyinka's lone voice in the midst of moral degeneration can sometimes seem quaint and unreal: an entity that bluntly discourages the establishment of a relationship with the Other. He becomes a caricature of the hero as the most unlikely and forbidding anti-hero. One certainly does not want to saunter down a broken provincial path seeking warmth and comfort from that fierce, uncompromising and unforgiving voice.

In a similar vein, other critics have noted that Soyinka is always the sole hero in all of his narratives. There invariably looms the figure of the hero as an all-time favourite or an insufferable cultural bugbear. The predictability of this persona sometimes becomes a trifle too heavy: a caricature that floats without an anchor and in urgent need of puncturing to plunge it back to earth. It appears that Soyinka is congenitally incapable of an inversion of persona to achieve a different set of results. All he has left is his unrelieved anger and self-righteousness as the mediating ingredients of his writings. With time, all of this can become rather wearisome.[22]

Concluding Reflections

Soyinka's strong views on crucial African political issues have always been integral to his work. In traditional Yoruba society, the *are* – artist and intellectual – served as both custodian of tradition and innovator. He lived an itinerant lifestyle in the manner of Lagbayi, the transcendental Yoruba sculptor, spreading and renewing culture, investigating the limits of knowledge, and affirming the verities of exilic existence. Wole Soyinka is a man of many gifts and preoccupations: leading African dramatist, engaging novelist, poet of the post-colonial African Renaissance, iconoclastic cineaste, indefatigable political activist, prisoner of conscience, musician with a singularly acidic social vision, translator of D.O. Fagunwa's universe of unique tales, defender of traditional African customs and values, and incomparable essayist of Africa's seemingly intractable existential predicament. Soyinka is in every sense an *are*, serving as a global public intellectual, proclaiming the values and virtues of Yoruba culture in a cosmopolitan idiom. In this way, he has revealed himself to be simultaneously both a custodian of culture and a vital innovator.

Derek Walcott: Black Power and "The Myth of My Own Self"

Vladimir Lucien

"He publishes everyday the newspaper of himself in the journal he
now keeps. The craftsman, the artisan, has become the writer. Crusoe
can now look at Crusoe as at another object. It is this act that saves his
sanity."[1]
— Derek Walcott, "The Figure of Crusoe"

"When I enter my house, it will be a tower.
There I will paint with blood and brain,
The myth of my own self"[2]
— Ozzy King, "The Myth of My Own Self"

Derek Walcott was born in Castries, St Lucia, on 23 January 1930, and died
on 17 March 2017. He was one of the Caribbean's most celebrated poets as well
as a prolific and influential playwright and, indisputably, one of the region's
most seminal thinkers. In 1992, he received the Nobel Prize for Literature, for
what the Swedish Academy described as "a poetic oeuvre of great luminosity,
sustained by a historical vision ... the outcome of a multicultural commitment".[3]
Having been born and raised in colonial St Lucia, Walcott sought from the
outset to challenge the depredations of colonialism and to reflect on existential
questions posed by it. These remained his main concerns throughout his career:
the supposed tension between Walcott's commitment to the Caribbean, and his
love and sense of belonging to some of what he inherited from the coloniser,

chief among these being the English language and its poetic tradition. This tension took on manifold manifestations throughout Walcott's life.

From an early age, Walcott proved himself a prodigy, publishing his first poem at 14 in a local newspaper and his first collection of poetry, *25 Poems* (self-published and financed by his mother), in 1948 at the age of 18. This was followed by another collection, *Epitaph for the Young*, the following year. Thereafter, Walcott published 25 books of poetry and wrote 25 plays, along with books of essays and other publications. In 1959 he founded the Trinidad Theatre Workshop (TTW), one of the most formidable theatre ensembles the Caribbean has ever seen. This was later followed by the founding of the Boston Playwrights' Theatre in 1981. Having lived and taught abroad for many years – including extended stints in the United States, and shorter stints later in Canada and Italy – and having for years written poems about his remote island with the intensity of vision and depth of understanding of language's inner magic, as British poet Robert Graves put it, Walcott made himself into an infrangible global figure, poet and grand citizen of the English language, as well as a literary icon of the Caribbean – the two worlds he claimed passionately in his work and life.

One of the things that marred my early reading of Derek Walcott's essay "The Muse of History" (1974) was what seemed to be an embittered tone. He seemed to be critiquing the ideals and proponents of Black Power and the revolution of consciousness that had swept through the Caribbean during the late 1960s and the 1970s. But Walcott here was in defence mode. For he had come under scrutiny, and was reviled by some during this period. The choice presented to him had to do with authenticity: to become authentically "black" by an abandonment of what was "non-black" – the culture of the coloniser. And being a choice of authenticity, this was also a choice of "reality". So, in the ultimatum posed to Walcott by the concept of Black Power, there was also the question of whether he would cease to be "real": whether, because he embraced a mixed heritage beyond his own black heritage, including what could be seen as the coloniser's, he would become obsolete, unintelligible, dismissed: become nothing.

The theme of "nothing" and "nothingness" has loomed over Caribbean discourses for decades, and is a charge that has been laid against the region both from within and without. The visiting British historian James Anthony Froude pronounced that "There are no people there in the true sense of the word, with a character and purpose of their own."[4] (See Cudjoe in this volume.) Decades later, the Trinidadian Nobel Literature laureate V.S. Naipaul would similarly proclaim: "History is built around achievement and creation and nothing was created in the West Indies."[5] In Naipaul's statement, and implicitly in Froude's, is the notion that, to operate outside a history that defined itself around "creation and achievement" – understood in a subjective way, of course – was to be nobody, half-made: to live half a life. The irony is that Black Power offered Walcott similarly despairing and limiting parameters of being. To Black Power, then, in defence of the self, Walcott responded acerbically:

> Those who peel from their own leprous flesh, their names,
> who chafe and nurture the scars of rusted chains,
> like primates favouring scabs, those who charge tickets
> for another free ride on the middle passage,
> those who explain to the peasant why he is African,
> their catamites and eunuchs banging tambourines,
> whores with slave bangles banging tambourines
> and the academics crouched like rats
> listening to tambourines ...[6]

The eminent Jamaican critic and poet Edward Baugh, in his essay "The West Indian Writer and His Quarrel with History" (1977), regarded "The Muse of History" as the "discursive theoretical twin of Chapter 22"[7] of Walcott's long poem "Another Life". Baugh noted that Chapter 22 was actually initially published as a stand-alone poem, entitled "The Muse of History at Rampanalgas". In my reading, however, I found Walcott's essay, in tone and argument, to be deeply related to the infamous Chapter 19 in which he excoriated and mocked Black Power, and pointed to the irony of similar degradation and limitations imposed on the black man by the espousal of an identical convention of history to that of the former colonisers and an obsession with being the arbiters of truth, definition, and "measuring" *within* the black race – just as the coloniser had:

> they measure the skulls with calipers
> and pronounce their measure
> of toms, of traitors, of traditionals and Afro-Saxons.
> They measure them carefully
> as others measured the teeth
> of men and horses, they measure and divide.[8]

I actually returned to Walcott's essay through American jazz artist Sun Ra. Ra did not mention Walcott, nor did he quote him. But he said something in a 1981 interview that threw me headlong into Walcott's essays in *What the Twilight Says*, specifically "The Muse of History". Ra warned:

> And a lot of things black people dealing with have proven to be not profitable. Of course, they try to base things on the truth, but the truth is no longer acceptable, you see. Not to the creator. Because when they took Christ and put him on the cross and he said I am the truth, they eliminated the truth. You see, you're dealing with cosmic equations so when he says I am the truth and they crucified him, they crucified truth. It doesn't exist anymore. So you can't use it. If you do you'll be just like it. So what you have now, you got to deal with the *myth*. Particularly the black race, they got to stop everything and realize whatever they doing is not profitable. Don't care if it's righteous. Don't care if it's the truth. It's not doing anything. So then they have to deal with something else. Deal with the myth. [9]

In returning to the argument that Walcott made in "The Muse of History", and the tone that marred my early reading of it, I realised that the two were connected. If Black Power did anything for Walcott, it was that its demands were read as attacks on his personhood, thereby making him exceedingly self-aware. He took the slights and criticisms of Black Power personally. And it is from this "personal" standpoint that Walcott mounted his resistance to the limitations posed by Black Power. Exiled within the self, his riposte emerged from both the limiting social and historical "truth" of himself that had been thrust upon him, and from an acknowledgement of a deeper, more visceral – even elemental – truth of his experience of being. It is through this collision between an imposed "social" history and a personal history that "The Muse of History" was born.

The Historical Self

For purity, then, for pure black Afro-Aryanism, only the unsoiled black is valid, and West Indianism is a taint, and other strains adulterate him. The extremists, the purists, are beginning to exercise those infections, so that a writer of "mixed", hence "degenerate", blood can be nothing stronger than a liberal. This will develop a rich individualism through a deeper bitterness, it will increase egocentricity and isolation, because such writers and poets already have more complex values. They will seem more imperialistic, nostalgic, and out of the impetus of the West Indian proletariat, because they cannot simplify intricacies of race and the thought of race. They will become hermits or rogue animals, increasingly exotic hybrids, broken bridges between two ancestries, Europe and the Third World of Africa and Asia; in other words, they will become islands.[10]

What seemed like Walcott's "historical self" can be encapsulated in these lines from "The Schooner Flight", but his entire writing life can be said, in one way or another, to be a confrontation between the self that history "dealt" him and the deeper self, with greater agency to create:

I know these islands from Monos to Nassau,
a rusty head sailor with sea-green eyes
that they nickname Shabine, the patois for
any red nigger, and I, Shabine, saw
when these slums of empire was paradise.
I'm just a red nigger who love the sea,
I had a sound colonial education,
I have Dutch, nigger, and English in me
and either I'm nobody, or I'm a nation.[11]

The present, the self created by the past, is accepted by Walcott. Throughout, his work finds a way of accepting some of the conditions that have tormented many artists and people in the region. Through its violence and vileness, without denying the current degradations with which it is connected, he recognised the creative potential of the past:

I think that precisely because of their limitations our early education must have ranked with the finest in the world. The grounding was rigid – Latin, Greek, and the essential masterpieces, but there was this elation of discovery. Shakespeare, Marlowe, Horace, and Vergil – these writers weren't jaded but immediate experiences. The atmosphere was competitive, creative. It was cruel, but it created our literature.[12]

Walcott recognises the past as a potentially creative force – even as it is destructive – but a creative force that is energised by faith. So that it is not Horace, Vergil, Marlowe and others who, for Walcott, created Caribbean literature, but the experience of colonial education, which is not merely the education offered, but the faith and elation of discovery with which it was received. As Walcott noted:

> I feel absolutely no shame in having endured the colonial experience. There was no obvious humiliation in it. In fact, I think that many of what are sneered at as colonial values are part of the strength of the West Indian psyche, a fusion of formalism with exuberance, a delight in both the precision and the power of language. We love rhetoric, and this has created a style, a panache about life that is particularly ours. Our most tragic folk songs and our most self-critical calypsos have a driving, life-asserting force. Combine that in our literature with a long experience of classical forms and you're bound to have something exhilarating.[13]

Instead of a focus on the degradations and contradictions of history, Walcott prioritised its creations – creations that somehow managed to balance, fuse and even utilise its contradictions. After all, he was one of its "contradictory" creations, "poisoned with the blood of both" black and white, two groups of people who, according to history, were separate, and not equal to each other (not even of the same species in some cases). But it was this history and its contradictions that allowed Walcott to begin to debunk the authoritative status of history, to accept the creative potential of the Caribbean past while rejecting it as the point of origin of all creativity. For, whether history tells of the valour of the Romans, or the blackness of the ancient Egyptians, what is often common in both of these approaches is the relinquishment of all creative power to the past as it is constructed in "history". History then constitutes a kind of tool for the powerful, a kind of propaganda meant to vindicate them by presenting history as objective, disinterested and, therefore, truthful. This leads Walcott, like Sun Ra, to reject truth, and recognise history as a "literature without morality",[14] and also to "reject the idea of history as time, for its original concept as myth".[15]

Walcott, then, not only scrutinised and rejected the structuring of history as *chronology* presented to him by both Black Power and Froude – history as the interpreter of present maladies – but also rejected its chief protagonists: political leaders of various stripes. The political powerlessness of the protagonists of the Caribbean people throughout history led Walcott to disregard the traditional leaders as the makers of history. In his 1974 essay "The Caribbean: Culture or Mimicry?", he noted:

> In the Caribbean we do not pretend to exercise power in the historical sense. I think that what our politicians define as power, the need for it, or the lack of it, should have another name; that, like America, what energizes our society is the *spiritual force* of a culture shaping itself, and it can do this without the formula of politics.[16]

Walcott's idea of power therefore moved from the political to the spiritual, the former engendered by the formation of nations, the latter by the free exercise of the will and the imagination. In critiquing some of the writers whom he refers to as the "new magnifiers of Africa", Walcott states that "for these their deepest loss is of the old gods, the fear that it is worship which has enslaved progress. Thus the humanism of politics replaces religion. They see such gods as part of the process of history, subjected like the tribe to cycles of achievement and despair."[17] Spiritual power therefore becomes the victim of political power, which is the power acknowledged by history, the power which is history's engine and generator. For Walcott, the societies of the recently enslaved should not invest themselves in a sense of history or "progress" that foregrounds political power as true power. For him "the future of West Indian militancy lies in his art",[18] and "our definitions of power must go beyond the immediately political".[19]

Something Out of Nothing

Naipaul's and Froude's *nothing* also proved to be useful for Walcott, for it allowed him to make of Caribbean history a myth – a myth of a truly New World; a myth of his own self. And it is this sense of the New World that reduces all servitude to, or reverence for, sociological and historical designations. In this elemental world, the key relationship is not between man and man, but between man and the mystery of the world before him (which includes other men):

> the possibility of the individual Caribbean man, African, European, or Asian in ancestry, the enormous, gently opening morning of his possibility, his body touched with dew, his nerves as subtilized to

sensation as the mimosa, his memory, whether of grandeur or of pain, gradually erasing itself as recurrent drizzles cleanse the ancestral or tribal markings from the coral skull, the possibility of a man and his language waking to wonder here.[20]

The possibility is demonstrated of perceiving the New World through mystery.

To add the history to this New World, according to Naipaul, would be to fill an emptiness. For elemental man, there was no emptiness except it were his own gaping awe at a new world. It awakens him to the presence of nature, to things beyond visible nature. Elemental man's awe liberates him from the narrow "human" category, to connect his being not only to the spiritual, but also to the natural history of the place – a deeper engagement of place than its "political history". Edward Baugh saw Walcott's transformation of the inherited nothing into something, in which he transforms the landscape itself into ancestors, as "an identification between the almond trees and the people, an identification already suggested by the adjacency of the fishermen and the trees. Setting history into the landscape."[21] Baugh quotes Walcott's commentary on his own poem "The Almond Trees" (1965), in which he states: "In [this] poem, trying to describe the absence of history, tradition, ruins, I saw the figures of ancient almond trees in a grove past Rampanalgas on the north coast [of Trinidad], as a grove of dead, transplanted, uprooted ancestors."[22]

The Spiritual Self

As Walcott himself noted: "It is this awe of the numinous, this elemental privilege of naming the New World which annihilates history in our great poets, an elation common to all of them, whether they are aligned by heritage to Crusoe and Prospero or to Friday and Caliban. They reject ethnic ancestry for faith in elemental man."[23]

So, what was Walcott's deeper sense of himself? As a writer and a creator, his experience seems to have presented his "self" as something permeable, in constant exchange with the ever-present past. Walcott's sense of himself, his work, was always a vocation. In some places, he claims it was a vocation he "received" from his father, who died young when Derek and his twin brother Roddy were only a year old. Walcott's father was both a budding watercolourist and a writer. For Derek, however, this "inheritance" is not his receiving something from the dead and gone, but is the living presence of the dead within him: his being possessed by the dead, by the so-called past. Of his father's death, Walcott intimated in an interview: "Now that didn't make me a morose, morbid child. Rather, in a sense, it gave me a kind of impetus and a strong sense of continuity. I felt that what had been cut off in him somehow was an extension that I was continuing."[24]

The convention of history that Walcott critiqued in "The Muse of History" gains its sense of certainty in the material presence of things. When things fail to exist materially, fail to assert a material presence, then they no longer have a claim to being "real", to being present. But clearly this is not the case for Walcott. This bestowal of his gift had come through the permeability of the self, the turning of the self into a kind of vessel, enacting a displacement or temporary annihilation of ego. This explains why Walcott had no qualms about imitation, about being inhabited by the presences of the old great writers, or even living ones, whatever their race. He was not concerned with originality, which was supposed to be more desirable than the condition of imitation, which Naipaul would have seen as mere "mimicry".

Neither would it have been tolerated by Froude who believed that true men had a "character and purpose of their own".[25] So this is how Walcott "felt" himself, his person: as a vessel, something permeable, something willing and made to be inhabited by presences other than his own ego – like his father's, and that of the great dead he knew of through his education and with which he had been surrounded. His idea of himself moved more and more towards that original sense, which he had as a young writer, of being a vessel:

What I described in *Another Life* – about being on the hill and feeling the sort of dissolution that happened – is a frequent experience in a younger writer. I felt this sweetness of melancholy, of a sense of mortality, or rather of immortality, a sense of gratitude both for what you feel is a gift and for the beauty of the earth, the beauty of life around us. When that's forceful in a young writer, it can make you cry. It's just clear tears; it's not grimacing or being contorted, it's just a flow that happens. The body feels it is melting into what it has seen. This continues in the poet. It may be repressed in some way, but I think we continue in all our lives to have that sense of melting, of the "I" not being important.[26]

Of his writing rituals, Walcott noted:

> I do know that if one thinks a poem is coming on – in spite of the noise of the typewriter, or the traffic outside the window, or whatever – you do make a retreat, a withdrawal into some kind of silence that cuts out everything around you. What you're taking on is really not a renewal of your identity but actually a renewal of your *anonymity*, so that what's in front of you becomes more important than what you are. Equally – and it may be a little pretentious-sounding to say it – sometimes if I feel that I have done good work I do pray, I do say thanks. It isn't often, of course. I don't do it every day. I'm not a monk, but if something does happen I say thanks because I feel that it is really a piece of luck, a kind of fleeting grace that has happened to one. Between the beginning and the ending and the actual composition that goes on, *there is a kind of trance that you hope to enter* where every aspect of your intellect is functioning simultaneously for the progress of the composition.[27]

This espousal of the spiritual self is directly connected to the convention of history that Walcott later articulated in "The Muse of History". This is why ideas of originality and imitation never bothered him much because he believed that these ideas gain relevance within a history based on *chronological* time, which sees originality as a preserve of the past. With myth, on the other hand, the present and the past are simultaneous with each other. Of African-American artist Romare Bearden, Walcott observed:

> It is a patronizing way of saying about, for instance, Romare's work: "Look at those black cutouts. They are like Greek vases." Yes, they may be like Greek vases, but they are *simultaneous* concepts, not *chronological* concepts. The black cutout of a diving figure is no more historical than the silhouette of a Greek athlete on a vase. It's not a question of where you stop, since you then have to go from the Greek silhouette back to the Egyptian profile, et cetera. *If you think of art merely in terms of chronology, you are going to be patronizing to certain cultures.* But if you think of art as a simultaneity that is inevitable in terms of certain people, then Joyce is a contemporary of Homer.[28]

This concept of simultaneity bestows authority on the creative potential of the present, of the artist, as much as the past, the historian. It further defends a region with a short history in comparison to its coloniser's much longer history, with a larger pile of "creation and achievement". Walcott's sense of continuity was as much a spiritual experience as it was a corporeal one – encouraged by his family and the circle of friends that his father had left behind. From very early on, he was considered to be a prodigy, and was keenly aware of it. In fact, Walcott allowed this to innervate him, and he was actively encouraged. As he noted: "In those days I would leave our house on Chaussée Road, equipped for such pilgrimages with a small, brown cardboard suitcase of clothes and painting and writing materials. I would bid my mother goodbye, and the cook would see me down to the country bus terminus on the wharf. I was going off alone into the country, 'en betassion', to write." [29]

With the audacity and precocity necessary in any young artist – particularly in a colony like St Lucia – Walcott also viewed himself as a contemporary of Homer, Vergil and the other classical writers. And his references to the Greek classical world and his casting of the Caribbean as the "New Aegean" expressed a general admiration for, and fascination with, that classical world. But this was also a belief that he was just as good as these writers, that they bore no authority over him on account of their age or for their being dead. The vision that the world was new was not only an intellectual conceit, but "a child's belief that the world is its own age". [30] And this vision of being simultaneous with the past made Homer not merely an ancient to be revered, but a contemporary of Walcott's:

"I saw you in London," I said, "sunning on the steps
of St. Martin-in-the-Fields, your dog-eared manuscript
clutched to your heaving chest. The queues at the bus stops
smiled at your seaman's shuffle, and a curate kicked
you until you waddled down to the summery Thames."

"That's because I'm a heathen. They don't know my age.
Even nightingales have forgotten their names.
The goat declines, head down with these rocks for a stage
bare of tragedy. The Aegean's chimera
is a camera, you get my drift, a drifter
is the hero of my book."

"I never read it,"
I said. "Not all the way through." [31]

485

Walcott's sense of time, then, registers no difference between his channelling of Homer and that of contemporaries such as the American poet Robert Lowell. For both Homer and Lowell are reducible to the basic unit of Walcott's reality, to the truly energising force in all cultures and histories which is spiritual. And since all cultures possess spirit, no one is more privileged or powerful than another.

Walcott's sense of himself as a child prodigy, his sense of having inherited his father's gift, his sense of being inhabited by presences, his sense of being Homer's contemporary, would have to constitute a kind of myth-making especially *because* of the dominant and ubiquitous understanding of history with which he was surrounded on all sides. His belief in the power of artists, that "the future of West Indian militancy lies in art",[32] would sound to many – accustomed to a history shaped by political figures of one variety or another – like the ravings and rantings of a madman. The renowned Jamaican writer Erna Brodber once told me that "God" provided for the enslaved an authority above man. The beauty of such a God lay in his pliability, for his existence to his supplicant was made possible through an enactment of faith, of myth-making, and a belief in such a myth's *reality* with the "tribal" faith, and the awe of elemental man. Not myth in the secular sense, not myth as noble ruin, but myth as the living and simultaneous presence of the past, myth as a collaborative creation between present and past.

Concluding Reflections

It strikes me now that the achievement of Walcott's essay lies in the very fact that it was personal. That it was engendered by a defence of personhood made it, in and of itself, a bid for freedom. That the strategies for physical, psychological, emotional and spiritual survival within the human person are activated not by a need to wrest truth from someone else and to have his truth dominate, but to attempt to utter a small but *personal* truth – a personal truth which is not up for debate, because it is personal, and no less real, no less true, for that. It is beneath and beyond a "political" truth or a "politics". It is the myth of one's own self.

Walcott was what would be considered a "mulatto" and he was made ever more conscious of this identity by apostles of Black Power. He lived in a predominantly black society, receiving an education that could be considered "white" or European. He wrote about black people – in English. He had balanced what the world had defined over time as separate things. But within him, there was no sense of contradiction, of irony and, thus, of shame. Asking him to choose was an assault on his sensibility, on his freedom, on himself. Walcott's essay is not perfect. It attempts at times to wrest truth from its interlocutors. It attempts to show their contradictions, and to assert its coherence as an idea *over* theirs. It attempts to justify itself by showing its intellectual integrity. However, towards the end of the essay, as if from exhaustion, the approach changes; the tone changes. It is as if, after having swung its fists to the point of exhaustion, the self offers all that it has left – itself. As Walcott notes:

> I accept this archipelago of the Americas. I say to the ancestor who sold me, and to the ancestor who bought me, I have no father, I want no such father, although I can understand you, black ghost, white ghost, when you both whisper "history", for if I attempt to forgive you both I am falling into your idea of history which justifies and explains and expiates, and it is not mine to forgive, my memory cannot summon any filial love, since your features are anonymous and erased and I have no wish and no power to pardon ... I, like the more honest of my race, give a strange thanks. I give the strange and bitter and yet ennobling thanks for the monumental groaning and soldering of two great worlds, like the halves of a fruit seamed by its own bitter juice, that exiled from your own Edens you have placed me in the wonder of another, and that was my inheritance and your gift.[33]

The lesson of Derek Walcott has nothing to do with the sense of history he proposes as revolutionary in "The Muse of History" but lies in his ability to create a world, and a vision of the world, out of the "accidents" of history that in one way made him, as well as from the exertion of his own imagination, faith and talent; his own capability to create the world that made sense *to* him and made sense *of* him. Black Power, in its own way, challenged Walcott to find *his* "truth", since the ideology was more than ready to articulate and foist its own ideas on him. And if Walcott's truth was anything, it was not in any ideology or doctrine that he found or founded, but in his untiring and stubborn need for his own sovereignty, for his *own* history, his own myth.

"So at the end," the Trinidadian novelist Earl Lovelace wrote in his moving elegy to Walcott in March 2017: "his followers embraced him not because they could follow where he led, or embrace what he said, but because in a way he had been all, been everything. And that is what he remained, a work in progress, guided by his own talent and genius and love."[34]

33
___

BUCHI EMECHETA: THE BURDEN OF EXILE

Louisa Uchum Egbunike

"Writing my autobiography is not going to be easy. This is because most of my early novels, articles, poems and short stories are, like my children, too close to my heart. They are too real. They are too me."[1]
–BUCHI EMECHETA, *HEAD ABOVE WATER*

NIGERIAN AUTHOR BUCHI EMECHETA'S writing can be described as a form of creative expression centred on experiential knowledge. The biographical details of Emecheta's life are present at the inception of her career as a novelist, visible in her debut novel *In the Ditch* (1972) and its 1974 prequel, *Second-Class Citizen*. These two novels, which were later published in a single volume as *Adah's Story*,[2] explore the struggles faced by Emecheta from her childhood in Lagos to her life as a single mother of five in London. When Buchi later penned her autobiography in 1986, *Head Above Water*, over a decade later, she made her readers aware of the multiple junctures between the imagined and the real in her writing, noting that she would "write episodically, touching lightly here and there on those incidents on which I dwelt in depth in my other books: *Second-Class Citizen, In the Ditch, The Bride Price, The Slave Girl, The Joys of Motherhood* and *Double Yoke*".[3] Thus, distinctions between biography and fiction become blurred as Emecheta's own lived experience – or the lived experiences of those she comes into contact with – is foundational in many of her books. A semblance of distance is created between Emecheta and her protagonists by her use of the novel form, a point on which she has reflected, stating that "although the work was fictitious, it drew heavily upon my personal experiences" so that "I was becoming more and more the black woman in the book, Adah. I *was* a second-class citizen."[4]

Emecheta's words reveal that her literature is not solely a conscious examination of her lived experience, but delves into aspects of her reality that only become apparent to her when she sees them reflected on the pages of her books.

Nostalgia for the Ancestral Home

In her writing, Buchi Emecheta's ideological project centres on foregrounding the lives of those whose narratives do not feature prominently in mainstream official histories. By examining the life of an orphan in Lagos, a girl sold into slavery in Onitsha, or a single mother in London; Emecheta captures the day-to-day reality of figures who are often located at the margins of society, consigned to the periphery due to their class, gender, race or ethnicity. In her own words, Emecheta describes her fiction thus: "What I am doing is writing social documentary novels, based upon what I have seen and experienced."[5] Her novels thus become a hybridised genre, drawing on sociology and non-fiction elements to provide the basis for her narratives. For the purpose of this essay, the intersection of Emecheta's life and works will be explored with specific reference to notions of home, community and belonging in a selection of her diaspora novels. The shifting temporal and physical locations of Emecheta's works at large demonstrate her capacity to engage with the changing notions of home. Particularly in works set within a diaspora – for example, the Ibusa community in Lagos, or Nigerians in London – the movement from one's ancestral home to another locale expands the composition of one's community as people are bound together by circumstances with elements of shared experiences. These communities often create networks of support that extend beyond a traceable common ancestry.

Buchi Emecheta's approach to writing represents the culmination of an academic background in sociology,[6] as well as the impact and influence of the oral stories she was told as a child. She describes the clear distinctions between the content of her formal education in British colonial schools in Nigeria, and that of tales told to her under the moonlight in her home town of Ibusa in eastern Nigeria. While her colonial education sought to elevate British imperialism, thereby affirming Britain's right to rule over Nigeria, the stories she was told by female family members affirmed not only Emecheta herself, but also those who came before her. As she noted:

Most of the events that happened before I was born had to be told to me by my mothers. The history of the British Empire and her greatness I learned from my English teachers at school in Lagos. But when it came to events that happened nearer home, concerning my ancestors and me in particular, I had to rely on the different versions told to me by my mothers.[7]

Emecheta goes on to describe the joy of being placed at the centre of a story told to a group of children by Nwakwaluzo Ogbuenyi, one of her aunts. In one episode, Ogbuenyi puts a series of questions to the group of children who have gathered around her, the answers to which gradually reveal who will feature at the centre of that evening's story-telling session. A young Buchi becomes overjoyed at the prospect of her own narrative being the focus of that evening's entertainment:

"Whose father walked seven lands and swam seven seas to fight and kill a bad man called Hitilah?"

"It's me," I whispered hoarsely, afraid of disturbing the quiet grip her voice was having on us.

"Who is our come-back mother Agbogo?"

"It's me." This time I could not restrain myself any longer. I stood up proudly and this movement of mine startled all my little relatives sitting there on the sand at Otinkpu. "It's her, it's her," their voices chorused. "It's me, it's me," I screamed intermittently."

"Who has a mother that can write and read like white people?"

By this time, I was dancing around singing "*O nmu. O mu.*" (It's me, it's me.)[8]

The excitement that young Buchi develops in the build-up to the delivery of her story is grounded in the public recognition of its importance by somebody both senior and well liked. This affirmation of Emecheta is bolstered by the collective excitement displayed by her peers. What initially may seem like an unremarkable episode in her life is, in fact, a foundational moment. There is space within the oral tradition for the narrative of Emecheta, as well as those in her family and her community. This validation of hearing her story told, and having her narrative given visibility by her aunt and others, not only permeates Buchi's writing, but becomes central to it. Her work thus serves to make her own narrative visible.

But like her "mothers", Emechata also sought to bring the stories of others into the light. This episode in story-telling provides a window into the nature and functions of Igbo cultural constructs of narrative. Literature serves the purpose of both entertainment and education. As I have argued elsewhere, "within the oral tradition, narratives comprise both creative and informative components. Art serves both an imaginative and socio-political function and so a conceptual divide was not drawn between literary and historical oral texts. It can include historical truths or it can be purely fictive."[9] Reading Emecheta's works in the light of the conventions of the oral tradition illuminates her approach to the narrative content of her novels. This moment in Buchi's life can be seen as an inaugural experience, not only in setting her on the path to a literary career, but also in shaping her perspective of what constitutes a good story.

Emecheta's career as a writer began after she had moved to London in 1962. As a Nigerian writing in London, her body of work has the capacity to speak to both continental Africa and its longstanding and more recent diaspora. Over the course of Emecheta's career, her work oscillated across time and space, from colonial Lagos to contemporary London. As such, her writings sit comfortably within both black British and African literary canons, with her two most celebrated novels – *Second-Class Citizen* and *The Joys of Motherhood* – often featuring on black British and African literature university syllabi. It is this sustained capacity across her oeuvre to engage with continental Africa and its diaspora that marks Emecheta's work out as Pan-African in its vision and scope. Within the different societies that she explores, there are recurrent thematic concerns: dislocation, displacement, and the sense of not belonging. We see her characters – primarily black females – struggling against the constraints that patriarchal society has placed upon them, as they seek to find a place to call home and a supportive community of their own. Given that many of her texts incorporate migration narratives – be it within the nation or across nations – there is a persistent engagement with competing ideas regarding the location of home. Emecheta's own narrative of migration, both as a child of Ibusa heritage living in Lagos and, later, as a Nigerian living in London, provides the basis for her engagement with this subject. Her time in Britain introduced her to a range of migratory narratives, including those of post-war Caribbean migrants in Britain. The Caribbean narrative of a double diaspora added further depth and dimension to Emecheta's writing on displacement, belonging and community. Home to many was not a single locale but consisted of multiple sites, some of which they had lived in, and others which they had imagined.

Emecheta's frequent references to Ibusa in her works set in both Lagos and London demonstrate the significance and reverence with which she regarded her ancestral home. The persistent engagement with the homeland of her characters speaks to a particular cultural assertion of home as the place of one's origins, above and beyond where one resides. In *Second-Class Citizen*, we are told that the "virtues of Ibuza were praised so much that Adah came to regard her being born in a God-forsaken place like Lagos as a misfortune".[10] Ibusa remains a strong presence in many of Emecheta's works, and while affirming the grounding which her home town has provided for her – in her documentary style of writing – her works engage with the process of creating one's home. In a scene in the novel *In the Ditch*, the categories of ancestral home and home in the diaspora collide, as Adah reads her new London home through an Ibusa lens, rendering the unfamiliar as familiar: "the Pussy Cat Mansions were built round a large compound. Adah called the open space a compound, remembering Africa."[11] This reminds us how the cultural specificity of our socialisation impacts upon how we read our surroundings, and how we interpret our experiences. This search for a connection to a particular homeland while abroad is extended in Emecheta's exploration of the Caribbean double diaspora narrative in Britain, in which an African homeland is sought and, in a particular way, is found.

Second-Class Citizen

Emecheta's second novel, *Second-Class Citizen*, centres on the story of Adah, who, as a young married woman with two small children, emigrates from Nigeria to join her husband in London. Eager to leave Nigeria immediately, Adah books first-class tickets for herself and her children. Surrounded by the "wives of diplomats and top white civil servants going home on leave", Adah realises that "life was changing fast", leading her erroneously to envisage that this was a "taste of what was to come".[12] This transatlantic sea voyage instead ushers in a life in which the emerging Nigerian class boundaries are undermined. On arrival in Britain, Adah is faced with adversities, compounded by her drastic reduction in status and social dislocation. While colonialism had imprinted a hierarchical structure that often negated pre-existing social organisations, privileging those with Western education, the relocation to Britain negates the social ascendance that Adah has achieved within Nigerian society. The swiftness in her social descent is captured in her stepping out of her first-class cabin on the ship, to set foot on British soil as a "second-class citizen". Adah is warned by her husband that "you can't discriminate against your own people, because we're all second-class".[13] It is the homogenising experience of life in England which frames Emecheta's rendering of the immigrant experience. This is most apparent in her trying to secure accommodation for her family, an experience which was "very short in London, especially for black people with children. Everyone is coming to London. The West Indians, the Pakistanis and even the Indians, so that African students are usually grouped together with them. We are all black, all coloured, and the only houses we can get are horrors like these."[14]

The commonality of experience for Commonwealth citizens creates larger categories of identification that extend beyond ethno-nation, country or continent, unified by a shared transnational history of British imperial rule, and consequently uniting these migrants in the land of their "colonial masters". The broadening of identities that Emecheta depicts signals the constructions of new identities fashioned to serve a protracted period in the diaspora. During the 1960s, the decade in which *Second-Class Citizen* is set, there had been a wave of decolonisation in British territories across the world. In this time, the British Empire had been substantially reduced in size, leaving a crop of newly independent countries with an emerging middle class, many of whom travelled to Britain in search of the golden fleece of education.[15]

In Britain, Adah undergoes a process of racialisation in which she is identified as black. The implication of this racialisation is that her experiences are now bound up with the experiences of people from many distinct parts of the world. This broadening of identity that Adah experiences is underscored by the use of race: a transnational and expansive marker of identification, which subsequently creates a shift in ideas of community and the collective. In the context of post-war Britain after 1945, the "politically black" identity construct created the possibility for cross-cultural unity in a climate of overt racism in British society. Broader but in some ways more fragile than previous modes of identification to which Adah had subscribed, political blackness created a bridge across the destinies and experiences of those who did not fit within the racial category of "white", and who – treated like a homogeneous "other" – sought strength and solidarity in their collective power. The British Nationality Act of 1948 gave people from British colonies and former colonies the right to citizenship, which meant that they could relocate to Britain and live as citizens of that country. For those who came to live in Britain, the realities of life stood in direct opposition to the image of the country portrayed in the British colonial educational system, delivered to children in the various seats of the imperial Raj. As a young girl, Adah had expressed the view in *Second-Class Citizen* that "going to the United Kingdom must surely be like paying God a visit".[16] It was from the collective experience of living in a British colony and receiving a colonial education, migrating to the "Motherland" and subsequently confronting the racism that beset their lives, which resulted in the solidarity shown by first-generation migrants who were racialised as "black." From the early 1960s onwards, successive governments in Westminster would increasingly restrict migration from former colonies to Britain, echoing the rising tide of xenophobia and racism in the nation.

Diasporas within Diasporas

It was in Britain that Emecheta first encountered people from the Caribbean. The interface of Caribbean and West African cultures became a subject of particular interest that she would explore in her writing. Caribbean post-war migration to Britain after 1945 was born out of the declining imperial power's need to replenish its workforce after the severe casualties suffered during the Second World War. The arrival of the *Empire Windrush* in Tilbury docks in London in the summer of 1948 marked the beginning of a sustained migration from the Caribbean. The presence of Caribbean people in Britain – who in the eyes of the law were British citizens – disrupted long-held notions of Britishness. The more visible presence of black and brown people in post-war British cities challenged the assumption that Britishness was synonymous with whiteness, thus creating a sense of unease among many of those in Britain whose views were aligned with the political right. With prominent politicians such as the Conservative parliamentarian Enoch Powell, openly calling for the repatriation of Commonwealth citizens living in Britain, anti-immigrant sentiment was palpable at both the level of government and in local communities in the form of racist verbal and physical abuse. For this generation, the pursuit of their rights as citizens began on their arrival in Britain in the late 1940s, and in the wake of the 2018 "Windrush scandal" it still remains incomplete.[17]

The second generation of Caribbean people in Britain would begin to identify as black British, and, as such, black British identity was heavily shaped by Caribbean culture and its intersections with British culture. Among the second and third generation of people from the Commonwealth living in Britain, there were shifting modes of identification, as their experiences were not bound together in the same way that their parents' or grandparents' experiences had been. Writing in the late 1980s, Guyanese-British intellectual Paul Gilroy noted: "The naming of 'races' here [in Britain] has recently undergone a significant shift. It has moved away from the political definitions of black based on the possibilities of Afro-Asian unity and towards more restricted alternative formulations which have confined the concept of blackness to people of African descent."[18] The changing tide in British society around the construction of "blackness" thus moved towards the notion of a common African ancestry.

It is at this point, when the idea of blackness within Britain began to encompass a form of unity that centred on heritage, that Emecheta wrote *Gwendolen* in 1989. The book captured the sentiment behind the collective destiny of people of African descent. Gwendolen is a young girl growing up in rural Jamaica who migrates to London, following her parents who had left for London several years before her. In the opening of the novel, Emecheta introduces visible markers of African heritage in her representation of Jamaica. This is done through both what are visible physiological markers of heritage – Gwendolen's father is described as "a big healthy 'African'" – and ideological markers of Jamaica's link to Africa through reference to the "Marcus Garvey Academy", the school that Gwendolen attended. Garvey, one of Jamaica's national heroes, campaigned for the return of people of African descent in the Americas to Africa itself, arguing that black people in these societies had not won their liberty (see Grant in this volume).

For Garveyites, Africa thus became the locale for emancipation. In spite of this particular cultural and ideological context, the characters in *Gwendolen* who do leave Jamaica travel to Britain, specifically London, the heart of the British Empire. While this form of Atlantic crossing does not follow the Garveyist ideal of reconnection with the African homeland, 1980s London is a melting pot of cultures that included settled Caribbean and African communities. *Gwendolen* examines the relationships forged between Jamaican and Nigerian characters, demonstrating that the reconnection between Africa and its diaspora that Garvey envisioned was also taking place in the metropolitan centres of Europe.

In *Gwendolen*, the migration of characters from Jamaica to Britain employed the rhetoric of British Empire, as they embark on their journey to the "moder kontry".[19] In so doing, Emecheta engages in a three-pronged discussion of motherhood, nationhood and belonging. Britain as "Mother" inevitably disappoints her children. Life in Britain proves trying, both in terms of structural inequalities in society and also within the more intimate family setting. Gwendolen is raped by her father, Winston, and bears a child from this abuse. Gwendolen's mother, Sonia, also fails initially to understand the situation at hand; the truth dawns on her only after her granddaughter is born, and her husband has died. Motherhood as an institution is interrogated in this novel, as Emecheta returns to a pertinent theme that has featured prominently throughout her work.

The circumstances of Gwendolen's daughter's birth, and the naming of the baby as Iyamide – Yoruba for "mother is here" – provide a particular commentary on mother–daughter dynamics. As Nigerian critic Chikwenye Okonjo Ogunyemi has noted: "Emecheta's final statement is bold and disquieting. She moves fiction and ethics to another realm by insisting that one's daughter should be one's sister (literally) and mother (metaphorically)."[20] In an episode in the closing of the novel, Gwendolen explains her name choice for her daughter to her mother: "Iyamide means 'My mother is here'. It is symbolic. It does not mean you're no longer my mother, it means everything I ever wanted, warmth, security, comfort, is all here in a female form."[21]

The representation of the mother figure, through the image of a baby girl, provides a new framework for engaging with the institution of motherhood. As Ogunyemi suggests, there is an expressed need to form a sisterhood that moves beyond ordinary patterns of familial relations. Emecheta's deliberate choice of name for this baby, born out of such troubling circumstances, interjects a sense of hope in a narrative replete with trauma. Emecheta also ensures that the figure which comes to personify hope and has a clear association with Africa is also female. Her Pan-African womanist conclusion to the novel highlights the centrality of unity among women of African descent in providing mutually supportive roles. The novel's conclusion also presents a return to the assertion that the convergences of Africa and its older diaspora can take place abroad. Iyamide is the child of a double diaspora: from Africa to the Caribbean to Britain. Her name signals a return to Africa symbolically and, figuratively speaking, "Mother Africa" is present with them in Britain. This reconnection has taken place and emerged in the most unlikely place – the product of traumatic sexual abuse. Unlike the "moder kontry", the tangible presence of Mother Africa expressed in "Iyamide" signals the comforting role of mother that neither biological mother (Sonia) nor "Motherland" (Britain) could provide. Thus, in Emecheta's re-engagement with the theme of motherhood, she locates Africa at the centre of a redemptive motherhood. It is worth noting that the novel is dedicated "to that woman in the Diaspora who refused to sever her umbilical cord with Africa".[22]

Stuart Hall (see Magubane in this volume), speaking about the Caribbean community in Britain, regarded the ideological and intellectual project of Jamaican-British photographer Armet Francis as seeking to find "a way of imposing an imaginary coherence on the experience of dispersal and fragmentation, which is the history of all enforced diasporas".[23] Francis and his contemporaries

> do this by representing or "figuring" Africa as the mother of these different civilisations. This Triangle is, after all, "centred" in Africa. Africa is the name of the missing term, the great aporia, which lies at the centre of our cultural identity and gives it a meaning which, until recently, it lacked. No one who looks at these textural images now, in the light of the history of transportation, slavery and migration, can fail to understand how the rift of separation, the "loss of Identity", which has been integral to the Caribbean experience only begins to be healed when these forgotten connections are once more set in place. Such texts restore an imaginary fullness or plentitude, to set against the broken rubric of our past.[24]

While Hall complicated this approach to what he describes as an "essentialised past", he identified the attempts of artists like Francis and Emecheta to bridge the diaspora divide. Emecheta, like Francis, found herself in a multicultural Britain in which she was confronted with the Caribbean migrant experience. Like Francis, her creative output provided a means by which to interrogate this history while attempting to make sense of the present. In *Gwendolen*, Emecheta aims to bring about a sense of resolution through representations of reconnections between Nigerian and Jamaican characters.

Other aspects in the text complicate the Pan-African ideal that Emecheta proposes in *Gwendolen*. In her decision to make Gwendolen's partner Greek, Buchi thereby acknowledges the varied cultural influences and intersections that are brought about when living in a multi-ethnic global city in the late twentieth century. Emecheta also complicates the Garveyist ideal of reconnection by bringing to the forefront some of the cultural distances and misunderstandings created by the historical divisions between Africa and its older diaspora. Sonia's initial reaction to the naming of Gwendolen's baby echoes the colonial language of "the primitivism of Africa", as she asks: "You give the baby uncivilized African voodoo name?" Gladys, a Nigerian friend of Sonia's, reflects: "when [will] these Caribbeans ... stop calling Africans uncivilized as if they were civilised themselves."[25] This contentious aspect of reconnecting forms part of Emecheta's documenting process. In *Head above Water* (1994), Emecheta noted:

> We were all black, yes. But my black experience was not the same as the type weathered by the members of the Seventies. We all came to Britain as economic refugees, but the experiences and expectations of the African were different from those of the Caribbean. I had to struggle and fight my way through libraries, colleges, universities and grant departments, while all most of them wanted was simply a good job. Most of the Africans in those days would take any job, however dirty, because they knew they were here to work their way through college. Most of them hoped to go home after their studies. The Caribbean wanted a good job, which he would hold just as if he were in the West Indies.[26]

While there had been a homogenising discourse in Britain when discussing African and Caribbean people, with all regarded as second-class citizens, there were underlying class differences among these groups that compounded cultural differences. Historically, Britain's main objective in recruiting workers from the Caribbean was in many instances, to help reinvigorate the declining imperial power's depleted workforce. As for West Africans, many had come to study in Britain with the intention of returning to their home countries to take up middle-class jobs in their newly independent or soon-to-be-independent nations.

The idea of return to Africa is introduced in *Gwendolen* and became a theme that Emecheta continued to explore in later works, *Kehinde* in 1994, and *The New Tribe* in 2000. In Buchi's own life, from 1980 to 1981, she held a visiting lecturership at the University of Calabar in Nigeria, which formed part of her personal exploration of the possibility of return. At the same time, in Emecheta's self-described documentary style of writing, she sought to "create literature for the present generation born here",[27] influenced to a certain extent by her children's experience of growing up in multicultural Britain. This provided one aspect of the purpose that Buchi felt as a writer, but this was superseded by her desire to return to her ancestral home in a physical and literary sense:

I could stay here and not travel or visit Africa and specialise in writing about the black problem in England. But I don't want to. I feel more at home writing about the clear sand of the mid-western Ibo land, the plaintive voice of the evening announcer and the emptiness of the Eke markets after the people and the dancers have gone.[28]

Concluding Reflections

Ibusa – the land of Emecheta's ancestors – is somewhere she had never lived. And yet this is the place Buchi felt most compelled to write about. Emecheta never returned permanently to live in Nigeria up to her death in January 2017 at the age of 72. Instead, like her works, she would frequently move between spaces. Living in Britain provided her with distance from her Ibusa culture and Lagos life, which facilitated her reflective writing. This distance was counterbalanced by a sense of needing to regenerate: "when I want to write about something, I usually go back home and sort of revitalize the Africanness or Nigerianness in me."[29] Emecheta's life and works demonstrate the multiplicity and complexity in the constructs of home and one's community, extending to the idea of return, which is not presented as definitive or absolute. It is through her multiple positioning that she brings about the diverse and complex nature of her work. Written from between spaces, Emecheta's novels encapsulate a range of voices in diverse societies grappling with divergent concerns, but, like herself, they seem always to be asking: Where is home, and who is my community?

34

Mariama Bâ: Pioneering Feminist

Ada Uzoamaka Azodo

"*Ce que le temps n'a pas voulu accorder à Mariama Bâ, elle l'a gagné dans le cœur des hommes.*" ("What time denied Mariama Bâ, she won in human hearts.")

— Mame Coumba Ndiaye[1]

"The life of Mariama Bâ gives an impression of absolute coherence. It is a destiny that follows a straight line: the old woman who dies in the 1980s, covered with honors, had remained faithful to her childhood dream."

— Simone Schwarz-Bart[2]

Mariama Bâ's childhood dream in the 1930s was to preserve the old city of Dakar: that mirror of the foundational Africa culture disappearing under the domination of the modern Africa of the *toubabs* (labourers).[3] Bâ envisioned a new Africa of the future exemplified by the openness of Dakar and its docks and ports to the world. As a child, notes Guadeloupian literary critic, playwright and novelist Simone Schwarz-Bart, "She wandered the streets of a city where deepest Africa knocked at every corner: Wolof drums; the poetic flights of the young women at the river; sails outstretched like butterfly wings; men and women from Galam, Niger, Sudan; bare bodies and elaborate coiffures; ornaments; shouts, calls; sudden passion and laughter – all this spoke to the little girl in a language she recognised as her own. All this beat with a pulse that she felt in her veins. Bâ would later write: "I was eight years old and I cried, Tam-tam, take me away."[4]

500

A Childhood in Dakar and Other Early Influences

In "*La fonction politique des littératures africaines écrites*"[5] ("The Political Functions of Written African Literatures"),[6] her theoretical essay and laudatory speech, Bâ justifies the political orientation of written African literatures from the 1930s to the 1960s as protest against the false identity imposed on Africa by the colonialists. The European assertion that Africa was barbaric, uncivilised, incapable of rational thinking and without history – according to scholars like British historian Hugh Trevor-Roper[7] – was so hurtful to African traditions, cultures and civilisations that even in the post-colonial era, Africa was still deemed to exist in a neo-colonial epoch. Despite political independence, its nations remained in the economic stranglehold of the global core–periphery economic system. Two eminent American geographers, Harm J. de Blij and Peter O. Muller, bemoaned the fate of the periphery-area countries of the South of the global economy *vis-à-vis* the core areas of the North in 1993: "They suffer far more than core-area countries do from environmental degradation, overpopulation and mismanagement. They possess inherited disadvantages that have grown, not lessened, over time. The widening gaps between enriching cores and persistently impoverished peripheries clearly are a threat to the future of the world."[8]

Mariama Bâ recognised that politics is about power relations and that politics and history are essential tools and means enabling committed African literature to shake up the very foundations of the colonial system in Africa. In order to counter the negative impact of the impoverishment and domination of colonial culture and the false identity imposed on Africans, some of them took recourse to valorising the African past. Others, including Senegal's Léopold Sédar Senghor, French Guiana's Léon Damas and Martinique's Aimé Césaire – and, later on, Nigeria's Abiola Irele and Mabel Segun and Martinique's Paulette Nardal – recognised the merits of the Négritude philosophy. Senegal's Cheikh Anta Diop, for his part, reaffirmed the existence of African civilisation, while Mariama Bâ saw the similarity between the role of the writer who employs the pen to examine the nature and extent of European domination of Africa and the calling of the freedom fighter who uses the gun to protest against racism. Hence, art for art's sake was not an option for the African writer, for art must be subordinated to politics.

Four main literary themes – racial inequality, gender inequity, cultural emancipation, and Western destruction of African societies and traditions

– are predominant in Bâ's work.[9] In the struggle for political independence, nationalism led to a proliferation of *coups d'état*, ethnic-fuelled conflicts and civil wars, resulting in a lack of democracy and government suppression of self-expression and free speech. Bigotry, despotism, authoritarianism, corruption and profligacy thus abounded. As guide to and consciousness-raiser for more effective socio-economic development, Bâ sought to provoke change by denouncing social ills, especially among the downtrodden, poor and disadvantaged. Customs, traditions and bad practices – when they did not reflect Africa's treasured cultural heritage – were not spared. In these roles, Bâ called on women to be in the forefront of writing political literature in order to fight gender discrimination, segregation, subordination, inequality and exploitation.

Born on 17 April 1929 into the noble Muslim Lébous family – the first inhabitants of the city of Dakar – Mariama Bâ and her sister Marguerite (Maguette) Bâ lost their mother very early on. It then fell to their conservative maternal grandparents, especially their grandmother, to raise them. In the family compound, there was a mosque where the poor flocked daily for material and spiritual succour. Niéle Bâ, Mariama's father, was born in 1892. Like his own father, Sarakholé Bâ, who was an interpreter in Saint-Louis for the French colonial administration before migrating to Dakar, Niéle was a career civil servant with the imperial administration. He was wedded to French traditions and protocol, and worked and travelled often throughout French West Africa. Niéle served as a *tirailleur* (infantryman) in the French army during the First World War (1914–18). Upon his return to Senegal, he first worked as a treasurer or teller, later becoming the deputy mayor of Dakar, and eventually Senegal's first minister of health in 1956. Niéle Bâ inculcated in Mariama a view of human relationships as equal. He wanted Mariama to be educated in the modern way in the French educational system, even as her grandmother pushed fervently for a traditional Senegalese education for young girls. Niéle Bâ won this battle, colluding with the principal of the Women's Teacher Training College at Rufisque, Madame Germaine Le Goff.

In 1943 Mariama took the common entrance examination for the École Normale des Jeunes Filles à Rufisque and came first of all the students who attempted the examination that year. She was admitted to the college for the 1943/4 school year, and excelled academically. In 1947, for her senior project,[10] she wrote a composition based on two lines of a poem from the collection *Mémoires* by François René de Chateaubriand, which the students were assigned and which they were asked to use to evoke their own place of birth:

Combien j'ai douce souvenance
Du joli lieu de ma naissance.[11]

[Ah, sweet remembrances
Of the beautiful place where I was born.]

Bâ's composition showed a student of great talent and ability, such that Madame Le Goff had it published as *"Petite patrie"* ("A Childhood in Dakar") in the journal *Notes Africaines.*[12] Later, the piece was republished in *Espri*, by the visiting French intellectual Emmanuel Mournier. Later, French writer Maurice Genevoix quoted passages from it in his travelogue on Africa. Indeed, the essay mirrored Bâ's ambivalence as an eight-year old girl engaged in a "game of mirrors",[13] according to Simone Schwarz-Bart, who further states: "The teenage girl described her childhood in Dakar, in her grandfather's compound – the family milieu, its feasts and famines, the sand in the hourglass days. She evoked the renunciation of those who knelt down and assimilated the French values that were then fashionable, and suddenly she erupted in what was to be the heartfelt cry of a generation: '*They have whitened my reason but my head is still black; and my blood, unreachable, still prances in my civilized veins.*'"[14] Mariama's life and work sought to help Africa rediscover its cultural roots, while leaving a window open to the world; to fight against prejudices and the constraints of tradition, customs and superstitions that kept women subjugated; to appreciate other civilisations without giving up one's own: to be rooted in Africa while remaining open to the world; to develop worldviews, cultivate personalities, strengthen a sense of identity, and develop universal moral values.[15] After Rufisque, Bâ attended the Lycée Van Vollenhoven (now Lycée Lamine Guèye), but her grandmother's death, soon after, stalled her academic dream. So, from 1947 to 1959, Mariama worked as a teacher in the Medina, the walled section of the city of Dakar set aside for indigenous populations.

A little after Bâ left the Teacher Training College at Rufisque, at about 20, she married her equally young husband, Bassirou (Bass). After about 20 months of marriage, Bâ found out that beyond the progressive ideas they both shared, Bassirou believed in the traditional customs that kept women down, in bondage and in servitude. As she put it, "It was not wedlock." Mariama noted that what she wanted to do was not leave her marriage, but rather to escape from the asphyxiation of her true self that yearned for freedom.[16] Then, soon after, Bâ married Abdoulaye (Ablaye) Ndiaye. According to Mariama, she and

Ablaye did not have much in common beyond the child they had had together, Mame Coumba Ndiaye. The marriage ended as abruptly as the first one. Then, Bâ married Obèye Diop-Tall, a young and passionate politician with whom she had nine children, including a pair of twins. The marriage lasted about twenty-five years. Mariama described this third marriage thus: "Intellectual fervour brought us together and that gave us the desire to go one step further."[17] Diop-Tall concurred, noting that the marriage failed as a result of their two opposing philosophies of life. He believed staunchly in a traditional division of labour in the family, contrary to Bâ's view of equality in sex and gender roles in the way she wanted to live her life.[18] Clearly, Mariama was torn between two poles: she could not put up with the self-centredness of men and their relegation of women to the periphery of society; but, at the same time, she could not abide the new individualism that French culture had brought to Senegal.[19] As Bâ saw it, marriage merely transferred a young girl from one man's house (her father's) to another man's (her husband's), where she was supposed to cook, clean, wash and iron her husband's *grand boubous* (flowing robes). As Schwarz-Bart noted: "When the time came, with or without her consent, [she would] slip into another family – her husband's."[20] At the end of her third marriage, the strain and stresses of the single parenting of nine children took a toll on her life. She fell ill with cancer for many years. Nonetheless, she was promoted to the position of inspector of schools, which she held until her death on 17 August 1981 at the age of 52.

As her children grew up and she grew tired of teaching during the late 1960s, Bâ went from ideology to activism, extending her struggles for women's rights in her personal life to participation in feminist organisations in her local community, empowering women through education, mutual aid, and social activities. First, she founded and managed a rather large traditional investment scheme, a *tontine*, which allowed her and other participants to benefit from an annuity scheme of mutual sharing and financial support.[21] Then, she joined the Federation of Senegal Women's Associations. Next, from 1979 to 1981, she was the secretary of the Dakar Soroptimist Club, a position that allowed her to pursue her passion for the emancipation of women. In her sparse but dense publications – *Une si longue lettre*,[22] "La Fonction politique des littératures africaines *écrites*" and *Un chant écarlate*[23] – Mariama gave voice to women; encouraged their self-esteem and self-confidence; promoted their self-fulfilment and economic opportunities; presented women's viewpoints; and pursued their desire to change laws and traditions that subjugated them, as well as customs and traditions that turned them into objects to be used and discarded by men at will. The "African Mother" trope was no longer an option, since it did not provide women with the respect they deserved. Bâ argued that women must be allowed space beside men as equal citizens engaged in a liberation struggle for Africa, because many women had contributed, and were still contributing, to national economic development, and ought to become proactive in civic life to regain their power. In 1976, at the age of 47, Bâ wrote a speech in honour of Madame Germaine Le Goff, the headmistress of Rufisque Women's Teacher Training College, to whom she attributed her awakening to her true racial and gender identity. Then, in 1979, Bâ addressed the Senegalese National Assembly on the occasion of the annual International Women's Day celebrations. The same year, she wrote an essay on polygyny, to commemorate the International Year of the Child.[24] Finally, in 1980, Mariama attended the Frankfurt Book Fair, where she was presented with the first Noma Prize for Publishing in Africa. There, she delivered a lecture on her essay on "The Political Functions of Written African Literatures and the Role of the African Writer".[25]

Two Pioneering Novels

Dakar – the city of Bâ's two novels written in her fifties – *Une si longue lettre* ("So Long a Letter") (1980) and *Un chant écarlate* ("Scarlet Song") (1981), is a dual city.[26] Survival in the African section only occurs through family ties, hope and steadfastness in the belief that everything will be alright in the end.[27] The novels mirror Marianne's life, her activism and her work.[28] In *Un chant écarlate* – published posthumously – which inscribes the legacy of Mariama in indelible ink in the hearts of the Pan-African literary world, Schwarz-Bart notes that Bâ "speaks, telling the oldest and yet the most extraordinary story in the world: how a woman can marry without having chosen her husband, how she can have children without having wanted them, how her own existence can be imposed on her like her fate, even though she feels free".[29] Schwarz-Bart continues: "She set fire to a certain kind of Islam, wherein the woman always follows the man, clinging to the hem of his robe even in her final ascent to heaven. She set fire to a certain African tradition, too often cited by men to justify a privilege or state of affairs completely out of date – for there is no, or at least there is no longer, any true happiness for women in polygamy. And she set fire to assimilation, the colonization of the soul that goes hand-in-hand with the colonization of countries and people."[30] Many of these ideas were already beginning to emerge in "A Childhood in Dakar" ("*Petite patrie*").[31] *Une si longue lettre*, in particular, captures complex subjects, including Africa at the crossroads between tradition and modernity, and the demands for future socio-economic progress on the continent. The book also examines the travails of abandoned women in the modern city of Dakar, women who suffer from "nervous conditions" due to multiple, complex and complicated symptoms arising from domestic abuse by the men in their lives. It engages the recurring themes of conflict between tradition and modernity in the city, where "post-modern" men clumsily combine their values and customs, arts and crafts, and traditional marriage rules with Islamic religion, which is often quoted out of context to suit their own selfish ends. The same themes recur in Bâ's second novel, *Un chant écarlate*, which is focused on the traditional marriage of a French woman to a Senegalese husband, who later takes a second wife, plunging the first wife into untold misery, suicidal thoughts, infanticide and other murderous acts.

Mariama Bâ and Traditional African Communal Values: Denouncing Taboos, Obsolete Morality, and Antiquated Laws

In relation to gender and racial politics, Bâ advocates embracing all that is good about African and European cultures. Firstly, in a community, everyone should take care of everyone else in the true spirit of African communalism,[32] what South Africans would call *Ubuntu*. In *Une si longue lettre*, the grandmothers of Ramatoulaye and her bosom friend Aïssatou daily exchange greetings across the compound fence that separates one homestead from the other. Communal living in sorrow and in happiness is neither materialistic nor individualistic. It encourages sharing and care of the disadvantaged. Religion is practised well, with neighbours taking care of each other. Bounty flows from the advantaged to the disadvantaged, so that each person lives without human indignity. Polygyny, according to laid-down rules, conserves respect and dignity for the older wives. For example, the senior wife has a say as to the choice of the next wife or wives. And men do not always acquire new wives due to lust, but to fulfil certain functions such as the care of a widow in the extended family and provision for the under-age children left behind by a father who dies too young. Marriage, therefore, has to be communal and men are raised to be responsible for their families.[33]

Bâ denounced taboos and "old morality and antiquated laws"[34] that contributed to the subjugation of women, subsumed individual needs within communal dictates that indoctrinated women and attempted to stop them from leaving an oppressive marriage with such sayings as "Children need their fathers or mothers", "You don't burn the tree that bears the fruit" or "Boys cannot succeed without their fathers".[35] Bâ also condemned the dispossession of widows by the extended family: property accumulated by a couple during their marriage reverted to the communal pool when the man died.[36] Not only did this trample on the personal dignity of a widow, but such a woman was treated as an object and as the property of her dead husband and his extended family.[37] Bâ disapproved of women being treated as a category, with no recognition given to individuality, personality, skill or experience, once she became a wife. This downside of Senegalese culture came to light in her novel on the death of Modou – the common husband of Ramatoulaye, schoolteacher and wife for thirty years – and Binetou – secondary school drop-out and wife for only five years. The extended family made no distinction between the two women. Even while Modou lived, he saw nothing wrong in mortgaging, for four million CFA francs, the house in which Ramatoulaye and their nine children had lived, the Villa Fallene, built by Société Immobilière du Cap-Vert (SICAP),[38] to pay for a luxurious flat for Binetou and her mother,[39] as was revealed by the Mirasse – the "stripping of the dead" ceremony – on the fourth day of Modou's funeral.[40] It was discovered that Ramatoulaye's name was not on the title deed of the house, although she and her husband Modou had worked hard as a couple and kept all their savings together to buy their home.

Furthermore, Bâ criticises the fact that people value death higher than life, as they often save money to give a relative a befitting burial, rather than spend it while the relative is still alive for hospitalisation and medicines to cure his or her illness.[41] Worse, the money collected at the funeral is taken away by the extended family, leaving the widow and children destitute. It is always in such abusive cases that women suffer oppression and indignity.[42]

The caste system also came under Mariama's scrutiny, for dividing the community between nobles and untouchables. The creative artist belongs to a working class, and should not eat at the same table as the master of noble stock.

Before the advent of Europeans, the artisan was a producer to be admired and reckoned with in traditional Africa.[43] The goldsmith's occupation sustained his family and every family member joined the guild of professionals, as soon as they were socialised into the community through the rite of passage of puberty and initiation.[44] For Bâ: "Each profession, intellectual or manual, deserves consideration, whether it requires painful physical effort or manual dexterity, wide knowledge or the patience of an ant."[45] Unfortunately, the new and modern French school brought about the disappearance of the elite of manual work, while being incapable of training Africans to replace them with new skills. The road to school is often too long and expensive. Although the youth can, in the long run, benefit from Western education, the schools cannot admit every child willing to attend. This obstacle places much demand on the youth, just when they are still attempting to consolidate their personalities. With the new school also come cults, drugs, vagrancy, sexual experimentation and promiscuity, giving rise to delinquency and unemployment among the youth. Bâ resoundingly condemns the hypocrisy of European colonialism which regarded Africans as inferior to Europeans. In *Un chant écarlate*, the malaise of the post-colonial era takes hold of the colonialists as well: they suffer from the ennui and depression of their own domination of others.[46]

How, then, can the African writer merge the good aspects of tradition and modernity, while dropping the bad, despite the hard work required? Mariama Bâ advocates resilience and commitment to throwing off the yoke and burden of colonisation. It is true that the pioneers of nationalism were killed or imprisoned, yet the next generation must not be daunted.[47] But, nationalism – while replacing French assimilationist policies – also introduced party politics and the division of the citizenry into classes and clashing ideologies "because of the constraints, the lies, the injustices that weigh down their conscience in return for ephemeral joys of change".[48] Furthermore, despite this sordid state of affairs, Senegalese embassies abroad, and foreign dignitaries invited back to Africa at great cost to the people, represent money wasted that could have gone towards establishing more schools, hospitals and salaries for wage earners.[49]

In terms of gender equity, polygyny is untenable, opines Bâ, especially as it is practised in the modern era, when men would marry a second wife without involving the first one, in utter disregard of her feelings and traditional mores. Men marry in response to their supposed "caveman's instincts" which drive them to take to bed as many females as possible, in order to sow their seeds and multiply their chances of prolonging their mortality.[50] Examples abound in *Une si longue lettre*, where everyone else in the community knows what is happening, except the women for whom it is of primary concern.[51] When it is not their basic instincts, men use tradition and religion, which they often misinterpret, but selectively forget the Koranic injunctions when they decide to abandon one wife and marry another.[52]

In advocating a new dawn of progress, Bâ asks several pertinent questions. Why is the ratio of males to females in the national assemblies of African nations so vastly uneven? Why are men afraid of women in politics, when they could stimulate discussions about a better humanity?[53] Why do men at once admire and fear educated and powerful women? Why is there no equal pay for equal work between the sexes in most countries of the world? Why are women lacking in opportunities to advance themselves individually and collectively? Why are women often still denied full suffrage by keeping them ignorant or by bullying them? Worse still, why are many women not conscious of their own predicament? Why do women not struggle for their rights, as laid down in the Family Code, aimed at restoring the dignity of women? How many women are aware of the constitutional changes that allow them to inherit property from their parents as well as to benefit from property acquired together with their husbands in marriage? How many women know that they now have the right to their own bodies?

Employing double-voicing as a critical strategy with Dauda Dieng, a gynandrist and one of her male characters, Mariama declares: "Women should no longer be decorative accessories, objects to be moved about, companions to be flattered or calmed with promises. Women are the nation's primary, fundamental root, from which all else grows and blossoms. Women must be encouraged to take keener interest in the destiny of the country."[54] Again, Bâ adds: "Developing a country is not easy. The more responsibility one has, the more one feels it; poverty breaks your heart, but you have no control over it. I am speaking of the whole range of material and moral poverty. Better living requires roads, decent houses, wells, clinics, medicines, seeds … Any project that enables regional investments and transformations is welcome."[55]

Bâ asks too: How then can nations merge economic liberation with political emancipation in Africa? How can women's struggles for liberation and education complement their quest for integration into the political and governing systems of their communities and countries? How can the neo-colonialism of Africa be tackled, so that democracy based on socialism, and adapted to the realities of life, can be achieved? That would be the way to regain liberty and open many doors for the disadvantaged and the poor. For that reason, the idea of a single party – as in Senegal – is not laudable, since it is impossible to express the diverse and divergent views of all citizens through one party. As Bâ noted: "If all individuals were made in the same mould, it would lead to an appalling collectivism. Differences produce conflicts, which may be beneficial to the development of a country if they occur among true patriots, whose only ambition is the happiness of the citizens."[56]

On the youth, Bâ opines that they need to be guided in their quest for their own self-identity. Town planners should make provision for recreational spaces and facilities for them, so that they are not forced to play in the streets, thereby endangering their lives.[57] Social ills and delinquencies should be eschewed, such as smoking, teenage pregnancy, drunkenness and immorality, for they cannot lead to the progress of the individual or the community.[58] Rhetorically, Mariama asks: "Does it mean that one can't have modernism without a lowering of moral standards?"[59] She suggests that young people should date openly, so as to "limit the damage" and consequently not to have to give up their education.[60] The youth, for their part, should exercise self-control, reason, choice, power and liberty, and should not abuse the privilege of sexual expression by neglecting their bodies, in essence their temple, which should be held in respect at all times. For Mariama, just because contraceptives are available to them does not mean they should abuse their sexual freedom. Otherwise, one becomes open to abuse by all and sundry, which could lead to degeneration to the level of an animal. Then, speaking specifically about, and to, women, Bâ concludes: "Each woman makes her life what she wants. A profligate woman is incompatible with morality. What does one gain from pleasures? Early ageing, debasement, no doubt about it."[61]

Concluding Reflections

Clearly, Mariama Bâ's legacy includes the institutional politics of family, workplace, school, religion, gender, sex, customs, traditions, state and nation. She recommends a future of progress anchored in foundational African cultural traditions and open to borrowings from other cultures that enhance African life. More than before, women should become part of this future, with courage and independence. No longer should they be afraid to be branded lion women, troublemakers, chaos-seekers and crazy,[62] when they choose to march in front because they are able to do things better than them.[63] On the contrary, women should hold up their heads, because they have education, skills and know-how to do and to dare. In the end, men and women should be there for each other – whether as individuals or communities in societies and nations. For where there is selfless love there is no discrimination, no dominance, and no subjugation, only empathy and compassion. Bâ concludes by praising the merits of love and gender equality:

> Love, imperfect as it may be in its context and expression, remains the natural link between these two beings. To love one another! If only each partner could move sincerely towards the other! If each could only melt into the other! If each would only accept the other's successes and failures! If each would only praise the other's qualities instead of listing his faults! If each could only correct bad habits without harping on about them! If each could penetrate the other's most secret haunts to forestall failure and be a support while tending to the evils that are repressed![64]

That was Mariama Bâ, from the beginning, and at her finest in older age, showing maturity and wisdom.

35

MICERE MUGO: MAKING LIFE SING IN PURSUIT OF UTU

Ndirangu Wachanga

THERE IS NO BIOGRAPHY that is more emblematic of Kenya's political, cultural and intellectual history, and the processes of becoming a nation, than that of Micere Githae Mugo. She made life sing in pursuit of Utu: that which makes us human.

Growing up during one of the most violent periods in Kenyan history, and coming of age at the end of the colonial occupation of the country, Micere's life has mirrored Kenya's failures and triumphs. Her career offers an inspiring diagnosis of the Kenyan condition, beginning with the crises of the pre-independence era in the 1950s involving the Mau Mau uprising and extending to the unresolved grievances that haunt contemporary Kenya such as ethnic divisions and electoral violence. In her own quiet way, Micere has been one of the most prominent custodians of Kenya's national conscience.

I have served as Mugo's authorised documentary biographer. From 2013, I travelled with her to her birthplace in Baricho in central Kenya; to her residence in Syracuse in upstate New York. During this period, I have conducted numerous interviews with her family members, students, academic colleagues, community members, and cultural and political activists.

Micere Mugo's life provides a window into the major historical, academic, cultural and political developments in Kenya, as well as the study of its literature and orature. Her cultural activism as well as her intellectual work has fashioned a space for creatively imagining Africa's history and herstory, which she has argued were repressed by colonialism and continue to be suppressed by neo-colonialism, imperialism and the oppressive designs of patriarchy.

For close to half a century, Mugo has been an eloquent voice in championing democracy and human rights in Kenya and beyond. She is regarded as one of Africa's leading writers, and one of the most significant post-colonial political, social and cultural thinkers produced by the continent. She has been widely recognised for her foundational role in the development of orature. In the humanities, she occupies a unique place in Africa's oral performance, cultural criticism and political activism. Her two celebrated plays,[1] two collections of poems,[2] and two collections of essays[3] about pre- and post-independence Kenya and Africa blend lyricism with uncompromising political and social commentary. A wordsmith *par excellence*, Mugo weaves her narratives with deep care for form and content. Her influential play with Ngũgĩ wa Thiong'o, *The Trial of Dedan Kimathi* (1976)[4] – involving one of the Mau Mau struggle's most prominent figures – served as a vehicle for her desire to transform an artistic production into a communal enterprise in subtle ways, thus enabling her to transcend critical literary barriers that often separate readers from a text and its context.

Mugo's inexorable commitment to artistic expression, education, democracy, representation, human rights and economic equality sparked the anger of the Kenyan governments of Jomo Kenyatta (1963–78) and Daniel arap Moi (1978–2002), triggering a series of political battles that subsequently forced her into exile in 1982.

A Difficult, Privileged Childhood

Micere (nicknamed Njũrĩ, and later baptised as Madeleine) was born on 12 December 1942 to an elite Kenyan family. She rose to become not only a carrier, but also a maker of Kenya's herstory. Her father, Richard Karuga Githae, was a schoolteacher and commissioner of the Boy Scouts in central Kenya. He was actively involved in the country's independence struggle, serving as an active member of the Kenya African Union (KAU), a forerunner of the Kenya African National Union (KANU). Richard Githae worked closely with the country's founding president, Jomo Kenyatta, in the late 1940s and early 1950s in organising rallies that conscientised the masses against British colonial rule. He later, curiously – given his anti-colonial antecedents – became a colonial senior chief. But when Githae refused to use methods of torture adopted by the British colonial rulers in fighting the Mau Mau uprising, he was arrested and imprisoned. Micere later explained how profoundly her father's imprisonment had affected her:

I cannot accurately recall the year [when her father was imprisoned], but I want to say it was either 1954, or 1955 ... At the time of my father's arrest and jailing, I was a boarder at the then prestigious government school for girls: Embu Girls' Intermediate School (Kangaru). We used to be allowed out on Saturday afternoons and would go out in uniform, returning in time for roll call.

One Saturday afternoon, I was called from my dormitory and told that I had family guests. On going out to meet them, I was elated to find out that it was my mother, Grace Njeri and her younger sister, *Tata* (Aunty) Joyce, who was a teacher in Gaturi, Mūrang'a. But their gloomy faces cut down my excitement. After embraces, my mother told me to go back into the dormitory and put on my uniform because they wanted to take me to Boma, the name Embu town was known by. It all didn't make sense, but on the way to Boma, they informed me that my father had been jailed and when they had visited him in jail earlier, he had asked for me. [At the time, my two elder sisters were miles away in Gatĩ Igũrũ boarding school, Mūgoiri, Mūrang'a.] Apparently, my father had been accused of double-dealing with the government and assisting Mau Mau adherents by refusing to torture villagers and their families to force them to confess their linkages with the fighters. He had been sacked as Senior Chief presiding over Mwea Division.

I remember speaking with my father from outside Embu jail, separated by what seemed unending rows of barbed wire. His hands were shackled and there were two guards on either side, plus many more swarming all over the place, all armed to the teeth. I was scared to death. We had to shout our conversation through the rolls of wire. At first I was just in shock and tongue-tied, but when the visit ended and the *askaris* [guards] escorted him back (I suppose to his cell), I simply broke down into tears and cried for so long that my mother and aunt were still begging me to dry my eyes as I waved them good-bye after they took me back to school.

I have no idea what lawyer fought for my father's release, but I heard he was released after legal intervention. I believe he was in jail for several months. He was then given some administrative job in Boma because I do remember that during my last two years at Embu Girls' School (1955/1956) and before joining Alliance Girls' High School in 1957 we lived in Embu town.[5]

Micere attended Baricho primary school, and developed a passion for education and reading as an exceptionally bright student. In 1952 she then went on to Embu Girls' Intermediate School in Kangaru, which admitted only the very best students in the region, before studying at another elite school, Alliance Girls' High School, between 1957 and 1960. At Alliance, Mugo was very active in sports and other extracurricular activities, performing with the school choir, joining the debating society, and engaging in drama and creative writing. She was sociable and appointed as the school's head girl. While at Alliance, Micere was sheltered from the unspeakable colonial violence taking place beyond the gates of the school. The British colonial government had deployed its most vicious measures following the militant demand of Kenya's liberation movement for independence. The Mau Mau demanded the release of Jomo Kenyatta and other detainees, the integration of public spaces and political independence. Among the first demands that the British conceded to the country's liberation movement was the integration of schools. This marked the beginning of powerful twists in Micere's life.

She was selected from Alliance Girls after her O-levels (then known as the Cambridge School Certificate) – along with an Indian girl, Kirpal Singh, from Agha Khan School in Nairobi – and enrolled at Limuru Girls' High School, a private white settler girls' school in Kenya's White Highlands in 1961. Micere and Kirpal then became experimental guinea pigs to test whether blacks and Asians could intellectually and cognitively match their white counterparts. This was Kenya's pre-independence era, and the country was organised along the lines of a colonial settler economy imbued with the racism of a four-tiered racial hierarchy: whites on top, followed by Asians, followed by Arabs and mixed-race "Coloureds", with blacks at the bottom of this perverse racial pyramid.

In an interview in 2014, Micere described her enrolment at Limuru Girls' High School:

It literally turned my world upside down. I was coming from Alliance Girls' High School where I was respected. Limuru, I knew, was going to be a hostile environment because some parents had actually removed their children from the school when the new liberal headmistress, Miss Veronica Owen, newly arrived from Malvern Girls' College in Britain, decided to be the first person to show the courage to engage in the process of integration. I didn't know anyone; I didn't have friends. It was a very lonely environment and I understood that I was walking into an antagonistic space. Knowing that a lot of students believed I was inferior to them and assumed that I couldn't perform at their level made the experience very painful.[6]

Limuru Girls was originally founded exclusively for the daughters of Kenya's white settlers and white colonial government officials, even though it later admitted students from other white communities such as missionaries from East Africa and elsewhere. Walking into the school compound, Micere was transgressing racially defined practices and conventions: a form of contravention that radically changed the psychology of, and the ordering of, the education system. Once inside, other girls isolated Mugo. Some even expressed shock that she would be using the same bathroom as them. Others wanted to move away from her dormitory. Yet others would simply walk away if she sat next to them in the dining hall.

Makerere and Canada

At Limuru Girls, all spaces were infested by covert, if not openly overt, acts of racial discrimination. As Micere later recalled: "I used to be extremely lonely and it was very painful. That period I got ... into a habit of reading extensively as I made friends with books and that is how I came across the literature of James Baldwin."[7] Baldwin's work and activism inspired Micere to recognise that her experiences of racism at Limuru were not unique.

Micere recalls that the school's headmistress, Veronica Owen, was quite supportive, as were a few other teachers. Outside the school, other progressive public figures had championed Mugo's enrolment at Limuru. They included Bishop Trevor Huddleston, the British anti-apartheid clergyman then based in neighbouring Tanganyika; Tom Mboya, an exceptionally shrewd Kenyan trade unionist and later cabinet minister; and Bishop Obadiah Kariuki, one of the first black Anglican bishops to be ordained in Kenya. They visited Micere at Limuru, reminding her that the experiment had significant consequences for the entire black community in Kenya, as well as for the country's independence movement. "It is as if our independence depended on Micere's performance," Kenyan writer Ngũgĩ wa Thiong'o noted in an interview in 2015.[8]

Ngũgĩ drew parallels between Micere's case and the experiences of the "Little Rock Nine", the African-American students who enrolled in an all-white school in Arkansas in 1957. But there were also key differences. As Ngũgĩ noted: "Those in Arkansas needed troops to ensure their entry. Micere did not need troops to ensure her enrolment. Those in Arkansas were nine. Micere Mugo was just one. For Kenya, she was the one."[9]

Despite the pain she endured, the loneliness she withstood, and the racism she confronted, Micere finished among the best students at Limuru in her A-levels. She obtained admission with a scholarship to study at Oxford University. She declined the offer and instead joined Makerere University College in Uganda in 1963 because "at that time, Makerere had acquired a reputation of almost mythical proportions. People graduating from Makerere were seen as gods and goddesses walking on the earth," she noted.[10]

Uganda had gained its independence in 1962, a year before Micere arrived in Makerere, where she graduated in 1966. Her relief was palpable when she arrived at an institution at which the majority of students were black. Ngũgĩ wa Thiong'o was Mugo's senior in the English Department in the university, and they worked together on *PenPoint*, the department's literary journal. Ngũgĩ was the editor and Micere served as assistant editor, before rising to become the first female editor of the journal.

After Makerere, Mugo went on to acquire many firsts: she was the first black deputy headmistress of Alliance Girls, her alma mater; and the first Kenyan to obtain a doctorate in literature in 1973 from the University of New Brunswick in Canada, with a thesis on the different visions of Africa in the works of Chinua Achebe, Margaret Laurence, Elspeth Huxley and Ngũgĩ wa Thiong'o.

While in Canada until 1973, Micere was actively involved in political movements fighting for the liberation of southern African countries such as Namibia, Angola, Mozambique, Zimbabwe and South Africa. She was also active in the Black Power Movement in the United States. This is how she met and forged strong friendships with such activists as Angela Davis and Assata Shakur, whom she later visited in Cuba.

The University of Nairobi

By the time Mugo joined the University of Nairobi in 1973, she had been nurtured by a tradition of struggle and emboldened by a culture of resistance. Arriving at Kenya's leading institution of higher learning, she became an active participant in the open and vibrant debates that defined the intellectual culture at the university during this transformative era. This was a period when intellectuals debated with political leaders; memorable clashes occurred involving Ali Mazrui, Julius Nyerere and Milton Obote.

The decade of the 1970s also witnessed a crisis as the initial euphoria that arose from the dreams of a new dawn was gradually dispelled. The unholy trinity of poverty, disease and illiteracy was ravaging Kenya's subaltern underclass, even as a tiny corrupt leadership class had emerged. Longstanding grievances remained unresolved and new ones were emerging. There was a widespread clamour for an alternative political order. Disillusionment had set in. If intellectuals had sought to present the paradoxes of the new country in the late 1960s, they fashioned a path to interrogate the future beyond these paradoxes in the 1970s. When Mugo was leaving for Canada in the late 1960s, there was a sense of optimism and sanguineness in Kenya. Her return to her native country in the 1970s was akin to a narrative of melancholy and disenchantment. Indeed, Kenya was a paradox: a country suffocating under the weight of disillusionment, but also energised by the vibrancy of intellectual debates that imagined the future beyond the failures of independence and the contractions of the neo-colony.

Still, at the University of Nairobi, there were significant changes following the call for the abolition of the English Department and its replacement with the Department of Literature after the curriculum transformation rebellion in 1969, led by Ngũgĩ wa Thiong'o, Taban Lo Liyong and Henry Owuor Anyumba.[11] The trio offered a new approach to challenging dominant ideas while suggesting other ways of thinking about Africa outside the established paradigms. It is not until 1973, when Ngũgĩ became the head of the department and Micere joined him, that the radical changes which had earlier been advocated were implemented. Mugo contributed immensely to the developments that placed Africa at the centre of a literary curriculum that integrated African, African-American, Caribbean, Indian, Latin American and Asian literatures in one department. This fundamentally changed the study of literature at Nairobi University, and contributed substantially to the post-colonial literary project across Africa and globally.

Kenyan academic Simon Gikandi was Micere's student between 1976 and 1979. In 2015, he described the inspiring role of his teacher thus:

I recall her lecturing to us, very young, would-be intellectuals, in what was then Education Theatre II. Or I remember sitting around a seminar table, at the Department of Literature, discussing South African writers, debating the implication of Alan Paton's liberalism or Alex La Guma's Marxism; disagreeing with her sometimes, partly agreeing with her other times, and completely agreeing with her many times.[12]

Micere had a tremendous influence in reforming Kenya's primary and secondary education system. She was not only the first African chief examiner of O-level and A-level literature in East Africa in the post-colonial era, but she was also part of the project that decolonised the curriculum in Kenya. She belonged to the group of academics who challenged older British interests that still controlled most institutions of cultural production, such as the British Cultural Centre and the Kenya National Theatre. Rather than reforming the education system through Kenya's Ministry of Education, Micere instead used her influence and position as an examiner and a scholar of literature to work closely with high school teachers. According to her, the biggest national educational projects between 1973 and 1982 included "overhauling the up to then colonial secondary school curricula, promoting drama and theatre in schools and colleges, increasing outreach to the communities outside the campus, applying individual and collective research to practical community needs and so on".[13]

Micere worked closely with Ngũgĩ in an intellectual relationship which culminated in their co-authoring the play *The Trial of Dedan Kimathi* in 1976.[14] According to Ngũgĩ, the play was a major intervention in the writing of Kenya's history and politics, particularly because the project sought to capture the aesthetics of resistance at the heart of contemporary Kenyan history, reversing the official trend of indifference and denial about the epic nature of Kenya's independence struggle and the heroic role that had been played by Dedan Kimathi. The attendance of Kimathi's wife and her children at the play's performance at the Kenya National Theatre in 1976 added to its success in attracting large audiences.

Micere played the role of Woman, the leading female character in the play, who was also a respected general and confidante of Field Marshal Dedan Kimathi. According to Gikandi:

the enactment of *The Trial of Dedan Kimathi* was not just the recovery of repressed voices, but what turned out to be a struggle over the meaning of history in the post-colony between the authorised voices of the new colonial elites who insisted on the need to forgive and forget and the claims of Kenyan people insisting on the primacy of their own local histories in the site of self-fashioning.[15]

Ironically, the success of the play marked the beginning of the state's suspicions about Mugo's and Ngũgĩ's intellectual relationship and collaboration. One of the more absurd charges was that they were interfering with the European theatre. In the four days of performance of this play at the Kenyan National Theatre to a packed house in 1976 – the only days allowed for the play – police in riot gear would conduct exercises at the nearby Central Police Station in a show of intimidation.

In December 1977 Ngũgĩ was detained without trial. Mugo remained at the university as one of the most senior faculty members. Symbolically, by jailing the country's leading writer, the government of Jomo Kenyatta was sending a message that no dissenting voice would be spared. But Mugo could not be intimidated, as she belonged to a group of radical intellectuals who, as she put it in 2015,

> decoded their language so that there was communication and dialogue with the students and members of their constituent communities. They organised out-reach symposia in schools and colleges. They became rebels. Important as these developments were, however, what these people often overlooked was the urgency of identifying tactics that would help them dodge the now widening net of repression, denial of academic freedom and abuse of human rights.[16]

In 1978 Mugo was elected dean of the Faculty of Arts at the University of Nairobi, the first woman dean in the country's history. Her campaign to become dean had been led by, among others, Peter Anyang Nyong'o, Michael Chege, Apollo Njonjo and Katama Mkangi. During the campaign, Micere was "plagued with all forms of intimidation, including stalking and life-threatening anonymous telephone calls".[17]

Still, she won the deanship, beating the state and administration-preferred candidate, Philip Mbithi. Her turbulent ascent to power marked the beginning of yet another tumultuous phase in her biography. As Mugo later noted in 2015:

> We were given to understand that the government ordered the university Registrar to nullify the elections immediately, which he did even though he

had been the election's returning officer and had publicly announced my victory. He issued an official bulletin announcing that he had appointed the defeated candidate to serve as Acting Dean until further notice. The activists issued a counter statement, with my consent, asserting that I was the elected Dean and would not step down. The CID (Criminal Investigation Department) police swung into action and threatened me with arrest if I did not step down. At times, they would coax me to resign, advising me that my activism was not befitting of a respectable woman.[18]

During this period, Mugo was constantly harassed, often receiving demeaning and sexually graphic messages on her home telephone. Holding such a position in the 1980s required much courage, especially at a time when powerful men were running the government. Although Mugo was viewed as an "enemy of the state," her brother-in-law, Jeremiah Kiereini, was an influential secretary to the cabinet at the time, and a close confidant of President Daniel arap Moi. In criticising the government and its policies, Mugo was accused of undermining members of her own family who were in positions of power. According to her brother-in-law, "I spoke to her many times. But I realised that I was not going to change her. I feared that she was going to be detained, and there was nothing I could have done to stop it."[19]

A Difficult Deanship

Had Mugo so chosen, she could have climbed to the top of Kenya's hierarchy of power, consorting with heads of state and dealing with the occupants of some of the most powerful positions in the country. But she chose to go beyond those privileges and think about larger issues not only in terms of pedagogy, but also in terms of the role of culture in development. By choosing a "people's path" to champion the interests of the masses rather than the elite, Mugo had become reprehensibly dangerous in the eyes of the elite and the state. By refusing the privileges of her class, Mugo had effectively committed class suicide.

Micere's unshakeable resolve to give up certain privileges for the greater good was demonstrated in her incorruptibility during her tenure as dean between 1979 and 1982. The Moi government offered her properties or positions that came with many privileges, but she declined all of these. She recounted one of these encounters:

At one point, the government offered me land up there in Naromoru, about 50 acres. I was actually called to go to [Minister of Land and Settlement] Mr. [Nicholas] Biwott's office in order to be given this gift from President Moi. While at the office, I told Mr. Biwott, "Thank you very much, I really appreciate it, but please can you give this piece of land to some of the landless people, especially the former Mau Mau fighters?" The next thing I knew was that I was being called in for questioning at the police station. "Look," interrogators yelled. "You were offered this piece of land by the president and you were very rude and you are now trying to tell him who to give it to. Who do you think you are?"

During the interrogation, if I didn't write what they wanted me to, I remember a number of times they would hold my head and bash it on the table. Many times, I would go blank. Later, during hospitalisation in London, I was to discover that a minor stroke I had been diagnosed with had come from these bashings. But I recovered sufficiently from the ordeal.[20]

The attempted coup in Kenya in August 1982 was the culmination of the violent intervention of the state in the cultural sphere. This event also signified the end of the university as an autonomous space for free thinking. The revolution that Mugo and others had fought for during the previous decade was interrupted. Mugo had just returned from England where she had been treated for a minor stroke. According to her brother-in-law, Kiereini, Micere was going to be detained,[21] as government agents viciously went after those it felt had contributed to the attempted coup. Mugo had not recovered fully from the stroke, and in order to avoid detention, she hurriedly left the country with her two young daughters, eight-year-old Mumbi and six-year-old-Njeri.

By exiling Micere and others such as Ngũgĩ wa Thiong'o and Alamin Mazrui, Kenya lost two generations of intellectuals responsible for vital African-centred and democratically driven projects of education. The Moi regime seemed oblivious to the positive role of intellectuals in society. Mugo and her group were not interested in political power; they were instead seeking to create a space where a democratically-driven project of education could take place. The university collapsed as an autonomous space of knowledge production. The nostalgia that developed for the 1970s – despite its economic and political problems – derived from a yearning for a past that had characterised the university as a centre of autonomous debates. When Mugo campaigned to become dean, there had been heated debates. What was unique about this, however, was that these debates were open. After the 1982 coup, the university became an extension of the government and its interests. Once the institution had lost its ideals, it became a functional place to be manipulated by politicians: a place to be seen, but not valued for the ideas that it produced. A president coming from a wedding on a Saturday afternoon could decide who taught what philosophy at the university, and decree which books could be studied in high school literature courses. Marxism was thus banned as a subject of study at all the country's universities.

American and Zimbabwean Exile

St Lawrence University in Canton, New York, offered Mugo a visiting professorship when she started her sojourn in exile in 1982. But after two years at St Lawrence, she decided to return to Africa. Her two young daughters had suffered racism, and were constantly bullied by some of their schoolmates. Mugo also felt "alienated, geographically, historically, and spiritually, from the heart of the struggle that my compatriots and patriots were waging at home".[22]

In 1984, Micere applied for and was offered a position as chair and professor of English at the University of Zambia. Excited, she packed all her belongings and shipped them to Lusaka. On the way to Zambia, accompanied by her two daughters, they made a stop-over in London where *The Trial of Dedan Kimathi* was being performed at the Commonwealth Centre. But while in London, Mugo was informed by the Zambian High Commission in London that the Kenyan government had contacted the Zambian government, requesting that she be denied landing rights in Lusaka. Mugo and her two children could therefore not proceed to Zambia. They were stranded in London. The situation became so dire that Micere had to send Mumbi and Njeri to Kenya, while she struggled to determine her next move. When the shipping agents in Zambia were contacted regarding Micere's goods, they said that they had never received them. She lost everything, from her extensive library collection to her daughters' precious toys.

Fortunately, Mugo had been involved as an activist in the liberation movements of southern Africa when she was a student in Canada. While she was at the University of Nairobi, she had also helped to send material to support the liberation movements in Zimbabwe and Mozambique. When Sally Mugabe, the Ghanaian wife of Zimbabwe's president, Robert Mugabe, learnt about Mugo's plight, she asked her to apply for a position at the University of Zimbabwe.

Mugo got the job, and made Harare her home for eight years. During her stay in Zimbabwe, Mugo needed a new passport. She applied for a new one after contacting Sally Kosgei, the Kenyan ambassador in Harare at the time. Mugo would never see her passport again. This was at the time when President Moi made the declaration that people like Mugo were not Kenyans. The Zimbabwean government came to Mugo's rescue by granting her Zimbabwean citizenship. Only in 2010 was her Kenyan citizenship finally restored.

After her sojourn in Harare, Micere returned to North America as a visiting professor at Cornell University in Ithaca, New York, during her sabbatical leave in 1992, before moving in 1993 to Syracuse University where she taught for 22 years until her retirement in 2015.

While patriarchy partly explains why Mugo was marginalised in the politics of literary canon formation, this sidelining also resulted from how she conducted her life. Micere was content to work behind the scenes. She willingly gave up the public platform so that she could do the work she preferred. She was not an admirer of the "cult of celebrity" and refused to be celebrated as a unique individual, particularly because of her commitment to the interests of the collective. At the University of Nairobi, when professors were standing on their seemingly untouchable pedestals, Mugo would be conversing with students in the institution's corridors.

Towards the end of the 1970s, Micere started to rethink the project of literature in relation to its audiences and sources. She became interested in orature at the time of political crisis in Kenya. Her significant work in this area was largely produced in Zimbabwean exile in the 1980s, and it revolved around the relationship between orature and democracy. Micere studied orature because she was looking for new avenues of using literature as a medium of democratisation. Once she became involved in orature in Zimbabwe, she started to see literature and literary criticism as a mode of performance. Observing her delivering a lecture, one notices a profound sense of commitment to performativity, which not only allows her ideas to be articulated powerfully, but also makes these ideas accessible since they are being performed. Micere studied orature and its intersection with democracy because she was committed to giving people a voice, which is one of the most important tools in the production of a culture of democratisation.

Concluding Reflections

One question that has haunted many students of Mugo's work is the source of her strength, since her life has so often been punctuated by protest, pain and persecutions. Like most women of her generation, Micere came of age at a very difficult time: the period of Kenya's emergency in the 1950s. Her poetry is reflective of the violence of that period in which most women had to summon their inner strength to survive. Most men were either in exile or fighting in the forest, or had been "swallowed" by the detention camps. Mugo's strength also came from her commitment to her work, an undying willingness to pursue a project to its logical conclusion. Furthermore, she seems to derive much strength from her own black community. When Micere moved to North America, she was heavily influenced by the Black Arts Movement, especially the power of community organisation. One of her major strengths is her ceaseless ability to create communities wherever she has lived.

Her life is defined by struggles, resilience, commitment, bravery, passion and, more importantly, honesty and forthrightness. If there have been attempts to frame her in other terms, it is precisely because Kenya's process of becoming has been defined by an unofficially sanctioned programme of forgetting. Micere's biography powerfully invites the Kenyan public to resist that urge to forget. This has been the case in most African countries where the official policy has promoted amnesia, and the public tends easily to buy into official histories urging them to forget certain incidents and remember only events that have been officially sanctioned. Micere's biography invites the public to re-examine the memory project. It encourages them to understand the present by examining the past.

Mugo's life, like those of other intellectuals, is an important historical archive. There is an emerging trend in Kenya in which elites are writing biographies or hiring biographers to write it for them. There seems to be a struggle to control the past and its meaning; attempts to recall and rewrite a certain history that fits the officially sanctioned project of remembering. More importantly, because of her work and the nature of her activism, Mugo was labelled a "dissident intellectual" by the Kenyan authorities. Her life provides us with an alternative approach which fashions a space for honest dialogue.

How does one move on after being forced to abandon a thriving intellectual space that one has nurtured? How does one forgive a system that destroys one's family and violently disrupts one's life? Micere's response to these fundamental questions was this:

> I used to be very angry and bitter. We were being silenced and methods of silencing were unspeakably cruel. But the regime would have been victorious if we all broke down and simply turned into nothing more than angry men and women. If I allowed myself to wade in bitterness, that would have been part of the defeat. I needed to forgive; to focus on what I believed was my right to live up to my conscience. I had to remind myself that part of the liberation process was not just to create a better world, but also to create better people of ourselves. [That involved] learning to humanise ourselves and be humane in the way we articulate our thoughts and treat others. I also learned the differences between systems and institutions, and agents functioning in them. The person who oppresses you as an agent of an oppressive system is also being dehumanised. Oppressive systems dehumanise their own agents as much as they seek to dehumanise those who resist oppression. If one, therefore, is to do any meaningful work of transformation, one must learn not only to liberate oneself, but also to remember that even the oppressor needs to be liberated.[23]

No one can endure such experiences without personal scars. Mugo has learnt to live with these scars, and accepted them without focusing on their negative aspects, thus turning them into "monuments of beauty".[24]

PART 8

THE MUSICAL ACTIVISTS

Miriam Makeba: Mama Africa

Nomsa Mwamuka

THROUGHOUT THE TWENTIETH CENTURY, various socio–political movements and leaders, including Pan Africanists, used culture as a weapon of resistance and as a unifying force in the quest for freedom from oppression. Ghana's Kwame Nkrumah spoke of the African Personality to express "cultural and social bonds which unite Africans and people of African descent"[1] (see Biney in this volume). Tanzania's Julius Nyerere regarded culture as a power: "the soul and spirit"[2] of the nation. Guinea-Bissau's Amílcar Cabral described culture as simultaneously "the fruit of a people's history and a determinant of history" as well as an "essential component" in liberation struggles[3] (see Rabaka in this volume). The Congo's Patrice Lumumba stated: "We have a culture of our own ... unparalleled moral and artistic values, an art of living and patterns of life that are ours alone ... these African splendours must be jealously preserved and developed."[4] Guinea's Sékou Touré turned his vision of *l'authenticité* – embracing African culture – into an official cultural policy of his government.[5] These calls to centre African culture and identity in liberation struggles included embracing the return to an ideological past where "music, songs, drama, storytelling, dance, drumming, drawing were used to rebel, agitate, communicate, educate and claim freedom".[6]

Artist, Activist and Pan-Africanist

Then Miriam Makeba – "Mama Africa" – came along. Through her music, songs, dance, style and image, and by virtue of being one of the first African artists to become visible in the international arena, she came to embody, symbolise and personify the Pan-Africanism and pride in African culture and identity that many of the aforementioned leaders were seeking.

From this perspective – focusing on Makeba's story and weaving it into the fabric of broader history – this essay explores the interrelationship between cultural expression, specifically music, and social dynamics. It explores how Makeba's experiences and activities on and off stage had an impact on her society, and, conversely, how her music and her life were shifted and shaped by various political and social movements of her era: from anti-colonialism to anti-apartheid, from civil rights and black nationalism to African nationalism and Pan-Africanism.

When she made her first professional appearance as a lead vocalist for the popular South African all-male band, the Manhattan Brothers, the bandleader proudly announced: "Introducing ... our own nut-brown baby ... Miriam Makeba." The year was 1952. The place was the black Johannesburg township of Soweto. Makeba was 20 years old. The following day, in the *Bantu World* newspaper, journalist Bloke Modisane effused about Miriam's performance, gushing: "She sings like a nightingale."[7] Little did anyone imagine that this powerful voice would resonate across the country, the continent and the world for five and a half more decades.

As Miriam Makeba's career progressed, she traversed the world. With her trips, her nicknames grew, as did her reputation. In the early 1960s, Miriam went from being nonchalantly tagged "The Click, Click Girl" to being declared "Africa's musical ambassador to the US".[8] In the late 1960s, she became "The Voice of Africa". In the 1970s, at a concert recorded live at the Théâtre des Champs-Elysées in Paris, she was dubbed *"l'Impératrice de la chanson africaine"* ("the Empress of African Song"). By the 1980s, Makeba needed little introduction. They simply called her "Mama Africa". The continent had claimed her. She, in turn, claimed Africa back.

Miriam Makeba was first and foremost an artist, a singer and a performer who, by harnessing the power of her gift – her voice, her songs, her music, her presence and, in essence, her culture – saw her life take on a political mantle. Makeba was secondly an activist. She sang and spoke out against injustices, vocalising against apartheid, and chanting for the independence of oppressed people across Africa. She used her voice for the social upliftment of black Africans, and for fundraising and consciousness-raising at social, cultural and political events.

Ultimately, Makeba was a Pan-Africanist, singing to the broad tenets of national consciousness, political and economic emancipation, historical and cultural awareness, pride and dignity. "Unify us, don't divide us," she sang on her hit single "West Wind" (1966). Much as she was bound by her South Africanness, Miriam chose to embrace her African heritage. However, when asked about her identity, Makeba declared herself to be a "citizen of the world".

This essay seeks to show the potential of art and culture in political activism. Miriam Makeba often protested: "I don't sing politics, I merely sing the truth."[9] What was her truth? Could she have avoided politics? I assess this through an analysis of Makeba's life, captured in three chronological and somewhat overlapping phases: South Africa (1930s–1959), America (1959–69), and Africa and the world (1970s–1990s), discovering how her music impacted on African and international society beyond her initial design.

South Africa: Birth and Beginnings

Miriam Zenzile Makeba was born on 4 March 1932 in Pretoria (Tshwane), South Africa, of Swati and Xhosa parentage. Her mother was a domestic worker who supplemented her income by "illegally" brewing traditional beer, *umqombothi*. Like many other women of her epoch, she was often arrested for this activity. Her father died when Miriam was six. She was sent to live with her grandmother, and raised as one of 21 grandchildren in a township where, while the family sought to stave off poverty, Miriam was buoyed by the strength of the women around her, as well as by the spirit of communalism within the black community.

Music, from the start, was central to Makeba's life. She would watch migrant labourers from neighbouring countries such as Bechuanaland (Botswana), Nyasaland (Malawi), Southern Rhodesia (Zimbabwe) and Tanganyika (Tanzania), as well as Xhosa and Pedi workers, playing their traditional songs and instruments on the streets.[10] They entertained and inspired her. Miriam enjoyed her mother's singing, and watched her play drums and the mouth organ. From her mother, who would later become a traditional healer (*sangoma*), Makeba learnt to sing spiritual and ancestral songs. Her brother played the saxophone and piano, collected records, and introduced Miriam to the jazz of black American divas Ella Fitzgerald and Billie Holiday. With these hybrid influences, Makeba "could sing in English before [she] could even speak it!"[11] She sang in church, at community functions, and at school where a choir director, Joseph Mothuba, once taught Miriam a song about oppression which went: "Wake up my people, let's get together, for the fault is within us."[12] Makeba was then 12 years old, but learnt at an early age that song could be a powerful weapon of protest. Her childhood was disrupted when, aged 13, money ran out, and her education ended. She was forced, like her mother, to become a domestic worker.

In 1948, Miriam was 16 when the National Party came to power. With this political development came oppressive apartheid laws that classified groups racially; outlawed miscegenation; imposed the carrying of identity passes; uprooted millions of people into ethnically designated townships and homelands ("Bantustans");[13] and legitimised the use of separate public amenities such as beaches, toilets and park benches. In 1953 the government introduced the Bantu Education Act which would have dire consequences for the black majority. Its chief architect, Hendrik Verwoerd, explained the Act as follows: "There is no place for the Bantu in the European community above the level of certain forms of labour. Until now he has been subjected to a school system which drew him away from his own community and misled him by showing him green pastures of European society in which he will not be allowed to graze."[14] In this environment, Miriam's life, like those of many other black people around her, was conflicted. Aged 18, she fell pregnant, was compelled to marry her mixed-race police officer boyfriend, James "Goolie" Kubayi, and became a mother. After suffering physical and emotional abuse at the hands of her husband, Miriam fled, child in hand, ultimately making her way to Johannesburg. The injustice, inequality, and racial and gender abuse that marked this early phase in her life would help shape Makeba's future activism.

In Johannesburg, Miriam's singing talent led to the world of professional music where – aside from harassment from township gangsters or *tsotsis* and the scorn of those who considered her career risqué – she made her way with hits that were played on Radio Bantu, and eventually across the continent. Rare for her times, Makeba was able to travel across Southern and Northern Rhodesia, to Mozambique, and to the Belgian Congo. She made a name for herself in the region despite many obstacles. Constantly in black newspapers, Makeba was widely photographed for her style, her music and her daring relationship with Indian balladeer Shunna "Sonny" Pillay, in contravention of apartheid's 1950 Immorality Act[15] and other laws. Shunna would soon become her second husband, though their marriage in 1959 would last only for a few months. After being cast in the lead role of the hit musical *King Kong* in 1958, Miriam's fame grew, and she was invited to star in a documentary shot clandestinely by American filmmaker Lionel Rogosin. Titled *Come Back, Africa*, the 1960 docufiction was scathingly critical of apartheid's racism and was not allowed to be screened in South Africa until shown at a security film festival in Durban in 1982 (which the police raided); in 1988, it was officially unbanned.[16]

While Miriam's career soared, the endemic horrors of apartheid persisted: roadblocks, curfews and police brutality, set against the backdrop of the Defiance Campaign of 1952, the launch of the Freedom Charter in Kliptown in 1955, and the 20,000-strong Women's March to the Union Buildings in Pretoria in 1956, with women singing, "*Wathint' abafazi, wathint' imbokodo* ... You strike a woman, you strike a rock."[17] In this climate of resistance, Makeba's music gained increasing political resonance. The lyrics of her first recording, "Lakutshon Ilanga" went: "The sun is setting, I cannot find you, I have been to the hospitals and jails",[18] highlighting how black lives were brutalised under apartheid. In 1956, at the memorial service of black journalist Henry Nxumalo, who had been killed on the streets of Sophiatown,[19] and later after the death of comedian Victor Mkhize, she and others sang "Sad Times, Bad Times", asking: "What have these men done wrong to deserve this fate?" In the latter part of the 1950s, as black communities were forcibly removed from their homes in Sophiatown and other urban areas,[20] the trauma and pain of lives disrupted was brought to the fore as Makeba sang Strike Vilakazi's lyrically ironical song "Meadowlands" (1956).[21] She also later recorded the deeply melancholic "Sophiatown is Gone" (1959). Other women would sing protest songs too, most notably Miriam's friend Dorothy Masuka, fearlessly vocalising against D.F. Malan, the South African prime minister, and in support of Patrice Lumumba. These songs ultimately forced Miriam into exile to escape police harassment. Audiences increasingly identified with the songs which expressed the despair and heartbreak of wanton deaths and the misery of the apartheid era. Politicisation was intensifying, and resistance against apartheid kept rising through music.

Venice, London, America

In September 1959 Makeba was invited to attend the premier of the docufiction *Come Back, Africa* at the Venice Film Festival. As the only black African woman on the red carpet, Miriam was a star attraction.[22] When the film won the Critics Award, her appeal widened. Her next stop on her journey was London, where she was introduced to African-American musician, actor and activist Harry

Belafonte, who facilitated her travel to America. In November 1959 Miriam arrived in New York in the full glare of the media. Her debut television appearance on *The Steve Allen Show*, with its viewership of 60 million people, was followed by a series of sold-out performances at upmarket venues.[23] She would meet and befriend artistic and cultural activists as diverse as Sidney Poitier, Duke Ellington, Diahann Carroll, Nina Simone, Marlon Brando, Miles Davis, Dizzy Gillespie, as well as radical African-American writers Maya Angelou (see Brown in this volume), James Baldwin and Langston Hughes.[24]

Makeba was the first African woman artist to be presented to a large viewership on American television. With her short natural hair, her songs and her dance styles, she was pioneering and different, noted as much for her sensuality as for her "exoticism".[25] She owned her idiosyncratic attitude and sharp wit, once wryly commenting as she introduced a song: "They call this 'The Click Song', because the Afrikaners don't know how to pronounce Qongqothwane."[26] Miriam demystified and decolonised perceptions of Africa, while retaining her Xhosa identity, her self-confidence and her soft-spoken intelligence. These qualities all proved to be beguiling as much to America's black nationalists as to those on the liberal left who "imagined" or felt they saw a little more about Africa through her.

The year 1960 – Makeba's first year in America – was one of dramatic personal and political changes. In South Africa, in March 1960, 69 black people were gunned down in anti-passbook demonstrations in what would become known as the "Sharpeville Massacre". The world was outraged. As violence escalated, political parties and activists were banned, thousands arrested, and many more forced into exile. Miriam found herself effectively exiled too; an exile and alienation that would last for 31 years. Exile fuelled her political activism.

In America, Makeba's music carried her from playing the college circuit to festivals, to New York's Carnegie Hall, even to performing at US president John F. Kennedy's "Birthday Salute" in May 1962. However, behind the glamorous life was another reality of America: racism, injustice, Jim Crow laws, poverty, Native Indian reservations and oppression similar to what she had experienced in South Africa. Working with Harry Belafonte, himself a vocal and financial proponent of the civil rights movement, Miriam participated in events with and for Martin Luther King Jr, performed at marches, and met activists like Malcolm X, whom she would later write a song about (see Daniels in this volume). She shared the stage with artists such as Pete Seeger, Leon Bibb[27] and the inimitable civil rights activist Odetta Holmes, who was labelled "the Voice of the Civil

Rights Movement". As 17 African countries gained their independence in the *annus mirabilis* of 1960, Miriam became acquainted with leaders of liberation movements from countries as diverse as Guinea, Ghana, Tanzania and Kenya. She performed at fundraising events for educational, cultural and political groupings such as Africa-American Friends of Africa, the American Committee on Africa (ACOA), and the African American Students Foundation (AASF).[28] This deepened Makeba's own political consciousness and sense of philanthropy. In 1966, with South African artists Hugh Masekela and Jonas Gwangwa, Miriam formed the Student Aid Association of South Africa (SASA) to provide scholarships for South African students in exile.[29]

After two years in America, and through her association with Kenyan trade unionist Tom Mboya, Miriam was invited to perform and assist in fundraising events throughout Kenya in 1962. From there, Makeba crossed over into the newly independent Tanzania where President Julius Nyerere, after learning about her statelessness when the apartheid government effectively stripped Miriam of her citizenship, honoured her with a Tanzanian passport. This was her first of nine others to follow. In May 1963 Miriam's profile was such that she was the only artist to be invited to perform at the launch of the Organisation of African Unity (OAU) in the Ethiopian capital of Addis Ababa. There she met several heads of state including Ethiopia's Haile Selassie, Ghana's Kwame Nkrumah, Zambia's Kenneth Kaunda, Guinea's Sékou Touré, Côte d'Ivoire's Félix Houphouet-Boigny, Senegal's Léopold Senghor and Egypt's Gamal Abdel Nasser. The concept of African unity had thus come alive for her.

Makeba's vocalism went beyond her music when, in July 1963, she was invited to speak before the UN Decolonization Committee. At the world body in New York, she boldly described South Africa as a "nightmare of police brutality and government terrorism".[30] The following year, at the height of the Rivonia Trial[31] of Nelson Mandela and other liberation fighters in South Africa, Miriam addressed the UN Special Committee against Apartheid, calling on all governments to "free political prisoners" and "boycott" South Africa. Pretoria reacted by banning her music.

Music was Makeba's power, and she harnessed it. In 1960 she released her eponymous first album, which demonstrated her versatility and artistry. The album compilation included the upbeat "Jikele Maweni – The Retreat Song", "a battle song", alongside Solomon Linda's "Mbube"; the Indonesian lullaby "Suliram"; the Caribbean lilt "The Naughty Little Flea"; the playful Austrian "One More Dance"; and "Malaika", a Swahili classic. On her second album,

The Many Voices of Miriam Makeba, released in 1962, she sang of local and regional socio-political issues: "Ngoma Kurila", a song of a mother comforting her hungry child, as there is nothing in the house to eat; "Liwa Wechi", a song of a wife bidding farewell to her husband as he leaves to work on the mines; and "Kilimanjaro", a hunting song to which she added the trademark "gum boot dance"[32] each time she performed it. The song "Khawuleza" harked back to the memory of Miriam's mother being arrested for brewing beer: "Khawuleza Mama ... Hurry up Mama. Look out Mama, there come the police, don't let them catch you."[33]

By the time Miriam recorded her third and fourth albums – *The World of Miriam* (1963) and *The Voice of Africa* (1964) – she had traversed the globe in sound, spirit and genre from calypso to ballads, *marabi* and pop – and sang about diverse issues from hunger, to migrant labour, war and motherhood.

Makeba's musical zenith was reached in 1966 when she and Harry Belafonte won the Grammy Award for Best Folk Recording for their album *An Evening with Belafonte/Makeba*. Miriam thus made history as the first African to win a Grammy (she had been nominated three times before).[34] The album reflected the spirit of Pan-Africanism: Africa meets the diaspora, and the Caribbean meets South Africa. Politically, Miriam's renditions of trade unionist Vuyisile Mini's[35] songs "Dubula" ("Shoot them") and "Beware Verwoerd", with the taunting lyrics "Naants' indod' emnyama, Verwoerd pasopa – Here comes the black man, watch out, Verwoerd" were courageous, direct and seditious. So, when her dance-craze-inducing "Pata" made it to the top ten of America's Billboard charts in 1967, peaking at number 7 in December 1967, with its lyrics – "Pata is the name of a dance we do down Johannesburg way",[36] though seemingly frivolous, the song kept apartheid South Africa and its horrors in the headlines.

Makeba also used language as a statement. Beyond singing in English, Sotho, Zulu or Xhosa, she consciously broadened her repertoire, learning songs in Swahili, Bambara, Fula, Malinke, French, Spanish and Portuguese. She enthralled her audience in Algeria when she sang the traditional praise song "Ifrikia" in Arabic. Makeba was an artist *with the people*, bridging a multicultural landscape. With her prowess of singing in multiple languages, she developed a technique of pre-introducing songs, allowing her to highlight anti-apartheid and pro-African issues. Out of principle, she refused to sing in Afrikaans.[37]

As the community of South African artists in exile expanded to include the trumpeter Hugh Masekela; musical couple Caiphus Semenya and Letta Mbulu; producer Jonas Gwangwa; jazz maestro Abdullah Ibrahim; vocalist Sathima Bea;

diverse writers and poets; and activists from South Africa's African National Congress (ANC) and the Pan Africanist Congress (PAC), cultural expression proved a powerful enhancer of national imagery. In the "imagined community"[38] of exile, the war against apartheid was deeply cultural. During this time, Makeba would marry fellow musician Hugh Masekela. Though he was ten years her junior, she had had an on-and-off relationship with him in South Africa. It was Miriam who, through Harry Belafonte, facilitated Masekela's travel to America. They formalised their relationship with a marriage that lasted from 1964 to 1966. Though the marriage was tempestuous and prone to infidelity, they remained bound by a common desire to see South Africa free. They composed, recorded and performed songs together for decades to come. Of his relationship with Miriam, Hugh Masekela noted: "When I met Miriam Makeba in 1955, no one in the world could sing as beautifully as she did. No woman in the world was more beautiful, kind, loving, generous, talented, prolific, humorous and proud of her people's heritage."[39] The pride in "her people's heritage" would be a beacon for other African artists to follow. Poignantly, Masekela himself would in later life gain the moniker "Father of South African Jazz". His political activism would find expression through his compositions such as "Stimela" (1974), an ode to the tribulations of migrant labourers toiling on South African mines and transported on trains from Namibia, Malawi, Zambia, Zimbabwe, Angola and Mozambique; and "Bring Him Back Home" (1987), which was a bold call for the release of Nelson Mandela. While the ravages of the politics of apartheid would continue to encroach on their personal lives, both Makeba and Masekela chose to demonstrate the power of resistance to oppression through music. Both vocally and physically embraced the positive values of Pan-Africanism.[40]

Africa and the World

From the late 1960s, Miriam's travels across Africa reinforced Kwame Nkrumah's Pan-African lament: "Ghana will not be free until all of Africa is liberated." Africa would become Miriam's home again. In 1967, she was invited to the Guinean capital of Conakry for the Quinzaine Artistique, a fortnight of musical events, with the aim of reviving traditional orchestras, theatre, ballet, ensembles and cultural activism. She was rapt.

There Makeba met Trinidadian-American activist Stokely Carmichael, whom, after a politics-infused relationship, she married in 1968. Carmichael's radicalism in the US civil rights movement – mobilising the "freedom rides", "sit-ins" and voter registration drives; working as president of the Student Nonviolent Coordinating Committee (SNCC); marching alongside Martin Luther King Jr; working with the Black Panther Party; appearing before the US House Committee on Un-American Activities; being arrested many times (over 27); and popularising the call for Black Power – were all defining revolutionary acts for Miriam.

The marriage proved to be controversial. It resulted in Makeba's shows, bookings and recordings being increasingly cancelled, and the pair facing constant surveillance from the US Federal Bureau of Investigation (FBI). In 1969, after a decade in America, Makeba and Carmichael relocated to Conakry to avoid the constant harassment of the American authorities.[41]

From Guinea, Miriam continued to record, working predominantly with Guinean musicians. Though living in West Africa and sidelined from America, her reach broadened exponentially. She now toured more often in Europe, performed in Asia, and even did shows in South America. Here she met Fidel Castro in Havana, who gave her a Cuban passport, and performed for President Salvador Allende in Chile just a few weeks prior to his assassination in September 1973. In Africa, Stokely Carmichael began to look beyond the concept of Black Power and embraced the Pan-African ideals of Sékou Touré and Kwame Nkrumah. In honour of these two great men who became his "spiritual and political mentors", Carmichael changed his name to Kwame Ture.[42] For Makeba, Guinea refashioned and sharpened her artistry.[43] Her image took on broader political connotations. In America, she had given emblematic visibility to the mantra "Black is Beautiful" and brought Africa into the global mainstream. From Conakry, she became more "trend-setting" with her *kaftans*, *boubous*, and *dashikis*; her stylish head-dresses, high hats, and beaded and braided hairstyles. She was *distinctly* African, a model for African womanhood, resilience and pride, and a metaphorical praise-singer and griot for the continent. Her Africanness magnified her impact.

Throughout the 1960s and 1970s cultural festivals became a significant component of political activism and a powerful vehicle for promoting solidarity. Makeba was in the midst of these developments. She performed at the first Pan-African Musical Cultural Festival in Algeria in 1969, where "musicians, dancers, horsemen, poets and painters, writers, film-makers, scholars, and political leaders ... sat alongside freedom fighters and veteran guerrillas, artists and academics ... Black Power advocates alongside Pan Africanists".[44] The premise behind the 1969 festival was that "liberation from colonial rule was as central to African unity as music was".[45]

In October 1974 Makeba was at the ringside for the "Rumble in the Jungle"[46] held in Zaire (the Democratic Republic of the Congo), the historic boxing match between George Foreman and Muhammad Ali. This too was a reinforcement of Pan-Africanism, a showcase of Black Power and African nationalism. B.B. King played alongside rumba maestro Franco, and James Brown belted out: "I'm Black and I'm Proud" before a stadium packed with an all-African audience. In June 1975 Miriam performed at the independence celebration of Mozambique: she sang "Aluta Continua", not just for Mozambique but for all of Africa. In January/February 1977, at the Second World Black and African Festival of Arts and Culture (FESTAC), held in Lagos, Nigeria, with 60,000 people in attendance and 50 nations represented, Miriam, *la pasionaria* of African liberation[47] – as a journalist famously tagged her – sat beside African-American legend Stevie Wonder, when his album *Songs in the Key of Life* won multiple Grammy Awards and bagged the much-vaunted Album of the Year award.

However, no matter where Miriam was, South Africa remained in her heart. In June 1976, in what was later termed the Soweto Uprising, South African police fired on unarmed students protesting against the imposition of Afrikaans as a language of instruction in schools. Violence spread across the country. An estimated 176 (with some figures up to 700) children[48] were killed, while thousands more were arrested, injured, maimed, tortured and brutalised. Many students fled into exile, among them Tsietsi Mashinini, a leader of the South African Students' Movement, who ultimately made his way to Conakry where Miriam's home would become an unofficial refuge for traumatised and emotionally damaged South African students in exile. Hugh Masekela penned the heart-wrenching homage "Soweto Blues",[49] with Makeba's resonating voice present to memorialise the atrocity. Fuelled by this incident, Miriam would make her voice heard on platforms beyond the music stage. In 1975 and 1976, as a delegate of the Guinean government, she spoke before the United Nations General Assembly, vociferously and fearlessly condemning apartheid's brutalities.

Throughout the late 1970s and 1980s, the unstoppable "winds of change"[50] continued to blow across the continent. Africa bled as struggles for liberation persisted, in Guinea-Bissau, Cape Verde, Mozambique, Zimbabwe and South Africa. Miriam bled too. On a personal level, her marriage to Carmichael would end in divorce after ten years in 1978.[51] A subsequent and fifth marriage to Bageot Bah from Guinea lasted from 1980 to 1985.[52] In 1984, Miriam – now a grandmother of three – lost her youngest grandson in Guinea. Shortly after his death, Miriam's only daughter, Sibongile "Bongi" Angela Makeba, a child from her first marriage, died in 1985 following complications during childbirth. Bongi Makeba was buried in Guinea. These tragic losses haunted Miriam for the rest of her life, and remain emblems of the sad consequences of her life in exile. Politically, the Africa that she loved had become unstable. She felt the pain of Patrice Lumumba's assassination in 1961; devastation at Kwame Nkrumah's overthrow in 1966, his exile and death in 1972; and despair as *coups d'état* erupted across the continent. In later years, leaders she once admired were branded dictators, among them her friend and benefactor, Sékou Touré.[53] In many quarters, Miriam was increasingly condemned for her political affiliations, and often she felt ostracised and maligned. Suffering her losses alone, and perhaps a bit disillusioned, after 16 years of living in Guinea, Makeba left the country. She relocated to Belgium in 1985, but her total commitment to seeing a free and independent South Africa and Africa remained undiminished.

Throughout her career Miriam had used her voice and her music to educate her audiences about injustices in South Africa and Africa. As calls for sanctions against apartheid South Africa amplified, Makeba was there. In December 1968 the United Nations had proposed resolutions to "suspend cultural, educational, sporting and all other exchanges with racist regimes and other institutions in South Africa which practiced apartheid".[54] Miriam strongly supported and spoke out in favour of the boycotts. By the 1980s, many more musicians, actors, playwrights, academics and writers around the world answered the call to boycott South Africa, thus affirming the interrelationship between, and the power of, the arts and culture in resistance politics. In 1987, Makeba would lend her voice to Paul Simon's "Graceland Tour" alongside Hugh Masekela, Ray Phiri and Ladysmith Black Mambazo. In 1988, when rock stars, jazz and pop musicians, and rap artists stood together at Wembley Stadium at a concert in honour of Nelson Mandela's 70th birthday – an event broadcast to about 600 million people around the world[55] – Miriam was also there. In the fight against apartheid, the interaction of popular culture, music and protest had ignited the global imagination and prompted activism on an international scale.

Concluding Reflections

In June 1990, after the unbanning of the ANC and the release of Nelson Mandela, Miriam Makeba and her music returned to South Africa after 31 years in exile. Her return was greeted with much fanfare, but she felt unappreciated by the new generation of young audiences and music lovers. After years of being uprooted from homes, first from South Africa, from America, then from Guinea, she lamented: "I hope I will not be erased again."[56] While she continued to tour and perform internationally, it would take her ten years before she released an album in the "new" South Africa. She significantly titled the 2000 album *Homeland*. It reinvigorated her, garnered her a Grammy Award nomination, and a new following in South Africa. Makeba was now truly and finally home.

Kenyan intellectual Micere Githae Mugo (see Wachanga in this volume) noted in her distinguished Julius Nyerere lecture in 2012: "The songs of Miriam Makeba Pan-Africanised and internationalised the anti-apartheid liberation struggle, reaching not just the world's dance floors but all corners of the globe."[57] Indeed, through her own world-consciousness and the varied life experiences that had propelled her, Miriam's voice reached beyond the confines of the anti-apartheid movement to wider human rights and global issues. She had discovered universalising values and embraced them. She was a social, cultural and political activist; holder of honorary citizenship status from ten different countries; a multiple international award winner;[58] and a recipient of eight honorary doctorates[59] from various institutions. A philanthropist and human rights activist, Miriam also founded the Miriam Makeba Rehabilitation Centre for Girls in South Africa in 1999, establishing a safe house for abused and abandoned girls, thereby demonstrating her commitment to women's rights. In the same year she was appointed a goodwill ambassador for the UN Food and Agricultural Organization (FAO),[60] and in 2001 she was appointed as South Africa's first official goodwill ambassador to Africa.[61]

However, what is most telling about Miriam Makeba was the way in which she lived out her last years. In 2005, Miriam, then aged 73, announced to the media that she would be retiring from the stage.[62] Her fans took heed of this and she received innumerable invitations to do "farewell shows" around the world. The tours would run for three years, taking her to countries she had visited during her career, including America and a momentous visit to Cuba to bid farewell to old friend Fidel Castro.[63] On 7 November 2008, Makeba was invited to perform in Castel Volturno, near Naples in Italy, as part of a human rights concert in support of the writer Roberto Saviano, who was living under threat of assassination from the Mafia because of his writing against them.[64] After singing for half an hour and rounding off her set with her signature tune, "Pata", Miriam collapsed as she left the stage, and died shortly afterwards of a heart attack at the age of 76.

Two things remain true of Miriam Makeba. Firstly, music was her life. In her 2004 autobiography, she prophetically quipped: "I will sing till the day I die"[65] – and she did. Secondly, Miriam lived, fought for, and stood up against, injustice all of her life and died as she had lived. Makeba lived her vision and life as an artist, activist, Pan-Africanist and true citizen of the world. Mama Africa's music left a resounding legacy, and an undeniable imprint on global resistance history.

BOB MARLEY: REVOLUTIONARY PROPHET OF AFRICAN UNITY

Clinton Hutton

> "How good and how pleasant it would be before God and man
> To see the unification of all Africans."[1]
>
> – BOB MARLEY

BOB MARLEY'S MUSIC REPRESENTS an impressive catalogue of ideas of the black experience and the framing of a Pan-African order germane to freedom, justice, redemption, sovereignty and development. This body of work is decidedly an instrument for decolonisation. It is rooted in the epistemology and ontology of Rastafari which itself is a form of Pan-Africanism. This involvement emerged from the creative weaving of an assemblage of aspects of the cultural, spiritual, aesthetic, linguistic and ideational complex of Jamaican people, catalysed by the coronation of the Ethiopian regent, Ras Tafari, as Emperor Haile Selassie I – in a global African Garveyite belief system – 15 years in the making. This essay explores and analyses the framing of being in Bob Marley's music as the basis for Pan-African agency and solidarity.

Jamaican popular music greatly influenced the national liberation struggles in southern Africa, as told to me by soldiers of the liberation movements. I was a member of the Jamaican delegation to the World Festival of Youth and Students in the Cuban capital of Havana in 1978. I met members of delegations from Namibia's South West Africa People's Organisation (SWAPO), Zimbabwe's Patriotic Front (PF) and South Africa's Umkhonto we Sizwe (MK), the military wing of the African National Congress (ANC). I met with young men of my age who were waging guerrilla warfare in southern Africa. They were as animated as we were to learn about each other's countries and cultures.

When these men – all dressed in military uniforms – heard that we were from Jamaica, they called out "Bob Marley" as a kind of greeting and salutation. They also greeted us with the names "Peter Tosh", "Jimmy Cliff" and a few others. These men told us that they marched to war singing Marley's and Tosh's songs. They explained to us that in times of vulnerability, sadness, loneliness, hope and triumph, it was these songs that sustained their struggles.

Bob Marley's Pan-African Roots

The cultural, political and philosophical genealogy of Bob Marley's Pan-Africanism is rooted in two traditions. The first resides in the Jamaican folk cultural, linguistic and belief system, evident in Revival, Kumina, Myaal, and Burru; the second is based on the Ethiopianist philosophy and opinions of Marcus Garvey, who founded the Universal Negro Improvement Association (UNIA) in Jamaica in 1914 (see Grant in this volume). Pan-Africanist consciousness, culture and agency in Jamaican popular music is formulated and articulated in Bob Marley's songs of freedom in several ways. The Pan-African being and agency was birthed and framed in a black anti-slavery cultural, ontological and epistemological complex of the folk in which Marley posits that he is his ancestors and his ancestors are him. This is expressed thus in the song, "Slave Driver/Catch A Fire", on the Wailers album, *Catch a Fire* thus:

> Every time I hear the crack of the whip
> My blood runs cold
> I remember on the slave ship
> How they brutalised our very souls.[2]

Bob Marley who was born of a white British soldier father and black Jamaican mother on 6 February 1945 – 107 years after slavery was abolished in Jamaica – reminisced about being on the slave ship with other captured Africans, where the traffickers merchandising in human beings, brutalised their "very souls". The slave ship thus became a symbol of immense ontological brutality and simultaneously the womb of Pan-Africanism, impoverishment and the cosmological roots of slavery reparation. At the time that he – along with the rest of the Wailers, released the *Catch a Fire* album in 1973 – 11 years after Jamaica had gained its independence from Britain, Marley sang on the title track: "Today they say we are free/Only to be chained to poverty".[3] The implication here is that neither the abolition of slavery nor political independence ended the chain of poverty that enslavement had imposed on Africans, living and ancestral. Hence the extent to which African people are free and sovereign in the post-colonial Jamaican state and society depends on the extent of the persistence of the legacy of slavery, as well as the extent of the cultivation of a Pan-African community to unite Jamaicans of African descent against "political tribalism" and fragmentation.

In "Redemption Song", from the 1980 *Uprising* album, Marley continues the theme and epistemology evident in the song "Slave Driver/Catch a Fire":

Old pirates yes, they rob I
Sold I to the merchant ship
Minutes after they took I
From the bottomless pit
But my hand was made strong
By the hand of the Almighty
We forward in this generation
Triumphantly.[4]

Here Marley states that he was captured (robbed), placed in a dungeon (bottomless pit), and sold into slavery (sold to the merchant ship). It was with the help of the Almighty that he survived slavery and arrived triumphantly "in this generation". Like the *Uroboros* (an ancient and traditional African symbol of eternity, denoted by a snake forming a circle by biting its tail) or the Congolese circular ritual drawing framing the crossroads, there is no end or beginning in the identity constructing complex which Marley frames in "Redemption Song." He is his ancestors and his ancestors are him.

In this song, Marley also cites a line from a speech made by Marcus Garvey: "Emancipate yourself from mental slavery/None but our selves can free our minds".[5] Like the chains of poverty that survived slavery and continue to shape black existence, so too the chains of mental enslavement fetter and distort the epistemology of being, agency, solidarity, freedom and sovereignty.

This episteme of the black folk in Bob Marley's music is not unique to him. When Peter Tosh – one of the original "Wailers" – sings in "Mystic Man": "I am a man of the past/Living in the present/Walking into the future",[6] he is evoking that principle of being: "I am my ancestors and my ancestors are me". So too, Burning Spear's "Slavery Days": "Do you remember the days of slavery/Do you remember the days of slavery/And they beat us/And they work us so hard".[7]

In this epistemic culture, the pronouns "I", "we", "us", "my" and "our" are used to connote the living and the living dead, the ancestor variously referred to in the Caribbean colloquim as *dopi*, *ori*, *jumbie*, *bonanj*, *neg ginin* and *nanm*. The ancestor is often spoken of in the present tense because her or his existence is not of a dead forgotten severed past, but an integral part of the evolving genealogical intercourse framed in "Slave Driver", "Redemption Song" and "Slavery Days". It is on this same basis that people of African descent in Jamaica and across the Caribbean offer libation to the ancestors and engage them in simple or complex feeding rituals, bringing them messages about the living, and engaging them in rituals of spirit possession.

The relationship between the living and the living dead during the enslavement of Africans in the Americas, was central to the genesis or the cosmological roots of freedom and Pan-Africanism. Enslaved Africans felt that the most likely way they could be free from slavery, was for their spirit-self, or soul to transmigrate. It was only with death that the spirit person was freed from his or her enslaved corporeal abode. With the proper funeral rituals, the spirit would go back to the ancestral homeland in Africa: free, sovereign and happy.

The transmigration freedom complex did not disappear with the abolition of slavery or even with the coming of independence in the Caribbean. It has become an important theme in traditional Rastafari music and Jamaican popular music. Bob Marley's 1977 *Exodus*: "We know where we are going/We know where we are from/We're leaving Babylon/We are going to our Father's land/Exodus…"[8] is one of those songs. So too The Wailers' "Rastaman Chant"; Bob Andy's "I've Got to Go Back Home"; The Abyssinians' "Satta Massagana"; Bunny Wailer's "Dreamland"; and Johnny Clarke's "Move Out of Babylon."[9]

Bob Marley's Pan-Africanism was forged in the crucible of a black cultural, ontological and philosophical upsurge by Rastafari in the 1960s and 1970s. This upsurge was significantly assisted by the visit to Jamaica in 1966 of Ethiopia's Haile Selassie I. It was not unrelated to the increasing restlessness of the younger, more radical sections of Jamaica's middle-class intellectuals and the working class. There was also the influence of the American Black Power movement, in the US in the 1960s and the significant rise of the national liberation struggles in African states such as Guinea-Bissau, Angola, Mozambique and South Africa.

Pan-African Rhythms

If there is one song that most epitomises Bob Marley's Pan-Africanism, it is "Africa Unite". This was a Garveyite Pan-Africanist text from the classic 1979 album *Survival*. This song expresses one of Marley's most profound hopes: "How good and how pleasant it would be/Before God and man/To see the unification of all Africans/As it's been said already/Let it be done."[10] In his 1979 performance of this song in Santa Barbara, US, Marley substituted "As it's been said already/Let it be done" with "Marcus Garvey said it/So let it be done". For Marley, whose mission was to enable Garvey's revolution, an important part of this unification mission was the repatriation of blacks in the diaspora back to the mother continent: "Africa unite/Cause we're moving right out of Babylon/And we're going to our Father's land."[11] Repatriation then is a goal of unification, an imperative of "Back to Africa" advocates for the development of "Global Africa".

Repatriation was and remains an important principle and goal of Rastafari. Bob Marley has been the religion's best-known global advocate: "We are the children of the Rasta man/We are the children of the Higher Man."[12] The Rasta man or Higher Man (Iya Man), of which Marley spoke, is Ras Tafari Makonen: the Ethiopian regent who was crowned Emperor Haile Selassie I in November 1930. This inspired four men, steeped in the Garveyite cultural and philosophical tradition – Leonard Howell, Joseph Hibbert, Archibald Dunkley and Robert Hinds – to found the Rastafari movement in Jamaica in the early 1930s, based on the deification of Rasta Tarari.[13]

For Bob Marley, the unity of Africans abroad in places like Jamaica, Barbados, the US and Brazil with those in Africa was an imperative "for the benefit of our people".[14] Unification would allow Africa to garner its creators: "Africa awaiting its creators."[15] This approach is based around shared ancestry, shared identity and a shared history of rupture, requiring the repair of the breach: "Africa you're my forefather cornerstone/Unite for the Africans abroad/Unite for the Africans a yard."[16]

Another song on the *Survival* album is "Zimbabwe". Marley's message here is unity and solidarity to protect the Zimbabwean revolution, its integrity and values from ethnic divisions and betrayal in order to ensure its triumph for the benefit of the country's citizens. Jamaica's reggae superstar regarded the liberation struggle in Zimbabwe as a Pan-African struggle of which he was a part: "Africans a liberate (Zimbabwe)/I an' I a liberate Zimbabwe". He refers to Zimbabweans as "my people" who are engaged in a struggle that was his own: "We'll have to fight/We gonna fight/Fight for our rights."[17]

Marley locates Rastafari (Natty/Natty Dread) at the centre of the liberation war: "Natty dread it (In a Zimbabwe)/Set it up in (Zimbabwe)/Mash it up in a Zimbabwe." He warns of the dangers of internal conflict in the liberation movement which he sees as endangering the struggle: "No more internal power struggle/...cause, I don't want my people to be contrary." He warns: "Divide and rule could tear us apart/In everyman's chest/There beats a heart/Soon we'll find out/Who is the real revolutionaries/And I don't want my people/To be tricked by mercenaries."[18] Here, mercenaries denote Africans who pretend to be revolutionaries, but are actually undermining the struggle of the people by putting their personal desires for power before the interests of the masses.

Imperial Revolution: Emperor Selassie I

Bob Marley's call for "war" against colonialism from the song of the same name on his 1976 album, *Rastaman Vibration,* reflects the theme of Pan-African unity and agency to facilitate the armed struggle as articulated in "Africa Unite" and "Zimbabwe". "War", however, differs from the songs in that its lyrical content is the melodious framing of a section of a speech made by Haile Selassie to the United Nations (UN) General Assembly in 1963. This was an appeal and a warning to the UN by independent African states and liberation movements to act against the colonial regimes in Africa. The part of the speech that became "War" went as follows:

> That until the philosophy which holds one race superior and another inferior is finally and permanently discredited and abandoned; That until there are no longer first-class and second-class citizens of any nation; That until the colour of a man's skin is of no more significance than the colour of his eyes; That until the basic human rights are equally guaranteed to all without regard to race; That until that day, the dream of lasting peace and world citizenship and the rule of international morality will remain but a fleeting illusion to be pursued but never attained; And until the ignoble and unhappy regimes that hold our brothers in Angola,

in Mozambique and in South Africa in subhuman bondage have been toppled and destroyed; ...Until that day the African continent will not know peace. We Africans will fight, if necessary and we know that we shall win, as we are confident in the victory of good over evil.[19]

In covering this part of Haile Selassie's speech, Bob Marley, along with Alan "Skill" Cole, constructs a melody and includes the refrain "war" and bridge words and lines, to produce a masterpiece anthem of a revolutionary call to arms.

Marley's use of the emperor's UN speech took his mission beyond the Pan-Africanism of the African continent, and globalised it to include the African diaspora. And so, the words, "We Africans will fight, if necessary" in Selassie's continental Pan-African speech, became a rousing call for liberation by Africans on the continent and in the diaspora in "War". The song became a clarion call for new generations of freedom fighters like those I had met in Havana during the 1978 Youth Conference for whom diaspora support had meant so much.

The category of songs represented on the *Survival* album such as "Africa Unite", "Zimbabwe" and "War" on the 1976 *Rastaman Vibration* album, focuses more on rallying and encouraging Pan-African forces to embrace the national liberation wars as their own. Peter Tosh penned and recorded more songs in this category than any other prominent Jamaican recording artist. Tosh advanced one of the most explicitly Garveyite Pan-African reasons for the ontological support of Africa's wars of liberation. In the song "Fight On", Tosh urges his brothers and sisters to fight on, because if Africa was not free, all Africans at home and abroad, would face re-enslavement.[20]

The Spirit of Marcus Garvey

What character, what psychological compass, what agency is required to win this struggle for national liberation and construct a creative sustainable Pan-African complex antithetical to re-enslavement and neo-colonialism? "Ride Natty Ride", on the 1979 *Survival* album, represents a category of songs which exudes this philosophy of being, and deems it an agential imperative of black liberation struggle. Indeed, this philosophy and vision of being was a central feature of Garvey's pedagogy and political campaign. Moreover, this character of being has long been articulated in the folk philosophical and cultural tradition of Jamaica as *talawa*. *Talawa* is the state of fortitude associated with the ontology, psychology and agency of the most persistent Jamaican personality for justice. Its unwavering destination entails victory against all odds.

In "Ride Natty Ride", Marley tells us about the story of the "job" or the struggle for freedom, justice, and sovereignty which constitutes the "mission" that Rastafari (Dready) has "got to fulfil". He notes that although the "greatest ambition" of the enemies is to see Natty fail (hurt), Rastafari who embodies the spirit of *talawa* "will survive in this world of competition/Cause no matter what they do/Natty keep on coming through/And no matter what they say/Dready de deh (is there) every day."[21]

In this struggle, Marley urges: "Have no fear, have no sorrow" for even though the forces of oppression have built "their world in great confusion/To force on us the devil's illusion", he is confident that "the stone that the builder refused/Shall be the head cornerstone" because "no matter what game they play", he insists, "We got something they could never take away". That something that could not be taken away is "the fire" (that ontology of hope, certainty, determination, perseverance and desire to overcome) which is "burning down everything" that the oppressors put in the way of Africans.[22]

For Marley, victory was certain for the agency of liberation:

Cause now the fire is out of control
Panic in the city, wicked
Weeping for their souls
Everywhere this fire is burning
Destroying and melting their gold
Destroying and wasting their souls.[23]

In another song, "I Know", on the *Confrontation* album, released posthumously in 1983, two years after his death, Marley embraces this fireman and freedom fighter persona as explicitly his own:

Many a time I sit and wonder why
This race so – so very hard to run
Then I say to my soul take courage
Battle to be won.[24]

A primary goal of Garvey was to cultivate this kind of personality in the African whom he refers to as the "New Negro". This African, Garvey argues, is just like himself, emancipated from mental slavery by embracing the philosophy of black consciousness and its liberating Pan-African episteme that enabled the imagination and agency of a pantheon of diaspora ancestors such as Toussaint L'Ouverture, Edward Blyden, Phillis Wheatley, Antonio Maceo, Frederick Douglass and Robert Love (see Introduction in this volume). What Marley has done is to include in the Garveyite ontological model, Haile Selassie as godhead, the basis of the faith, fortitude and determination expressed above and articulated below in Marley's song, "Forever Loving Jah" from the 1980 *Uprising* album:

Some say see them walking up the street
They say we are going wrong to all the people we meet
But we won't worry
We won't shed no tears
We found a way to cast away the fears
Forever yeah.[25]

The fears that have been cast away to allow for the reconstitution of the spirit of *talawa* in the age of African national liberation are expressed thus:

So Oldman River don't cry for me
I've got a running stream of love you see
So no matter what stages
Oh stages, stages, stages they put us through
We'll never be blue
No matter what rages
Oh rages, changes, rages they put us through
We'll never be blue[26]

The expression of faith and determination that is evident in the above narrative framed by Marley, resulted from the decades of countless rituals of divination of Haile Selassie in Rasta camps and other assemblages of Rastafari across Jamaica. In these rituals, the weaving of an invocating sonic, linguistic, literary, aesthetic, epistemic and ontological redemptive liberating spiritual complex took shape, and became the philosophical and creative ethos of Marley. It is within this cultural complex that the Jamaican superstar was able to find the language to express his faith and determination to be free and sovereign: "We'll be forever loving Jah/...Forever, and ever/Yes and forever...cause, there is no end."[27]

This spiritual complex of courage, perseverance, dignity and hope forged in rituals of deifying Haile Selassie, which Marley articulates with such beautiful unflinching certainty in his lyrical poetry, is not without its antecedents in the history and culture of Afro-Caribbean spirituality and resistance. In this tradition, the essential qualities of the divinity or spirit tend to be borne by the warrior/healer spirit.

This tradition was also evident in a more secular form in Marcus Garvey's UNIA movement. Apparently influenced by the First World War (1914–1918) in which tens of thousands of African Americans and other people of African descent from colonies in the Caribbean and Africa served, that military experience was mobilised to shape the mood, discipline, cohesion, political direction and tenor of the UNIA. In many parades, marches and meetings, Garvey and members of the executive of the UNIA – along with specially constituted units of UNIA militants, dressed in military uniform and swords – could be seen in New York.

This Garveyite-Ethiopianist tradition, as well as the *Myaal* cum Revival and *Kumina* traditions, were, to a significant degree, responsible for shaping the culture and identity of courage and fortitude in Rastafari. Haile Selassie played a special role in this regard. Shortly after the birth of the Rastafarian movement in the early 1930s, Benito Mussolini's Italian army invaded Ethiopia in 1935. This led to massive demonstrations in the Jamaican capital of Kingston in which Rastafarians and Garveyites played a pivotal role. Some Jamaicans volunteered to travel to Ethiopia to fight against the Fascist invaders, but were not allowed to do so by the British colonial authorities in Jamaica.

It is not uncommon to see Rastafarians wearing military uniform in the style worn by Haile Selassie since in Rastafari cosmology, Selassie had become a warrior god. In Rastafarian iconography, the photo of Selassie, with his left foot on an unexploded Italian bomb taken shortly after an Italian bombardment near Addis Ababa in the 1930s, is highly regarded. So too, the photo of the Ethiopian emperor manning an anti-aircraft gun at the Battle of Maychew in March 1936. Indeed, this photo is reprinted on Bob Marley's 1979 *Survival* album jacket. Both photographs are signifiers of the ontology of courage, fortitude and steadfastness articulated in songs like "Ride Natty Ride". Also on the *Survival* album cover is a photo of members of the Wailers dressed in military uniform in a setting that suggests a guerrilla encampment.

There is another category of Marley songs such as "Music Gonna Teach/ Music Lesson". The concern here is with the nature of the sources, methods, content and role of knowledge in shaping education and pedagogy for a consciousness, identity and agency consistent with freedom, sovereignty and development. In all of this, the teaching of history is so critical to the extent that the following quote from Garvey is included on the *Survival* album jacket: "A people without the knowledge of their past, origin and culture is like a tree without roots."[28] In "Music Gonna Teach", Marley sings:

> Music gonna teach them one lesson...
> Teach them about Marco Polo
> Teach the good youth Christopher Columbus
> How these wicked men
> Rob, cheat, kill the poor in our defence of this land
> Heard they're from this far land
> The colour of our skin made us understand
> Why this teaching of Marco Polo?
> Couldn't it be one of them great Africans?[29]

Concluding Reflections

For Bob Marley, the twin impact of the neo-colonial church and school continued to mire African peoples in a culture of colonial episteme and deception aimed at preserving the chains of mental slavery and frustrating struggles for freedom and sovereignty, while perpetuating a neo-colonial state. In "Babylon System" on the *Survival* album, Marley thus extolled the liberating qualities of the episteme of mental freedom: "We refused to be what you wanted us to be/We are what we are and that's the way it's going to be."[30]

For Marley, the masses of the people of Jamaica after independence in August 1962 – despite having only black and brown faces in government – were yet to be liberated from mental slavery because the principal agents of socialisation – especially the church and the education system – continued to foster too much of a colonial epistemology. The independence elites were: "Building church and university/Deceiving the people continually."[31] Marley advanced the same theme in "Crazy Baldhead" on the 1976 *Rastaman Vibration* album.

Build your penitentiaries. We build your schools
Brainwash education to make us the fools
Hatred your reward for our love
Telling us of your God above.[32]

For Marley, the post-colonial state was a neo-colonial state in which – like the colonial state – the reward for the labour, creativity and imagination of the masses was in heaven, what Jimmy Cliff described as "a pie up in the sky, just waiting for me when I die".[33] Bob Marley thus not only stood unabashedly for the removal of the colonial system, he was also promoting the creation of a free, sovereign society in which the masses got their just rewards on earth.

Fela Anikulapo-Kuti: A Felasophy[1] of Kalakuta[2] Republic and African Citizenship

Sola Olorunyomi

I no go gree make my brother hungry, make I no talk
I no go gree make my brother homeless, make I no talk
My Papa talk, My Mama talk, My Grandpapa talk, My grandmama
talk
Those wey no talk wey dem dey?[3]

[I will not be silent while my brother is hungry
I will not be silent while my brother is homeless
Just a family tradition that we speak back
What became of those who kept mute?]

CALL THIS NIGERIAN MUSICAL SUPERSTAR Fela Anikulapo-Kuti's viewpoint on art and life, his philosophy or – in the lingo of the affectionate "down street" – Felasophy. As conceived by the iconoclastic Nigerian musician, Afrobeat is primarily a cultural and political musical practice or, better still, an aesthetics of cultural politics.[4] Its performance is equally characterised by the creation of a liberal cultural space that is admissive of a free discourse of society's fears, doubts and inhibitions: be it governance, sex or the yearnings of restive youth in general. Thus, Afrobeat is not simply a musical rhythm, but a rhythm of alterity, achieved largely in song and musical text, and also through cultural and political action. Afrobeat incorporates the amalgam ideology of Fela's "Kalakuta

Republic" commune and the creative excesses of his Afrika Shrine in Lagos. In these enclaves, Fela tried to live out some of his dreams, as far as the national political authorities would tolerate them. These were, for him, channels of communication as well as ways of representing distance from the homogenising ordering of society.

Early Beginnings

Fela Anikulapo-Kuti was born Olufela Ransome-Kuti, as the fourth of five children, to an Egba family in south-western Nigeria on 15 October 1938. His father, the Reverend Israel Oludotun Ransome-Kuti, was married to Funmilayo Thomas. A number of factors helped to shape Fela's musical and cultural performance and lifestyle. Since about 1830, the Egba have been concentrated in the metropolis of Abeokuta and along the districts around the River Ogun in present-day Ogun state. Even though hemmed in between the Oyo Empire and the British, who would soon arrive on the coast, the Egba early on sought autonomy and – led by Lisabi, their national hero – rebelled against Oyo hegemony and fought a reprisal team sent from the Oyo Kingdom, forcing them to retreat.

The contexts of both family and nationality played a vital role in shaping Fela's upbringing. You could indeed say that music and rebellion were intertwined in the family history. Fela's grandfather Josiah Ransome-Kuti was a musician who had recorded in the London studio of EMI early in the twentieth century. By the turn of the century, he had teamed up with other choirmasters to start rejecting the domination of Yoruba Christian hymns by European compositional principles, and replacing them with a much more African texture of composition, progression and even melody. Fela's father, Israel Ransome-Kuti, was also an accomplished musician, aside from being an educationist and clergyman. Fela's mother was an activist who was part of the global Pan-African political elite. Together, the Ransome-Kuti parents dedicated their time to struggling for African liberation and Nigerian independence. From interacting with Fela, and reading some of his interviews, it is clear he was obviously immensely proud of the heritage that was bequeathed to him.

Translating the Pan-African vision of his youth into music, however, took a while after many unsuccessful attempts, which included experimentation with American soul-style music and the Highlife, which dominated the West African scene by the 1950s. The striving to evolve other layers of contemporary African music styles had always been part of the effort of that generation of young Nigerians who enrolled in music schools in England in the 1950s and early 1960s.

While an older generation of music scholars such as Adam Fiberesima, Akin Euba, Sam Akpabot and Laz Ekwueme studied classical music and worked in radio, television or academia, another group including Fela studied popular music and dance. In this latter group were also Wole Bucknor and Briddy Wright. These musicians became involved in diverse musical forms: European jazz, rhythm and blues, rock 'n' roll, and the emerging music of the 1960s. As a remote influence, the jazz music of Miles Davis, John Coltrane, Sonny Rollins and Charles Mingus – with whom they occasionally had jam sessions – came to have an impact on their musical styles. This trend was later noticed in Fela's composition. However, their focus was largely on Highlife, an attitude informed by their conviction that the new musical form had to be rhythm-driven with a heavy percussion. For Fela, the solution to this search did not emerge until many years later when he suddenly realised that he was playing to empty halls, and that his music did not reflect his new consciousness. It was during his 1969 American visit – and meeting Sandra Izsadore, the African-American girlfriend who greatly influenced his music and political consciousness – that the Afrobeat superstar finally decided on a new rhythm, as he recalled to his Afro-Cuban biographer Carlos Moore:

I said to myself, 'How do Africans sing songs? They sing with chants. Now let me chant into this song: la-la-la-aaa ...' Looking for the right beat I remembered this very old guy I'd met in London: Ambrose Campbell. He used to play African music with a special beat. I used that beat to write my tune man.[5]

Fela as Ebami Eda: "The Strange One"

Incidents in which Fela contested hegemonic laws were quite diverse and not always obvious. By "law", I am referring to normative discursive practices in general and the institutions that support them. This often volatile terrain was Fela's regular polemical turf, where he tried to re-imagine the continent in relation to itself and others. Fela's imagined universe, of which Africa was its epicentre, takes off from an idyllic "Renaissance Africa" with a scribal culture. He makes this manifest through his lyrical narratives. Fela arrives with an omnibus baggage that testifies against conventional attitudes to education, gender, technology, power, life and death in contemporary Africa. In displacing the colonial narrative of the African story, Fela replaced it with a Pan-African grand narrative that tended to romanticise the continent's pre-colonial experience, especially in relation to class stratification and internal ideological polarities.

Though he challenged the statute books in court, Fela's regular site of struggle was in positing alternative ways of living and actually living in alterity to traditional norms. In the first place, he created a communal residence – the "Kalakuta Republic" – and partook in sharing with "brethrens" and other residents. For the Nigerian state and its prebendal elite, this was regarded as dangerous, as these symbolic actions portended a humanism that the state could not afford its own citizens.[6] Worse still, to emphasise communality already in the 1970s – in an age when the state promoted the ideology of private property, and members of the political class engaged in fierce primitive accumulation of capital deriving from oil wealth – it was only going to be a matter of time before the state challenged Fela's claims in the most brutal fashion.

Then, there was the idea of an autonomous "Republic" within a supposedly Federal Republic of Nigeria which was incapable of guaranteeing the primary conditions of republicanism: a society of equal citizens with equal access to socio-economic and political rights, even in its most cynical bourgeois sense. A linguistic dispute had thus been provoked. The semantic field of the quarrel could also be noticed at the Afrika Shrine, Fela's active place of worship since the 1970s, which was accorded the same reverence as orthodox Islam and Christianity, which were the state's official religions. Nigeria's political elite continues to encourage the liturgy of these two global monotheistic religions by consciously cultivating both their leadership and congregations, at times by building mosques and churches, even if this is against the expectations of a secular state, as enshrined in the 1999 Nigerian Constitution. The state thus expects a measure of cooperation from these institutions, part of which includes preaching the ideology of acquiescence.

But with Fela comes a ribaldry of Afrobeat worship at the Afrika Shrine with a liturgy so decentred and dynamic that the state could not vouch for it.

Rather than the selective acquiescence in "the will of Allah" or Jesus Christ's pacifism of "turning the other cheek," the chief priest of worship here is full of anger, as spokesperson of Africa's ancestors who have asked him to denounce the treachery and debauchery of the continent's corpulent post-independence elite.

By appearing in his underwear, though only within his own residence, and by daring to suggest and remind people of the ordinariness of life, in a society where clothing – especially the military khaki – served the semiotics of power, Fela seemed to have been marked for extinction by the state. His entire career would be dogged by the sheer wish to defend this alterity. Fela smoked marijuana and encouraged society to acknowledge it as a medicinal Nigerian natural grass (NNG) – rather than the banned Indian hemp, thereby confounding the state's counsels, who, on checking their statute books, could not find any trace of such a term as Nigerian natural grass. This peculiar individual was thus regarded as an enigma, a corrupter of youth. The state and its representative agencies seemed to have reached this consensus, and Fela was marked out for repressive treatment.

Recruits for Revolution Day

The Nigerian state has been generally more wary of the core Fela fan, as it is through her or him that the ideology of Afrobeat is often expressed in social action. This may include confrontation with the physical coercive apparatus of the state. Fela has challenged the legitimacy of Nigerian laws on several occasions, the most memorable being the 1977 Kalakuta incident when his Agege Motor Road residence in Lagos was burned down by General Olusegun Obasanjo's soldiers from Abalti Barracks, resulting in the "Coffin for Head of State" aftermath, when Fela dumped a replica of his mother's coffin at Dodan Barracks, then the seat of government.

Many groups sustained this sense of resistance culture through fan-bonding, especially during tours with Fela's "Egypt '80" band. His communal sensibility further encouraged this, as many fans would have their transport fares underwritten by the management of the band. Fans also greeted each other in a variety of ways: by clasping each other's hands in a doubled "high five", with the clenched-fist Black Power salute, or simply by exchanging a gentle clenched-fist shake, often repeating the motion a couple of times while mumbling "rootsman", in an apparent syncretism with Rastafarians and reggae fans (see Hutton in this volume). The bonding experience is, at times, expressed in sharing moments to smoke marijuana, engaging in heated debates on national and international resistance politics, or simply "moonlighting".

Until Fela's Shrine was invaded and occupied by units of Nigeria's National Drug Law Enforcement Agency (NDLEA) in 1997, it had gathered together regular habitués. A dynamic informal trading sector within the shrine and in the adjoining streets also flourished during this era. The variety of trade included food vendors, water hawkers, drinking bars, and a myriad of kiosks offering cigarettes, marijuana, chewing gum, perfumes, and the like for sale. For traders operating within the shrine, a mandatory tax of three naira per day was paid, but by 1997 the rate had moved to twenty naira. There was not to be any tax exemption and revenue generated was channelled into the collective pool of "chop money".

Both at the Shrine and in Fela's residence, there were constant habitués who were essentially made up of the primary fans, who may include the general hustler, the gambler, the irate student or, to some extent, lower cadres of the Nigerian military, and the lunch-time executive who has only made a quick dash down the street to "drag" a quick puff of the banned marijuana weed. All mingled in Fela's Shrine, attempting to create a levelling culture and, to a considerable degree, all aspired towards this new culture code.

The essential habitué was ideologically syncretic and also somewhat malleable. Because his vision was highly messianic, the character of his consciousness was basically informed by the political hero figure, which, in this case, was Fela. The *habitué* hovers between the quest for private material advancement and a belief in social change that may not necessarily have been backed by any revolutionary organisational strategy.

In this dispensation, the habitué inhabits some "imaginative inner dimensions"[7] where long-term strategy could become easily expendable, where solutions come in spatial-spiritual dimensions, and where the energy for change could be deferred to an amalgam god who may come in the garb of Ṣàngó, Chiwota, Amadioha, Osiris or even more recent ancestors. Between puffs of his marijuana, the habitué muses, "one day go be one day": a phrase with the oblique sense of the biblical Judgment Day, denoting a concern for a quick resolution of social crises. In this instance, though, it is a rather secular sense of judgment day when the underprivileged will partake in restructuring political and economic imbalances in society occasioned by the Nigerian state and its monotheistical Constitution.[8]

Anarchy and the Kalakuta Republic

The Kalakuta Republic in its heyday drew its citizenry from the widest imaginable places. Members of the commune included the undergraduate, the secondary school drop-out, the repressed but artistically talented youth, the jobseeker, the rebelling ward of an elite, and the simply adventurous from such far-flung places as Ghana, Togo, Equatorial Guinea and Zaire (now the Democratic Republic of the Congo [DRC]). There were also the black brothers and sisters from the African diaspora in the Americas and the Caribbean. All commingled in their individual search for laughter and the desire to break out of institutions of containment. Though they soon learnt to develop a sense of personality, and take part in the never-ending debates about the "African Revolution", and some even became instant recruits to combat despotic regimes, they nonetheless all subscribed to a new form of institutional containment, which Kalakuta turned out to be, with its own idiosyncratic rules and social organisation.

The day-to-day running of Fela's band and the commune was based on a variety of organisational structures that overlapped. The different modes of structure and mechanisms of control corresponded to what Irish philosopher, Charles Handy, identified in 1970[9] as the power, role, task and person cultures, or, as British theorist, John Child, identified them in 1984,[10] as the personal centralised, bureaucratic, output and cultural controls.

Both within the commune and the band, Fela played the focal role, with other members having to fit in, and taking their cues for their duties and obligations from him, the player of this substantially melodramatic role. Fela played the part of a counter-culture hero, but at the same time resisted the image of the commercial superstar. He was content simply to be acknowledged as an artist with a strong folk sentiment. He buttressed his role choice through the way he lived and the ideals that he preached: an austere sense of dress, the clenched Black Power fist salute, the chain-smoking and a linguistic choice of colloquial vernacular that often confounded. This social mode of behaviour constituted the grand rules that generally defined the attitude of members of the organisation and its fans, who could be seen to replicate them over time.

In strict organisational terms, Fela was central to this movement by operating a minimalist bureaucracy and thereby having to delegate power to the different strands of sub-authorities such as band leaders and supervisors (in the case of the commune). As a result of this limited bureaucratic practice and an aura-dependent code of conduct, quite frequently there arose conflicting role assumptions. All you had to do to justify your claim, it seemed, was to legitimise your position by assuming what Fela's attitude would be on a particular issue. The centrality of Fela to the structure and the privileges emanated from two sources. As the founder of the group, with the passage of time, he sustained its crests and troughs in the face of state hostility, which eventually earned him an "idiosyncrasy credit", and consequently stage members of the group came to offer a freely given devotion and loyalty to him as the central figure. This attitude largely derived from what many fans saw in Fela as a personality with a deep sense of self-denial and a readiness to share. There was also a knowledge of the fact of someone from a middle-class background having integrated with the subculture, and thereby committed "class suicide". Fela was a consistent advocate of human rights which did not suggest a sense of personal gain. His commune and band members recognised these sacrifices, and in a moment of personal contemplation, you could hear a resident or member of the band sighing and exclaiming: "Ah! Fela don try o!"

But such an avowed loyalty by the group – which might include fans and a highly expectant civil population who sought to invest in a messianic figure – created its own contradictions. The first problem that arose was one of an uncritical relationship with this central figure such that, rather than being criticised, his errors were consistently rationalised, and individuals with dissenting views were invariably tagged as "saboteurs" or even "agents", especially since the group's primary antagonist was the Nigerian state and its coercive agencies. This structure thus sustained Fela's indulgence and those of members of his group, especially the young women around the commune with whom he regularly engaged in casual sex. This way, the Nietzschean dictum of God-as-the-supreme-nihilist becomes applicable to Fela – the Chief Priest himself – for, as the German philosopher noted: "when a god climbs to the top of the mountain and there is no path to break and thereby becomes responsible to himself ... God becomes the supreme nihilist".[11]

This limited role of the bureaucratic culture in the group derived both from political expediency and from Fela's artistic temperament. He seemed to personify the pure will that found itself hemmed in by societal requirements of structure and ordering. And Fela's continual conflicts with political authorities right from his first arrest in 1974 until his death from an AIDS-related illness in August 1997 hardly left room for a different outlook in this free-willing spirit.

Another side to the commune's mode of organisation was evident in the use of the task culture, which emphasised getting the job done. Unlike in the case of power culture, acknowledgment came not by a balance of influence as much as by the ability to deliver. This was a more representative team culture and influence based on expert power and individual assiduity to the team; and it was one whose absence was hardly conceivable in musical production by a group.

Each of these disparate management cultures have had to be used, either singly or in combination depending on the particular circumstances in which the organisation found itself. Properly speaking, the flimsy bureaucratic structure that later came to typify the group was, to a large extent, accentuated by the 1977 destruction of Kalakuta Republic. As with the 1984 incident when Fela was jailed by the regime of Generals Muhammadu Buhari and Tunde Idiagbon or, between 1996 and 1997, by General Sani Abacha, these extreme situations exposed the bare bureaucratic base of the organisation. External interventions were always resorted to, in order to substitute for the absence of the central figure: Fela. Since there was hardly room during such events for a properly functioning organisational chart, a new central figure invariably arose. In 1984, Fela's activist brother, Beko Ransome-Kuti (a medical doctor), took over the band and supervised the commune while Fela's son Femi became the lead singer of the Egypt '80 band. What explained fan and member loyalty to policies enunciated by Ransome-Kuti on behalf of the group was sympathy for his activism as a scourge of Nigeria's military, and a human rights advocate in his own right. But as always in such situations, Beko remained an external figure, not having the same "sacred" authority as the displaced central figure.

Self-Crusading Revolutionary Africanist

From the early 1990s onwards, Fela's personal bibliography on Pan-Africanism included a substantial number of earlier thinkers and texts often cited from the early twentieth century. He read, assimilated and entered into polemical debates on these issues, citing copious literature to the amazement of many Nigerians and foreigners who had not had the benefit of this aspect of Fela's inclination. Three texts by Kwame Nkrumah (see Biney in this volume) correspond to the development of Fela's conception of an African identity: *Consciensism*; *Africa Must Unite*; and *Neo-colonialism: The Last Stage of Imperialism*.[12]

A radical departure here was that Fela had a concept of Africa as a black continent. Even when he sought to move into a non-racial category of Africa, he did not move too far from this initial conception. The attempt to transcend the racially based category in his interpersonal relationships was symbolised by his mode of signing his personal letters with the phrase – "best African wishes" rather than the "best black wishes" of the 1970s.[13] Fela also attempted to grapple with this identity in his attitude to the Négritude movement (see Irele in this volume). According to him, Négritudists thought along the same line as Ghana's J.K. Aggrey and his theory about the black and white keys of the piano. For Fela, Négritude did not give black people their full expression.[14]

In spite of this claim, there was still a sense in which Fela was undoubtedly in agreement with certain strands of the Négritude movement such as those represented by Martinique's Aimé Césaire and Jules Monnerot, and Senegal's Léopold Senghor and Birago Diop, to the extent that they sought – in spite of being different hues of socialists – to "determine a strategy for promoting the *individuality* of African culture".[15] Thus, theoretically, Fela agreed on the individuality of the black man, but rejected the binary postulations of his vocation and the potential that preoccupied Senghor's imagination. This can only be said to be a theoretical concession because, quite often, the implications of some of Fela's positions placed him in this same Négritude mould. The distinction he tried to make between "technology" and "naturalogy", for example, suggested that the African was incapable of quantitative and analytical knowledge, even though Fela, as an individual, was a self-evident negation of this stereotype.

Fela's perspectives presented a romantic image of the African, a particular type of African who did not agree to being integrated into the Western cultural maelstrom. And this African was a very simple, non-complex type, one in the Rousseauesque African golden age fantasia of "perfect liberty, equality and fraternity".[16] Hence, Fela's choice was for "naturalogy" not technology, the latter being derived from the insatiate lust for profit rather than genuine progress and concern for the individual. But in adopting this approach, Fela sometimes went to the extreme of denying universal references of certain knowledge production, of which the African was also part creator, by branding them as "Western". Ultimately, Fela's African has distanced the self from a society in which he or she is not in control: this African appears to be overwhelmed by the "interference" factor of colonialism.

Another rung of the African identity debate is the sort of distinctions made by Kenyan intellectual, Ali Mazrui, has, since the mid-1970s, put forth the idea of a "triple heritage" – borrowed from Edward Blyden (see Khadiagala in this volume) and Kwame Nkrumah (see Biney in this volume) – which can be explained by the prevalence of Western (and Christian), Oriental (and Islamic) and indigenous values on the continent. However, African-American intellectual Molefi Asante, like Fela, had rebutted this claim, arguing that the African context is better captured by a description that acknowledges only "one heritage": the indigenous. The "two major invasions" are thus Western and Judaeo-Christian, and Oriental and Islamic.[17] Again, we see here a problem of definition arising from a difference in the paradigms deployed. Is Africa being defined by geography, race, religious values or even language?

Yet another strand in this debate was Fela's conception of citizenship in the context of defining an African identity. From his perspective, all Negro Africans would qualify as citizens of the continent, even if colonial intervention had reduced them to ethnic citizens. And as Ugandan scholar, Mahmood Mamdani, has aptly noted in the case of the Equatorial region of Africa, the colonising forces assumed citizenship while "Natives were said to belong NOT to any civic space, but to an ethnic space".[18] Discussed in relation to post-nineteenth-century European colonising forces, Fela's position was quite clear: they were neither citizens nor did they belong to an ethnic space, even when they might have usurped citizenship rights as settlers.

Fela rejected the qualification of any black African in the continent as belonging to anything less than a civic space. In other words, no black African should be regarded as a native settler, a somewhat contradictory term which could also no longer be based on a racial, but on an ethnic category, as Mamdani suggested. Arising from this observation, Fela – as usual, ahead of his time – advocated the inclusion of the black diaspora in the Organisation of African Unity (OAU), now the African Union (AU). The AU finally recognised the diaspora as a sixth region in its 2000 Constitutive Act. It is also this reading that informed Fela's support for Biafran secessionists during the Nigerian civil war (1967–70). Fela read the incidents of the *araba* (secession), after thousands of Igbos had been massacred in northern Nigeria on the eve of the civil war, as an Igbo (re)classification of themselves as native settlers. The Igbo thus became an ethnic stranger, as against a redefined indigenous ethnic citizen, a privilege which the predominant Hausa–Fulani groups had extended to non-Igbos during the riots of 1966 in northern Nigeria.

In application to the entire continent, Fela's position is quite tenuous and an appropriate way to describe it is that he regarded non-Negro Africans as native settlers in so far as they sought to redefine Africa away from its indigenous values. In relation to Arab Africa in particular, Fela's position was the hybrid of an anthropological and ideological reading. The anthropological stemmed from his articulation of the concept of the indigenous, more or less, as those who first peopled the continent, hence his naming of his band, Egypt '80. Ideologically, there could hardly be any room for accommodation once such groups also exhibited an extroverted settler mentality by partaking in an ideology of a superior racial complex, or were implicated in black enslavement by Arabs across the Sahara.

However, what made Fela's position challenging was that he fused certain animistic structures with a diasporic image of Africa, so that the old ancestors of ancient times were now replaced by a new set of ancestors such as Kwame Nkrumah, Patrice Lumumba, W.E.B. Du Bois (see Morris in this volume), Marcus Garvey (see Grant in this volume) and Malcolm X (see Daniels in this volume), who were determinate in their thinking and whose ideas were accessible. By bringing together these diverse, identifiable African ancestors to build a common image, Fela demonstrated a clear preference for the continental rather than ethnic ancestor. This distinction between the nationalist and the continentalist underscored the Afrobeat "universalist" conception of Africa – what in the discourse of African philosophy would be described as "unanimism": an African culture that is unitary and to which all Africans subscribe.

This explains why Fela never came to terms with the idea of national and regional boundaries on the continent, and the sense of ease with which he intervened through his lyrics and physical intervention in local politics, especially in the West African sub-region. This is what the Ghanaian police in the early 1980s might have had in mind when Fela was taken to the Adabraka police station in Accra after he challenged a Lebanese, whom he had deemed a settler and who was violating the rights of a Ghanaian trader. Fela would casually point at commonalities in the languages of many West African and African groups.

This attitude, for Fela, meant that you had cultures with their formal integrity relating across many interactive spaces in a manner that made it possible for them to share ideas through contact predating the colonial encounter. He was specific about the indices of this unanimity, one of which was cultural values in terms of the ways in which Africans lived. One of the interesting ironies of this outlook was that, while being an advocate of the working class, Fela quite often adopted a very peasant view of lived experience. For example, he would emphasise the choice of a chewing stick over a toothbrush, or eating with bare hands rather than with European cutlery, striving to be as "natural" as possible.

In his thrust towards an aesthetics of the unanimist, Fela compared well to two other African performing artists: the Abidjan-based Cameroonian Werewere Liking, and Nigerian Nobel laureate Wole Soyinka (see Osha in this volume), who was Fela's cousin. With Soyinka, this comes to bear in his *Ogun Abibiman* (1976),[19] in which his experimental fusion of a mythical figure, Ogun (the Yoruba god of iron and creativity) and a more contemporary ancestor, the Zulu king Chaka, explored a timeless mutuality of these figures. In addition, Fela also related the idea of being African to the idea of the original or early man who is free and unencumbered by conventions and apparatuses of containment. This is the central theme of his song "Africa: Centre of the World". His music from the 1971 *Jeun Koku* ("Eat until you Die") album keeps pointing at that element of authenticity, the purity of the human as a person free to act and create. Without asserting it in any clear theoretical frame, Fela subscribed to solarism and its climatic influence on culture. He often noted the "natural" warmth of the African, which he contrasted to the European, whom he found to be rather cold. Fela was thus, in this sense, attributing a certain happy-go-luckiness to the sun, which put a sparkle in every situation. This also had echoes of Négritude.

The circumscription of the dream of a self-conscious Africa arising from the weak nature of its economy led Fela to suggestions of causative factors similar to those once espoused by Tanzanian scholar A.M. Babu in "the inherited backwardness from the primitive structure of colonial economy, failed attempts to formulate policies for restructuring these economies after independence, and a proliferation of weak and self-seeking leadership and coup makers".[20]

Concluding Reflections

In spite of his forays into political group organisational efforts, Fela was essentially in the mould of the Russian anarchist Mikhail Bakunin. Not believing in the "Other's" grand narrative, he settled for the Foucauldian single issue of interventionist symbolic actions: challenging individual instances of oppression, standing up for a Ghanaian trader cheated by a Lebanese, snatching the helmet of a rude policeman, and commissioning a driver to cruise around town with a Mercedes-Benz fixed with a carriage to transport fuel in order to trivialise a symbol of societal elitism. This interventionist stance is often achieved in Fela's lyrical discourse as the troubadour and quester for truth. It usually comes off as "me Fela I challenge", as we find in his 1985 album, *Army Arrangement*. Having frequently succeeded in a lumpen mode of advocacy, Fela elevated the form into a theory of living.

Anarchism here does not suggest the absence of organisation. Fela's sense of anarchism is simply a commitment to freedom in a specific manner that was not going to make compromises just because convention required him to do so. He was a man who used his own authority and exercised it effectively. People respected and deferred to him, and that gave him the freedom to act outside the code that he had created for his followers. The primary and general fan followed Fela, but he was hardly himself a follower, at least not of an immediate, visible authority. Those whom he supposedly "followed" were highly rarefied ancestors: Nkrumah, Lumumba, Garvey, Du Bois and Malcolm X. Though there was a mythical conception of authority to which Fela related, here on earth – and surely in his Republic – he remained the boss.

In relation to the broad sense of organisation of civil society, the most that Fela could tolerate was the "minimal state", one in which citizens ought to be treated as "inviolate individuals, who may not be used in certain ways by others as means or tools or instruments or resources".[21] He shared certain basic ideas with many radical thinkers of the century in identifying layers of contradictions between labour and capital; imperialism and the developing world; private property and social production; and the necessity to abolish the state. Through Fela's examples and precepts, he invariably affirms Lenin's 1917 thesis in *State and Revolution* that "So long as there is the state there is no freedom. When there is freedom there will be no state".[22] But these are ideas equally shared by anarchists. In addition to Fela's disdain for structure and organisation, even when he created them for contingency purposes, his soul was essentially etched in the lines of anarchism's leading French polemicist, Pierre-Joseph Proudhon, who had identified some of the state's domestic "inconveniences" in the fact that "To be governed is to be watched, inspected, spied upon, directed, law-driven, numbered, regulated, enrolled, indoctrinated, preached at, controlled, checked, estimated, valued, censured, commanded, by creatures who have neither the right nor the wisdom nor the virtue to do so ... That is government; that is justice; that is its morality."[23]

Fela Anikulapo-Kuti need not have been self-conscious about theoretical anarchism, either as philosophically deriving from the Hegelian axiom of the "negation of negation", or as a perspective of the necessity for the absence of a central authority. All the organisations that he helped to create were aimed at first distancing themselves from authority, before disrupting what that authority considered to be the norm. Ever since his youth, Fela had hankered after the displacement of central authority when he founded The Planless Society and The Planless Times Publication: institutions that were promptly banned by his school authorities.

Fela's Afrobeat legacy continues today through the music of his sons, Femi and Seun. The 2009 Broadway show *Fela!*, which was staged in New York and Europe – and directed by African-American, Bill T. Jones – ensured Fela's posthumous immortality. Nigerian director Bolanle Austen Peters later directed *Fela and the Kalakuta Queens* (2017) and *Fela's Republic and the Kalakuta Queens* (2019), which both engage with his complex relationship with his wives. These musicals were staged in Lagos, Abuja, Tshwane (Pretoria) and Cairo to widespread acclaim. Today, Fela lies buried in the compound of his home in the Lagos suburb of Ikeja, which has been converted into the Kalakuta Museum.

NOTES

CHAPTER 1

1   I would like to thank Hilary Beckles, Selwyn Cudjoe and Gilbert Khadiagala for extremely useful comments on this Introduction; and also express my profound gratitude to Patrick Gomes, Anthony Gonzales and Annita Montoute for similarly helpful comments on the sections on the Caribbean.
    J.F. Ade Ajayi, "The Atlantic Slave Trade and Africa", in Toyin Falola (ed.), *Tradition and Change in Africa: The Essays of J.F. Ade Ajayi* (Trenton and Asmara: Africa World Press, 2000), pp. 295–6.

2   Though the Caribbean is usually considered part of the Americas, we distinguish it here as a region from the Americas, which here covers the United States and South America. "Africa" is also sometimes used broadly to include the diaspora.

3   "Diva" is used here to connote a "goddess" or supremely talented woman.

4   Hakim Adi, *Pan-Africanism: A History* (London: Bloomsbury Academic, 2018), p. 2.

5   Adi, *Pan-Africanism*, pp. 2–25. See also, Kadiatu Kanneh, *African Identities: Race, Nation and Culture in Ethnography, Pan-Africanism and Black Identities* (London: Routledge, 1998); Ali A. Mazrui, *Towards a Pax Africana: A Study of Ideology and Ambition* (Chicago: University of Chicago Press, 1967); Olisanwuche Esedebe, *Pan-Africanism: The Idea and Movement, 1776–1991* (Washington DC: Howard University Press, 2007); Tunde Babawale, Akin Alao and Tony Onwumah (eds), *Pan-Africanism, and the Integration of Continental Africa and Diaspora Africa*, volume 2 (Lagos: Centre for Black and African Arts and Civilization, 2011); Samuel Oloruntoba, *Africa and Its Diaspora: History, Identities and Economy* (Ibadan and Texas: Pan-African University Press, 2017).

6   Guy Martin, *African Political Thought* (New York: Palgrave Macmillan, 2012).

7   Adi, *Pan-Africanism*.

8   Hakim Adi and Marika Sherwood, *Pan-African History: Political Figures from Africa and the Diaspora since 1787* (London and New York: Routledge, 2003).

9   Reiland Rabaka (ed.), *Routledge Handbook of Pan-Africanism* (Abingdon-on-Thames: Routledge, 2020).

10 I thank Selwyn Cudjoe for editorial contributions to this paragraph and the next.

11 Derek Walcott, "Tribute to C.L.R. James", in Selwyn R. Cudjoe and William E. Cain (eds), *C.L.R. James: His Intellectual Legacies* (Amherst: University of Massachusetts Press, 1995), p. 38.

12 Ole J. Benedictow, "The Black Death: The Greatest Catastrophe Ever", *History Today*, 3

(March 2005), www.historytoday.com; and BBC History Extra, *"Black Death Facts: Your Guide to the 'Worst Catastrophe in Recorded History'"*, 23 March 2020, www.historyextra.com.

13 See Linda M. Heywood, *Njinga of Angola: Africa's Warrior Queen* (Cambridge and London: Harvard University Press, 2017).

14 Ajayi, "The Atlantic Slave Trade and Africa", p. 288.

15 Horace Campbell, *Rasta and Resistance: From Marcus Garvey to Walter Rodney* (Trenton: Africa World Press, 1987), pp. 12, 15.

16 Campbell, *Rasta and Resistance*, p. 15.

17 I have relied for this analysis on Walter Rodney, *How Europe Underdeveloped Africa* (Washington DC: Howard University Press, 1982; originally published London: Bogle-L'Ouverture Publications and Dar es Salaam: Tanzanian Publishing House, 1972), pp. 98–100.

18 This paragraph and the next have drawn from Eric Williams, *Capitalism and Slavery* (Chapel Hill: University of North Carolina Press, 1944), pp. 30–50.

19 Williams, *Capitalism and Slavery*, p. 39.

20 Ajayi, "The Atlantic Slave Trade and Africa", p. 288.

21 See, for example, Emmanuel Akyeampong, "History, Memory, Slave-Trade and Slavery in Anlo", *Slavery and Abolition*, 22, 3 (December 2001), pp. 1–24.

22 Hilary McD. Beckles, *Britain's Black Debt* (Jamaica, Barbados, and Trinidad and Tobago: University of the West Indies, Press, 2013), p. 168.

23 Rodney, *How Europe Underdeveloped Africa*, p. 102.

24 Campbell, *Rasta and Resistance*, p. 13.

25 Ajayi, "The Atlantic Slave Trade and Africa", pp. 291–2.

26 I have summarised much of the information in this paragraph and the following two from Campbell, *Rasta and Resistance*, pp. 19–30; see also C.L.R. James, *A History of Pan-African Revolt* (Oakland: PM Press, 2012 [1938]).

27 C.L.R. James, *The Black Jacobins: Toussaint L'Ouverture and the San Domingo Revolution* (New York: Vintage Books, 1989 [1938]).

28 This information is taken from the 2013 Public Broadcasting Service (PBS) documentary by Henry Louis Gates, Jr, *The African Americans: Many Rivers to Cross*, Episode 2: "The Age of Slavery (1780–1860)", and Episode 3: "Into the Fire (1861–1896)".

29 Micere Mugo, "Art, Artists and the Flowering of Pan-Africana Liberated Zones", in Issa Shivji (ed.), *Reimagining Pan-Africanism: Distinguished Mwalimu Nyerere Lecture Series 2009–2013* (Dar es Salaam: Mkuki Na Nyota, 2015), p. 178.

30 W.E.B. Du Bois, *The Souls of Black Folk* (New York, London, and Johannesburg: Penguin, 1996 [1903]).

31 See Abiola Irele, "Black Utopia I: Slavery and Providence", in Abiola Irele, *The African Scholar and Other Essays* (Ibadan: Bookcraft, 2019), pp. 137–9.

32 Amiri Baraka (previously LeRoi Jones), *Blues People: Negro Music in White America* (New York and London: Harper, 1963), p. 17.

33 Baraka, *Blues People*, pp. 17–31.

34 See Maya Angelou, *I Know Why the Caged Bird Sings* (New York: Random House, 1969).

35 Cited in Theresa Singleton and Marcos André Torres de Souza, "Archaelogies of the African Diaspora: Brazil, Cuba, and the United States", in Teresita Majewski and David Gaimster (eds), *International Handbook of Historical Archaeology* (New York: Springer, 2009), p. 450; and Ana Lucia Araújo, "Slavery and the Atlantic Slave Trade in Brazil and Cuba from an Afro-Atlantic Perspective", *Almanack*, 12 (January/April 2016), p. 1.

36 Araújo, "Slavery and the Atlantic Slave Trade in Brazil and Cuba from an Afro-Atlantic Perspective", pp. 1–5.

37 Singleton and de Souza, "Archaeologies of the African Diaspora,' p. 457.
38 See Jacob U. Gordon, "Yoruba Cosmology and Culture in Brazil: A Study of African Survivals in the New World", *Journal of Black Studies*, 10, 2 (December 1979), pp. 231–44; and Henry Louis Gates's PBS documentary *Black in Latin America*, "Brazil: A Racial Paradise?", 2011.
39 See Shubi L. Ishemo, "From Africa to Cuba: An Historical Analysis of the Sociedad Secreta Abakuá (Ñañiguismo)", *Review of African Political Economy*, 29, 92 (June 2002), pp. 253–72.
40 See Henry Louis Gates's PBS documentary *Black in Latin America*, "Cuba: The Next Revolution", 2011.
41 This section draws from Adekeye Adebajo, *The Curse of Berlin: Africa after the Cold War* (New York: Oxford University Press, 2013 [2010]), "Introduction: Bismarck's Sorcery and Africa's Three Magic Kingdoms", pp. 1–27.
42 Ali A. Mazrui, "Black Berlin and the Curse of Fragmentation: From Bismarck to Obama", Preface in Adebajo, *The Curse of Berlin*, pp. ix–xxviii.
43 Jan Morris, *Pax Britannica: The Climax of an Empire* (New York: Harcourt Brace, 1968), p. 110.
44 Quoted in V.Y. Mudimbe, "E.W. Blyden's Legacy and Questions", in V.Y. Mudimbe, *The Invention of Africa: Gnosis, Philosophy, and the Order of Knowledge* (Bloomington: Indiana University Press, 1988), p. 108.
45 Quoted in Ali A. Mazrui, *The African Condition: A Political Diagnosis* (Cambridge: Cambridge University Press, 1980), p. 88.
46 See A. Adu Boahen, "Africa and the Colonial Challenge", in A. Adu Boahen (ed.), *General History of Africa*, vol. 7, *Africa under Colonial Domination, 1880–1935* (Berkeley: University of California Press, 1985), pp. 1–18.
47 Mazrui, *The African Condition*, p. 95.
48 My summary of the Berlin Conference in this section relies largely on the narratives in Thomas Pakenham, *The Scramble for Africa: White Man's Conquest of the Dark Continent from 1876 to 1912* (New York: Avon, 1991), pp. 239–55; Wm. Roger Louis, "The Berlin Congo Conference and the (Non-) Partition of Africa, 1884–1885", in Wm. Roger Louis, *Ends of British Imperialism: The Scramble for Empire, Suez, and Decolonization* (London: Tauris, 2006), pp. 75–126; and G.N. Uzoigwe, "The Results of the Berlin West Africa Conference: An Assessment", in Stig Förster, Wolfgang J. Mommsen, and Ronald Robinson (eds), *Bismarck, Europe, and Africa: The Berlin Africa Conference, 1884–1885, and the Onset of Partition* (Oxford: Oxford University Press, 1988), pp. 543–4.
49 See Adam Hochschild, *King Leopold's Ghost: A Story of Greed, Terror, and Heroism in Colonial Africa* (London: Pan Macmillan, 1998).
50 Quoted in J.F. Ade Ajayi, "Colonialism: An Episode in African History", in Falola, *Tradition and Change in Africa*, p. 174, n.12.
51 Quoted in Uzoigwe, "The Results of the Berlin West Africa Conference", pp. 543–4.
52 This point is made in Bernard Makhosezwe Magubane, *The Ties That Bind: African-American Consciousness of Africa* (Trenton: Africa World Press, 1987), p. 135.
53 See John C. Shields (eds), *The Collected Works of Phillis Wheatley* (New York: Oxford University Press, 1988).
54 Quoted in Irele, *The African Scholar*, p. 137.
55 This paragraph is drawn from Adi, *Pan-Africanism*, pp. 6–7.
56 This paragraph draws from Adi, *Pan-Africanism*, p. 10.
57 Hollis R. Lynch, *Edward Wilmot Blyden: Pan-Negro Patriot 1832–1912* (Oxford and New York: Oxford University Press, 1967), p. 3.

58 Edward Wilmot Blyden, *Christianity, Islam and the Negro Race* (Monrovia: Black Classic Press, 1888).

59 Irele, "Black Utopia", p. 151.

60 Quoted in Mudimbe, "E.W. Blyden's Legacy and Questions", p. 133.

61 Quoted in Colin Legum, *Pan-Africanism* (London: Pall Mall Press, 1962), p. 21.

62 Quoted in Lynch, *Edward Wilmot Blyden*, p. 6.

63 Mudimbe, "E.W. Blyden's Legacy and Questions", pp. 100, 116.

64 Adi, *Pan-Africanism*, p. 25.

65 Adi, *Pan-Africanism*, pp. 21–2.

66 Quoted in Geoffrey Barraclough, "The Revolt against the West", in Prasenjit Duara (ed.), *Decolonization: Perspectives from Now and Then* (London: Routledge, 2004), p. 118.

67 See Tajudeen Abdul-Raheem, "Introduction: Reclaiming Africa for Africans: Pan-Africanism, 1900–1994", in Tajudeen Abdul-Raheem (ed.), *Pan-Africanism: Politics, Economy, and Social Change in the Twenty-First Century* (London: Pluto, 1996), pp. 1–30.

68 Magubane, *The Ties That Bind*, p. 125.

69 Legum, "Pan-Africanism", pp. 28–9.

70 Adekeye Adebajo, "Facing Up to Woodrow Wilson's True Legacy," *Times Literary Supplement*, online version, August 2020 (thetls.co.uk).

71 Legum, "Pan-Africanism", p. 26.

72 See Colin Grant, *Negro with a Hat: The Rise and Fall of Marcus Garvey* (Oxford: Oxford University Press, 2008).

73 See, for example, W.E.B. Du Bois, "Manifesto of the Second Pan-African Congress", in Eric J. Sundquist (ed.), *The Oxford W.E.B. Du Bois Reader* (New York and Oxford: Oxford University Press, 1996), pp. 640–4.

74 Legum, "Pan-Africanism", pp. 29–30.

75 Kwame Nkrumah, *Ghana: The Autobiography of Kwame Nkrumah* (London: Panaf, 1957), p. 53.

76 Legum, "Pan-Africanism", pp. 31–2.

77 Kwame Nkrumah, *Africa Must Unite* (London: Panaf, 1963), pp. 150–72.

78 Julius Nyerere, "A United States of Africa", *Journal of Modern African Studies*, 1, 1 (1963), p. 1.

79 Nyerere, "A United States of Africa", pp. 1–6.

80 Léopold Senghor, "Some Thoughts on Africa: A Continent in Development", *International Affairs*, 38, 2 (April 1962), p. 189.

81 Senghor, "Some Thoughts on Africa", pp. 189–95.

82 See, for example, Yassin El-Ayouty (ed.), *The Organization of African Unity after Thirty Years* (New York: Praeger Publishers, 1994); Gino Naldi, *The Organization of African Unity* (London: Mansell, 1989); Salim Ahmed Salim, "The OAU Role in Conflict Management", in Olara Otunnu and Michael Doyle (eds), *Peacemaking and Peacekeeping for the New Century* (Maryland and Oxford: Rowman and Littlefield, 1998), pp. 245–53; and Amadu Sesay, Olusola Ojo and Orobola Fasehun, *The OAU after Twenty Years* (Boulder: Westview Press, 1984).

83 Immanuel Wallerstein, *The Politics of Unity* (New York: Vintage Books, 1967), p. 7.

84 This section builds on Adekeye Adebajo, "Africa, African Americans and the Avuncular Sam", *Africa Today*, 50, 3 (Spring 2004), pp. 93–110.

85 Robert Johnson, *Returning Home: A Century of African-American Repatriation* (Trenton and Asmara: Africa World Press, 2005), pp. 2–4.

86 Randall Robinson, *The Debt: What America Owes to Blacks* (New York and London: Penguin Books, 2000), p. 210.

87 Quoted in Adi, *Pan-Africanism*, p. 11.

88 Irele, "Black Utopia", p. 147.

89 Quoted in Adi, *Pan-Africanism*, p. 13.

90 This information draws from the 2013 PBS documentary by Henry Louis Gates, *The African Americans: Many Rivers to Cross*, Episode 2: "The Age of Slavery (1780–1860)", and Episode 3: "Into the Fire (1861–1896)".

91 Equal Justice Initiative, Alabama, US, *Lynching in America: Confronting the Legacy of Racial Terror*, third edition, 2017.

92 See, for example, Elliot P. Skinner, *African Americans and US Policy toward Africa 1850– 1924: In Defense of Black Nationality* (Washington DC: Howard University Press, 1992).

93 See, for example, James Baldwin, *Notes of a Native Son* (Boston: Beacon Press, 1955); and Paul Robeson, *Here I Stand* (Boston: Beacon Press, 1958).

94 See, for example, Winston James, *Holding Aloft the Banner of Ethiopia* (London and New York: Verso, 1998).

95 See Henry Louis Gates, Jr, *Thirteen Ways of Looking at a Black Man* (New York: Vintage Books, 1998), pp. 123–54.

96 See Joseph E. Harris (in collaboration with Slimane Zeghidour), "Africa and Its Diaspora since 1935", in Ali A. Mazrui (ed.), *Africa: Africa since 1935*, General History of Africa vol. VIII (Berkeley: University of California Press, 1993), pp. 705–23.

97 See Adekeye Adebajo, "Africa and the United States: A History of Malign Neglect", in Dawn Nagar and Charles Mutasa (eds), *Africa and the World: Bilateral and Multilateral International Diplomacy* (London: I.B. Tauris, 2018) pp. 27–50.

98 Ali A. Mazrui, "Africa Entrapped: Between the Protestant Ethic and the Legacy of Westphalia", in Hedley Bull and Adam Watson (eds), *The Expansion of International Society* (Oxford: Clarendon Press, 1984), pp. 293–5.

99 Francis M. Deng, *Identity, Diversity, and Constitutionalism in Africa* (Washington DC: US Institute of Peace, 2008), p. 3. See also Mahmood Mamdani, *Citizen and Subject: Contemporary Africa and the Legacy of Late Colonialism* (Kampala: Fountain, 1996).

100 See Basil Davidson, *The Black Man's Burden: Africa and the Curse of the Nation State* (New York: Times Books, 1992), pp. 162–96.

101 Mazrui, *Towards a Pax Africana*.

102 Samuel E. Finer, *The Man on Horseback: The Role of the Military in Politics* (London: Pall Mall, 1962).

103 See Yoichi Mine, "The Political Element in the Works of W. Arthur Lewis: The 1954 Lewis Model and African Development", *Developing Economies*, XLIV (3 September 2006), pp. 329–55.

104 See, for example, Adekeye Adebajo, "The Pharaoh and the Prophet: Boutros Boutros-Ghali and Kofi Annan", in Adebajo *The Curse of Berlin*, pp. 77–97.

105 Franklin W. Knight, "Introduction", in Gordon Lewis, *The Growth of the Modern West Indies* (Kingston and Miami: Ian Randle Publishers, 2004 [1968]), p. xxx.

106 This paragraph and the next two have mainly drawn from Wouter Veenendaal and Jack Corbett, "Clientelism in Small States: How Smallness Influences Patron-Client Networks in the Caribbean and the Pacific", *Democratization*, 27, 1 (2020), pp.61-80; and Paul Sutton, "Caribbean Politics: A Matter of Diversity", *Social Education*, vol. 64, no. 2, March 2000, pp. 78--81.

107 See Haroon Siddique, "'Baby Doc' Duvalier's Escape into Exile", *The Guardian* (London), 17 January 2011, www.the guardian.com.

108 Eric Hobsbawn, *The Age of Empire, 1875–1914* (London: Abacus, 1994 [1987]), pp. 63–6.

109 "Making Africa Work", *The Economist*, 16 April 2016, p. 7. See also Thandika Mkandawire, "Can Africa Turn from Recovery to Development?", *Current History*, 113, 763 (May 2014), pp. 171–7.

110 Rodney, *How Europe Underdeveloped Africa.*

111 Knight, "Introduction", p. xx.

112 I have drawn in this paragraph and the following from Gordon D. Lewis, *The Growth of the Modern West Indies*, pp. 391–411.

113 See Arthur Hazlewood, "The End of the East African Community: What Are the Lessons for Regional Integration Schemes?" *Journal of Common Market Studies*, XVIII, 1 (September 1979), pp. 40–58; Agrippa T. Mugomba, "Regional Organisations and African Underdevelopment: The Collapse of the East African Community", *Journal of Modern African Studies*, 16, 2 (June 1978), pp. 261–72; Joseph S. Nye, "East African Economic Integration", *Journal of Modern African Studies*, 1, 4 (December 1963), pp. 475–502; and Christian P. Potholm, "Who Killed Cock Robin? Perceptions Concerning the Breakup of the East African Community", *World Affairs*, 142, 1 (Summer 1979), pp. 45–56.

114 Norman Girvan, "Reinventing CARICOM: A Question of Survival", *Social and Economic Studies*, 50, 2 (June 2001), p. 189.

115 Girvan, "Reinventing CARICOM", pp. 189–94.

116 Norman Girvan, "The Quest for Regional Integration in the Caribbean: Successes and Challenges", speaking notes, United Nations (UN) Economic Commission for Latin America and the Caribbean (ECLAC) Caribbean Development Roundtable, Port of Spain, Trinidad and Tobago, 13 September 2011.

117 This paragraph has drawn from Jessica Byron, "Developmental Regionalism in Crisis? Rethinking CARICOM, Deepening Relations with Latin America", *Caribbean Journal of International Relations and Diplomacy*, 2, 4 (December 2014), pp. 29–32.

118 This paragraph draws from Annita Montoute, "CARICOM's External Engagements: Prospects and Challenges for Caribbean Regional Integration and Development", Policy Brief, the German Marshall Fund of the United States, May 2015, pp. 1–7.

119 This paragraph has drawn from Byron, "Developmental Regionalism in Crisis?", pp. 38–42.

120 Byron, "Developmental Regionalism in Crisis?", p. 24.

121 See Norman Girvan and Annita Montoute, "The EU and the Caribbean: The Necessity of Unity", pp. 79–110; and Anthony Peter Gonzales, "The Caribbean–EU Economic Partnership Agreement: A Caribbean Perspective", pp. 181–209, both in Annita Montoute and Kudrat Virk (eds), *The ACP Group and the EU Development Partnership: Beyond the North–South Debate* (New York: Palgrave Macmillan, 2017).

122 See Shridath Ramphal, "The Primacy of Institutionalised Unity Is Key to the Georgetown Agreement", Keynote speech delivered at the policy seminar in Barbados on 26–27 March 2019 "Revisiting the Georgetown Agreement: Comparative Region-Building in Africa, the Caribbean, and the Pacific", hosted by the ACP secretariat; CARICOM; the University of Johannesburg's Institute for Pan-African Thought and Conversation (IPATC); and the University of the West Indies Shridath Ramphal Centre.

123 Adebayo Adedeji, "ECOWAS: A Retrospective Journey", in Adekeye Adebajo and Ismail Rashid (eds), *West Africa's Security Challenges: Building Peace in a Troubled Region* (Boulder and London: Lynne Rienner, 2004), p. 46.

124 Wallerstein, *The Politics of Unity*, p. 15.

125 See, for example, Wole Soyinka, *The Burden of Memory: The Muse of Forgiveness* (Cape Town, Oxford and New York: Oxford University Press, 1999), pp. 93–194.

126 Quoted in Ali A. Mazrui, "Africa Entrapped", p. 296.

127 Quoted in Ubang P. Ugor, "Reparation, Reconciliation and Négritude Poetics in Soyinka's *The Burden of Memory, The Muse of Forgiveness*", in Onookome Okome (ed.), *Ogun's*

Children: The Literature and Politics of Wole Soyinka since the Nobel (Trenton and Asmara: Africa World Press, 2004), p. 273.

128 Quoted in Legum, *Pan-Africanism*, p. 16.

129 Kweku Ampiah kindly shared his unpublished paper on "Kizomba: Redefining Angolan Identity through Music, Dance and Style".

130 See, for example, Pierre Barrot (ed.), *Nollywood: The Video Phenomenon in Nigeria* (Oxford: Currey, 2008); John Haynes, *Nollywood: The Creation of Nigerian Film Genres* (Ibadan: Bookcraft, 2017, first published by the University of Chicago in 2016); and Odia Ofeimum, "In Defence of the Films We Have Made", *Chimurenga*, no. 8 (2006), pp. 44–54.

131 Matthias Krings and Onookome Okome, "Nollywood and Its Diaspora: An Introduction", in Matthias Krings and Onookome Okome (eds), *Global Nollywood: The Transnational Dimensions of an African Video Industry* (Bloomington and Indianapolis: Indiana University Press, 2013), p. 1.

132 This paragraph has drawn from Jane Bryce, "'African Movies' in Barbados: Proximate Experiences of Fear and Desire", in Krings and Okome, *Global Nollywood*, pp. 223–44.

133 Cited in Beckles, *Britain's Black Debt*, p. 163.

134 Robinson, *The Debt*, pp. 199–216.

135 Robinson, *The Debt*, pp. 199–208.

136 Robinson, *The Debt*, pp. 199–234.

137 John Eligon, Audra D.S. Buruch, Dionne Searcey and Richard A. Oppel Jr, "Black Americans Face Alarming Rates of Coronavirus Infection in Some States", *New York Times*, 14 April 2020, www.nytimes.com.

138 Beckles, *Britain's Black Debt*, p. 2.

139 Beckles, *Britain's Black Debt*, pp. 163–71.

140 Severin Carrell, "Glasgow University to Pay £20m in Slave Trade Reparations", *The Guardian* (London), 23 August 2019, www.the guardian.com.

141 J.F. Ade Ajayi, "The Crusade for Reparations", in Toyin Falola (ed.), *Tradition and Change in Africa*, p. 339.

142 Ajayi, "The Crusade for Reparations", pp. 337–49.

143 Blyden, *Christianity, Islam and the Negro Race*.

144 See Ali A. Mazrui, *The Africans: A Triple Heritage* (London: BBC Publications, 1986); and the nine-part documentary.

145 Maya Angelou, *All God's Children Need Travelling Shoes* (London: Virago, 2008).

146 Quoted in Nemata Amelia Ibitayo Blyden, *African Americans and Africa: A New History* (New Haven and London: Yale University Press, 2019), p. 4.

147 Quoted in Blyden, *African Americans and Africa*, p. 9.

148 "The Other African-Americans", *The Economist*, 19 October 2019, pp. 38–9.

149 For these points in the paragraph I thank Blyden, *African Americans and Africa*, p. 205.

150 See, for example, Derrick Bell, *Faces at the Bottom of the Well: The Permanence of Racism* (New York: Basic Books, 1992); Orlando Patterson, *Rituals of Blood: Consequences of Slavery in Two American Centuries* (New York: Perseus Books, 1998); and Robinson, *The Debt*.

151 Toni Morrison, "The Slavebody and the Blackbody", in Toni Morrison, *The Source of Self-Regard: Selected Essays, Speeches, and Meditations* (New York: Alfred A. Knopf, 2019), p. 74.

152 Ali A. Mazrui, *The Trial of Christopher Okigbo* (New York: Third Press, 1971).

153 Quoted in Wallerstein, *Africa: The Politics of Unity*, p. 67.

CHAPTER 2

1   See Hilary Beckles, *The First Slave Society: Britain's "Barbarity Time" in Barbados, 1636–1876* (Kingston: University of the West Indies Press, 2016); Robin Blackburn, *The Overthrow of Colonial Slavery, 1776–1848* (London: Verso Books, 1988); and V.P. Franklin, *Black Self Determination: A Cultural History of African-American Resistance* (New York: Lawrence Hill Book, 1992).

2   See the classic study by C.L.R. James, *The Black Jacobins: Toussaint L'Ouverture and the San Domingo Revolution* (New York: Vintage Books, 1989 [1938]); and Nick Nesbit, *Universal Emancipation: The Haitian Revolution and the Radical Enlightenment* (Charlottesville: University of Virginia Press, 2008).

3   A.J. Cameron, *The Berbice Uprising, 1763* (Georgetown: Caribbean Press, 2013); J.J. Hartsinck, "Berbice Revolt of 1763", *Journal of the British Guiana Museum and Zoo*, 20 (1958); and Alvin Thompson, *Colonialism and Underdevelopment in Guyana, 1500–1803* (Bridgetown: Carib Research, 1987).

4   See, for example, Philip D. Curtin, *The Atlantic Slave Trade: A Census* (Wisconsin: University of Wisconsin Press, 1972).

5   See, for example, Paul Gilroy, *The Black Atlantic: Modernity and Double-Consciousness* (Cambridge: Harvard University Press, 1993); Kwasi Konadu, *The Akan Diaspora in the Americas* (London: Oxford University Press, 2010); and Sidney Lemelle and Robin Kelly (eds), *Imagining Home: Class and Culture and Nationalism in the African Diaspora* (London: Verso Books, 1994.)

6   Horace Campbell, *Rasta and Resistance: Marcus Garvey to Walter Rodney* (Trenton and Asmara: Africa World Press, 1987); and Winston James, *Holding Aloft the Banner of Ethiopia: Caribbean Radicalism in the Early 20th Century* (Chapel Hill: University of North Carolina Press, 1998).

7   See Frantz Fanon, *The Wretched of the Earth* (New York: Grove Press, 1963); and Alistair Horne, *A Savage War of Peace: Algeria 1954–1962* (London: Macmillan, 1977).

8   See, for example, Peter Katjavivi, *A History of Resistance in Namibia* (London: James Currey, 1988); William Minter, *Apartheid's Contras: An Inquiry into the Roots of War in Angola and Mozambique* (London, New Jersey and Johannesburg: Zed Books and Witwatersrand University Press, 1994); and Chris Saunders, "UN Peacekeeping in Southern Africa: Namibia, Angola and Mozambique", in Adekeye Adebajo (ed.), *From Global Apartheid to Global Village: Africa and the United Nations* (Scottsville: University of KwaZulu-Natal Press, 2009), pp. 269–81.

9   See, for example, K.G. Davies, *The Royal African Company* (London: Longman, 1957).

10 See, for example, Malegapuru William Makgoba (ed.), *African Renaissance: The New Struggle* (Cape Town: Tafelberg, 1999).

11 See Makgoba, *African Renaissance*. For some critiques of Mbeki's Renaissance vision, see Jimi O. Adesina, Yao Graham, and Adebayo Olukoshi (eds), *Africa and Development Challenges in the New Millennium: The NEPAD Debate* (Dakar: CODESRIA, 2006); Patrick Bond (ed.), *Fanon's Warning: A Civil Society Reader on the New Partnership for Africa's Development*, 2nd edn (Asmara: Africa World Press, 2005); and Peter Vale and Sipho Maseko, "Thabo Mbeki, South Africa and the Idea of an African Renaissance", in Sean Jacobs and Richard Calland (eds), *Thabo Mbeki's World: The Politics and Ideology of the South African President* (Pietermaritzburg: University of Natal Press, 2002).

12 See, for example, Clara Carvalho, "Africa and Portugal", in Dawn Nagar and Charles Mutasa (eds), *Africa and The World: Bilateral and Multilateral International Diplomacy* (New York: Palgrave Macmillan, 2018), pp. 143–65.

13 See, for example, Francis Kornegay, "The AU and Africa's Three Diasporas", in John Akokpari, Angela Ndinga-Muvumba and Tim Murithi (eds), *The African Union and Its*

Institutions (Johannesburg: Jacana, 2008), pp. 333–54.

14 See Ali A. Mazrui, *The Africans: A Triple Heritage* (London: BBC Books, 1986).

CHAPTER 3

1 Benyamin Neuberger, "Early African Nationalism, Judaism and Zionism: Edward Wilmot Blyden", *Jewish Social Studies*, 47, 2 (1985), p. 151.

2 Hollis Ralph Lynch, "Edward Wilmot Blyden: Pioneer West African Nationalist", *Journal of African History*, 3 (1965), p. 237. See also Lynch's magisterial work, *Edward Wilmot Blyden, Pan-Negro Patriot, 1832–1912* (London: Oxford University Press, 1967).

3 Thomas H. Henriksen, "African Intellectual Influences on Black Americans: The Role of Edward W. Blyden", *Phylon*, 36, 3 (1973), p. 280.

4 Lynch, "Edward Wilmot Blyden", pp. 2–3.

5 Charles Collyer, "Edward Wilmot Blyden: A Correspondent of William Ewart Gladstone", *Journal of Negro History*, 35, 1 (January 1950), p. 75.

6 Collyer, "Edward Wilmot Blyden", p. 39.

7 Edward Wilmot Blyden, *Christianity, Islam and the Negro Race* (Monrovia: Black Classic Press, 1888), p. 276.

8 *The West African University: Correspondence between Edward W. Blyden and His Excellency J. Pope-Hennessy, Administrator-in-Chief of the West African Settlements* (Freetown: Negro Printing Office, 1872), p. 17.

9 Neuberger, "Early African Nationalism, Judaism, and Zionism", p. 153.

10 Andrew Billingsley, "Edward Blyden: Apostle of Blackness", *Black Scholar* (December 1970), p. 3.

11 Edward Wilmot Blyden, "Africa and the Africans", in Albert G. Mosley (ed.), *African Philosophy: Selected Writings* (Princeton: Prentice Hall, 1968), pp. 7–29; Yu M. Frenkel, "Edward Blyden and the Concept of African Personality", *African Affairs*, 73, 292 (1974), pp. 277–89; and Robert July, "Nineteenth-Century Négritude: Edward Wilmot Blyden", *Journal of African History*, 5, 1 (1963), pp. 73–86.

12 Abiola Irele, "The Correspondence of Edward Wilmot Blyden (1832–1912)", *Présence Africaine*, 114 (1980), p. 186.

13 Frenkel, "Edward Blyden and the Concept of African Personality", pp. 282–4.

14 Blyden, *Christianity, Islam, and the Negro Race*, p. 124.

15 Blyden, *Christianity, Islam, and the Negro Race*, p. 129.

16 Billingsley, "Edward Blyden", p. 7.

17 Billingsley, "Edward Blyden", p. 7.

18 Billingsley, "Edward Blyden", p. 7.

19 Billingsley, "Edward Blyden", p. 11.

20 Billingsley, "Edward Blyden", p. 11.

21 *The West African University*, p. 3.

22 *The West African University*, p. 13.

23 *The West African University*, p. 2.

24 *The West African University*, p. 14.

25 Billingsley, "Edward Blyden", p. 9.

26 Lynch, "Edward W. Blyden", pp. 380–1; and Henriksen, "African Intellectual Influences on Black Americans", p. 282.

27 Lynch, "Edward Wilmot Blyden", pp. 380–1; and Billingsley, "Edward Blyden", pp. 8–9.

28 Lynch, "Edward Wilmot Blyden", pp. 84–5.

29 *The West African University*, p. 14. Blyden further saw the university as the place to restore, in some measure, "the strength and self-respect that the Negro had lost", p. 14.

30 *The West African University*, p. 12.
31 Christopher Fyfe, Introduction to Blyden's *Christianity, Islam, and the Negro Race* (London: Pall Mall, 1967).
32 Frenkel, "Edward Blyden and the Concept of African Personality", pp. 284–5; and Lynch, "Edward Wilmot Blyden", p. 211.
33 Lynch, "Edward Wilmot Blyden", p. 211.
34 Lynch, "Edward Wilmot Blyden", p. 214.
35 Lynch, "Edward Wilmot Blyden", p. 373.
36 Judson M. Lyon, "Edward Blyden: Liberian Independence and African Nationalism, 1903–1909", *Phylon*, 41, 1 (1980), p. 48.
37 Billingsley, "Edward Blyden", p. 6.
38 Lyon, "Edward Blyden".
39 Lyon, "Edward Blyden", p. 37; and Lynch, *Edward Wilmot Blyden*, p. 374. As Lyon further stated: "Blyden was convinced that the integrity of African culture was more important to Africa's future than Liberia's continued independence", p. 41.
40 Lynch, "Edward Blyden", p. 379.
41 Valentin-Yves Mudimbe, *The Invention of Africa: Gnosis, Philosophy, and the Order of Knowledge* (London: James Currey), p. 98.
42 Irele, "The Correspondence of Edward Wilmot Blyden", p. 188.

CHAPTER 4

1   See William Francis Allen, Charles Pickard Ware and Lucy McKim Garrison (eds), *Slave Songs of the United States* (New York: A. Simpson & Co., 1867).
2   Aldon Douglas Morris, *The Origins of the Civil Rights Movement: Black Communities Organizing for Change* (New York: Free Press, 1984).
3   William Edward Burghardt Du Bois, *The Souls of Black Folk* (Oxford: Oxford University Press, 2008 [1903]).
4   See W.E.B. Du Bois, *The Early Beginning of the Pan-African Movement, June 20, 1958*, W.E.B. Du Bois Papers (MS 312), Special Collections and University Archive, University Libraries, Amherst, University of Massachusetts.
5   Martin Luther King, *Honoring Dr. Du Bois* (Moscow: YCL, 1968).
6   William Edward Burghardt Du Bois, *Dusk of Dawn: An Essay towards an Autobiography of a Race Concept*, edited by Henry Louis Gates (Oxford: Oxford University Press, 2007 [1940]).
7   Du Bois, *The Souls of Black Folk*.
8   Karida L. Brown, "The 'Hidden Injuries" of School Desegregation: Cultural Trauma and Transforming African American Identities", *American Journal of Cultural Sociology*, 4, 2 (2016), pp. 196–220.
9   Du Bois, *The Souls of Black Folk*.
10 William Edward Burghardt Du Bois, *The Philadelphia Negro* (Millwood, New York: Kraus-Thomson, 1973 [1899]).
11 Aldon D. Morris, *The Scholar Denied: WEB Du Bois and the Birth of Modern Sociology* (Oakland: University of California Press, 2015).
12 King, *Honoring Dr. Du Bois*.
13 King, *Honoring Dr. Du Bois*.
14 King, *Honoring Dr. Du Bois*.
15 See, for example, Adekeye Adebajo, *The Curse of Berlin: Africa after the Cold War* (New York: Columbia University Press, and Scottsville: University of KwaZulu-Natal Press, 2010).

16 Minkah Makalani, "African and African Diasporan Transformations in the 20th Century: Pan-Africanism", The New York Public Library, *Africana Age* (2011), http://exhibitions. nypl.org/africanaage/essay-pan-africanism.html.

17 Makalani, "African and African Diasporan Transformations in the 20th Century".

18 William Edward Burghardt Du Bois, *The Conservation of Races* (Washington, DC: American Negro Academy, 1897).

19 Du Bois, *The Conservation of Races*.

20 Du Bois, *The Conservation of Races*.

21 Du Bois, *The Conservation of Races*.

22 Du Bois, *Dusk of Dawn*.

23 William Edward Burghardt Du Bois, "To the Nations of the World", Lecture delivered at the First Pan-African Conference in 1900.

24 William Edward Burghardt Du Bois, "To the World: Manifesto of the Second Pan-African Congress", *The Crisis*, 23, 1 (November 1921).

25 William Edward Burghardt Du Bois and Eugene Floyd Dubois, "Basal Metabolism in Health and Disease", *Southern Medical Journal*, 20, 6 (1927), p. 497.

26 William Edward Burghardt Du Bois, *The Crisis*, 27, 2 (December 1923).

27 Kwame Nkrumah, Radio Address in 1963, Ghana.

28 Kwame Nkrumah, Radio Address in 1963, Ghana.

29 William Edward Burghardt Du Bois, *WEB Du Bois Speaks: 1920–1963, with a Tribute, by Kwame Nkrumah* (New York: Pathfinder Press, 1970).

30 Kwame Nkrumah, "Nkrumah's Tribute to Dr. W.E.B. Du Bois", Accra, 29 August 1963.

31 Nkrumah, "Nkrumah's Tribute to Dr. W.E.B. Du Bois".

CHAPTER 5

1   John Edward Bruce, "Impressions of Marcus Garvey", Bruce Papers, Schomburg Centre, no. 1885 (1922), pp. 5–14.

2   Ralph Crowder, *John Edward Bruce: Politician, Journalist and Self-Trained Historian of the African Diaspora* (New York: New York University Press, 2004), p. 136.

3   Ralph Ellison, *Invisible Man* (New York: Penguin, 1952), p. 296.

4   David Levering Lewis, *When Harlem Was in Vogue* (New York: Alfred A. Knopf, 1981), p. xxviii.

5   A popular, if disparaging, Jamaican phrase for the working class. Author interview with the Jamaican writer Viv Adams, June 2006.

6   Amy Jacques Garvey (comp.), *The Philosophy and Opinions of Marcus Garvey, or, Africa for the Africans* (Dover, MA: The Majority Press, 1986), p. 38.

7   Edward Wilmot Blyden, *Christianity, Islam and the Negro Race* (London: Black Classic Press, 1888).

8   *Black Man*, 21 May 1929.

9   Andrew Hull Foote commanded the ship *Scott Perry* off the African coast. His book, *Africa and the American Flag* (New York: D. Appleton & Co., 1854), influenced the US public against the trafficking of slaves.

10 Edward Blyden to William Coppinger (secretary of the American Colonization Society), 3 October 1887. Also cited in Hollis R. Lynch, *Edward Wilmot Blyden: Pan-Negro Patriot* (London, Oxford University Press, 1967), p. 121.

11 This article was printed in the *Tourist* in June 1914. It is reproduced in Robert A. Hill, *The Marcus Garvey and Universal Negro Improvement Association Papers: November 1927–August 1940*, vol. 1 (California: University of California Press, 1983), p. 40.

12 Hill, *The Marcus Garvey and Universal Negro Improvement Association Papers*, vol. 1, p. 4.

13 Robert A. Hill, *The Marcus Garvey and Universal Negro Improvement Association Papers: November 1927–August 1940*, vol. 7 (California: University of California Press, 1991), p. 206.

14 *New York Times*, 3 December 1918.

15 *Negro World*, 5 April 1919, cited in Hill, *The Marcus Garvey and Universal Negro Improvement Association Papers*, vol. 1, pp. 394–9.

16 Hill, *The Marcus Garvey and Universal Negro Improvement Association Papers*, vol. 2 (California: University of California Press, 1983), p. 477.

17 Hill, *The Marcus Garvey and Universal Negro Improvement Association Papers*, vol. 2, p. 206.

18 *Negro World*, Editorial, 6 December 1919.

19 John Henrik Clarke (ed.), *Marcus Garvey and the Vision of Africa* (New York: Vintage, 1974), p. 142.

20 Hill, *The Marcus Garvey and Universal Negro Improvement Association Papers*, vol. 2, pp. 559–60.

21 William Edward Burghardt Du Bois, "The Negro and Radical Thought", *Crisis*, 22, 2 (1921), p. 204.

22 Psalm 68:31, King James Bible.

23 *Black Man*, July 1935.

24 *Black Man*, July 1935.

25 *Black Man*, July 1935.

26 Hill, *The Marcus Garvey and Universal Negro Improvement Association Papers*, vol. 7, p. 663.

27 Hill, *The Marcus Garvey and Universal Negro Improvement Association Papers*, vol. 7, p. 663.

28 Hill, *The Marcus Garvey and Universal Negro Improvement Association Papers*, vol. 6 (California: University of California Press, 1989), p. 98.

CHAPTER 6

1   For a discussion on the principles of Pan-Africanism, see Ali A. Mazrui, *Towards a Pax Africana: A Study of Ideology and Ambition* (London: Weidenfeld and Nicolson, 1967).

2   George Padmore, *The Life and Struggles of Negro Toilers* (London: Red International of Labour Unions, 1931).

3   George Padmore, *History of the Pan-African Congress: Colonial and Coloured Unity, a Programme of Action* (London: Hammersmith Bookshop, 1963), pp. 16–17.

4   Padmore, *History of the Pan-African Congress*, p. 22.

5   Padmore, *History of the Pan-African Congress*, p. 22.

6   George Padmore, *How Britain Rules Africa* (London: Wishart Books, 1936).

7   George Padmore, *Africa and World Peace* (London: M. Secker and Warburg, 1937).

8   George Padmore, *The White Man's Duty* (London: W.H. Allen, 1942).

9   George Padmore (ed.), *The Voice of Coloured Labour* (Manchester: Panaf Service, 1945).

10 George Shepperson and St Clare Drake, "The Fifth Pan-African Congress, 1945 and the All African People's Congress, 1958", *Contributions in Black Studies: A Journal of African and Afro-American Studies*, 8, 5 (September 2008), pp. 35–66.

11 Padmore, *History of the Pan-African Congress*, p. 55.

12 Padmore, *History of the Pan-African Congress*, p. 55.

13 Padmore, *History of the Pan-African Congress*, p. 56.

14 Olisanwuche Esedebe, *Pan-Africanism: The Idea and Movement, 1776–1991* (Washington D.C.: Howard University Press, 2007), p. 147.

15 Esedebe, *Pan-Africanism*, p. 147.

16 George Padmore, *Pan-Africanism or Communism? The Coming Struggle for Africa* (London: Dobson, 1956).

17 Guy Martin, *African Political Thought* (New York: Palgrave Macmillan, 2012), p. 58.

18 See, for example, Adekeye Adebajo, *The Curse of Berlin: Africa after the Cold War* (New York: Oxford University Press, 2013; New York: Columbia University Press; and Scottsville: University of KwaZulu-Natal Press, 2010).

CHAPTER 7

1 Ula Y. Taylor, "Intellectual Pan-African Feminists: Amy Ashwood-Garvey and Amy Jacques-Garvey", in Charles M. Payne and Adam Green (eds), *Time Longer Than Rope: A Century of African American Activism, 1850–1950* (New York: New York University Press, 2003), p. 180.

2 Tony Martin, *Amy Ashwood Garvey: Pan-Africanist, Feminist, and Mrs Marcus Garvey No. 1 or, A Tale of Two Amys* (Dover: The Majority Press, 2007).

3 Others would include Adelaide Casley-Hayford of Sierra Leone and Una Marson of Jamaica.

4 Tony Martin reports that there was some confusion about that date, since another birthdate, 18 January 1895, was also used on her passport. See Martin, *Amy Ashwood Garvey*, p. 16.

5 Martin, *Amy Ashwood Garvey*, p. 17.

6 Ula Taylor describes this as "the prestigious Westwood Boarding School for Girls". See Taylor, "Intellectual Pan-African Feminists", p. 181.

7 Martin, *Amy Ashwood Garvey*, p. 17.

8 Amy Ashwood Garvey, "The Birth of the United Negro Improvement Association", in Tony Martin (ed.), *The Pan-African Connection: From Slavery to Garvey and Beyond* (Wellesley: The Majority Press, 1983), p. 223.

9 Taylor, *Intellectual Pan-African Feminists*, p. 181.

10 Ashwood Garvey, "The Birth of the United Negro Improvement Association", pp. 220–5.

11 Ashwood Garvey, "The Birth of the United Negro Improvement Association", p. 225.

12 Martin, *Amy Ashwood Garvey*, p. 22.

13 Martin, *Amy Ashwood Garvey*, p. 67.

14 This was influenced by the British Red Cross

15 Robert Abraham Hill, *The Marcus Garvey and Universal Negro Improvement Association Papers*, vol. I, (Berkeley, CA: University of California Press, 1983), pp. 112–13; and pp. 128 and 161.

16 Judith Stein, *The World of Marcus Garvey: Race and Class in Modern Society* (Baton Rouge: Louisiana State University Press, 1986), pp. 33–6.

17 Martin, *The Pan-African Connection*, p. 220.

18 Hill, *The Marcus Garvey and Universal Negro Improvement Association Papers*, vol. I, p. 32.

19 Lionel Yard, *Biography of Amy Ashwood Garvey, 1897–1969: Co-Founder of the Universal Negro Improvement Association* (New York: Associated Publishers, 1988), p. 45.

20 Martin, *Amy Ashwood Garvey*, p. 37.

21 On street-strolling, see Ula Taylor, "Street Strollers: Grounding the Theory of Black Women Intellectuals", *Afro-Americans on New York Life and History*, 30, 2 (July 2006), pp. 153–71.

22 Taylor, "Street Strollers", p. 158.

23 Yard, *Biography of Amy Ashwood Garvey*, p. 43; Martin, *Amy Ashwood Garvey*, p. 38.

24 Fitz Andre Baptiste, *Amy Ashwood Garvey and Afro-West Indian Labor in the United States*

Emergency Farm and War Industries' Programs of World War II, 1943–1945 (2005), p. 18, PureHost-d30046191-emigre123/archive 02/f baptiste.htm.

25 Yard, *Biography of Amy Ashwood Garvey*, p. 43; Martin, *Amy Ashwood Garvey*, pp. 49–50.
26 Martin, *Amy Ashwood Garvey*, pp. 38–40.
27 Martin, *Amy Ashwood Garvey*, p. 38
28 Martin, *Amy Ashwood Garvey*, pp. 39–40
29 Yard, *Biography of Amy Ashwood Garvey*, p. 61.
30 Minkah Makalani, "An International African Opinion: Amy Ashwood Garvey and C.L.R. James in Black Radical London", in Davarian L. Baldwin and Minkah Makalani (eds), *Escape from New York: The New Negro Renaissance Beyond Harlem* (Minneapolis: University of Minnesota Press, 2013), pp. 77–9.
31 Hakim Adi, "The Nigerian Progress Union", mimeo, n.d., p. 3.
32 Adi, "The Nigerian Progress Union", p. 3.
33 She had earlier been given the name Adeyola after Solanke's sister. See Hakim Adi, "The Nigerian Progress Union", p. 4.
34 Adi notes that Henry Carr, a former resident of Nigeria and supporter of the NPU, wrote to Du Bois in the US to ask him to help the NPU's fundraising efforts. Adi, "The Nigerian Progress Union", pp. 5–6.
35 Cited in Martin, *Amy Ashwood Garvey*, p. 88.
36 Members included Nnamdi Azikiwe, Obafemi Awolowo and H.O. Davies of Nigeria; Joseph Appiah, F.R. Kankam-Boadu and Nii Odoi Annan of Ghana; and E.S. Beoku-Betts of Sierra Leone. See F.R. Kankam-Boadu, "The West African Students' Union", in Hakim Adi and Marika Sherwood (eds), *The 1945 Manchester Pan-African Congress Revisited* (London: New Beacon Books, 1995), p. 162.
37 Makalani, "An International African Opinion", p. 88.
38 Also known as the IAFA, International African Friends of Abyssinia.
39 Makalani, "An International African Opinion", p. 88.
40 Kelvin Yelvington, "The War in Ethiopia and Trinidad", in Bridget Brereton and Kevin Yelvington (eds), *The Colonial Caribbean in Transition: Essays on Post-Emancipation Social and Cultural History* (Kingston: University of the West Indies Press and University Press of Florida, 1999).
41 Makalani, "An International African Opinion", p. 89.
42 Makalani, "An International African Opinion", p. 90.
43 Amy Jacques, then back in Jamaica, was invited, but was unable to attend. She suggested to George Padmore two important resolutions to be considered. See Martin, *Amy Ashwood Garvey*, pp. 198–9.
44 Frederick Robert Kankam-Boadu and Earnest Marke, "Reminiscences", in Adi and Sherwood (eds.), *The 1945 Manchester Pan-African Congress Revisited*, pp. 33–40.
45 George Padmore (ed.), *History of the Pan-African Congress* (1963), reprinted in Adi and Sherwood (eds.), *The 1945 Manchester Pan-African Congress Revisited*, pp. 51–124.
46 Padmore, *History of the Pan-African Congress*, p. 98.
47 Yard, *Biography of Amy Ashwood Garvey*, p. 134.
48 Martin, *Amy Ashwood Garvey*, p. 222.
49 Martin, Amy Ashwood Garvey, p. 212
50 Martin, *Amy Ashwood Garvey*, p. 212.
51 Yard, *Biography of Amy Ashwood Garvey*, p. 141.
52 Yard, *Biography of Amy Ashwood Garvey*, p. 142.
53 Yard, *Biography of Amy Ashwood Garvey*, p. 142.
54 Apparently, the full book was to have been published in 1954. This preview was published in 1953 in Port of Spain, Trinidad and Tobago, during Amy Ashwood's visit there.

55 This Declaration stated that Ashwood would have to appear in person to collect her Certificate of Citizenship in two years' time. See Martin, *Amy Ashwood Garvey*, p. 201.

56 Martin, Amy Ashwood Garvey, p. 227

57 Martin, *Amy Ashwood Garvey*, pp. 216–20.

58 Yard, *Biography of Amy Ashwood Garvey*, p. 166.

59 Yard, *Biography of Amy Ashwood Garvey*, pp. 180–1.

60 Martin, *Amy Ashwood Garvey*, p. 227.

61 Ashwood's travels in the Caribbean, return to London to establish the Afro-Women's Centre, and her subsequent return to the US in 1967–9, and support of Adam Clayton Powell's political efforts, are not the subject of this chapter.

62 Carole Boyce-Davies, "Enduring Legacies of Mrs Garvey No. 1", *Proudflesh*, Issue 6 (2007), p. 8, https://www.africaknowledgeproject.org/index.php/proudflesh/article/view/164.

CHAPTER 8

1 This chapter builds on Bongani Ngqulunga, *The Man Who Founded the ANC: A Biography of Pixley ka Isaka Seme* (Cape Town: Penguin Books, 2017).

2 Pixley Seme, "The Regeneration of Africa", *Columbia Monthly*, 3, 6 (April 1906).

3 Seme, "The Regeneration of Africa".

4 Seme, "The Regeneration of Africa".

5 Although Seme neither mentioned the name of the black professor nor the university in question, it is highly probable that he was referring to Anton Wilhelm Amo who was originally from what is today known as Ghana and who became the professor of philosophy at the universities of Halle and Jena in the 1700s.

6 Seme, "The Regeneration of Africa".

7 Seme, "The Regeneration of Africa".

8 Seme, "The Regeneration of Africa".

9 Seme, "The Regeneration of Africa".

10 Wilson Jeremiah Moses (ed.), *Classical Black Nationalism: From the American Revolution to Marcus Garvey* (New York: New York University Press, 1996), p. 172.

11 Moses, *Classical Black Nationalism*, p. 292.

12 Moses, *Classical Black Nationalism*, p. 293.

13 Moses, *Classical Black Nationalism*, p. 173.

14 Moses, *Classical Black Nationalism*, p. 174.

15 The italics and exclamation mark are Seme's.

16 Leonard Harris and Charles Molesworth, *Alain L. Locke: The Biography of a Philosopher* (Chicago: University of Chicago Press, 2010), p. 71.

17 See, for instance, Theophilus E.S. Scholes, *The British Empire and Alliances, or Britain's Duty to Her Colonies and Subject Races* (London: British Library, Historical Print Editions, 2011 [1899]). See also Theophilus E.S. Scholes, *Chamberlain and Chamberlainism: His Fiscal Proposals and Colonial Policy* (London: John Long Publisher, 1903).

18 Scholes's letter to Locke can be found in Jeffrey Green, *Black Edwardians: Black People in Britain, 1901–1914* (London and Portland: Frank Cass, 1998).

19 *Ilanga lase Natal*, 20 October 1911.

20 *Bantu World*, 23 June 1951.

21 *Inkundla ya Bantu*, 30 June 1951.

22 The *Bantu World*, 23 June 1951.

23 *Ilanga lase Natal*, 5 and 12 April 1929.

24 Hilda Kuper, *Sobhuza II, Ngwenyama and King of Swaziland: The Story of an Hereditary Ruler and His Country* (Cape Town: Africana Publishers, 1978).

25 Record of the court decision, University of South Africa library, F47356.

CHAPTER 9

1 Ali Al'amin Mazrui, "Nkrumah: The Leninist Czar", in Ali Al'amin Mazrui and Willy Mutunga, *Debating the African Condition: Mazrui and His Critics* (Trenton: Africa World Press, 2003), p. 30.

2 Ali Al'amin Mazrui, *Nkrumah's Legacy and Africa's Triple Heritage between Globalization and Counter-Terrorism* (Accra: Ghana University Press, 2004), p. 4.

3 Mazrui, "Nkrumah", p. 11.

4 Mazrui, "Nkrumah", p. 12.

5 Mazrui, "Nkrumah", p. 12.

6 Mazrui, "Nkrumah", p. 17.

7 Nkrumah, *Towards Colonial Freedom* (London: Panaf Books, 1947).

8 Mazrui, "Nkrumah", p. 23.

9 Mazrui, "Nkrumah", p. 25; Ama Biney, *The Political and Social Thought of Kwame Nkrumah* (New York: Palgrave Macmillan, 2011). Even in exile in Guinea-Conakry, Nkrumah continued to live an ascetic lifestyle with few, if any luxuries (p. 159). It is also entirely fictitious that Nkrumah "amassed a private fortune both inside and outside the country", as asserted in Albert Kwesi Ocran, *A Myth is Broken: An Account of the Ghana Coup d'Etat of 24 February 1966* (London: Longman, 1968), p. 20.

10 Michael O. West provides an interesting analysis of the debate in his "Kwame Nkrumah and Ali Mazrui: An Analysis of the 1967 *Transition* Debate".

11 M.O. West, "Kwame Nkrumah and Ali Mazrui: An Analysis of the 1967 *Transition* Debate", *Journal of Pan African Studies*, 8, 6 (September 2015), p. 125. This is a good review of the debate initiated by Mazrui.

12 Mazrui, *Nkrumah's Legacy and Africa's Triple Heritage between Globalization and Counter Terrorism*, p. 3.

13 Mazrui, *Nkrumah's Legacy and Africa's Triple Heritage between Globalization and Counter Terrorism*, p. 4.

14 Mazrui, *Nkrumah's Legacy and Africa's Triple Heritage between Globalization and Counter Terrorism*, p. 5.

15 Mazrui, *Nkrumah's Legacy and Africa's Triple Heritage between Globalization and Counter Terrorism*, p. 5.

16 Mazrui, *Nkrumah's Legacy and Africa's Triple Heritage between Globalization and Counter Terrorism*, p. 5.

17 Mazrui, *Nkrumah's Legacy and Africa's Triple Heritage between Globalization and Counter Terrorism*, p. 4.

18 Mazrui, *Nkrumah's Legacy and Africa's Triple Heritage between Globalization and Counter Terrorism*, p. 6.

19 Aristide R. Zolberg, *Creating Political Order: The Party-States of West Africa* (Chicago: Rand McNally, 1966), p. 39.

20 Zolberg, *Creating Political Order*, pp. 19–27.

21 Zolberg, *Creating Political Order*, pp. 44–45.

22 Zolberg, *Creating Political Order*, p. 50.

23 Zolberg, *Creating Political Order*, p. 51.

24 Zolberg, *Creating Political Order*, p. 55.

25 Zolberg, *Creating Political Order*, p. 86.

26 Zolberg, *Creating Political Order*, p. 86. See also Martial Joseph Ahipeaud, "Elite Ideologies and the Politics of Media: A Critical History of Ivoirien Elite Ideologies and Their Press from the Brazzaville Conference to the December 24th 1999 Military Coup" (PhD thesis, University of London, 2003), p. 155.

27 H.M. Basner was a white South African communist and journalist living in Ghana in the 1960s. His incomplete memoirs are at the Institute of Commonwealth Studies, University of London, Bas/2/91.

28 Zolberg, *Creating Political Order*, p. 82.

29 Mazrui, *Nkrumah's Legacy and Africa's Triple Heritage between Globalization and Counter Terrorism*, p. 5.

30 Biney, *The Political and Social Thought of Kwame Nkrumah*, pp. 99–118.

31 Ama Biney, "Ghana's Contribution to the Anti-Apartheid Struggle: 1958–1994", in *The Road to Democracy in South Africa*, vol. 5 (Tshwane: Unisa Press, 2013), pp. 88–91; see also Biney, *The Political and Social Thought of Kwame Nkrumah*, pp. 144–8.

32 For example, Nkrumah's appointment of Ambassador A.Y.K. Djin to the Congo during the country's crisis. Djin not only lacked diplomatic experience, but also did not speak French. See Biney, *The Political and Social Thought of Kwame Nkrumah*, pp. 144–8. In addition, there were numerous CPP careerist officials who used the party to line their own pockets.

33 Ama Biney conducted the interview with former president of Algeria, Ahmed Ben Bella, on 23 January 1999 at Friends House in London.

34 Peter T. Omari and Nii Amaa Ollennu, *Kwame Nkrumah: The Anatomy of an African Dictatorship* (London: C. Hurst & Company, 1970), p. 2.

35 Ocran, *A Myth is Broken*, p. 93.

36 Mazrui, *Nkrumah's Legacy and Africa's Triple Heritage between Globalization and Counter Terrorism*, p. 4.

37 See *The Autobiography of Malcolm X with the assistance of Alex Haley* (London: Penguin Books, 1966), p. 467.

38 Kevin Kelly Gaines, *American Africans in Ghana: Black Expatriates and the Civil Rights Era* (Chapel Hill: University of North Carolina Press, 2006).

39 Omari, *Kwame Nkrumah*, p. 169.

40 See "Education in Ghana, 1951–1966", in Kwame Arhin (eds), *The Life and Work of Kwame Nkrumah: Papers of a Symposium Organized by the Institute of African Studies, University of Ghana* (Legon: Africa World Press, 1993), pp. 53–82.

41 See, for example, Naaborle Sackeyfio, *Energy Politics and Rural Development in Sub-Saharan Africa: The Case of Ghana* (New York: Palgrave MacMillan, 2018).

42 Takyiwaa Manuh, "Women and their Organisations during the Convention People's Party Period", in *The Life and World of Kwame Nkrumah* (1991), p. 109.

43 Manuh, "Women and their Organisations during the Convention People's Party Period", p. 109.

44 Jean Marie Allman, "The Disappearing of Hannah Kudjoe: Nationalism, Feminism, and the Tyrannies of History", *Journal of Women's History*, 21, 3 (2009), p. 15. This interesting article sheds some insight on the reasons for the disappearance of Kudjoe from Ghana's nationalist narrative.

45 Allman, "The Disappearing of Hannah Kudjoe", p. 15.

46 Allman, "The Disappearing of Hannah Kudjoe", p. 17.

47 Manuh, "Women and their Organisations during the Convention People's Party Period", p. 117.

48 Tawia Adamafio, *By Nkrumah's Side: The Labour and the Wounds* (Accra: Westcoast, 1982).

Tawia Adamafio was general secretary of the CPP and in 1960 was appointed minister of information until he was accused of being one of the co-conspirators in the August 1962 assassination attempt on Nkrumah.

49 Biney, *The Political and Social Thought of Kwame Nkrumah*, p. 88.

50 Adamafio, *By Nkrumah's Side*, pp. 117–18.

51 Cited in Issa G. Shivji, *Silences in NGO Discourse: The Role and Future of NGOs in Africa* (Oxford: Fahamu, 2007), p. 13.

52 Shivji, *Silences in NGO Discourse*, p. 13.

53 Kwame Nkrumah, *Autobiography of Kwame Nkrumah* (London: Panaf Books, 1973), pp. vii–viii.

54 Mazrui, *Nkrumah's Legacy and Africa's Triple Heritage between Globalization and Counter Terrorism*, p. 22.

55 Biney, "Ghana's Contribution to the Anti-Apartheid Struggle: 1958–1994", pp. 79–119.

56 Prime Minister's Midnight Speech on the eve of independence, 6 March 1957, box 154-14 folder 21, Kwame Nkrumah Papers at the Moorland-Spingarn Research Center, Howard University.

57 Kwesi Armah, *Peace without Power: Ghana's Foreign Policy 1957–66* (Accra: Ghana University Press, 2004), p. 187. The author served in Nkrumah's government as high commissioner in London and also as minister for trade.

CHAPTER 10

1 This chapter builds on Adekeye Adebajo, *Thabo Mbeki: Africa's Philosopher-King* (Johannesburg: Jacana Media, 2016; and Athens: Ohio University Press, 2016).

2 Melissa Lane, "Philosopher King", *Britannica Online Encyclopedia* (www.britannica.com).

3 Quoted in Mark Kingwell, "Why Every Government Should Keep an Empty Seat for a Philosopher King," *The Guardian* (London), 10 May 2012 (www.theguardian.com).

4 Kingwell, "Why Every Government Should Keep an Empty Seat for a Philosopher King."

5 For accounts on Thabo Mbeki's leadership and thinking, see Mark Gevisser, *Thabo Mbeki: A Dream Deferred* (Johannesburg: Jonathan Ball, 2007); Daryl Glaser (ed.), *Mbeki and After: Reflections on the Legacy of Thabo Mbeki* (Johannesburg: Wits University Press, 2010); William Mervin Gumede, *Thabo Mbeki and the Battle for the Soul of the ANC* (Cape Town: Zebra, 2005); Adrian Hadland and Jovial Rantao, *The Life and Times of Thabo Mbeki* (Rivonia: Zebra, 1999); Sean Jacobs and Richard Calland (eds), *Thabo Mbeki's World: The Politics and Ideology of the South African President* (Pietermaritzburg: University of Natal Press, 2002); Lucky Mathebe, *Bound by Tradition: The World of Thabo Mbeki* (Tshwane: University of South Africa Press, 2001); Mukanda Mulemfo, *Thabo Mbeki and the African Renaissance* (Tshwane: Actua, 2000); Brian Pottinger, *The Mbeki Legacy* (Cape Town: Zebra, 2008); Ronald Suresh Roberts, *Fit to Govern: The Native Intelligence of Thabo Mbeki* (Johannesburg: STE, 2007); Sifiso Mxolisi Ndlovu and Miranda Strydom (eds), *The Thabo Mbeki I Know* (Johannesburg: Picador Africa, 2016); and Barney Pityana (ed.), *Building Blocks Towards an African Century: Essays in Honour of Thabo Mbeki*, (Johannesburg: Real African Publishers, 2018).

6 See Adekeye Adebajo, "Mbeki: A Nkrumahist Renaissance?", in Adekeye Adebajo, *The Curse of Berlin: Africa after the Cold War* (New York: Columbia University Press; London: Hurst; Scottsville: University of KwaZulu-Natal Press, 2010), pp. 233–59.

7 Pixley Seme, "The Regeneration of Africa", Columbia University, New York, 5 April 1906 (www.anc.org.za).

8 Quoted in Gevisser, *Thabo Mbeki*, p. 221.

9 Gevisser, *Thabo Mbeki*, p. 264.

10 Thabo Mbeki, *Mahube: The Dawning of the Dawn. Speeches, Lectures, and Tributes* (Braamfontein: Skotaville Media, 2001), pp. 4–5.

11 Thabo Mbeki, *Africa: The Time Has Come* (Cape Town: Tafelberg and Mafube, 1998), pp. 31–32.

12 Mbeki, "Prologue", *Africa*, p. xv.

13 Peter Vale and Sipho Maseko, "Thabo Mbeki, South Africa and the Idea of an African Renaissance", in Sean Jacobs and Richard Calland (eds), *Thabo Mbeki's World: The Politics and Ideology of the South African President* (Pietermaritzburg: University of Natal Press, 2002), p. 124.

14 Gevisser, *Thabo Mbeki*, p. 374.

15 Gevisser, *Thabo Mbeki*, p. 387.

16 Confidential correspondence.

17 Thabo Mbeki, "Africa's Moment of Hope." Opening Address at the Launch of the African Union, Durban, 9 July 2002, in Mbeki, *Africa: Define Yourself* (Cape Town: Tafelberg, 2002), p. 186.

18 See, for example, Adekeye Adebajo, Adebayo Adedeji and Chris Landsberg (eds), *South Africa in Africa: The Post-Apartheid Era* (Pietermaritzburg: UKZN Press, 2007); Chris Alden and Garth Le Pere, *South Africa's Post-Apartheid Foreign Policy: From Reconciliation to Revival?* Adelphi Paper no. 362 (London: Institute for Strategic Studies, 2003).

19 See United Nations (UN), *Report of the UN Secretary-General on Burundi*, UN Doc. S/2004/210, 16 March 2004.

20 See, for example, Devon Curtis, "South Africa: 'Exporting Peace' to the Great Lakes Region", in Adebajo, Adedeji and Landsberg (eds), *South Africa in Africa*, pp. 253–73; Gilbert M. Khadiagala, "UN Peacekeeping in the Great Lakes Region: The DRC, Rwanda, and Burundi", in Adekeye Adebajo (ed.), *From Global Apartheid to Global Village: Africa and the United Nations* (Scottsville: UKZN Press, 2009), pp. 305–22; Chris Landsberg, "South Africa", in Gilbert M. Khadiagala (ed.), *Security Dynamics in Africa's Great Lakes* (Boulder, CO: Rienner, 2006), pp. 121–40; René Lemarchand, "Region–Building in Central Africa", in Daniel H. Levine and Dawn Nagar (eds), *Region-Building in Africa: Political and Economic Challenges* (New York: Palgrave Macmillan, 2016), pp. 231–44.

21 See Adebayo Adedeji, "NEPAD's African Peer Review Mechanism: Progress and Prospects", in John Akokpari, Angela Ndinga-Muvumba and Tim Murithi (eds), *The African Union and its Institutions* (Johannesburg: Jacana Media, 2008), pp. 241–269.

22 Thabo Mbeki, "Africa's Time Has Come." Address to the Corporate Council on Africa's Attracting Capital to Africa Summit, Chantilly, Virginia, US, 19–22 April 1997, in Mbeki, *Africa: The Time Has Come*, p. 200.

23 Mbeki, "Africa's Time Has Come", p. 201.

24 Joseph Conrad, *The Heart of Darkness* (New York: Tribeca Books, 2010, first published in 1902).

25 Mbeki, "Africa's Time Has Come", p. 201.

26 Thabo Mbeki "Partnership Africa", in Mbeki, *Africa: The Time Has Come*, p. 205.

27 Mbeki "Partnership Africa", p. 206.

28 Thabo Mbeki, "Moving the Frontiers of Knowledge", The University of the State of Bahia, Brazil, 14 December 2000, in Mbeki, *Mahube*, p. 179.

29 Mbeki, "Moving the Frontiers of Knowledge", pp. 179–180.

30 Mbeki, "Moving the Frontiers of Knowledge", p. 180.

31 Mbeki, "Moving the Frontiers of Knowledge", p. 182.

32 Mbeki, "Moving the Frontiers of Knowledge", p. 183.

33 Mbeki, "Moving the Frontiers of Knowledge", p. 184.

34 Thabo Mbeki, "Am I My Brother's Keeper?", Oliver Tambo Inaugural Lecture, Washington D.C., 23 May 2000, in Mbeki, *Mahube*, p. 70.
35 Thabo Mbeki, "The African Renaissance: Africans Defining Themselves." Address at the University of Havana, Cuba, 27 March 2001, in Thabo Mbeki, *Africa: Define Yourself*, p. 72.
36 Mbeki, "The African Renaissance", p. 73.
37 Mbeki, "The African Renaissance", p. 75.
38 Thabo Mbeki, "Ending Racism in the World". The World Conference against Racism, Racial Discrimination, Xenophobia and Related Intolerance. Durban, 31 August 2001, in Mbeki, *Mahube*, pp. 129–30.
39 Mbeki, "Ending Racism in the World", p. 130.
40 See Glaser (ed.), *Mbeki and After*.

CHAPTER 11

1   He was the youngest headmaster of a public school in Jamaica's history. See Herbert George Helps, "Dudley Thompson's Rich Legacy: A Brighter Legal Mind Was Hard to Find", *Jamaican Observer*, 22 January 2012, http://www.jamaicaobserver.com/news/Dudley-Thompson-s-rich-legacy_10609879, accessed on 7 May 2018.
2   Dudley Thompson, *From Kingston to Kenya: The Making of a Pan-Africanist Lawyer* (Dover, MA: The Majority Press, 1993), pp. 52–120.
3   See foreword by Rex Nettleford in Thompson, *From Kingston to Kenya*, p. viii.
4   Keebie McFarlane, "Dudley Was, Above All, a Superb Advocate", *Jamaican Observer*, 15 May 2018, http://www.jamaicaobserver.com/columns/Dudley-was--above-all--a-superb-advocate_10650343, accessed on 27 May 2018.
5   Horace Campbell, "Dudley Thompson: A Fighter for Socialism and African Unity", *Pambazuka News*, 8 February 2012, https://www.pambazuka.org/governance/dudley-thompson-fighter-socialism-and-african-unity, accessed on 27 May 2018.
6   See Walter Rodney, *How Europe Underdeveloped Africa* (Dar-es-Salaam: Tanzanian Publishing House, 1973), http://abahlali.org/files/3295358-walter-rodney.pdf, accessed on 27 May 2018.
7   J.E. Inikori, "Measuring the Atlantic Slave Trade: A Rejoinder", *Journal of African History*, 17, 4 (1976).
8   See Robert Johnson, Jr (ed.), *Fighting for Africa: The Pan-African Contributions of Ambassador Dudley J. Thompson and Bill Sutherland* (Maryland: United Press of America, 2010), p. 2.
9   He also became Queen's Counsel in 1962.
10 C. Fred Bergsten, *A New OPEC in Bauxite* (Washington, DC: Brookings Institution, 1976).
11 Helps, "Dudley Thompson's Rich Legacy".
12 David Gonzalez, "A Killing Shocks Jamaicans into Soul-Searching", *New York Times*, 18 October 1999, https://www.nytimes.com/1999/10/18/world/a-killing-shocks-jamaicans-into-soul-searching.html, accessed on 7 May 2018.
13 Campbell, "Dudley Thompson: A Fighter for Socialism and African Unity".
14 But Thompson also recognised that Africans living in the diaspora have been so cut off from the continent that it might be a struggle for them to "rejoin". See Helps, "Dudley Thompson's Rich Legacy".
15 The sections on the WADU statement are from *Africology: The Journal of Pan African Studies*, 10, 1 (March 2017), p. 410. See also Hassimi Oumarou Maiga, *Balancing Written History with Oral Traditions: The Legacy of the Songhoy People* (New York: Routledge, 2010), pp. 175–6.

16 "Holocaust Survivors, Family to Get Money from $60 M Fund", *New York Post*, 5 December 2014, https://nypost.com/2014/12/05/holocaust-survivors-family-to-get-money-from-60m-fund/, accessed on 7 May 2018.

17 David R. Francis, "Compensating Victims of War: Ottawa Hears Redress Claims of Japanese-Canadians", *Christian Science Monitor*, 14 April 1988, https://www.csmonitor.com/1988/0414/djacan.html, accessed on 7 May 2018.

18 David Reese, "Feds Spend $1 Billion on Land for Native American Tribes", *Courthouse News Service*, 17 November 2017, https://www.courthousenews.com/feds-spend-1-billion-land-native-american-tribes/, accessed on 8 May 2018.

19 "Poland Puts Berlin's WWII Bill at 440 Billion Euros", *Japan Times*, 23 March 2018, https://www.japantimes.co.jp/news/2018/03/23/world/poland-puts-berlins-wwii-bill-440-billion-euros/#.WrSddZNubJM, accessed on 8 May 2018.

20 Paul Lewis, "Canada About to Sign Major Land Agreement with Eskimos", *New York Times*, 21 August 1989, https://www.nytimes.com/1989/08/21/world/canada-about-to-sign-major-land-agreement-with-eskimos.html, accessed on 8 May 2018.

21 Debora Steel and Cheryl Petten, "Compensation Package Announced", *Saskatchewan Sage*, 10, 3 (2005), http://ammsa.com/publications/saskatchewan-sage/compensation-package-announced, accessed on 8 May 2018; Anthony Depalma, "Canada's Indigenous Tribes Receive Formal Apology", *New York Times*, 8 June 1998, https://www.nytimes.com/1998/01/08/world/canada-s-indigenous-tribes-receive-formal-apology.html, accessed on 8 May 2018.

22 See, for example, Hilary Beckles, *Britain's Black Debt: Reparations for Caribbean Slavery and Native Genocide* (Jamaica, Barbados, and Trinidad and Tobago: University of the West Indies Press, 2013), pp. 1–23.

23 Dudley Thompson, "The Debt Has Not Been Paid, the Accounts Have Not Been Settled", *African Studies Quarterly*, 2, 4 (1999).

24 See Anthony Gifford, "The Legal Basis of the Claim for Slavery Reparations", *Human Rights* (Spring 2000), p. 16.

25 See Brendan Wolfe, "Slave Ships and the Middle Passage", *Encyclopaedia Virginia*, 9 July 2018, https://www.encyclopediavirginia.org/slave ships and the middle passage.

26 See http://avalon.law.yale.edu/imt/judlawre.asp.

27 Lord Anthony Gifford, "Pipe Dream or Necessary Atonement", *Index on Citizenship* (2007), pp. 92–3.

28 Gifford, "The Legal Basis of the Claim for Slavery Reparations", p. 18.

29 "Researchers Highlight the Impact of Slavery on Health and Disease", *Newsblog*, 8 June 2012, http://blogs.nature.com/news/2012/07/researchers-highlight-the-impact-of-slavery-on-health-and-disease.html; see also Hilary Beckles and Verene Shepherd (eds), *Caribbean Slave Society and Economy: A Student Reader* (Kingston, Jamaica: Ian Randle, 1991).

30 Francisco Sastre, Patricia Rojas, Elena Cyrus, Mario De La Rosa and Aysha H. Khoury, "Improving the Health Status of Caribbean People: Recommendations from the Triangulating on Health Equity Summit", *Global Health Promotion*, 21, 3 (18 March 2014), pp. 19–28.

31 Kenneth F. Kiple and Virginia Himmelsteib King, *Another Dimension to the Black Diaspora: Diet, Disease and Racism* (London: Cambridge University Press, 1981), pp. 80–100.

32 Jose Santos Woss and Aristotle Jones, "Mass Incarceration and the Legacy of Slavery", Friends Committee on National Legislation, 10 October 2016, https://www.fcnl.org/updates/mass-incarceration-and-the-legacy-of-slavery-329, accessed on 27 May 2018.

33 See the Abuja Declaration, http://www.shaka.mistral.co.uk/abujaProclamation.htm,

accessed on 8 May 2018.

34   The quotes in this paragraph are taken directly from the 1993 Abuja Declaration.

35   Thompson, "The Debt Has Not Been Paid, the Accounts Have Not Been Settled", pp. 19–25.

36   As quoted in "Farewell Dudley Thompson: Champion of the Race", *Jamaican Observer*, 13 February 2012, http://www.jamaicaobserver.com/news/Farewell-Dudley-Thompson---champion-of-the-Race_5810015, accessed on 27 May 2018.

37   See Chris McGreal, "Africans Back Down at UN Race Talks", *The Guardian*, 9 September 2001, https://www.theguardian.com/world/2001/sep/09/race.chrismcgreal, accessed on 8 May 2018.

38   On this point, see Stephanie Wolfe, *The Politics of Reparations and Apologies* (New York: Springer, 2014), p. 78.

39   Thompson expressed the wish to live to 100 in the hope that by that time Africa would have officially become the United States of Africa. See Helps, "Dudley Thompson's Rich Legacy".

40   Helps, "Dudley Thompson's Rich Legacy".

Chapter 12

1   This chapter builds on Adekeye Adebajo, "Boutros Boutros-Ghali", in Manuel Fröhlich and Abiodun Williams (eds), *The UN Secretary-General and the Security Council: A Dynamic Relationship* (Oxford: Oxford University Press, 2018), pp. 138–59.

2   Adekeye Adebajo, *UN Peacekeeping in Africa: From the Suez Crisis to the Sudan Conflicts* (London and Boulder: Lynne Rienner Publishers, 2011).

3   Paul Lewis, "Africans Pressing Bid for UN Post", *New York Times*, 22 October 1991, http://www.nytimes.com; Paul Lewis, "Security Council Selects Egyptian for Top UN Post", *New York Times*, 22 November 1991; and Boutros Boutros-Ghali, *Unvanquished: A US–UN Saga* (New York: Random, 1999), pp. 7–13.

4   Brian Urquhart, "The Evolution of the Secretary-General", in Simon Chesterman (ed.), *Secretary or General? The UN Secretary-General in World Politics* (Cambridge: Cambridge University Press, 2007), p. 27.

5   Marrack Goulding, "The UN Secretary-General", in David M. Malone (ed.), *The UN Security Council: From the Cold War to the 21st Century* (Boulder: Lynne Rienner Publishers, 2004), p. 276.

6   Boutros Boutros-Ghali, *Egypt's Road to Jerusalem: A Diplomat's Story of the Struggle for Peace in the Middle East* (New York: Random, 1997).

7   Goulding, "The UN Secretary-General".

8   Chinmaya R. Gharekhan, *The Horseshoe Table: An Inside View of the UN Security Council* (New Delhi: Longman, 2006), p. 25.

9   Stanley Meisler, "Dateline UN: A New Hammarskjöld?", *Foreign Policy*, 98 (Spring 1995), p. 186.

10   Meisler, "Dateline UN: A New Hammarskjöld?", p. 181.

11   Gharekhan, *The Horseshoe Table*, p. 303.

12   Peter Wallensteen, *Dag Hammarskjöld* (Stockholm: Swedish Institute, 2004); and Brian Urquhart, *Hammarskjöld* (New York: Knopf, 1972).

13   David Hannay, *New World Disorder: The UN after the Cold War – An Insider's View* (London: Tauris, 2009), p. 76.

14   David M. Malone, "Introduction", in Malone (ed.), *The UN Security Council*.

15   See the detailed coverage of these events in Stephen Burgess, *The United Nations under Boutros Boutros-Ghali, 1992–1997* (Lanham: Scarecrow Press, 2002).

16 Boutros-Ghali, *Unvanquished*, p. 192.
17 United Nations, Department of Public Information, "Secretary-General, in Lecture at Oxford, Speaks of Globalization, Fragmentation and Consequent Responsibilities on UN", UN Doc. SG/SM/5870/Rev.1, 12 January 1996.
18 Quoted in Anthony F. Lang Jr, "A Realist in the Utopian City: Boutros Boutros-Ghali's Ethical Framework and Its Impact", in Kent J. Kille (ed.), *The UN Secretary-General and Moral Authority: Ethics and Religion in International Leadership* (Washington, DC: Georgetown University Press, 2007), p. 265.
19 Quoted in Meisler, "Dateline UN: A New Hammarskjöld?", p. 181.
20 See, for example, Rupert Smith, "The Security Council and the Bosnian Conflict: A Practitioner's View", in Vaughan Lowe, Adam Roberts, Jennifer Welsh and Dominik Zaum (eds), *The United Nations Security Council and War: The Evolution of Thought and Practice since 1945* (Oxford: Oxford University Press, 2008), pp. 442–51.
21 Gharekhan, *The Horseshoe Table*, p. 293.
22 Boutros-Ghali, *Unvanquished*.
23 Gharekhan, *The Horseshoe Table*, p. 248.
24 Marrick Goulding, *Peacemonger* (London: Murray, 2000), p. 18.
25 Henry Anyidoho, *Guns over Kigali* (Accra: Woeli, 1999); Turid Laegreid, "UN Peacekeeping in Rwanda", in Howard Adelman and Astri Suhrke (eds), *The Path of a Genocide: The Rwanda Crisis, from Uganda to Zaire* (New Brunswick: Transaction, 1999), pp. 231–51; Linda Melvern, *A People Betrayed: The Role of the West in Rwanda's Genocide* (London: Zed Books, 2000); and Gérard Prunier, *The Rwandan Crisis: History of a Genocide* (New York: Columbia University Press, 1995).
26 Melvern, *A People Betrayed*, p .93.
27 Michael Barnett, "Review Essay: Unvanquished", *Global Governance*, 5, 4 (October–December 1999), p. 517.
28 Cited in Lang, "A Realist in the Utopian City", p. 291.
29 Associated Press, "Former UN Secretary-General Boutros Boutros-Ghali Dies", 16 February 2016.
30 Melvern, *A People Betrayed*, p. 159. See also Ibrahim A. Gambari, "Rwanda: An African Perspective", in Malone (eds), *The UN Security Council*, pp. 512–20.
31 Boutros-Ghali, *Unvanquished*, p. 138.
32 Kofi Annan (with Nader Mousavizadeh), *Interventions: A Life in War and Peace* (New York: Penguin Press, 2012), p. 138.
33 Annan, *Interventions*, pp. 38, 44, and 137–8.
34 Goulding, *Peacemonger*, p. 190.
35 See, for example, Lise Morjé Howard, *UN Peacekeeping in Civil Wars* (Cambridge: Cambridge University Press, 2008), pp. 35–42.
36 Gharekhan, *The Horseshoe Table*, p. 224.
37 Boutros Boutros-Ghali, *An Agenda for Peace: Preventive Diplomacy, Peacemaking, and Peacekeeping*. Report of the Secretary-General Pursuant to the Statement Adopted by the Summit Meeting of the Security Council on 31 January 1992 (New York: United Nations, www.un.org.za).
38 Quoted in Lang, "A Realist in the Utopian City", p. 274.
39 See United Nations, *An Agenda for Peace*.
40 See, for example, Devon Curtis and Gwinyayi A. Dzinesa (eds), *Peacebuilding, Power, and Politics in Africa* (Athens: Ohio University Press, 2013).
41 Boutros Boutros-Ghali, "The Diplomatic Role of the United Nations Secretary-General", Cyril Foster Lecture, Oxford University, 15 January 1996.

42 Annan, *Interventions*, p. 138.

43 See James Traub, *The Best Intentions: Kofi Annan and the UN in the Era of American World Power* (New York: Farrar, Straus, and Giroux, 2006).

44 See two informative biographies on Annan: Stanley Meisler, *Kofi Annan: A Man of Peace in a World of War* (Hoboken, New Jersey: Wiley, 2007); and Traub, *The Best Intentions*.

45 For an insightful account of this saga, see Douglas A. Yates, "The UN Educational, Scientific and Cultural Organisation", in Adekeye Adebajo (ed.), *From Global Apartheid to Global Village: Africa and the United Nations* (Scottsville: University of KwaZulu-Natal Press, 2009), pp. 481–98.

46 Quoted in Gharekhan, *The Horseshoe Table*, p. 112.

47 Barnett, "Review Essay: *Unvanquished*", pp. 519–20.

48 Luck, "The Secretary-General in a Unipolar World", in Chesterman, *Secretary or General?*, pp. 220–2.

49 Mats Berdal, "Humanity's Mirror", Review Essay, *Survival*, 50 (October–November 2008), p. 181.

50 Goulding, "The UN Secretary-General", p. 272.

51 Boutros-Ghali, *Unvanquished*.

CHAPTER 13

1   Alex Haley, *The Autobiography of Malcolm X* (New York: Ballantine, 1992).

2   http://entertainment.time.com/2011/08/30/all-time-100-best-nonfiction-books/slide/the-autobiography-of-malcolm-x-as-told-to-alex-haley/.

3   Manning Marable, *Malcolm X: A Life of Reinvention* (New York: Viking Penguin, 2011).

4   See a mild example of the fierceness of the controversy in "Manning Marable's Controversial New Biography Refuels Debate on Life and Legacy of Malcolm X", https://www.democracynow.org/2011/5/19/manning_marables_controversial_new_biography_refuels; Herb Boyd, Ron Daniels, Maulana Karenga and Haki R. Madhubuti (eds), *By Any Means Necessary: Malcolm X; Real, Not Reinvented* (Chicago: Third World Press, 2012).

5   See "Free Breakfast for Children", https://en.wikipedia.org/wiki/Free_Breakfast_for_Children.

6   See Malcolm X, "Message to Grassroots", http://teachingamericanhistory.org/library/document/message-to-grassroots/, 10 November 1963.

7   See Marable, *Malcolm X*, p. 406, for Malcolm's "romance with Africa itself, its beauty, diversity, and complexity. It was the African people who had embraced Malcolm as their own long-lost son."

8   See Lee A. Daniels "Martin Luther King, Jr: The Great Provocateur", in Adekeye Adebajo (ed.), *Africa's Peacemakers: Nobel Peace Laureates of African Descent* (London: Zed Books, 2013), pp. 106–10.

9   Maya Angelou, *All God's Children Need Traveling Shoes* (London: Virago Books, 2008 [1986]; and New York: Vintage ebooks), loc. 1642–873.

10 Angelou, *All Gods Children Need Travel Shoes*, loc. 1810.

11 Angelou, *All Gods Children Need Travel Shoes*, loc. 1642.

12 Angelou, *All Gods Children Need Travel Shoes*, loc. 1677–81.

13 See Taylor Branch, *Parting the Waters: America in the King Years 1954–63* (New York: Simon & Shuster, 1988), pp. 209–13, and pp. 902–4.

14 See https://en.wikipedia.org/wiki/McCarthyism.

15 See Donald Bogle, *Toms, Coons, Mulattoes, Mammies, and Bucks: An Interpretive History of Blacks in American Films* (London: Bloomsbury Publishing, 2001); "African-American Representation in Hollywood", https://en.wikipedia.org/wiki/African-American_

representation_in_Hollywood.

16 See Peniel E. Joseph, *Waiting 'til the Midnight Hour: A Narrative History of Black Power in America* (London: Macmillan, 2007); and Henry Louis Gates and Kevin Michael Burke, *Still I Rise: Black America since MLK* (New York: HarperCollins, 2015), pp. 2–54.

17 Marable, *Malcolm X*, pp. 84–90.

18 Marable, *Malcolm X*, pp. 16–24.

19 Charles Eric Lincoln, *The Black Muslims in America* (Michigan: Wm. B. Eerdmans Publishing, 1994), pp. 105–6.

20 See Malcolm X, "After the Bombing" speech on 14 February 1965, Detroit, Michigan, in *Malcolm X Speaks: Selected Speeches and Statements* (New York: Grove Press, 1965), pp. 155–77.

21 See Daniels, "Martin Luther King Jr", pp. 100–18.

22 See Isabel Wilkerson, "The Warmth of Other Suns: The Epic Story of America's Great Migration", *African Diaspora Archaeology Newsletter*, 13, 4 (2010), p. 25; and "Great Migration (African American)", https://en.wikipedia.org/wiki/Great_Migration_(African_American).

23 "The Second Great Migration", http://www.inmotionaame.org/print.cfm;jsessionid=f83044466145872931 5793?migration=9&bhcp=1. See also: "Great Migration", https://en.wikipedia.org/wiki/Great_Migration_(African_American).

24 Daniels, "Martin Luther King, Jr", pp. 111–12.

25 Haley, "*The Autobiography of Malcolm X*, p. 406.

26 Marable, *Malcolm X*, pp. 85–6.

27 For a brief description of the challenge-demeanor dynamic, see Daniels, "Martin Luther King, Jr: The Great Provocateur", pp. 5 and 12. For a full discussion, see Martin Kilson, *Transformation of the African American Intelligentsia, 1880–2012* (Cambridge and London: Harvard University Press, 2014), pp. 44–85.

28 Lincoln, *The Black Muslims in America*, pp. 102–3.

29 See Elise C. Boddie, "Philando Castile and the Terror of an Ordinary Day", https://mobile.nytimes.com/2017/06/20/opinion/philando-castile-and-the-terror-of-an-ordinary-day.html?mcubz=0. Elise Boddie wrote of the "everyday racism" that blacks of all social classes face openly on a normal basis. It takes little effort to imagine how much more numerous such "minor" incidents there were before the mid-1960s.

30 Daniels, "Martin Luther King Jr", pp. 106–9.

Chapter 14

1 Maya Angelou, *The Heart of a Woman* (London: Virago, 2008 [1981]).

2 Maya Angelou, *All God's Children Need Travelling Shoes* (London: Virago, 2008 [1981]).

3 Relying on Angelou's autobiographies is not to make use of them as objective historical records of fact. Rather, her autobiographies, like other forms of the genre of creative nonfiction (i.e. literary journalism, memoir, personal essay), are valuable in that they are meant to offer recollections of events that exist in the official historical record, from the author's specific, albeit subjective, point of view. "The [writing] may indeed be subjective, but it is still concerned with people who have really lived and events that have really happened, presenting history as a matter of personal significance as well as public record in a way that more objective reports – providing 'just the facts' – could never hope to." William Bradley, "The Ethical Exhibitionist's Agenda: Honesty and Fairness in Creative Nonfiction", *College English*, 70, 2 (2007), p. 204, https://doi.org/10.2307/25472261.

4 Acclaimed in 1965 as one of the "four most celebrated Negro comedians" in the US, along with Bill Cosby, Dick Gregory and Nipsy Russell. See "Comedians: They Have

Overcome", *Time*, 5 February 1965.

5   Angelou's accession to this significant position of leadership was atypical for a woman. It is worth noting that Rustin, who selected her for the role, was a gay man.

6   Evelyn Brooks Higginbotham, *Righteous Discontent: The Women's Movement in the Black Baptist Church, 1880–1920* (Massachusetts: Harvard University Press, 1994).

7   Kimberly Foster, "Wrestling with Respectability in the Age of #BlackLivesMatter: A Dialogue", http://www.forharriet.com/2015/10/wrestling-with-respectability-in-age-of.html#axzz4hzSH44nc.

8   Christina Simmons, "Women's Power in Sex Radical Challenges to Marriage in the Early-Twentieth-Century United States", *Feminist Studies*, 29, 1 (2003), pp. 169–98, http://www.jstor.org/stable/3178485.

9   Angelou, *The Heart of a Woman*, 176.

10 Angelou, *The Heart of a Woman*, 176.

11 Angelou, *The Heart of a Woman*, p. 123.

12 Angelou, *The Heart of a Woman*, pp. 123–4.

13 Angelou, *The Heart of a Woman*, p. 124.

14 Angelou, *The Heart of a Woman*, p. 125.

15 Angelou, *The Heart of a Woman*, p. 125.

16 Angelou, *The Heart of a Woman*, pp. 127–9.

17 Angelou, *The Heart of a Woman*, p. 131.

18 Angelou, *The Heart of a Woman*, p. 151.

19 Angelou, *The Heart of a Woman*, p. 151.

20 Angelou, *The Heart of a Woman*, p. 151.

21 Angelou, *The Heart of a Woman*, p. 151.

22 Angelou, *The Heart of a Woman*, pp. 146–7.

23 Angelou, *The Heart of a Woman*, p. 179.

24 Angelou, *The Heart of a Woman*, p. 180.

25 Angelou, *The Heart of a Woman*, p. 122.

26 Angelou, *The Heart of a Woman*, pp. 121–2.

27 Angelou, *The Heart of a Woman*, p. 186.

28 The *New York Times* stated that there were 200 protesters. See "Riot in Gallery Halts U.N. Debate: American Negroes Ejected after Invading Session", *New York Times*, 16 February 1961, pp. A1 and 10. Angelou, however, writes that the protesters numbered in the thousands. See Angelou, *The Heart of a Woman*, p. 194.

29 Hickner identifies other participating organisations as the United African Nationalist Movement, the Liberation Committee for Africa, South Africa's Pan Africanist Congress (PAC), the Universal African Legion, the International Muslim Society, the Brooklyn-based United Sons and Daughters of Africa, and the Order of Damballah Ouedo. See Jamie Elizabeth Hickner, "'History Will One Day Have Its Say': Patrice Lumumba and the Black Freedom Movement" (Purdue University, 2011), p. 199.

30 Angelou records the number of blacks in the auditorium as 75, the *New York Times* states 60 persons were in the UN gallery. See Angelou, *The Heart of a Woman*, p. 198; *New York Times*, "Riot in Gallery Halts U.N. Debate", p. A1.

31 Angelou, *The Heart of a Woman*, p. 209.

32 See, for example, Lee A. Daniels, "Martin Luther King, Jr: The Great Provocateur", in Adekeye Adebajo (ed.), *Africa's Peacemakers: Nobel Peace Laureates of African Descent* (London: Zed Books, 2013), pp. 100–18.

33 Angelou, *The Heart of a Woman*, p. 211.

34 Angelou, *The Heart of a Woman*, p. 209.

35 Angelou, *The Heart of a Woman*, p. 209.

36 Angelou, *The Heart of a Woman*, p. 211.

37 Angelou, *The Heart of a Woman*, pp. 210–11.

38 The NAACP's Roy Wilkins stated that the protests did not "represent either the sentiment or the tactics of American Negroes". Ralph Bunche, a prominent diplomat, political scientist, and first African-American recipient of the Nobel Peace Prize (1950), accused the protest organisers of "hooliganism" and denied that they represented African-American opinion. See Brenda Gayle Plummer, *Rising Wind: Black Americans and U.S. Foreign Affairs, 1935–1960* (Chapel Hill: University of North Carolina Press, 1996), p. 303.

39 Angelou recalls seeing the unknown man take responsibility on the evening news. See Angelou, *The Heart of a Woman*, p. 209.

40 Angelou, *The Heart of a Woman*, p. 302.

41 Tavis Smiley, *My Journey with Maya* (New York: Little, Brown, 2015), p. 61.

42 Angelou, *All God's Children Need Travelling Shoes*, p. 145.

43 Smiley, *My Journey with Maya*, p. 63.

44 Angelou, *The Heart of a Woman*, pp. 211–12.

45 Angelou, *All God's Children Need Travelling Shoes*, p. 162.

46 Maya Angelou, *A Song Flung Up to Heaven* (reprint, New York: Random House, 2002), p. 4.

47 Smiley, *My Journey with Maya*, p. 64.

CHAPTER 15

1 Ajamu Nangwaya, "Dr. Walter Rodney: Revolutionary Intellectual, Socialist, Pan-Africanist and Historian", *Global Research*, 14 October 2016, pp. 4–5; and Walter Rodney Foundation, "Walter Rodney and Works", http://www.walterrodneyfoundation.org/biography/.

2 Nangwaya, "Dr. Walter Rodney".

3 Nangwaya, "Dr. Walter Rodney", p. 12.

4 Winston McGowan, "Walter Rodney the Historian", *Journal of Caribbean History*, 39, 2 (2005), p. 129.

5 Nangwaya, "Dr. Walter Rodney", p. 1.

6 Nangwaya, "Dr. Walter Rodney", p. 3.

7 Horace Campbell, "Walter Rodney and Pan-Africanism Today", Presentation, Africana Studies Research Centre, Cornell University, Ithaca, New York Africana Colloquium Series, 28 September 2005, pp. 12–13.

8 Nangwaya, "Dr. Walter Rodney", p. 3.

9 McGowan, "Walter Rodney the Historian", pp. 126–7.

10 McGowan, "Walter Rodney the Historian", p. 126.

11 McGowan, "Walter Rodney the Historian", pp. 127.

12 McGowan, "Walter Rodney the Historian", pp. 127.

13 Rupert Lewis, "Walter Rodney: 1968 Revisited", *Social and Economic Studies*, 43, 3 (1994), pp. 39–40.

14 McGowan, "Walter Rodney the Historian", pp. 126–7.

15 Campbell, "Walter Rodney and Pan-Africanism Today", p. 4.

16 Twelfth Annual Walter Rodney Symposium, "Hungry Nation, Hungry World", Atlanta University Centre, 20 and 21 March 2015, p. 3.

17 Campbell, "Walter Rodney and Pan-Africanism Today", p. 4.

18 Twelfth Annual Walter Rodney Symposium, p. 3.

19 Campbell, "Walter Rodney and Pan-Africanism Today", p. 4.
20 Walter Rodney, *Guyanese Sugar Plantations in the Late Nineteenth Century: A Contemporary Description from the "Argosy"* (Georgetown: Release Publishers, 1979). See Campbell, "Walter Rodney and Pan-Africanism Today", p. 12.
21 McGowan, "Walter Rodney the Historian", p. 127.
22 Walter Rodney, *Groundings with My Brothers* (London: Bogle-L'Ouverture Publications, 1969), p. 51.
23 McGowan, "Walter Rodney the Historian", p. 127.
24 Walter Rodney, "Interview", *Black Scholar*, 6, 3 (1974), p. 38.
25 Campbell, "Walter Rodney and Pan-Africanism Today", p. 3.
26 Robert A. Hill, "Walter Rodney on Pan-Africanism", *Ufahamu: A Journal of African Studies*, 12, 3 (1983), pp. 15–16.
27 Jeffrey D. Howison, "Walter Rodney, African Studies and the Study of Africa", *Ankara University Journal of African Studies*, 1, 1 (2011), p. 44.
28 Kurt B. Young, "Walter Rodney's Pan African Nationalism", *Peace Review: A Journal of Social Justice*, 20, 4 (2008), p. 488.
29 Campbell, "Walter Rodney and Pan-Africanism Today", p. 12.
30 Rodney, *Guyanese Sugar Plantations in the Late Nineteenth Century*.
31 Howison, "Walter Rodney, African Studies and the Study of Africa", p. 50.
32 Howison, "Walter Rodney, African Studies and the Study of Africa", p. 47.
33 Howison, "Walter Rodney, African Studies and the Study of Africa", p. 46.
34 Howison, "Walter Rodney, African Studies and the Study of Africa", p. 46.
35 Young, "Walter Rodney's Pan African Nationalism", p. 489.
36 W.E.B. Du Bois, (1966). *Black Reconstruction in America* (New York: Harcourt Brace & Company, 1966 [1935]).
37 Howison, "Walter Rodney, African Studies and the Study of Africa", pp. 48–9.
38 Hill, "Walter Rodney on Pan- Africanism", p. 15.
39 Viola Mattavous-Bly, "Walter Rodney and Africa", *Journal of Black Studies*, 16, 2 (1985), p. 115.
40 Young, "Walter Rodney's Pan African Nationalism", pp. 489-90.
41 Hill, "Walter Rodney on Pan- Africanism", p. 14.
42 Hill, "Walter Rodney on Pan- Africanism", p. 14.
43 Hill, "Walter Rodney on Pan- Africanism", pp. 14–15.
44 Hill, "Walter Rodney Walter Rodney on Pan-Africanism", p. 20.
45 Campbell, "Walter Rodney and Pan-Africanism Today", p. 7; and Hill, "Walter Rodney", p. 19.
46 Campbell, "Walter Rodney and Pan-Africanism Today", p. 19.
47 Campbell, "Walter Rodney and Pan-Africanism Today", p. 19.
48 Campbell, "Walter Rodney and Pan-Africanism Today", p. 17.
49 Walter Rodney, "Aspects of the International Class Struggle in Africa, the Caribbean and America", in Horace Campbell (ed.), *Pan- Africanism: Struggle against Neo-Colonialism and Imperialism. Documents of the Sixth Pan-African Congress* (Toronto: Afro-Carib Publications, 1975), p. 1.
50 Walter Rodney, *Walter Rodney Speaks* (New Jersey: Africa World Press, 1990), p. 3.
51 Rodney, "Interview", p. 39
52 Rodney, "Interview", p. 40.
53 Rodney, "Interview", p. 40.
54 Hill, "Walter Rodney", p. 22.
55 Rodney, "Aspects of the International Class Struggle in Africa", p. 1.

56 Rodney, "Aspects of the International Class Struggle in Africa", p. 2.
57 Rodney, "Interview", p. 40.
58 Rodney, "Aspects of the International Class Struggle", p. 7.
59 Rodney, "Interview", p. 40.
60 Rodney, "Interview", p. 40.
61 Rodney, "Aspects of the International Class Struggle in Africa", p. 5.
62 Rodney, "Aspects of the International Class Struggle in Africa", p. 2.
63 Rodney, "Interview", p. 41.
64 Rodney, *Groundings with My Brothers*, p. 56.
65 Rodney, *Groundings with My Brothers*, p. 56.
66 Rodney, *Groundings with My Brothers*, p. 58.
67 Rodney, *How Europe Underdeveloped Africa*, p. 75.
68 Rodney, *How Europe Underdeveloped Africa*, p. 75.
69 Horace Campbell, "The Impact of Walter Rodney and Progressive Scholars on the Dar es Salaam School", *Social and Economic Studies*, 40, 2 (1991), p. 103.
70 Howison, "Walter Rodney, African Studies and the Study of Africa", p. 58.
71 Campbell, "The Impact of Walter Rodney", pp. 101–2.
72 Campbell, "The Impact of Walter Rodney", p. 101.
73 Toyin Fayola, *Nationalism and African Intellectuals* (Rochester, NY: University of Rochester Press, 2001), p. 252.
74 Trevor Campbell, "The Making of an Organic Intellectual: Walter Rodney (1942–1980)", *Latin American Perspectives*, 8, 1 (Winter 1981), pp. 56–7.
75 Howison, "Walter Rodney, African Studies and the Study of Africa", p. 54; and Rupert Lewis, "Walter Rodney", p. 8.
76 Lewis, "Walter Rodney", p. 8.
77 Lewis, "Walter Rodney", p. 21.
78 Lewis, "Walter Rodney", pp. 21–2.
79 Howison, "Walter Rodney, African Studies and the Study of Africa", p. 53.
80 See, for example, Norman Girvan and Annita Montoute, "The EU and the Caribbean: The Necessity of Unity", in Annita Montoute and Kudrat Virk (eds), *The ACP Group and the EU Development Partnership: Beyond the North–South Debate* (Cham: Palgrave Macmillan, 2017), pp. 79–110.

CHAPTER 16

1 Interview with Angela Davis, "My Political Life has Been Informed by the Struggle in South Africa", in Ainehi Edoro, *Johannesburg Salon*, 8 (2014), pp. 1–3, http://www.jwtc.org.za/resources/docs/salon-volume-8/20_Vol8.pdf.
2 Dikgang Moseneke, "Courage of Principle: Reflections on the 30th Anniversary of the Assassination of Ruth First", *Constitutional Court Review*, 5 (2015), pp. 91–100, http://www.constitutionalcourtreview.co.za/wp-content/uploads/2015/08/Courage-of-Principle.pdf.
3 Ronald Segal, "Ruth First: A Memorial Address", *Review of African Political Economy*, 9, 25 (September and December 1982), p. 54, http://www.jstor.org/stable/3998094.
4 Gillian Slovo, *Every Secret Thing* (London: Little, Brown, 2009), ch. 4, Kindle edition, loc. 474.
5 Albie Sachs, Address at Ruth First Memorial, "A Revolutionary Life: Ruth First 1925–1982", Senate House, University of London, June 2012, http://www.ruthfirstpapers.org.uk/symposium.
6 See Diana Collecott, "Ruth First 1925–1982", Ruth First Educational Trust (Durham: University of Durham Press, 2011), p. 3, https://community.dur.ac.uk/ruthfirst.trust/

Ruth%20First%20by%20Diana%20Collecott.pdf.

7 See "Traces of Truth: Documents Relating to the South African Truth and Reconciliation Commission", Wits Historical Papers and South African History Archive Project, http://truth.wwl.wits.ac.za/cat_descr.php?cat=3.

8 See also Jonathan Ancer, *Spy: Uncovering Craig Williamson* (Johannesburg: Jacana Media, 2017), ch. 31, Kindle edition, loc. 3176 and 3177. Williamson and Raven also received amnesty for the parcel bomb murder of Jeanette and six-year-old Katryn Schoon in Lubango, Angola, on 28 June 1984. The Slovo and Schoon families opposed Williamson's amnesty, unsuccessfully, although their legal team argued that Williamson had not shown full disclosure and neither First nor Schoon were "legitimate targets" (i.e. in the armed struggle) and the murders were therefore disproportionate to the killers' political objective. After the amnesty decision the families launched a judicial review, later abandoned for reasons related to the Schoon family's circumstances.

9 Gillian Slovo, *Portrait of an Activist: Ruth First and the South African Struggle* (Texas: University of Texas Press, 2007), p. 21, https://law.utexas.edu/wp-content/uploads/sites/31/2016/04/Slovo_Gillian.pdf.

10 Ali A. Mazrui, "Pan-Africanism, from Poetry to Power", *Issue: A Journal of Opinion*, 23, 1 (Winter–Spring 1995), pp. 35–8, http://www.jstor.org/stable/1166980.

11 Ruth First, *The Barrel of a Gun: Political Power in Africa and the Coup d'Etat* (London: Allen Lane, 1970), p. ix. Also republished by Ruth First Papers Project; University of the Western Cape-Robben Island and Centro de Estudos Africanos, Universidade Eduardo Mondlane (2012), http://sas-space.sas.ac.uk/id/eprint/3622.

12 Don Pinnock, "Her Life", in *Ruth First: Voices of Liberation* (Cape Town: Human Sciences Research Council Press, 2012), p. 4, http://www.hsrcpress.ac.za/product.php?productid=2292.

13 Slovo, *Portrait* of an *Activist*, p. 3.

14 "Comrade Ruth First, Obituary", *Sechaba* (October 1982), p. 27, http://disa.ukzn.ac.za/sites/default/files/pdf_files/art19740600.043.049a.pdf.

15 Despite its gagging and her banning, Ruth First continued to work for its incarnations, *Clarion, People's World, Advance* and *New Age*. See Alan Wieder, *Ruth First and Joe Slovo in the War against Apartheid* (New York: Monthly Review Press, 2019), p. 71.

16 Ruth First, "Our Duty, as We See It", in Pinnock, *Ruth First*, p. 82.

17 Pinnock, *Ruth First*, pp. 11–12.

18 Angela Y. Davis, Introduction to Ruth First, *117 Days: An Account of Confinement and Interrogation under the South African Ninety Day Detention Law* (New York: Penguin Books, 2009 [1965]), p. 14.

19 Davis, *Introduction*, p. 46.

20 Alan Wieder, "Ruth First as Educator: An Untold Story", *Southern African Review of Education*, 17, 1 (January 2011), p. 90, https://journals.co.za/content/sare/17/1.

21 Wieder, "Ruth First as Educator", p. 92.

22 Barbara Harlow, "Public Spheres, Personal Papers, Pedagogical Practices: Ruth First's Academic Postings to/from Dar es Salaam and Maputo", *Africa Development*, 35, 4 (2010), p. 48, Council for the Development of Social Science Research in Africa, Dakar, Senegal, http://pro.ovh.net/~codesria/spip.php?article1434. Harlow notes that First's term coincided with the presence of prominent Africanists including Walter Rodney, Mahmood Mamdani, Archie Mafeje, John Saul, Jacques Depelchin, Terence Ranger and Issa Shivji.

23 First's single-author publications include *South West Africa* (Baltimore: Penguin Books, 1963); *117 Days*; *The Barrel of a Gun*; *Portugal's Wars in Africa* (London: International

Defence and Aid Fund, 1971); *Libya: The Elusive Revolution* (London: Penguin, 1974; New York: Penguin, 1975); and *Black Gold: The Mozambican Miner, Proletarian and Peasant* (Brighton, Sussex: Harvester Press; New York: St Martin's Press, 1983). First's co-authored books include: Ruth First, Jonathan Steele and Christabel Gurney, *The South African Connection: Western Investment in Apartheid* (London: Maurice Temple Smith, 1972); and Ruth First and Ann Scott, *Olive Schreiner: A Biography* (New York: Schocken, 1980). Her edited books include: Ronald Segal, Ruth First and International Court of Justice (eds), *South West Africa: Travesty of Trust. The Expert Papers and Findings of the International Conference on South West Africa, Oxford, 23–26 March 1966* (London: Deutsch, 1967); and Nelson Mandela, *No Easy Walk to Freedom* (London: Heinemann, 1965), to which she contributed a foreword to the 1978 edition. She assisted in editing Oginga Odinga, *Not Yet Uhuru: The Autobiography of Oginga Odinga* (London: Heinemann, African Writers Series, 1980); and Govan Mbeki, *The Peasants' Revolt* (London: Penguin African Library, 1964; London: International Defence and Aid Fund, 1984), to which she contributed the preface.

24 Gillian Slovo, *Every Secret Thing*, loc. 474.

25 Moseneke, "Courage of Principle", p. 94.

26 Barbara Harlow, "Looked Class, Talked Red: Sketches of Ruth First and Redlined Africa", *Meridian*, 3, 1 (2002), p. 249, http://www.jstor.org/stable/40338555.

27 Albie Sachs, Address at Ruth First Memorial, University of London, June 2012, http://www.ruthfirstpapers.org.uk/symposium.

28 Davis, "Introduction", p. 40.

29 Davis, "Introduction", p. 35.

30 Ralph Miliband, "Ruth First", *Socialist Register*, 19 (1982), p. 314, https://www.marxists.org/archive/miliband/1982/xx/ruthfirst.htm.

31 Nelson Mandela, "Conversation with Richard Stengel", in *Conversations with Myself* (London: Pan Macmillan, 2011), p. 52.

32 Pallo Z. Jordan, "Ruth First Memorial Lecture, University of the Witwatersrand", South African History Online (8 August 2000), http://www.sahistory.org.za/archive/ruth-first-memorial-lecture-pallo-jordan-28-august-2000-south-africa.

33 Anna Maria Gentili, "Ruth First: Internationalist Activist, Researcher and Teacher: The Long Road to Mozambique", *Review of African Political Economy*, 41, 139, (2014), p. 109, http://dx.doi.org/10.1080/03056244.2014.878081.

34 Jordan, "Ruth First Memorial Lecture".

35 Gavin Peter Williams, "Ruth First: Political Journalist, Researcher and Teacher", *Journal of Contemporary African Studies*, 32, 1 (2014), p. 3.

36 Ruth First, *Barrel of a Gun*, p. 8.

37 Gentili, "Ruth First: Internationalist Activist, Researcher and Teacher", p. 109.

38 See Gavin Williams, Leo Zeilig, Janet Bujra and Gary Littlejohn, "Não vamos esquecer (We will not forget)", Editorial, *Review of African Political Economy*, 41, 139 (2014), p. 9, http://dx.doi.org/10.1080/03056244.2014.885486.

39 Chris Saunders, "Some Roots of Anti-Colonial Historical Writing about Namibia", *Journal of Namibian Studies*, 3 (2008), pp. 83–93, http://namibian-studies.com/index.php/JNS/article/view/103.

40 Ruth First, *South West Africa* (Harmondsworth: Penguin Books, 1963), p. 13.

41 First, *South West Africa*, p. 234.

42 First, *South West Africa*, p. 238.

43 First, *South West Africa*, p. 241.

44 First, *Barrel of a Gun*, p. ix.

45 First, *Barrel of a Gun*, p. 441.

46 First, *Barrel of a Gun*, p. 6.

47 First, *Barrel of a Gun*, pp. 411–13.

48 First, *Barrel of a Gun*, p. 452.

49 First, *Barrel of a Gun*, p. 461.

50 First, *Barrel of a Gun*, p. 90.

51 First, *Barrel of a Gun*, p. 442.

52 First, *Barrel of a Gun*, p. 218.

53 First, *Barrel of a Gun*, p. 187.

54 First, *Barrel of a Gun*, p. 197.

55 First, *Barrel of a Gun*, p. 438.

56 First, *Barrel of a Gun*, p. 102.

57 First, *Barrel of a Gun*, p. 419.

58 Shula Marks, "Ruth First: A Tribute", *Journal of Southern African Studies*, 10, 1 (October 1983), pp. 123–8, http://www.jstor.org/stable/2636820.

59 Ruth First, *Libya*, p. 22; and Ruth First Papers, Institute of Commonwealth Studies, http://www.ruthfirstpapers.org.uk/term/cluster/libya-elusive-revolution.

60 First, *Libya*, p. 19.

61 First, *Libya*, p. 18.

62 First, *Libya*, p. 256.

63 First, *Libya*, p. 255.

64 First, *Libya*, p. 256.

65 Aquino de Bragança and Bridget O'Laughlin, "The Work of Ruth First in the Centre of African Studies: The Development Course", *Review (Fernand Braudel Center)*, 8, 2 (1984), p. 160, http://www.jstor.org/stable/40240984.

66 Marc Wuyts, "Ruth First and the Mozambican Miner", *Review of African Political Economy*, 41, 139 (2014), p. 60, http://dx.doi.org/10.1080/03056244.2014.878077.

67 Williams, Zeilig, Bujra and Littlejohn, "Não vamos esquecer (We will not forget)", p. 7.

68 Colin Darch, "Remembering Ruth First at the CEA", *Review of African Political Economy*, 41, 139 (2014), p. 41, http://dx.doi.org/10.1080/03056244.2014.878075.

69 Harold Wolpe, "The Liberation Struggle and Research", *Review of African Political Economy*, 32 (April 1985), pp. 75–6, http://www.jstor.org/stable/4005709.

70 De Bragança and O'Laughlin, "The Work of Ruth First in the Centre of African Studies", p. 167. See also Williams, Zeilig, Bujra and Gary Littlejohn, "Não vamos esquecer (We will not forget)", p. 8.

71 See Marc Wuyts, "Ruth First and the Mozambican Miner", p. 67.

72 First, *Black Gold*.

73 See also De Bragança and O'Laughlin, "The Work of Ruth First in the Centre of African Studies: The Development Course", p. 166.

74 Gentili, "Ruth First", p. 114.

75 See De Bragança and O'Laughlin, "The Work of Ruth First in the Centre of African Studies", p. 162.

76 Tebello Letsekha, "Ruth First: Lessons for a New Generation of African Scholars", *Education and Skills Development* (Cape Town: Human Sciences Research Council, 2014), http://repository.hsrc.ac.za/handle/20.500.11910/1936.

CHAPTER 17

1 This chapter builds on Janice Golding, "Wangari Maathai: The Earth Mother" in Adekeye Adebajo (ed.), *Africa's Peacemakers: Nobel Peace Laureates of African Descent* (London:

Zed Publishers, 2014), pp. 235–56.

2   The Nobel Prize Organisation, "The Nobel Peace Prize 2004: Award Ceremony Speech", http://www.nobelprize.org/nobel_prizes/peace/laureates/2004/presentation-speech. html.

3   See Judith Hicks Stiehm, *Champions for Peace: Women Winners of the Nobel Peace Prize* (Lanham, Rowman and Littlefield, 2006).

4   The Nobel Prize Organisation, "The Nobel Peace Prize 2004: Award Ceremony Speech."

5   Right Livelihood Award, http://www.rightlivelihood.org/maathai.html.

6   The Greek *Gaia* concept personifies "Planet Earth" as a living organism or spirit.

7   Wangari Maathai, *Unbowed: A Memoir* (New York: Knopf, 2006). See also Judith Hicks Stiehm, "Wangari Muta Maathai: Kenya's 'Green Doctor'", in Stiehm, *Champions for Peace*, pp. 201–17.

8   See, for example, William Beinart, "African History and Environmental History", *African Affairs*, 99 (2000), pp. 269–302.

9   L. Aguilar Revelo, I. Castañeda and H. Salazar, *In Search of the Lost Gender: Equity in Protected Areas* (International Union for the Conservation of Nature [IUCN], World Commission on Protected Areas, 2008).

10 Maathai, *Unbowed*. See also Stiehm, "Wangari Muta Maathai: Kenya's 'Green Doctor'", p. 146.

11 Adekeye Adebajo, "Ellen Johnson Sirleaf: The Iron Lady", in Adebajo (ed.), *Africa's Peacemakers*, pp. 281–99.

12 Adekeye Adebajo, "Leymah Gbowee: The Prayerful Peace Warrior", in Adebajo (ed.), *Africa's Peacemakers*, pp. 300–17.

13 Wangari Maathai, *The Green Belt Movement: Sharing the Approach and the Experience* (New York: Lantern, 2004).

14 Maathai, *The Green Belt Movement*.

15 *Green Belt Movement*, 18 May 2019. http://www.greenbeltmovement.org/what-we-do/ see-where-we-work.

16 Maathai, *Unbowed*. It therefore must have come as a great surprise to Maathai when, in 1990, Daniel arap Moi was listed on UNEP's "Global 500 Roll of Honour" for "planting trees and erecting gabions".

17 Stockholm Conference, The United Nations Conference on the Human Environment (also known as the Stockholm Conference) was convened under UN auspices and held in Stockholm, Sweden, on 5–16 June 1972. http://www.unep.org/Documents. Multilingual/Default.asp?documentid=97.

18 The Brundtland Commission, *Report of the World Commission on Environment and Development: Our Common Future* (United Nations General Assembly Resolution 42/187, 1987), http://www.un-documents.net/wced-ocf.htm.

19 Gro Harlem Brundtland, *Our Common Future* (Oxford: Oxford University Press, 1987).

20 See Press Statement: Achim Steiner, United Nations Environment Programme (UNEP), 26 September 2011. http://www.un.org.za/unep-pays-tribute-to-professor-wangari-maathai/

21 Funds totalling over $200 million were provided by the Norwegian and British governments for the Congo Basin Fund, which was managed by the African Development Bank.

22 Wangari Maathai, "State of the Congo Basin", in *The Challenge for Africa: A New Vision* (London: Heinemann, 2009), pp. 260–73.

23 United Nations Environment Programme (UNEP), *Plant for the Planet: Billion Tree Campaign*, 2008.http://wedocs.unep.org/bitstream/handle/20.500.11822/7661/-Plant%20 for%20the%20Planet_%20%20The%20Billion%20Tree%20Campaign-2008810.pd-

f?sequence=5&isAllowed=y

24 *Green Belt Movement*, 18 May 2019. http://www.greenbeltmovement.org/what-we-do/
    see-where-we-work .

25 Trillion Trees Campaign. https://www.trilliontrees.org/

26 See, for example, Charles Mutasa, "A Critical Appraisal of the African Union–ECOSOCC
    Civil Society Interface", in John Akokpari, Angela Ndinga-Muvumba and Tim Murithi
    (eds), *The African Union and Its Institutions* (Johannesburg: Jacana Media, 2008), pp. 291–306.

27 Camilla Toulman, *Climate Change in Africa* (London: Zed Books, 2009).

28 See the media release preceding the African Union summit, Malabo, Equatorial Guinea,
    held on 29 June 2011, http://nobelwomensinitiative.org/2011/06/media-release-
    wangari-maathai-calls-on-au-leaders-to-take-action-on-climate-change.

29 Nobel Women's Initiative, http://www.nobelwomensinitiative.org.

30 Ken Saro-Wiwa, *Genocide in Nigeria: The Ogoni Tragedy* (London: Saros International,
    1992). See also Ike Okonta and Oronto Douglas, *Where Vultures Feast: Shell, Human
    Rights and Oil in the Niger Delta* (San Francisco: Sierra Club, 2001).

31 Wangari Maathai, "Deficits: Indebtedness and Unfair Trade", in Wangari Maathai, *The
    Challenge for Africa* (London: Arrow Books), pp. 83–110.

32 Al Gore, *Earth in the Balance: Ecology and the Human Spirit* (Boston: Houghton Mifflin,
    1992), p. 407.

33 "Ten Questions: Wangari Maathai", *Time*, 10 October 2004, http://content.time.com/
    time/magazine/article/0,9171,901041018-713166,00.html.

CHAPTER 18

1 Ben Nnamdi Azikiwe, "Africa Speaks", *The Hilltop* (Howard University newspaper), 7
    November 1928, p. 3.

2 Randall Robinson, *Defending the Spirit: A Black Life in America* (London and New York:
    Penguin, 1998), p. 243.

3 Azikiwe, "Africa Speaks", p. 3.

4 Azikiwe, "Africa Speaks", p. 3.

5 Jacqueline Trescott, "Randall Robinson, Witness for Africa", *Washington Post*, 4 June 1983,
    https://www.washingtonpost.com/archive/lifestyle/1983/06/04/randall-robinson-
    witness-for-africa/5af9cca3-a79d-4423-a229-b0c56b38fb0f/.

6 *Mwalimu* is Swahili for "teacher". Tanzania's President Julius Nyerere was called
    Mwalimu. A former teacher by profession, he conceived of nation-building as both a
    political project and an educational project.

7 Trescott, "Witness for Africa".

8 Robinson, *Defending the Spirit*, p. 20.

9 Frantz Fanon, *The Wretched of the Earth* (New York: Grove Press, 1968).

10 Cyril Lionel Robert James, *The Black Jacobins: Toussaint L'Ouverture and the San Domingo
    Revolution* (London: Secker and Warburg, 1938).

11 William Edward Burghardt Du Bois, *The Souls of Black Folk* (Oxford: Oxford University
    Press, 2008 [1903]).

12 Robinson, *Defending the Spirit*, p. 69.

13 This discussion of Randall Robinson's years in Boston draws heavily on R. Joseph Parrott,
    "Boycott Gulf! Angolan Oil and the Black Power Roots of American Anti-Apartheid
    Organizing", *Modern American History* (2018), pp. 1–26.

14 Parrott, "Boycott Gulf!", p. 8.

15 SARF focused on eight African countries dominated by European minorities: Angola,
    Mozambique, Guinea-Bissau, Cape Verde, São Tomé and Príncipe, Rhodesia (Zimbabwe),

South Africa and South West Africa (Namibia).

16 Randall Robinson to A. Taylor, 27 March 1970, Brenda Randolph Papers, Michigan State University, cited by Parrott, "Boycott Gulf!", p. 8.

17 Mohammed Sahnoun, "Nyerere, the Organisation of African Unity and Liberation", *Pambazuka News*, 13 October 2009, https://www.pambazuka.org/pan-africanism/ nyerere-organization-african-unity-and-liberation.

18 J. Brooks Spector, "Randall Robinson and the Legacy of TransAfrica", *Daily Maverick*, 1 May 2019 (South Africa), https://www.dailymaverick.co.za/article/2012-05-01-randall-robinson-and-the-legacy-of-transafrica/#.Wl6ZNiOZOYU.

19 Robinson, *Defending the Spirit*, p. 78.

20 Charles Diggs, Jr, "Action Manifesto", *Issue*, 2, 1 (Spring 1972), pp. 52–60.

21 Robert Eggert, "Black Students Seize Mass Hall", *Harvard Crimson*, 29 April 1972, https://www.thecrimson.com/article/1972/4/20/black-students-seize-mass-hall-pthe/?page=single; Paula A. Engelmayer, "A Fortnight to Remember", 12 May 1982, *Harvard Crimson*, https://dev.thecrimson.com/article/1982/5/12/a-fortnight-to-remember-pbtbhe-latter/?page=1.

22 "Harvard Study Examines Angola Role", *New York Times*, 6 October 1972, https://www.nytimes.com/1972/10/06/archives/harvard-study-examines-angola-role.html.

23 Robinson, *Defending the Spirit*, pp. 90–3.

24 Brenda Gayle Plummer, *In Search of Power: African-Americans in the Era of Decolonization, 1955–1974* (Cambridge and New York: Cambridge University Press, 2013).

25 Interview with Sylvia Hill, by William Minter (interviewer), Washington DC, 12 August 2004, http://www.noeasyvictories.org/interviews/int16_hill.php.

26 The Congressional Black Caucus, "The African-American Manifesto on Southern Africa", *Black Scholar*, 8, 4 (January–February 1977), pp. 27–32.

27 Created in 1979 by the cable television industry as a non-profit public service, C-Span televises proceedings of the US federal government, along with other public affairs programming.

28 Jennifer Bailey Woodard and Teresa Mastin, "Black Womanhood: *Essence* and its Treatment of Stereotypical Images of Black Women", *Journal of Black Studies*, 36, 2 (November 2005), pp. 264–81.

29 Earl G. Graves, "Champion of Justice", *Black Enterprise*, 25, 4 (November 1994), p. 13.

30 "Tribute to Randall Robinson", 3 December 2001, Washington DC, video, C-Span.org, https://www.c-span.org/video/?167603-1/tribute-randall-robinson.

31 Randall Robinson, personal communications with the author.

32 The journal received grants from the Carnegie Corporation, the New World Foundation, the Africa Fund, the William Penn Foundation, the Tides Foundation, and the Links Foundation.

33 Hope Lewis, professor of law and founder of Northeastern University Law School's Programme on Human Rights and the Global Economy, was funded by fellowships in Women's Law and Public Policy (1986–7) and Public Interest Law (1987–8). Makau wa Mutua, formerly dean of the University of Buffalo Law School, received fellowship support from Harvard Law School's Human Rights Program (1986). Ibrahim Gassama, Frank Nash Professor of Law at the University of Oregon, was a research fellow while serving as TransAfrica's legislative director (1994).

34 Mary Frances Berry, "Anatomy of a Resistance: How the Free South Africa Movement Succeeded", Salon.com, 11 March 2018, https://www.salon.com/2018/03/11/anatomy-of-a-resistance-how-the-free-south-africa-movement-succeeded/.

35 Alvin B. Tillery Jr, *Between Homeland and the Motherland: Africa, US Foreign Policy, and*

Black Leadership in America (Ithaca and London: Cornell University Press, 2011), p. 139.

36   Parrott, "Boycott Gulf!", p. 24.

37   President Ronald Reagan's veto was overridden in the House by a vote of 313 to 82 and in the Senate by a vote of 78 to 21.

38   Rachel Cooper, "Top 10 Think Tanks in Washington DC", https://www.tripsavvy.com/top-think-tanks-in-washington-dc-1038694.

39   Karen DeWitt, "Black Lobby Group to Include Foreign Policy", *New York Times*, 6 June 1993, https://www.nytimes.com/1993/06/06/world/black-lobby-group-to-include-foreign-policy.html.

40   Frank McCoy, "TransAfrica Explores New Challenges", *Black Enterprise*, 23, 1 (August 1992), pp. 52–61.

41   DeWitt, "Black Lobby Group to Include Foreign Policy".

42   "Dedication Reception, Arthur Ashe Foreign Policy Library", *C-Span Sunday Journal*, 6 June 1993, https://www.c-span.org/video/?42310-1/span-sunday-journal.

43   "Voter News Service Exit Poll", reported in *New York Times*, 10 November 1996, p. 28.

44   George Moose's previous assignments included ambassador to Benin and Senegal, as well as ambassador to the UN office in Geneva.

45   In 1995 Susan Rice became senior director for African affairs on the NSC and was promoted in 1997 to assistant secretary of state for African affairs.

46   TransAfrica Forum Scholars Council Foreign Policy Brief, "Rethinking US Foreign Assistance", *TransAfrica Forum*, 9, 4 (1993), pp. 9–23.

47   George E. Moose, "The Clinton Administration's Africa Policy Agenda", speech given at the TransAfrica Forum Annual Foreign Policy Conference, 4 June 1993, Washington DC, https://www.c-span.org/video/?43300-1/transafrica-forum.

48   *Taegan Goodard's Political Dictionary*, "Triangulation", https://politicaldictionary.com/words/triangulation/.

49   Michelle Alexander, *The New Jim Crow: Mass Incarceration in the Age of Colorblindness* (New York: New Press, 2010); Jennifer Mittelstadt, *From Welfare to Workfare: The Unintended Consequences of Liberal Reform, 1945–1965* (Chapel Hill: University of North Carolina Press, 2005); and National Security Archive, State Department cable to US/UN, 29 September 1993, Secretary of State to US Mission to the UN, https://nsarchive2.gwu.edu/NSAEBB/NSAEBB511/.

50   Frank Newport, "President Clinton's Job Approval Averages by Race, Gallup Polls", cited in "Blacks and Whites Continue to Differ Sharply over Obama", *Politics*, 3 August 2010, https://news.gallup.com/poll/141725/blacks-whites-continue-differ-sharply-obama.aspx.

51   Robert C. Smith, *Ronald W. Walters and the Fight for Black Power, 1969–2010* (Albany: State University of New York Press, 2018); and Ronald Walters and Robert C. Smith, *African American Leadership* (Albany: State University of New York Press, 1997).

52   Robinson, *Defending the Spirit*, p. 270.

53   Robinson, *Defending the Spirt*, p. 189

54   Randall Robinson, *Public Policy Issues of the 1990s*, Roundtable discussion with Brian Lamb, 17 December 1991, https://www.c-span.org/video/?23531-1/public-policy-issues-1990s.

55   Interview with Sylvia Hill, by William Minter (interviewer), Washington DC, 12 August 2004, http://www.noeasyvictories.org/interviews/int16_hill.php.

56   Berry, *Anatomy of a Resistance*.

57   Adam Habib and Rupert Taylor, "South Africa: Anti-Apartheid NGOs in Transition", *Volantas: International Journal of Voluntary Nonprofit Organizations*, 10, 1 (1999), pp. 78–9.

58 Moeletsi Mbeki, "How US Sees Political Favours", *The Star* (South Africa), 14 February 1997.

59 Financial Package, TransAfrica Forum board meeting, 6 June 1993.

60 Robinson, *Defending the Spirit*, pp. 188–9.

61 Robinson, *Defending the Spirit*, p. 271.

62 C-Span, "Tribute to Randall Robinson", https://www.c-span.org/video/?167603-1/tribute-randall-robinson.

63 C-Span, "Tribute to Randall Robinson", https://www.c-span.org/video/?167603-1/tribute-randall-robinson.

64 Robinson, *Defending the Spirit*, p. xx.

65 Randall Robinson, *Quitting America: The Departure of a Black Man from his Native Land* (London and New York: Penguin, 2000).

66 Randall Robinson, *The Debt: What America Owes to Blacks* (London and New York: Penguin, 2001).

67 Randall Robinson, *The Reckoning: What Blacks Owe to Each Other* (London and New York: Penguin, 2002).

CHAPTER 19

1 Cyril Lionel Robert James, "The Making of a Caribbean People", Lecture given in Montreal, 1966, published in David Austin (ed.), *You Don't Play with Revolution: The Montreal Lectures of C.L.R. James* (Oakland, CA: AK Press, 2009).

2 "French Count Gives Lopinot Its Name", *Express*, Trinidad, 17 June 2013.

3 *Trinidad Slave Register*, Folio, 1813, T 71/501, 194.

4 Cyril Lionel Robert James, *Beyond a Boundary* (New York: Pantheon Books, 1963), p. 13.

5 Among other things, the Rules of the Society mandated (3rd): All persons are eligible for membership whose conduct is of a becoming character, who appear in decent apparel, and are introduced by any two members of the Society; (13th): No Gentleman shall be allowed to sing, whistle, smoke, or wear his hat, during his stay in the Reading Room; (14th): No Books to be introduced to the Society without the knowledge and approbation of the Committee, or other Officers.

6 L.B. Tronchin, "Charles Wm. Warner and His Times", *Public Opinion*, 28 September 1888.

7 Cyril Lionel Robert James, "The West Indian Intellectual", in John Jacob Thomas, *Froudacity: West Indian Fables by James Anthony Froude* (London: New Beacon Books, 1889), pp. 24, 27.

8 James Anthony Froude, *The English in the West Indies, or, The Bow of Ulysses* (New York: Charles Scribner's, 1900 [1888]), p. 96.

9 Cyril Lionel Robert James, "Michel Maxwell Philip: 1829–1889", in Reinhard Sander (ed.), *From Trinidad: An Anthology of Early West Indian Writing* (New York: Africana Publishing Company, 1978), p. 266.

10 William H. Gamble, *Trinidad Historical and Descriptive* (London: Yates and Alexander, 1866), p. 39.

11 Froude, *The English in the West Indies, or, The Bow of Ulysses*, p. 56.

12 Froude, *The English in the West Indies, or, The Bow of Ulysses*, p. 57.

13 Thomas, *Froudacity*.

14 Thomas, *Froudacity*, p. 26.

15 Thomas, *Froudacity*, p. 57.

16 Thomas, *Froudacity*, p. 142.

17 Thomas, *Froudacity*, p. 134.

18 See Selwyn R. Cudjoe, "Plumbing His Caribbean Roots", in David Featherstone, Christopher Gair, Christian Høgsbjerg and Andrew Smith (eds), *Marxism, Colonialism and Cricket: C.L.R. James's Beyond a Boundary* (Durham: Duke University Press, 2018).

19 Austin (ed.), *You Don't Play with Revolution*, p. 219.

20 Cyril Lionel Robert James, *The Black Jacobins: Toussaint L'Ouverture and the San Domingo Revolution* (London: Secker and Warburg, 1938).

21 Cudjoe, "Plumbing His Caribbean Roots", p. 218.

22 Tariq Ali and Cyril Lionel Robert James, "A Conversation", *Socialist Challenge*, 3 July 1980, p. 9.

23 Al Richardson, Clarence Chrysostom and Anna Grimshaw, "C.L.R. James and British Trotskyism: An Interview", *Socialist Platform Ltd*, 8 June and 16 November 1986, pp. 4–15.

24 Richardson, Chrysostom and Grimshaw, "C. L. R. James and British Trotskyism", p. 5.

25 Richardson, Chrysostom and Grimshaw, "C. L. R. James and British Trotskyism", p. 5.

26 Thomas, *Froudacity*, p. 45.

27 *Cyril Lionel Robert James and British Trotskyism: An Interview* (London: Socialist Platform Ltd, 1987).

28 Quoted in Selwyn Reginald Cudjoe and William Cain (eds), *C.L.R. James: His Intellectual Legacies* (Amherst: University of Massachusetts Press, 1995), p. 26.

29 Cyril Lionel Robert James, *Notes on Dialectics: Hegel, Marx, Lenin* (London: Allison & Busby, 1980 [1948]), p. 15.

30 *Cyril Lionel Robert James and British Trotskyism: An Interview*, p. 6.

31 See Cudjoe and Cain, *C.L.R. James*.

32 Cyril Lionel Robert James, *Party Politics in the West Indies* (San Juan: Vedic Enterprises, 1962), p. 4.

33 Austin, *You Don't Play with Revolution*, p. 218.

34 Cudjoe, "Plumbing His Caribbean Roots".

35 James, *Beyond a Boundary*, p. 246.

36 Cyril Lionel Reginald James, *At the Rendezvous of Victory: Selected Writings* (London: Allison & Busby, 1984), p. 251.

37 James, *Beyond a Boundary*, 255.

38 Aucher Warner, *Sir Thomas Warner, Pioneer of the West Indies: A Chronicle of His Family* (London, 1933).

39 Timothy J.L. Chandler, "Sir Pelham Warner [1873–1963]", in John Nauright and Charles Parrish (eds), *Sports around the World: History, Culture and Practices* (Santa Barbara: ABC-CLIO, 2012), p. 207.

40 Warner, *Sir Thomas Warner*, pp. 133–4.

41 James, "Preface", *Beyond a Boundary*, p. xxi.

42 Christian Høgsbjerg, *C.L.R. James in Imperial Britain* (Durham: Duke University Press, 2014), pp. 17–18.

43 Høgsbjerg, *C.L.R. James in Imperial Britain*, p. 6.

44 See Selwyn Reginald Cudjoe, *Beyond Boundaries: The Intellectual Tradition of Trinidad and Tobago in the Nineteenth Century* (Wellesley: Calaloux Publications, 2003).

45 Aimé Césaire, *Notebook of a Return to the Native Land*, transl. and ed. Clayton Eshlean and Annette Smith (Middletown, CT: Wesleyan University Press, 2001), p. xiii.

46 Austin, *You Don't Play with Revolution*, p. 218.

47 James, *Party Politics in the West Indies*, pp. 171–2.

48 Hannibal Price, "De la rehabilitation de la race noire par le République d'Haiti", quoted in G.R. Coulthard, *Race and Colour in Caribbean Literature* (New York: Oxford University Press, 1962), p. 63.

CHAPTER 20

1 W. Arthur Lewis, *Growth and Fluctuations, 1870–1913* (London: George Allen and Unwin, 1978), p. 76.

2 Gerald M. Meier, "Sir Arthur Lewis and Development-Fifty Years On", The VII Sir Arthur Lewis Memorial Lecture from the Eastern Caribbean Central Bank, Kingstown, St Vincent and the Grenadines, 6 November 2002, https://www.eccb-centralbank.org/content-manager/documents/download/155.

3 Walter Rodney, *Walter Rodney Speaks: The Making of an African Intellectual* (Trenton: Africa World Press, 1990), p. 113.

4 Norman Girvan, "Sir Arthur Lewis: A Man of His Time; and a Man Ahead of His Time", *Journal of Eastern Caribbean Studies*, 34, 4 (2009), p. 84.

5 W. Arthur Lewis, quoted in Kari Polanyi Levitt, "W. Arthur Lewis: Pioneer of Development Economics", UN Chronicle, XLV, 1 (2008), https://www.un.org/en/chronicle/article/w-arthur-lewis-pioneer-development-economics.

6 Girvan, "Sir Arthur Lewis", p. 86.

7 Mark Figueroa, "W. Arthur Lewis: Mild Afro-Saxon or Militant Antiracist? Lessons from His Struggles and Disparagement by Other Black Power Advocates", in Clinton A. Hutton, Maziki Thame and Jermaine McCalpin (eds), *Caribbean Reasonings: Rupert Lewis and the Black Intellectual Tradition* (Kingston: Ian Randle, 2018), p. 266.

8 Figueroa, "W. Arthur Lewis: Mild Afro-Saxon or Militant Antiracist?", p. 266.

9 Yoichi Mine, "The Political Element in the Works of W. Arthur Lewis: The 1954 Lewis Model and African Development", *Developing Economies*, 44, 3 (2006), p. 333.

10 Mine, "The Political Elements in the Works of W. Arthur Lewis", p. 351.

11 W. Arthur Lewis, *Politics in West Africa* (Toronto and New York: Oxford University Press, 1965), p. 11.

12 Mine, "The Political Elements in the Works of W. Arthur Lewis", p. 330.

13 Mine, "The Political Elements in the Works of W. Arthur Lewis", p. 336.

14 Mine, "The Political Elements in the Works of W. Arthur Lewis", p. 341.

15 W. Arthur Lewis, Michael Scott, Martin Wright and Colin Legum, *Attitude to Africa* (Harmondsworth: Penguin Books, 1951), as quoted in Mine, "The Political Elements in the Works of W. Arthur Lewis", p. 343.

16 Eastern Caribbean Central Bank, *Economic Theory and Development Options for the Caribbean: The Sir Arthur Lewis Memorial Lectures 1996–2005* (Kingston: Ian Randle, 2007), p. xvi.

17 Ravi Kanbur, "W. Arthur Lewis and the Roots of Ghanaian Economic Policy: Working Paper", Charles H. Dyson School of Applied Economics and Management, Cornell University, 4 April 2016.

18 Correspondence between Selwyn-Clarke and Lewis quoted by Figueroa, "Arthur Lewis: Mild Afro Saxon or Militant Anti-Racist?", p. 263.

19 Robert L. Tignor, "Ghana: Lessons from Nkrumah's Fallout with His Economic Advisor", Excerpt from *W. Arthur Lewis and the Birth of Development Economics* (Princeton: Princeton University Press, 2006) as presented on *The Conversation* website on 1 March 2016, https://theconversation.com/ghana-lessons-from-nkrumahs-fallout-with-his-economic-adviser-53233.

20 Mine, "The Political Elements in the Works of W. Arthur Lewis", pp. 342–3.

21 Tignor, *W. Arthur Lewis and the Birth of Development Economics*, pp. 181–3.

22 Letter from Lewis dated 11 December 1958, quoted in Tignor, *W. Arthur Lewis and the Birth of Development Economics*, p. 171.

23 The pamphlet being referred to here is *Politics in West Africa* which Lewis wrote for

"emotional reasons". It was his way of addressing his concerns about Ghana's political decline; see Tignor, *W. Arthur Lewis and the Birth of Development Economics*, p. 207.

24 Figueroa, "Arthur Lewis: Mild Afro-Saxon or Militant Anti-Racist?", p. 263.

25 W. Arthur Lewis, *Some Aspects of Economic Development* (London: George Allen and Unwin, 1969), quoted in Mine, "The Political Elements in the Works of W. Arthur Lewis", p. 346.

26 W. Arthur Lewis, *Politics in West Africa* (Toronto & New York: Oxford University Press, 1965), quoted in Mine, "The Political Elements in the Works of W. Arthur Lewis", p. 346.

27 Mine, "The Political Elements in the Works of W. Arthur Lewis", pp. 346–9.

28 Arthur Lewis quoted in Mine, "The Political Elements in the Works of W. Arthur Lewis", p. 348.

29 W. Arthur Lewis, "On Being Different", in O. Nigel Bolland, *The Birth of Caribbean Civilisation: A Century of Ideas about Culture and Identity, Nation and Society* (Kingston: Ian Randle, 2004), p. 520.

30 W. Arthur Lewis, *The Evolution of the International Economic Order* (Princeton: Princeton University Press, 1978), pp. 71–2.

31 Eastern Caribbean Central Bank, *Economic Theory and Development Options for the Caribbean*, p. xi.

32 Kari Polanyi Levitt, "The Right to Development", in Eastern Caribbean Central Bank, *Economic Theory and Development Options for the Caribbean*, pp. 84–5.

33 W. Arthur Lewis, "On Being Different", p. 520.

34 Girvan, "Sir Arthur Lewis", p. 82.

35 Caribbean Development Bank, "Sir Wm. Arthur Lewis: President 1970–1973", https://www.caribank.org/about-us/bank-organisation/president.

36 Figueroa, "Arthur Lewis: Mild Afro Saxon or Militant Anti-Racist?", p. 264.

37 *The West Indies Federation*, CARICOM Caribbean Community, August 2019, https://caricom.org/community/the-west-indies-federation/.

38 Arthur Lewis, *The Agony of the Eight* (Bridgetown: Advocate Commercial Printery, 1965).

39 Agreement Establishing the Caribbean Development Bank, 26 January 1970, Ch. VI, Article 35, http://www.caribank.org/uploads/2012/03/agreement.pdf.

40 "Keep Politics Out, Urges Sir Neville", *Nation News*, 18 November 2014, http://www.nationnews.com/nationnews/news/59480/politics-urges-sir-neville.

41 Girvan, "Sir Arthur Lewis", p. 98.

42 Girvan, "Sir Arthur Lewis", p. 98.

43 W. Arthur Lewis, "The Industrialization of the West Indies", in Dennis Pantin (ed.), *The Caribbean Economy: A Reader* (Kingston: Ian Randle, 1950), p. 43.

CHAPTER 21

1 See foreword by Kwame Anthony Appiah to Chinua Achebe's *The African Trilogy: Things Fall Apart, Arrow of God, No Longer at Ease* (London: Penguin, 2007).

2 Ali A. Mazrui, *The African Condition: A Diagnosis* (Cambridge: Cambridge University Press, 1980).

3 Yu M. Frenkel, "Edward Blyden and the Concept of African Personality", *African Affairs*, 73, 292 (1974), pp. 277–89.

4 Cheick Tidjane Thiam, *Return to the Kingdom of Childhood: Re-Envisioning the Legacy and Philosophical Relevance of Négritude* (Columbus: Ohio State University Press, 2014); and Gary Wilder, *Freedom Time: Négritude, Decolonization, and the Future of the World* (Durham and London: Duke University Press, 2015).

5 Kwame Nkrumah, *Consciencism: Philosophy and the Ideology for Decolonization* (New York:

St Martin's Press, 1970); Paul Tiyambe Zeleza, "The Invention of African Identities and Languages: The Discursive and Developmental Implications", in O.F. Arasanyin and M.A. Pemberton (eds), Selected Proceedings of the 36th Annual Conference on African Linguistics: Shifting the Centre of Africanism in Language Politics and Economic Globalization (Somerville, MA: Cascadilla Proceeding Project, 2006), pp. 14–26.

6   Valentin-Yves Mudimbe, *The Idea of Africa* (Oxford: James Currey, 1994); and Valentin-Yves Mudimbe, *The Invention of Africa: Gnosis, Philosophy and the Order of Knowledge* (Bloomington and Indianapolis: Indiana University Press, 1998).

7   Ngũgĩ wa Thiong'o, *Something Torn and New: An African Renaissance* (New York: Basic Civitas Books, 2009).

8   Zeleza, "The Invention of African Identities and Languages", p. 16.

9   Melville Jean Herskovits, "Does Africa Exist?" in Symposium on Africa (Wellesley College, Wellesley, Mass, 1960), pp. 1–13.

10 Ali Al'amin Mazrui, "On the Concept of 'We Are All Africans'", *American Political Science Review*, 57, 1 (1963), pp. 24–57.

11 Mazrui, "On the Concept of 'We Are All Africans'"; Ngũgĩ wa Thiong'o, *Something Torn and New*.

12 Seifudein Adem, "Ali A. Mazrui, the Post-colonial Theorist", *African Studies Review*, 57, 1 (April, 2014), pp. 135–52.

13 Zeleza, "The Invention of African Identities and Languages", p. 20.

14 Wole Soyinka, "Triple Tropes of Trickery", *Transition*, 54 (1991), pp. 179–83.

15 Zeleza, "The Invention of African Identities and Languages", p. 20.

16 See Soyinka, "Triple Tropes of Trickery".

17 Mazrui, *The African Condition*; Ali Al'amin Mazrui, T*he Africans: A Triple Heritage* (London: BBC Publications, 1986); Sabelo Jeremiah Ndlovu-Gatsheni, *Empire, Global Coloniality and African Subjectivity* (New York and Oxford: Berghahn Books, 2013); and Sabelo Jeremiah Ndlovu-Gatsheni, *Coloniality of Power in Postcolonial Africa: Myths of Decolonization* (Dakar: CODESRIA Book Series, 2013).

18 Richard Lewis Gordon, *An Introduction to Africana Philosophy* (Cambridge: Cambridge University Press, 2008), p. 204.

19 Gordon, *An Introduction to Africana Philosophy*, p. 207.

20 Wole Soyinka, *Of Africa* (New Haven and London: Yale University Press, 2012), p. 27.

21 Soyinka, *Of Africa*, p. 48.

22 Valentin-Yves Mudimbe, *On African Faultlines: Meditations on Alterity Politics* (Scottsville: University of KwaZulu-Natal Press, 2013), p. 11.

23 Nelson Maldonado-Torres, "On Coloniality of Being: Contributions to the Development of a Concept", *Cultural Studies*, 21, 2/3 (2007), pp. 240–70.

24 W.E.B. Du Bois, *The Souls of Black Folk* (New York: New American Library, 1982).

25 Boaventura de Sousa Santos, "Beyond Abyssal Thinking: From Global Lines to Ecologies of Knowledges", *Review*, XXX, 1 (2007), pp. 45–89.

26 Robert William July, *The Origins of Modern African Thought: Its Development in West Africa during the Nineteenth and Twentieth Centuries* (London: Faber & Faber, 1968); Pieter Boele van Hensbroek, *Political Discourse in African Thought, 1860 to the Present* (Westport, CT: Praeger, 1999); Toyin Falola, *Nationalism and African Intellectuals* (Rochester, NY: University of Rochester Press, 2001); Nicholas Creary (ed.), *African Intellectuals and Decolonization* (Athens: Ohio University Press, 2012); and Ngũgĩ wa Thiong'o, *Something Torn and New*.

27 Quoted in Pal Ahluwalia, *Politics and Post-Colonial Theory: African Inflections* (London and New York: Routledge, 2001), p. 68.

28 Archie Mafeje, "Africanity: A Combative Ontology", in Renaat Devisch and Francis Beng Nyamnjoh (eds), *The Postcolonial Turn: Re-Imagining Anthropology and Africa* (Bamenda and Leiden: Langaa and African Studies Centre, 2011), pp. 31–2.

29 Ndlovu-Gatsheni, "Genealogies and Lineages of Coloniality in Africa".

30 Edward Said, *Culture and Imperialism* (New York: Vintage Books, 1994), p. 24.

31 Mazrui, *The Africans*, p. 13.

32 Mazrui, *The Africans*, p. 13.

33 Mazrui, *The Africans*, p. 13.

34 Mazrui, *The Africans*, p. 13.

35 Mazrui, *The Africans*, p. 13.

36 Arnold Temu and Bonaventure Swai, *Historians and Africanist History: A Critique: Post-Colonial Historiography Examined* (London: Zed Books, 1981); Paul E. Lovejoy, "The Ibadan School and Its Critics", in Bogumil Jewsiewicki and David Newbury (eds), *African Historiographies* (London: Sage Publications, 1986), pp. 197–205; and Paul Tiyambe Zeleza, *Manufacturing African Studies and Crises* (Dakar: CODESRIA Book Series 1997).

37 Mazrui, *The Africans*, p. 20.

38 Mazrui, *The Africans*, p. 12.

39 Mazrui, *The Africans*, p. 12.

40 Mazrui, *The Africans*, p. 21.

41 Mazrui, *The African Condition*, p. 34.

42 Mazrui, *The Africans*, p. 21.

43 Mazrui, *The Africans*, p. 21.

44 Mazrui, *The Africans*, p. 295.

45 Mazrui, *The Africans*, p. 295.

46 Mazrui, *The African Condition*.

47 Mazrui, *The African Condition*, p. 34.

48 Mazrui, *The African Condition*, p. 34.

49 Wai Fah Chen (ed.), *Limit Analysis and Soil Plasticity* (Netherlands: Elsevier, 2013).

50 Samuel Makinda, "Leadership in Africa: A Contextual Essay", in Alamin Mazrui and Willy Mutunga (eds), *Governance and Leadership: Debating the African Condition: Mazrui and His Critics*, vol. 2 (Trenton: Africa World Press, 2004), pp. 3–10.

51 Ali Al'amin Mazrui, "Pro-Democracy Uprisings in Africa's Experience: From Sharpeville to Benghazi", Unpublished paper presented at the African Studies Centre at the University of Free State, Bloemfontein, South Africa, 2011, p. 1.

52 Seifudein Adem, "ASR Focus on Ali A Mazrui: Introduction", *African Studies Review*, 57, 1 (2014), pp. 131–3.

CHAPTER 22

1 Stuart Hall, *Familiar Stranger: A Life between Two Islands* (Durham: Duke, 2017), p. 95.

2 Hall, *Familiar Stranger*, p. 13.

3 Hall, *Familiar Stranger*, p. 15.

4 Hall, *Familiar Stranger*, p. 16.

5 Hall, *Familiar Stranger*, p. 47.

6 Stuart Hall, "Cultural Studies and Its Theoretical Legacies", in David Morley and Kuan-hsing Chen, *Stuart Hall: Critical Dialogues in Cultural Studies* (Abingdon: Routledge, 1996), p. 263.

7 Hall, *Familiar Stranger*, p. 3.

8 Hall, *Familiar Stranger*, p.3.

9 Hall, "Cultural Studies", p. 232.

10 Hall, *Familiar Stranger*, p. 239.

11 Hall, *Familiar Stranger*, p. 264.

12 Bill Ashcroft, Gareth Griffiths and Helen Tiffin, *The Empire Writes Back: Theory and Practice in Post-colonial Literatures* (New York: Routledge, 1989).

13 Hall, "Cultural Studies", p. 264.

14 Hall, *Familiar Stranger*, p. 236.

15 Hall, *Familiar Stranger*, p. 227.

16 Hall, *Familiar Stranger*, p. 241.

17 Hall, "Cultural Studies", p. 265.

18 Kuan-hsing Chen, "The Formation of a Diasporic Intellectual: An Interview with Stuart Hall", in Morley and Chen, *Stuart Hall*, p. 25.

19 Hall, *Familiar Stranger*, p. 25.

20 Hall, *Familiar Stranger*, p. 27.

21 Hall, *Familiar Stranger*, p.4.

22 Hall, *Familiar Stranger*, p. 5.

23 Chen, "Interview", p. 490.

24 Hall, *Familiar Stranger*, p. 27.

25 Hall, *Familiar Stranger*, p. 46.

26 Hall, *Familiar Stranger*, p. 18.

27 Hall, *Familiar Stranger*, p. 48.

28 Hall, *Familiar Stranger*, p. 165.

29 Hall, *Familiar Stranger*, p. 260.

30 Hall, *Familiar Stranger*, p. 16.

31 Hall, *Familiar Stranger*, p. 260.

32 Hall, *Familiar Stranger*, p. 261.

33 Hall, *Familiar Stranger*, p. 4.

34 Hall, *Familiar Stranger*, p. 98.

35 Hall, "Cultural Studies", p. 264.

36 Hall, *Familiar Stranger*, p. 248.

37 Hall, *Familiar Stranger*, p. 248.

38 Hall, *Familiar Stranger*, p. 249.

39 Hall, *Familiar Stranger*, p. 250.

40 Stuart Hall, "New Ethnicities", in Morley and Chen, *Stuart Hall*, p. 441.

41 Hall, *Familiar Stranger*, p. 172.

42 Hall, *Familiar Stranger*, p.174.

43 Hall, *Familiar Stranger*, p. 2814.

44 Chen, "Interview", p. 494.

45 Hall, *Familiar Stranger*, p. 198.

46 C. Wright Mills, *The Sociological Imagination* (New York: Grove, 1959), p. 3.

47 Mills, *The Sociological Imagination*, p. 6.

48 Hall, *Familiar Stranger*, p. 16.

49 Hall, *Familiar Stranger*, p. 198.

50 Morley and Chen, *Stuart Hall*, p. 15.

51 Gurminder K. Bhambra, *Rethinking Modernity: Postcolonailism and the Sociological Imagination* (New York: Palgrave, 2007); Julian Go, *Postcolonial Sociologies: A Reader* (Bingley: Emerald, 2016); George Steinmetz, *Sociology and Empire: The Imperial Entanglements of a Discipline* (Durham: Duke, 2013).

52 Chen, "Interview", p. 490.

53 Hall, "Cultural Studies", p. 265.

54 Stuart Hall, "Gramsci's Relevance for the Study of Race and Ethnicity", in Morley and Chen, *Stuart Hall*, p. 435.

55 Hall, "Gramsci's Relevance", p. 437

56 Hall, "Gramsci's Relevance", p. 437.

57 Hall, "Gramsci's Relevance", p. 439.

58 Stuart Hall, "The Problem of Ideology: Marxism without Guarantees", in *Morley* and Chen, *Stuart Hall*, p. 29.

59 *Hall, Familiar Stranger*, p. 42.

60 Stuart, Hall, "A Sense of Classlessness", in *The Great Moving Right Show and Other Essays* (Durham: Duke University Press, 2017), p. 37.

61 Stuart Hall, Chas Critcher, Tony Jefferson, John Clark and Brian Roberts, *Policing the Crisis: 'Mugging', the State, and Law and Order* (London: Macmillan, 1978).

62 Sally Davidson, David Featherstone and Bill Schwartz, "Introduction", in *The Great Moving Right Show and Other Essays*, p. 10.

63 Kevin B. Anderson, *Marx at the Margins: On Nationalism, Ethnicity, and Non-Western Societies* (Chicago: Chicago Review Place, 2017).

64 Anderson, *Marx at the Margins*, p. 74.

65 Gustave Beaumont, *Marie: or Slavery in the United States* (Baltimore: Johns Hopkins, 1999).

66 Quoted in Anderson, *Marx at the Margins*, p. 299.

67 Hall, "New Ethnicities", p. 443.

68 Hall, "New Ethnicities", p. 443.

69 Hall, "New Ethnicities", p. 443.

70 Hall, *Familiar Stranger*, p. 200.

71 Hall, *Familiar Stranger*, p. 272.

CHAPTER 23

1 This quote comes from a blurb on the cover of the book by Amos Sawyer, Afeikhena Jerome and Ejeviome Eloho Otobo (eds), *African Development in the 21st Century: Adebayo Adedeji's Theories and Contributions* (Trenton, New Jersey: Africa World Press, 2015).

2 See African Union High Level Panel, Audit of the African Union, Addis Ababa, 2007.

3 Irma Adelman, "Fallacies in Development Theory and Their Implications for Policy", in Gerald M. Meier and Joseph E. Stiglitz (eds), *Frontiers of Development Economics: The Future in Perspective* (New York: Oxford University Press, 2001), pp. 103–34.

4 Olu Ajakaiye and Afeikhena Jerome, "Public–Private Interface for Inclusive Development in Africa", in Célestin Monga and Justin Yifu Lin (eds), *The Oxford Handbook of Africa and Economics, vol. 1: Context and Concepts* (Oxford: Oxford University Press, 2015), pp. 536–52.

5 See Meier and Stiglitz, *Frontiers of Development Economics*.

6 Chenery Hollis, Montek Singh Ahluwalia, Jack Duloy, C.L.G. Bell and Richard Jolly (eds), *Redistribution with Growth: Policies to Improve Income Distribution in Developing Countries in the Context of Economic Growth* (New York: Oxford University Press, 1974).

7 Paul M. Romer, "Increasing Returns and Long-Run Growth", *Journal of Political Economy*, 94, 5 (1986), pp. 1002–37.

8 Ian Malcolm David Little, *Economic Development: Theory, Policy and International Relations* (New York: Basic Books, 1982).

9 Ajakaiye and Jerome, "Public–Private Interface for Inclusive Development in Africa", pp. 536–52.

10 See, for example, Bruce Currie-Alder, Ravi Kanbur, David M. Malone and Rohinton

Medhora (eds), *International Development: Ideas, Experience and Prospects* (Oxford: Oxford University Press, 2014).

11 World Bank, *From Poor Areas to Poor People: China's Evolving Poverty Reduction Agenda: An Assessment of Poverty and Inequality in China*, Report no. 47349-CN China, Poverty Reduction and Economic Management Department East Asia and Pacific Region (World Bank, Washington DC, 2009).

12 Dani Rodrik, "Diagnostics before Prescription", *Journal of Economic Perspectives*, 24, 3 (2010), pp. 33–44.

13 Daron Acemoglu and James A. Robinson, *Why Nations Fail: The Origins of Power, Prosperity and Poverty* (Germiston: Crown Business, 2013).

14 Pranab Bardhan, "State and Development: The Need for a Reappraisal of the Current Literature", *Journal of Economic Literature*, 54, 3 (2016), pp. 862–92.

15 UNECA was established by the UN Economic and Social Council (ECOSOC) in 1958 as one of the global body's five regional commissions. The ECA's mandate is to promote the economic and social development of its member states, foster intra-regional integration and promote international cooperation for Africa's development.

16 See Samuel K.B. Asante, *African Development: Adebayo Adedeji's Alternative Strategies* (London: Hans Zell Publications, 1991), p. 232.

17 Angola, Mozambique, Namibia, Seychelles, and Zimbabwe were not yet independent at the time.

18 See Richard Jolly, "Contemporary Perspectives on the Lagos Plan of Action and Structural Adjustment in the 1980s", in Sawyer, Jerome and Otobo (eds), *African Development in the 21st Century*, pp. 17–27.

19 For details, see Adebayo Adedeji, *Towards a Dynamic African Economy: Selected Speeches and Lectures 1975–1986*, compiled and arranged by Jeggan C. Senghor (London, Frank Cass, 1989), p. 82.

20 World Bank, *Accelerated Development in Sub-Saharan Africa: An Agenda for Action* (Washington DC, 1981).

21 See Afeikhena Jerome, Oluyele Akinkugbe and Francis Chigunta, "Africa's Development Agenda after the Global Economic and Financial Crisis", in Sawyer, Jerome and Otobo (eds), *African Development in the 21st Century*, pp. 159–87.

22 Thandika Mkandawire and Charles C. Soludo, *Our Continent, Our Future: African Perspectives on Structural Adjustment* (Dakar: CODESRIA/Africa World Press/IDRC, 1999).

23 World Bank, *Adjustment in Africa: Reforms, Results and the Road Ahead* (World Bank, Washington DC, 2004).

24 Adekeye Adebajo, "A Tale of Two Prophets: Jean Monnet and Adebayo Adedeji", in Sawyer, Jerome and Otobo (eds), *African Development in the 21st Century*, pp. 77–90.

25 Afeikhena Jerome and David Nabena, "Infrastructure and Regional Integration in Africa", in Daniel H. Levine and Dawn Nagar (eds), *Region-Building in Africa: Political and Economic Challenges* (New York: Palgrave Macmillan, 2016), pp. 89–108.

26 His honorary degrees include: Doctor of Letters, Ahmadu Bello University, 1976; Honorary Doctor of Laws, University of Dalhousie, 1984; Honorary Doctor of Laws, University of Zambia, 1984; Honorary Doctor of Laws, University of Calabar, 1987; Doctor of Science, Obafemi Awolowo University, 1989; Doctor of Science, University of Ibadan, 1997; Doctor of Science, Ogun State University, 1998; and Doctor of Science, University of Johannesburg, 2008.

27 Reginald Cline-Cole, "Adebayo Adedeji", in David Simon (ed.), *Fifty Key Thinkers on Development* (Oxford and New York: Routledge, 2006), pp. 3–9.

28   Sawyer, Jerome and Otobo (eds), *African Development in the 21st Century*.
29   See Joaquim Alberto Chissano, "Foreword", in Sawyer, Jerome and Otobo (eds), *African Development in the 21st Century*, pp. xiii–xv.

CHAPTER 24

1   Frantz Fanon, *The Wretched of the Earth* (New York: Grove Press, 1968), p. 315.
2   Frantz Fanon, *Toward the African Revolution* (New York: Grove Press, 1967), pp. 177–8.
3   David Macey, *Frantz Fanon: A Life* (London: Granta Books, 2000), p. 155.
4   David Caute, *Fanon* (New York: Viking Press, 1970), p. 16; cf. Irene Gendzier, *Frantz Fanon: A Critical Study* (New York: Pantheon, 1973), p. xiv: "It was in the Algerian Revolution that Fanon became a militant."
5   Frantz Fanon, *Toward the African Revolution* (New York: Grove Press, 1968), p. 54.
6   Macey, *Frantz Fanon*, p. 369; see also pp. 435–45.
7   See Eric Stokes, "Traditional Resistance Movements and Afro-Asian Nationalism: The Context of the 1857 Mutiny Rebellion in Asia", *Past and Present*, 48 (August 1970), p. 100: "Whatever its emotive origins in the writings of Fanon, the newer interpretation has been pioneered for modern historical scholarship by work on those regions, notably East and Central Africa and the Congo where the roots of the modern-educated elite and modern-style politics are shallowest."
8   On the distinction between "bourgeois" and "proletarian" nations, see Claude Ake, *Revolutionary Pressures in Africa* (London: Zed Books, 1978).
9   Frantz Fanon, *Black Skin, White Masks* (New York: Grove Press, 1967), p. 222.
10   Fanon, *Black Skin, White Masks*, p. 89.
11   Fanon, *Black Skin, White Masks*, p. 222 [emphasis in original].
12   Quoted in Sheldon Wolin, *Politics and Vision: Continuity and Innovation in Western Political Thought* (Boston: Little, Brown and Co., 1960), p. 221, note 90.
13   See Christopher Rowland (ed.), *Cambridge Companion to Liberation Theology* (Cambridge: Cambridge University Press, 1999), chs. 1, 9-11.
14   Jean Khalfa and Robert Young (eds), *Frantz Fanon: Alienation and Freedom* (London: Bloomsbury Publishing, 2018). Recent books on Fanon include Anthony C. Allesandrini, *Frantz Fanon: Critical Perspectives* (Abingdon: Routledge, 1999); Alice Cherki, *Frantz Fanon: A Portrait* (New York: Cornell University Press, 2006); Peter Hudis, *Frantz Fanon, Philosopher of the Barricades* (London: Pluto Press, 2015); Nigel Gibson, *Fanonian Practices in South Africa* (Durban: University of KwaZulu-Natal Press, 2011); and Lewis R. Gordon, *What Fanon Said: A Philosophical Introduction to His Life and Thought* (New York: Fordham University Press, 2015).
15   Adam Shatz, "Where Life is Seized", *London Review of Books*, 39, 2 (29 January 2017), p. 27.
16   Roger Southall, *Liberation Movements in Power: Party and State in Southern Africa* (Suffolk: James Currey, 2016), p. 12.
17   The references are to the US editions of the three books as follows: *Studies in a Dying Colonialism*, 1967; *Towards the African Revolution*, 1967; and *The Wretched of the Earth*, 1968, all published by Grove Press.
18   See United Nations Economic Commission for Africa, *Capturing the Twenty-First Century: African Peer Review Mechanism (APRM) Best Practices and Lessons Learned*, Part II, pp. 16–73. See also L. Adele Jinadu, *Social Science and Development: Ethiopia, Mozambique, Tanzania and Zimbabwe* (Stockholm: Swedish Agency for Cooperation with Developing Countries [SAREC], 1984); and Claude Ake, *Social Science and Imperialism: The Theory of Development* (Ibadan: University of Ibadan Press, 1979).

19 See Oluwaseun Tella and Shireen Motala (eds), *From Ivory Towers to Ebony Towers: Transforming Humanities Curricula in South Africa, Africa and African-American Studies* (Johannesburg: Jacana Media, 2020).

20 See Claude Ake, *Democracy and Development in Africa* (Washington, DC: The Brookings Institution, 1995); Severine Rugumamu, "Globalization, Liberalization and Africa's Marginalization", AAPS Occasional Paper Series, 4, no. 1, 1999; Kwame Ninsin, "Globalization and the Future of Africa", AAPS Occasional Paper Series, 4, no. 1, 2000; Tukumbi Lumumba-Kasongo, "Globalization, Capitalism, Liberal Democracy and the Search for New Development Paradigms in Africa", AAPS Occasional Paper Series, 5, no. 1, 2001; and Dani W. Nabudere, "The Epistemological and Methodological Foundations for an All-Inclusive Research Paradigm in the Search for Global Knowledge", AAPS Occasional Paper Series, 6, no. 1, 2002.

21 Fanon, *Black Skin, White Masks*, p. 229 [emphasis in original].

22 Claude Ake, "Editorial: Raison d'être", *African Journal of Political Economy*, 1 (1986), p. 3.

23 Paul Tiyambe Zeleza and Adebayo Olukoshi (eds), *African Universities in the Twenty-First Century*, 1 and 2 (Dakar: CODESRIA, 2004).

24 W.E.B. Du Bois, *The Negro Problem* (New York: J. Potts and Co., 1903); Kwame Nkrumah, *Consciencism: Philosophy and Ideology for Decolonization and Development, with Particular Reference to the African Revolution* (New York: Monthly Review Press, 1964); and Amilcar Cabral, *Selected Speeches of Amilcar Cabral* (New York: Monthly Review Press, 1973).

25 Dani Nabudere, "Introduction" in Dani Nabudere (ed.), *Globalisation and the Post-Colonial African State* (Harare: AAPS Books, 2000), p. 4.

26 On the distinction between "bourgeois" and "proletarian" nations, see Ake, *Revolutionary Pressures in Africa*.

27 Fanon, *Wretched of the Earth*, pp. 98–102.

28 See Adebayo Adedeji, "The Economic Commission for Africa", in Adekeye Adebajo (ed.), *From Global Apartheid to Global Village: Africa and the United Nations* (Scottsville: University of KwaZulu-Natal Press, 2009), pp. 373–98.

29 See Herbert Marcuse, "Re-Examination of the Concept of Revolution", in Raymond Klibansky (ed.), *Contemporary Philosophy*, 4 (1968–1971), pp. 424–32.

30 For example, J.S. Coleman and C.G. Rosberg, *Political Parties and National Integration in Tropical Africa* (Berkeley: University of California Press, 1964). See also Ake, *Social Science as Imperialism*; and Richard L. Sklar, "Political Science and National Integration: A Radical Approach", *Journal of Modern African Studies*, 5, 1 (May 1967).

31 Fanon, *Wretched of the Earth*, p. 166.

32 Fanon, *Wretched of the Earth*, p. 166.

33 Fanon, *Wretched of the Earth*, pp. 166, 224, where referring to the experience of petty traders from Dahomey (now Benin Republic) and Upper Volta (now Burkina Faso) in Côte d'Ivoire, Fanon regretfully observed that "from nationalism we have passed to ultra-nationalism, to chauvinism, and finally to racism".

34 "Because the various means whereby decolonisation has been carried out have appeared in many different aspects, reason hesitates to say which is a true decolonisation and which a false one." Fanon, *Wretched of the Earth*, p. 143.

35 "The theoretical question … whether or not the bourgeois stage can be skipped … ought to be answered in the field of revolutionary action, and not by logic." Fanon, *Wretched of the Earth*, p. 175.

36 Fanon, *Black Skin, White Masks*, p. 232.

37 "Because we want an independent and renovated Algeria, we believe we cannot rise and liberate oneself in one area and sink in another." Fanon, *A Dying Colonialism*, p. 25. See

also Simone de Beauvoir, *Force of Circumstance* (London: Andre Deutsch and Weidenfeld and Nicholson, 1965), p. 595, where she claims, on the basis of her discussions with him, that Fanon knew, and was concerned about, contradictions, dissensions, liquidations and intrigues within the FLN.

38 See African Charter on Human and Peoples' Rights, 1981/86; the New Partnership for Africa's Development (NEPAD) Declaration, 2001; Constitutive Charter of the African Union, 2000/2001; the African Union Declaration on Democracy, Political, Economic and Corporate Governance, 2002; and the African Union Charter on Democracy, Elections and Governance, 2007. See also Christof Heyns and Magnus Killander (eds), *Compendium of Key Human Rights Documents of the African Union*, 3rd edn (Tshwane: Pretoria University Law Press, 2007).

39 "The people must understand what is at stake. Public business ought to be the business of the public. So the necessity of creating a large number of well-informed nuclei at the bottom crops up again. Too often, we are content to establish national organisations at the top and always in the capital." Fanon, *Wretched of the Earth*, p. 194. See also Fanon, *Wretched of the Earth*, p. 209, where he argued that "nationalising the intermediary sector means organizing wholesale and retail cooperatives on a democratic basis. It also means decentralising these cooperatives by getting the mass of the people interested in the ordering of public affairs."

40 This argument is developed in Adele Jinadu, "Governance and Development in Africa", in Charles Mutasa and Mark Paterson (eds), *Africa and the Millennium Development Goals: Progress Problems, and Prospects* (Lanham: Rowman and Littlefield, 2015), pp. 51–66. See also Grant Masterson, Kojo Busia and Adele Jinadu (eds), *Peering the Peers: Civil Society and the African Peer Review Mechanism* (Johannesburg: Electoral Institute of Southern Africa, 2010), chs. 2 and 4.

41 Fanon, *Black Skin, White Masks*, p. 232.

42 Fanon, *The Wretched of the Earth*, p. 251

43 Fanon, *The Wretched of the Earth*, p. 255.

CHAPTER 25

1 Olufemi Taiwo, "Cabral", in Robert L. Arrington (ed.), *A Companion to the Philosophers* (Malden: Blackwell, 1999), p. 6.

2 Tsenay Serequeberhan (ed.), *African Philosophy: The Essential Readings* (New York: Paragon House, 1991), p. 20.

3 For further discussion of Cabral's life and legacy, see Mario de Andrade, *Amílcar Cabral: Essai de biographie politique* (Paris: François Maspero, 1980); Jean-Claude Andreini and Marie-Claude Lambert, *La Guinée-Bissau: D'Amílcar Cabral à la reconstruction nationale* (Paris: L'Harmattan, 1978); Aquino de Bragança, *Amílcar Cabral* (Lisbon: Iniciativas Editorias, 1976); José Pedro Castanheira, *Qui a fait tuer Amílcar Cabral?* (Paris: L'Harmattan, 2003); Patrick Chabal, *Amílcar Cabral: Revolutionary Leadership and People's War* (Cambridge: Cambridge University Press, 1983); Ronald H. Chilcote, *Amílcar Cabral's Revolutionary Theory and Practice* (Boulder, CO: Lynne Rienner, 1991); Carlos Comitini, *Amílcar Cabral: The Weapon of Theory* (Rio de Janeiro: CODESRIA, 1980); John Fobanjong and Thomas Ranuga (eds), *The Life, Thought and Legacy of Cape Verde's Freedom Fighter Amílcar Cabral (1924–1973): Essays on His Liberation Philosophy* (Lewiston, NY: Mellen Press, 2006); Carlos Lopes (ed.), *Africa's Contemporary Challenges: The Legacy of Amílcar Cabral* (London: Routledge, 2010); Jock McCulloch, *In the Twilight of Revolution: The Political Theory of Amílcar Cabral* (London: Routledge and Kegan Paul, 1983); Anatolïi Vladimirovich Nikanorov, *Amílcar Cabral* (Moscow: Novosti

Press, 1973); Oscar Oramas, *Amílcar Cabral: Para além do seu tempo* (Praia: Universidade de Cabo Verde Press, 1998); Dessalegn Rahmato, *Cabral and the Problem of the African Revolution* (Addis Ababa: Addis Ababa University Press, 1982); and Paul Khalil Saucier (ed.), *A Luta Continua: (Re)Introducing Amílcar Cabral to a New Generation of Thinkers* (Trenton, NJ: Africa World Press, 2016).

4   On Cabral's concept of "return to the source", see Amílcar Cabral, *Return to the Source: Selected Speeches of Amílcar Cabral* (New York: Monthly Review Press, 1973); Charles F. Peterson, "Returning to the African Core: Cabral and the Erasure of the Colonized Elite", in Charles F. Peterson, *Du Bois, Fanon, Cabral: The Margins of Elite Anti-Colonial Leadership* (Lanham: Lexington Books, 2007), pp. 115–38; and Tsenay Serequeberhan, "Amílcar Cabral's 'Return to the Source': A Reading", in Saucier, *A Luta Continua: (Re)Introducing Amílcar Cabral to a New Generation of Thinkers*, pp. 69–85. For further discussion of Cabral's conceptions of revolutionary decolonisation and revolutionary re-Africanisation, see Cabral, *Return to the Source*, pp. 39–56, esp. 43–5.

5   Amílcar Cabral, *Unity and Struggle: Speeches and Writings of Amílcar Cabral* (New York: Monthly Review Press), pp. 151–2.

6   Cabral, *Unity and Struggle*, p. 152. On Frantz Fanon's concepts of revolutionary decolonisation and revolutionary self-defensive violence, see Reiland Rabaka, *Forms of Fanonism: Frantz Fanon's Critical Theory and the Dialectics of Decolonization* (Lanham: Rowman and Littlefield, 2010), pp. 97–144.

7   Cabral, *Unity and Struggle*, p. 143.

8   Cabral, *Return to the Source*, p. 63, all emphases in original. For further discussion of Aimé Césaire's conception of "return", see Reiland Rabaka, *The Négritude Movement: W.E.B. Du Bois, Leon Damas, Aimé Césaire, Leopold Senghor, Frantz Fanon and the Evolution of an Insurgent Idea* (Lanham: Rowman and Littlefield, 2015), pp. 149–96.

9   Cabral, *Return to the Source*, p. 63.

10 Karenga, "The African Intellectual and the Problem of Class Suicide", pp. 93–104.

11 Cabral, *Return to the Source*, p. 63.

12 On the Africana tradition of critical theory, see Reiland Rabaka, "Africana Critical Theory of Contemporary Society: Ruminations on Radical Politics, Social Theory and Africana Philosophy", in Molefi Kete Asante and Maulana Karenga (eds), *The Handbook of Black Studies* (Thousand Oaks, CA: Sage, 2006), pp. 130–51.

13 Tsenay Serequeberhan, *The Hermeneutics of African Philosophy: Horizon and Discourse* (New York: Routledge, 1994), p. 107.

14 Amilcar Cabral, *National Liberation and Culture: The Eduardo Mondlane Memorial Lecture*, trans. Maureen Webster (Syracuse: Syracuse University Press, 1970), *passim*; and Amilcar Cabral, "The Role of Culture in the Struggle", in Amilcar Cabral, *Resistance and Decolonization*, trans. and ed. Dan Wood (Lanham: Rowman and Littlefield International, 2016), pp. 159–80.

15 For further discussion of Africanité, see Rabaka, *The Négritude Movement*, pp. 200–24.

16 Frantz Fanon, *The Wretched of the Earth*, trans. Constance Farrington (New York: Grove, 1968), pp. 36–7.

17 Serequeberhan, *The Hermeneutics of African Philosophy*, pp. 102–15.

18 Fanon, *The Wretched of the Earth*, p. 232.

19 Cabral, *Return to the Source*, p. 68, all emphases in original.

20 Frantz Fanon, *Black Skin, White Masks*, trans. Charles Lam Markmann (New York: Grove, 1967), pp. 17–40.

21 Cabral, *Resistance and Decolonization*, pp. 75–156; Amilcar Cabral, *Our People Are Our Mountains: Amilcar Cabral on Guinean Revolution* (Nottingham: Russell Press, 1971);

Cabral, *Revolution in Guinea*; Fanon, *The Wretched of the Earth*, pp. 206–48; and Rabaka, *Concepts of Cabralism*, pp. 183–218; and Rabaka, *Forms of Fanonism*, pp. 271–304.

22 Cabral, *Unity and Struggle*, p. 143. On Cabral's conception of the "weapon of theory", see Amilcar Cabral, "The Weapon of Theory", in Amilcar Cabral, *Revolution in Guinea: Selected Texts*, trans. and ed. Richard Handyside (New York: Monthly Review Press, 1972), pp. 90–111.

23 Amílcar Cabral, *La Descolonizacion del Africa Portuguesa: Guinea-Bissau*, trans. Victor Fischman (Buenos Aires: Ediciones Periferia, 1975); and Rabaka, *Concepts of Cabralism*, pp. 183–218.

24 Cabral, *Unity and Struggle*, p. 150.

25 Cabral, *Unity and Struggle*, p. 150.

26 Cabral, *Revolution in Guinea*, pp. 134–51; Timothy W. Luke, "Cabral's Marxism: An African Strategy for Socialist Development", *Studies in Comparative Communism*, 14, 4 (1981), pp. 307–30; Bernard Magubane, "Amílcar Cabral: Evolution of Revolutionary Thought", *Ufahamu: A Journal of African Studies*, 2, 2 (1981), pp. 71–87; and Charles McCollester, "The Political Thought of Amílcar Cabral", *Monthly Review*, 24, 10 (1973), pp. 10–21.

27 Cabral, *Return to the Source*, p. 55, all emphases in original.

28 Cabral, *Resistance and Decolonization*, pp. 75–156; Chabal, *Amílcar Cabral*, pp. 167–87; Ameth Lo, "Amílcar Cabral and the Pan-African Revolution", in Firoze Manji and Bill Fletcher (eds), *Claim No Easy Victories: The Legacy of Amílcar Cabral* (Dakar, Senegal: CODESRIA/Daraja Press, 2013), pp. 61–78; and Olufemi Taiwo, "Cabral, Culture, Progress, and the Metaphysics of Difference", in Manji and Fletcher (eds), *Claim No Easy Victories*, pp. 355–64.

29 See Fanon, *The Wretched of the Earth*, pp. 35–95; Rabaka, *Forms of Fanonism*, pp. 97–215; and Rabaka, *Concepts of Cabralism*, pp. 113–42.

30 Rabaka, *Concepts of Cabralism*, pp. 151–251.

31 Cabral, *Return to the Source*, pp. 62–9; McCulloch, *In the Twilight of Revolution*, pp. 82–91; and Rabaka, *Concepts of Cabralism*, pp. 220–31.

32 Cabral, *Resistance and Decolonization*, pp. 75–179; Cabral, *Return to the Source*, pp. 39–69; Cabral, *Revolution in Guinea*, pp. 90–126; Cabral, *Unity and Struggle*, pp. 28–82; Davidson, "On Revolutionary Nationalism"; Hubbard, "Culture and History in a Revolutionary Context"; and Luke, "Cabral's Marxism."

33 Cabral, *Return to the Source*, pp. 62–9; Chabal, *Amílcar Cabral*, pp. 182–7.

34 Cabral, *Return to the Source*, pp. 75–92; Cabral, *Revolution in Guinea*, pp. 76–85, 152–64; Cabral, *Unity and Struggle*, pp. 160–73.

35 Fanon, *The Wretched of the Earth*, p. 233.

36 Herbert Marcuse, "A Revolution in Values", in Herbert Marcuse, *Towards a Critical Theory of Society: Collected Papers of Herbert Marcuse*, vol. 2, ed. Douglas Kellner (New York: Routledge, 2001), pp. 193–201; and Fanon, *The Wretched of the Earth*, p. 36.

37 Herbert Marcuse, "Cultural Revolution", pp. 121–62; Herbert Marcuse, "Liberation from the Affluent Society", in Stephen E. Bronner and Douglas Kellner (eds), *Critical Theory and Society: A Reader* (New York: Routledge, 1989), pp. 276–87.

38 Cabral, *Unity and Struggle*, pp. 56–7.

39 Cabral, "The Role of Culture in the Struggle", pp. 159–79. See also Peter Karibe Mendy, "Amílcar Cabral and the Liberation of Guinea-Bissau: Context, Challenges, and Lessons for Effective African Leadership", *African Identities*, 4, 1 (2006), pp. 7–21.

40 Cabral, *Resistance and Decolonization*, pp. 115–38; Chabal, *Amílcar Cabral*, pp. 188–219; McCulloch, *In the Twilight of Revolution*, pp. 82–91; and Alexis Wick, "Manifestations of

Nationhood in the Writings of Amílcar Cabral", *African Identities*, 4, 1 (2006), pp. 45–70.

41 Cabral, *Return to the Source*, p. 42.

42 Chabal, *Amílcar Cabral*, pp. 182–7.

43 Chabal, *Amílcar Cabral*, p. 187.

44 Chabal, *Amílcar Cabral*, pp. 182–7.

CHAPTER 26

1 This essay builds on the Steve Biko lecture that I delivered at the London School of Economics and Political Science (LSE) under the title: "Black Consciousness, Black Theology, Student Activism, and the Shaping of the New South Africa", on 9 October 2012.

2 *The Steve Biko Memorial Lectures 2000–2008* (Johannesburg: Pan Macmillan, 2017).

3 Xolela Mangcu, *Biko: A Life* (London: IB Tauris, 2014).

4 Mobogo Percy More, *Biko: Philosophy, Identity and Liberation* (Cape Town: HSRC Press, 2017) but see also Ian M. MacQueen: *Black Consciousness and Progressive Movements under Apartheid* (Pietermaritzburg: UKZN Press, 2018).

5 NUSAS was a student organisation founded on liberal principles. The culture and practice had been that while NUSAS leaders rejected apartheid, they did not actively oppose universities that imposed the law in this manner. Among students there was an unwritten code that defied the law. It was that ambiguity that Biko challenged.

6 Baruch Hirson, *Year of Fire, Year of Ash: The Soweto Revolt, Roots of a Revolution* (London: Zed Books, 2016 [1979]).

7 Frank Talk, "I Write What I Like", *SASO Newsletter*, 2, 1 (January/February 1972), p. 10.

8 Mabogo Percy More, "Locating Frantz Fanon in Post-Apartheid South Africa", *Journal of Asian and African Studies*, 52, 2 (2017), pp. 127-.

9 Frederick G. Weiss (ed.), *Hegel: The Essential Writings* (New York: Harper, 1975), p. 5.

10 Weiss, *Hegel*, p. 13.

11 Herbert Marcuse, *One-Dimensional Man: Studies in the Ideology of Advanced Industrial Society*, second edition (Boston: Beacon Press, 1991 [1964]).

12 Note the dialogue and discussion between Marcuse and Bryan Magee published in *Men of Ideas: Some Creators of Contemporary Philosophy* (London: BBC, 1978), pp. 62–73. This may well have been the last interview by Herbert Marcuse, who died in America in 1979.

13 Frantz Fanon, *The Wretched of the Earth* (New York: Grove Press, 1968).

14 Lewis R. Gordon, *What Fanon Said: A Philosophical Introduction to His Life and Thought* (New York: Fordham University Press, 2015). The following work has also investigated the interface between Fanon and Black Consciousness in South Africa: Nigel C. Gibson, *Fanonian Practices in South Africa: From Steve Biko to Abahlali baseMjondolo* (Pietermaritzburg: UKZN Press, 2011).

15 Frantz Fanon, *Black Skin, White Masks* (New York: Grove Press, 1967 [1952]).

16 Michael Neocosmos, *Thinking Freedom in Africa: Towards a Theory of Emancipatory Politics* (Johannesburg: Wits University Press, 2016) places Steve Biko and Black Consciousness firmly in the mould of the politics of liberation in South Africa.

17 Emmanuel Chukwudi Eze, *Reason, Memory and Politics* (Tshwane: University of South Africa, 2008).

18 Eze, *Reason, Memory and Politics*.

19 Eze, *Reason, Memory and Politics*, p. 66.

20 Eze, *Reason, Memory and Politics*, p. 67.

21 Steve Biko, *I Write What I Like* (Johannesburg: Picador Africa, 2008 [1978]), pp. 29–35.

22 Biko, *I Write What I Like*, p. 3.

23 Biko, *I Write What I Like*, p. 31.
24 Biko, *I Write What I Like*, p. 108.
25 Section 1(a) of the Constitution of the Republic of South Africa, 1996.
26 Malesela John Lamola, "Biko, Hegel and the End of Black Consciousness: A Historico-Philosophical Discourse on South African Racism", *Journal of Southern African Studies*, 42, 2 (2016), pp. 183–94.
27 Lamola, "Biko, Hegel and the End of Black Consciousness", pp. 183–94.
28 Lamola, "Biko, Hegel and the End of Black Consciousness".
29 Lamola, "Biko, Hegel and the End of Black Consciousness".
30 Lamola, "Biko, Hegel and the End of Black Consciousness".
31 Teresa M. Redd, *Revelations: An Anthology of Expository Essays by and about Blacks* (London: Pearson Custom Publishing, 2002), p. 461.
32 Redd, *Revelations*, p. 461.

CHAPTER 27

1 See for example Paulin J. Hountondji, "Knowledge as a Development Issue", in Kwasi Wired (ed.), *A Companion to African Philosophy* (Oxford: Blackwell, 2004), pp. 529–37; and Paulin J. Hountondji, "Global Knowledge: Imbalances and Current Tasks", in Guy Neave (ed.), *Knowledge, Power and Dissent: Critical Perspectives on Higher Education and Research in Knowledge Society* (Paris: UNESCO Publishing, 2006), pp. 41–60.
2 In a famous article, "Four Trends in Africa Philosophy", Henry Odera Oruka suggests, post-Hountondji's critique, that African Philosophy manifests itself as Ethnophilosophy, Sage Philosophy, Nationalistic-Political Philosophy and Professional-Academic Philosophy. See Alwin Diemer (ed.), *Philosophy in the Present Situation in Africa* (Weisbaden: Franz Steiner Erlgh, 1981), pp. 45–56.
3 Paulin J. Hountondji, *African Philosophy: Myth and Reality*, trans. Henri Evans and Jonathan Rée, 2nd edn (Bloomington: Indiana University Press, 1996), originally published as *Sur la "philosophie africaine": Critique de l'ethnophilosophie* (Paris: François Maspero, 1977).
4 Paulin J. Hountondji, *The Struggle for Meaning: Reflections on Philosophy, Culture and Democracy in Africa*, trans. John Conteh-Morgan (Athens: Ohio University Press, 2002), p. xi.
5 Paulin J. Hountondji, "Knowledge of Africa, Knowledge by Africans: Two Perspectives on African Studies", *RCCS Annual Review: An Online Journal for the Social Sciences and the Humanities*, issue no. 1 (2009), http://www.ces.uc.pt/publicacoes/annualreview/.
6 Frederick Ochieng'-Odhiambo, "The African Intellectual: Hountondji and After", *Radical Philosophy*, 164 (November/December 2010), pp. 25–37.
7 Hountondji refers to "modes of existence of the forms of knowledge", in *Struggle for Meaning*, p. 26.
8 In Klaus Gottstein and Götz Link (eds), *Cultural Development, Science and Technology in Sub-Saharan Africa* (Baden-Baden: Nomos Verlagsgesellschaft, 1986), pp. 109–13.
9 Paulin J. Hountondji, "Knowledge as Development Issue", in Kwasi Wiredu (ed.), *A Companion to African Philosophy* (Oxford: Blackwell, 2004), pp. 529–37.
10 See Paulin J. Hountondji, "Knowledge Appropriation in a Post-Colonial Context", in Catherine A. Odora-Hoppers (ed.), *Indigenous Knowledge and the Integration of Knowledge Systems: Towards a Philosophy of Articulation* (Cape Town: New Africa Books, 2002), pp. 23–38.
11 Archibald Mafeje, *Anthropology and Independent Africans: Suicide or End of an Era?* (Dakar: Council for the Development of Social Science Research in Africa, 1996).

12 Ngũgĩ wa Thiong'o, *Decolonising the Mind: The Politics of Language in African Literature* (Nairobi: Heinemann Kenya, 1986).

13 Literally meaning "On African Philosophy: A Critique of Ethnophilosophy".

14 Kwame A. Appiah in the preface to Hountondji, *Struggle for Meaning*, p. ix.

15 Barry Hallen, *A Short History of African Philosophy* (Bloomington: Indiana University Press, 2001), pp. 68–71.

16 Hountondji, *Myth and Reality*, p. 34.

17 Hountondji, *Myth and Reality*, p. vii.

18 Jacques Derrida, *Writing and Difference*, trans. Alan Bass (Chicago: Chicago University Press, 1978 [1967]).

19 Hountondji, *Myth and Reality*, p. viii.

20 Hountondji, *Myth and Reality*, p. viii.

21 Hountondji, *Struggle for Meaning*.

22 In Hountondji, *Struggle for Meaning*, pp. 80–5.

23 Paulin J. Hountondji, "Le Mythe de la philosophie spontanée", *Cahiers Philosophiques Africains*, 1 (1972), pp. 107–42.

24 Louis Althusser, *Philosophy and the Spontaneous Philosophy of the Scientists and Other Essays*, trans. George Elliot (London: Verso, 1990 [1967]).

25 Paulin J. Hountondji, "The Myth of Spontaneous Philosophy", *Conséquence: Revue du Conseil Interafricain de Philosophie*, no.1 (1974), pp. 11–37.

26 Bruce B. Janz, "The Folds in Paulin Hountondji's 'African Philosophy, Myth and Reality'", *Philosophical Papers*, 39, 1 (2010), p. 120 .

27 Louis Althusser, *For Marx* (Harmondsworth: Penguin Press, 1969), p. 19.

28 Hountondji, *Struggle for Meaning*, p. 137.

29 Hountondji "Knowledge of Africa, Knowledge by Africans", p. 4.

30 Hountondji, *Myth and Reality*, p. 53.

31 Hountondji, *Myth and Reality*, p. 53.

32 Hountondji, *Myth and Reality*, p. 33.

33 Kwame Gyekye, *An Essay on African Philosophical Thought: The Akan Conceptual Scheme*, 2nd edn (Cambridge: Cambridge University Press, 1995 [1987]).

34 Henry Odera Oruka, *Sage Philosophy: Indigenous Thinkers and Modern Debate on African Philosophy* (Nairobi: ACTS Press, 1991).

35 Hountondji, *Myth and Reality*, p. 38.

36 Hountondji, *Struggle for Meaning*, p. 73.

37 Hountondji, *Struggle for Meaning*, p. 35.

38 Hountondji, "Knowledge of Africa, Knowledge by Africans", p. 8.

39 Hountondji, "Knowledge of Africa, Knowledge by Africans", p. 8.

40 Hountondji, "Knowledge of Africa, Knowledge by Africans", p. 8.

41 Althusser, *For Marx*, pp. 17–18.

42 Paulin J. Hountondji (ed.), *Economie et société au Bénin*, preface by Samir Amin (Paris: L'Harmattan, 2000).

43 Kwame Nkrumah, *Consciencism: Philosophy and Ideology for Decolonization* (London: Panaf Books, 1964).

44 Hountondji, *Myth and Reality*, pp. 131–40.

45 Hountondji, *Myth and Reality*, pp. 141–56.

46 Kwame Nkrumah, "African Socialism Revisited", in *Africa: National and Social Revolution: Collection of Papers Read at the Cairo Seminar* (Prague: Peace and Socialism Publishers, 1967), www.marxists.org/subject/africa/nkrumah/1967/african-socialism-revisited.htm.

47 Hountondji, "Knowledge of Africa, Knowledge by Africans", p. 10.
48 Paulin Hountondji, "From the Ethnosciences to Ethnophilosophy: The Thesis Project of Kwame Nkrumah", *Research in African Literatures*, 28, 4 (1998), pp. 112–20.
49 Quoted in Hountondji, *Struggle for Meaning*, p. 165.
50 Hountondji, *Struggle for Meaning*, p. xi.
51 Dismas A. Masolo, *Self and Community in a Changing World* (Bloomington: Indiana University Press, 2010).
52 Janz, "The Folds in Paulin Hountondji's 'African Philosophy, Myth and Reality'", pp. 117–34.
53 Janz, "The Folds in Paulin Hountondji" p.122.
54 Janz, "The Folds in Paulin Hountondji" p.134.
55 Janz, "The Folds in Paulin Hountondji", p. 120.
56 Janz, "The Folds in Paulin Hountondji", p. 132.
57 Janz, "The Folds in Paulin Hountondji", p. 124.
58 Hountondji, *Struggle for Meaning*, p. 11.
59 Janz, "The Folds in Paulin Hountondji", p. 67.
60 See M. John Lamola, "Marxism as a Science of Interpretation: Beyond Althusser", *South African Journal of Philosophy*, 32, 2 (2013), pp. 187–96.
61 See "epistemological break" in http://www.oxfordreference.com/view/10.1093/oi/authority.20110803095755104.
62 Hountondji, *Struggle for Meaning*, p. 71.
63 Hountondji, *Myth and Reality*, p. 75.
64 Karl Marx, *Capital: A Critical Analysis of Capitalist Production*, vol. 1 (London: Lawrence and Wishart, 1974 [1867].
65 Hountondji, *Struggle for Meaning*, p. 9.
66 Hountondji, *Struggle for Meaning*, p. 31.
67 Hountondji, *Struggle for Meaning*, p. 53.
68 Hountondji, *Struggle for Meaning*, p. 53.
69 Hountondji, "Knowledge of Africa, Knowledge by Africans", p. 12.
70 Hountondji, "Knowledge of Africa, Knowledge by Africans", p. xx.
71 Hountondji, *Myth and Reality*, p. 12.

CHAPTER 28

1 See Evan Mwangi, "Gender, Unreliable Oral Narration and the Untranslated Preface in Ngũgĩ wa Thiong'o's *Devil on the Cross*", *Research in African Literatures*, 38, 4 (2007).
2 See Emmanuel Chukwudi Eze, "Modern Western Philosophy and African Colonialism", in Emmanuel Chukwudi Eze, *African Philosophy: An Anthology* (Massachusetts: Blackwell, 1998).
3 See Léopold Senghor, "We Are All Cultural Half-Castes", *Présence Africaine*, 1956, pp. xiii–v.
4 Bernadette Cailler, "The Impossible Ecstasy: An Analysis of V.Y. Mudimbe's *Déchirures*", *Research in African Literatures*, 24, 4 (1993), p. 15.
5 See Barry Hallen, "Contemporary Anglophone African Philosophy: A Survey", in Kwasi Wiredu, *A Companion to African Philosophy* (Oxford: Blackwell Publishing, 2007), p. 118.
6 Hallen, "Contemporary Anglophone African Philosophy", p. 118.
7 See D.C. Makinson, "The Paradox of the Preface", *Analysis*, 25, 6 (1965), p. 205.
8 V.Y. Mudimbe, *Déchirures* (Kinshasa: Editions du Mont Noir, 1971), p. 6.
9 See the end of Ama Ata Aidoo's preface to *African Love Stories: An Anthology* (Banbury: Ayebia Clarke, 2006), p. vi.

10 See Chinua Achebe, "The Writer as Novelist", in *Morning Yet on Creation Day* (New York: Garden City, 1975).

11 V.Y. Mudimbe takes up this issue more directly in his novel *Shaba deux: Les Carnets de Mère Marie-Gertrude* (Paris: Présence Africaine, 1989), while in their introduction to *The Mudimbe Reader* (Charlottesville: University of Virginia Press, 2016), Pierre-Philippe Fraiture and Daniel Orrells discuss Mudimbe's opposition to Mobutu's project of nationalisation in Zaïre.

12 Isidore Okpewho explains the fundamentals of African oral literature in *African Oral Literature: Backgrounds, Character, and Continuity* (Bloomington: Indiana University Press, 1992).

13 V.Y. Mudimbe recounts how he left his family home at an early age to join a Benedictine seminary; V.Y. Mudimbe, *Parables and Fables: Exegesis, Textuality, and Politics in Central Africa* (Madison: University of Wisconsin Press, 1991), p. 94. He expands further on this issue in Mudimbe, *Tales of Faith: Religion as Political Performance in Central Africa* (New York: Continuum International Publishing Group, 1997).

14 See Mudimbe, *Déchirures*, p. 6.

15 See Cailler, "The Impossible Ecstasy", p. 16.

16 Cailler, "The Impossible Ecstasy", p. 16.

17 See Neil Lazarus, "Representation and Terror in V.Y. Mudimbe", *Journal of African Cultural Studies*, 17, 1 (2005), p. 90.

18 These critiques run through V.Y. Mudimbe, *The Invention of Africa: Gnosis, Philosophy and the Order of Knowledge* (Bloomington: Indiana University Press, 1988), and V.Y. Mudimbe, *The Idea of Africa* (Bloomington: Indiana University Press, 1994).

19 See Cailler, "The Impossible Ecstasy", pp. 16–17.

20 Mudimbe, *The Invention of Africa*, p. 154.

21 Chinua Achebe: *Things Fall Apart* (London: Heinemann, 1958).

22 V.Y. Mudimbe's *Shaba deux: Les Carnets de Mère Marie-Gertrude* is about a Zaïrean nun who is abandoned by her white colleagues after she involves herself in the conflicts that marked the country in the late 1970s. In "African Gnosis: Philosophy and the Order of Knowledge", *African Studies Review*, 28, 3 (1985), Mudimbe explicitly identifies religion as an effective cloak of the colonising enterprise. In both cases, Mudimbe demonises the role of Western religion.

23 For seminal perspectives on this classic debate, see Obi Wali, "The Dead End of African Literature?", *Transition*, 10 (1963); Ngũgĩ wa Thiong'o, *Decolonising the Mind: The Politics of Language in African Literature* (London: James Currey, 1986); and Chinua Achebe, "The African Writer and the English Language", in *Morning Yet on Creation Day* (New York: Garden City, 1975).

CHAPTER 29

1   Kwame Anthony Appiah, *In My Father's House: Africa in the Philosophy of Culture* (New York: Oxford University Press, 1992).

2   Appiah, *In My Father's House*, p. 25.

3   Kwame Anthony Appiah, *Cosmopolitanism: Ethics in a World of Strangers* (London: Allen Lane, 2006), p. 104.

4   Appiah, *Cosmopolitanism*, p. 104.

5   Appiah, *Cosmopolitanism*, p. 113.

6   Appiah, *In My Father's House*, p. 45.

7   Appiah, *In My Father's House*, pp. 20–5.

8   Appiah, *In My Father's House*, p. 20.

9   Appiah, *In My Father's House*, p. 107.
10 Emmanuel Akyeampong, "The Power of Constructed Identities? Thinking through Ethnicity in Africa", *Institute of African Studies Research Review* (University of Ghana, Legon), New Series, 22, 2 (2006).
11 Appiah, *Cosmopolitanism*, p. 322.
12 Appiah, *In My Father's House*, p. 26.
13 Appiah, *In My Father's House*, p. 14.
14 Appiah, *In My Father's House*, p. 14.
15 Appiah, *In My Father's House*, p. 13.
16 Appiah, *In My Father's House*, p. 15.
17 Appiah, *In My Father's House*, p. 13.
18 Appiah, *In My Father's House*, p. 107.
19 Appiah, *In My Father's House*, p. 17.
20 Appiah, *In My Father's House*, p. 45.
21 William Edward Burghardt Du Bois, *The Souls of Black Folk* (New York: Penguin Books, 1996 [1903]), p. 178.
22 William Edward Burghardt Du Bois, *Dusk of Dawn: An Essay Toward an Autobiography of a Race Concept* (Philadelphia: University of Pennsylvania Press, 1980 [1940]), p. 31.
23 Appiah, *In My Father's House*, p. 45.
24 Appiah, *In My Father's House*, ch. 2.
25 Kwame Anthony Appiah, "Liberalism, Individualism and Identity", *Critical Inquiry*, 27, 2 (Winter 2001), pp. 305–32.
26 Appiah, "Liberalism, Individualism, and Identity", p. 331.
27 Appiah, *In My Father's House*, p. 45.
28 Appiah, *In My Father's House*, p. 45.
29 Appiah, *In My Father's House*, p. 45.
30 Malcolm X, *The Autobiography of Malcolm X* (London: Penguin Books, 1978 [1965]), pp. 465–6.
31 Kwame Nkrumah, *Ghana: The Autobiography of Kwame Nkrumah* (London: Panaf, 1957), p. 12.
32 Tajudeen Abdul-Raheem (ed.), *Pan-Africanism: Politics, Economy and Social Change in the Twenty-First Century* (New York: New York University Press, 1996).
33 Kwadwo Afari-Gyan, "Kwame Nkrumah, George Padmore and W.E.B. Du Bois", *Institute of African Studies Research Review* (University of Ghana, Legon), 7, 1&2 (1991), p. 7
34 Appiah, *In My Father's House*, p. 45.
35 Nkrumah, *Ghana*, p. 152.
36 Nkrumah, *Ghana*, p. 153.
37 Appiah, *In My Father's House*, p. 19.
38 Marcus Garvey, *The Philosophy and Opinions of Marcus Garvey, or, Africa for the African* (New York: Universal Publishing House, 1923).
39 Nkrumah, Autobiography *of Kwame Nkrumah*, pp. 153–4.
40 Nkrumah, *Autobiography of Kwame Nkrumah*, pp. 153–4.
41 Nkrumah, *Autobiography of Kwame Nkrumah*, p. 12.
42 Du Bois, *Dusk of Dawn*, pp. 192–3.
43 Wilson Jeremiah Moses, *Alexander Crummell: A Study of Civilization and Discontent* (New York: Oxford University Press, 1989), p. 228.
44 Malcolm X, *The Autobiography of Malcolm X*, p. 470; and Malcolm X and Tahar Gaid, Digital Howard, Howard University, https://dh.howard.edu/pp_negatives/1881/, accessed 14 May 2019.

45 Appiah, *In My Father's House*, p. 19.
46 Appiah, *In My Father's House*, p. 19.
47 Du Bois, *Dusk of Dawn*, p. 294.
48 Du Bois, *Dusk of Dawn*, p. 294.
49 Du Bois, *Dusk of Dawn*, pp. 290–1.
50 Appiah, *In My Father's House*, p. 19.
51 Appiah, *In My Father's House*, p. 19.
52 Appiah, "Liberalism, Individualism and Identity", p. 331.
53 Appiah, "Liberalism, Individualism and Identity", p. 331.
54 Appiah, "Liberalism, Individualism and Identity", p. 331.
55 Appiah, "Liberalism, Individualism and Identity", p. 331. See also Horace Campbell, "Pan Africanism in the Twenty-First Century", in Abdul-Raheem, *Pan-Africanism*, pp. 212–28.
56 Appiah, "Liberalism, Individualism, and Identity", p. 331.
57 CLAGS (Center for LGBTQ Studies), *Queer Afropolitans: Mark Gevisser and Kwame Anthony Appiah in Conversation*, The Graduate Center, CUNY, New York, 6 May 2014, https://www.youtube.com/watch?v=ggSfFsDvUHA.
58 Appiah, "Liberalism, Individualism and Identity", p. 331.
59 Appiah, *In My Father's House*, p. 17.
60 Appiah, *In My Father's House*, p. 19
61 Appiah, "Liberalism, Individualism and Identity", p. 311.
62 Appiah, *Cosmopolitanism*, p. 104.
63 Du Bois, *Dusk of Dawn*, p. 275.
64 Homi K. Bhabha, "Race, Time and the Revision of Modernity", in Bill Ashcroft, Gareth Griffiths and Helen Tiffin (eds), *The Post-Colonial Studies Reader* (London and New York: Routledge, 2006), pp. 219–23.

CHAPTER 30

1   See Liliane Kesteloot, *Les Ecrivains noirs de langue française* (Brussels: Institute of Sociology of the Free University of Brussels, 1963); and Donna V. Jones, *The Racial Discourses of Life Philosophies: Négritude, Vitalism and Modernity* (New York: Columbia University Press, 2010).
2   See Naomi Mills Garrett, *The Renaissance of Haitian Poetry* (Paris: Présence Africaine, 1963).
3   Aimé Césaire, *Aimé Césaire: The Collected Poetry*, translated by Clayton Eshleman and Annette Smith (Berkeley: University of California Press, 1983), p. 101.
4   See Léopold Sédar Senghor, *Anthologie de la nouvelle poésie nègre et malgache de langue française* (Paris: Presses Universitaires de France, 1948).
5   Léopold Sédar Senghor, *Chants d'ombre* (Paris: Seuil, 1956 [1945]).
6   Léopold Sédar Senghor, *Nocturnes* (London: Heinemann, 1969).
7   Senghor, *Nocturnes*.
8   Léopold Sédar Senghor, *Hosties noires* (Paris: Seuil, 1948).
9   Senghor, *Hosties noires*.
10 See Léopold Sédar Senghor, *The Collected Poetry of Léopold Senghor*, translated with an Introduction by Melvin Dixon (Charlottesville: University of Virginia press, 1991).
11 See Senghor, *The Collected Poetry of Léopold Senghor*.
12 See Catherine Awoundja Nasata, *L'Épopée des peuples noirs* (Yaoundé: Editions CLE, 2016).
13 Léopold Sédar Senghor, *Liberté 1: Négritude et humanisme* (Paris: Seuil, 1964).

14 Léopold Sédar Senghor, *Liberté 1: Négritude et humanisme*; *Liberté 2: Nation et voie africaine du socialisme* (Paris: Seuil, 1971); *Liberté 3: Négritude et civilisation de universel* (Paris: Seuil, 1977); *Liberté 4: Socialisme et planification* (Paris: Seuil, 1983); and *Liberté 5: Le Dialogue des cultures* (Paris: Seuil, 1993).

15 Léopold Sédar Senghor, *Pierre Teilhard de Chardin et la politique africaine* (Paris: Seuil, 1962).

16 Léopold Sédar Senghor, "Ce que l'homme noir apporte", in Claude Nordey (ed.), *L'Homme de couleur* (Paris: Coll. Présences Plon, 1939), p. 295.

17 See Olaudah Equiano, *The Life of Olaudah Equiano, or, Gustavus Vassa, the African* (London: Heinemann, 1967 [1789]).

18 See Hollis Lynch, *Edward Wilmot Blyden, Pan-Negro Patriot, 1832–1912* (London: Oxford University Press, 1967).

19 See, for example, Ousmane Kane, *Beyond Timbuktu: An Intellectual History of Muslim West Africa* (Cambridge, MA: Harvard University Press, 2017).

20 Pixley Seme, "The Regeneration of Africa", Address at Columbia University, New York, 5 April 1906, www.anc.org.za.

21 Sol Plaatje, *Mhudi* (Cape Town: Penguin, 2006 [1930]).

22 Zakes Mda, *The Heart of Redness* (New York: Farrar, Straus and Giroux, 2002).

23 See Cheikh Anta Diop, *African Origins of Civilization: Myth or Reality* (Chicago: Lawrence Hill Books, 1974).

24 Ezekiel Mphahlele, *The African Image* (London: Faber, 1974).

25 Wole Soyinka, "And after the Narcissist", *African Forum*, 1, 4 (Spring 1966), pp. 53–64.

26 Wole Soyinka, "The Fourth Stage: Through the Mysteries of Ogun to the Origin of Yoruba Tragedy", in *Art, Dialogue and Outrage: Essays on Literature and Culture* (New York: Pantheon Books, 1993), pp. 27–39.

27 Steve Biko, *I Write What I Like* (New York and London: Penguin, 1988, first published in 1978), pp.116–7.

28 Biko, *I Write What I Like*, p. 117.

29 See, for example, Thabo Mbeki, "Prologue", in Malegapuru William Makgoba (ed.), *African Renaissance* (Cape Town: Mafube and Tafelberg, 1999), pp. xiii–xxi.

30 Reiland Rabaka. *The Négritude Movement* (Lanham: Lexington Books, 2015).

31 V.Y. Mudimbe: *The Invention of Africa: Gnosis, Philosophy, and the Order of Knowledge* (Bloomington: Indiana University Press, 1988).

CHAPTER 31

1 Chinua Achebe made this remark to the Nigerian media shortly after Wole Soyinka won the Nobel Prize for Literature in 1986.

2 Wole Soyinka, *The Interpreters* (London; Andre Deutsch, 1965).

3 Wole Soyinka, *The Burden of Memory, the Muse of Forgiveness* (New York: Oxford University Press, 1999), p. 90.

4 See Wole Soyinka, *The Man Died* (London: Penguin, 1972).

5 This famous dismissive remark was made in response to the publication of *Myth, Literature and the African World*.

6 See Wole Soyinka, *Myth, Literature and the African World* (Cambridge: Cambridge University Press, 1976).

7 See Wole Soyinka, *Aké: The Years of Childhood* (New York: Random House, 1982).

8 See Chinweizu Ibekwe, Jamie Onwuchekwa and Ihechukwu Madubuike, *Towards the Decolonization of African Literature: African Fiction and Poetry and Their Critics* (London: KPI, 1980).

9   See Wole Soyinka, *Isara: A Voyage around Essay* (New York: Random House, 1989); and *Ibadan: The Penkelemes Years – A Memoir, 1945–1965* (London: Methuen, 1994).

10 Soyinka, *The Burden of Memory, the Muse of Forgiveness*, pp. 26–7.

11 Soyinka, *The Burden of Memory, the Muse of Forgiveness*, p. 31.

12 Soyinka, *The Burden of Memory, the Muse of Forgiveness*, pp. 38–9.

13 Soyinka, *The Burden of Memory, the Muse of Forgiveness*, p. 40.

14 Soyinka, *The Burden of Memory, the Muse of Forgiveness*, p. 40.

15 Soyinka, *The Burden of Memory, the Muse of Forgiveness*, pp. 71–2.

16 Wole Soyinka, *Harmattan Haze on an African Spring* (Ibadan: Bookcraft, 2012), p. 62.

17 Soyinka, *Harmattan Haze on an African Spring*, p. 73.

18 This section builds on Sanya Osha, "Rage against That Good Night", *Africa Review of Books*, 12, 2 (September 2016).

19 Wole Soyinka, *Between Defective Memory and the Public Lie: A Personal Odyssey in the Republic of Liars* (Ibadan: Bookcraft, 2015), p. 35.

20 Soyinka, *Harmattan Haze on an African Spring*, p. 23.

21 Wole Soyinka, *King Baabu* (London: Methuen, 2002).

22 See Osha, "Rage against That Good Night".

Chapter 32

1   Derek Walcott, "The Figure of Crusoe", in Robert D. Hamner (ed.), *Critical Perspectives on Derek Walcott* (Washington, DC: Three Continents Press, 1993), p. 38.

2   Ozzy King, "The Myth of My Own Self", *Moko*, 7 (November 2015), p. 109

3   The Nobel Prize in Literature, 1992, https://www.nobelprize.org/prizes/literature/1992/summary/.

4   James Anthony Froude, *The English in the West Indies: or, The Bow of Ulysses* (London: Longman's, Green, 1888), p. 306.

5   Vidiadhar Surajprasad Naipaul, *The Middle Passage* (Harmondsworth: Penguin, 1969), p. 29.

6   Derek Walcott, "Another Life", in *Collected Poems 1948–1984* (New York: Farrar, Straus and Giroux, 1988), p. 269.

7   Edward Baugh, "The West Indian Writer and His Quarrel with History", *Small Axe: A Journal of Criticism* (2012), p. 71.

8   Walcott, "Another Life", p. 270.

9   Sun Ra, "Detroit Black Journal: Sun Ra" (1981), YouTube video, https://www.youtube.com/watch?v=mNgwzY0KzlM.

10 Derek Walcott, "The Muse of History", in *What the Twilight Says* (London: Faber and Faber, 1998), p. 56.

11 Derek Walcott, "The Schooner Flight", in *Collected Poems 1948–1984*, p. 346.

12 Derek Walcott, "Meanings", in *Savacou*, 2 (1970), p. 51.

13 Walcott, "Meanings", p. 51.

14 Walcott, "The Muse of History", p. 37.

15 Walcott, "The Muse of History", p. 37.

16 Derek Walcott, "The Caribbean: Culture or Mimicry", in Hamner (ed.), *Critical Perspectives on Derek Walcott*, p. 57.

17 Walcott, "The Muse of History", pp. 42–3.

18 Walcott, "What the Twilight Says", p. 16.

19 Walcott, "The Caribbean: Culture or Mimicry", p. 52.

20 Walcott, "The Muse of History", p. 53.

21 Baugh, "The West Indian Writer and his Quarrel with History", p. 70.

22 Baugh, "The West Indian Writer and His Quarrel with History", p. 71.

23 Walcott, "The Muse of History", p. 40.

24 Derek Walcott, "The Art of Poetry no. 37", interview with Edward Hirsch, *Paris Review*, 7, https://www.theparisreview.org/interviews/2719/derek-walcott-the-art-of-poetry-no-37-derek-walcott.

25 Froude, *The English in the West Indies*, p. 306

26 Walcott, "The Art of Poetry no. 37".

27 Walcott, "The Art of Poetry no. 37".

28 Rachael D. Friedman, "Call and Response: Derek Walcott's Collaboration with Homer in His 'The Odyssey': A Stage Version", *Arethusa*, 48, 1 (2015), p. 59 (emphasis mine).

29 Derek Walcott, "Leaving School", in Hamner, *Critical Perspectives on Derek Walcott*, pp. 24–32.

30 Walcott, "What the Twilight Says", p. 6.

31 Derek Walcott, *Omeros* (New York: Farrar, Straus and Giroux, 1992), pp. 282–3.

32 Walcott, "What the Twilight Says", p. 16.

33 Walcott, "The Muse of History", p. 64.

34 Earl Lovelace, "A Work in Progress", Speech delivered in Port of Spain, Trinidad, 18 March 2017.

Chapter 33

1 Buchi Emecheta, *Head above Water* (Oxford: Heinemann, 1994).

2 In this chapter, when discussing *In the Ditch* and *Second-Class Citizen*, I will quote from *Adah's Story*.

3 Emecheta, *Head above Water*, p.1.

4 Emecheta, *Head above Water*, p. 6.

5 Buchi Emecheta, "A Nigerian Writer Living in London", *Kunapipi*, 4, 1 (1982), p. 117.

6 Buchi Emecheta held a degree in sociology.

7 Emecheta, *Head above Water*, p. 6.

8 Emecheta, *Head above Water*, pp. 7–8.

9 Louisa Uchum Egbunike, "Narrating the Past: Orality, History and the Production of Knowledge in the Works of Chimamanda Ngozi Adichie", in Ernest Emenyonu (ed.), *A Companion to Chimamanda Ngozi Adichie* (Woodbridge: James Currey, 2017), p. 18.

10 Buchi Emecheta, *Adah's Story: A Novel* (London: Allison and Busby, 1983), p. 9.

11 Emecheta, *Adah's Story*, p. 156.

12 Emecheta, *Adah's Story*, p. 31.

13 Emecheta, *Adah's Story*, p. 35.

14 Emecheta, *Adah's Story*, p. 34.

15 In addition to this, in post-Second World War Britain, requests were made in Jamaican newspapers for people to come and work in Britain as part of the country's post-war reconstruction. Many Caribbean people settled in Britain, and so these Jamaican/Caribbean communities constituted part of this "homogenised" diaspora, although the initial motivations for migration were for work rather than for study.

16 Emecheta, *Adah's Story*, p. 9.

17 The 'Windrush scandal' refers to the deportation of members of the 'Windrush generation' after Theresa May at the Home Office sought to create a 'hostile environment' for so-called 'illegal immigrants'. Changes to Britain's immigration policy in 2012 left some members of the Windrush generation vulnerable to deportation or unable to access welfare even though they had the right to live and work in Britain and the right to access public services. When the immigration policy changes were announced, the Home Office was made aware of the impact the changes would have on some members of the Windrush

generation. Their decision to proceed in spite of these warnings indicates that the rights of the Windrush generation has not yet been fully realised. See, for example, Colin Grant, *Homecoming: Voices of the Windrush Generation* (London: Jonathan Cape, 2019).

18   Paul Gilroy, *There Ain't No Black in the Union Jack* (Chicago: University of Chicago Press, 1991), p. 39.

19   Buchi Emecheta, *Gwendolen* (London: Flamingo, 1989), p. 41.

20   Chikwenye Okonjo, *Africa Wo/man Palava: The Nigerian Novel by Women* (Chicago: University of Chicago Press, 1996), p. 278.

21   Emecheta, *Gwendolen*, p. 237.

22   Emecheta, *Gwendolen*.

23   Stuart Hall, "Cultural Identity and Diaspora", in J. Rutherford (ed.), *Identity: Community, Culture, Difference* (London: Lawrence and Wishart, 1990), p. 395.

24   Hall, "Cultural Identity and Diaspora", p. 395.

25   Emecheta, *Gwendolen*, p. 237.

26   Emecheta, *Head above Water*, p. 140.

27   Buchi Emecheta, "The Dilemma of Being in between Two Cultures", in Raoul Granqvist and John Stotesbury (eds), *African Voices: Interviews with Thirteen African Writers* (Sydney: Dangaroo Press, 1989).

28   Emecheta, "A Nigerian Writer Living in London", p. 123.

29   Oladipo Joseph Ogundele, "A Conversation with Dr. Buchi Emecheta", in Marie Umeh (ed.), *Emerging Perspectives on Buchi Emecheta* (Trenton: Africa World Press, 1996), p. 450.

CHAPTER 34

1   Mame Coumba Ndiaye, *Mariama Bâ ou les allées d'un destin* (Dakar: Nouvelles Éditions du Sénégal, 2007), p. 260.

2   Simone Schwarz-Bart and André Schwarz-Bart, *In Praise of Black Women, vol. 3: Modern African Women* (translation of *Hommage à la femme noire: Femmes africaines modernes* by Rose-Myriam Réjouis and Val Vinokurov), (Madison: Modus Vivendi Publications, University of Wisconsin Press, 2003), p. 94.

3   It was said that the colonial masters paid the Senegalese "two bobs" for slave wage for their labour. The Senegalese then learnt to call them derogatively "the people of two bobs", or simply "les toubabs".

4   Schwarz-Bart and Schwarz-Bart, *In Praise of Black Women*, p. 98.

5   Mariama Bâ, "La fonction politique des littératures Africaines écrites", Écritures française dans le monde, 5, 3 (1981), pp. 3–7. Translated as "The Political Functions of Written African Literatures", in Ada Uzoamaka Azodo (ed.), *Emerging Perspectives on Mariama Bâ: Feminism, Postcolonialism, Feminism, and Postmodernism* (Trenton: African World Press, 2003), pp. 411–16.

6   Azodo, *Emerging Perspectives on Mariama Bâ*, pp. 411–16.

7   Cited in Ali A. Mazrui, *The African Condition: A Political Diagnosis* (Cambridge and New York: Cambridge University Press, 1980), p. 6.

8   Harm J. de Blij and Peter O. Muller (eds), *Geography, Regions and Concepts* (New York: John Wiley and Sons, 1993), p. 42. See also Azodo, "The Multifaceted Aidoo: Ideologue, Scholar, Writer and Woman", in *Emerging Perspectives on Ama Ata Aidoo*, p. 402.

9   Ada Uzoamaka Azodo, *African Feminisms in the Global Arena: Gender, Class, Ethnicity and Race*, (Glassboro, NJ: Goldline and Jacobs, 2019). This work argues that race and gender together are oppressive to women in the world.

10   This piece would later be published with a more succinct title as "Petite patrie" ("A Dakar Childhood").

11 François René de Chateaubriand (1768–1848) or François-René, Vicomte de Chateaubriand, a writer, politician, diplomat and historian, descendant of an old aristocratic family from Brittany, who was the founder of Romanticism in French literature. François René de Chateaubriand was also a royalist, who defended Catholicism in *Genie du christianisme*, in an era when some intellectuals turned against the church. His works include the autobiography *Mémoires d'outre-tombe*, which was published posthumously in 1849–50.

12 *Notes Africaines*, 35 (July 1947), pp. 16–17. See also Azodo, *Emerging Perspectives on Mariama Bâ*, p. 420, and *Mariama Bâ ou les allés d'un destin*, pp. 179-89, which focuses on what Senegal was like before the advent of European colonialism, as well as Bâ's castigation of the French assimilationist policy in French West Africa in general.

13 Schwarz-Bart and Schwarz-Bart, *In Praise of Black Women*, p. 102.

14 Schwarz-Bart and Schwarz-Bart, *In Praise of Black Women*, p. 100.

15 Mariama Bâ, *Une si longue lettre* (Dakar: Nouvelles Éditions Africaines, 1980), p. 16.

16 Ndiaye, *Mariama Bâ ou les allées d'un destin*, p. 47.

17 Ndiaye, *Mariama Bâ ou les allées d'un destin*, p. 54.

18 Reported by Ndiaye, in *Mariama Bâ ou les allées d'un destin*, pp. 140-1.

19 Mame Coumba Ndiaye in *Mariama Bâ ou les allées d'un destin*, p. 46, reports Mariama Bâ's ambivalence because of the tensions created in her by tradition and modernity, which in the long run affected her love life, which invariably ended before it even started.

20 Schwarz-Bart and Schwarz-Bart, *In Praise of Black Women*, p. 96.

21 This is a form of investment in finance and insurance industry in which, when an investor dies, his or her share of the investment is divided among the other remaining investors.

22 Bâ, *Une si longue lettre*. Translated by Modupé Bodé-Thomas as Mariama Bâ, *So Long a Letter* (Ibadan and London: Heinemann, 1980).

23 Mariama Bâ, *Un chant écarlate* (Dakar: Les Nouvelles Éditions Africaines, 1984); and Mariama Bâ, *Scarlet Song* (New York: Longman, 1981).

24 Ndiaye, *Mariama Bâ ou les allées d'un destin*, pp. 158-63.

25 Bâ, "La fonction politique des littératures Africaines écrites", pp. 3–7.

26 John J. Macionis and Vincent N. Parrillo, *Cities and Urban Life* (New York: Pearson Education, Inc., 2017).

27 Melville J. Herskovits, *The Human Factor in Changing Africa* (New York: Routledge, 2013 [1962]).

28 See Omofolabo Ajayi-Soyinka, "Négritude, Feminism and the Quest for Identity: Re-Reading Mariama Bâ's *So Long a Letter*", in Azodo (ed.), *Emerging Perspectives on Mariama Bâ*, pp. 153–74.

29 Schwarz-Bart and Schwarz-Bart, *In Praise of Black Women*, p. 102.

30 Schwarz-Bart and Schwarz-Bart, *In Praise of Black Women*, p. 102.

31 Schwarz-Bart and Schwarz-Bart, *In Praise of Black Women*, p. 98.

32 Bâ, *Une si longue lettre*, p. 1.

33 Bâ, *Une si longue lettre*, p. 17.

34 Bâ, *Une si longue lettre*, p. 31.

35 Bâ, *Une si longue lettre*, p. 32.

36 Bâ, *Une si longue lettre*, p. 4.

37 Bâ, *Une si longue lettre*, p. 4.

38 SICAP (many times written simply as "Sicap") is a "privatised" real estate company that builds luxurious homes and villas in and around Dakar, Senegal.

39 SICAP homes, compared to those of HLM (Habitations-à-loyer-modéré) – subsidised (project) housing for the poor and underprivileged – are luxury homes and villas of grand standing. Some of the many Sicap areas in and around Dakar in Senegal include, but are

not limited to, Sicap Amitié 3, Dieupeul, Mermoz, Baobab, Grand Mbao, Karak, Rue Dix, Keur-Massar, Lac Rose, Sacré Coeur and Liberté.

40 Bâ, *Une si longue lettre*, p. 10.
41 Bâ, *Une si longue lettre*, pp. 6–7.
42 Bâ, *Une si longue lettre*, p. 8.
43 Bâ, *Une si longue lettre*, p. 18.
44 Bâ, *Une si longue lettre*, p. 19.
45 Bâ, *Une si longue lettre*, p. 24.
46 Bâ, *Un chant écarlate*, p. 28.
47 Bâ, *Une si longue lettre*, p. 25.
48 Bâ, *Une si longue lettre*, p. 72.
49 Bâ, *Une si longue lettre*, p. 26.
50 Bâ, *Une si longue lettre*, p. 35.
51 Bâ, *Une si longue lettre*, pp. 36–9.
52 Bâ, *Une si longue lettre*, pp. 54–5.
53 Bâ, *Une si longue lettre*, p. 64.
54 Bâ, *Une si longue lettre*, p. 64.
55 Bâ, *Une si longue lettre*, p. 65.
56 Bâ, *Une si longue lettre*, p. 67.
57 Bâ, *Une si longue lettre*, pp. 82, 84.
58 Bâ, *Une si longue lettre*, pp. 59–81.
59 Bâ, *Une si longue lettre*, p. 81
60 Bâ, *Une si longue lettre*, p. 92.
61 Bâ, *Une si longue lettre*, p. 92.
62 Bâ, *Une si longue lettre*, p. 93.
63 See Ada Uzoamaka Azodo, "Di-Feminism: An Indigenous Feminist Theory with Broad Claims for Ndigbo", in *f: Journal of Transatlantic Studies*, 5, 1 & 2 (2016). In this treatise, "Agụnwanyị", to the Igbo of south-east Nigeria, is a lion-woman – not a lioness, the killer queen – due to her intelligence, capability, courage, ability and hard work. See also "Di-Feminism: Valorizing the Indigenous Igbo Concept of Agụnwanyị", in Azodo (ed.), *African Feminisms in the Global Arena*, pp. 7–61.
64 Bâ, *Une si longue lettre*, p. 94.

Chapter 35

1 Micere Mugo's plays include *The Long Illness of Ex-Chief Kiti* (Nairobi: East African Literature Bureau, 1976); and Ngũgĩ wa Thiong'o and Micere Mugo, *The Trail of Dedan Kimathi* (Nairobi and London: Heinemann, 1976).
2 Micere Mugo's two collections of poems are *Daughter of My People, Sing* (Nairobi: East African Literature Bureau, 1976); and *My Mother's Songs and Other Poems* (Nairobi: East African Educational Publishers, 1994).
3 Micere Mugo's major critical essays include *Visions of Africa: The Fiction of Chinua Achebe, Margaret Laurence, Elspeth Huxley and Ngũgĩ wa Thiong'o* (Nairobi: East African Educational Publishers, 1978); and *Writing and Speaking from the Heart of My Mind* (Trenton: Africa World Press, 2012).
4 wa Thiong'o and Mugo, *The Trial of Dedan Kimathi*.
5 Author interview with Micere Githae Mugo, Nairobi, Kenya, August 2016.
6 Author interview with Micere Mugo, Indianapolis, US, November 2014.
7 Author interview with Micere Mugo, Indianapolis, US, November 2014.
8 Author interview with Ngũgĩ wa Thiong'o, Syracuse, US, April 2015.

9   Author interview with Ngũgĩ wa Thiong'o, Syracuse, US, April 2015.

10 Author interview with Ngũgĩ wa Thiong'o, Syracuse, US, April 2015.

11 See, for example, Chris Wanjala, "The Development of Contemporary Literature in East Africa", in Oluwaseun Tella and Shireen Motala (eds), *From Ivory Towers to Ebony Towers: Transforming Humanities Curricula in South Africa, Africa and African-American Studies* (Johannesburg: Jacana Media, 2020), pp. 314–26.

12 Author interview with Simon Gikandi, Syracuse, US, April 2015.

13 Mugo, *Writing and Speaking from the Heart of My Mind*.

14 Ngũgĩ wa Thiong'o and Mugo, *The Trial of Dedan Kimathi*.

15 Author interview with Simon Gikandi, Syracuse, US, April 2015.

16 Mugo, *Writing and Speaking from the Heart of My Mind*.

17 Mugo, *Writing and Speaking from the Heart of My Mind*.

18 Mugo, *Writing and Speaking from the Heart of My Mind*.

19 Author interview with Jeremiah Kiereini, Nairobi, Kenya, August 2016.

20 Author interview with Micere Mugo, Indianapolis, US, November 2014.

21 Author interview with Jeremiah Kiereini, Nairobi, Kenya, August 2016.

22 Mugo, *Writing and Speaking from the Heart of My Mind*.

23 Author interview with Micere Mugo, Syracuse, US, October 2014.

24 Author interview with Micere Mugo, Syracuse, US, October 2014.

CHAPTER 36

1   Zizwe D. Poe, "Kwame Nkrumah's Contribution to Pan-African Agency", in *Kwame Nkrumah's Contribution to Pan-Africanism: An Afrocentric Analysis* (New York: Routledge, 2003).

2   Issa Shivji (ed.), *Reimagining Pan-Africanism: Distinguished Mwalimu Nyerere Lecture Series 2009–2013* (Dar es Salaam: Mkuki Na Nyota, 2015).

3   Amilcar Cabral, "National liberation and Culture", *Transition*, 45 (1974), pp. 12–17.

4   Guy Martin, *African Political Thought* (New York: Springer, 2012); Nyeyere speech on 10 June 1962 titled "Culture, the Soul of the Nation".

5   Graeme Counsel, "Digitising and Archiving Syliphone Recordings in Guinea", *Australasian Review of African Studies*, 30, 1 (2009), p. 144; and Graeme Counsel, "The Music Archives of Guinea: Nationalism and its Representation under Sékou Touré", African Studies Association of Australasia and the Pacific, 36th Annual Conference Perth, Australia, 26–28 November 2013.

6   Micere Mugo, "Art, Artists and the Flowering of Pan-Africana Liberated Zones", in Shivji (ed.), *Reimagining Pan-Africanism*, p.190.

7   Ruth Feldstein, *How It Feels to Be Free: Black Women Entertainers and the Civil Rights Movement* (London: Oxford University Press, 2013).

8   Robert Shelton, "2,800 Hear Concert by Miriam Makeba", *New York Times*, 22 April 1963.

9   Miriam Makeba and Nomsa Mwamuka. *Makeba: The Miriam Makeba Story* (Johannesburg: STE, 2005).

10 Ruth First, "The Gold of Migrant Labour", *Review of African Political Economy*, 25 (1982), pp. 5–21, www.jstor.org/stable/3998090.

11 Makeba and Mwamuka, *Makeba*, p. 6.

12 Richard Harrington, "Makeba and the Song of Exodus: The Long-Exiled South African Singer Looks Back on Unfinished Journey", *Washington Post*, 17 February 1988.

13 Natives Resettlement Act 19 of 1954 gave the apartheid government power to remove black Africans from any area. This Act, for example, effected the removal of black Africans from Sophiatown to Soweto, the Southwest Township.

14 See listing of apartheid laws, https://www.sahistory.org.za/article/apartheid-legislation-1850s-1970s.

15 See https://www.sahistory.org.za/dated-event/commencement-immorality-act.

16 See Lionel Rogosin's diaries, in Lionel Rogosin, *Come Back, Africa: Lionel Rogosin – A Man Possessed* (Johannesburg: STE Publishers, 2004). See also the official Lionel Rogosin website: www.lionelrogosin.org.

17 See http://www.sahistory.org.za/dated-event/20-000-women-march-union-buildings-protest-pass-laws.

18 Harrington, "Makeba and the Song of Exodus".

19 See http://www.sahistory.org.za/people/henry-mr-drum-nxumalo.

20 See https://www.sahistory.org.za/article/forced-removals-south-africa.

21 See https://www.revolvy.com/page/Meadowlands-%28song%29; and Anne Schumann, "The Beat that Beat Apartheid: The Role of Music in the Resistance against Apartheid in South Africa", *Wiener Zeitschrift für Kritische Afrikastudien*, 14, 8 (2008), pp. 17–39.

22 "Miriam Star of Venice", *Drum*, October 1959, p. 65.

23 Feldstein, *How It Feels to Be Free*.

24 Miriam Makeba and James Hall, *Makeba: My Story* (New York: New American Library, 1987).

25 Milton Bracker, *New York Times*, 28 February 1960.

26 The *Steve Allen Show* aired on NBC at 8 pm. Makeba appeared on 30 November 1959.

27 See http://africanactivist.msu.edu/document_metadata.php?objectid=32-130-111C.

28 See http://africanactivist.msu.edu/asearch.php?keyword=Miriam%20Makeba.

29 Ntongela Masilela, "An Appreciation", New Africa Movement, 18 November 2008, http://pzacad.pitzer.edu/nam/sophia/writers/makeba/makebaA.htm.

30 See http://www.suedafrika.org/en/news-archive/newsarchive-details/.

31 See http://www.suedafrika.org/en/news-archive/newsarchive-details/.

32 Gumboot dancing was seen as tool of resistance among mineworkers. See, for example, Jane Osborne, "The Gumboot Dance: An Historical, Socio-Economic and Cultural Perspective", *South African Theatre Journal*, 4, 2 (1990), pp. 50–79, DOI: 10.1080/10137548.1990.9688012.

33 See liner notes: *Miriam Makeba* 1960 (RCA Victor Label); and *Many Voices of Miriam Makeba* 1962 studio album (LP Kapp KL1274).

34 See the official page of the Grammy Awards, https://www.grammy.com/grammys/artists/miriam-makeba.

35 To read about Vuyisile Mini, see https://www.sahistory.org.za/sites/default/files/Mini%20Vuyisile.pdf.

36 Gwen Ansell, *Soweto Blues: Jazz, Popular Music and Politics in South Africa* (Johannesburg: Jacana Media, 2005); Rob Allingham, "From 'Noma Kumnyama' to 'Pata': A History", *African Music: Journal of the International Library of African Music*, 8, 3 (November 2009), pp. 117–31.

37 Lee Zhito, "Makeba Too Hip for Ciro's," *Billboard*, 31 October 1960, p. 52.

38 Benedict Anderson, *Imagined Communities: Reflections on the Origin and Spread of Nationalism* (London: Verso Books, 1983), pp. 6–7.

39 Hugh Masekela, and Michael D. Cheers, *Still Grazing: The Musical Journey of Hugh Masekela* (New York: Crown Publishers, 2004).

40 See Hugh Masekela obituary in *The Guardian* (London), 23 January 2018, https://www.theguardian.com/music/2018/jan/23/hugh-masekela-obituary. Hugh Masekela spent 31 years in exile, making homes in the US, Guinea, Zaire (now the DRC), Liberia, Ghana, Nigeria and Botswana.

41 See "American Public Media: Say it Plain – A Century of Great African Speeches", Introduction to the recording of a speech by Stokely Carmichael at the University of California, Berkeley, 22 October 1966, http://americanradioworks.publicradio.org/features/blackspeech/scarmichael-2.html.

42 Stokeley Carmichael, *Ready for Revolution: The Life and Struggles of Stokely Carmichael (Kwame Ture)* (New York: Scribner, 2003).

43 In Guinea, Miriam Makeba immersed herself in the local culture, performing with local musician and singing traditional songs. Yair Hashachar, "Playing the Backbeat in Conakry: Miriam Makeba and the Cultural Politics of Sékou Touré's Guinea, 1968–1986", *Social Dynamics*, 43, 2 (2017), pp. 259–73.

44 Kathleen Neal Cleaver, "Art and Revolution: Black Power at the 1969 Pan-African Cultural Festival", in Sylviane A. Diouf and Komozi Woodward (eds), *Black Power 50* (New York: New Press, 2016).

45 Cleaver, "Art and Revolution".

46 Lewis A. Erenberg, "Rumble in the Jungle: Muhammad Ali vs. George Foreman in the Age of Global Spectacle", *Journal of Sport History*, 39, 1 (2012), pp. 81–97.

47 C.R. Jonathan, "FESTAC: Upbeat Finale", *Washington Post*, 14 February 1977, https://www.washingtonpost.com/archive/lifestyle/1977/02/14/festac-upbeat-finale/.

48 See https://www.sahistory.org.za/topic/june-16-soweto-youth-uprising-casualties.

49 Carol A. Muller, "The New African Diaspora, the Built Environment and the Past in Jazz", *Ethnomusicology Forum*, 15, 1 (June 2006), pp. 63–86.

50 See https://www.sahistory.org.za/archive/wind-change-speech-made-south-africa-parliament-3-february-1960-harold-macmillan.

51 Tyler Fleming, "A Marriage of Inconvenience: Miriam Makeba's Relationship with Stokely Carmichael and Her Music Career in the United States", *Safundi*, 17, 3 (2016), pp. 312–38.

52 Makeba, *Makeba, My Story*, p. 180.

53 Rajen Harshe, "Guinea under Sékou Touré", *Economic and Political Weekly*, 19, 15 (1984), pp. 624–6.

54 Michael C. Beaubien, "The Cultural Boycott of South Africa", *Africa Today*, 29, 4 (1982), pp. 5–16.

55 See https://www.sahistory.org.za/dated-event/british-anti-apartheid-movement-hosts-concert-mandela.

56 Hank Bordowitz, *Noise of the World: Non-Western Musicians in Their Own Words* (Brooklyn, NY: Soft Skull Press, 2004), p. 248.

57 Shivji (ed.), *Reimagining Pan-Africanism*.

58 Other awards included the Dag Hammarskjöld Peace Prize from Sweden (1988), the Légion d'honneur from France (2002) and the Polar Music Prize from Sweden (2002).

59 *Musicus*, 31, 1 (January 2003), pp. 100–3.

60 See http://www.fao.org/tempref/GI/Reserved/ambassadors/finalVersion/amb/makeba_en.htm.

61 See http://www.dirco.gov.za/foreign/Multilateral/profiles/ambassador.htm.

62 See https://www.sahistory.org.za/people/miriam-makeba.

63 See https://www.cubanet.org/htdocs/CNews/y05/oct05/10e11.htm.

64 See the interview with John Hooper, *The Guardian* (London), 1 November 2008, https://www.theguardian.com/world/2008/nov/01/italy-gomorrah-roberto-saviano.

65 Makeba and Mwamuka, *Makeba*, p. 208.

CHAPTER 37

1 Bob Marley and the Wailers, "Africa Unite", *Survival* (album) (Kingston: Island/Tuff Gong, 1979).

2 Bob Marley and the Wailers, "Slave Driver/Catch a Fire", *Catch a Fire* (album) (Kingston: Island Record Inc./Tuff Gong, 1973).

3 Bob Marley and the Wailers, "Slave Driver/Catch a Fire."

4   Bob Marley and the Wailers, "Redemption Song", *Uprising* (album) (Kingston: Tuff Gong, 1980).

5   Bob Marley and the Wailers, "Redemption Song."

6   Peter Tosh, "Mystic Man", *Mystic Man* (album) (Kingston: Rolling Stones Record/ EMI/Intel Diplo, 1979).

7   Burning Spear, "Slavery Days," *Marcus Garvey* (album) (Kingston: Island, 1975).

8   Bob Marley and the Wailers, "Exodus", *Exodus* (album) (Kingston and London: Island/ Tuff Gong, 1977).

9   The Wailers, "Rasta Man Chant", *Burnin'* (album) (Kingston and London: Island/Tuff Gong, 1973); Bob Andy, "I've Got To Go Back Home" (vinyl 7" 45 RPM single) (Jamaica: Coxsone Records, 1967); The Abyssinians, "Satta Massagana", *Satta Massagana* (album) (Jamaica: Jam Sounds/Heartbeat, 1976); Bunny Wailer, "Dreamland", *Black Heart Man* (album) (Kingston: Solomonic/Island, 1976); and Johnny Clarke, "Move Out of Babylon" (vinyl 7" 45 RPM single) (Horse-Hoss United Kingdom [UK], 1975).

10   Bob Marley and the Wailers, "Africa Unite".

11   Bob Marley and the Wailers, "Africa Unite".

12   Bob Marley and the Wailers, "Africa Unite".

13   See Clinton Hutton, "Leonard Howell Announcing God: The Conditions That Gave Birth to Rastafari in Jamaica", in Clinton A. Hutton, Michael A Barnett, D. A. Dunkley and Jahlani A. H. Niaah (eds), *Leonard Percival Howell and the Genesis of Rastafari* (Kingston, Bridgetown, and Port of Spain: The University of The West Indies Press, 2015), pp. 9–52.

14   Bob Marley and the Wailers, "Africa Unite".

15   Bob Marley and the Wailers, "Africa Unite".

16   Bob Marley and the Wailers, "Africa Unite".

17   Bob Marley and the Wailers, "Zimbabwe", *Survival* (album) (Kingston: Island/Tuff Gong, 1979).

18   Bob Marley and the Wailers, "Zimbabwe".

19   This 1963 United Nations' speech by H.I.M. Haile Selassie can be found at Rastafari. tv/1963-haile-selassie-war-speech-inspired-bob-marley-famous-war-song.

20   Peter Tosh, "Fight On", *Mystic Man* (album).

21   Bob Marley and the Wailers, "Ride Natty Ride", *Survival* (album) (Kingston: Island/Tuff Gong, 1979).

22   Bob Marley and the Wailers, "Ride Natty Ride".

23   Bob Marley and the Wailers, "Ride Natty Ride".

24   Bob Marley and the Wailers, "I Know", *Confrontation* (album) (Kingston: Tuff Gong, 1983).

25   Bob Marley and the Wailers, "Forever Loving Jah", *Uprising* (album) (Kingston: Tuff Gong/Island, 1980).

26   Bob Marley and the Wailers, "Forever Loving Jah".

27   Bob Marley and the Wailers, "Forever Loving Jah".

28   Bob Marley and the Wailers, *Survival* (album) (Kingston: Island/Tuff Gong, 1979).

29   Bob Marley and the Wailers, "Music Gonna Teach (aka Music Lesson)", *Grooving Kingston 12*, CD boxset, disc 3, (US: Universal Music, 2004).

30   Bob Marley and the Wailers, "Babylon System", *Survival* (album) (Kingston: Island/Tuff Gong, 1979).

31   Bob Marley and the Wailers, "Babylon System".

32   Bob Marley and The Wailers, "Crazy Baldhead", *Rastaman Vibration* (album) (Kingston: Island/Tuff Gong, 1976).

33   Jimmy Cliff, *The Harder They Come* (Island, 1972).

CHAPTER 38

1   Felasophy is a neologism coined by Afrobeat fans to cover Fela's general ideas and philosophy.

2   Fela's communal residence of Kalakuta was created out of the desire to accommodate Africans fleeing persecution. Kalakuta was derived from the name of his prison cell in Lagos in 1974. He also noted and justified its Swahili inflection of "rascally". The word "republic" was later added to it because Fela disagreed with the Federal Republic of Nigeria being created by Lord Lugard, an Englishman. The exigency of political activism led to Fela having to live in many places, but his more notable residences in Lagos are chronologically: Kalakuta I, number 14A Agege Motor Road; Kalakuta II, number 1 Atinuke Olabanji Street, Ikeja; and Kalakuta III, number 7 Gbemisola Street, Ikeja.

3   Fela Anikulapo-Kuti and the Africa 70, *No Agreement* (LP Decca AfrodisiaDWAPS2039, 1978).

4   Sola Olorunyomi, *Afrobeat! Fela and the Imagined Continent* (Asmara and Trenton: Africa World Press, 2003).

5   Carlos Moore, *Fela: This Bitch of a Life* (Abuja: Cassava Republic, 2010 [1982]), p. 94.

6   This had less to do with how much members of the household were paid, which was indeed barely on subsistence level, but more as a statement symbolised by the very act of Fela's lifestyle.

7   A similar experience is described by Dick Hebdige in "Reggae, Rastas and Rudies" in James Curran, Michael Gurevitch and Janet Woollacott (eds), *Mass Communication and Society* (London: Edward Arnold, 1977), pp. 427–39.

8   Curran, Gurevitch and Woollacott (eds), *Mass Communication and Society*. A similar experience of the Rastafarian subculture has been documented.

9   Charles Handy, *The Gods of Management: The Changing Work of Organisation* (London: Arrow Books, 1991).

10   John Child, *Organisation: A Guide to Problems and Practice* (London: Harper and Row, 1984).

11   See Friederich Nietzsche, *The Birth of Tragedy and the Genealogy of Morals* (New York: Doubleday, 1956), pp. 96–7.

12   The three books by Kwame Nkrumah cited in the essay are *Africa Must Unite* (London: Panaf, 1963); *Consciencism: Philosophy and Ideology for Decolonization* (London: Panaf, 1964); and *Neo-colonialism: The Last Stage of Imperialism* (London: Panaf, 1970 [1965]).

13   Information from Fela's correspondence.

14   See Lasisi Buraimo, "Fela Anikulapo-Kuti: A Misunderstood Poet", University of Ibadan, Nigeria, Department of English, BA project, 1980.

15   See V.Y. Mudimbe, *The Invention of Africa* (Bloomington: Indiana University Press, 1988), p. 86. The emphasis in this quote is the author's.

16   Thomas Hodgkin, *Nationalism in Colonial Africa* (New York: New York University Press, 1957), pp. 174–5.

17   See *ANA Review* (last quarter, 1995), a quarterly publication of the Association of Nigerian Authors.

18   Mahmood Mamdani, "When Does a Settler Become a Native? Reflections on the Colonial Roots of Citizenship in Equatorial and Southern Africa", Inaugural Lecture, University of Cape Town, Centre for African Studies, 1998.

19   Wole Soyinka, *Ogun Abibiman* (London: Rex Collings, 1976).

20   See Abdulrahman Mohamed Babu, "The New World Disorder: Which Way Africa?" in Tajudeen Abdul-Raheem (ed.), *Pan Africanism: Politics, Economy and Social Change in the Twenty-First Century* (London: Pluto Press, 1996), p. 90.

21   See Robert Norzick, *Anarchy, State and Utopia* (New York: Basic Books, 1974), p. 334.

22 Vladimir Lenin, *The State and Revolution* (Moscow: Progress Publishers, 1985 [1917]), p. 91.
23 See John Beverly Robinson's translation of Pierre-Joseph Proudhon, *General Ideas of the Revolution* (London: Freedom Press, 1923), pp. 293–4.

INDEX

This index is arranged word by word.